D1308549

GrantFinder

The complete guide to postgraduate funding worldwide

Arts and Humanities

GrantFinder

The complete guide to postgraduate funding worldwide

Arts and Humanities

© Macmillan Reference Ltd, 2000

The publishers of GrantFinder cannot undertake any correspondence in relation to grants listed in this volume.

While every care has been taken in compiling the information contained in this publication, the publishers accept no responsibility for any errors or omissions therein.

Published in the United States and Canada by

ST. MARTIN'S PRESS, INC.

175 Fifth Avenue, New York

NY 10010

ISBN 0-312-22893-7
ISSN 1526-0895

Published in Great Britain by

MACMILLAN REFERENCE LTD

25 Eccleston Place, London, SW1W 9NF

Basingstoke and Oxford

Companies and representatives throughout the world.

British Library Cataloguing in Publication Data
GrantFinder
Arts and humanities

1. Student aid
2. Graduate students - Scholarships, fellowships, etc.
3. Arts - Research grants
4. Humanities - Research grants
I. Waterlows Specialist Information Publishing
378.3
ISBN 0-333-777301

Typeset by Macmillan Reference Ltd

Printed and bound in Great Britain by Antony Rowe Ltd, Chippenham, Wiltshire

Visit our website: http://www.macmillan-reference.co.uk

CONTENTS

HOW TO USE GRANTFINDER

For ease of use, GrantFinder is divided into four sections:

• The Grants
• Subject and Eligibility Guide to Awards
• Index of Awards
• Index of Awarding Organisations

The Grants

Information in this section is supplied directly by the awarding organisations. Entries are arranged alphabetically by name of organisation, and awards are listed alphabetically within the awarding organisation. This section includes details on subject area, eligibility, purpose, type, numbers offered, frequency, value, length of study, study establishment, country of study, and application procedure. Full contact details appear with each awarding organisation and also appended to individual awards where additional addresses are given.

Subject and Eligibility Guide to Awards

Awards can be located through the Subject and Eligibility Guide to Awards. This section allows the user to find an award within a specific subject area. GrantFinder uses a list of subjects endorsed by the International Association of Universities (IAU), the information centre on higher education, located at UNESCO, Paris (please see pp. 394 for the complete subject list). It is further subdivided into eligibility by nationality. Thereafter, awards are listed alphabetically within their designated category, along with a page reference where full details of the award can be found.

Index of Awards

All awards are indexed alphabetically with a page reference.

Index of Awarding Organisations

A complete list of all awarding organisations, with country name and page reference.

AMERICAN PHILOSOPHICAL SOCIETY

104 S Fifth Street, Philadelphia, PA, 19106-3387, United States of America
www: http://www.amphilsoc.org
Contact: Committee on Research

General Research Grant Program

Subjects: Scholarly research.
Eligibility: Applicants are normally expected to have a doctorate, but applications are considered from persons whose publications display equivalent scholarly achievement. Grants are rarely made to persons who have held the doctorate less than a year, and never for predoctoral study or research. It is the Society's long-standing practice to encourage younger scholars. The Committee will seldom approve more than two grants to the same person within any five-year period. Applicants may be residents of the United States, American citizens on the staffs of foreign institutions,

---

GENERAL

Any Country

AIA College of Fellows Grant, 13
The AIA/AAF Scholarship for Advanced Study and Research, 13
Alexander S Onassis Programme of Research Grants, 7
Alexander S Onassis Research Grants, 7
Board of Architects of New South Wales Research Grant, 56

THE GRANTS

AAUW EDUCATIONAL FOUNDATION

Department 60
2201 North Dodge Street, Iowa City, IA, 52243-4030, United States of America
Tel: (1) 319 337 1716 ext 60
www: http://www.aauw.org
Contact: Grants Management Officer

AAUW is composed of three corporations: the Association, a 150,000-member organisation with more than 1,500 branches nationwide that lobbies and advocates for education and equity; the AAUW Educational Foundation, which funds pioneering research on girls and education, community action projects, and fellowships and grants for outstanding women around the globe; and the AAUW Legal Advocacy Fund, which provides funds and a support system for women seeking judicial redress for sex discrimination in higher education.

AAUW Educational Foundation American Fellowships

Subjects: All subjects.
Eligibility: Applicants must be US citizens.
Level of Study: Doctorate, Postdoctorate.
Purpose: To offset a scholar's living expenses while she completes her final year of dissertation writing; or, to increase the number of women in tenure-track faculty positions and promote equality for women in higher education.
Type: Fellowship.
Frequency: Annual.
Value: US$15,000 for the Dissertation Award; US$27,000 for Postdoctoral Research Leave Award; and US$5,250 for the Research Publication Grant.
Length of Study: 1 year.
Country of Study: USA.
Application Procedure: Application package includes an application form, narrative autobiography, CV, statement of project, transcripts, three letters of recommendation and a filing fee.
Closing Date: November 15th.

AAUW International Fellowships Program

Subjects: All subjects.
Eligibility: Open to women who are not US citizens or permanent residents. Must hold a US bachelor's degree or equivalent. Must be planning to return to their home country upon completion of degree/research. English proficiency required.
Level of Study: Doctorate, Postdoctorate, Postgraduate, Professional development.
Purpose: To award women who are not US citizens or permanent residents studying at the graduate or postgraduate level or for research beyond the Bachelor's level.
Type: Fellowship.
No. of awards offered: 45.

Frequency: Annual.
Value: US$16,000 for the Fellowship Award; US$5,000-7,000 (limited number available) for the Community Action Grants.
Length of Study: 1 year.
Study Establishment: Any accredited institution.
Country of Study: USA.
Application Procedure: Application must be filled out for each year applying. Applications must be obtained through our customer service centre between August 1st and November 15th. Three letters of recommendation, transcripts, TOEFL scores (min 550) are also required.
Closing Date: January 15th.
Additional Information: These awards are non-renewable.

Career Development Grants

Subjects: All subjects.
Eligibility: Open to all, yet special consideration is given to AAUW members, women of colour, women pursuing their advanced degree or credentials in non-traditional fields. Applicants must be US citizens or permanent residents whose last degree was received before June 30th 1994. Candidates eligible for another AAUW Educational Foundation fellowship or grant programme are not eligible for Career Development Grants.
Purpose: To support women who currently hold a Bachelor's degree and who are preparing for a career in advancement, career change, or to re-enter the work force.
Type: Grant.
No. of awards offered: Approx. 75 in two categories: Academic Grants and Professional Development Institute Grants.
Value: US$2,000-8,000.
Closing Date: Postmark deadline January 2nd.
Additional Information: The two categories are as follows: Academic Grants - provide support for course work towards a Master's degree or specialised training in technical or professional fields. Course work must be undertaken at a fully accredited two or four year college, university or technical school licensed, accredited, or approved by the US Department of Veterans Affairs; and Professional Development Institute Grants - support women's participation in professional institutes.

Community Action Grants

Subjects: All subjects.
Eligibility: Applicants must be women who are US citizens or permanent residents. Special consideration will be given to AAUW branch and state applicants who seek partners for collaborative projects. Collaborators can include local schools or school districts, businesses and other community based organisations.
Purpose: To provide seed money to individual women and AAUW branches and states for innovative programmes or non-degree research projects that promote education and equity for women and girls.
Type: Grant.
No. of awards offered: Approx. 40.
Value: US$2,000-$7,000 for one-year projects; US$5,000-$10,000 for two-year projects.

Length of Study: 1 or 2 years.
Application Procedure: Please write for details.
Closing Date: February 1st.
Additional Information: Two types of grants are available: one year grants for short term projects; topic areas are unrestricted but should have a clearly defined educational activity; two year grants are for longer term programmes and are restricted to projects focused on K-12 girls achievement in maths, science, and technology. Funds support planning activities and coalition building during the first year and implementation and evaluation the following year.

ACADEMY OF MOTION PICTURE ARTS AND SCIENCES

8949 Wilshire Boulevard, Beverly Hills, CA, 90211-1972, United States of America
Tel: (1) 310 247 3059
Email: nicholl@oscars.org
www: http://www.oscars.org/nicholl
Contact: Grants Management Officer

The Academy of Motion Picture Arts and Sciences annually presents Academy Awards for motion picture artistic achievement. The Academy Film Archive is a leader in preservation and restoration and the Academy's Margaret Herrick Library holds a vast array of film-related materials. The Student Academy Awards honours achievements by talented student film-makers.

Don and Gee Nicholl Fellowships in Screenwriting

Subjects: Screenwriting.
Eligibility: Open to writers in English who have not sold or optioned a screen or teleplay or the story for a screen or teleplay.
Level of Study: Unrestricted.
Purpose: To foster the development of new writers.
Type: Fellowship.
No. of awards offered: Up to 5.
Frequency: Annual.
Value: US$25,000.
Country of Study: Any country.
Application Procedure: Please send a stamped, self-addressed business-size envelope for further details (after January 1st), or visit the website to print an application form.
Closing Date: May 1st.
Additional Information: The Fellowships are not to be used to pursue undergraduate or graduate college degrees. In addition to the Academy Awards or Oscars (no monetary value) and the Nicholl Fellowships, the Academy offers Student Film Awards for films completed by students at an accredited college or university.

ACADIA UNIVERSITY

Division of Research and Graduate Studies, Wolfville, NS, B0P 1X0, Canada
Tel: (1) 902 542 1498
Fax: (1) 902 585 1078
Email: peter.mcleod@acadiau.ca
www: http://www.ace.acadiau.ca/gradstud/gradhome.htm
Contact: Mr Peter McLeod, Director of Research and Graduate Studies

Acadia University is primarily an undergraduate institution providing a liberal education based on the highest standards. The university provides a scholarly community that aims to ensure a broadening life experience for students, faculty, and staff.

Acadia Graduate Teaching Assistantships

Subjects: English, political science, sociology, biology, chemistry, computer science, geology, psychology, education.
Eligibility: Open to those registered as full-time graduate students at Acadia University.
Level of Study: Postgraduate.
Purpose: To support graduate students.
Type: Assistantships.
No. of awards offered: Limited.
Frequency: Annual.
Value: Approx. C$8,000.
Length of Study: 1 or 2 years.
Study Establishment: Acadia University, Division of Research and Graduate Studies.
Country of Study: Canada.
Application Procedure: There is no application form. Please write for details.
Closing Date: February 1st.
Additional Information: A recipient of a graduate teaching assistantship should expect to undertake certain duties during the academic year, up to a maximum of eight hours per week, as a condition of tenure of the award. The specific duties are to be established by agreement at the beginning of each academic year.

ADOLPH AND ESTHER GOTTLIEB FOUNDATION, INC.

380 West Broadway, New York, NY, 10012, United States of America
Tel: (1) 212 226 0581
Fax: (1) 212 226 0584
www: http://www.pacrim.ca/~naimiroy/anvil/gr-gottl.htm
Contact: Ms Sheila Ross, Grants Manager

The Adolph and Esther Gottlieb Foundation is a non-profit corporation registered with the state of New York. It was established to award financial aid to mature creative painters and sculptors.

Gottlieb Foundation Emergency Assistance Grants

Subjects: Painting, sculpture, printmaking.
Eligibility: Open to artists who can demonstrate a minimum of 10 years' involvement in a mature phase of their work and who do not have the resources to meet the costs incurred by a catastrophic event.
Level of Study: Unrestricted.
Purpose: To provide interim financial assistance to creative visual artists (painters, sculptors and printmakers) whose need is the result of unforeseen catastrophic events, eg. fire, flood or emergency medical expenses.
Type: Grant.
No. of awards offered: Varies.
Frequency: Varies, depending on funds available.
Value: Up to US$10,000; US$4,000 is typical, on a one-time basis only.
Country of Study: Any country.
Application Procedure: Application form must be completed and submitted with documentation of situation (such as bills) and professional references.
Closing Date: Please write for details.
Additional Information: The disciplines of film, photography, or related forms are not eligible unless the work involves directly, or can be interpreted as, painting or sculpture. 'Maturity' is based on the level of technical, intellectual and creative development of the artist. The programme does not cover general indebtedness, dental work, unemployment, capital improvements, long-term disabilities, or project funding.

Gottlieb Foundation Individual Support Grants

Subjects: Painting, sculpting, printmaking.
Eligibility: Open to creative painters, sculptors, and printmakers who have been in a mature phase of their work for at least 20 years and require financial assistance to continue this work. US residency is not required.
Level of Study: Unrestricted.
Purpose: To recognise and support serious, fully committed painters, sculptors and printmakers, who have been working in a mature phase of their art for at least 20 years and are in financial need.
Type: Grant.
No. of awards offered: 10.
Frequency: Annual.
Value: Varies.
Length of Study: 12 months.
Country of Study: Any country.
Application Procedure: Applicants must submit a written request for an application form, which must then be completed and submitted with slides to document twenty years of mature work, narrative statement and financial information.
Closing Date: December 15th. Awards are distributed the following March.
Additional Information: Artists who have been awarded a grant must allow one year to elapse before re-application. Only first-person written requests for application forms will be honoured.

AFRICA EDUCATIONAL TRUST

Small Grants Project
38 King Street, London, WC2E 8JS, England
Tel: (44) 171 836 5075
Fax: (44) 171 379 0090
Email: mbrophy@aet.win-uk.net
www: http://www.africaeducationaltrust.mcmail.com
Contact: Director

Africa Educational Trust Emergency Grants

Subjects: All subjects.
Eligibility: Open to students from Africa studying in the UK. The applicant must have run into unexpected difficulties at the end of his or her course for which the small level of grant will, by itself or in conjunction with other grants, solve the problem. Most awards are made on a humanitarian basis. Academic considerations are more important at the postgraduate and research levels.
Level of Study: Unrestricted.
Purpose: To provide one-off grants on an emergency basis to students from Africa studying in the UK.
Type: Emergency Grant.
No. of awards offered: 30.
Frequency: Monthly.
Value: £100-£600.
Length of Study: Final year.
Country of Study: United Kingdom.
Additional Information: Applications should be made by post or via a third party (such as a student welfare officer). Emergency Grants are provided at any time of year. The Trust will also consider contributions towards conference fees.

Emergency and Small Grants for Students from Africa

Subjects: All subjects.
Eligibility: Applicants should be studying in the UK and hold a student's visa.
Purpose: To support students in the final four months of their course who need a small amount of money to help them complete their studies.
Type: Grant.
No. of awards offered: Varies.
Value: Maximum £800.
Length of Study: Final 4 months of their course.
Application Procedure: Please write for details.

Full and Part Time Scholarships

Subjects: All subjects.
Eligibility: Criteria varies for year to year, please write for details.
Type: Scholarship.
No. of awards offered: Varies.
Frequency: As available.
Value: Covers transport costs, fees and books.
Country of Study: Europe and Africa.

Application Procedure: Criteria varies from year to year, please write for details.
Closing Date: Criteria varies from year to year, please write for details.

AFRO-ASIAN INSTITUTE IN VIENNA AND CATHOLIC WOMEN'S LEAGUE OF AUSTRIA

Student Division
Türkenstrasse 3, Vienna, A-1090, Austria
Tel: (43) 1 222 31 05 145 213
Fax: (43) 1 222 31 05 145 312
Email: aai.wien@magnet.at
Contact: Mr Markus Pleschko, Study Advisor

The AAI's major function is to aid students from third world countries. Presently the AAI provide services for more than 5,000 students from developing countries, and count as an acknowledged contribution to Austrian development aid.

One World Scholarship Program

Subjects: All subjects.
Eligibility: Open to nationals of developing countries in Africa, Asia and Latin America who are between the ages of 18 and 35, and who have had adequate previous study or vocational practice in the specific field for which the scholarship is applied.
Level of Study: Unrestricted.
Purpose: To promote cultural exchange, international development and international co-operation aid.
Type: Scholarship.
No. of awards offered: Varies.
Frequency: Annual.
Value: 2,500-7,000 Austrian Schillings each month.
Study Establishment: Universities (Vienna, Linz, Innsbruck).
Country of Study: Austria.
Application Procedure: Please contact the Institute personally, for an application form.
Closing Date: April 1st to 30th, for the following academic year.
Additional Information: It is preferred that candidates are able to speak German. Only those in financial need will be considered, and applicability of the special branch of study or training in the applicant's home country is essential. It is expected that scholars will return to their home country after studying. Good, and sometimes excellent, study results are also required. Preference is given to applicants from the least developed countries. It is one of AAI's essential aims to establish a 'partnership' contact between assisted students and the Scholarship donor which continues beyond the termination of studies. Only personal applications will be considered. Only about 10% of the applicants can be accepted. Only written applications are accepted.

ALEXANDER GRAHAM BELL ASSOCIATION FOR THE DEAF

3417 Volta Place NW, Washington, DC, 20007, United States of America
Tel: (1) 202 337 5220
www: http://www.agbell.org/
Contact: Ms Elissa M Brooks, Public Relations

The Alexander Graham Bell Association for the Deaf is a nonprofit membership organisation that was established in 1890 to empower persons who are hearing impaired to function independently by promoting universal rights and optimal opportunities to learn to use, maintain, and improve all aspects of their verbal communications, including their abilities to speak, speechread, use residual hearing, and process both spoken and written language.

Alexander Graham Bell Scholarship Awards

Subjects: All subjects.
Eligibility: Open to auditory-oral students born with profound hearing loss (80 dB loss in the better ear, average), or a severe hearing loss (60 to 80 dB loss), who experienced such a loss before acquiring language. Candidates must use speech and residual hearing and/or speech-reading as their preferred customary form of communication and demonstrate a potential for leadership. In addition, applicants must have applied to, or already be enrolled full time in, a regular college or university programme for hearing students.
Level of Study: Unrestricted.
Purpose: To encourage severely or profoundly hearing-impaired students to attend regular hearing colleges.
Type: Scholarship.
No. of awards offered: Varies.
Frequency: Annual.
Value: US$250-US$1,000.
Country of Study: USA.
Application Procedure: Requests for application must be received, in writing, by December 1st. Photocopies of applications are not accepted.
Closing Date: March 15th.

ALEXANDER S ONASSIS PUBLIC BENEFIT FOUNDATION

56 Amalias Ave, Athens, GR-10558, Greece
Tel: (30) 1 3310900
Fax: (30) 1 3236044
Email: pubrel@onassis.gr
www: http://www.onassis.gr
Contact: Mr Stelio Papadimitriou, President

The Foundation establishes and supports public benefit projects, offers services and makes contributions to other public benefit institutions for medical care, education, literature, religion, science, research, journalism, art, cultural matters, history, archaeology and sport. It also awards prizes, grants and scholarships to both Greeks and foreigners.

Alexander S Onassis Programme of Research Grants

Subjects: Humanistic and political sciences, architecture, fine arts, law and education.
Eligibility: Open to non-Greeks from any country. Also open to scholars of Greek descent or citizenship, provided they have followed a professional career for at least ten years in a university or research institute outside Greece. There is an age limit of 55 years.
Level of Study: Postdoctorate, Professional development.
Purpose: To support non-Greek university professors at all levels and university researchers (PhD holders and above) who wish to conduct research in Greece.
Type: Grant.
No. of awards offered: 5.
Frequency: Annual.
Value: 300,000 Greek Drachmas per month, plus accommodation in a furnished apartment, plus a round-trip air ticket (economy class).
Length of Study: Up to 6 months.
Country of Study: Greece.
Application Procedure: Application form is required which contains all other documentation that has to be submitted to the Foundation.
Closing Date: January 30th.
Additional Information: Please submit applications to: 7 Aeschinou Street, 10558 Athens, Greece.

Alexander S Onassis Research Grants

Subjects: Humanistic and political sciences, architecture, fine arts, law and education.
Eligibility: Open to non-Greeks from any country. Scholars of Greek citizenship or descent are also eligible provided they have followed a professional academic career for at least ten years in a university or research institute outside Greece.
Level of Study: Professional development.
Purpose: To support non-Greek academicians and university full professors who wish to conduct research in Greece.
Type: Grant.
No. of awards offered: 5.
Frequency: Annual.
Value: 350,000 Drachmas. If the grantee is accompanied by his/her spouse, the amount is increased to 500,000 Drachmas or pro rata for the period of the spouse's stay, and two round-trip air tickets (business class) for the grantee and his/her spouse, plus hotel accommodation (room and breakfast).
Length of Study: 1 month.
Country of Study: Greece.
Application Procedure: Nomination form to be completed. This contains other documentation which has to be submitted to the Foundation.
Closing Date: January 30th.
Additional Information: Nominations should be submitted to: 7 Aeschinou Street, 10558 Athens, Greece.

Onassis Programme of Postgraduate Research Scholarships

Subjects: Humanistic and political sciences, architecture and fine arts.
Eligibility: Open to non-Greeks from any country or students (Master's or PhD level) who are of Greek descent or citizenship, who have obtained a degree abroad and who have been permanently residing outside Greece for more than fifteen years. There is an age limit of 40 years old.
Level of Study: Doctorate, Postgraduate.
Purpose: To support non-Greek postgraduate students studying in or outside Greece who wish to collect material, visit libraries and attend classes in Greek universities. Also to support postgraduate students or PhD candidates who are of Greek descent or citizenship who have obtained a degree abroad, and who have been permanently residing abroad for more than fifteen years.
Type: Scholarship.
No. of awards offered: 10.
Frequency: Annual.
Value: 200,000 Greek Drachmas per month, plus hotel accommodation, plus a round-trip air ticket (economy class).
Length of Study: Up to 12 months.
Country of Study: Greece.
Application Procedure: Application to be completed containing other documentation which is to be submitted to the Foundation.
Closing Date: January 30th.
Additional Information: Submit applications to: 7 Aeschinou Street, 10558 Athens, Greece.

ALEXANDER VON HUMBOLDT FOUNDATION

Jean-Paul Strasse 12, Bonn, Bad Godesberg, D-53173, Germany
Tel: (49) 228 833 0126
Fax: (49) 228 833 212
Email: post@avh.de
www: http://www.avh.de
Telex: 885 627
Contact: Dr Heide Radlanski

The Humboldt Foundation grants research fellowships to foreign scholars who hold doctorates and have not yet reached the age of 40, and research awards to internationally recognised foreign scholars of any age, enabling them to spend a lengthy period of research in the Federal Republic of Germany.

Federal Chancellor Scholarship

Subjects: Arts and humanities, business administration and management, fine and applied arts, mass communication and information science, medicine, recreation, welfare, protective services, religion and theology, social and behavioural sciences.
Eligibility: Open to US citizens only.

Level of Study: Postgraduate.
Purpose: To maintain and foster a close relationship between the USA and Germany by sponsoring individuals who demonstrate the potential of playing a pivotal role in the future development of this relationship.
Type: Scholarship.
No. of awards offered: 10.
Frequency: Annual.
Value: DM3,000-DM5,000 per month plus travel costs.
Length of Study: 12 months.
Study Establishment: Academic or other research institutions.
Country of Study: Germany.
Application Procedure: Application form must be completed; available from Bonn or Washington office.
Closing Date: October 31st, for next academic year.

Feodor Lynen Research Fellowships for German Scholars

Subjects: All academic fields.
Eligibility: Open to German nationals.
Level of Study: Postdoctorate.
Purpose: To enable highly-qualified German scholars (of less than 38 years of age) to conduct research of their choice at home institutions of non-German recipients of Humboldt fellowships and prizes.
Type: Fellowship.
No. of awards offered: Up to 150.
Frequency: Annual.
Value: DM4,000-DM5,000 per month (joint financing by Humboldt Foundation and host institute is required).
Length of Study: 1-4 years.
Study Establishment: Research institutions or universities.
Country of Study: Any, except Germany.
Application Procedure: Application form is required, available from Bonn and Washington addresses.
Closing Date: February 15th, June 15th, October 15th.

Humboldt Research Award for Foreign Scholars

Subjects: All subjects.
Eligibility: Open to all nationalities except Germans.
Level of Study: Postdoctorate.
Purpose: To enable internationally recognised foreign scholars to conduct research on a project of their choice in Germany.
Type: Research Prize.
No. of awards offered: Up to 200.
Frequency: Annual.
Value: Between DM20,000 and DM150,000 plus travel costs.
Length of Study: 4-12 months.
Study Establishment: Universities, research institutions.
Country of Study: Germany.
Application Procedure: Eminent German scholars propose candidates directly to the Foundation in Bonn. Direct applications are not accepted.
Closing Date: No deadline; nominations are accepted throughout the year.
Additional Information: Selection committee meetings are held twice per year, in March and October.

Japan Society for the Promotion of Science (JSPS) Research Fellowships

Subjects: All academic fields.
Eligibility: Open to German nationals only.
Level of Study: Postdoctorate.
Purpose: To enable highly-qualified German scholars (of less than 38 years of age), to carry out research projects of their own choice at universities or non-university research institutions in Japan.
Type: Fellowship.
No. of awards offered: 25.
Frequency: Annual.
Value: 270,000 Yen plus travel and housing allowance.
Length of Study: 12-24 months.
Study Establishment: University or other research institution.
Country of Study: Japan.
Application Procedure: Application form must be completed.
Closing Date: February 15th, June 15th, October 15th.

Konrad Adenauer Research Award

Subjects: Humanities, social sciences.
Eligibility: Open to highly qualified Canadian scholars, whose research work in the humanities or in the social sciences has brought them international recognition and who belong to the group of leading scholars in their respective area of specialisation. The award will be made regardless of the age, race, religion or sex of the applicants.
Level of Study: Postdoctorate.
Purpose: To promote academic relations between Canada and the Federal Republic of Germany.
Type: Research Grant.
No. of awards offered: 1.
Frequency: Annual.
Value: DM20,000-DM150,000. The Humboldt Foundation will pay the return travel costs once only for award winners and family members (provided the latter stay with them in Germany for at least six months) between Canada and Germany. Medical and accident insurance may be provided for the award winners (and family members) if requested.
Length of Study: 1 year.
Study Establishment: German research institutes.
Country of Study: Germany.
Application Procedure: Self-application cannot be accepted. Candidates should be nominated by their universities and their dossiers should be sent to the Awards Co-ordinator. Nomination forms and information may also be requested from the Awards Co-ordinator.
Closing Date: December 1st.
Additional Information: Nominations will be made jointly by the Royal Society of Canada and the University of Toronto, and submitted to the Humboldt Foundation. At least two candidates should be nominated each year.

For further information contact:

The Royal Society of Canada
225 Metcalfe Street
Suite 308, Ottawa, ON, K2P 1P9, Canada
Contact: Mrs Kathy Riikonen, Awards Co-ordinator

Max-Planck Award for International Co-operation

Subjects: All academic fields.
Eligibility: Open to scholars of all disciplines and nations.
Level of Study: Postdoctorate, Professional development.
Purpose: To enable internationally recognised foreign and German scholars to conduct long-term co-operative research.
Type: Research Prize.
No. of awards offered: 12.
Frequency: Annual.
Value: Up to DM250,000.
Length of Study: 3-5 years.
Country of Study: Germany.
Application Procedure: Nomination by presidents of German universities, academies of sciences, Max-Planck Society, corporations of large research establishments, Fraunhofer Society, German Research Association, former prize holders, and selection committee members.
Closing Date: April 15th.
Additional Information: Selection occurs once per year.

Postdoctoral Humboldt Research Fellowships

Subjects: Postdoctoral academic research in any subject.
Eligibility: Open to persons of any nationality other than German, up to 40 years of age, who have obtained a PhD degree or equivalent, who can furnish proof of independent research and can submit academic publications. Candidates in the arts and humanities should possess sound German language ability. Those in the natural, medical and engineering sciences should possess English language ability. (German language courses at the Goethe Institute in Germany for 2-4 months may be available prior to commencement of the Research Fellowship). Candidates should already have established relations with a German research institute where the project can be realised.
Level of Study: Postdoctorate.
Purpose: To provide opportunities for young, highly qualified scholars from abroad to carry out research projects of their own choice in Germany.
Type: Research Fellowship.
No. of awards offered: Approx. 500.
Frequency: Annual.
Value: DM3,600-DM4,400 per month, plus travel allowance for Research Fellow only, and dependant's allowance.
Length of Study: 6-12 months, with the possibility of extension for a limited number of months.
Study Establishment: Universities or research institutions in Germany.
Country of Study: Germany.
Application Procedure: Application form must be completed (available from Bonn or Washington office); submit completed forms and application documents to Bonn office at least five months before selection committee meeting, during which the decision is to be made.
Closing Date: No specified deadline, applications can be accepted at any time.
Additional Information: Applications should be forwarded directly to the Foundation or through diplomatic or consular offices of the Federal Republic of Germany in the candidates' respective countries. The Foundation also offers up to 150 Feodor Lynen Research Fellowships to German postdoctoral researchers to foster co-operation with former Humboldt Fellows and Award-holders abroad.

Science and Technology Agency (STA) Research Fellowships

Subjects: All academic fields.
Eligibility: Open to German nationals only.
Level of Study: Postdoctorate.
Purpose: To enable highly-qualified German scholars up to the age of 38 to carry out research projects of their own choice at non-university research institutions in Japan.
Type: Fellowship.
No. of awards offered: 10.
Frequency: Annual.
Value: 270,000 Yen plus travel and housing allowance.
Length of Study: 6-24 months.
Study Establishment: Non-university research institution.
Country of Study: Japan.
Application Procedure: Application form must be completed.
Closing Date: February 15th, June 15th, October 15th.

ALL SAINTS EDUCATIONAL TRUST

St Katherine Cree Church
86 Leadenhall Street, London, EC3A 3DH, England
Tel: (44) 171 283 4485
Fax: (44) 171 283 2920
www: http://ats.edu/index.html
Contact: Mr Alfred W Bush, The Secretary

All Saints Educational Trust Corporate Awards

Subjects: Research in and the development of education, particularly religious education, home economics and kindred subjects, and multi-cultural and inter-faith education.
Purpose: To offer assistance to individuals and institutions within certain specified terms of reference.
Type: Award.
Length of Study: Not more than 5 years.
Application Procedure: Applications should be sent to the secretary of the Trust.
Closing Date: January 31st.

All Saints Educational Trust Personal Awards

Subjects: Religious education, home economics, multicultural education.
Eligibility: Open to individuals over 18 years of age who are, or intend to become, teachers. Grants for research are open to individuals. Study must take place in the United Kingdom.
Level of Study: Unrestricted.

Purpose: To enable persons who are, or intend to become teachers or to work in certain capacities associated with education in home economics and kindred subjects, and in religious subjects.
Type: Grant.
Frequency: Annual.
Value: Varies, but normally in the range of £500-£2,000.
Length of Study: 1-3 years.
Study Establishment: Recognised educational institutions in the United Kingdom.
Country of Study: United Kingdom.
Application Procedure: All applications must be submitted on forms available from the Secretary of the Trust.
Closing Date: January 31st.
Additional Information: Enquiries should not be delayed until the offer of a place on a course of study has been confirmed. Late applications cannot be considered.

AMERICA-ISRAEL CULTURAL FOUNDATION

32 Allenby Road, Tel Aviv, 63325, Israel
Tel: (972) 3 517 4177
Fax: (972) 3 517 8991
Email: aicf@netvision. net.il
www: http://aicf.webnet.org
Contact: Mr Benny Gal-Ed, General Director

The America-Israel Cultural Foundation began as the Norman Fund, music lovers who set out to rescue Jewish musicians from Europe, resettle them in Palestine and help establish a symphony orchestra. Through the hectic years that followed, the Fund supported more and more cultural institutions. In 1957, the Fund became the America-Israel Cultural Foundation with a new mission of supporting individual creative and performing artists.

Sharett Scholarship Program

Subjects: Performing arts, design, film and television.
Eligibility: Open to Israeli citizens only.
Level of Study: Unrestricted.
Purpose: To provide scholarships to students whose major field is one of the following: art & design, music, dance, theatre, film & TV - following annual auditions.
Type: Scholarship.
No. of awards offered: Approx. 500.
Frequency: Annual.
Value: US$750 - US$2,000.
Length of Study: Varies.
Country of Study: Any country.
Application Procedure: Application form must be completed and submitted with recommendations and pre-required repertoire. Application forms are available from February 1st of each year.
Closing Date: March 15th.
Additional Information: The Programme is revised on an annual basis. For more detailed information please contact the America-Israel Cultural Foundation after February 1st.

AMERICAN ACADEMY OF ARTS AND LETTERS

633 West 155th Street, New York, NY, 10032-7599, United States of America
Tel: (1) 212 368 5900
Fax: (1) 212 491 4615
Contact: Grants Management Officer

Richard Rodgers Awards for the Musical Theater

Subjects: Musical theater.
Eligibility: Open to US citizens or permanent residents.
Level of Study: Professional development.
Purpose: To encourage the development of the musical theater by subsidising productions and staged readings by a not-for-profit theater in New York City of a work by American composers and writers who are not already established in the field of musical theater.
Type: Subsidy.
No. of awards offered: Varies.
Value: Varies.
Country of Study: USA.
Application Procedure: A self-addressed stamped envelope should accompany requests for further information. Applications are available in the spring and composers/authors should send tapes and scripts with applications.
Closing Date: Usually November 1st.
Additional Information: Awards are given to professional level works. Musicals being entered should be ready for reading or production by a theatre company in New York City.

AMERICAN ACCORDION MUSICOLOGICAL SOCIETY

334 South Broadway, Pitman, NJ, 08071, United States of America
Tel: (1) 609 854 6628
Contact: Mr Stanley Darrow, Secretary

The Society sponsors an annual accordion festival which is held each March.

American Accordion Musicological Society Music Competition Contest

Subjects: Musical composition.
Eligibility: Open to any composer acquainted with the various types of accordion. There are no restrictions in regard to age or nationality.
Level of Study: Professional development.
Purpose: To encourage composers to write classical accordion music.
Type: Contest.
No. of awards offered: 4.
Frequency: Annual.

Value: Amateur Award of US$100 and Professional Award of US$500; paid in a lump sum.
Length of Study: Competition takes place the first weekend in March each year.
Country of Study: Any country.
Closing Date: September 30th.
Additional Information: Applicants competing for the Professional Award should have at least one composition already published.

AMERICAN ANTIQUARIAN SOCIETY (AAS)

185 Salisbury Street, Worcester, MA, 01609-1634, United States of America
Tel: (1) 508 755 5221
Fax: (1) 508 754 9069
Email: cfs@mwa.org
Contact: Mr John B Hench, Vice President for Academic and Public Programs

AAS American Society for Eighteenth-Century Studies Fellowships

Subjects: American eighteenth-century studies.
Eligibility: Open to suitably qualified scholars. Degree candidates are not eligible. Membership in ASECS is required upon taking up an award, but not for making an application.
Level of Study: Postdoctorate.
Type: Fellowship.
No. of awards offered: 1-2.
Frequency: Annual.
Value: US$950 per month.
Length of Study: 1-2 months.
Study Establishment: The Society's library in Worcester, Massachusetts.
Country of Study: USA.
Closing Date: January 15th.

AAS National Endowment for the Humanities Visiting Fellowships

Subjects: Early American history and culture.
Eligibility: Fellowships may not be awarded to degree candidates or for study leading to advanced degrees; nor may they be granted to foreign nationals unless they have been resident in the USA for at least three years immediately prior to receiving the award.
Level of Study: Postdoctorate.
Purpose: To make the Society's research facilities more readily available to qualified scholars.
Type: Fellowship.
No. of awards offered: 2+.
Frequency: Annual.
Value: The maximum available stipend is US$30,000.
Length of Study: 6-12 months, or 4-5 months.
Study Establishment: The Society's library in Worcester, Massachusetts.

Country of Study: USA.
Closing Date: January 15th.
Additional Information: Fellows may not accept teaching assignments or undertake any other major activities during the tenure of the award. Other major fellowships, except sabbaticals or grants from the Fellow's own institution, may not be held concurrently with a Fellowship.

AAS Northeast Modern Language Association Fellowship

Subjects: American literary studies.
Purpose: To support research in American Literary studies through 1876.
Type: Fellowship.
Value: $950 per month.
Length of Study: 1-3 months.
Application Procedure: Fellow's are selected on the basis of the applicant's scholarly qualifications, the scholarly significance or importance of the project, and the appropriateness of the proposed study to the Society's collections. Application packets providing full details about the fellowships, including certain restrictions that apply for some categories, must be requested before an application is made. Please email or phone with inquiries and requests for application materials.

Joyce A Tracy Fellowship

Subjects: Early American history and culture.
Level of Study: Doctorate, Postdoctorate.
Purpose: To support research on newspapers or magazines for projects using these resources as primary documentation.
Type: Fellowship.
No. of awards offered: 1.
Frequency: Annual.
Value: US$950 per month.
Length of Study: 1-2 months.
Study Establishment: The Society's library in Worcester, Massachusetts.
Country of Study: USA.
Application Procedure: Write for further information.
Closing Date: January 15th.

Kate B and Hall J Peterson Fellowships

Subjects: Early American history through 1876.
Eligibility: Open to individuals engaged in scholarly research and writing, including foreign nationals and persons at work on doctoral theses.
Level of Study: Doctorate, Postdoctorate.
Purpose: To enable persons who might not otherwise be able to do so, to travel to the Society in order to make use of its research facilities.
Type: Fellowship.
No. of awards offered: 6-10.
Frequency: Annual.
Value: US$950 per month.
Length of Study: 1-3 months.
Study Establishment: The Society.

Country of Study: USA.
Closing Date: January 15th.

Mellon Postdoctoral Research Fellowships

Subjects: All subjects.
Eligibility: Applicants selected on the basis of their scholarly qualifications, the scholarly significance to the project, and the appropriateness of the proposed study to the Society's collections.
Purpose: To provide support for residence in the Society's library.
Type: Fellowship.
Value: Maximum stipend $35,000.
Length of Study: An academic year - 9 or 10 months in residence at the Society's Library.
Application Procedure: Application packets providing full details about the fellowships, including certain restrictions that apply for some categories must be requested before an appliation is made. Please phone or email with enquiries and requests for application materials.

Stephen Botein Fellowship

Subjects: The history of the book in American culture.
Eligibility: Open to suitably qualified scholars.
Level of Study: Doctorate, Postdoctorate.
Type: Fellowship.
No. of awards offered: 1-2.
Frequency: Annual.
Value: US$950 per month.
Length of Study: Up to 2 months.
Study Establishment: The Society's library.
Country of Study: USA.
Closing Date: January 15th.

AMERICAN COUNCIL OF LEARNED SOCIETIES

228 East 45th Street, New York, NY, 10017, United States of America
Tel: (1) 212 697 1505 ext 136
Fax: (1) 212 949 8058
Email: grants@acls.org
www: http://www.acls.org
Contact: Grants Management Officer

Chinese Fellowships for Scholarly Development

Subjects: Social sciences and the humanities.
Eligibility: Open to Chinese scholars with the MA, PhD or equivalent.
Level of Study: Postgraduate.
Purpose: To support Chinese scholars undertaking research in the USA.
Type: Fellowship.
No. of awards offered: Varies.
Frequency: Annual.

Value: Varies.
Length of Study: 1 semester.
Study Establishment: Approved US universities or research institutions.
Country of Study: USA.
Application Procedure: Candidates must be nominated by the US host. Chinese scholars cannot apply directly, and scholars involved in a degree programme are not eligible.
Closing Date: October 31st.
Additional Information: This programme was formerly administered by the Washington office of the Committee on Scholarly Communication with China.

National Programme for Advanced Study and Research in China

Subjects: Social sciences and the humanities.
Eligibility: Scholars conducting research on China, who are US citizens or permanent residents of the US.
Level of Study: Doctorate, Postgraduate.
Purpose: The graduate programme and the research programme support individuals enrolled in a social sciences or humanities programmeme, to carry out research on China.
Type: Research Grant.
No. of awards offered: Varies.
Frequency: Annual.
Value: Not specified.
Length of Study: Eleven months for the Graduate Programme and from 4-12 months for the Research Programme.
Study Establishment: A Chinese university or research institute.
Country of Study: China.
Application Procedure: Please write for details.
Closing Date: The application deadline for both programmes is October 15th.
Additional Information: These programs were formerly administered by the Washington offfice of the Committee on Scholarly Communication with China.

AMERICAN HISTORICAL ASSOCIATION

400 A Street SE, Washington, DC, 20003, United States of America
Tel: (1) 202 544 2422
Fax: (1) 202 544 8307
Email: aha@theaha.org
www: http://www.theaha.org
Contact: Mr Andrew L Schulkin, Administrative Assistant

Albert J Beveridge Grant

Subjects: History of the Western hemisphere.
Eligibility: Open to AHA members only.
Level of Study: Doctorate, Postdoctorate, Postgraduate.
Purpose: To support research in the history of the Western hemisphere.

Type: Grant.
No. of awards offered: Varies.
Frequency: Annual.
Value: Not to exceed US$1,000.
Country of Study: Any country.
Application Procedure: Please contact the AHA for details.
Closing Date: February 1st.

Bernadotte E Schmitt Grants

Subjects: History of Europe, Asia and Africa.
Eligibility: Open to AHA members only.
Level of Study: Doctorate, Postdoctorate, Postgraduate.
Purpose: To support research in the history of Europe, Asia and Africa.
Type: Grant.
No. of awards offered: Varies.
Frequency: Annual.
Value: Up to US$1,000.
Country of Study: Any country.
Application Procedure: Contact the American Historical Association for details.
Closing Date: September 15th.

J Franklin Jameson Fellowship

Subjects: Research in the collections of the Library of Congress.
Eligibility: Open to suitably qualified applicants of any nationality.
Level of Study: Postdoctorate, Postgraduate.
Purpose: To support significant scholarly research, by young historians, in the collections of the Library of Congress.
Type: Fellowship.
No. of awards offered: 1.
Frequency: Annual.
Value: US$10,000.
Length of Study: 1 semester.
Country of Study: USA.
Application Procedure: Please contact the AHA for details.
Closing Date: February 1st.

Littleton-Griswold Research Grant

Subjects: American legal history, law and society.
Eligibility: Open to AHA members only.
Level of Study: Doctorate, Postdoctorate, Postgraduate.
Purpose: To support research in American legal history and the field of law and society.
Type: Research Grant.
No. of awards offered: Varies.
Frequency: Annual.
Value: Up to US$1,000.
Country of Study: Any country.
Application Procedure: Please contact the AHA for details.
Closing Date: February 1st.

AMERICAN INSTITUTE OF ARCHITECTS (AIA)

1735 New York Avenue NW, Washington, DC, 20006, United States of America
Tel: (1) 202 626 7300
Fax: (1) 202 626 7468
www: http://www.aiaonline.com
Contact: College of Fellows Grant Program Director

AIA College of Fellows Grant

Subjects: Architecture and town planning.
Eligibility: There are no restrictions on eligibility.
Level of Study: Unrestricted.
Purpose: To support architecturally related projects which advance the profession of architecture and promote the purposes of the AIA. To promote the public awareness of architecture and to provide programmes which advise and mentor young architects.
Type: Grant.
No. of awards offered: 1.
Frequency: Annual.
Value: US$5,000-US$10,000.
Length of Study: 1 year.
Country of Study: Any country.
Application Procedure: An application form must be completed; there is a processing fee of US$50. Please address all applications to the Director, College of Fellows Grant Program, the American Institute of Architects.
Closing Date: January.
Additional Information: Grantees are required to acknowledge the COF in publications and promotional materials.

The AIA/AAF Scholarship for Advanced Study and Research

Subjects: Architecture.
Eligibility: Applicants must have a professional degree in architecture.
Level of Study: Postgraduate.
Purpose: To support projects that advance the education of architects and the architecture profession.
Type: Scholarship.
No. of awards offered: Varies, up to 20.
Frequency: Annual.
Study Establishment: US university.
Country of Study: USA.
Application Procedure: Applicants must submit an application, transcripts, budget, letters of recommendation, and a project proposal. Please address all applications to The American Architectural Foundation, the American Institute of Architects.
Closing Date: February 15th.

AIA/AHA Graduate Fellowship in Health Facility Planning and Design

Subjects: Health facility planning and design.
Eligibility: The applicant must hold a degree from an accredited school of architecture, must be a citizen of the US, Canada or Mexico, and must be English speaking.
Level of Study: Postgraduate.
Purpose: To support architecture students pursuing education in the planning and design of health care facilities.
Type: Fellowship.
No. of awards offered: Multiple.
Frequency: Annual.
Value: A total amount of US$22,000 is currently available for the fellowship program.
Length of Study: Normally the fellowship period is limited to 1 year. An exception to this requirement may be granted in special cases.
Country of Study: USA.
Application Procedure: The application consists of: an application form, four letters of recommendation, completed "Deans Form", and official transcripts of academic work. Please address all applications to the Academy of Architecture for Health, the American Institute of Architects.
Closing Date: January 15th.
Additional Information: There are three options available for this program: graduate study, independent graduate-level or professional study, travel and study with in-residence research.

AMERICAN INSTITUTE OF INDIAN STUDIES (AIIS)

1130 E 59th Street, Chicago, IL, 60637, United States of America
Tel: (1) 773 702 8638
Fax: (1) 773 702 6636
Email: aiis@uchicago.edu
www: http://www.kaldarshan.arts.ohio-state.edu/aiis/aiishomepage.htm
Contact: The Fellowships Officer

The AIIS is a consortium of American colleges and universities that supports the understanding of India, its people, and cultures. AIIS offers a range of fellowships for research in India. It also supports individuals studying the performing arts, operates language programs in India, and offers research facilities to scholars in India.

AIIS Senior Performing and Creative Arts Fellowships

Subjects: Performing and creative arts.
Eligibility: Open to accomplished practitioners of the performing arts of India and creative artists who demonstrate that study in India would enhance their skills, develop their capabilities to teach or perform in the USA, enhance American involvement with India's artistic traditions, and strengthen their links with peers in India.

Level of Study: Unrestricted.
Type: Fellowship.
Frequency: Annual.
Country of Study: India.
Application Procedure: Please write for further information.
Closing Date: July 1st.

AMERICAN MUSIC CENTER, INC.

30 West 26th Street
Suite 1001, New York, NY, 10010-2011, United States of America
Tel: (1) 212 366 5260
Fax: (1) 212 366 5265
Email: center@amc.net
www: http://www.amc.net
Contact: Ms Lisa Kang, Grants Manager

The American Music Center is a non-profit organisation dedicated to the building of a community for new American concert music and jazz.

Margaret Fairbank Jory Copying Assistance Program

Subjects: Musical composition.
Eligibility: Open to American composers/members of the American Music Center. Funds are available for copying parts for the première performance of large-scale works for four or more instrumental and/or vocal parts. The composer must have a written commitment for at least one public performance of the work by a professional ensemble of recognised artistic merit.
Level of Study: Professional development.
Purpose: To assist composers with copying expenses for a première performance.
Type: Grant.
No. of awards offered: Approx. 75.
Frequency: Three times each year.
Country of Study: Any country.
Application Procedure: An application form must be completed and submitted with supporting materials.
Closing Date: February 1st, May 1st, October 1st.

AMERICAN MUSICOLOGICAL SOCIETY

Department of Music
201 S 34th Street, Philadelphia, PA, 19104-6313, United States of America
Tel: (1) 215 898 8698
Fax: (1) 215 573 3673
Email: ams@sas.upenn
www: http://musdra.ucdavis.edu/document/ams/ams.html/
Contact: Mr Robert Judd, Executive Director

The American Musicological Society was founded in 1934 as a non-profit organisation, with the aim of advancing research in the various fields of music as a branch of learning and scholarship. In 1951 the Society became a constituent member of the American Council of Learned Societies.

Alfred Einstein Award

Subjects: Musicology.
Eligibility: Open to citizens or permanent residents of Canada or the United States.
Level of Study: Professional development.
Purpose: To honour a musicological article of exceptional merit by a scholar in the early stages of his or her career.
Type: Award.
No. of awards offered: 1.
Value: US$400 and a certificate.
Application Procedure: The committee will entertain articles from any individual, including eligible authors who are encouraged to nominate their own articles. Nominations should include the name of the author, the title of the article, and the name and year of the periodical or other collection in which it was published. A CV will also be required.
Closing Date: June 1st.

For further information contact:

Department of Music
Yale University
Box 4030, New Haven, CT, 06520-4030, United States of America
Contact: Mr Robert P Morgan, Chair

AMS 50 Dissertation Fellowship

Subjects: Any field of musical research.
Eligibility: Open to full-time students registered for a doctorate at a North American university, in good standing, who have completed all formal degree requirements except the dissertation at the time of full application. Open to all students without regard to nationality, race, religion or gender.
Level of Study: Doctorate, Postgraduate.
Purpose: To encourage research in the various fields of music as a branch of learning and scholarship.
Type: Fellowship.
No. of awards offered: Varies.
Frequency: Annual.
Value: US$12,000.
Country of Study: USA or Canada.
Application Procedure: Preliminary application forms will be sent via the Directors of Graduate Study at all doctorate granting institutions in North America; they will also be available directly from the Society. Applications should include a CV, certification of enrolment and degree completed, and two supporting letters from faculty members, one of whom is the principal adviser of the dissertation. A detailed dissertation prospectus and a completed chapter or comparable written work on the dissertation should accompany the full application. All documents should be submitted in triplicate.
Closing Date: January 15th or October 15th (these dates may change so please check before applying).

Additional Information: Any submission for a doctoral degree in which the emphasis is on musical scholarship is eligible. The award is not intended for support of early stages of research; it is expected that a recipient's dissertation will be completed within the fellowship year. An equivalent major award from another source may not normally be held concurrently unless the AMS award is accepted on an honorary basis.

For further information contact:

University of Iowa, Iowa City, IA, 52242, United States of America
Contact: Mr Thomas Christensen, AMS 50 Chair
or
201 South 34th Street, Philadelphia, PA, 19104, United States of America
Contact: Grants Management Officer

The Howard Mayer Brown Fellowship

Subjects: Musicology.
Eligibility: Candidates must have completed at least one year of academic work at an institution with a graduate programme in musicology and who intends to complete a PhD in the field. There are no restrictions on age or sex.
Level of Study: Postgraduate.
Purpose: The fellowship is intended to increase the presence of minority scholars and teachers in musicology.
Type: Fellowship.
Frequency: Every two years.
Value: US$12,000.
Length of Study: 1 year.
Study Establishment: An institution which has a graduate programme in musicology.
Country of Study: USA or Canada.
Application Procedure: Nominations may come from a faculty member of the institution at which the student is enrolled, from a member of the AMS at another institution or directly from the student. Supporting documents should include: a letter summarising academic background, letters of support from three faculty members, and samples of the applicants work, such as term papers or any published material.
Closing Date: April 1st of the year in which the fellowship is awarded.
Additional Information: The AMS encourages the institution at which the recipient is pursuing his or her degree to offer continuing financial support.

For further information contact:

University of California
Irvine
School of the Arts
Music Department, Irvine, CA, 92697-2775, United States of America
Contact: Ms Rae Linda Brown, The Chair of the Committee

The Noah Greenberg Award

Subjects: Musicology.
Eligibility: Both scholars and performers may apply. Applicants need not be members of the Society.
Level of Study: Professional development.
Purpose: The Award is intended as a grant-in-aid to stimulate active co-operation between scholars and performers by recognising and fostering outstanding contributions to historical performing practices.
Type: Award.
No. of awards offered: 1-2.
Frequency: Annual.
Value: US$2,000.
Application Procedure: The applicant must submit in triplicate, a description of the project, a detailed budget, and supporting materials such as articles or tapes of performances which are relevant to the project. Applications must be sent to the Chair of the Noah Greenberg Award Committee.
Closing Date: School of Music.

For further information contact:

School of Music
University of Minnesota
2106 Fourth Street South, Minneapolis, MN, 55455, United States of America
Tel: (1) 612 624 5093
Contact: Professor Vern Sutton, Chair

The Otto Kinkeldey Award

Subjects: Musicology.
Eligibility: The work must be published during the previous year in any language and in any country by a scholar who is a citizen or permanent resident of Canada or the United States.
Level of Study: Professional development.
Purpose: To award the work of musicological scholarship such as a major book, edition, or other piece of scholarship that best exemplifies the highest quality of orginality, interpretation, logic and clarity of thought and communication.
Type: Award.
Value: US$400 and a certificate.
Application Procedure: Nominations, including self-nominations, and submissions are not requested for this Award. Please write for details.

For further information contact:

Washington University Campus
Campus Box 1032, St Louis, MO, 63130-4899, United States of America
Contact: Mr Craig A Monson, Committee Chair

The Paul A Pisk Prize

Subjects: Any field of musicology.
Eligibility: Open to graduate students whose abstracts have been submitted to the Programme Committee of the Society and papers accepted for inclusion in the Annual Meeting. Open to all students without regard to nationality, race, religion, or gender.
Level of Study: Postgraduate.
Purpose: To encourage scholarship by graduate students in musicology.
Type: Prize.
No. of awards offered: 1.
Frequency: Annual.
Value: US$1,000.
Country of Study: USA or Canada.
Application Procedure: Applicants should submit 5 copies of the complete text paper to the Chair of the Pisk Prize Committee. The submission must be accompanied by a statement from the students academic adviser affirming graduate student status as of the applicant.

For further information contact:

School of Fine Arts
Department of Music
University of Wisconsin
Milwaukee
Box 413, Milwaukee, WI, 53201-0413, United States of America
Contact: Mr Mitchell P Brauner, Chair

The Philip Brett Award

Subjects: Musicology.
Eligibility: Work must be completed during the previous two academic years (ending June 30th), in any country and in any language.
Purpose: To honour an exceptional musicological work such as, a published article, book, edition, annotated translation, a paper read at a conference, and teaching materials in the field of gay, lesbian, bisexual, transgender/transsexual studies.
Type: Award.
Value: $500 and a certificate.
Country of Study: Any country.
Application Procedure: Nominations are accepted from any individual and should include five copies of the following information: the name of the scholar, a description of the work and a statement to the effect that the work was completed during the previous two academic years.
Closing Date: July 1st.

For further information contact:

Department of Music
Hamilton College, Clinton, NY, 13323-1295, United States of America
Contact: Ms Lydia Hamessley, Chair of the Award Committee

AMERICAN NUMISMATIC SOCIETY (ANS)

Broadway at 155th Street, New York, NY, 10032, United States of America
Tel: (1) 212 234 3130
Fax: (1) 212 234 3381
Email: info@amnumsoc.org
www: http://www.amnumsoc2.org
Contact: Chief Curator

The mission of the American Numismatic Society is to be the pre-eminent national institution advancing the study and appreciation of coins, medals and related objects of all cultures as historical and artistic documents by, maintaining the foremost numismatic collection and library, supporting scholarly research and publications, and sponsoring educational and interpretative programmes for diverse audiences.

ANS Fellowship in Roman Studies

Subjects: Ancient Civilisations.
Eligibility: Applicants must be American citizens affiliated with a North American institution of higher learning and must demonstrate academic competence and submit a detailed proposal of their work. There is no minimum age or degree requirement, but it is expected that the work proposed will lead to publication and teaching. The work undertaken may or may not be in pusuit of a higher degree, but preference will be given to those seeking advanced degrees.
Level of Study: Unrestricted.
Purpose: To promote the use of the ANS collection and library in connection with studies of the Roman world.
Type: Fellowship.
No. of awards offered: 1.
Frequency: Annual.
Value: Up to US$5,000.
Length of Study: 1 year.
Country of Study: USA.
Application Procedure: Application form and references are required.
Closing Date: March 1st.
Additional Information: email: metcalf@amnumsoc.org.

AMERICAN ORIENTAL SOCIETY

Hatcher Graduate Library
University of Michigan, Ann Arbor, MI, 48109-1205, United States of America
Tel: (1) 734 747 4760
Email: sleemart@umich.edu
www: http://www.umich.edu/~jrodgers/
Contact: Grants Management Officer

The American Oriental Society is primarily concerned with the encouragement of basic research in the languages and literatures of Asia.

Louise Wallace Hackney Fellowship

Subjects: Chinese art, with special relation to painting, and the translation into English of works on the subject.
Eligibility: Open to US citizens who are doctoral or postdoctoral students and have successfully completed at least three years of Chinese language study at a recognised university, and have some knowledge or training in art.
Level of Study: Doctorate, Postdoctorate.
Purpose: To remind scholars that Chinese art, like all art, is not a disembodied creation, but the outgrowth of the life and culture from which it has sprung. It is requested that scholars give special attention to this approach in their study.
Type: Fellowship.
No. of awards offered: 1.
Frequency: Annual.
Value: US$8,000.
Length of Study: 1 year.
Study Establishment: Any institution where paintings and adequate language guidance are available.
Country of Study: Any country.
Application Procedure: All applicants should submit the following materials in duplicate: a transcript of their undergraduate and graduate coursework; a statement of personal finances; a four page summary of the proposed project to be undertaken including details of expense; and no less than three letters of recommendation.
Closing Date: March 1st.
Additional Information: In no case shall a Fellowship be awarded to scholars of well recognised standing, but shall be given to either men or women who show aptitude or promise in the said field of learning. It is possible to apply for a renewal of the Fellowship, but it may not be done in consecutive years.

AMERICAN PHILOSOPHICAL ASSOCIATION

University of Delaware, Newark, DE, 19716, United States of America
Tel: (1) 302 831 1112
Fax: (1) 302 831 8690
www: http://www.udel.edu/apa
Contact: Ms Leslie Walsh, Assistant to the Director

The American Philosophical Association was founded in 1900 to promote the exchange of ideas among philosophers; to encourage creative and scholarly activity in philosophy; to facilitate the professional work and teaching of philosophers; and to represent philosophy as a discipline.

APA Book and Article Prizes

Subjects: Philosophy.
Purpose: To award a book prize and an article prize awarded in alternating years.
Type: Prize.
No. of awards offered: 1.
Frequency: Annual.

Value: Book Prize US$4,000; Article Prize US$2,000.
Application Procedure: Please write for more information or contact our website.
Additional Information: Awarded with the help of the Matchette Foundation and private contributions.

Baumgardt Memorial Lecture

Subjects: Philosophy.
Eligibility: Open to candidates of any nationality, working in any country, whose work has some bearing on the philosophical interests of the late David Baumgardt.
Level of Study: Postgraduate.
No. of awards offered: 1.
Frequency: Every five years.
Value: US$5,000.
Country of Study: Any country.
Application Procedure: Please write for details or visit our website.

Edinburgh Fellowship

Subjects: Philosophy.
Eligibility: Open to suitably qualified scholars of any nationality.
Level of Study: Postgraduate.
Type: Fellowship.
No. of awards offered: 1.
Frequency: Annual.
Value: To cover the cost of a study and secretarial support.
Length of Study: 3-5 months.
Study Establishment: Institute for Advanced Studies in the Humanities, University of Edinburgh, Scotland.
Country of Study: Scotland.
Application Procedure: Please write for details or visit our website.

Frank Chapman Sharp Memorial Prize

Subjects: The philosophy of war and peace.
Eligibility: Open to writers of unpublished essays or monographs on the philosophy of war and peace.
Level of Study: Postgraduate.
Purpose: To recognise unpublished work in philosophy.
No. of awards offered: 1.
Frequency: Every two years (odd-numbered years).
Value: US$1,500.
Country of Study: Any country.
Application Procedure: Please write for details or visit our website.

Rockefeller Prize

Subjects: Philosophy.
Eligibility: Open to non-academically affiliated philosophers.
Level of Study: Postgraduate.
Purpose: To recognise unpublished work in philosophy by non-academically affiliated philosophers.
No. of awards offered: 1.
Frequency: Every two years.

Value: US$1,000.
Country of Study: Any country.
Application Procedure: Please write for details or visit our website.
Additional Information: The prize is funded by the Rockefeller Foundation.

AMERICAN PHILOSOPHICAL SOCIETY

104 S Fifth Street, Philadelphia, PA, 19106-3387, United States of America
www: http://www.amphilsoc.org
Contact: Committee on Research

General Research Grant Program

Subjects: Scholarly research.
Eligibility: Applicants are normally expected to have a doctorate, but applications are considered from persons whose publications display equivalent scholarly achievement. Grants are rarely made to persons who have held the doctorate less than a year, and never for predoctoral study or research. It is the Society's long-standing practice to encourage younger scholars. The Committee will seldom approve more than two grants to the same person within any five-year period. Applicants may be residents of the United States, American citizens on the staffs of foreign institutions, and foreign nationals whose research can only be carried out in the United States. Institutions are not eligible to apply. Applicants expecting to conduct interviews in a foreign language must possess sufficient competence in that language, and be able to read and translate all source materials.
Purpose: To contribute towards the cost of scholarly research in all areas of knowledge except those in which support by government or corporate enterprise is more appropriate. Scholarly research, as the term is used here, covers most kinds of scholarly inquiry by individuals leading to publication. It does not include journalistic or other writing for general readership; the preparation of textbooks, casebooks, anthologies, or other materials for use by students; or the work of creative and performing artists.
Type: Grant.
Value: The maximum grant is US$6,000. If an applicant receives an award for the same project from another granting institution, the Society will consider limiting its award to costs that are not covered by the other grant. Eligible expenses include living costs while away from home (lodging, meals and local transportation) up to a maximum of US$65 per day. Costs may exceed this amount, but the request to the Society must stay within these guidelines. Microfilms, photo-reproductions which will enable the work to be done more efficiently. The Society may request that such reproductions be deposited in an appropriate institution when the research is complete. Consumable supplies, not normally available at the applicant's institution (for proposals in the natural sciences; see section E for non-eligible items). Necessary

foreign and domestic travel at the lowest available rate, to a research site distant from the applicant's place of residence by more than 75 miles. US$0.25 per mile is allowed for fuel. Non-eligible expenses: the Society offers no funds for conference support, scholarships, financial aid for study, work already done, or costs of publication. The Society does not make grants to replace salary during a leave of absence, or earnings from summer teaching, pay living expenses at current place of residence, pay costs of travel to conferences, workshops or study groups, or to take up a visiting position, whether in the United States or abroad, pay consultant fees, or the cost of trips to consult with other scholars, pay for typing, secretarial services or office supplies (e.g. notebooks, computer diskettes, stationery, etc), telephone, fax charges, postage, purchase permanent equipment, such as books, cameras, laboratory apparatus, tape recorders, etc, pay research assistants, translators, or for transcription or encoding assistance, pay overhead or indirect costs to any institution.

Application Procedure: Requests for application forms must indicate eligibility of both applicant and project; state the nature of the research (e.g. laboratory, archival, fieldwork) and proposed use of the grant (e.g. travel, purchase of microfilm, etc). Foreign nationals must specify the objects of their research, only available in the United States (e.g. indigenous plants, archival materials, architectural sites, etc.). Include a self-addressed mailing label. If forms are downloaded from the website, please verify that page-format is maintained; be sure to print enough copies of the form for the letters of support.

Closing Date: October 1st for a January decision; December 1st for a March decision; October 1st for a January decision; December 1st for a March decision; March 1st for a June decision.

Additional Information: If an award is made and accepted, the recipient is required to provide the Society with a 250-word report on the research accomplished during tenure of the grant, and a one-page financial statement.

Phillips Fund Grants for North Native American Research

Subjects: Linguistics and ethnohistory.
Eligibility: Applicants may be graduate students who have passed their qualifying examinations for either the Master's or Doctorate degrees. Postdoctoral applicants are eligible.
Purpose: For research in North Native American linguistics and ethno-history, i.e. the continental United States and Canada.
Value: The average award is about US$1,200; grants rarely exceed US$1,500. Covers travel, tapes, and informants' fees; not for general maintenance or the purchase of permanent equipment.
Length of Study: Ordinarily given for 1 year.
Application Procedure: Applications are due no later than March 1st. A complete application includes all information requested on the form, in the correct number of copies, and three confidential letters supporting the application. It is the applicant's responsibility to verify that all materials reached the Society on time. Requests for forms must indicate eligibility of both applicant and project; and state whether the field of research is linguistics or ethnohistory. Include a self-addressed mailing label. Applications should be addressed to Phillips Fund for Native American Research at the main address.
Closing Date: March 1st.
Additional Information: If an award is made and accepted, the recipient is required to provide the American Philosophical Society Library with a brief formal report and copies of any tape recordings, transcriptions, microfilms, etc, which may be acquired in the process of the grant-funded research.

Sabbatical Award for the Humanities and Social Sciences

Subjects: Humanities and social sciences.
Eligibility: The Sabbatical Fellowship is open to mid-career faculty of universities and 4-year colleges in the United States who have been granted a sabbatical/research year, but for whom financial support from the parent institution is available for only the first half of the year. Candidates must not have had a financially supported leave during the past three years. At the discretion of the review panels, the fellowship may be used to supplement another external award of similar purpose. The total external support cannot exceed the half-year salary. The Society encourages candidates to use the resources of the American Philosophical Society Library, but this is not a requirement of the fellowship. There is no restriction on where the Fellow resides during the fellowship year, but an indication of the appropriateness of the available library resources should be given.
Purpose: To support the second half of an awarded sabbatical year.
Type: Award.
Frequency: Annual.
Value: The Sabbatical Fellowship carries a stipend of US$30,000.
Length of Study: Tenure of the fellowship is for the second half of the academic year.
Application Procedure: Applications consist of eight collated sets of the following: cover sheet, giving the following information: name of applicant in full, last name in capital letters, mailing address, telephone numbers, email address, date and place of birth, title of project, indication choice of review panel, humanities or social sciences, name, address, and telephone number of three persons who will write letters of support, not more than one from the parent institution; letter from a university official, approving leave for sabbatical/research year, statement of the project, giving work accomplished to date, sources used or to be examined, methodology and interpretive framework, and stating how the work will increase or modify current knowledge of the subject; explain why a full year of leave will represent a major scholarly advantage. The statement must not exceed 4 double-spaced typed pages (1000 words). Type name, date, and title of project at the top of the first page, and last name in capital letters in upper left corner of each page. Applicant's

curriculum vitae and list of publications; indicate with an asterisk the publications which are particularly significant to the present proposal; include reprints of articles so designated. Three letters of support, to be sent separately by the referees, postmarked no later than December 15th.
Closing Date: December 15th.

AMERICAN RESEARCH INSTITUTE IN TURKEY (ARIT)

c/o University Museum
33rd and Spruce Streets, Philadelphia, PA, 19104-6324,
United States of America
Tel: (1) 215 898 3474
Fax: (1) 215 898 0657
Email: leinwand@sas.upenn.edu
www: http://mec.sas.upenn.edu/arit
Contact: Ms Nancy Leinwand

ARIT's main aim is to support scholarly research in all fields of the humanities and social sciences in Turkey through administering fellowship programs at the doctoral and postdoctoral level, and through maintaining research centres in Ankara and Istanbul.

ARIT Humanities and Social Science Fellowships

Subjects: All fields of the humanities and social sciences.
Eligibility: Open to US citizens and permanent residents, or others, affiliated with US or Canadian institutions of higher learning.
Level of Study: Doctorate, Postdoctorate.
Purpose: To encourage research in Turkey in ancient, medieval and modern times.
Type: Fellowship.
No. of awards offered: 6-12.
Frequency: Annual.
Value: Varies; dependent on the length of the study period.
Length of Study: 2-12 months; renewable only in exceptional cases.
Study Establishment: ARIT maintains two research establishments in Ankara and Istanbul, Turkey.
Country of Study: Turkey.
Application Procedure: Application form, transcript (where relevant), references, and project statement must be submitted.
Closing Date: November 15th.

ARIT Language Fellowships

Subjects: (Spoken) Turkish language.
Eligibility: Open to graduate students enrolled in, a degree programme of Turkish or related language and area studies. Applicants must be US citizens or permanent residents and have at least two years of college level Turkish language study or its equivalent.
Level of Study: Postgraduate.

Purpose: To provide students with the opportunity of studying Turkish language at all levels.
Type: Fellowship.
No. of awards offered: 10-15.
Frequency: Annual.
Value: Tuition, travel and a maintenance stipend of varying amounts.
Length of Study: 8 weeks during July and August, plus additional travel time.
Study Establishment: Bosphorus University, Istanbul.
Country of Study: Turkey.
Application Procedure: Application form, statement, references and exam must be submitted.
Closing Date: February 15th.

For further information contact:

ARIT Summer Fellowship Program
Center for the Study of Islamic Societies and Civilizations
Washington University
Campus Box 1230
One Brookings Drive, St Louis, MO, 63130-4899, United States of America
Tel: (1) 314 935 5166
Fax: (1) 314 935 7462
Contact: Ms Iris Wright

ARIT/NEH Fellowships for the Humanities in Turkey

Subjects: All subjects of the humanities and interdisciplinary approaches - art, archaeology, language, history, etc.
Eligibility: Open to US citizens or permanent residents who have completed a doctoral degree. Independent scholars are considered.
Level of Study: Postdoctorate.
Purpose: To fund research in all fields of the humanities in Turkey; to support longer-term projects by scholars in the early years of their careers.
Type: Fellowship.
No. of awards offered: 2-4.
Frequency: Annually, dependent on funds available.
Value: Salary replacement of up to US$30,000 for 12 months.
Length of Study: 4-12 months.
Study Establishment: ARIT maintains two research institutes in Turkey: ARIT-Istanbul and ARIT-Ankara.
Country of Study: Turkey.
Application Procedure: Application form, project statement and references must be submitted.
Closing Date: November 15th.

Kress/ARIT Graduate Fellowship

Subjects: Art history, archaeology.
Eligibility: Doctoral candidates affiliated with US or Canadian institutions.
Level of Study: Doctorate.
Purpose: To fund doctoral dissertation research in Turkey in the fields of art history and archaeology.
Type: Fellowship.
No. of awards offered: 2-4.

Frequency: Annual, if funds are available.
Value: US$3,500-US$13,500.
Length of Study: 4-12 months.
Study Establishment: ARIT centres in Ankara and Istanbul.
Country of Study: Turkey.
Application Procedure: An application form must be submitted, accompanied by three letters of recommendation.
Closing Date: November 15th.

Mellon Research Fellowship

Subjects: Humanities and social sciences.
Eligibility: Open to Bulgarian, Czech, Slovak, Polish, Hungarian, and Romanian nationals residing in same countries.
Level of Study: Postdoctorate.
Purpose: To bring east-central European scholars to Turkey to carry out research in humanities and social sciences.
Type: Fellowship.
No. of awards offered: 3-4.
Frequency: Annual, if funds are available.
Value: Up to US$10,500.
Length of Study: 2-3 months.
Study Establishment: ARIT maintains two research centres in Istanbul and Ankara,Turkey.
Country of Study: Turkey.
Application Procedure: Application form, project statement, and references must be submitted.
Closing Date: March 5th.

AMERICAN SCHOOL OF CLASSICAL STUDIES AT ATHENS (ASCSA)

6-8 Charlton Street, Princeton, NJ, 08540, United States of America
Tel: (1) 609 683 0800
Fax: (1) 609 924 0578
Email: ascsa@ascsa.org
www: http://www.ascsa.org
Contact: Committee on Admission and Fellowship

Established in 1881, the American School of Classical Studies at Athens offers both graduate students and scholars the opportunity to study Greek civilisation at first hand, in Greece. The ASCSA supports and encourages the teaching of archaeology, art, history, language, and the literature of Greece from early times to the present.

ASCSA Fellowships

Subjects: Classical philology and archaeology, post-classical Greek studies or a related field.
Eligibility: Open to students at colleges or universities in the US or Canada who have a BA but not a PhD, and who are preparing for an advanced degree in classical studies or a related field.
Level of Study: Postgraduate.

Type: Fellowship.
No. of awards offered: 7.
Frequency: Annual.
Value: US$7,840 stipend plus fees, room and partial board.
Length of Study: 1 academic year.
Study Establishment: American School of Classical Studies at Athens.
Country of Study: Greece.
Application Procedure: Applications are judged on the basis of credentials and competitive examinations in Greek language, history and archaeology. Fulbright Fellowships are also sometimes available for work at the School. Application to the School must be made simultaneously with the application for a Fulbright grant. Two Fellowships may not be held concurrently.
Closing Date: January 5th.

ASCSA Research Fellow in Faunal Studies

Subjects: Biological and life sciences, archaeological sciences.
Eligibility: Please write for details.
Level of Study: Doctorate, Postdoctorate, Postgraduate.
Purpose: To study faunal remains from archaeological contexts in Greece.
Type: Fellowship.
No. of awards offered: 1.
Frequency: Annual.
Value: Stipend of US$13,000 to US$25,000, depending on seniority and experience.
Length of Study: 1 academic year.
Study Establishment: The Malcolm H Wiener Research Laboratory for Archaeological Scienceat the American School of Classical Studies at Athens.
Country of Study: Greece.
Application Procedure: A detailed (under three pages) project submission to include: aim, scope and significance of the project; timetable including publication schedule; methodology to be used; project bibliography; copies of permits to study proposed material; and a CV and two letters of recommendation must be submitted to the office.
Closing Date: February 5th.

ASCSA Research Fellow in Geoarchaeology

Subjects: Earth and geological sciences, archaeological sciences.
Eligibility: Please write for details.
Level of Study: Doctorate, Postdoctorate, Postgraduate.
Purpose: To support research on a geo-archaeological topic in Greece.
Type: Fellowship.
No. of awards offered: 1.
Frequency: Annual.
Value: Stipend of US$13,000 to US$25,000 depending on seniority and experience.
Length of Study: 1 academic year.
Study Establishment: The Malcolm H. Wiener Laboratory at the American School of Classical Studies at Athens.
Country of Study: Greece.

Application Procedure: A detailed project submission, CV and two letters of recommendation must be submitted to the office. These can be obtained by writing or contacting in the website.
Closing Date: February 5th.

ASCSA Summer Sessions

Subjects: Archaeology, with emphasis on the topography and antiquities of Greece.
Eligibility: Open to graduate and advanced undergraduate students and high school and college teachers.
Level of Study: Postgraduate, Undergraduate.
Purpose: Designed for those who wish to become acquainted with Greece and its antiques in a limited time, and to improve their understanding of the relationship between the country (its monuments, landscape and climate) and its history, literature and culture.
Type: Scholarship.
No. of awards offered: 5.
Frequency: Annual.
Value: To cover tuition, room and partial board (US$2,950).
Length of Study: 6 weeks.
Study Establishment: At one of the two Summer Sessions of the School in Athens.
Country of Study: Greece.
Application Procedure: Please submit application form, transcripts, and letters of recommendation.
Closing Date: February 15th.
Additional Information: Applications should be made to the Committee on the Summer Sessions.

J Lawrence Angel Fellowship in Human Skeletal Studies

Subjects: Biological and life sciences, archaeological sciences.
Eligibility: Please write for details.
Level of Study: Doctorate, Postdoctorate, Postgraduate.
Purpose: To study human skeletal remains from archaeological contexts in Greece.
Type: Fellowship.
No. of awards offered: 1.
Frequency: Annual.
Value: Stipend of US$13,000 to US$25,000 depending on seniority and experience.
Length of Study: 1 academic year.
Study Establishment: The Malcolm H Wiener Laboratory at the American School of Classical Studies at Athens.
Country of Study: Greece.
Application Procedure: A detailed project submission, CV and two letters of recommendation must be submitted. These can be obtained by writing, or visiting the School's website.
Closing Date: February 5th.
Additional Information: Enquiries can be directed to: The Malcolm H. Wiener Laboratory, American School of Classical Studies at Athens, 54 Souidias Street, Athens GR 106-76, Greece. Tel: 30 1 723 63 13, Fax: 30 1 729 4047.

Jacob Hirsh Fellowship

Subjects: Pre-classical, classical, or post-classical archaeology.
Eligibility: Open to graduate students of US or Israeli institutions writing a dissertation, or to recent PhD graduates completing a project, such as a dissertation for publication. Applications will be judged on the basis of appropriate credentials, including referees.
Level of Study: Postdoctorate, Postgraduate.
Type: Fellowship.
No. of awards offered: 1.
Frequency: Annual.
Value: US$7,840 stipend plus room and partial board.
Length of Study: 1 academic year; not renewable.
Study Establishment: American School of Classical Studies at Athens.
Country of Study: Greece.
Application Procedure: Please submit three letters of recommendation, transcripts, and detailed description of project to be pursued in Greece. Candidate must apply for membership at the school simultaneously with application for the Hirsch.
Closing Date: January 31st.

M Alison Frantz Fellowship in Post-Classical Studies at The Gennadius Library (formerly known as the Gennadeion Fellowship)

Subjects: Post-classical studies in late antiquity, Byzantine studies, post-Byzantine studies, modern Greek studies.
Eligibility: Open to PhD candidates or recent PhDs from a US or Canadian institution. Candidates must show a need to use the Gennadius Library.
Level of Study: Doctorate, Postdoctorate.
Type: Fellowship.
No. of awards offered: 1.
Frequency: Annual.
Value: US$7,840 stipend plus fees, room and partial board.
Length of Study: 1 academic year.
Study Establishment: The American School of Classical Studies at Athens, Gennadius Library.
Country of Study: Greece.
Application Procedure: Please submit CV, project description, and two letters of support.
Closing Date: January 31st.

NEH Senior Research Fellowship

Subjects: Ancient, classical, and post-classical studies, including but not limited to, history, philosophy, language, art and archaeology of Greece and the Greek World, art history, literature, philology, architecture, archaeology, anthropology, metallurgy, and environmental studies, from pre-historic times to present.
Eligibility: Open to postdoctoral scholars who are US Citizens or foreign nationals who have lived in the US for the three years immediately preceeding the application deadline.
Level of Study: Postdoctorate.
Type: Fellowship.
No. of awards offered: 1.

Frequency: Annual.
Value: Stipend of no more than US$30,000.
Length of Study: 1 academic year.
Study Establishment: American School of Classical Studies at Athens.
Country of Study: Greece.
Application Procedure: Please write for details or visit our website at http://www.asca.org.
Closing Date: November 15th.

Samuel H Kress Fellowship in Classical Art History

Subjects: Classical art history.
Eligibility: Open to students from US or Canadian institutions who have completed one year at the school.
Level of Study: Postgraduate.
Type: Fellowship.
No. of awards offered: 1.
Frequency: Annual.
Value: Varies.
Length of Study: 1 academic year.
Study Establishment: The American School of Classical Studies in Athens.
Country of Study: Greece.
Application Procedure: Please write to the director of the school in Athens for further information.
Closing Date: March 1st.

For further information contact:

54 Soudias Street, Athens, 106 76, Greece
Contact: Director of the School

Samuel H Kress Joint Athens-Jerusalem Fellowship

Subjects: Classical studies, or ancient or post-classical art history, architecture and archaeology.
Eligibility: Open to any nationality yet they must be at a college or university in the US or Canada.
Level of Study: Postgraduate.
Purpose: To enable doctoral students to do research in Greece and Israel in the same academic year and to promote better understanding of inter-relationships between the cultures, languages, literature, and history of the Aegean and the Near East.
Type: Fellowship.
No. of awards offered: 1.
Frequency: Annual.
Value: Stipend of US$5,500 and room and partial board at each of the two institutions.
Length of Study: 1 academic year.
Study Establishment: American School of Classical Studies at Athens and the W.F. Albright Institute of Archaeological Research, Jerusalem.
Country of Study: Greece or Israel.
Application Procedure: Please write for details.
Closing Date: October 30th.

For further information contact:

Albright Institute
c/o American Schools of Oriental Research
656 Beacon
5th Floor, Boston, MA, 02215, United States of America
Tel: (1) 617 353 6570
Fax: (1) 617 353 6575

AMERICAN SCHOOLS OF ORIENTAL RESEARCH (ASOR)

656 Beacon Street
5th Floor, Boston, MA, 02215-2010, United States of America
Tel: (1) 617 353 6570
Fax: (1) 617 353 6575
Email: asor@bu.edu
www: http://www.asor.org
Contact: Director

AIAR Annual Professorship

Subjects: Near Eastern archaeology, geography, history and Biblical studies.
Eligibility: Open to qualified applicants of any nationality.
Level of Study: Postdoctorate.
Purpose: To support studies in Near Eastern archaeology, geography, history and biblical studies.
Type: Professorship.
No. of awards offered: 1.
Frequency: Annual.
Value: US$10,000 plus US$13,000 for room and half-board for appointee and spouse at the Institute (additional funding may be available via USIA for an appointee who is a US citizen).
Length of Study: 9-12 months.
Study Establishment: The W F Albright Institute of Archaeological Research, Jerusalem.
Country of Study: Israel.
Application Procedure: Please write for details.
Closing Date: October 16th.
Additional Information: The professorship period should be continuous, without frequent trips outside the country.

AIAR Islamic Studies Fellowship

Subjects: Islamic archaeology, art and architecture.
Eligibility: Candidates must have expertise in research and teaching in Islamic archaeology, art and architecture.
Level of Study: Postgraduate.
Type: Fellowship.
No. of awards offered: 1.
Frequency: Annual.
Value: US$20,000. The stipend is US$12,200 with the remainder for room and half board at the Institute.
Length of Study: 1 year.
Study Establishment: W F Albright Institute of Archaeological Research in Jerusalem.

Country of Study: Israel.
Application Procedure: Please write for details.
Closing Date: October 16th.
Additional Information: During the period of the appointment, the Fellow will teach regular courses in the Master's degree programme at the Institute for Islamic Archaeology in Jerusalem, as well as conduct seminars at the Albright and other local academic institutions.

Andrew W Mellon Foundation Fellowships

Subjects: Humanities.
Eligibility: Open to Czech, Hungarian, Polish and Slovak scholars who have obtained a doctorate by the time the fellowship is awarded.
Level of Study: Postdoctorate.
Purpose: To support Czech, Hungarian, Polish and Slovak scholars.
Type: Fellowship.
No. of awards offered: 3.
Frequency: Annual.
Value: US$34,500 for the three awards.
Length of Study: 3 months.
Study Establishment: W F Albright Institute of Archaeological Research in Jerusalem (if room is available).
Country of Study: Israel.
Application Procedure: Please write for details.
Closing Date: April 1st.
Additional Information: Candidates should not be permanently resident outside the four countries concerned.

ASOR Mesopotamian Fellowship

Subjects: Mesopotamian civilisation.
Eligibility: Open to pre and postdoctoral scholars.
Level of Study: Doctorate, Postdoctorate.
Purpose: To support field or museum research in ancient Mesopotamian civilisation.
Type: Fellowship.
No. of awards offered: 1.
Frequency: Annual.
Value: US$5,000.
Length of Study: 3-6 months.
Study Establishment: American Schools of Oriental Research.
Country of Study: Any country.
Application Procedure: Please write for further details.
Closing Date: February 1st.

Council of American Overseas Research Centers (CAORC) Fellowships for Advanced Multi-Country Research

Subjects: Multi-country significance in the fields of humanities, social sciences, and related natural sciences in countries in the Near and Middle East and South Asia.
Eligibility: Open to doctoral candidates and established scholars with US citizenship are eligible to apply.
Level of Study: Doctorate.
Type: Fellowship.

No. of awards offered: 8.
Frequency: Annual.
Value: US$6,000 plus an additional US$3,000 for travel.
Study Establishment: W F Albright Institute of Archeological Research in Jerusalem.
Country of Study: Near and Middle East Asia and South Asia.
Application Procedure: Please write for details.
Closing Date: December 31st.
Additional Information: Preference will be given to candidates examining comparative or cross-regional questions requiring research in two or more countries.

For further information contact:

CAORC
Smithsonian Institution
1c 3123 MRC 705, Washington, DC, 20560, United States of America
Contact: Grants Management Officer

George A Barton Fellowship

Subjects: Near Eastern archaeology, geography, history and Biblical studies.
Eligibility: Open to seminarians, predoctoral students and recent PhD recipients specialising in the appropriate subject fields. This award may not be used during the summer.
Level of Study: Doctorate, Postdoctorate, Postgraduate.
Type: Fellowship.
No. of awards offered: 1.
Frequency: Annual.
Value: US$5,000. The stipend is US$2,000 and the remainder covers room and half board at the Institute.
Length of Study: 4-5 months.
Study Establishment: W F Albright Institute of Archaeological Research in Jerusalem.
Country of Study: Israel.
Application Procedure: Please write for details.
Closing Date: October 16th.
Additional Information: The research period should be continuous, without frequent trips outside the country.

Kress Fellowship in the Art and Archaeology of Jordan

Subjects: History of art is defined to include art history, archaeology, architectural history, and in some cases classical studies. A topic should be focused on some aspect of the artistic legacy of a specific culture, site, or period.
Eligibility: Applicants must be American PhD candidates or those matriculated at US institutions.
Level of Study: Doctorate.
Purpose: To support students completing dissertation research in an art historical topic.
Type: Fellowship.
No. of awards offered: 1+.
Frequency: Annual.
Value: US$14,000 maximum.
Length of Study: 3-6 months.

Study Establishment: The American Center of Oriental Research, Amman.
Country of Study: Jordan.
Application Procedure: Please write for details.
Closing Date: February 1st.

NEH Fellowship

Subjects: Archaeology, anthropology, geography, ancient history, philology, epigraphy, Biblical studies, Islamic studies, religion, art history, literature, philosophy or related disciplines.
Eligibility: Open to scholars in Near Eastern studies holding a PhD, who are US citizens or alien residents residing in the country for the last three years.
Level of Study: Postdoctorate.
Purpose: To support scholars who hold a PhD.
Type: Fellowship.
No. of awards offered: 2.
Frequency: Annual.
Value: US$30,000 for each award.
Length of Study: 1 year.
Study Establishment: W F Albright Institute of Archaeological Research, Jerusalem.
Country of Study: Israel.
Application Procedure: Please write for details.
Closing Date: October 16th.
Additional Information: The research period should be continuous, without frequent trips outside the country.

NEH Postdoctoral Fellowships

Subjects: Humanistic topics, ancient or modern.
Eligibility: Open to US citizens and permanent residents who hold a PhD.
Level of Study: Postdoctorate.
Purpose: To support postdoctoral research at the Cyprus American Archaeological Research Institute (CAARI) in Nicosia.
Type: Fellowship.
No. of awards offered: 1+.
Frequency: Annual.
Value: US$30,000.
Length of Study: 6-12 months.
Study Establishment: CAARI in Nicosia, Cyprus.
Country of Study: Cyprus.
Application Procedure: Please write for details.
Closing Date: January 15th.

NEH Postdoctoral Research Award

Subjects: Fields of study include - languages (both modern and classical), linguistics, literature, history, jurisprudence, philosophy, archaeology, comparative religion, ethics, the history, criticism, and theory of the arts.
Eligibility: Open to US citizens or foreign nationals who are living in the USA.
Level of Study: Postdoctorate.
Purpose: To support postdoctoral scholars.
Type: Fellowship.
No. of awards offered: 2.

Frequency: Annual.
Value: $30,000 maximum.
Length of Study: 4 months.
Study Establishment: The American Center of Oriental Research, Amman.
Country of Study: Jordan.
Application Procedure: Please write for details.
Closing Date: February 1st.

NMERTP Predoctoral Fellowships

Subjects: Fields of study include - anthropology, economics, history, international relations, journalism, and political science.
Eligibility: Open to US citizens only.
Level of Study: Predoctorate.
Purpose: To support students with little or no previous experience in the Middle East.
Type: Fellowship.
No. of awards offered: 2+.
Frequency: Annual.
Value: US$9,200 maximum.
Length of Study: 2-4 months.
Study Establishment: The American Center of Oriental Research, Amman.
Country of Study: Jordan.
Application Procedure: Please write for details.
Closing Date: February 1st.

NMERTP Senior Postdoctoral Research Grants

Subjects: Social sciences, humanities and associated disciplines relating to the Middle East.
Eligibility: Open to senior postdoctoral scholars who are US citizens.
Level of Study: Postdoctorate.
Purpose: To support scholars pursuing research or publication projects in the social sciences, humanities, and associated disciplines relating to the Middle East.
Type: Research Grant.
No. of awards offered: 2+.
Frequency: Annual.
Value: US$35,600 maximum.
Length of Study: 4-9 months.
Study Establishment: The American Center of Oriental Research, Amman.
Country of Study: Jordan.
Application Procedure: Please write for details.
Closing Date: February 1st.
Additional Information: Preference will be given to scholars with limited prior experience in the Middle East.

Samuel H Kress Fellowship

Subjects: Architecture, art history and archaeology.
Eligibility: Open to US citizens only.
Level of Study: Doctorate.
Purpose: To support dissertation research.
Type: Fellowship.
No. of awards offered: 1.
Frequency: Annual.

Value: US$16,500; the stipend is for US$9,800 and the remainder is for room and half board at the Institute.
Length of Study: 10 months.
Study Establishment: W F Albright Institute of Archaeological Research, Jerusalem.
Country of Study: Israel.
Application Procedure: Please write for details.
Closing Date: October 16th.
Additional Information: The research period should be continuous, without frequent trips outside the country.

Samuel H Kress Joint Athens-Jerusalem Fellowship

Subjects: Art history, architecture, archaeology, and classical studies.
Eligibility: Open to predoctoral students who are US citizens.
Level of Study: Doctorate.
Purpose: To support predoctoral students.
Type: Fellowship.
No. of awards offered: 1.
Frequency: Annual.
Value: US$15,000. The stipend is US$8,300 and the remainder covers room and board at the two institutions.
Length of Study: 10 months (5 months in Athens, 5 months in Jerusalem).
Study Establishment: American School of Classical Studies in Athens, W F Albright Institute of Archaeological Research in Jerusalem.
Country of Study: Greece or Israel.
Application Procedure: Please write for details.
Closing Date: October 30th.

United States Information Agency (USIA) Fellowships

Subjects: Humanities and social sciences.
Eligibility: Open to predoctoral students and postdoctoral scholars of US nationality.
Level of Study: Doctorate, Postdoctorate.
Purpose: To support students undertaking study in the fields of humanities and social sciences.
Type: Fellowship.
No. of awards offered: 5+.
Frequency: Annual.
Value: US$14,000 maximum.
Length of Study: 2-6 months.
Study Establishment: The American Center of Oriental Research, Amman.
Country of Study: Jordan.
Application Procedure: Please write for details.
Closing Date: February 1st.

AMERICAN SOCIETY OF INTERIOR DESIGNERS EDUCATIONAL FOUNDATION, INC (ASID)

608 Massachusetts Avenue NE, Washington, DC, 20002-6006, United States of America
Tel: (1) 202 546 3480
Fax: (1) 202 546 3240
Email: iholly@asid.org
www: http://www.asid.org
Contact: Ms Iris Holly, Communications Manager

ASID/Joel Polsky-Fixtures Furniture Academic Achievement Award

Subjects: Interior design.
Eligibility: Open to applicants of any nationality.
Level of Study: Postgraduate, Undergraduate.
Purpose: To recognise an outstanding undergraduate or graduate student's interior design research or thesis project.
Type: Prize.
No. of awards offered: 1.
Frequency: Annual.
Value: US$1,000.
Country of Study: Any country.
Application Procedure: Please write for details.
Closing Date: March 15th.
Additional Information: Entries will be judged on actual content, breadth of material, comprehensive coverage of topic, innovative subject matter and bibliography/references.

ASID/Joel Polsky-Fixtures Furniture Prize

Subjects: Interior design.
Level of Study: Unrestricted.
Purpose: To recognise outstanding academic contributions to the discipline of interior design through literature or visual communication.
Type: Prize.
No. of awards offered: 1.
Frequency: Annual.
Value: US$1,000.
Country of Study: Any country.
Application Procedure: Please write for details.
Closing Date: March 15th.
Additional Information: Entries should address the needs of the public, designers, and students on such topics as educational research, behavioural science, business practice, design process, theory, or other technical subjects. Material will be judged on innovative subject matter, comprehensive coverage of topic, organisation, graphic presentation, and bibliography/references.

ASID/Mabelle Wilhelmina Boldt Memorial Scholarship

Subjects: Interior design.
Eligibility: Applicants must have been practising designers for a period of at least five years prior to returning to graduate level.
Level of Study: Graduate.
Purpose: To support students who are enrolled in a graduate level interior design programme at a degree-granting institution.
Type: Scholarship.
No. of awards offered: 1.
Frequency: Annual.
Value: US$2,000.
Study Establishment: A degree-granting institution.
Country of Study: Any country.
Application Procedure: Please write for details.
Closing Date: March 5th.
Additional Information: The scholarship will be awarded on the basis of academic/creative accomplishment, as demonstrated by school transcripts and a letter of recommendation.

THE AMERICAN UNIVERSITY IN CAIRO

113 Kasr El Aini Street
PO Box 2511, Cairo, 11511, Egypt
Tel: (20) 2 357 5530
Fax: (20) 2 355 7565
Email: aucgrad@aucegypt.edu
www: http://www.aucegypt.edu/graduate
Contact: Office of International Graduate Studies

AUC provides quality higher and continuing education for students from Egypt and the surrounding region. The University is an independent, non-profit, apolitical, non-sectarian and equal opportunity institution. English is the primary language of instruction. The University is accredited in the US by the Commission of Higher Education of the Middle States Association of Colleges and Schools.

African Graduate Fellowship

Subjects: Arts and humanities, business administration, engineering and information science.
Eligibility: Open to sub-Saharan nationals with a Bachelor's degree. Must be proficient in the English language. Academic record of not less than an overall GPA of 3.0 on a 4.0 scale or equivalent.
Level of Study: Graduate.
Purpose: To enable outstanding young men and women from sub-Saharan Africa to study at AUC.
Type: Tuition waiver.
No. of awards offered: 10.
Frequency: Annual.
Value: US$9,250 per academic year.
Length of Study: 2 years.

Study Establishment: AUC only.
Country of Study: Egypt.
Application Procedure: Application form and supporting documents are available from address shown at the Office of Graduate Studies and Research.
Closing Date: February 1st.
Additional Information: Fellowships offered to nationals of African nations not including Egyptians.

Assistantships

Subjects: Art and humanities, business administration, engineering and information science.
Eligibility: Fully accepted graduate students enrolled in two or more courses or actively involved in thesis work are given preference over those not enrolled in the graduate program. Applicants who have completed their MA or MS, are preparing for a PhD, and have or are receiving academic degree training may also receive assistantships.
Level of Study: Graduate.
Purpose: Awards made to graduate-level teaching or research assistants who do not receive tuition waivers.
Type: Award.
Frequency: Three times each year.
Value: Holders of a Master's degree receive monthly stipends of LE29 per hour of load per week. Bachelor's degree holders receive monthly stipends of LE24 per hour of load per week.
Length of Study: 1 semester, renewable.
Country of Study: Egypt.
Application Procedure: Application for teaching and research studentships is made to the department.
Closing Date: September 1st, January 1st, June 1st.

Ryoichi Sasakawa Young Leaders Graduate Scholarship

Subjects: Arts and humanities.
Eligibility: Applicants should have a Bachelor's degree, 3.4 GPA or above.
Level of Study: Graduate.
Purpose: To award grants to outstanding young men and women for the pursuit of graduate studies at AUC.
Type: Tuition waiver and stipend.
No. of awards offered: 3.
Frequency: Annual.
Value: US$12,000 per academic year.
Length of Study: 2 years.
Study Establishment: AUC only.
Country of Study: Egypt.
Application Procedure: Applicant must request application. Please write for details to the Office of the Provost at the above address.
Closing Date: February 1st.

University Fellowships

Subjects: Art and humanities, business administration and management, engineering, mass communication and information, mathematics and computer science, social and behavioural sciences.

Eligibility: Students who have an undergraduate GPA of at least 3.2 or its equivalent, enrolled in no less than six credits of course work or actively engaged in thesis research.
Level of Study: Graduate.
Type: Fellowship.
Frequency: Annual.
Value: US$3,000 per year, student services and activities fee and LE152 monthly for ten months.
Length of Study: Renewed every semester and may be renewed for a maximum period of 2 years.
Country of Study: Egypt.
Application Procedure: Applications are available from the department of major in May.
Closing Date: June.

Writing Center Graduate Fellowships

Subjects: English, grammar, education and native language, literacy education, teaching and learning.
Eligibility: Students who are fully admissable to the graduate programme in English and Comparative Literature at AUC and who have a BA degree with a minimum overall grade point average of 3.2 or its equivalent.
Level of Study: Graduate.
Purpose: To provide recipients with valuable teaching and academic experience and involve them as tutors in AUC's Writing Centre.
Type: Fellowship.
Frequency: Annual.
Value: US$3,000 per year, student services and activities fee and LE 200 monthly for ten months.
Length of Study: Renewed every semester and maybe renewed for a maximum period of 2 years. The fellowship may cover a summer session.
Country of Study: Egypt.
Application Procedure: Please write for details to The Chair of the Department of English and Comparative Literature, and The Office of Graduate Studies and Research.
Closing Date: End of April.

THE AMERICAN-SCANDINAVIAN FOUNDATION (ASF)

15 East 65th Street, New York, NY, 10021, United States of America
Tel: (1) 212 879 9779
Fax: (1) 212 249 3444
Email: grants@amscan.org
www: http://www.amscan.org
Contact: Ms Ellen B McKey, Director of Fellowships and Grants

The American-Scandinavian Foundation is a publicly supported, non-profit organisation that promotes international understanding through educational and cultural exchange between the United States and Denmark, Finland, Iceland, Norway and Sweden.

ASF Translation Prize

Subjects: Translation.
Eligibility: Open to translators of any nationality.
Level of Study: Unrestricted.
Purpose: To award the best English translation of poetry, fiction, drama or literary prose written by a Scandinavian author since 1800.
Type: Translation Prize.
No. of awards offered: 1.
Frequency: Annual.
Value: US$2,000, plus publication of an excerpt in an issue of 'Scandinavian Review' and a commemorative bronze medallion.
Country of Study: Scandinavian countries.
Application Procedure: An entry should consist of: four legible copies of the translation, including a title page and a table of contents for the proposed book of which the manuscript submitted is a part; one copy of the work(s) in the original language; a separate sheet containing the name, address and telephone number of the translator and the title and author of the manuscript with the original language specified; and a letter or other document signed by the author, the author's agent or the author's estate granting permission for the translation to be entered in this competition and published in 'Scandinavian Review'.
Closing Date: June 3rd.
Additional Information: The Inger Sjoberg Prize of US$500 will be offered annually for the Honorable Mention entry.

Fellowships and Grants for Study and Research in Scandinavia

Subjects: All subjects.
Eligibility: Open to US citizens or permanent residents.
Level of Study: Doctorate, Postdoctorate, Professional development.
Purpose: To encourage advanced study and research, and increase understanding between the USA and Scandinavia.
Type: Fellowship.
No. of awards offered: 25-30.
Frequency: Annual.
Value: US$3,000-US$15,000.
Length of Study: 1 year maximum.
Country of Study: Denmark, Finland, Iceland, Norway or Sweden.
Application Procedure: Please submit application form, three references, plus US$10 application fee.
Closing Date: November 1st.
Additional Information: For further information please contact Ellen McKey (Email: grants@amscan.org).

ANGLO-AUSTRIAN MUSIC SOCIETY

Richard Tauber Memorial Scholarship Committee
46 Queen Anne's Gate, London, SW1H 9AU, England
Tel: (44) 171 222 0366
Fax: (44) 171 233 0293
Email: aas@angloaustrian.demon.co.uk
www: http://www.angloaustrian.org.uk
Contact: The Secretary

The Anglo-Austrian Music Society promotes lectures and concerts and is closely associated with its parent organisation, The Anglo-Austrian Society, which was founded in 1944 to promote friendship and understanding between the people of Great Britain and Austria through personal contacts, educational programmes and cultural exchanges.

Richard Tauber Prize

Subjects: Vocal musical performance.
Eligibility: Open to British and Austrian residents, singers who are men between the ages of 21 and 32 or women between the ages of 21 and 30.
Level of Study: Postgraduate.
Purpose: To enable a British or Austrian singer to travel and study in order to broaden his or her musical experience prior to giving a public recital in London under the auspices of the Anglo-Austrian Music Society.
Type: Prize.
No. of awards offered: 1.
Frequency: Every two years, next in 2000.
Value: A cash prize of £2,500 to be used in whatever way the winner prefers to further his/her career as a singer, or to study a language, or become acquainted with the Austrian or British musical scene. Advice to this end will be available from the Anglo-Austrian Music Society if required. There will also be a Wigmore Hall recital for the winner.
Length of Study: An unlimited period.
Country of Study: Any country.
Application Procedure: Application form must be completed.
Closing Date: February.
Additional Information: Preliminary auditions are held in London and Vienna in March. A public final audition is held in London in April or May. Applicants attend the preliminary auditions at their own expense.

THE ANGLO-DANISH SOCIETY

Danewood
4 Daleside, Gerrards Cross, Buckinghamshire, SL9 7JF, England
Tel: (44) 1753 884846
Contact: Mrs A M Eastwood, Secretary

The Society exists to promote closer understanding between the United Kingdom and Denmark. It provides a forum in which Britons and Danes can meet one another.

The Anglo-Danish (London) Scholarships

Subjects: Other things being equal, candidates whose study topics are of specific value to Anglo-Danish cultural/scientific interests will be preferred.
Eligibility: Open to graduates of Danish nationality.
Level of Study: Doctorate, Postdoctorate, Postgraduate, Professional development.
Purpose: To promote Anglo-Danish relations.
Type: Scholarship.
No. of awards offered: 4-6.
Frequency: Dependent on funds available.
Value: £175 per month for a maximum of six months.
Length of Study: Maximum 6 month grant.
Study Establishment: UK university for Danish graduates and Danish university for British graduates.
Country of Study: United Kingdom or Denmark.
Application Procedure: Application forms are required. These are available from the Secretary, between October 1st and December 31st. Please enclose a stamped addressed envelope or international reply coupon.
Closing Date: January 12th.

The Denmark Liberation Scholarships

Subjects: Other things being equal, candidates whose study topics are of specific value to Anglo-Danish cultural/scientific interests will be preferred.
Eligibility: Open to graduates of British nationality only.
Level of Study: Doctorate, Postdoctorate, Postgraduate, Professional development.
Purpose: To promote Anglo-Danish relations.
Type: Scholarship.
No. of awards offered: 4-6.
Frequency: Annual.
Value: One major award of £9,000, and others at £6,000 each.
Length of Study: A minimum of 6 months.
Study Establishment: A Danish University or other approved institution.
Country of Study: Denmark.
Application Procedure: Application forms are required to be completed. These are available between October 1st and December 31st from the Secretary. Please enclose a stamped addressed envelope or international reply coupon.
Closing Date: January 12th.

ANGLO-JEWISH ASSOCIATION

Commonwealth House
(5th Floor)
1-19 New Oxford Street, London, WC1A 1NF, England
Tel: (44) 171 404 2111
Fax: (44) 171 404 2611
Contact: The Secretary

Anglo-Jewish Association Bursary

Subjects: All subjects.
Eligibility: Open to Jewish students of any nationality.

Level of Study: Postgraduate, Undergraduate.
Purpose: To assist students in full-time education in financial need.
Type: Bursary.
No. of awards offered: 100-120.
Frequency: Annual.
Value: Up to £2000 per year.
Country of Study: United Kingdom.
Application Procedure: Applicant must write formal letter of application in the first instance.
Closing Date: May 31st.

THE ARCHAEOLOGICAL INSTITUTE OF AMERICA

656 Beacon Street, Boston, MA, 02215-2010, United States of America
Tel: (1) 617 353 9361
Fax: (1) 617 353 6550
Email: aia@bu.edu
www: http://csaws.brynmawr.edu:443/aia.html
Contact: Mr Domenico Composto, Staff Intern

The Archaeological Institute of America (AIA) is dedicated to the encouragement and support of archaeological research and publication and to the protection of the world's cultural heritage. The AIA is a non-profit cultural and educational organisation chartered by the US Congress and has more than 10,000 members around the world.

Anna C and Oliver C Colburn Fellowship

Subjects: Archaeology.
Eligibility: Competition is open to United States or Canadian citizens or permanent residents. Current officers and members of the Governing Board of the Institute are not eligible for this award.
Level of Study: Postgraduate.
Purpose: To fund study.
Type: Fellowship.
No. of awards offered: 1.
Frequency: Annual.
Value: US$11,000.
Length of Study: 1 year.
Country of Study: Any country.
Application Procedure: Please contact the AIA for an application form.
Closing Date: February.
Additional Information: Other major fellowships may not be held during the requested tenure of the Colburn award.

Harriet and Leon Pomerance Fellowship

Subjects: Archaeology.
Eligibility: Applicants must be residents of the United States or Canada. Current officers and members of the Governing Board of the Institute are not eligible for this award.
Level of Study: Unrestricted.

Purpose: To enable a person to work on an individual project of a scholarly nature related to Aegean Bronze Age Archaeology.
Type: Fellowship.
No. of awards offered: 1.
Frequency: Annual.
Value: US$3,000.
Length of Study: 1 academic year.
Country of Study: Any country, preference given to Mediterranean region.
Application Procedure: Please contact the AIA office for an application form.
Closing Date: November.

Helen M Woodruff Fellowship

Subjects: Archaeology and classical studies.
Eligibility: Competition is open to citizens or permanent residents of the United States. Current officers and members of the Governing Board of the Institute are not eligible for this award.
Level of Study: Doctorate, Postdoctorate.
Purpose: To fund research.
Type: Fellowship.
No. of awards offered: 1.
Frequency: Annual.
Study Establishment: The American Academy in Rome.
Country of Study: Italy.
Application Procedure: Further information and application forms are available from: The American Academy in Rome, 7 East 60th Street, New York, NY 10022, USA.
Additional Information: At the conclusion of the Fellowship tenure, Woodruff recipients must submit a report to the President of the Institute and the President of the American Academy in Rome.

Kenan T Erim Award

Subjects: Archaeology.
Eligibility: Open to scholars working on Aphrodisias material. Current officers and members of the Governing Board of the Institute are not eligible for this award.
Level of Study: Postgraduate.
Purpose: To fund study.
No. of awards offered: 1.
Frequency: Annual.
Value: US$4,000.
Country of Study: Any country.
Application Procedure: Please contact the AIA office for an application form.
Closing Date: November.
Additional Information: If the project involves work at Aphrodisias, candidates must submit written approval from the Field Director with their applications. Recipients of the Erim Award must submit a final report to the President of the AIA which will be forwarded to the President of the American Friends of Aphrodisias.

Olivia James Traveling Fellowship

Subjects: Classics, sculpture, architecture, archaeology and history.
Eligibility: Open to citizens or permanent residents of the United States. Current officers and members of the Governing Board of the Institute are not eligible for this award.
Level of Study: Doctorate, Postdoctorate.
Purpose: Travel and study.
Type: Fellowship.
No. of awards offered: 1.
Frequency: Annual.
Value: US$15,000.
Length of Study: At least 6 months.
Country of Study: Greece, the Aegean Islands, Sicily, Southern Italy, Asia Minor or Mesopotamia.
Application Procedure: Please contact the AIA office for an application form.
Closing Date: November.
Additional Information: Preference will be given to individuals engaged in dissertation research, or to recent recipients of the PhD. The award is not intended to support field excavation projects. Recipients may not hold other major fellowships during the requested tenure of the Olivia James award.

ARISTOTLE UNIVERSITY OF THESSALONIKI

School of Modern Greek Language
University Campus, Thessaloniki, GR-54006, Greece
Tel: (30) 31 99 6726
Fax: (30) 31 99 6725
www: http://www.auth.gr/
Contact: Mr Ioannis Vassiliou, Public & International Relations Office Director

Aristotle University of Thessaloniki Scholarships

Subjects: Modern Greek language.
Eligibility: Open to foreign citizens as well as those of Greek origin, who hold at least a high school diploma.
Level of Study: Unrestricted.
Purpose: To encourage foreigners to learn the modern Greek language.
Type: Scholarship.
No. of awards offered: 40.
Frequency: Annual.
Value: Dr75,000 in total.
Length of Study: 1 month.
Country of Study: Greece.
Application Procedure: Application forms are available from the Public and International Relations Office.
Closing Date: April 30th.
Additional Information: Application forms are available on request.

ARTHUR RUBINSTEIN INTERNATIONAL MUSIC SOCIETY

12 Huberman St, Tel Aviv, 64075, Israel
Tel: (972) 3 6856684
Fax: (972) 3 6854924
Email: competition@arims.org.il
www: http://www.arims.org.il
Contact: Mr Jan Jacob Bistritzky, Director

The Arthur Rubinstein International Music Society was founded by Jan Jacob Bistritzky in 1980 in tribute to the artistry of Arthur Rubinstein (1887-1982) and to maintain his spiritual and artistic heritage in the art of the piano. The Society organises and finances the Arthur Rubinstein International Piano Master Competition; the Hommage a Rubinstein worldwide concert series and festivals; awards scholarships; runs music courses and master classes; organises lectures, seminars, exhibitions, film shows and memorial festivals; and issues publications and recordings.

Arthur Rubinstein International Piano Master Competition

Subjects: Piano.
Eligibility: Candidates must be 18-32 years of age.
Level of Study: Professional development.
Purpose: To reward talented pianists with the capacity for multifaceted creative interpretation of composers, ranging from the pre-classic to the contemporary era.
Type: Prize.
No. of awards offered: 10.
Frequency: Every three years.
Value: First Prize: Competition Gold Medal plus US$25,000, RX 3 Grand Piano by Kawai Piano Co, concert tour of the Far East, courtesy of Yamaha Co; Second Prize: Competition Silver Medal plus US$15,000; Third Prize: Competition Bronze medal plus US$10,000; Fourth, Fifth and Sixth Prizes: US$3,000 each. Additional prizes: Audience Favorite Prize and concert engagements.
Country of Study: Any country.
Application Procedure: Please write for details.

THE ARTS COUNCIL OF ENGLAND

14 Great Peter Street, London, SW1P 3NQ, England
Tel: (44) 171 333 0100
Fax: (44) 171 973 6590
Email: enquiries@artscouncil.org.uk
www: http://www.artscouncil.org.uk
Contact: Information Officer

The Arts Council of England receives public money from the Government to support and develop the arts in England. From these funds the Arts Council provides regular grants to arts organisations and artists.

Arts Council Drama Grants

Subjects: Drama - writing or performance.
Eligibility: Open to playwrights and performers.
Level of Study: Professional development.
Purpose: To support drama productions and events.
Type: Grant.
No. of awards offered: Varies.
Frequency: Annual.
Value: Varies.
Country of Study: United Kingdom.
Application Procedure: Please contact the Drama Department for an application form. (tel: (44) 171 973 6479; email: info.drama@artscouncil.org.uk).
Additional Information: Grants include small scale touring and project funds; theatre writing schemes and traineeships.

Arts Council Independent Dance Project Grants

Subjects: Dance.
Eligibility: Open only to professional groups and soloists. Applications cannot be accepted for the following: a programme of work lasting 52 weeks; separate capital costs, for example vans or equipment; companies already receiving revenue subsidy from the Dance Department of the Arts Council. Applications for performances (and for projects initiated) in Scotland, Northern Ireland or Wales should be made to the Arts Councils of those countries. Priority will be given to companies planning to make and premiere new work outside London.
Level of Study: Professional development.
Purpose: To enable the making of innovative high quality performance work, research and development, promoter/artists collaborations, and dance training.
Type: Project Grant.
No. of awards offered: Varies.
Frequency: Twice a year.
Value: Varies.
Country of Study: United Kingdom.
Application Procedure: Please contact Janet Stephenson, Assistant Dance Officer. (tel: (44) 171 973 6485; e-mail: info.dance@artscouncil.org.uk).
Additional Information: Awards include making and touring of dance works, including revivals; research and development; promoter/artists collaborations; and dance training.

Arts Council Literature Awards

Subjects: Poetry, fiction, literary autobiography and biography, writing for young people.
Eligibility: Open to writers resident in England and writing in English. The applicant must be a previously published author of a creative work, published in book form.
Level of Study: Professional development.
Purpose: To help published writers at a crucial stage of their career who need finance for a period of concentrated work on their next book.
Type: Bursary.
No. of awards offered: 15.
Frequency: Annual.

Value: £7,000.
Country of Study: United Kingdom.
Application Procedure: Please contact the office for application details (tel: (44) 171 973 6442; e-mail: info.literature@artscouncil.org.uk).
Additional Information: The awards include literature touring; translation scheme; writer's awards scheme; the Raymond Williams Community Publishing Prize; independent initiatives applications; publishing, education, and broadcasting awards.

Arts Council of England Combined Arts

Subjects: Arts.
Level of Study: Professional development.
Purpose: To encourage and support innovative and high quality combined arts projects, and to provide research and development opportunities for both individual artists and groups of artists working in inter-disciplinary ways.
No. of awards offered: Varies.
Frequency: Annual.
Value: Varies.
Country of Study: United Kingdom.
Application Procedure: For application details please contact the office (tel: (44) 171 973 6573, e-mail: info.combinedarts@artscouncil.org.uk).
Closing Date: Please write for details.
Additional Information: Awards include the Combined Arts Project Fund; International Initiatives Fund; Live Art and Inter-Disciplinary Practice Commission Scheme; Live Art and Inter-Disciplinary Practice Travel and Research Fund; and the Notting Hill Carnival Costume Mass Bands Scheme.

Arts Council of England Music Grants

Subjects: Composition, commissioning, recording, music theatre development.
Eligibility: Open to suitably qualified musicians.
Level of Study: Professional development.
Purpose: To support artists undertaking projects in all music areas.
Type: Grant.
No. of awards offered: Approx. 10.
Frequency: Annual.
Country of Study: United Kingdom.
Application Procedure: For application details please contact the office (tel: (44) 171 973 6495, e-mail: info.music@artscouncil.org.uk).
Closing Date: Varies - please contact the Arts Council office for individual deadlines.
Additional Information: Awards include opera and music theatre projects; improvised music touring; London-based chamber orchestras; Composer/Creative Musician in Association Fund; African, Caribbean and Asian music touring; jazz touring; New Music Commission Support Scheme; Early Music Projects; and Larger Period Ensembles Touring and Development Fund.

Arts Council of England Visual Arts

Subjects: The visual arts.
Level of Study: Professional development.

Purpose: To support artists undertaking projects in varying visual arts disciplines.
No. of awards offered: Varies.
Frequency: Annual.
Value: Up to £25,000.
Country of Study: United Kingdom.
Application Procedure: Please contact the office for application details (tel: (44) 171 973 6470, e-mail: info.visualart@artscouncil.org.uk).
Closing Date: Please write for details.
Additional Information: The awards include Architecture Grants; Artist's Film and Video National Fund for Exhibition and Initiatives; Artist's Film and Video National Fund for Production; Artist's First Time Publications; Artist's in Sites for Learning Grants; Exhibition Development Awards; Exhibition Production Awards; Exhibition Research Awards; Media Publications; Small Grants for New Media; and symposia.

ARTS COUNCIL OF IRELAND

70 Merrion Square, Dublin, 2, Ireland
Tel: (353) 1 661 1840
Fax: (353) 1 676 1320
Contact: Ms Tara Byrne

The Arts Council awards grants in dance, drama, film and video, literature, music, and the visual arts.

Artflight Arts Council-Aer Lingus Travel Awards

Subjects: Creative arts, interpretative arts, arts administration.
Eligibility: Open to creative and interpretative artists in all fields, administrators, producers and directors of Irish birth or residence. Artflights are intended to assist those individuals who have a stated reason to travel and do not have the financial resources to do so.
Level of Study: Professional development.
Purpose: To offer opportunities to people working in the arts to travel outside of Ireland.
No. of awards offered: Varies.
Value: To cover the cost of the return fare to any destination on the Aer Lingus network.
Country of Study: Any country.
Application Procedure: Please complete an application form and supply an up to date CV; for visual artists no more than ten copies of slides and accompanying slide list is needed; supporting documentation, (letter of invitation, confirmation of acceptance on course, relevant correspondance or other materials) with your application.
Additional Information: Successful applicants must satisfy the Council that there is an artistic benefit to them and that their work as a whole will improve as a result of the travel award. In the case of an administrator, there must be a benefit to the applicant's employer or associated organisation. Full details are given in a special brochure.

The Arts Council of Ireland Composers Commission Scheme

Subjects: Music composition.
Eligibility: Open to promoters of music events such as music societies, associations, festivals, established performing groups, instrumental ensembles and choral groups. Applicants must be Irish citizens.
Level of Study: Professional development.
Purpose: To enable promoters of music events to commission work from a composer of their choice.
No. of awards offered: Varies.
Frequency: As required.
Value: Varies.
Country of Study: Any country.
Application Procedure: Please apply to the Contemporary Music Centre, 95 Lower Baggot Street, Dublin 2.
Closing Date: To be announced.

Arts Council of Ireland Travel Awards to Creative Artists

Subjects: Visual arts, writing, composition.
Eligibility: Open to applicants of Irish birth or residence.
Level of Study: Professional development.
Purpose: To allow artists and arts workers to expand their artistic experience.
Type: Award.
No. of awards offered: Varies.
Frequency: Three times each year.
Value: IR£1,500 maximum.
Length of Study: Normally for courses or projects of not more than 3 months duration.
Country of Study: Any country.
Application Procedure: The standard application form should be completed and is available on request.
Closing Date: February 26th, May 14th, October 1st.
Additional Information: Travel awards are not intended for persons wishing to pursue degree or diploma courses in educational institutions.

The Macaulay Fellowship

Subjects: On a rotating basis - visual arts (2000), music (2001).
Eligibility: Open to applicants born in Ireland and under 30 years of age on June 30th in the year of application (or under 35 in exceptional circumstances).
Level of Study: Unrestricted.
Purpose: To further the liberal education of young creative artists.
Type: Fellowship.
No. of awards offered: 1.
Frequency: Annual.
Value: Approximately IR£3,500.
Country of Study: Any country.
Application Procedure: Applicants are expected to submit detailed plans on how they would use the award and indicate

the extent to which arrangements have been put in place. The standard application form must be completed and is available on request.
Closing Date: April 23rd.

The Marten Toonder Award

Subjects: On a rotating basis - music (2000), literature (2001), visual arts (2002).
Eligibility: Open to applicants of Irish birth or residence.
Level of Study: Unrestricted.
Purpose: To honour an artist of established reputation.
No. of awards offered: 1.
Frequency: Annual.
Value: Approximately IR£4,000.
Country of Study: Any country.
Application Procedure: Applicants are required to complete an application form, which is available on request from the Council. They must also enclose a detailed CV, 12 slides and supporting documentation.
Closing Date: April 23rd.

ARTS COUNCIL OF NORTHERN IRELAND

MacNeice House
77 Malone Road, Belfast, BT9 6AQ, Northern Ireland
Tel: (44) 1232 385200
Fax: (44) 1232 661715
Contact: Awards

Alice Berger Hammerschlag Trust Award

Subjects: Visual arts.
Eligibility: Open to candidates normally resident in Northern Ireland or the Republic of Ireland who are practising in one of the visual or plastic arts.
Level of Study: Professional development.
Purpose: To assist young and unappreciated artists.
Type: Travel Grant.
No. of awards offered: 1.
Frequency: Annual.
Value: £1,000.
Country of Study: Any country.
Application Procedure: Applicants must complete an application form and produce slides.
Closing Date: April.
Additional Information: The Trust is a charity set up to honour the late Alice Berger Hammerschlag and to continue her work.

Arts Council of Northern Ireland Annual Award

Subjects: Any field of the arts.
Eligibility: Open to artists who contribute regularly to the artistic activities of the community, with residency in Northern Ireland of at least one year. Open to previous award holders. Registered students are not eligible to apply for visual arts

awards. There are no stipulated age limits.
Level of Study: Professional development.
Purpose: To enable the artist to achieve objectives for specific projects or for the acquisition of equipment or materials. Awards may also be made for travel; for attending masterclasses; or for short-term training courses.
No. of awards offered: Varies.
Frequency: Annual.
Value: £12,000 (for guidance only).
Country of Study: Any country.
Application Procedure: Applicants must complete an application form and produce slides.
Closing Date: April.
Additional Information: Not intended for courses of vocational training leading to professional qualifications.

Bass Ireland Arts Awards

Subjects: Art.
Eligibility: Open to artists working in any field of the arts, resident in Northern Ireland for at least one year.
Level of Study: Professional development.
Purpose: To encourage the enrichment of the cultural scene in Northern Ireland.
No. of awards offered: 1.
Frequency: Annual.
Value: £5,000.
Country of Study: Any country.
Application Procedure: Applicants must complete and application form.
Closing Date: August.
Additional Information: The Awards are part of Bass Ireland's commitment to supporting the arts.

British School at Rome Fellowship

Subjects: Painting, sculpture.
Eligibility: Open to artists resident in Northern Ireland or the Republic of Ireland for a period of at least one year, or domiciled elsewhere but contributing regularly to the artistic activity of the community. There is no stipulated age limit.
Level of Study: Professional development.
Purpose: To provide working and living accommodation for visual arts scholars for the period of fellowship in the British School at Rome.
Type: Fellowship.
No. of awards offered: 1.
Frequency: Dependent on available studio space.
Value: £10,000 from the Arts Council to the British School to cover costs; £4,500 of this to the Fellow as stipend, and for materials allowance and travel expenses within Italy.
Length of Study: 1 year.
Study Establishment: The British School at Rome.
Country of Study: Italy.
Closing Date: April.

George Campbell Travel Award

Subjects: Visual arts.
Eligibility: Open to artists resident in Northern Ireland or the Republic of Ireland. Particular attention is given to artists who

wish to work on attachment to an art college, museum or organisation. There is no age limit.
Level of Study: Professional development.
Purpose: In memory of the painter, George Campbell. Instituted to celebrate his special relationship with both parts of Ireland and the strong cultural contact he developed with Spain.
Type: Travel Grant.
No. of awards offered: 1.
Frequency: Annual.
Value: £1,000.
Country of Study: Spain.
Application Procedure: Applicants must complete an application form and produce slides.
Closing Date: April.
Additional Information: Awarded to Northern and Southern artists in alternate years.

The Milliken Brothers Award

Subjects: Art, drawing, painting.
Eligibility: Applicants must be resident in Northern Ireland or the Republic of Ireland for a period of at least one year, or domiciled elsewhere but contributing regularly to the activity of the community. There is no age limit and students are not eligible.
Level of Study: Professional development.
Purpose: To support and develop a body of work prior to an exhibition which may be of significance to the applicant's career.
Type: Grant.
Frequency: Annual.
Value: £1,000 for the purchase of fine art materials.
Application Procedure: Applicants must complete an application form. The application should be accompanied by slides or photographs of not more than 15 examples of the applicant's most recent work.
Closing Date: May 4th.

New York Fellowship

Subjects: Visual arts.
Eligibility: Open to artists resident in Northern Ireland or the Republic of Ireland for a period of at least one year, or domiciled elsewhere but contributing regularly to the artistic activity of the community. There is no stipulated age limit.
Level of Study: Professional development.
Purpose: To establish workspace for professional foreign artists in the US which, in turn, offers valuable exposure for these artists.
Type: Fellowship.
No. of awards offered: 2.
Frequency: Annual.
Value: To cover stipend, air fare and studio rent.
Length of Study: 1 year.
Country of Study: USA.
Application Procedure: Applicants must complete an application form and produce slides.
Closing Date: March.
Additional Information: Funded by Arts Councils and Ireland-America Arts Exchange.

Thomas Dammann Junior Memorial Trust

Subjects: Visual arts.
Eligibility: Open to students resident in Northern Ireland and the Republic of Ireland, and registered for a postgraduate or undergraduate award at a third level institution. Also open to applicants pursuing serious academic research outside of normal educational institutions. Previous award winners may reapply.
Level of Study: Postgraduate, Undergraduate.
Purpose: To enable students to travel abroad to visit exhibitions, museums, galleries and buildings of architectural importance.
Type: Travel Bursary.
No. of awards offered: 20.
Frequency: Annual.
Value: Up to IR£2,000.
Country of Study: Any country.
Application Procedure: Applicants must complete an application form and submit two references.
Closing Date: February.

ARTS COUNCIL OF WALES

Museum Place, Cardiff, CF1 3NX, Wales
Tel: (44) 1222 394711
Fax: (44) 1222 221447
Email: information@ccc-acw.org.uk
www: http://www.ccc-acw.org.uk
Contact: Mr Michael Baker, Artform Development Director

The Arts Council of Wales is the national organisation with specific responsibility for the funding and development of the arts in Wales. Most of its funds come from the Welsh Office, but it also receives funds from local authorities, the Crafts Council, and other sources.

Arts Council of Wales Awards for Advanced Study in Music

Subjects: Instrumental and voice.
Eligibility: Open to singers and instrumentalists under 28 years of age on February 1st in the year of application, who were born and educated in Wales, or who have been permanently resident in Wales for at least two years.
Level of Study: Professional development.
Purpose: To provide opportunity for advanced study.
Type: Study Grant.
No. of awards offered: Limited.
Frequency: Annual.
Value: Varies.
Country of Study: Any country.
Application Procedure: Enquiries should be addressed to the Director of the Music Department at Artform Development Division (Performing Arts), Cardiff office.
Closing Date: February 1st.

Arts Council of Wales Commissions to Composers

Subjects: Composition.
Eligibility: Commissions will be offered to composers of any nationality, providing the first performance will be in Wales.
Level of Study: Professional development.
Purpose: To commission new works.
Type: Commissions to composers.
No. of awards offered: Varies.
Frequency: Annual.
Value: Towards the cost of the Commission fee.
Country of Study: Any country.
Application Procedure: The Council will respond to applications from organisations and musicians who are able to guarantee the first performance of a new work. Enquiries should be addressed to the Artform Development Division, (Performing Arts), Cardiff office.
Closing Date: January 11th.

Arts Council of Wales Grants for Artists

Subjects: Visual arts.
Eligibility: Open to visual artists who live and/or work in Wales for at least nine months of the year, and have been out of full-time education for at least two years.
Level of Study: Professional development.
Purpose: In support of career development, acquisition of skills, travel and work with other practitioners.
Type: Research/Travel Grant.
No. of awards offered: Varies.
Frequency: Twice a year.
Value: Varies.
Country of Study: Any country.
Application Procedure: Application form must be completed; expanded proposal submitted; and visual evidence of recent work must be shown.
Closing Date: May 4th, October 5th.
Additional Information: Enquiries should be directed to Tessa Hartog.

Arts Council of Wales Grants to Dancers

Subjects: Dance projects.
Eligibility: Open to dancers and choreographers for projects taking place in Wales.
Level of Study: Unrestricted.
Purpose: To create new works of choreography and to commission new works of choreography.
Type: Grant.
No. of awards offered: Varies.
Frequency: Annual.
Value: Varies.
Country of Study: Wales.
Application Procedure: Please contact Artform Development Division (Performing Arts) at the Arts Council of Wales for further details.
Closing Date: Grants will be made throughout the year.

Arts for All

Subjects: Priority will be given to those projects which are aimed at young people, involve targeted community development or training within the arts.
Purpose: To support projects that encourage people to enjoy the arts or take part in the arts.
Length of Study: Up to 3 years.
Application Procedure: Please contact the Lottery Division, Cardiff, Carmarthen and Colwyn Bat offices for further information.
Closing Date: Applications may be submitted at any time during the year, although deadlines are due to be introduced so please check before applying.

Capital Grants

Subjects: Performing arts and related subjects.
Purpose: To enable building development and purchase of equipment, such as staging equipment. Also for feature film script development and production funding.
Type: Grant.
Application Procedure: Please contact Lottery Division, Cardiff, Carmarthen and Colwyn Bay offices for more details.
Closing Date: Applications may be submitted at any time during the year but please check before applying.

Grants to Periodicals, The Franchise Scheme

Subjects: Writing, readership, literature.
Purpose: Support is given to periodicals based in Wales, in Welsh or English, to provide an outlet for new work and to extend the readership for literature.
Type: Grant.
Length of Study: 3 years.
Application Procedure: Please contact Artform Development Division (Literature), Cardiff Office for more information.
Closing Date: November.

Indicvidual Craftspeople Awards

Subjects: Craft.
Purpose: For individual craftspeople who have had their own workshop for more than two years to assist with the development of skills and the creative process, to undertake a specific project, to develop work and techniques or to buy time out to research new work.
Type: Award.
No. of awards offered: Varies.
Frequency: Annual.
Application Procedure: Please contact Artform Development Division, (Visual Arts and craft), Cardiff office for more details.
Closing Date: August 20th.

Individual Professional Visual Artists Awards

Subjects: Visual arts.
Eligibility: Applicants should have been permanently domiciled in Wales for at least two years and have been out of full time education for at least five years.

Purpose: For individual professional visual artists to develop their work in particular by releasing them from their normal commitments.
Application Procedure: Please contact Artform Development Division, (Visual Arts and craft), Cardiff office for more details.
Closing Date: June 7th.

Inter-link

Subjects: The arts.
Eligibility: Open to presenters and promoters.
Purpose: To stimulate the touring of international arts into Wales and to encourage collaborative projects over the course of the tour.
Application Procedure: Please write to the International Office in Cardiff, for further information.
Closing Date: January 16th.

Inter-Reece

Subjects: The arts.
Purpose: To encourage contact with producers and presenters in countries outside the UK with a view to future collaborations.
Value: Financial assistance.
Country of Study: Any country except the UK.
Application Procedure: Please contact the International Office in Cardiff for further information.
Closing Date: Applications may be submitted throughout the year.

Literature Projects Fund

Subjects: Priority is currently given to small festivals and story-telling.
Purpose: For small scale projects in any area of literary promotion for which funding is not already available, with the aim of encouraging initiative and diversity. Priority is currently given to small festivals and story-telling.
Type: Project Grant.
Application Procedure: Please contact Artform Development Division (Literature), Cardiff office, for more details.
Closing Date: March 1st, June 1st, September 1st, December 1st.

New Visual Artists

Subjects: Visual arts.
Purpose: To assist new visual artists who are about to embark on professional practice.
Type: Award.
No. of awards offered: 15-20.
Frequency: Six times per year.
Value: To help establish a studio, research contacts and potential markets. Awards of up to £500 will be made six times a year.
Application Procedure: Please contact Artform Development Division, (Visual Arts and Craft), Cardiff office for more details.

Closing Date: April 23rd, June 18th, August 20th, October 22nd, December 17th, February 20th.

Production Grants for Individual Books

Subjects: Writing.
Level of Study: Professional development.
Purpose: Support for the production of literary books of Welsh interest or by writers living in Wales. Includes writing for both children and adults.
Type: Grant.
No. of awards offered: Varies.
Frequency: Annual.
Application Procedure: Please contact Artform Development Division (Literature), Cardiff office for more details.
Closing Date: February 1st and July 1st.

Trainee Director and Associate Director Bursaries

Subjects: Theatre direction.
Eligibility: The grants are to assist students normally resident in Wales.
Purpose: To help aspiring and experienced professional theatre directors in Wales gain training and further experience through residential training opprtunities.
Type: Bursary.
Application Procedure: Please contact Artform Development Division (Performing Arts), Cardiff office for more details.
Closing Date: January 11th.

Training Grants to Individuals

Subjects: Theatre.
Eligibility: Open to theatre professionals based in Wales.
Purpose: To encourage theatre professionals based in Wales to use in-service training opportntities to develop new skills and extend professional horizons.
Type: Grant.
No. of awards offered: Varies.
Frequency: Annual.
Value: Financial assistance.
Application Procedure: Please contact Artform Development Division (Performing Arts), Cardiff office for more details.
Closing Date: Applications may be submitted throughout the year.

Translation Grants

Subjects: Translation.
Eligibility: Applications are welcome from publishers anywhere in the world.
Purpose: Support for the commissioning of translations in Welsh or English.
Type: Grant.
No. of awards offered: Varies.
Frequency: Annual.
Application Procedure: Please contact Artform Development Division (Literature), Cardiff office for more details.
Closing Date: Applications may be submitted at any time.

Visual Arts Project Fund

Subjects: Fine and applied arts.
Eligibility: Open to artists living or working in Wales for at least nine months of the year.
Level of Study: Postgraduate.
Purpose: To support new one-off initiatives in the visual arts in Wales, including a wide range of activities.
Type: Grant.
No. of awards offered: Varies.
Frequency: Annual.
Country of Study: Any country.
Application Procedure: Application form must be supported by visual evidence of work and expanded proposal.
Closing Date: May 3rd, October 4th, January 17th.

Writers' Bursaries, Enabling Grants and Travel Awards

Subjects: Writing.
Purpose: Bursaries for several writers living in Wales or writing in Welsh, enabling them to devote more time to writing. Awards are also available for disabled writers, for travel and research and to promote international exchange.
Type: Bursaries, Grants and Travel Awards.
Application Procedure: Please contact Artform Development Division (Literature), Cardiff office for information.
Closing Date: November 30th.

Writers' Critical Service

Subjects: Development of writing skills.
Eligibility: Open to any writer in Welsh and any writers in English living in Wales.
Purpose: The Service provides assessments of writers' work to help them develop their skills.
No. of awards offered: Varies.
Application Procedure: A small fee is payable. Please contact Artform Development Division (Literature), Cardiff office, for more details.
Closing Date: Applications may be submitted throughout the year.

Writers' on Tour and Literature Residences

Subjects: Literary topics.
Purpose: To provide financial support towards visits by writers to schools, colleges, libraries, voluntary groups/organisations and other societies.
Type: Residency.
No. of awards offered: Varies.
Frequency: Annual.
Application Procedure: Please write for details.
Closing Date: Applications can be made at any time during the year, but must be made at least a month before the proposed date.

For further information contact:

Academi
Mount Studart House
Mount Stuart Square, Cardiff, CF1 6DQ, Wales
Tel: (44) 1222 472266

ARTS MANAGEMENT

Station House
Rawson Place
790 George Street, Sydney, NSW, 2000, Australia
Tel: (61) 2 9212 5066
Fax: (61) 2 9211 7762
Email: vbraden@ozemail.com.au
Contact: Ms Claudia Crosariol

Arts Management administrates and organises various artistic scholarships and awards in the fields of opera, singing, instrumental music, prose, poetry, ballet, architecture, sculpture and painting.

The Kathleen Mitchell Award

Subjects: Literature.
Eligibility: Entries must be published during the two years previous to the award, the entrant must be resident in Australia during the twelve months preceding the entry date, and must be under 30 years in the year such entry is published.
Purpose: To encourage the advancement and betterment of Australian literature.
Type: Award.
No. of awards offered: 1.
Frequency: Every two years.
Value: A$4,000.
Application Procedure: An entry form must be submitted by the closing date.
Closing Date: Last Friday in January.

Lady Mollie Askin Ballet Travelling Scholarship

Subjects: Dancing, classical ballet.
Eligibility: Open to Australian citizens who are between the ages of 17 and 30 as at the closing date for entries for the award.
Level of Study: Unrestricted.
Purpose: To support the furtherance of culture and the advancement of education in Australia and elsewhere. To be awarded by the Trustees to Australian citizens who shall be adjudged to be of outstanding ability and promise in ballet.
Type: Scholarship.
No. of awards offered: 1.
Frequency: Every two years.
Value: A$15,000.
Length of Study: Over 2 years.
Country of Study: Any country.

Application Procedure: Please submit application forms by the due date, together with the documents and enclosures specified - five photos, VHS, video, three references, CV, certificates, and birth certificate.
Closing Date: Applications are accepted at any time.

The Marten Bequest Travelling Scholarships

Subjects: Instrumental music, painting, singing, sculpture, architecture, ballet, prose, poetry, acting.
Eligibility: Applicants must have been born in Australia, and be between the ages of 21 and 35 (17-35 for ballet).
Level of Study: Unrestricted.
Purpose: To augment a scholar's own resources towards affording them a cultural education by means of a travelling scholarship.
Type: Scholarship.
No. of awards offered: 6.
Frequency: Annual.
Value: A$18,000 over two years.
Length of Study: 2 years.
Country of Study: Any country.
Application Procedure: Applicants should submit an application form, study outline and supporting material.
Closing Date: Last Friday in October.

Portia Geach Memorial Award

Subjects: Fine and applied arts.
Eligibility: Entrants must be female Australian residents who are either Australian born or naturalised, or British born. Works must be executed entirely in the previous year.
Purpose: To award the best portraits painted from life of some man or woman distinguished in art, letters or the sciences by any female artists.
Type: Award.
No. of awards offered: 1.
Frequency: Annual.
Value: A$18,000.
Application Procedure: An entry fee and application form must be submitted by the closing date.
Closing Date: Last Friday in August for entry forms.

Sir Robert Askin Operatic Travelling Scholarship

Subjects: Operatic singing.
Eligibility: Applicants must be male Australian citizens, between the ages of 18 and 30 at the time of application.
Level of Study: Unrestricted.
Purpose: To support the furtherance of culture and the advancement of education in Australia and elsewhere, to be awarded by the Trustees to male Australian citizens of outstanding ability and promise as an operatic singer.
Type: Scholarship.
No. of awards offered: 1.
Frequency: Every two years.
Length of Study: Over 2 years.
Country of Study: Any country.

Application Procedure: Please send completed application forms with the specified documents and enclosures - birth certificate, Australian Citizen certificate, CV, certificates, three references, photographs, and reviews.

ARTS MANAGEMENT PTY LIMITED

Station House
Rawson Place
790 George Street, Sydney, NSW, 2000, Australia
Tel: (61) 2 9212 5066
Fax: (61) 2 9211 7762
Email: vbraden@ozemail.com.au
Contact: Ms Louise Roberts, Associate Director

Miles Franklin Literary Award

Subjects: Authorship. The prize is directed to be awarded for the novel of the year which is of highest literary merit and which must present Australian life in any of its phases. If there is no novel worthy of the prize, then the award will be given to the author of a play.
Eligibility: Eligible genres include farce, musical comedy, biographies, collections of short stories. Poetry and childrens books are not eligible. The work must have been published in the year preceeding the award.
Level of Study: Unrestricted.
Purpose: To award a novel or play first published in the year preceding the award, which presents Australian life in any of its phases.
Type: Award.
No. of awards offered: 1.
Frequency: Annual.
Value: A$28,000.
Country of Study: Any country.
Application Procedure: Entry forms and entries must be received by the closing date.
Closing Date: January 31st.

THE ASCAP FOUNDATION

One Lincoln Plaza, New York, NY, 10023, United States of America
Tel: (1) 212 621 6327
Fax: (1) 212 721 0956
Email: frichard@ascap.com
www: http://www.ascap.com
Contact: Ms Frances Richard

ASCAP Grants to Young Composers

Subjects: Music composition.
Eligibility: Open to US citizens or permanent residents of the USA who have not reached their 30th birthday by March 15th in the year of competition.

Level of Study: Unrestricted.
Purpose: To encourage composers, up to the age of 30, and to provide recognition, appreciation and monetary awards to gifted, emerging talents.
Type: Cash Award.
No. of awards offered: Varies from year to year.
Frequency: Annual.
Value: From US$250 to US$2,500.
Country of Study: Any country.
Application Procedure: Application required and reference letter encouraged.
Closing Date: March 15th.

ASIAN CULTURAL COUNCIL

437 Madison Avenue
37th Floor, New York, NY, 10022, United States of America
Tel: (1) 212 812 4300
Fax: (1) 212 812 4299
Contact: Mr Ralph Samuelson

The Asian Cultural Council supports cultural exchange in the visual and performing arts between the United States and the countries of Asia. The emphasis of the ACC's programme is on providing individual fellowships to artists, scholars and specialists from Asia undertaking research, study, and creative work in the USA. Grants are also made to Americans pursuing similar work in Asia.

Asian Cultural Council Fellowship Grants Program

Subjects: Visual and performing arts.
Eligibility: Open to individuals from East and Southeast Asia (Burma to Japan) and US citizens or permanent residents.
Level of Study: Doctorate, Postdoctorate, Postgraduate, Professional development.
Purpose: To provide fellowship opportunities for research, training, travel and creative work.
No. of awards offered: Approx. 100.
Frequency: Annual.
Value: Varies.
Length of Study: From 1 month to 1 year.
Country of Study: Asians to travel to the USA, Americans to travel to Asia.
Application Procedure: Interested individuals and institutions should send a brief project description to the Council. If the proposal falls within the Council's guidelines, application forms will be forwarded to individual candidates or more detailed information will be requested from institutional applicants.
Closing Date: February 1st, August 1st.
Additional Information: Artists seeking aid for personal exhibitions or performances and students enrolled in undergraduate degree programmes cannot be considered.

ASSOCIATED BOARD OF THE ROYAL SCHOOLS OF MUSIC

14 Bedford Square, London, WC1B 3JG, England
Tel: (44) 171 637 0234
Fax: (44) 171 436 4520
Email: abrsm@abrsm.ac.uk
www: http://www.abrsm.ac.uk
Contact: Mr T P Pleates, Director of Finance and Administration

The Associated Board of the Royal Schools of Music is the world's leading provider of graded music examinations with over 500,000 candidates each year in over 80 countries. It is also a major music publisher and a provider of professional development courses and seminars for music teachers.

Associated Board of the Royal Schools of Music Scholarships

Subjects: Instrumental and vocal.
Eligibility: Open to students, normally between the ages of 17 and 26, except in certain circumstances, for example courses for singers and in-service teachers courses.
Level of Study: Postgraduate, Professional development, Undergraduate.
Purpose: To enable exceptionally talented young musicians to study at one of the four Royal Schools of Music.
Type: Scholarship.
No. of awards offered: Varies.
Frequency: Annual.
Value: Full course fees, contribution to air travel and £3,000 per year towards living expenses.
Length of Study: From 1 term to 4 years, according to designated course.
Study Establishment: Either the Royal Academy of Music, the Royal College of Music, the Royal Northern College of Music or the Royal Scottish Academy of Music and Drama.
Country of Study: United Kingdom.
Application Procedure: Applicants must submit an application form, health certificate, exam marks, forms, testimonials, and an authenticated cassette tape of recent performance.
Closing Date: December 31st preceding year of entry.
Additional Information: Entries can be received from any of the countries where the Associated Board organises examinations. Candidates must have a good standard of general education and must normally have qualified by passing, with distinction, Grade 8 in a practical examination of the Board's, the Advanced Certificate or the LRSM diploma, plus one other practical examination of the Board's above Grade 5. Candidates should apply to the Board's representative in their own country or directly to the Board in London.

ASSOCIATION OF AFRICAN UNIVERSITIES

PO Box 5744, Accra-North, Ghana
Tel: (233) 21 77 44 95
Fax: (233) 21 77 48 21
Email: program@aau.org
www: http:// www.aau.org
Telex: 2284Adua GH
Contact: Mr Gof Ekhajuere, Senior Program Officer

DAAD/AAU Graduate Education Scholarship

Subjects: All subjects except social sciences.
Eligibility: Applicants must be junior members of African universities, be less than 36 years old, and have a bachelor's degree or equivalent.
Level of Study: Doctorate, Postgraduate.
Purpose: To contribute to the capacity building of African universities, by enabling junior staff members to undertake graduate education in African universities.
Type: Scholarship.
No. of awards offered: 10.
Frequency: Annual.
Value: Approximately US$3,000-US$10,000 per year.
Length of Study: 2-4 years.
Study Establishment: African universities.
Country of Study: Africa.
Application Procedure: The AAU invites approximately 20 universities to apply and provides them with application forms. The universities nominate one candidate each and the AAU then selects 10. Students wishing to apply have to make enquiries in their university department to establish whether their university has been selected to take part in the scheme.
Closing Date: July 31st.

ASSOCIATION OF COMMONWEALTH UNIVERSITIES

John Foster House
36 Gordon Square, London, WC1H 0PF, England
Tel: (44) 171 387 8572
Fax: (44) 171 387 2655
www: http://www.acu.ac.uk/
Contact: Awards Division

The Association of Commonwealth Universities (ACU), founded in 1913, is the oldest international association of universities in the world. It is incorporated by royal charter and Her Majesty the Queen, Head of the Commonwealth, is its patron. The aim of the Association is to promote, in various practical ways, contact and co-operation between its member institutions: by encouraging and supporting the movement of academic and administrative staff and students from one country of the Commonwealth to another; by providing information about universities; by organising meetings; and by hosting a higher education management service.

Times Higher Education Supplement Exchange Fellowship

Subjects: All subjects.
Eligibility: Open to academic, administrative, professional or library staff of ACU member universities in developing countries.
Level of Study: Professional development.
Purpose: To enable the recipient to obtain further experience at another university in a Commonwealth developing country; undertake a short study tour of at least one Commonwealth developing country; and visit another university in a Commonwealth developing country to realise a specific developmental objective.
Type: Fellowship.
No. of awards offered: 1.
Frequency: Annual.
Value: Up to £3,000.
Length of Study: Up to 3 months.
Study Establishment: Universities in Commonwealth countries.
Country of Study: Developing countries of the Commonwealth, other than the recipient's own country.
Application Procedure: Applications should be made through the Vice Chancellor's office of the candidate's university.
Closing Date: End of May.

ASSOCIATION OF INTERNATIONAL EDUCATION, JAPAN (AIEJ)

4-5-29 Komaba
Meguro-ku, Tokyo, 153, Japan
Tel: (81) 3 5454 5213
Fax: (81) 3 5454 5233
Contact: Mr Naoko Kadowaki, Student Affairs Division

The AIEJ was founded in 1957 with the aim of advancing international exchange in education. The Association is financed mainly by government services as the central organisation in carrying out projects relating to international education under the auspices of the Japanese Ministry of Education, universities and other educational institutions.

AIEJ Honors Scholarships

Subjects: All subjects.
Eligibility: Open to self-supporting foreign students studying in a university graduate school, junior college, college of technology or special training college in Japan who display excellence in their academic work and character and who are deemed to be in need of economic assistance during their stay in Japan.

Level of Study: Postgraduate, Undergraduate.
Type: Scholarship.
No. of awards offered: Approx. 8,540.
Frequency: Annual.
Value: Y70,000 per month (for graduate students); Y49,000 per month for undergraduate students).
Length of Study: 1 year.
Study Establishment: A graduate school in Japan. University, Junior College (2 year), College of Technology, Special Training College.
Country of Study: Japan.
Application Procedure: Candidates should apply through their school in Japan.
Closing Date: Specified by each school.

ASSOCIATION OF RHODES SCHOLARS IN AUSTRALIA

University of Melbourne, Parkville, VIC, 3052, Australia
Tel: (61) 3 9344 6937
Fax: (61) 3 9347 6739
Email: g.swafford@research.unimelb.edu.au
www: http://www.unimelb.edu.au
Contact: Dr Glenn Swafford, General Manager of Research

The Association of Teachers and Lecturers is the leading professional organisation and trade union for teachers and lecturers with over 150,000 members in England, Wales and Northern Ireland. The Association is committed to protecting and promoting the interests of its members and maintaining the highest quality professional support for them.

Association of Rhodes Scholars in Australia Travel Bursary

Subjects: All subjects.
Eligibility: Open to graduates of a Commonwealth university approved by the committee administering the scholarship, who are currently enrolled as a research higher degree student at their home university. Applicants must be Commonwealth citizens and may not be graduates of an Australian or New Zealand university.
Level of Study: Postgraduate.
Purpose: To enable an overseas Commonwealth student to undertake research for six months at one or more universities in Australia.
Type: Travel Bursary.
No. of awards offered: 1.
Frequency: Dependent on funds available.
Value: Currently A$9,000 including travel expenses and monthly stipend.
Length of Study: 6 months.
Study Establishment: A university.
Country of Study: Australia.
Application Procedure: Information and application forms are available through the internet site.
Closing Date: As advertised.

ASSOCIATION OF UNIVERSITIES AND COLLEGES OF CANADA

International and Canadian Programs Division
350 Albert Street
Suite 600, Ottawa, ON, K1R 1B1, Canada
Tel: (1) 613 563 1236
Fax: (1) 613 563 9745
Email: mleger@aucc.ca
www: http://www.aucc.ca
Contact: Canadian Awards Program

The Association of Universities and Colleges of Canada is a non-profit, non-governmental association that represents Canadian universities at home and abroad. The Association's mandate is to foster and promote the interests of higher education in the firm belief that strong universities are vital to the prosperity and well-being of Canada.

Canada-Taiwan Scholarships Programme

Subjects: Mandarin language training.
Eligibility: Canadian university students.
Purpose: This programme allows 10 Canadian university students to travel to Taiwan each year for Mandarin language training.
Type: Scholarship.
No. of awards offered: 10.
Value: Return airfare to Taiwan, tuition and monthly allowance.
Length of Study: 12 months.
Study Establishment: Tenable at the Mandarin Training Center of the National Taiwan Normal University.
Country of Study: Taiwan.
Application Procedure: For more information contact Jeanne Gallagher.
Closing Date: March 27th.

Frank Knox Memorial Fellowships at Harvard University

Subjects: Arts and sciences (including engineering), business administration, dental medicine, design, divinity, education, law, medicine, public administration and public health.
Eligibility: Open to Canadian citizens or permanent residents who have recently graduated or are about to graduate from a university or college in Canada which is a member, or affiliated to a member, of AUCC. No application is considered from a student already in the USA, although applications will be considered from recent graduates who are working in the United States and will be applying to the MBA programme.
Level of Study: Postgraduate.
Type: Fellowship.
No. of awards offered: Up to 2.
Frequency: Annual.
Value: US$15,500 plus tuition fees and student health insurance..
Length of Study: 1 academic year.
Study Establishment: Harvard University, Cambridge, Massachusetts.

Country of Study: USA.

Application Procedure: Each candidate must apply directly to the graduate school of his or her choice. Candidates are responsible for gaining admission to Harvard University by the deadline set by the various faculties. For more information and application forms contact Alison Craig or download information and application form from the website.

Closing Date: February 1st (postmarked).

Additional Information: Fellows may not accept any other grant for the award period unless approved by the Committee on General Scholarships and the Sheldon Fund of Harvard University. Candidates applying to the School of Business Administration are required to take the Admissions Test for Graduate Study in Business in October or January. This may be arranged by contacting the Educational Testing Service, Box 966, Princeton, NJ, 08540, USA. Normally two months' notice should be given to ETS.

The Paul Sargent Memorial Linguistic Scholarship Program

Subjects: All fields at the Master's level, preferably with previous exposure to an oriental language.

Eligibility: Candidates must be Canadian citizens at the time of application and must hold a bachelor's degree either at the major or minor level, in the language concerned, with a high record of academic achievement. Applicants must have at least an intermediate level of competence in an Oriental language (the minimum proficiency required would be a consistent A- in language courses).

Level of Study: Postgraduate.

Purpose: To assist postgradaute level students in languages.

Type: Scholarship.

No. of awards offered: 2.

Value: US$12,000.

Length of Study: 2 years.

Study Establishment: Tenable at any Canadian university which is a member, or affiliated with a member, of AUCC.

Application Procedure: For more information and application forms contact Alison Craig.

Closing Date: January 6th.

Programme Canadien de bourses de la Francophonie

Subjects: All disciplines likely to contribute to the development of the scholar's country are eligible, with the exception of studies in medicine and dentistry.

Eligibility: Scholars must be fluent in written and oral French. There is no age limit; however, candidates must have completed their previous degree within five years prior to application.

Purpose: The programme is administered by the Association of Universities and Colleges of Canada for scholars studying in provinces other than Quebec at universities which offer programmes in French, and by the Direction de la co-opération, ministère de l'Éducation, Governement du Québec, for scholars studying in Quebec.

No. of awards offered: Determined annually by CIDA.

Value: The scholarship includes transportation to Canada and return trip home, tuition fees, installation allowance, living allowance, and books allowance. Scholars are invited to an information session upon arrival in Canada and a pre-departure session at the end of their studies.

Length of Study: 1 year, renewable up to the normal duration of the degree sought.

Country of Study: France.

Application Procedure: Application forms can be requested from the government authorities responsible for the pre-selection in the scholar's country of citizenship or at the responsible Canadian diplomatic mission. For more information contact Jeanne Gallagher.

Closing Date: Applications must be submitted by the authorities of the scholar's country to the responsible Canadian diplomatic mission before December 15th.

ATLANTIC SCHOOL OF THEOLOGY

640 Fracklyn Street, Halifax, NS, B3H 3B5, Canada
Tel: (1) 902 423 6801
Fax: (1) 902 492 4048
Email: dmaclachlan@astheology.ns.ca
www: http://www.astheology.ns.ca
Contact: Academic Dean

The Atlantic School of Theology is an ecumenical university committed to excellence in graduate level theological education and research and in formation for Christian ministries, lay and ordained, in church and society, primarily in Atlantic Canada.

The Evelyn Hilchie Betts Memorial Fellowship

Subjects: Any subject offered at the Atlantic School of Theology.

Eligibility: Open to ordained clergy (male or female) from developing countries, who are interested in theological education in an ecumenical atmosphere and are able to speak and write in the English language. Applicants must be interested in living and working in a Christian community and willing to share their work and experiences with the Canadian church.

Level of Study: Postgraduate.

Purpose: To enable ordained clergy from the Third World to study at the School and thereby to introduce persons from other Christian communities to the church and theological education in Canada and to share their context with the School.

Type: Fellowship.

No. of awards offered: 1.

Frequency: Every 4-5 years - next anticipated award 2001-2002.

Value: Approximately C$15,000. Pays for transportation, tuition, room and board.

Length of Study: 1 academic year.

Study Establishment: The Atlantic School of Theology in Halifax, Nova Scotia.

Country of Study: Canada.

Application Procedure: Application and letters of reference must be submitted.
Closing Date: December 31st, 2000.

AUSTRALIAN ACADEMY OF THE HUMANITIES

GPO Box 93, Canberra, ACT, 2601, Australia
Tel: (61) 2 6248 7744
Fax: (61) 2 6248 6287
Email: yvonne.gentry@anu.edu.au
www: http://www.asap.unimelb.edu.au/aas/naf/aah.htm
Contact: The Secretariat

The AAH was established under Royal Charter in 1969 for the advancement of the scholarship and of interest in and understanding of the humanities. Humanities disciplines include, but are not limited to; history, classics. english, european languages and cultures, Asian studies, philosophy, the arts, linguistics, prehistory and archaeology, and cultural and communications studies.

Australian Academy of the Humanities Travelling Fellowships

Subjects: Humanities.
Eligibility: Open to scholars resident in Australia working in the field of humanities.
Level of Study: Unrestricted.
Purpose: To enable short-term study abroad.
Type: Fellowship.
No. of awards offered: 5.
Frequency: Annual.
Value: A$2,500 each.
Length of Study: At least 6 weeks.
Study Establishment: An appropriate research centre.
Country of Study: Outside Australia.
Application Procedure: Please write for details.
Closing Date: July 30th.
Additional Information: Research projects should be near a state of completion.

AUSTRALIAN FEDERATION OF UNIVERSITY WOMEN - VICTORIA

PO Box 816, Mount Eliza, VIC, 3930, Australia
www: http://www.vicnet.net.au/afuwvic/
Contact: Honorary Scholarship Secretary

AFUW Victoria Endowment Scholarship, Lady Leitch Scholarship

Subjects: All subjects.
Eligibility: Open to women graduates who are members of the Australian Federation of University Women, or its international affiliates who are graduates of Australian Universities (Endowment Scholarship). Lady Leitch is open to AFUW/IFUW members.
Level of Study: Doctorate, Postdoctorate, Postgraduate, Professional development.
Purpose: To assist advanced study or research.
Type: Scholarship.
No. of awards offered: 2.
Frequency: Annual - AFUW Victoria, every two years - Lady Leitch.
Value: Approximately A$5,000 for each award.
Length of Study: 1 year.
Country of Study: Any country.
Application Procedure: Application form must be completed, with documentation on university qualifications, names of three referees, and membership of AFUW or affiliate.
Closing Date: March 1st.
Additional Information: Application forms are available on AFUW-Vic website.

THE AUSTRALIAN FEDERATION OF UNIVERSITY WOMEN, SOUTH AUSTRALIA, INC TRUST FUND (AFUW)

GPO Box 634, Adelaide, SA, 5001, Australia
Contact: Fellowships Trustee

The AFUW's main activity is directed at assisting women in tertiary education in Australia via bursaries. Funds for the bursaries are raised through volunteer work, academic dress hire, donations and bequests.

The AFUW-SA Inc Trust Fund Bursary

Subjects: All subjects.
Eligibility: Applications are invited from women enrolled for coursework Master's degrees at an Australian university, who have a good Honours degree or equivalent, have completed at least one year of postgraduate research (not including an Honours year), and are Australian citizens who are not in full-time paid employment or on fully-paid study leave during the tenure of the bursary.
Level of Study: Postgraduate.
Purpose: To assist women to complete Master's degrees by coursework.
Type: Bursary.
No. of awards offered: 1.
Frequency: Annual.
Value: Up to A$3,000; runners-up may receive awards of less than bursary amount.
Length of Study: Bursary must be used within 12 months of date of award.
Study Establishment: A recognised Australian tertiary institution.

Country of Study: Australia.
Application Procedure: The following must accompany the completed application form: evidence of enrolment at the institution at which the qualification is to be obtained; copies of official transcripts; CV, including employment record and list of publications.
Closing Date: March 1st.

Barbara Crase Bursary

Subjects: All subjects.
Eligibility: Open to women or men of any nationality; applicants must have completed one year of postgraduate research, excluding Honours year.
Level of Study: Doctorate, Postgraduate.
Purpose: To assist in completion of a Master's or PhD research degree.
Type: Bursary.
No. of awards offered: 1.
Frequency: Annual.
Value: A$2,500.
Length of Study: Bursary must be used within 12 months of date of award.
Study Establishment: A South Australian university.
Country of Study: Australia.
Application Procedure: Please write for details.
Closing Date: March 1st.

Cathy Candler Bursary

Subjects: All subjects.
Eligibility: Open to women or men of any nationality; applicants must have completed one year of postgraduate research, excluding Honours year.
Level of Study: Doctorate, Postgraduate.
Purpose: To assist in completion of a Master's or PhD degree by research.
Type: Bursary.
No. of awards offered: 1.
Frequency: Annual.
Value: A$2,500.
Length of Study: Bursary must be used within 12 months of date of award.
Study Establishment: A South Australian university.
Country of Study: Australia.
Application Procedure: Please write for details.
Closing Date: March 1st.

Diamond Jubilee Bursary

Subjects: All subjects.
Eligibility: Open to women or men of any nationality.
Level of Study: Postgraduate.
Purpose: To assist in completion of a Master's degree by coursework.
Type: Bursary.
No. of awards offered: 1.
Frequency: Annual.
Value: A$2,000.
Length of Study: Bursary must be used within 12 months of the date of award.

Study Establishment: A South Australian university.
Country of Study: Australia.
Application Procedure: Please write for details.

Doreen McCarthy Bursary

Subjects: All subjects.
Eligibility: Open to women or men any nationality; applicants must have completed one year of postgraduate research, excluding Honours year.
Level of Study: Doctorate, Postgraduate.
Purpose: To assist in completion of a Master's or PhD degree by research.
Type: Bursary.
No. of awards offered: 1.
Frequency: Annual.
Value: A$2,500.
Length of Study: Bursary must be used within 12 months of date of award.
Study Establishment: A South Australian university.
Country of Study: Australia.
Application Procedure: Please write for details.
Closing Date: March 1st.

Padnendadlu Bursary

Subjects: All subjects.
Eligibility: Must be an Australian indigenous woman.
Level of Study: Postgraduate.
Purpose: To assist in completion of a postgraduate degree by research.
Type: Bursary.
No. of awards offered: 1 but runners up may be awarded less than the bursary amount.
Frequency: Annual.
Value: A$2,500.
Study Establishment: A South Australian university.
Country of Study: Australia.
Application Procedure: Please write for details.
Closing Date: March 1st.

Thenie Baddams Bursary and Jean Gilmore Bursary

Subjects: All subjects.
Eligibility: Open to women graduates who are enrolled at an Australian tertiary institution and have completed at least one year of postgraduate research, excluding honours year. Applicants must hold a good Honours degree or equivalent, and not be not in full-time paid employment or study leave during tenure.
Level of Study: Postgraduate.
Purpose: To assist women to complete a Master's or PhD degree, by research.
Type: Bursary.
No. of awards offered: 2.
Frequency: Annual.
Value: Up to A$6,000 each; however runners-up can be awarded a lesser amount.

Length of Study: Bursary must be used within 12 months of date of award.
Study Establishment: A recognised Australian higher education institution.
Country of Study: Any country.
Application Procedure: Applications must include: completed application form; evidence of enrolment at the institution where the qualification is to be obtained; copies of official transcripts; curriculum vitae, including employment record and list of publications. There is a A$12.00 lodgement fee.
Closing Date: March 1st.

THE AUSTRALIAN GOVERNMENT

The University of Newcastle, Callaghan, NSW, 2308, Australia
Tel: (61) 49 21 6537
Fax: (61) 49 21 6908
Contact: P H Farley, Research Branch Director

The University of Newcastle ranks ninth out of thirty-six Australian universities, in research. There are twelve special research centres, over fifty research programmes of international standing and 900 research candidates spread over ten faculties including: Architecture Building and Design, Arts and Social Science, Economics and Commerce, Education, Engineering, Law Medicine and Health Sciences, Music, Nursing Science and Mathematics.

Australian Government Postgraduate Awards

Subjects: All academic disciplines.
Eligibility: Open to Australian citizens and permanent residents who have lived in Australia for 12 months prior to application. Applicants must have completed four years of full-time undergraduate study and gained a first class Honours, or equivalent award.
Level of Study: Doctorate, Postgraduate.
Purpose: To support students undertaking full-time higher research degree programmes at Australian universities.
Type: Research Grant, Research Scholarship.
No. of awards offered: Approx. 40.
Frequency: Annual.
Value: Living allowance of approximately A$16,000 per year tax exempt and index-linked, plus allowances for relocation and thesis production and exemption of HECS payments.
Length of Study: 2 years full-time study for research Master's candidates, or 3 years full-time for PhD candidates.
Country of Study: Australia.
Application Procedure: Application form must be completed.
Closing Date: October 31st.

AUSTRALIAN INSTITUTE OF ABORIGINAL AND TORRES STRAIT ISLANDER STUDIES

GPO Box 553, Canberra, ACT, 2601, Australia
Tel: (61) 6 246 1157
Fax: (61) 6 249 7714
Email: fbb@aiatsis.gov.au
www: http://www.aiatsis.gov.au
Contact: Director of Research

AIATSIS is a federally funded organisation central in Aboriginal and Torres Strait Islander research. Its principal function is to promote Australian Aboriginal and Torres Strait Islander studies. A staff of 60, directed by the Principal, engages in a range of services through the Research Program, the Research Grants Program, the archives and production team, and the library.

AIATSIS Research Grants

Subjects: Health, human biology, social anthropology, linguistics, ethnomusicology, material culture, rock art, prehistory, ethnobotany, psychology, education and Aboriginal history including oral history, native title, indigenous land use agreements.
Eligibility: Open to nationals of any country.
Level of Study: Unrestricted.
Purpose: To promote research into Aboriginal and Torres Strait Islander Studies.
Type: Research Grant.
No. of awards offered: Varies according to application and availablilty of funds.
Frequency: Annual.
Value: No predetermined value.
Length of Study: 12 months maximum.
Country of Study: Australia.
Application Procedure: Application form must be completed. Application form available from Research Administrator tel: 6 246 1145 or visit the AIATSIS website.
Closing Date: January 31st.
Additional Information: Permission to conduct research project must be obtained from the appropriate Aboriginal or Torres Strait Island community or organisation.

AUSTRALIAN MUSICAL FOUNDATION

Richards Butler 6
Beafort House
15 St Botolph St, London, EC3A 7EC, England
Tel: (44) 171 247 6555
Fax: (44) 171 257 5091
Contact: Mr John Emmett, Secretary

AMF Award

Subjects: Any aspect of musical study chosen by the recipient.

Eligibility: Open to Australian singers and instrumentalists under 30 years of age who are resident in Australia or the UK.
Level of Study: Unrestricted.
Purpose: To finance further studies.
No. of awards offered: Up to 3.
Frequency: Annual.
Value: £10,000.
Length of Study: 2 years; the second year is subject to assessment.
Country of Study: European countries.
Application Procedure: Application forms and demo cassette need to be submitted before the end of April each year. Applications must be sent to Mr John Emmett (Secretary).
Closing Date: End of April.
Additional Information: Applications are considered in the first instance by the Foundation Committee, with a panel of adjudicators making the final choice. It is stressed that this award is intended for musicians of merit and ability. The Foundation will also take into account, how applicants propose to use the award, should they win, to further their careers.

AUSTRALIAN NATIONAL UNIVERSITY

Canberra, ACT, 0200, Australia
Tel: (61) 6 249 2700
Fax: (61) 6 248 0054
Email: administraton.hrc@anu.edu.au
www: http://www.anu.edu.au/hrc
Contact: Humanities Research Centre

The Australian National University was founded by the Australian Government in 1946 as Australia's only completely research-oriented university. It comprises eight research schools, six teaching faculties, a graduate school and over a dozen other academic schools or centres.

Aboriginal and Torred Strait Islander Scholarship

Subjects: All subjects.
Eligibility: Awarded to an indigenous Australian who is an Aboriginal or Torres Strait Islander.
Level of Study: Doctorate, Postgraduate.
Purpose: To assist and Aboriginal or Torres Strait Islander to undertake a graduate diploma or master degree course, or a course leading to a PhD.
Type: Scholarship.
No. of awards offered: Varies.
Frequency: Annual.
Value: A$15,888 stipend per annum.
Length of Study: Dependent on the course to which the scholarship applies.
Country of Study: Australia.
Application Procedure: Please write for details.
Closing Date: October 31st.

ANU Alumni Association Country Specific PhD Scholarships

Subjects: All subjects.
Eligibility: Open to nationals from Malaysia, Thailand and Singapore.
Level of Study: Doctorate.
Purpose: To assist students from Malaysia, Singapore and Thailand with study in Australia.
Type: Scholarship.
No. of awards offered: 3- one to a candidate from each of the eligible countries.
Value: A$15,888 basic stipend perannum, tax free.
Length of Study: Normally tenable for 3 years renewable for 6 months.
Country of Study: Australia.
Application Procedure: Please write for details.
Closing Date: August 30th.

ANU Masters Degree Scholarships (The Faculties)

Subjects: All subjects.
Eligibility: Applicants must hold a Bachelors degree with at least upper second class honours, and, if wishing to undertake degree by research only, must have proven capability for research.
Level of Study: Postgraduate.
Purpose: To assist study in most graduate school programmes for courses leading to a Masters degree by research, by coursework or by coursework and research.
Type: Scholarship.
No. of awards offered: Varies.
Frequency: Annual.
Value: Basic stipend of A$15,888 per annum tax free; an additional allowance for dependant children of married international scholars, travel to Canberra (excluding international part of the airfare for those recruited from overseas) and a grant for the reimbursement of some removal expenses.
Length of Study: 1 year.
Study Establishment: The Faculties.
Country of Study: Australia.
Application Procedure: Please write for details.
Closing Date: October 31st for citizens/permanent residents of New Zealand and Australia; August 30th for international applicants.

ANU PhD Scholarships

Subjects: All subjects.
Eligibility: Please write for details.
Level of Study: Postgraduate.
Purpose: To assist research.
Type: Scholarship.
No. of awards offered: Varies.
Value: Stipend of $A15,888 per annum tax free, and if applicable, an additional allowance for dependent children of unmarried international scholars. Economy travel to Canberra and a grant for the reimbursement of some removal expenses.

Length of Study: 3 years, renewable for six months.
Country of Study: Australia.
Application Procedure: Please write for details.
Closing Date: October 31st for citizens/permanent residents of Australia and New Zealand; August 30th for international students.

Australian National University Visiting Fellowships

Subjects: The HRC interprets the humanities generously, recognising that new methods of theoretical enquiry have done much to break down the traditional distinction between the humanities and the social sciences, recognising too, the importance of establishing dialogue between the humanities and the natural and technological sciences and the creative arts.
Eligibility: Open to candidates of any nationality who are at the postdoctoral level.
Level of Study: Postdoctorate.
Purpose: To provide scholars with time to pursue their own work in congenial and stimulating surroundings.
Type: Fellowship.
No. of awards offered: Up to 20.
Frequency: Annual.
Value: Return economy airfare, plus a weekly stipend for a maximum of 13 weeks.
Length of Study: 3-12 months; not renewable.
Study Establishment: The Humanities Research Centre at the University.
Country of Study: Australia.
Application Procedure: Formal application available from the website.
Closing Date: October 31st.
Additional Information: Fellows are required to spend at least three-quarters of their time in residence at the Centre.

Graduate School Scholarships

Subjects: All subjects.
Eligibility: Restricted to those who are on the Order of Merit list for Australian Postgraduate Awards.
Level of Study: Graduate, Postgraduate.
Purpose: To fund graduate study.
Type: Scholarship.
Value: Stipend of A$15,888 per annum tax free, travel to Canberra from within Australia and a grant for the reimbursement of some removal expenses.
Country of Study: Australia.
Application Procedure: Please write for details.
Closing Date: October 31st.

Re-entry Scholarships for Women

Subjects: All subjects.
Eligibility: Applicants must be Australian citizens or permanent residents. The scholarship may be awarded to undertake a Master's degree course or a PhD and applicants must hold qualifications appropriate to the level of course for which they wish to apply.
Level of Study: Doctorate, Postgraduate.

Purpose: To assist women graduates who wish to resume their studies after a break of at least three years since formal enrolment in a university course, the break normally being due to fulfilment of family obligations.
Type: Scholarship.
No. of awards offered: Varies.
Frequency: Annual.
Value: A$15,888 per annum.
Length of Study: Tenure is dependent upon the course to which the scholarship applies.
Country of Study: Australia.
Application Procedure: An application must be submitted along with a letter setting out the applicants case for award of the scholarship and indicating their circumstances in terms of the eligibility criteria.
Closing Date: September 30th.

Scholarships for International Students Only

Subjects: All subjects.
Eligibility: Many students come from developing countries under the Australian Government's foreign aid programme which is administered by the Australian Agency for International Development (AusAID).
Level of Study: Doctorate, Postgraduate.
Purpose: To assist international students to study in Australia.
Type: Scholarship.
No. of awards offered: Varies.
Value: Some scholarships cover full tuition, living costs and travel, others cover tuition fees only.
Country of Study: Australia.
Application Procedure: Please write for details.
Closing Date: October 30th.

Tuition Fee Scholarships

Subjects: All subjects.
Eligibility: Awarded to those on the Overseas Postgraduate Research Scholarship (OPRS) Order of Merit list.
Level of Study: Doctorate, Postgraduate.
Purpose: Tuition waiver fee scholarships awarded to candidates on the OPRS Order of Merit list.
Type: Scholarship.
No. of awards offered: Varies.
Value: Covers course fee.
Country of Study: Australia.
Application Procedure: Please write for details.

AUSTRALIAN WAR MEMORIAL

GPO Box 345, Canberra, ACT, 2601, Australia
Tel: (61) 6 243 4257
Fax: (61) 6 243 4325
Email: peter.londay@awm.gov.au
www: http://www.adfa.oz.au/~awm/
Contact: The Research Grants Officer

The Australian War Memorial commemorates the sacrifice of those Australians who died in war. The mission is to assist

Australians to remember, interpret and understand the Australian experience of war and its enduring impact on Australian society.

John Treloar Grants-in-Aid

Subjects: Australian military history.
Eligibility: Open to applications assessed on the following criteria: the quality of the applicant; the quality of the project; and the potential contribution to Australian military history.
Level of Study: Unrestricted.
Purpose: To assist research into Australian military history.
Type: Grant-in-Aid.
No. of awards offered: 10-20.
Frequency: Annual.
Value: Up to A$6,000 to help cover costs such as photocopying, research assistance, travel, accommodation, and oral history.
Length of Study: 1 year.
Study Establishment: Tenable anywhere.
Country of Study: Any country.
Application Procedure: Application form and attachments to be completed by late June in year before the grants are awarded. Applications should be addressed to the Research Grants Officer at the Military History Section of Australian War Memorial.
Closing Date: June of the year prior to the award.

AUSTRALIAN-AMERICAN EDUCATIONAL FOUNDATION

GPO Box 1559, Canberra, ACT, 2601, Australia
Tel: (61) 2 6247 9331
Fax: (61) 2 6247 6554
Email: lindy@aaef.anu.edu.au
www: http://www.sunsite.anu.edu.au/education/fulbright
Contact: Program and Development Officer

The Australian-American Educational Foundation is a bi-national commission. The major objective of the Foundation is to further mutual understanding between the peoples of Australia and the United States through educational exchanges. The Foundation also provides information for Australians wishing to study in the United States.

Fulbright Awards

Subjects: All subjects.
Eligibility: Open to Australian postgraduate and postdoctoral students, senior scholars and professionals.
Level of Study: Doctorate, Postdoctorate, Postgraduate, Professional development.
No. of awards offered: Up to 16.
Frequency: Annual.
Value: Postgraduate students: up to A$32,530; postdoctoral fellows: up to A$38,890; senior scholars: up to A$28,350; professionals: up to A$17,600.

Length of Study: Varies.
Country of Study: USA.
Application Procedure: Application form must be completed, three referees' reports (included in the application form), documentation of citizenship and qualifications must be submitted. Additional information and an application form are available on the website.
Closing Date: September 30th.

Fulbright Postdoctoral Fellowships

Subjects: All subjects.
Eligibility: Open to Australian citizens by birth or naturalisation; naturalised citizens must provide a certificate of Australian citizenship with their application, and native-born Australians must provide a copy of their birth certificate. Those holding dual US/Australian citizenship are not eligible for this award. Applicants should have recently completed their PhD, normally less than three years prior to application, although those who have completed their PhD four to five years prior to application will be considered.
Level of Study: Postdoctorate.
Purpose: To enable those who have recently completed their PhD to conduct postdoctoral research, further their professional training, or lecture at a university.
Type: Scholarship.
No. of awards offered: Up to 2.
Frequency: Annual.
Value: Up to A$38,890.
Length of Study: 3-12 months.
Study Establishment: A university, college, research establishment or reputable private practice.
Country of Study: USA.
Application Procedure: An application form must be completed, three referees reports (included in the application form), documentation of citizenship and qualifications must be submitted. Additional Information are available on the website.
Closing Date: September 30th.

Fulbright Postgraduate Student Award for Aboriginal and Torres Strait Islander People

Subjects: All subjects.
Eligibility: Open to people of Aboriginal and Torres Strait Islander descent.
Level of Study: Postgraduate.
Purpose: To enable candidates to undertake an approved course of study for an American higher degree, or engage in research relevant to an Australian higher degree.
Type: Scholarship.
No. of awards offered: 1.
Frequency: Annually, dependent on funds available.
Value: Up to A$32,530.
Length of Study: 8-12 months funded; up to a further 4 years unfunded.
Study Establishment: An accredited institution.
Country of Study: USA.

Application Procedure: Application form, three referees' reports (included in application form), documentation of citizenship and qualifications must be submitted. Additional information and an application form can be obtained from the website.
Closing Date: September 30th.

Fulbright Postgraduate Student Award for the Visual and Performing Arts

Subjects: Fine and applied arts.
Eligibility: Open to Australian citizens. Those holding dual US/Australian citizenship are ineligible for an award.
Level of Study: Doctorate, Postgraduate, Professional development.
Purpose: To enable candidates to undertake a higher degree, or carry out research towards an Australian higher degree.
No. of awards offered: 1.
Frequency: Annually, dependent on funds available.
Value: Up to A$32,530.
Length of Study: 8-12 months funded; up to a further 4 years unfunded.
Country of Study: USA.
Application Procedure: Application form, three referees' reports (forms included in application form), documentation of citizenship and qualifications must be submitted. Additional information and an application form are available on the website.
Closing Date: September 30th.

Fulbright Postgraduate Studentships

Subjects: All subjects.
Eligibility: Open to Australian citizens by birth or naturalisation; naturalised citizens must provide a certificate of Australian citizenship with their application, and native-born Australians must provide a copy of their birth certificate. Those holding dual US/Australian citizenship are ineligible for this award. Applicants must be graduates.
Level of Study: Doctorate, Postgraduate.
Purpose: To enable students to undertake an approved course of study for an American higher degree or its equivalent, or to engage in research relevant to an Australian higher degree.
Type: Scholarship.
No. of awards offered: Up to 8.
Frequency: Annual.
Value: Up to A$32,530.
Length of Study: 8-12 months, renewable for a maximum of 5 years, but without additional allowance.
Study Establishment: An accredited US institution.
Country of Study: USA.
Application Procedure: Application form must be completed, three referees' reports (included in the application form), and documentation of citizenship and qualifications must be submitted. Additional Information and an application form are available from the website.
Closing Date: September 30th.
Additional Information: As the Award does not include any provision for maintenance payments, applicants must be able to demonstrate that they have sufficient financial resources to support themselves and any dependants during their stay in the USA.

Fulbright Professional Award

Subjects: Open to all professional fields.
Eligibility: Open to Australian citizens, resident in Australia, with a record of achievement, and are poised for advancement to a senior management or policy role. Those who hold dual US/Australian citizenship are ineligible for this award.
Level of Study: Professional development.
Purpose: To support applicants undertaking a programme of professional development.
Type: Fellowship.
No. of awards offered: 1.
Frequency: Annual.
Value: Up to A$17,600.
Length of Study: 3-4 months between July and June; programs of longer duration may be proposed but without additional funding.
Country of Study: USA.
Application Procedure: Application form must be completed, three referees' reports (included in the application form), and documentation of citizenship and qualifications must be submitted. Additional information and an application form are available from the website.
Closing Date: September 30th.
Additional Information: Programs should include an academic as well as a practical aspect.

Fulbright Senior Awards

Subjects: All subjects.
Eligibility: Open to Australian citizens by birth or naturalisation; naturalised citizens must provide a certificate of Australian citizenship with their application, and native-born Australians must provide a copy of their birth certificate. Those holding dual US/Australian citizenship are not eligible for this award. Applicants should be either scholars of established reputation working in an academic institution who intend to teach or research in the USA; leaders in the arts (for example music, drama, visual arts); or senior members of the academically based professions who are currently engaged in the private practice of their profession.
Level of Study: Professional development.
Purpose: To teach, undertake research, be an invited speaker, or visit institutions within their field.
No. of awards offered: 2.
Frequency: Annual.
Value: Up to A$28,350.
Length of Study: 4-6 months.
Study Establishment: A university, college, research establishment or reputable private organisation.
Country of Study: USA.
Application Procedure: Application form must be completed, three referees' reports (included in application form), and documentation of citizenship and qualifications must be submitted. Additional information and an application form are available from the website.
Closing Date: September 30th.

AUSTRIAN SCIENCE FUND

Weyringergasse 35, Vienna, A-1040, Austria
Tel: (43) 1 505 67 40
Fax: (43) 1 505 67 39
Email: maruska@mails.fwf.univie.ac.at
www: http://www.fwf.ac.at
Contact: Ms Monica Maruska

The FWF strives to advance basic research in Austria. The mandate of its' sister organisation, the Industrial Research Promotion Fund (FFF) which was established at the same time, is to deal with applied research and development.

Charlotte Bühler Habilitation Fellowships

Subjects: All subjects.
Eligibility: Female scientists up to the age of 40.
Level of Study: Postdoctorate.
Purpose: To support and encourage young female scientists to become future university lecturers.
Type: A variable number of Fellowships.
No. of awards offered: Varies.
Frequency: Annual.
Value: Approx. AS 390,000 per fellowship per annum. Includes up to AS25,000 per annum for travel and other expenses.
Length of Study: 12-24 months.
Application Procedure: Please write for details, or refer to the website.
Closing Date: Applications are accepted at any time.

Contribution to Publishing Costs

Subjects: All subjects.
Eligibility: Young scholars at doctoral or post doctoral level.
Purpose: To provide financial assistance for scholars publishing their work by providing subsidy (fundable or non-refundable) and interest free loans.
Type: Grant.
No. of awards offered: Varies.
Frequency: Annual.
Value: Dependent on the actual printing costs - not in excess of 70% of the technical production costs.
Application Procedure: Please contact the Austrian Science Fund for further details and an application form, or visit the website.
Closing Date: Applications can be submitted at any time.

Erwin Schrödinger Fellowships

Subjects: All subjects.
Eligibility: Highly qualified Austrian citizens up to the age of 35 who are Austrian nationals or permanent residents of Austria.
Level of Study: Postdoctorate.
Purpose: To offer highly qualified Austrian citizens the opportunity to work in leading foreign research institutions and research programmes.
Type: A variable number of Fellowships.
No. of awards offered: Varies.

Value: Approx. AS290,000 per fellowship per annum.
Length of Study: At least 10 months, maximum 24 months.
Study Establishment: Universities or research institutions worldwide.
Country of Study: Any country except Austria.
Application Procedure: Please write for details, or refer to the website.
Closing Date: Applications are accepted at any time.

Graduate Programme (WK)

Subjects: Regulatory mechanisms in molecular and cellular biology.
Eligibility: Candidates must be highly qualified PhD students or scientists at Austrian universities and non-university, non-profit research institution.
Level of Study: Research.
Purpose: To promote centres of scientific research in a particular field of enquiry.
Type: Research Grant.
Frequency: Varies.
Value: 10-15 work contracts for PhD students as well as equipment, travel and other costs (such as the organisation of workshops), depending on the number of participants.
Length of Study: Varies. The grant is subject to reviews at 3 year intervals to decide whether it is extended or terminated after a specified period.
Study Establishment: Vienna university.
Application Procedure: Please write for details, or refer to the website.
Closing Date: Please write for details.

Impulse Projects

Subjects: All subjects.
Eligibility: Postdoctoral students.
Level of Study: Professional development.
Purpose: To increase the number of research and development orientated businesses in Austria to create jobs for young researchers in the research and development departments of Austrian countries.
Type: Internship.
Frequency: Annual.
Value: AS504,000 per annum; AS125,000 per annum for any external services required.
Length of Study: Up to 2 years.
Study Establishment: Any company or business willing to participate in the project.
Country of Study: Austria.
Application Procedure: Please contact the Austrian Science Fund for further details and an application form.
Closing Date: Applications can be submitted at any time.

Individual Projects

Subjects: All subjects.
Eligibility: The merit of an individual research project is evaluated based on a peer review system. More than 2000 referees, virtually all from outside Austria, are requested to submit reviews each year.
Level of Study: Research.

Purpose: To offer qualified individuals research projects of up to 36 months in duration.
Type: A variable number of Grants.
No. of awards offered: Varies.
Frequency: Annual.
Value: Up to AS200,000 per individual.
Length of Study: Up to 36 months.
Application Procedure: Please write for details.
Closing Date: Please write for details.

Joint Research Programmes

Subjects: All subjects.
Eligibility: Decisions on whether to fund Joint Research Programmes are taken by the FWF Board once a year in autumn.
Level of Study: Research.
Purpose: To co-ordinate and focus the national potential on a particular topic. The objective is to solve interdisciplinary problems through inter-institutional co-operation in ambitious research projects of medium to long term duration.
Type: A variable number of Grants.
No. of awards offered: Varies.
Frequency: Annual.
Value: Approx. AS7 million per year.
Length of Study: Up to 5 years.
Study Establishment: Various research facilities across Austria with participation by universities in Germany and Switzerland.
Country of Study: Austria, Germany and Switzerland.
Application Procedure: Concepts can be submitted at any time. Guidelines for application are available from the Austrian Science Fund or from the website. For further information please contact the office responsible for the proposed field of research.
Closing Date: Concepts are accepted at any time.

Lise Meitner Fellowships

Subjects: All subjects.
Eligibility: Highly qualified foreign scientists up to the age of 35.
Level of Study: Postdoctorate.
Purpose: To offer highly qualified foreign scientists the opportunity of carrying out research in Austria and to enhance the Austrian scientific community through international contacts.
Type: A variable number of Fellowships.
No. of awards offered: Varies.
Frequency: Annual.
Value: Approx. AS385,000 per fellowship per annum.
Study Establishment: Austrian universities or research institutions.
Country of Study: Austria.
Application Procedure: Application forms and guidelines are available from the Austrian Science Fund or from the website.
Closing Date: Applications are accepted at any time.

Special Research Programmes

Subjects: All subjects.
Eligibility: Highly qualified research teams.
Level of Study: Research.
Purpose: To establish a centre of excellence at Austrian colleges and universities.
Type: A variable number of Grants.
No. of awards offered: Varies.
Frequency: Annual.
Value: Approx. AS16 million per project.
Length of Study: 2 to 5 years.
Study Establishment: Colleges and universities across Austria.
Country of Study: Austria.
Application Procedure: Information for application is available from the Austrian Science Fund or from the website.
Closing Date: Concepts can be submitted at any time.

START Programme

Subjects: All subjects.
Eligibility: Excellent young scientists from all disciplines up to the age of 36, who are Austrian nationals or permanent residents of Austria. Preferably candidates will have spent some time conducting academic research abroad.
Level of Study: Doctorate, Postdoctorate, Research.
Purpose: To offer excellent young scientists from all disciplines the opportunity to plan their research work in greater detail.
Type: Award.
No. of awards offered: Up to 5.
Frequency: Annual.
Value: AS1.5 million to AS2.5 million per award.
Length of Study: Up to 6 years.
Study Establishment: Austrian universities or research institutes.
Country of Study: Austria.
Application Procedure: Submission of the application form, together with a detailed research proposal and a reference from the Head of Department. Four copies of the applications are to be submitted in English. Application forms and further information are available from Monika Maruska, Austrians Science Foundation, tel: 43 1 505 67 40 27, email maruska@mails.fwf.univie.ac.at. Further information is also available from the website: http://www.fwf.ac.at.
Closing Date: November 16th.

Wittgenstein Award

Subjects: All subjects.
Eligibility: Scientists from all disciplines who have an international reputation in their field. Scientists must not be over 50 year of age, and must be Austrian nationals or permanent residents of Austria.
Level of Study: Postdoctorate.
Purpose: To guarantee maximum freedom and flexibility to researchers from all disciplines undertaking cutting edge research, and to facilitate the exceptional progress of their scientific performance.
Type: Award.

No. of awards offered: 1-2.
Frequency: Annual.
Value: AS10million-AS20million, according to individual requirements.
Length of Study: 5 years.
Study Establishment: Austrian universities or research institutes.
Application Procedure: Nominations to be submitted by officers from the Austrian Science Fund or past Wittgenstein Award winners, self nominations are not accepted.
Closing Date: Applications are accepted at any time.

THE BANFF CENTRE FOR THE ARTS

School of Fine Arts
Box 1020
Station 28, Banff, AB, T0L 0C0, Canada
Tel: (1) 403 762 6180
Fax: (1) 403 762 6345
Email: arts_info@banffcentre.ab.ca
www: http://www.banffcentre.ab.ca/
Contact: Ms Susan Adams, Associate Registrar

The Banff Centre for the Arts is Canada's only multi-disciplinary arts environment devoted to professional development and lifelong learning for artists. Acceptance is based on adjudication of submitted materials and/or audition.

Banff Centre Scholarships

Subjects: Studio art, photography, ceramics, performance art, video art, theatre production and design, stage management, opera, singing, dance, drama, music, writing, creative non-fiction and cultural journalism, publishing, media arts, television and video, audio recording, computer applications and research.
Eligibility: Open to advanced students who have been accepted for a residency at the Banff Centre.
Level of Study: Postgraduate.
Purpose: To provide financial assistance to deserving artists for a residency at the Banff Centre.
Type: Scholarship.
No. of awards offered: Varies.
Frequency: Annual.
Value: A major contribution towards tuition.
Length of Study: Courses of various lengths.
Study Establishment: The Banff Centre for the Arts.
Country of Study: Canada.
Application Procedure: A completed application form must be submitted, accompanied by requested documentation.
Closing Date: Varies according to programme.

BEIT TRUST (ZIMBABWE, ZAMBIA & MALAWI)

Beit Trust Fellowships
PO Box 76, Chisipite, Harare, Zimbabwe
Tel: (263) 4 96132
Fax: (263) 494046
Contact: Secretary to the Advisory Board

Beit Trust Postgraduate Fellowships

Subjects: All subjects.
Eligibility: Open to persons under 30 years of age (35 in the case of medical doctors) who are university graduates domiciled in Zambia (4 fellowships), Zimbabwe (4 fellowships), or Malawi (2 fellowships).
Level of Study: Postgraduate.
Purpose: To support postgraduate study or research.
Type: Fellowship.
No. of awards offered: 10.
Frequency: Annual.
Value: Personal allowance and fees (variable); plus book, clothing, thesis and departure allowances.
Length of Study: 2 years; possibly renewable for a further year.
Study Establishment: Approved universities and other institutions.
Country of Study: United Kingdom, Ireland or South Africa.
Application Procedure: Application form must be completed.
Closing Date: September 30th.

BELGIAN-AMERICAN EDUCATIONAL FOUNDATION, INC.

195 Church Street, New Haven, CT, 06510, United States of America
Tel: (1) 203 777 5765
Email: emile.boulpaep@yale.edu
Contact: The President

Belgian-American Educational Foundation Graduate Fellowships for Study in Belgium

Subjects: Agriculture, forestry and fishery, architecture and town planning, arts and humanities, business administration and management, education and teacher training, engineering, fine and applied arts, home economics, law, mass communication and information science, mathematics and computer science, medical sciences, natural sciences recreation, welfare, protective services, religion and theology, social and behavioural sciences, transport and communications.
Eligibility: Open to US citizens, preferably under 30 years of age, with a speaking and reading knowledge of Dutch, French or German. The candidate must have a Master's or

equivalent degree or be working towards a PhD or equivalent degree.
Level of Study: Doctorate, Postgraduate.
Type: Fellowship.
No. of awards offered: 10.
Frequency: Annual.
Value: US$12,000, which includes round-travel expenses, lodging and living expenses, as well as tuition and enrolment fees.
Length of Study: 1 academic year.
Study Establishment: A Belgian university or other academic institution of higher learning.
Country of Study: Belgium.
Application Procedure: Application form must be completed.
Closing Date: January 31st.

Belgian-American Educational Foundation Graduate Fellowships for Study in the USA

Subjects: All subjects.
Eligibility: Open to Belgian nationals. Applicants must have a good command of the English language.
Level of Study: Doctorate, Postgraduate.
Type: Fellowship.
Frequency: Annual.
Value: US$30,000.
Length of Study: 1 year.
Study Establishment: An American University.
Country of Study: USA.
Application Procedure: Application form must be completed, and 3-5 letters of reference must be submitted.
Closing Date: October 31st.
Additional Information: The stipend consists of a fixed sum to cover living expenses, purchase of books, and similar. In addition, the Foundation pays for tuition and health insurance at the American university. Fellows are expected to stay in the USA for a full academic year.

For further information contact:

Egmonstraat 11 rue d'Egmont, Brussels, B-1050, Belgium
Tel: (32) 2 513 59 55
Fax: (32) 2 672 53 81
Contact: The Secretary

Postgraduate Fellowships for Study in the USA

Subjects: All subjects.
Eligibility: Open to Belgian nationals. Applicants must have a good command of the English language.
Level of Study: Postgraduate.
Type: Fellowship.
Frequency: Annual.
Value: US$15,000.
Length of Study: 1 year.
Study Establishment: An American university.
Country of Study: USA.
Application Procedure: Application form must be completed, and 3-5 letters of reference must be submitted.
Closing Date: October 31st.

Additional Information: The stipend consists of a fixed sum to cover living expenses, purchase of books, and similar. In addition, the Foundation pays for health insurance at the American institution. Fellows are expected to stay in the USA for a full academic year.

For further information contact:

Egmontstraat 11 rue d'Egmont, Brussels, B-1050, Belgium
Tel: (32) 2 513 59 55
Fax: (32) 2 672 53 81
Contact: The Secretary

BEVERLY HILLS THEATRE GUILD

2815 North Beechwood Drive, Los Angeles, CA, 90068, United States of America
Tel: (1) 323 465 2703
Contact: Mr Marcella Meharg, Co-ordinator

The Beverly Hills Theatre Guild was established in 1977 to bring fine theatrical performances to the community; to develop and maintain community interest in the theatre; to stimulate children's participation in theatre; to enrich the theatrical experiences of senior adults; and to encourage and discover talent through annual Playwright Competitions.

Julie Harris Playwright Award Competition

Subjects: Playwriting.
Eligibility: Open to US playwrights. The award is made for an original, unpublished full-length play. Musicals, short one-act plays, adaptations, translations and plays that have previously been submitted, or have won other competitions are ineligible.
Level of Study: Unrestricted.
Purpose: To encourage and provide recognition to aspiring and/or established American playwrights.
Type: Competition.
No. of awards offered: 3.
Frequency: Annual.
Value: First award US$5,000 (June Moray Award); second award US$2,000 (Janet and Maxwell Salter Award); third award US$1,000 (Dr Henry and Lilian Nesburn Award).
Country of Study: Any country.
Application Procedure: Play entry must be submitted according to guidelines and with application form - both are available upon request with a SASE.
Closing Date: August 1st to November 1st (Postmarked).

Marilyn Hall Award

Subjects: Drama.
Eligibility: Open to US playwrights. The award is made for an original, unpublished play written for youth audiences of 7-14 years of age.
Level of Study: Unrestricted.

Purpose: To encourage the writing of plays specifically for young audiences.
Type: Prize.
No. of awards offered: 2.
Frequency: Annual.
Value: US$1,000: (US$750 winner; US$250 runner-up).
Country of Study: Any country.
Application Procedure: For enquiries, information and guidelines send an SASE to the Guild marked Children's Play Competition.
Closing Date: Only entries postmarked from January 15th through to the last day of February of the competition year will be accepted.
Additional Information: Winners will be announced in June of each year.

BFWG CHARITABLE FOUNDATION (FORMERLY CROSBY HALL)

28 Great James Street, London, WC1N 3ES, England
Tel: (44) 171 404 6447
Fax: (44) 171 404 6505
Email: bfwg.charity@btinternet.com
Contact: Ms Jean V Collett, Company Secretary

Offers grants to help woman graduates with their living expenses (not fees) while registered for study or research at an approved institution of higher education in Great Britain. The criteria for awarding grants are the proven needs of the applicants and their academic calibre.

BFWG Charitable Foundation and Emergency Grants

Subjects: All subjects.
Eligibility: Open to graduate women who have completed their first year of graduate or doctoral study or research. There is no restriction on nationality.
Level of Study: Doctorate, Postdoctorate, Postgraduate.
Purpose: Main Foundation Grants are to assist women graduates who have difficulty meeting their living expenses while studying or researching at approved institutions of higher education in Great Britain; Emergency Grants are to assist graduate women facing a financial crisis which may prevent them completing an academic year's study.
Type: Grant.
No. of awards offered: Approx. 50-60 Foundation Grants and approx. 50-60 Emergency Grants.
Frequency: Foundation Grants - annually. Emergency Grants - three times per year.
Value: Foundation Grants - will not exceed £2,500; Emergency Grants - no grant is likely to exceed £500.
Length of Study: Support for courses that exceed 12 months full-time.
Study Establishment: Approved institutions in Great Britain.
Country of Study: United Kingdom.

Application Procedure: Completed application forms, two references, copy of graduate certificate, evidence of acceptance for the year, a cheque for £12, or for £5 in the case of emergency grants;and a brief summary of thesis if applicable for foundation grants.
Closing Date: Foundation Grants - March 31st; Emergency Grants - February 17th, April 16th and June 15th.

Theodora Bosanquet Bursary

Subjects: English literature and history.
Eligibility: Open to women only.
Level of Study: Doctorate, Postdoctorate, Postgraduate.
Purpose: To support women postgraduate students who are carrying out research in English literature or history requiring the use of libraries, and archives in London.
Type: Bursary.
No. of awards offered: 1-2.
Frequency: Annual.
Value: Up to £600.
Length of Study: Up to 4 weeks.
Study Establishment: London Hall of Residence.
Country of Study: United Kingdom.
Application Procedure: Request for application should be sent to the Clerk of the Trustees, accompanied by a stamped, self addressed envelope or International Reply Coupons.
Closing Date: November 15th.

BIBLIOGRAPHICAL SOCIETY OF AMERICA

PO Box 1537
Lenox Hill Station, New York, NY, 10021, United States of America
Tel: (1) 212 452 2710
Fax: (1) 212 452 2710
Email: bibsocamer@aol.com
www: http://www.cla.sc.edu/engl/bsa
Contact: The Secretary

The Bibliographical Society of America (BSA) invites applications for its annual short-term fellowship program, which supports bibliographical inquiry as well as research in the history of the book trades and in publishing history.

BSA Fellowship Program

Subjects: Eligible topics may concentrate on books and documents in any field, but should focus on the book or manuscript (the physical object) as historical evidence. Such topics may include establishing a text or studying the history of book production, publication, distribution, collecting or reading. Enumerative listings do not fall within the scope of this program.
Eligibility: This programme is open to applicants of any nationality.
Level of Study: Doctorate, Postdoctorate, Postgraduate.

Purpose: To support bibliographical inquiry and research in the history of the book trades and publishing.
Type: Fellowship.
No. of awards offered: 8.
Frequency: Annual.
Value: US$1,500 per month.
Length of Study: 1-2 months.
Country of Study: Any country.
Application Procedure: An application form must be completed and the original plus six photocopies must be posted to the chairman of the Fellowship Committee at the Bibliographical Society of America. This application and three supporting letters of recommendation must be received by the deadline.
Closing Date: December 1st.
Additional Information: For information about membership in the society, contact the Executive Secretary.

BLUES HEAVEN FOUNDATION, INC.

2120 S Michigan Avenue, Chicago, IL, 60616, United States of America
Tel: (1) 312 808 1286
Contact: Grants Management Officer

Muddy Waters Scholarship

Subjects: Music, music education, Afro-American studies, folklore, performing arts, arts management, journalism, radio/TV/film.
Eligibility: Open to students with full-time enrolment status in a Chicago area college or university. Students must be in at least their first year of undergraduate studies or graduate programme.
Level of Study: Graduate, Undergraduate.
Type: Scholarship.
No. of awards offered: 1.
Frequency: Annual.
Value: US$2,000.
Study Establishment: A Chicago area college or university.
Country of Study: USA.
Application Procedure: Applications are available beginning in February for the upcoming academic year. Please write for details.
Closing Date: The application deadline is April 30th for announcement May 30th. Funds are made available for the following fall semester, upon documentation of enrolment.
Additional Information: The scholarship award shall be governed by the applicant's scholastic aptitude and extracurricular involvement, including grade point average, honours programs, and memberships. Eligibility will be based on projected expenses, student and family income. Special consideration will be given to applicants demonstrating need for financial assistance.

BOARD OF ARCHITECTS OF NEW SOUTH WALES

3 Manning Street, Potts Point, NSW, 2011, Australia
Tel: (61) 2 9356 4900
Fax: (61) 2 9357 4780
Email: boansw@ozemail.com.au
Contact: Registrar

Board of Architects of New South Wales Research Grant

Subjects: Any architectural topic approved by the Board.
Eligibility: Open to candidates who are registered as architects in New South Wales.
Level of Study: Professional development.
Purpose: To undertake research on a topic approved by the Board to contribute to the advancement of architecture.
Type: Research Grant.
No. of awards offered: 1.
Frequency: Every two years.
Value: A$6,000.
Length of Study: 1 year.
Country of Study: Any country.
Application Procedure: Please write for details.
Closing Date: April 30th.
Additional Information: A report is to be submitted upon completion of tenure.

Byera Hadley Travelling Scholarship, Postgraduate Scholarship, Student Scholarship

Subjects: Architecture.
Eligibility: Open only to graduates or students of four accredited schools of architecture in New South Wales. Applicants must be Australian citizens.
Level of Study: Postgraduate, Undergraduate.
Purpose: To undertake a course of study or research or other activity approved by the Board as contributing to the advancement of architecture.
Type: Scholarship.
No. of awards offered: 1 postgraduate, 1 graduate, 4 undergraduate.
Frequency: Annual.
Value: Total value of combined awards: A$65,000.
Country of Study: Any country.
Application Procedure: Please write for details.
Closing Date: Postgraduate and Graduate Scholarship: July 30th; Student Scholarship: to be announced.
Additional Information: A report suitable for publication to be submitted within three years (maximum) of the date of the award.

BOISE FOUNDATION

c/o Royal Academy of Music
Marylebone Road, London, NW1 5HT, England
Contact: Ms Jean Shannon, Honorary Secretary

Boise Foundation Scholarships

Subjects: Music practical.
Eligibility: Open to musical students of any nationality and under 30 years of age who are ordinarily resident in the UK or Republic of Ireland, or who are Commonwealth citizens temporarily resident in the UK for their musical education, or who are foreign nationals who have been resident in the UK for at least three years prior to commencing musical training.
Level of Study: Postgraduate.
Purpose: To enable vocalists or performing artists on any musical instrument to further their musical education.
Type: Scholarship.
No. of awards offered: 1-2.
Frequency: Every two years.
Value: Up to £5,000.
Study Establishment: Musical centres either in the UK or abroad, subject to the approval of the Scholar's plan of study by the Trustees of the Foundation.
Country of Study: Any country.
Application Procedure: Application form must be completed and signed by nominator. Awards are made on the basis of a competitive audition for which candidates must be nominated; names of nominators are available on request from the Foundation Secretary.
Closing Date: Early March in the year of the award.
Additional Information: All enquiries in writing only, please.

THE BOSTON SOCIETY OF ARCHITECTS

52 Broad Street
4th Floor, Boston, MA, 02109-4301, United States of America
Tel: (1) 617 951 1433
Fax: (1) 617 951 0845
Contact: The Awards Committee

The Boston Society of Architects (BSA) is the American Institute of Architects (AIA) chapter in eastern Massachusetts. It is the regional professional association of over 2,000 architects and 1,000 Affiliate members and is the largest chapter of the AIA. The BSA's Affiliate members include engineers, contractors, client/owners, public officials, other allied professionals, students, and lay-people. The BSA administers many programmes that enhance the public understanding of design as well as the practice of architecture. Since its establishment in 1867, the BSA has been committed to uniting the profession in fellowship and to making the profession of ever-increasing service to society.

Rotch Traveling Scholarship

Subjects: Architecture.
Eligibility: Open to US architects who are under 35 years of age on March 10th of the year of competition and have a degree from an accredited school of architecture plus one full year of professional experience in an architectural office.
Level of Study: Professional development.
Purpose: To provide young architects the opportunity for travel and study in foreign countries.
Type: Fellowship.
No. of awards offered: 1-2.
Frequency: Annual.
Value: A stipend of US$30,000.
Length of Study: 8 months.
Country of Study: Outside USA.
Application Procedure: Please submit a written request for an application form.
Closing Date: January 1st for application requests.
Additional Information: The Scholar is selected through a two-stage design competition. The one year of professional experience required should be completed prior to the beginning of the preliminary competition. Scholars are required to return to the USA after the duration of the Scholarship and submit a report of their travels.

BRADFORD CHAMBER OF COMMERCE AND INDUSTRY

Phoenix House
Rushton Avenue, Bradford, B03 7BH, England
Tel: (44) 1274 772777
Fax: (44) 1274 771123
Email: chamber@strosei.co.uk
www: http://www.sensei.co.uk/leedschamcomm
Contact: Miss T L Frost

The Bradford Chamber of Commerce and Industry represents member companies in the Bradford and District area. It works with local partners to develop the economic health of the district and has a major voice within the British Chamber of Commerce movement in order to promote the needs of local business on a national basis.

John Speak Trust Scholarships

Subjects: Modern languages.
Eligibility: Open to British-born nationals intending to follow a career connected with the export trade of the UK, who are over 18 years of age. A sound, basic knowledge of a language is required.
Level of Study: Professional development.
Purpose: To promote British trade abroad by assisting people in perfecting a basic knowledge of a foreign language.
Type: Scholarship.
No. of awards offered: Approx. 4.
Frequency: Three times each year.
Value: Approximately £1,800.

Length of Study: Abroad for 6 months, or 3 months if a candidate's knowledge of a language is advanced; not renewable.
Country of Study: Any non-English speaking country.
Closing Date: February 28th, May 31st, October 31st.

BRANDON UNIVERSITY

School of Music, Brandon, MB, R7A 6A9, Canada
Tel: (1) 204 727 7388
Fax: (1) 204 728 6839
Email: music@brandonu.ca
www: http://www.brandonu.ca/
Contact: Professor Robert Richardson, Graduate Music Programs

Brandon University is linked to the international community through the exchange of people and ideas. At an informal level, faculty may collaborate with researchers from around the world in pursuit of knowledge in their respective disciplines. In addition, the university has a number of joint programmes and exchange opportunities with institutions in other countries.

Brandon University Graduate Assistantships

Subjects: Music education, performance and literature (piano and strings).
Eligibility: Open to candidates with a Bachelor's degree in music or music education with a minimum grade point average of 3.0 during the final year.
Level of Study: Graduate.
Purpose: To afford graduate students the opportunity to gain professional experience while studying, and to provide monetary assistance.
No. of awards offered: 4-8.
Frequency: Annual.
Value: Up to C$6,500.
Length of Study: 1 year.
Study Establishment: School of Music, Brandon University.
Country of Study: Canada.
Closing Date: May 1st.
Additional Information: Candidates for the performance and literature major are also required to show, by audition, high potential as performers. For the music education major, candidates should have adequate related professional experience, preferably teaching.

BREAD LOAF WRITER'S CONFERENCE

Middlebury College, Middlebury, VT, 05753, United States of America
Tel: (1) 802 443 5286
Fax: (1) 802 443 2087
Email: blwc@mail.middlebury.edu
Contact: Mrs Carol Knauss

The Conferences' central purpose is to create a community in which a dialogue of converging literary voices can be sustained.

Bread Loaf Writer's Conference Fellowships and Scholarships

Subjects: Fiction, non-fiction, poetry.
Eligibility: Open to persons nominated by a publisher, editor, agent, established writer, or teacher of writing. Candidates for fellowships are assumed to have published a book or to have had a book-length manuscript accepted for publication. Candidates for scholarship assistance will have had articles published in periodicals. There are no restrictions regarding nationality or citizenship. All writing must be submitted in English.
Level of Study: Unrestricted.
Purpose: To provide both recognition for established writers and writers who show unusual promise, and an atmosphere in which writing can be discussed and criticised intensively.
Type: Fellowship, Scholarship.
No. of awards offered: Varies.
Frequency: Annual.
Value: Fellowships carry no cash value but cover all regular charges at the Conference. Scholarships cover full or partial tuition.
Length of Study: Eleven days.
Study Establishment: The Bread Loaf campus, Middlebury College, Vermont.
Country of Study: USA.
Application Procedure: Application form must be completed.
Closing Date: April 1st.

THE BRITISH ACADEMY

10 Carlton House Terrace, London, SW1Y 5AH, England
Tel: (44) 171 969 5200
Fax: (44) 171 969 5300
Email: secretary@britac.ac.uk
www: http://www.britac3.britac.ac.uk
Contact: Dr Ken Emond, Assistant Secretary (Research Projects and Posts)

The British Academy is the premier national learned society in the UK devoted to the promotion of advanced research and scholarships in the humanities and social sciences. It seeks to achieve this primary purpose in a number of ways through research grants and other awards, sponsorship of research projects, award of prizes and medals and through publications.

British Academy Major International Conference Grant

Subjects: Humanities and social sciences.
Eligibility: Open to organisers of major international conferences in the UK.
Level of Study: Postdoctorate.
Purpose: To help meet the costs of organising major international congresses in Britain, but only where either the congress is one of an established series, and where it is clearly the British turn to host the conference, or the conference celebrates a particular event and is on a very substantial scale.
Type: Grant.
Frequency: Annual.
Value: Between £10,000 and £15,000 a year for 2 or 3 years prior to conference.
Country of Study: United Kingdom.
Application Procedure: Two-stage consideration procedure. Application by letter with appropriate supporting documentation in the first instance.
Closing Date: None specified. Consult Research Grants Department, British Academy, for guidance.

British Academy Overseas Conference Grants

Subjects: Humanities and social sciences.
Eligibility: Open to scholars presenting an academic paper.
Level of Study: Postdoctorate.
Purpose: To help meet the costs of travel by British scholars to overseas conferences or similar gatherings. Awards will be contributions to travel expenses only.
Type: Grant.
No. of awards offered: Varies.
Frequency: Dependent on funds available, four times a year.
Value: Usually restricted to a maximum of £650.
Country of Study: Any country.
Application Procedure: Applications to be submitted on prescribed form.
Closing Date: End of October, January, March, and May.
Additional Information: Applicants must be resident in the UK.

British Academy Small Personal Research Grants

Subjects: All humanities and social science subjects.
Eligibility: Applicants must be resident in the UK.
Level of Study: Postdoctorate.
Purpose: For original research at postdoctoral level.
Type: Grant.
No. of awards offered: Up to 500.
Frequency: Four times per year.
Value: Maximum £5,000, but on average £2,500. Grants are personal to the applicant, and solely for the costs of the research itself; there is no element of salary or maintenance to the applicant.

Country of Study: Any country.
Closing Date: End of September, November, February and April.

British Academy Visiting Professorships for Overseas Scholars

Subjects: Humanities and social sciences.
Eligibility: Candidates for nomination must be either established scholars of distinction or younger people who show great promise and who would benefit from time to pursue their research in the UK.
Level of Study: Postdoctorate.
Purpose: To enable distinguished scholars from overseas to spend time in the UK to pursue their personal research.
Type: Professorship/Fellowship.
No. of awards offered: Varies.
Frequency: Annual.
Value: Travel expenses to the UK, and subsistence up to a maximum of £700 per week. Normal maximum length of visit one month, but applications for longer periods will be considered.
Country of Study: United Kingdom.
Application Procedure: Applications to be submitted on the prescribed form, by the British sponsor. Sponsors must undertake to make all administrative arrangements on behalf of the visitor. Applications are considered in February, in respect of visits to take place during the following financial year. Applications directly from foreign scholars will not be accepted.
Closing Date: December 31st. It may be possible to entertain applications at other times of the year, but the Academy's aim is to allocate the available funds in one go.

British Conference Grants

Subjects: Humanities and social sciences.
Eligibility: Applicants must be UK citizens applying on behalf of an academic living outside the UK.
Level of Study: Postdoctorate.
Purpose: To help meet the expenses of conferences held in Britain.
Type: Grant.
Frequency: Four times per year.
Value: Between £500 and £2,000.
Country of Study: United Kingdom.
Application Procedure: Applications to be submitted on prescribed form.
Closing Date: End of September, November, February and April.

Elisabeth Barker Fund

Subjects: Recent European history, particularly of East and Central Europe.
Eligibility: Open to scholars of postdoctoral or equivalent status ordinarily resident in the UK. Applicants need not be British nationals.
Level of Study: Postdoctorate.
Purpose: To support research or small conferences.

Type: Research Grant.
No. of awards offered: Up to 6.
Frequency: Annually, considered up to four times a year.
Value: Up to £1,000.
Country of Study: Europe.
Closing Date: September 30th, December 31st, February 28th and April 30th.
Additional Information: Applicants must be resident in the UK.

Neil Ker Memorial Fund

Subjects: Western medieval manuscripts, particularly those of British interest.
Eligibility: Open to both younger and established scholars of any nationality for research at postdoctoral level.
Level of Study: Postdoctorate.
Purpose: To promote the study of Western medieval manuscripts.
Type: Grant.
No. of awards offered: Varies, depending on funds available.
Frequency: Annual.
Value: Approximately £1,000.
Country of Study: Any country.
Closing Date: End of February.

Thank-Offering to Britain Fellowships

Subjects: Topics of an economic, industrial, social, political, literary or historical character relating to the British Isles. Preference will be given to projects in the modern period.
Eligibility: Open to persons ordinarily resident in the UK, and of postdoctoral status. Candidates should be in mid-career and must be employed at a UK university in an established teaching post.
Level of Study: Postdoctorate.
Purpose: To fund a research fellowship.
Type: Fellowship.
No. of awards offered: 1.
Frequency: Annual.
Value: Within the first two points of the Grade A university lecturers' scale.
Length of Study: Normally for 1 year.
Country of Study: United Kingdom.
Application Procedure: Applications must be completed on prescirbed form.
Closing Date: July 31st.
Additional Information: The award pays for a replacement to undertake the teaching and administrative duties of the award holders for one year.

BRITISH ASSOCIATION FOR AMERICAN STUDIES (BAAS)

American Studies Dept
University of Hull, Hull, HU6 7RX, England
Tel: (44) 1482 465303
Fax: (44) 1482 465303
Email: j.virden@anstuds.hull.ac.uk
www: http://human.ntu.ac.uk/baas
Contact: Dr Jenel Virden, Secretary (STA)

The British Association for American Studies was established in 1955 to promote research and teaching in all aspects of American Studies. The Association organises annual conferences, as well as specialist regional meetings for students, teachers, and researchers. It also publishes the Journal of American Studies, in co-operation with Cambridge University Press; BAAS Paperbacks, with Keele University Press; and British Records Relating to America in Microform, with Microform Publishing.

BAAS Short Term Awards

Subjects: US culture and society.
Eligibility: Open to UK citizens. Preference is given to young scholars, particularly postgraduates.
Level of Study: Doctorate, Postdoctorate, Postgraduate, Professional development.
Purpose: To fund travel to the USA for research purposes.
No. of awards offered: 3-4.
Frequency: Annual.
Value: £400.
Study Establishment: Anywhere in the USA.
Country of Study: USA.
Application Procedure: Application form must be completed; available from listed contacts.
Closing Date: September 30th.

BRITISH ASSOCIATION FOR CANADIAN STUDIES (BACS)

21 George Square, Edinburgh, EH8 9LD, Scotland
Tel: (44) 131 662 1117
Fax: (44) 131 662 1118
Email: jodie.robson@ed.ac.uk
www: http://www.iccs-ciec.ca/info/assoc/e-eng.html
Contact: Ms Jodie Robson

In response to the growing academic interest in Canada, BACS was established in 1975. Its aim is to foster teaching and research on Canada by locating study resources in Britain, facilitating travel and exchange schemes for professorial staff, and ensuring that the expertise of Canadian scholars who visit the United Kingdom is put to effective use.

Principal activities include publication of the British Journal of Canadian Studies and the BACS Newsletter, and organisation of the association's annual multidisciplinary conference, which attracts scholars from Canada and Europe as well as from the UK.

Prix du Québec

Subjects: Humanities and social sciences.
Level of Study: Doctorate, Postdoctorate, Professional development.
Purpose: To assist British Academics carrying out research related to Québec in the areas of the humanities and social sciences. The award seeks to encourage projects which incorporate Québec in a comparative approach.
Type: Award.
No. of awards offered: 2.
Frequency: Annual.
Value: £1,000.
Application Procedure: Guidelines for applicants are available from Jodie Robson, Administrative Secretary, BACS.
Closing Date: February 1st.
Additional Information: One award will be given to doctoral and post-doctoral students, and one award will be give to full-time teaching staff.

THE BRITISH COUNCIL

Science and Public Affairs
Hahnenstrasse 6, Koln, D-50667, Germany
Tel: (49) 221 20644 30
Fax: (49) 221 20644 55
Contact: Grants Management Officer

The purpose of the British Council is to promote a wider knowledge of the United Kingdom and the English language and to encourage cultural, scientific, technological and educational co-operation between the United Kingdom and other countries. The Council pursues its purpose through cultural relations and the provision of development assistance.

British-German Academic Research Collaboration (ARC) Programme

Subjects: All subjects.
Eligibility: Applications are invited from research groups in publicly-funded institutions in both the higher and non-higher education sectors. All areas of research are eligible, including the social sciences and humanities. Preference will be given to research projects which also provide research training opportunities for younger scientists.
Purpose: To increase collaboration between research groups in the United Kingdom and Germany.
Type: Travel Grant.
Frequency: Annual.
Country of Study: United Kingdom or Germany.

Application Procedure: Further information and application forms are available. British applicants should contact the British Council and German applicants should contact the German Academic Exchange Service, Section 313, Kennedyallee 50, D-53175 Bonn, Germany, tel (49) 228 882 0/236, fax (49) 228 882 551.
Closing Date: December 31st.
Additional Information: ARC can support research groups in the United Kingdom and Germany working in related fields for exploratory visits to establish the potential for research collaboration, and visits which are part of an agreed collaborative research project. For more information please contact the Science and Public Affairs Department , tel (49) 221 20644 15.

For further information contact:

The British Council
Science and Public Affairs
Hahnenstrasse 6, Koln, 50667, Germany
Tel: (49) 221 20644 15
Fax: (49) 221 20644 55

THE BRITISH COUNCIL

British Embassy
3100 Massachusetts Avenue NW, Washington, DC, 20008, United States of America
Tel: (1) 202 588 7830
Fax: (1) 202 588 7918
Email: study.uk@bc-washingtondc.bcouncil.org
www: http://www.britishcouncil-usa.org
Contact: Cultural Department

The British Council is Britain's international network for education, culture, and development services. It co-ordinates the Marshall Scholarships Programme in the USA.

British Marshall Scholarships

Subjects: All subjects.
Eligibility: Open only to United States citizens. Must be graduates of four-year accredited US college or university course with a minimum GPA of 3.7 and must have graduated within the last two years.
Level of Study: Postgraduate, Undergraduate.
Purpose: To enable United States college graduates of high ability to study for a degree - at either postgraduate or undergraduate level - at any UK university.
Type: Scholarship.
No. of awards offered: Up to 40.
Frequency: Annual.
Value: Covers all tuition fees, a living allowance and book allowance for two years.
Length of Study: 2-3 years.
Study Establishment: Any UK university.
Country of Study: United Kingdom.

Application Procedure: Application forms available from the British Council at the British Embassy in Washington DC, or British Consulates in Boston, Chicago, Atlanta, Houston, and San Francisco. For information on on-line applications please refer to the website.

Closing Date: October (in year preceding take up of award).

For further information contact:

Suite 2700
Marquis One Tower
245 Peachtree Centre Avenue, Atlanta, GA, 30303, United States of America
Tel: (1) 524 5856
Contact: British Consulate General

or

Federal Reserve Plaza
600 Atlantic Avenue, Boston, MA, 02210, United States of America
Tel: (1) 248 9555
Contact: British Consulate General

or

Suite 1600
The Wrigley Building
400 N Michigan Avenue, Chicago, IL, 60611, United States of America
Tel: (1) 346 1810
Contact: British Consulate General

or

First Interstate Bank Building
Suite 1900
1000 Louisiana, Houston, TX, 77002, United States of America
Tel: (1) 659 6270
Contact: British Consulate General

or

845 Third Avenue, New York, NY, 10022, United States of America
Tel: (1) 752 5747
Contact: British Information Services

or

1 Sansome Street
Suite 850, San Francisco, CA, 94104, United States of America
Tel: (1) 981 3030
Contact: British Consulate General

BRITISH FEDERATION OF WOMEN GRADUATES (BFWG)

4 Mandeville Courtyard
142 Battersea Park Road, London, SW11 4NB, England
Tel: (44) 171 498 8037
Fax: (44) 171 498 8037
www: http://homepages.wyenet.co.uk/bfwg
Contact: The Secretary

BFWG promotes women's opportunities in education and public life; works as part of an international organisation to improve the lives of women and girls; fosters local, national, and international friendship; and offers scholarships for postgraduate research.

AAUW/IFUW International Fellowships

Subjects: Research in any subject. Preference will be given to women who show prior commitment to the advancement of women and girls through civic, community, or professional work.

Eligibility: Women applicants must be a member of BFWG or another national federation or association of IFUW. It is a condition that the candidate will have started her second year of research at least (to which her application refers) at the time of the application and must be studying for three or more years. Taught Master's degrees do not count as research, though research done for a MPhil may count on the assumption that it will be upgraded to a PhD.

Level of Study: Postgraduate.
Type: Fellowship.
No. of awards offered: 6.
Frequency: Annual.
Value: Approximately US$15,000. The fellowships do not cover travel.
Length of Study: 12 months.
Country of Study: USA.
Application Procedure: Applicants studying in the UK should write for details enclosing a C5 stamped addressed envelope. Applicants must apply through their respective federation or association. A list of IFUW national federations can be sent on request.
Closing Date: December 1st in the year preceding the competition.

For further information contact:

AAUW Educational Foundation
Fellowships and Grants
PO Box 4030, Iowa City, IA, 52243-4030, United States of America

AFUW Georgina Sweet Fellowship

Subjects: Research in any subject.
Eligibility: Women applicants must be members of BFWG. It is a condition that the candidate will have started her second year of research at least (to which her application refers) at the time of application and must be studying for three years or more. Taught Master's degrees do not count as research, though research done for a MPhil may count on the assumption that it will be upgraded to a PhD.
Level of Study: Postgraduate, Research.
Type: Fellowship.
No. of awards offered: 1.
Frequency: Every two years.
Value: Approximately A$4,500. The fellowship does not cover travel.
Length of Study: 4-12 months.
Study Establishment: An Australian university.
Country of Study: Australia.

Application Procedure: Please write for details including a C5 stamped addressed envelope.
Closing Date: Early September in the year preceding the competition.
Additional Information: Recipients must submit a written report within six months of concluding the research.

For further information contact:

AFUW
PO Box 14
Bullcreek, WA, 6149, Australia

Australian Capital Territory Bursary

Subjects: All subjects.
Eligibility: Women applicants must be a member of BFWG or another national federation or association or IFUW. It is a condition that the candidate will have started her second year of research (to which her application refers) at least at the time of the application, and must be studying for three or more years. Taught Master's degrees do not count as research, though research done for a MPhil may count on the assumption that it will be upgraded to a PhD.
Level of Study: Postgraduate, Research.
Type: Bursary.
No. of awards offered: 1.
Frequency: Annual.
Value: AUS$1,000.
Length of Study: 3 months.
Study Establishment: Canberra.
Country of Study: Australia.
Application Procedure: Applicants should write for details enclosing a C5 stamped addressed envelope. Applicants must apply through their respective Federation or Association, and members of BFWG may apply for consideration by BFWG. A list of IFUW national federations can be sent upon request.
Closing Date: July 31st.

For further information contact:

AFUW-ACT Inc
GPO Box 520, Canberra, ACT, 201, Australia
Contact: The Fellowship Convener

BFWG Scholarships

Subjects: All subjects.
Eligibility: Candidates not of UK nationality but whose studies take place in the UK are eligible. They would not be eligible however, if they lived outside the UK and planned to continue to study out of the UK. It is a condition that the candidate will have started her second year of research (to which her application refers) at least at the time of the application and must be studying for three or more years. Taught Master's degrees do not count as research, although research completed for a MPhil may count on the assumption that it will be upgraded to a PhD.
Level of Study: Postgraduate, Research.
Purpose: To assist postgraduate research.
Type: Scholarship.

No. of awards offered: 1+.
Frequency: Annual.
Value: £750-£1,000.
Country of Study: United Kingdom.
Application Procedure: Applicants studying in the UK should write for details enclosing a C5 stamped addressed envelope. Overseas applicants must include two international reply coupons.
Closing Date: Early September in the year preceding the competition.
Additional Information: Recipients must submit a written report within six months of concluding the research.

IFUW International Fellowships

Subjects: Research in any subject.
Eligibility: Woman applicants must be a member of BFWG or another national federation or Association of IFUW. It is a condition that the candidate will have started her second year of research at least (to which her application refers) at the time of the application and must be studying for three or more years. Taught Master's degrees do not count as research, although research undertaken may count on the assumption that it will be updated to a PhD.
Level of Study: Postgraduate.
Type: Fellowship.
No. of awards offered: 7+.
Frequency: Every two years.
Value: Varies. The award does not cover travel.
Length of Study: 8 months.
Country of Study: Any country.
Application Procedure: Applicants studying in the UK should write for details enclosing a C5 stamped addressed envelope to BFWG. Applicants must apply through their respective federation or association. A list of national federations can be sent on request.
Closing Date: Early September in the year preceding the competition.
Additional Information: Recipients must submit a written report within 6 months of concluding the research.

For further information contact:

IFUW Headquarters
8 rue de l'Ancien-Port, Geneva, CH 1201, Switzerland
Tel: (41) 22 731 23 80
Fax: (41) 22 738 04 40
Contact: Grants Management Officer

JAUW International Fellowships

Subjects: Research in any subject.
Eligibility: Women applicants must be a member of BFWG or another national federation or association or IFUW. It is a condition that the candidate will have started her second year of research at least (to which her application refers) at the time of the application and must be studying for three or more years. Taught Master's degrees do not count as research, though research done for a MPhil may count on the assumption that it will be upgraded to a PhD.
Level of Study: Postgraduate, Research.

Type: Fellowship.
No. of awards offered: 1+.
Frequency: Annual.
Value: Y600,000. The fellowships do not cover travel.
Length of Study: 3 months.
Study Establishment: A Japanese institution.
Country of Study: Japan.
Application Procedure: Applicants should write for details enclosing a C5 stamped addressed envelope. Applicants must apply through their respective Federation or Association, and members of BFWG may apply for consideration by BFWG. A list of IFUW national federations can be sent upon request.
Closing Date: Early September in the year preceding the competition.
Additional Information: Recipients must submit a written report within six months of concluding their research.

For further information contact:

8 rue de l'Ancien Port, Geneva, CH 1201, Switzerland
Contact: International Federation of University Women

Kathleen Hall Memorial Fellowships

Subjects: Research in any subject.
Eligibility: People from countries with a low per capita income are eligible. They should be candidates not of UK nationality but whose studies take place in the UK. It is a condition that the candidate will have started her second year of research (to which her application refers) at least at the time of application and must be studying for three or more years. Taught Master's degrees do not count as research, although research undertaken for a MPhil may count on the assumption that it will be upgraded to a PhD.
Level of Study: Postgraduate, Research.
Type: Fellowship.
No. of awards offered: 1+.
Frequency: Annual.
Value: Approx. £1,000.
Country of Study: United Kingdom.
Application Procedure: Applicants studying in the UK should write for details enclosing a C5 stamped addressed envelope, while overseas applicants must include two international reply coupons.
Closing Date: Early September in the year including the competition.
Additional Information: The recipient must submit a written report within six months of concluding the research.

M H Joseph Prize

Subjects: Architecture or engineering.
Eligibility: Candidates not of UK nationality but whose studies take place in the UK are eligible. It is a condition that the candidate will have started her second year of research at least (to which her application refers) at the time of the application and must be studying for three or more years. Taught Master's degrees do not count as research, though research being done for a MPhil may count on the assumption that it will be upgraded to a PhD.

Level of Study: Postgraduate, Research.
Type: Prize.
No. of awards offered: 1.
Frequency: Annual.
Value: £500.
Study Establishment: A university or institution of university status in the United Kingdom.
Country of Study: United Kingdom.
Application Procedure: Applicants studying in the UK should write for details enclosing a C5 stamped addressed envelope. Overseas applicants must include two international mail coupons.
Closing Date: Early September in the year preceding the competition.
Additional Information: The recipient must submit a written report within six months of concluding the research.

Margaret K B Day Memorial Scholarships

Subjects: Research in any subject.
Eligibility: Candidates not of UK nationality but whose studies take place in the UK are eligible. (They would not be eligible however, if they lived out of the UK and planned to continue to study out of the UK). It is a condition that the candidate will have started her second year of research at least (to which her application refers) at the time of application and must be studying for at least three or more years. Taught Master's degrees do not count as research, though research undertaken for a MPhil may count on the assumption that it will be upgraded to a PhD.
Level of Study: Postgraduate, Research.
Purpose: To assist postgraduate research.
Type: Scholarship.
No. of awards offered: 1+.
Frequency: Annual.
Value: £1,000.
Country of Study: United Kingdom.
Application Procedure: Applicants studying in the UK should write for details enclosing a C5 stamped addressed envelope. Overseas applicants must include two international reply coupons.
Closing Date: Early September in the year preceding the competition.

Victorian Beatrice Fincher Scholarship

Subjects: Research in any subject that will benefit mankind.
Eligibility: Women applicants must be members of BFWG or another national federation or association of IFUW. A list of IFUW national federations can be sent upon request. It is a condition that the candidate will have started her second year of research at least (to which her application refers) at the time of application and must be studying for three or more years. Taught Master's degrees do not count as research, although research done for a MPhil may count on the assumption that it will be upgraded to a PhD.
Level of Study: Postgraduate, Research.
Type: Scholarship.
No. of awards offered: 1.
Frequency: Annual.

Value: Approximately A$5,000. The scholarship does not cover travel.
Country of Study: Any country.
Application Procedure: Applicants should write for details enclosing two international reply coupons.
Closing Date: March 1st in the year preceding the competition.
Additional Information: Recipients must submit a written report within six months of concluding the research.

For further information contact:

AFUW (Vic) Inc
PO Box 816, Mount Eliza, VIC, 3930, Australia
Contact: The Scholarship Secretary

Western Australian Bursaries

Subjects: Research in any subject.
Eligibility: Woman applicants must be members of BFWG or another national federation or association of IFUW. A list of IFUW national federations is available upon request. It is a condition that the candidate will have started her second year of research at least (to which her application refers) at the time of application and must be studying for three or more years. Taught Master's degrees do not count as research, though research done for a MPhil may count on the assumption that it will be upgraded to a PhD.
Level of Study: Postgraduate, Research.
Type: Bursary.
No. of awards offered: 1+.
Frequency: Annual.
Value: Approximately A$1,500-A$2,750. The bursaries do not cover travel.
Length of Study: 12 months.
Country of Study: Australia.
Application Procedure: Applicants should write for details enclosing two international reply coupons.
Closing Date: July 31st in the year preceding the competition.
Additional Information: Recipients must submit a written report within six months of concluding the research.

For further information contact:

AFUW (WA) Inc
PO Box 48, Nedlands, WA, 6909, Australia
Contact: The Bursary Liason Officer

BRITISH INSTITUTE IN EASTERN AFRICA

PO Box 30710, Nairobi, Kenya
Tel: (254) 2 43330
Fax: (254) 2 43365
Email: britinst@insightkenya.com
Contact: Director

The Institute encourages research by individual scholars, and works closely with the universities, museums and antiquities services of the eastern African countries. It is based in Nairobi where it maintains a centre for field research and a comprehensive reference library.

British Institute in Eastern Africa Research Studentships and Graduate Attachments

Subjects: Pre-colonial history and archaeology in East Africa - field research.
Eligibility: Open to citizens of East African countries, the UK and the Commonwealth who are over 21 years of age. Candidates should have a BA or equivalent degree and graduate or undergraduate training in African studies, archaeology or social anthropology.
Level of Study: Postgraduate.
Type: Studentship, Graduate Attachment.
No. of awards offered: Varies.
Value: Varies.
Country of Study: Kenya, Tanzania, Uganda and other Eastern African countries.
Closing Date: Normally May 1st.
Additional Information: Small grants and assistance may be offered on a discretionary basis to scholars of other nationalities. Archaeological students may be required to assist in excavation carried out by the Institute's staff. Details of activities are published in the Archaeology Abroad bulletin.

BRITISH INSTITUTE IN PARIS

University of London
Senate House
Malet Street, London, WC1E 7HU, England
Tel: (44) 171 862 8656
Fax: (44) 171 862 8655
Email: campos@ext.jussieu.fr
www: http://www.bip.lon.ac.uk
Contact: London Secretary

The British Institute in Paris is a teaching and research institute of London University specialising in English and French studies, translation and language pedagogy.

Quinn, Nathan and Edmond Scholarships

Subjects: French studies.
Eligibility: Open to citizens of the EU and Commonwealth countries, who are graduates and possess sufficient knowledge of French to pursue their proposed studies.
Level of Study: Doctorate, Postdoctorate, Postgraduate.
Purpose: To assist postgraduate research in France.
Type: Scholarship, junior research fellowship.
No. of awards offered: 2.
Frequency: Scholarship, annual; junior research fellowship, every two years.
Value: Scholarship, £450 per month; junior research fellowship, £500 per month (for 9 months per annum).
Length of Study: Scholarship, 3-6 months; junior research fellowship, up to 3 years.
Study Establishment: In Paris.

Country of Study: France.
Application Procedure: Applications should be accompanied by a written recommendation from the candidate's professor or tutor. The name of one academic referee must be given.
Closing Date: March 15th.
Additional Information: Scholarships cannot be held concurrently with other major awards. The scholarships are intended for research and not for those following taught courses.

BRITISH INSTITUTE OF ARCHAEOLOGY AT ANKARA

Senate House
Malet Street, London, WC1E 7HU, England
Tel: (44) 171 862 8734
Fax: (44) 171 862 8734
Contact: G Coulthard

The Institute was founded in 1948 and exists to undertake, promote, and encourage British Research into archaeology and related subjects in Turkey.

British Institute of Archaeology at Ankara Research Grants

Subjects: Archaeology and related subjects.
Eligibility: Open to citizens of the UK or other Commonwealth countries, who are qualified to undertake advanced research. Preference is given to research projects in areas in which the Institute is already interested.
Level of Study: Doctorate, Postdoctorate, Postgraduate.
Purpose: To aid research into all periods of Turkish archaeology.
Type: Research Grant.
No. of awards offered: Varies.
Frequency: Annual.
Value: Determined individually in regard to the level of work involved, qualifications and seniority of the applicant, and any other relevant factors.
Length of Study: Determined individually.
Study Establishment: At the Ankara institute or at other centres.
Country of Study: Turkey.
Application Procedure: Application form must be completed.
Closing Date: November 1st.
Additional Information: Application forms are obtainable from the Assistant Secretary.

British Institute of Archaeology at Ankara Travel Grants

Subjects: Archaeology and related subjects.
Eligibility: Open to graduates or undergraduates who are nationals of the UK or a Commonwealth country.

Level of Study: Doctorate, Postdoctorate, Postgraduate, Undergraduate.
Purpose: To enable students of archaeology or other relevant subjects to travel to and from Turkey for the purpose of familiarising themselves with its archaeology and geography, and to visit its sites and museums.
Type: Travel Grant.
No. of awards offered: Varies.
Frequency: Annual.
Value: Up to £500 paid in one lump sum.
Country of Study: Turkey.
Application Procedure: There is no application form; applicants must submit CV, itinerary, costing, and two references.
Closing Date: February 1st, but prospective candidates should check before applying.

THE BRITISH LIBRARY

2 Sheraton Street, London, W1V 4BH, England
Tel: (44) 171 412 7044
Fax: (44) 171 412 7251
Email: bnbrf@bl.uk
www: http://www.bl.uk/services/ric/research/bnbrfint.html
Contact: BNB Research Fund Secretariat

The BNBRF was established in 1975 following the transfer of the British National Bibliography to the British Library. It supports research in the book and information worlds of interest to its member organisations.

BNB Research Fund

Subjects: The three areas of particular interest are the study of the relations between bookseller, librarian and publisher, the general theme of publications and their use within the community, and the impact of new technology on all aspects of the book world.
Eligibility: Applications are open to all, but the subject of the research is restricted to the UK and awards are only payable in UK.
Level of Study: Unrestricted.
Purpose: To support research into the book and information worlds in the UK.
Type: Research Grant.
No. of awards offered: Varies.
Frequency: Three times per year.
Value: Varies.
Length of Study: Varies.
Country of Study: United Kingdom.
Application Procedure: Booklet available; outline proposals welcomed.
Closing Date: Three closing dates each year; details available from the Secretary.

Additional Information: The Fund has limited resources and directs its efforts towards areas which do not qualify for research funding from other sources. Money cannot be allocated however, for the preparation of historical bibliographies, nor to support students in undertaking graduate or postgraduate courses. The Fund is administered by a committee whose members represent the Library Association, Publishers' Association, Booksellers' Association, Book Trust, British Council, Royal Society, Aslib, the Joint Committee of the Five Copyright Libraries and the British Library.

For further information contact:

Library and Information Commission
19-29 Woburn Place, London, WC1H 0LU, England
Tel: (44) 171 273 8700

The Helen Wallis Fellowship

Subjects: History and the history of cartography, preferably with an international dimension.
Eligibility: Please write for details.
Level of Study: Postdoctorate.
Purpose: To promote the extended and complimentary use of the British Library's book and cartographic collections in historical investigation.
Type: Fellowship.
No. of awards offered: 1.
Frequency: Annual.
Value: £300.
Length of Study: 6-12 months.
Study Establishment: British Library, London.
Country of Study: United Kingdom.
Application Procedure: Submit a letter, indicating the proposed period and outlining the research project, together with a full curriculum vitae and the names of three references to: The Map Librarian, British Library, 96 Euston Road, London NW1 2DB.
Closing Date: May 1st.
Additional Information: The award honours the memory of Dr Helen Wallis, OBE, (1924-1995), Map Librarian at the British Museum and then the British Library (1967-1986).

BRITISH SCHOOL AT ATHENS

Odos Souedias 52, Athens, GR-10676, Greece
Tel: (30) 1 721 0974
Fax: (30) 1 723 6560
Email: bsadmin@eexi.qr
www: http://www.bsa.gla.ac.uk
Contact: Assistant Director

The British School at Athens provides facilities for research into the archaeology, architecture, art, history, language, literature, religion and topography of Greece in ancient, medieval and modern times. It consists of a hostel, library, archive, museum, the Fitch Laboratory for Archaelolgical Science, and a second base at Knossos for excavation and research.

Hector and Elizabeth Catling Bursary

Subjects: Research in Greek studies - archaeology, art, history, language, literature, religion, ethnography, anthropology, geography of any period, and all branches of archaeological science.
Eligibility: Open to researchers of British, Irish or Commonwealth nationality.
Level of Study: Doctorate, Postdoctorate, Postgraduate.
Type: Bursary.
No. of awards offered: 1 or 2.
Frequency: Annual, if funds are available.
Value: Up to a maximum of £500 per bursar, to assist in travel and maintenance costs incurred in fieldwork, to pay for the use of scientific or other specialised equipment in or outside a laboratory in Greece or elsewhere, and to buy necessary supplies. The bursary is not intended for publication costs, nor can it be awarded to an excavation or field survey team.
Study Establishment: British School at Athens.
Country of Study: Greece or Cyprus.
Application Procedure: There are no application forms. Applicants should send a CV and state concisely the nature of the intended work, a breakdown of budget, the amount requested from the Fund, and how this will be spent. Applications should include two sealed letters of reference. Bursary holders must submit a short report to the Committee on completion of the project. Recipients cannot reapply to the Fund the following year.
Closing Date: December 15th for notification by end of February.

Macmillan-Rodewald Studentship, School Studentship, Cary Studentship

Subjects: Research into the archaeology, architecture, art, history, language, literature, religion or topography of Greece in ancient, medieval or modern times.
Eligibility: Open to graduates of British, Irish or Commonwealth nationality.
Level of Study: Doctorate, Postdoctorate, Postgraduate.
Type: Studentship.
No. of awards offered: 3.
Frequency: Annual.
Value: Grant awards related to British Academy postgraduate award levels.
Length of Study: 1 year; renewable on reapplication.
Study Establishment: British School at Athens.
Country of Study: Greece.
Application Procedure: Applicants should submit a CV and a statement of their proposed course of study with reasons for pursuing it in Greece. Applications should include the names of two referees.
Closing Date: May 1st.
Additional Information: The student is required to spend a minimum of eight months in Greece, normally residing in the School when in Athens, and to undertake such duties in and for the School as the Director enjoins.

THE BRITISH SCHOOL AT ROME (BSR)

Via Gramsci 61, Rome, I-00197, Italy
Tel: (390) 6 32 64 939
Fax: (390) 6 32 21 201
Email: bsr@britac.ac.uk
www: http://www.britac.ac.uk/institutues/rome
Contact: Dr Gill Clark, Publications Manager

The British School at Rome is an interdisciplinary research centre for the humanities, visual arts, and architecture. Each year the School offers a range of awards in its principal fields of interest. These interests are further promoted by public lectures, conferences, publications, archaeological research and an excellent reference library.

Abbey Awards in Painting

Subjects: Painting.
Eligibility: Open to mid-career painters with an established record of achievement.
Type: Research Grant.
Value: £480 per month plus £180 travel allowance.
Length of Study: 1-3 month residencies.
Application Procedure: There is an application fee of £10.
Closing Date: January 30th.

For further information contact:

PO Box 5, Rhayder Powys, LD6 5WA, Wales
Contact: Ms Faith Clark, Abbey Awards Administrator

Abbey Scholarship in Painting

Subjects: Painting.
Eligibility: Open to US, UK or Commonwealth citizens of either sex.
Level of Study: Unrestricted.
Purpose: To give exceptionally promising emergent painters the opportunity to work in Rome.
Type: Scholarship.
No. of awards offered: 1.
Frequency: Annual.
Value: £4,500, plus board and lodging at BSR.
Length of Study: 9 months.
Study Establishment: The British School at Rome.
Country of Study: Italy.
Application Procedure: Application form must be completed.
Closing Date: Early December.

Balsdon Fellowship

Subjects: Archaeology, art history, history and literature of Italy.
Eligibility: Open to established scholars normally in post in a UK university.
Level of Study: Postdoctorate.
Purpose: To enable senior scholars engaged in research to spend a period in Rome to further their studies.

Type: Fellowship.
No. of awards offered: 1.
Frequency: Annual.
Value: £650 plus board and lodging at BSR.
Length of Study: 3 months.
Study Establishment: BSR.
Country of Study: Italy.
Application Procedure: Application form must be completed.
Closing Date: Early January.

For further information contact:

The British School at Rome
at The British Academy
10 Carlton House Terrace, London, SW1Y 5AH, England
Tel: (44) 171 969 5202
Fax: (44) 171 969 5401

BSR Archaeological Fieldwork Support

Subjects: Archaeological excavation, post-excavation and research projects in Italy.
Eligibility: Open to individuals or teams from British and Commonwealth universities.
Level of Study: Postdoctorate.
Purpose: To support archaeological projects undertaken in Italy.
Type: Research Facilities and Equipment.
No. of awards offered: Varies.
Frequency: Annual.
Value: Varies. Priority will be given to projects undertaken in collaboration with the School.
Country of Study: Italy.
Application Procedure: Applicants should contact the BSR Assistant Director (Archaeology) at the main address.

BSR Rome Awards in Archaeology, History and Letters

Subjects: Archaeology, art history, history and literature of Italy.
Eligibility: Open to candidates of either sex who are of British or Commonwealth nationality or residence. Applicants will normally have begun a programme of research in the general field for which the award is being sought, whether or not registered for a higher degree. The awards are not normally suitable for people in established posts.
Level of Study: Doctorate, Postdoctorate, Postgraduate.
Purpose: For research on the archaeology, art history, history and literature of Italy.
Type: Grant.
No. of awards offered: Varies.
Frequency: Annual.
Value: £150 per month, plus £180 travel, plus board and lodging at BSR.
Length of Study: 1-4 months.
Study Establishment: The BSR.
Country of Study: Italy.

Application Procedure: Application form must be completed.
Closing Date: Early January.

For further information contact:

The British School at Rome
at The British Academy
10 Carlton House, London, SW1Y 5AH, England
Tel: (44) 171 969 5202
Fax: (44) 171 969 5401

Geoffrey Jellicoe Scholarship in Landscape Architecture

Subjects: Contemporary design in the landscape.
Eligibility: Open to recent graduates and individuals in mid-career who wish to pursue a topic with direct bearing on contemporary design in the landscape. The scholarship is not confined to landscape architects.
Level of Study: Professional development.
Purpose: To allow recent graduates and individuals in mid-career to pursue a topic with direct bearing on contemporary design in the landscape.
Type: Research Grant.
Value: £550 per month.
Length of Study: 4 month residency (September-December).
Application Procedure: Please write for details.
Closing Date: January.

For further information contact:

The Landscape Foundation
17 Bowling Green Lane, London, EC1 0BD, England

Henry Moore Sculpture Fellowship at the BSR

Subjects: Fine and applied arts, sculpture.
Eligibility: Open to UK or Commonwealth nationals or residents of either sex.
Level of Study: Unrestricted.
Purpose: To enable well-established sculptors to spend 3 months in Rome.
Type: Fellowship.
No. of awards offered: 1.
Frequency: Annual.
Value: £2,000 per month plus board and lodging at BSR.
Length of Study: 3 months.
Study Establishment: The British School at Rome.
Country of Study: Italy.
Application Procedure: Please apply to BSR for precise procedure.
Closing Date: January.

For further information contact:

The British School at Rome
at The British Academy
10 Carlton House Terrace, London, SW1Y 5AH, England
Tel: (44) 171 969 5202
Fax: (44) 171 969 5401

Hugh Last Fellowship

Subjects: Classical antiquity.
Eligibility: Open to established scholars normally in post in a UK university.
Level of Study: Postdoctorate.
Purpose: To enable established scholars to collect research material concerning classical antiquity.
Type: Fellowship.
No. of awards offered: 1-2.
Frequency: Annual.
Value: Board and lodging at BSR plus research grant.
Length of Study: 1-4 months.
Study Establishment: BSR.
Country of Study: Italy.
Application Procedure: Application form must be completed.
Closing Date: Early January.

For further information contact:

The British School at Rome
at The British Academy
10 Carlton House Terrace, London, SW1Y 5AH, England
Tel: (44) 171 969 5202
Fax: (44) 171 969 5401

Paul Mellon Centre Rome Fellowship

Subjects: Anglo-Italian cultural and artitistic relations.
Eligibility: Open to established scholars in the UK, US or elsewhere. Applicants should have fairly fluent Italian.
Purpose: For research on the Grand Tour or on Anglo-Italian cultural and artistic relations.
Type: Research Grant.
Value: £1,000 per month plus travel allowance.
Length of Study: 6 month residency, inc. full board.
Application Procedure: Please contact the Paul Mellon Centre for Studies in British Art.
Closing Date: January 15th.

For further information contact:

The Paul Mellon Centre for Studies in British Art
16 Bedford Square, London, WC1B 3JA, England
Tel: (44) 171 580 0311
Fax: (44) 171 636 6730

RIBA Rome Scholarship in Architecture and Urbanism

Subjects: Architecture and urbanism relevant to Rome and Italy.
Eligibility: Open to architects and students of architecture and associated disciplines of at least post-diploma level.
Purpose: To allow architects and students of architecture to pursue projects in architecture and urbanism relevant to Rome and Italy.
Type: Research and Travel Grant.
No. of awards offered: 1-2.
Value: £500 per month plus board and lodging at BSR.
Length of Study: 3-9 month residencies.

Study Establishment: The British School at Rome.
Country of Study: Italy.
Application Procedure: There is an application fee of £25. Application forms are available from BSR Registrar.
Closing Date: Early December.

For further information contact:

The British School at Rome
The British Academy
10 Carlton House Terrace, London, SW1Y 5AH, England
Tel: (44) 171 969 5202
Fax: (44) 171 969 5401

Rome Scholarships in Ancient, Medieval and Later Italian Studies

Subjects: Archaeology, art history, history and literature of Italy.
Eligibility: Open to UK or Commonwealth citizens/residents of either sex. Applicants should normally have begun a programme of research in the general field for which the scholarship is being sought, whether or not registered for a higher degree.
Level of Study: Doctorate, Postdoctorate, Postgraduate.
Purpose: For research on the archaeology, art history, history and literature of Italy.
Type: Scholarship.
Frequency: Annual.
Value: £4,000 (plus board and lodging at BSR).
Length of Study: 9 months.
Study Establishment: The British School at Rome.
Country of Study: Italy.
Application Procedure: Application form must be completed.
Closing Date: Early January.

For further information contact:

The British School at Rome
at The British Academy
10 Carlton House, London, SW1y 5AH, England
Tel: (44) 171 969 5202
Fax: (44) 171 969 5401

Rome Scholarships in the Fine Arts

Subjects: Painting, printmaking, sculpture, and other suitable media.
Eligibility: Open to UK or Commonwealth citizens and residents of either sex.
Level of Study: Postgraduate.
Purpose: To give emerging and early/mid-career artists the opportunity of working in Rome.
Type: Scholarship.
No. of awards offered: 1-2.
Frequency: Annual.
Value: £500 per month.
Length of Study: 3-6 months.
Study Establishment: The British School at Rome.
Country of Study: Italy.

Application Procedure: Application form must be completed.
Closing Date: Early December.

For further information contact:

The British School at Rome
The British Academy
10 Carlton House Terrace, London, SW1Y 5AH, England
Tel: (44) 171 969 5202
Fax: (44) 171 969 5401

Sargant Fellowship

Subjects: Sculpture, drawing and painting, architecture and town planning.
Eligibility: Open to British and Commonwealth citizens and nationals of either sex.
Level of Study: Unrestricted.
Purpose: To enable distinguished artists and architects to spend 3-9 months in Rome developing their work.
Type: Fellowship.
No. of awards offered: Varies.
Frequency: Annual.
Value: £1,000 per month plus £500 travel plus board and lodging at BSR.
Length of Study: 3-9 months.
Study Establishment: BSR.
Country of Study: Italy.
Application Procedure: Please apply to BSR for precise procedure.
Closing Date: January.

For further information contact:

The British School at Rome
at The British Academy
10 Carlton House Terrace, London, SW1Y 5AH, England
Tel: (44) 171 969 5202
Fax: (44) 171 969 5401

Wingate Rome Scholarship in the Fine Arts

Subjects: Painting, printmaking, sculpture and other suitable media.
Eligibility: Open to UK Commonwealth and nationals and residents.
Level of Study: Postgraduate.
Purpose: To give emerging and early/mid-career artists the opportunity of working in Rome.
Type: Scholarship.
No. of awards offered: 1-2.
Frequency: Annual.
Value: £500 per month plus board and lodging at the BSR.
Length of Study: 3-6 months.
Study Establishment: The British School at Rome.
Country of Study: Italy.
Application Procedure: Application form must be completed.
Closing Date: Early December.

For further information contact:

The British School at Rome
at the British Academy
10 Carlton House Terrace, London, SW1Y 5AH, England
Tel: (44) 171 969 5202
Fax: (44) 171 969 5401

BRITISH SCHOOL OF ARCHAEOLOGY IN IRAQ

31-34 Gordon Square, London, WC1H 0PY, England
Tel: (44) 171 733 8912
www: http://www.britac.ac.uk
Contact: Honorary Secretary

The School's aim is to encourage and support the study of, and research relating to, the archaeology, history and languages of Iraq and neighbouring countries including E Syria and the Gulf, from the earliest times to the end of the 17th century AD.

British School of Archaeology in Iraq Grants

Subjects: Archaeology, history and languages of Iraq and neighbouring countries from the earliest time to AD1700.
Eligibility: Open to residents of the UK or Commonwealth citizens who are postgraduates with a knowledge of Western-Asiatic archaeology.
Level of Study: Postdoctorate, Postgraduate.
Purpose: To support research in the archaeology, history and languages of Iraq.
Type: Grant.
No. of awards offered: Varies.
Frequency: Annual.
Value: Usually between £500 and £3,000, depending on the nature of the research.
Length of Study: 1 academic year.
Country of Study: Normally Iraq, when possible, for at least some of the period of tenure. Until work in Iraq can be resumed, grants are available for studying primary material outside Iraq, whether in the field or in museums.
Application Procedure: For grants up to £1,000, there is no application form, for grants of £1,000 or more, information and application forms are available from the Secretary.
Closing Date: March 31st and September 30th for grants up to £1,000; September 30th for grants £1,000 or more.
Additional Information: Two references are required. Details of the British School of Archaeology in Iraq are available on the website under Institutes Overseas and Sponsored Societies.

THE BRITISH SCHOOLS AND UNIVERSITIES FOUNDATION, INC. (BSUF)

6 Windmill Hill
Hampstead, London, NW3 6RU, England
Tel: (44) 171 435 4648
Contact: Mrs S Wiltshire, UK Representative BSUF

The British Schools and Universities Foundation makes grants to educational, scientific or literary institutes in the UK and in member nations of the British Commonwealth. The Foundation also fosters the education and academic work of American scholars and students at British institutions and vice versa. It also provides a way for the US tax payer to make tax deductible gifts to the UK for colleges and schools.

British Schools and Universities Foundation, Inc. Scholarships

Subjects: All subjects.
Eligibility: Open to scholars from US, UK, Australia, Canada, and New Zealand.
Level of Study: Doctorate, Postgraduate, Professional development.
Purpose: To promote, foster and assist the education and academic work of British scholars and students at American educational institutions, and of American scholars and students at British educational institutions.
Type: Scholarship.
No. of awards offered: 4-6.
Frequency: Annual.
Value: US$12,500 maximum.
Length of Study: 2 years maximum.
Study Establishment: US educational institutions (UK candidates) or UK educational institutions (US candidates).
Country of Study: USA or United Kingdom.
Application Procedure: Application form can be obtained from representative. Please enclose SAE with request.
Closing Date: March 1st, for an award to commence the following September.

May and Ward

Subjects: All subjects.
Eligibility: Applicants must provide a strong rationale for attending an institution abroad and give evidence if possible. They must be attending or be graduates (usually) of an accredited institute of learning.
Level of Study: Doctorate, Graduate, Postgraduate, Predoctorate, Professional development, Research.
Purpose: To support US scholars at UK educational, literary and scientific institutions and vice versa.
Type: Scholarship.
No. of awards offered: 4-6.
Frequency: Annual.
Value: $12,500 annually.
Length of Study: 1-2 years.
Study Establishment: College, University or Research establishment.

Country of Study: USA or UK.

Application Procedure: For application form and guidelines apply to BSVF representative if in the UK at the London address and if in the USA at the New York address.

Closing Date: March 1st.

For further information contact:

BSVF
Suite 1006
575 Madison Ave, New York, NY, 10022-2511, United States of America

THE BROADCASTING CORPORATIONS OF THE FEDERAL REPUBLIC OF GERMANY

International Music Competition
Bayerischer Rundfunk, Munich, D-80300, Germany
Tel: (49) 89 5900 2471
Fax: (49) 89 5900 3573
Email: ard.conc@br-mail.de
Contact: Secretariat

International Music Competition of the ARD

Subjects: Music, categories vary annually.

Eligibility: Open to musicians of any nationality. They must be born in or between the years 1969 and 1982 if they play the piano, violin, horn or organ.

Purpose: This International Music Competition is intended for a selection of young musicians who must be at concert standard.

Type: Competition.

No. of awards offered: The competition includes either 4 or 5 categories. For each category 3 prizes are offered.

Frequency: Annual.

Study Establishment: Conservatories, university schools of music, music academies, but also advanced private studies.

Country of Study: Any country.

Application Procedure: A completed application form. An audio cassette may also be required. Please write for further details.

Closing Date: April 23rd.

Additional Information: There is an entry fee of DM150 per soloist; DM200 for duos; DM240 for trios; DM270 for quartets; DM300 for quintets.

Prize Winner of the International Music Competition of the ARD

Subjects: Music.

Eligibility: Applicants must be born between the years 1969 and 1982 and be at concert standard in one of the following instruments piano, violin, horn, organ.

Purpose: This International Music Competition is intended to support and award a selection of young musicians who are at concert standard.

Type: Prize.

No. of awards offered: The competition includes either 4 or 5 categories. For each category 3 prizes are offered.

Frequency: Annual.

Study Establishment: Conservatories, university schools of music, and music academies, but also advanced private studies.

Country of Study: Any country.

Application Procedure: Candidates must complete an application form.

Closing Date: April 23rd.

THE BROSS FOUNDATION, LAKE FOREST COLLEGE

Religion Department
555 North Sheridan, Lake Forest, IL, 60045, United States of America
Tel: (1) 847 735 5175
Fax: (1) 847 735 6192
Contact: Mr Ron Miller

Bross Prize

Subjects: The relationship between any discipline and the Christian religion.

Eligibility: There are no eligibility restrictions.

Level of Study: Unrestricted.

Purpose: To award the best unpublished manuscripts.

Type: Cash Prize.

No. of awards offered: 3.

Frequency: Every ten years.

Value: This is dependent on funds. In 1990, first prize US$15,000; second prize, US$7,500; third prize US$4,000.

Country of Study: Any country.

Application Procedure: Three copies of manuscript must be submitted.

Closing Date: September 2000.

Additional Information: Manuscript must be at least 50,000 words.

BUDAPEST INTERNATIONAL MUSIC COMPETITION

Interart Festivalcenter
PO Box 80
Bp V Vörösmarty Ter 1, Budapest, H-1366, Hungary
Tel: (36) 1 317 9838
Fax: (36) 1 317 9910
Contact: Ms Maria Liszkay, Secretary

The Budapest Music Competitions have been held since 1933. The most important competitions are organised by Interart Festivalcenter, for various instruments.

Budapest International Music Competition

Subjects: Organ, performance and composition (improvisation).
Eligibility: Open to young artists of all nationalities under 32 years of age.
Level of Study: Professional development.
Purpose: To hold a competition in memory of Ferenc Liszt.
Type: Competition.
No. of awards offered: 3.
Frequency: Annual.
Value: Total of US$10,000.
Country of Study: Any country.
Application Procedure: Application form must be completed and other documentation submitted; please contact the office for further details.
Closing Date: April 30th.

BUNAC

16 Bowling Green Lane, London, EC1R 0BD, England
Tel: (44) 171 251 3472
Fax: (44) 171 251 0215
Email: bunac@easynet.co.uk
www: http://www.bunac.org.uk/
Contact: Ms Jenna Peters

BUNAC Educational Scholarship Trust (BEST)

Subjects: Any subject. Some awards are specifically for sports and geography-related courses.
Eligibility: Open to British citizens who have recently (within the last five years) graduated from a British university. Candidates must have a first degree.
Level of Study: Postgraduate.
Purpose: To help further Anglo-American understanding.
Type: Scholarship.
No. of awards offered: 10.
Frequency: Annual.
Value: From a total of US$25,000. Usually approx. US$2,000.
Length of Study: From 3 months to 3 years.

Study Establishment: A North American university or college.
Country of Study: USA or Canada.
Application Procedure: Application forms are available on request (from January each year).
Closing Date: March 25th.

THE BUNTING INSTITUTE OF RADCLIFFE COLLEGE

34 Concord Avenue, Cambridge, MA, 02138, United States of America
Tel: (1) 617 495 8212
Fax: (1) 617 495 8136
Email: bunting_fellowships@radcliffe.harvard.edu
www: http://www.radcliffe.edu
Contact: Fellowships Co-ordinator

The Mary Ingraham Bunting Institute was founded in 1960 as the Radcliffe Institute for Independent Study. The Institute is a multidisciplinary research centre for women scholars, scientists, artists, and writers and is one of the major centres for advanced study in the United States.

Berkshire Summer Fellowship

Subjects: Any field of history.
Eligibility: Open to women historians at the postdoctoral level working in any field of history. Preference is given to junior scholars and to those who do not normally have access to Boston area resources.
Level of Study: Postdoctorate.
Purpose: The programme seeks to support women of exceptional promise and demonstrated accomplishment who wish to pursue independent work in academic and professional fields.
Type: Fellowship.
No. of awards offered: 1.
Frequency: Annual.
Value: US$3,500.
Length of Study: 1 summer.
Country of Study: USA.
Closing Date: January 15th.
Additional Information: Applications are judged on the quality and significance of the proposed project, the applicant's record of achievement, and the difference the fellowship might make in advancing the applicant's career. The Bunting Institute is a multidisciplinary programme for women scholars, scientists, artists, and writers. Office or studio space, auditing privileges, and access to libraries and most other resources of Radcliffe and Harvard are provided. Residence in the Boston area is required during the fellowship appointment. Fellows are expected to present their work in progress at public colloquia.

Bunting Fellowship

Subjects: Any discipline, including creative writing, visual and performing arts.
Eligibility: Open to women scholars in any field, with receipt of a doctorate or appropriate terminal degree at least two years prior to appointment, women creative writers, and visual or performing artists with a record of significant accomplishment and equivalent professional experience (special eligibility requirements apply to creative artists).
Level of Study: Postdoctorate.
Purpose: The programme seeks to support women of exceptional promise and demonstrated accomplishment who wish to pursue independent work in professional and academic fields and in the creative arts.
Type: Fellowship.
No. of awards offered: 8-10.
Frequency: Annual.
Value: US$36,500 for a year appointment starting September 15th. Bunting Fellows may not simultaneously hold another major fellowship which provides more than US$20,000.
Length of Study: 1 year.
Country of Study: USA.
Closing Date: October 1st.
Additional Information: Applications are judged on the quality and significance of the proposed project, the applicant's record of accomplishment, and the difference the fellowship might make in advancing the applicant's career. The Bunting Institute is a multidisciplinary programme for women scholars, scientists, artists, and writers. Office or studio space, auditing privileges, and access to libraries and most other resources of Radcliffe and Harvard are provided. Residence in the Boston area is required during the fellowship appointment. Fellows are expected to present their work in progress at public colloquia or in exhibitions.

Bunting Institute Affiliation

Subjects: All subjects.
Eligibility: Open to women scholars in any field, with receipt of a doctorate or appropriate terminal degree at least two years prior to appointment, and with a record of significant accomplishment. Women holding or seeking grants or fellowships from other sources are invited to apply. Radcliffe College and the Bunting Institute are unable to serve as the fiscal agent of, or assist in the development and management of, other awards. We issue a special invitation for proposals with public policy implications.
Level of Study: Postdoctorate.
Purpose: The programme seeks to support women of exceptional promise and demonstrated accomplishment.
Type: Affiliations.
No. of awards offered: 10-20.
Frequency: Annual.

Value: This appointment is without stipend, includes office space and other resources available to all Fellows.
Length of Study: 1 semester, or 1 academic year.
Country of Study: USA.
Closing Date: October 1st.
Additional Information: Applications are judged on the quality and significance of the proposed project, the applicant's record of accomplishment, and the difference the fellowship might make in advancing the applicant's career. The Bunting Institute is a multidisciplinary programme for women scholars, scientists, artists, and writers. Office or studio space, auditing privileges, and access to libraries and most other resources of Radcliffe and Harvard are provided. Residence in the Boston area is required during the fellowship appointment. Fellows are expected to present their work in progress.

THE CALEDONIAN RESEARCH FOUNDATION

The Carnegie Trust for the Universities of Scotland
Cameron House
Abbey Park Place, Dunfermline, Fife, KY12 7PZ, Scotland
Tel: (44) 1383 622148
Fax: (44) 1383 622149
Email: carnegie.trust@ed.ac.uk
www: http://www.geo.ed.ac.uk/carnegie/carnegies.html
Contact: The Secretary and Treasurer

Caledonian Scholarship

Subjects: All subjects in the university curriculum. At least one scholarship each year is made in a non-scientific discipline.
Eligibility: Open to persons possessing a first class honours degree from a Scottish University.
Level of Study: Postgraduate.
Purpose: To support postgraduate research in any subject.
Type: Scholarship.
No. of awards offered: 2-3.
Frequency: Annual.
Value: £6,877 (in 1998/99) plus tuition fees and allowances.
Length of Study: A maximum of 3 years, subject to annual review.
Study Establishment: Any university in Scotland.
Country of Study: United Kingdom.
Application Procedure: Please write for details.
Closing Date: March 15th.
Additional Information: Considered along with Carnegie Scholarships.

CALOUSTE GULBENKIAN FOUNDATION (INTERNATIONAL DEPARTMENT)

Av de Berna 45, Lisbon, P-1093, Portugal
Tel: (351) 793 51 31
Fax: (351) 793 51 39
Telex: 63768 GULBEN P
Contact: The Director

Calouste Gulbenkian Foundation (International Department) Research Fellowships

Subjects: Humanities.
Eligibility: Open to postgraduates of foreign nationality.
Level of Study: Postgraduate.
Purpose: To stimulate research and specialisation on themes relating to Portuguese culture, namely in the field of humanities.
Type: Fellowship.
No. of awards offered: Limited.
Frequency: Annual.
Value: Varies.
Length of Study: A maximum of 12 months.
Country of Study: Portugal.
Application Procedure: Application form must be completed.
Closing Date: October 31st.
Additional Information: In the selection of applications, the Foundation will bear in mind the importance and originality of the work proposed to promote Portuguese culture, or cultural exchange between the candidate's country of origin and Portugal.

THE CAMARGO FOUNDATION

BP 75, Cassis Cedex, F-13714, France
Tel: (33) 4 4201 1157
Fax: (33) 4 4201 3657
Contact: Mr Michael Perina, Executive Director

Camargo Fellowships

Subjects: Humanities and social sciences.
Eligibility: Open to: members of university and college faculties who wish to pursue special studies whilst on leave from their institutions; teachers and independent scholars; graduate students whose academic residence and general examination requirements have been met and for whom a stay in France would be beneficial in completing the dissertation required for their degree; and writers, visual artists, photographers and composers with specific projects to complete.
Level of Study: Doctorate, Postgraduate, Professional development, Independent Scholars.

Purpose: To assist scholars who wish to pursue projects in the humanities and social sciences related to French and Francophone cultures.
Type: Residency.
No. of awards offered: Varies, 20-26.
Frequency: Annual.
Value: The Foundation offers eleven furnished apartments and a reference library, a darkroom, an atelier, and a music composition studio, at no cost.
Length of Study: Varies.
Study Establishment: Camargo Foundation study center in Cassis.
Country of Study: France.
Application Procedure: Candidates are required to submit an application form, CV, and a detailed description of their projects, not to exceed 1,000 words.
Closing Date: February 1st for the following academic year.
Additional Information: A written report will be required at the end of the stay.

For further information contact:

125 Park Square Court
400 Sibley Street, St Paul, MN, 55101-1928, United States of America
Tel: (1) 612 290 2237
Contact: Ms Sheryl Mousley

CAMBRIDGE COMMONWEALTH TRUST, CAMBRIDGE OVERSEAS TRUST AND ASSOCIATED TRUSTS

PO Box 252, Cambridge, CB2 1TZ, England
Tel: (44) 1223 323322
Fax: (44) 1223 351449
Email: egs10@cam.ac.uk

Arab-British Chamber Charitable Foundation Scholarships

Subjects: All subjects.
Eligibility: The Trusts cannot admit students to the University or any of its Colleges. Applicants for awards from the Trusts must therefore also apply to the University of Cambridge and be offered a place at Cambridge in the normal way. All applicants must have a first class or high second class honours degree, or equivalent and normally be under 26. For citizens of Algeria, Comoro Islands, Djibouti, Egypt, Jordan, Mauritania, Morocco, Palestine, Somalia, Sudan, Syria, Tunisia and the Yemen.
Type: Scholarship.
No. of awards offered: 5.
Frequency: Annual.
Value: The scholarships will cover the University Composition Fee at the overseas rate, approved College fees, a maintenance allowance sufficient for a single student, a contribution top a return economy airfare.

Length of Study: 1 year.
Study Establishment: Cambridge University.
Country of Study: United Kingdom.
Application Procedure: Candidates must complete a Preliminary Application Form, which can be obtained from local universities, offices of the British Council or, the main address. Completed application forms must be returned to the main address. Candidates short-listed will be sent forms for admission to the University of Cambridge and a scholarship application form. These forms must be returned to The Board of Graduate Studies.
Closing Date: September 21st, a full year in advance of the proposed entry date to Cambridge for preliminary application, January 31st for actual application.

For further information contact:

The Board of Graduate Studies
4 Mill Lane, Cambridge, CB2 1TZ, England
Contact: The Secretary

Blue Circle Cambridge Scholarship

Subjects: All subjects.
Eligibility: The Trusts cannot admit students to the University or any of its Colleges. Applicants for awards from the Trusts must therefore also apply to the University of Cambridge and be offered a place at Cambridge in the normal way. All applicants must have a first class or high second class honours degree, or equivalent and normally be under 26. This scholarship is for students from Nigeria.
Level of Study: Doctorate.
Type: Scholarship.
No. of awards offered: 1.
Frequency: Annual.
Length of Study: Tenable for up to 3 years.
Study Establishment: Cambridge University.
Country of Study: United Kingdom.
Application Procedure: Preliminary application forms for these scholarships can be obtained from Blue Circle Industries PLC, PO Box 1001, Lagos and should be returned to this address by September 1st.

Britain-Australia Bicentennial Scholarships

Subjects: All subjects.
Eligibility: The Trusts cannot admit students to the University or any of its Colleges. Applicants for awards from the Trusts must therefore also apply to the University of Cambridge and be offered a place at Cambridge in the normal way. All applicants must have a first class or high second class honours degree, or equivalent and normally be under 26. Open to students from Australia.
Level of Study: Postgraduate.
Purpose: To assist one year taught postgraduate courses.
Type: Scholarship.
No. of awards offered: 2.
Frequency: Annual.
Study Establishment: Jesus College, Cambridge.
Country of Study: United Kingdom.

Application Procedure: Application form for the scholarship will be sent out to eligible candidates once the completed form for admission to the University of Cambridge has reached the Board of Graduate Studies.
Closing Date: Scholarship forms must be returned by April 30th.

For further information contact:

The Board for Graduate Studies
4 Mill Lane, Cambridge, CB2 1TZ, England
Contact: The Secretary

British Chevening Cambridge Scholarship - Namibia

Subjects: All subjects.
Eligibility: The Trusts cannot admit students to the University or any of its Colleges. Applicants for awards from the Trusts must therefore also apply to the University of Cambridge and be offered a place at Cambridge in the normal way. All applicants must have a first class or high second class honours degree, or equivalent and normally be under 26. For students from Namibia.
Level of Study: Postgraduate.
Type: Scholarship.
No. of awards offered: 1.
Frequency: Annual.
Value: Scholarships will cover the University Composition Fee at the overseas rate; approved College fees; a maintenance allowance sufficient for a single student.
Length of Study: 1 year.
Study Establishment: Cambridge University.
Country of Study: United Kingdom.
Application Procedure: Candidates must complete a Preliminary Application Form, which can be obtained from local universities, offices of the British Council or, the main address. Completed application forms must be returned to the main address. Candidates short-listed will be sent forms for admission to the University of Cambridge and a scholarship application form. These forms must be returned to The Board of Graduate Studies.
Closing Date: September 21st, a full year in advance of the proposed entry date to Cambridge for preliminary application, January 31st for actual application.

For further information contact:

The Board of Graduate Studies
4 Mill Lane, Cambridge, CB2 1TZ, England
Contact: The Secretary

British Chevening Cambridge Scholarship for PhD Study - Mexico

Subjects: All subjects.
Eligibility: The Trusts cannot admit students to the University or any of its Colleges. Applicants for awards from the Trusts must therefore also apply to the University of Cambridge and be offered a place at Cambridge in the normal way. All applicants must have a first class or high second class honours degree, or equivalent and normally be under 26.

Successfully nominated for an ORS award which pays the difference between the home and overseas rate of the University Composition Fee.
Level of Study: Doctorate.
Purpose: To assist study towards a PhD.
Type: Scholarship.
No. of awards offered: 1.
Frequency: Annual.
Value: Scholarships will cover the University Composition Fee at the overseas rate; approved College fees; a maintenance allowance sufficient for a single student.
Length of Study: Tenable for up to 3 years.
Study Establishment: Cambridge University.
Country of Study: United Kingdom.
Application Procedure: All candidates for this scholarship must complete a Preliminary Application Form which can only be obtained from the British Council, Mexico City.

For further information contact:

British Council
Maestro Antonio Caso 127
Col San Rafael
Delegacion Cuauhtemoc
Apartado postal 30-588, Mexico City, 06470 DF, Mexico

British Chevening Cambridge Scholarship for Postgraduate Study - Australia

Subjects: All subjects.
Eligibility: The Trusts cannot admit students to the University or any of its Colleges. Applicants for awards from the Trusts must therefore also apply to the University of Cambridge and be offered a place at Cambridge in the normal way. All applicants must have a first class or high second class honours degree, or equivalent and normally be under 26. For students from Australia.
Level of Study: Postgraduate.
Purpose: To assist with one year taught postgraduate courses.
Type: Scholarship.
No. of awards offered: 4.
Frequency: Annual.
Study Establishment: Cambridge University.
Country of Study: United Kingdom.
Closing Date: Scholarship forms must be returned by April 30th.

For further information contact:

The Board for Graduate Studies
4 Mill Lane, Cambridge, CN2 1TZ, England
Contact: The Secretary

British Chevening Cambridge Scholarship for Postgraduate Study - Cyprus

Subjects: All subjects.
Eligibility: The Trusts cannot admit students to the University or any of its Colleges. Applicants for awards from the Trusts must therefore also apply to the University of Cambridge and be offered a place at Cambridge in the normal way. All applicants must have a first class or high second class honours degree, or equivalent and normally be under 26. Applicants must pass a medical examination, and sign an undertaking with the Cyprus Scholarship Board to return to work in Cyprus for a minimum of three years which may be deferred if, for example, the scholar obtains a subsequent award for further studies. Candidates who are currently receiving, or who have received a British Award within the past three years, are not normally eligible for this scholarship.
Level of Study: Postgraduate.
Purpose: To assist study towards one year taught postgraduate courses of study.
Type: Scholarship.
No. of awards offered: 3.
Frequency: Annual.
Value: Scholarships will cover the University Composition Fee at the overseas rate; approved College fees; a maintenance allowance sufficient for a single student; a contribution to a return economy airfare.
Length of Study: 1 year.
Study Establishment: Cambridge University.
Country of Study: United Kingdom.
Application Procedure: Candidates must complete a Preliminary Application Form, which can be obtained from local universities, offices of the British Council or the main address. Completed application forms must be returned to the main address. Candidates short-listed will be sent forms for admission to the University of Cambridge and a scholarship application form. These forms must be returned to The Board of Graduate Studies.
Closing Date: September 21st, a full year in advance of the proposed entry date to Cambridge for preliminary application, January 31st for actual application.

For further information contact:

The Board of Graduate Studies
4 Mill Lane, Cambridge, CB2 1TZ, England
Contact: The Secretary

British Chevening Cambridge Scholarship for Postgraduate Study - East and West Africa

Subjects: All subjects.
Eligibility: The Trusts cannot admit students to the University or any of its Colleges. Applicants for awards from the Trusts must therefore also apply to the University of Cambridge and be offered a place at Cambridge in the normal way. All applicants must have a first class or high second class honours degree, or equivalent and normally be under 26. For students from Ghana, Sierra Leone, Tanzania and Uganda.
Level of Study: Postgraduate.
Type: Scholarship.
No. of awards offered: Up to 7: 3 to Ghana, 1 to Sierra Leone, 1 to Tanzania, 1 to Uganda.
Frequency: Annual.
Study Establishment: Cambridge University.
Country of Study: United Kingdom.
Application Procedure: Candidates must complete a Preliminary Application Form, which can be obtained from local universities, offices of the British Council or the main

address. Completed application forms must be returned to the main address. Candidates short-listed will be sent forms for admission to the University of Cambridge and a scholarship application form. These forms must be returned to The Board of Graduate Studies.

Closing Date: September 21st, a full year in advance of the proposed entry date to Cambridge for preliminary application, January 31st for actual application.

For further information contact:

The Board of Graduate Studies
4 Mill Lane, Cambridge, CB2 1TZ, England
Contact: The Secretary

British Chevening Cambridge Scholarship for Study Towards a PhD - Uganda

Subjects: All subjects.
Eligibility: The Trusts cannot admit students to the University or any of its Colleges. Applicants for awards from the Trusts must therefore also apply to the University of Cambridge and be offered a place at Cambridge in the normal way. All applicants must have a first class or high second class honours degree, or equivalent and normally be under 26. This scholarship is for students from Uganda.
Level of Study: Doctorate.
Purpose: To assist students for study towards a PhD.
Type: Scholarship.
No. of awards offered: 1.
Frequency: Annual.
Study Establishment: Cambridge University.
Country of Study: United Kingdom.
Application Procedure: Candidates must complete a Preliminary Application, which can be obtained from local universities, offices of the British Council or, the main address. Completed application forms must be returned to the main address. Candidates short-listed will be sent forms for admission to the University of Cambridge and a Scholarship application form. These forms must be returned to The Board of Graduate Studies.
Closing Date: September 21st, a full year in advance of the proposed entry date to Cambridge for preliminary application, January 31st for actual application.

For further information contact:

The Board of Graduate Studies
4 Mill Lane, Cambridge, CB2 1RZ, England
Contact: The Secretary

British Chevening Cambridge Scholarships - Chile

Subjects: All subjects.
Eligibility: The Trusts cannot admit students to the University or any of its Colleges. Applicants for awards from the Trusts must therefore also apply to the University of Cambridge and be offered a place at Cambridge in the normal way. All applicants must have a first class or high second class honours degree, or equivalent and normally be under 26. For a student from Chile.

Level of Study: Postgraduate.
Type: Scholarship.
No. of awards offered: 1.
Frequency: Annual.
Value: Scholarships will cover the University Composition Fee at the overseas rate; approved College fees; a maintenance allowance sufficient for a single student.
Length of Study: 1 year.
Study Establishment: Cambridge University.
Country of Study: United Kingdom.
Application Procedure: Candidates for this scholarship must apply directly to the British Council, Chile.
Closing Date: July 15th of the year before the year of entry.

For further information contact:

British Council
Eliodoro Yanez 832, Santiago de Chile, Chile

British Chevening Cambridge Scholarships - Eastern Europe

Subjects: All subjects.
Eligibility: The Trusts cannot admit students to the University or any of its Colleges. Applicants for awards from the Trusts must therefore also apply to the University of Cambridge and be offered a place at Cambridge in the normal way. All applicants must have a first class or high second class honours degree, or equivalent and normally be under 26. For students from Poland, Romania and Yugoslavia.
Level of Study: Postgraduate.
Purpose: To assist students studying for one year taught postgraduate courses.
Type: Scholarship.
No. of awards offered: Up to 6.
Frequency: Annual.
Value: Scholarships will cover the University Composition Fee at the overseas rate; approved College fees; a maintenance allowance sufficient for a single student.
Length of Study: 1 year.
Study Establishment: Cambridge University.
Country of Study: United Kingdom.
Application Procedure: Candidates must complete a Preliminary Application Form, which can be obtained from local universities, offices of the British Council or the main address. Completed application forms must be returned to the main address. Candidates short-listed will be sent forms for admission to the University of Cambridge and a scholarship application form. These forms must be returned to The Board of Graduate Studies.
Closing Date: September 21st, a full year in advance of the proposed entry date to Cambridge for preliminary application, January 31st for actual application.

For further information contact:

The Board of Graduate Studies
4 Mill Lane, Cambridge, CB2 1TZ, England
Contact: The Secretary

British Chevening Cambridge Scholarships - Hong Kong

Subjects: All subjects.
Eligibility: The Trusts cannot admit students to the University or any of its Colleges. Applicants for awards from the Trusts must therefore also apply to the University of Cambridge and be offered a place at Cambridge in the normal way. All applicants must have a first class or high second class honours degree, or equivalent and normally be under 26. For students from Hong Kong.
Level of Study: Postgraduate.
Purpose: To assist one year taught postgraduate study.
Type: Scholarship.
No. of awards offered: Up to 8.
Frequency: Annual.
Value: Scholarships will cover the University Composition Fee at the overseas rate; approved College fees; a maintenance allowance sufficient for a single student.
Length of Study: 1 year.
Study Establishment: Cambridge University.
Country of Study: United Kingdom.
Application Procedure: Candidates must complete a Preliminary Application Form, which can be obtained from local universities, offices of the British Council or the main address. Completed application forms must be returned to the main address. Candidates short-listed will be sent forms for admission to the University of Cambridge and a scholarship application form. These forms must be returned to The Board of Graduate Studies.
Closing Date: September 21st, a full year in advance of the proposed entry date to Cambridge for preliminary application, January 31st for actual application.

For further information contact:

The Board of Graduate Studies
4 Mill Lane, Cambridge, CB2 1TZ, England
Contact: The Secretary

British Chevening Cambridge Scholarships - Indonesia

Subjects: All subjects.
Eligibility: The Trusts cannot admit students to the University or any of its Colleges. Applicants for awards from the Trusts must therefore also apply to the University of Cambridge and be offered a place at Cambridge in the normal way. All applicants must have a first class or high second class honours degree or equivalent and normally be under 26. For students from Indonesia.
Level of Study: Postgraduate.
Purpose: To assist students with one year taught postgraduate courses of study.
Type: Scholarship.
No. of awards offered: 3.

Frequency: Annual.
Value: Scholarships will cover the University Composition Fee at the overseas rate; approved College fees; a maintenance allowance sufficient for a single student.
Length of Study: 1 year.
Study Establishment: Cambridge University.
Country of Study: United Kingdom.
Application Procedure: Candidates for these scholarships must apply directly to the British Embassy in Indonesia.
Closing Date: September 21st, a full year in advance of the proposed entry date to Cambridge for preliminary application, January 31st for actual application.

For further information contact:

British Embassy
Jalan M H Thamrin 75, Jakarta, 10310, Indonesia

British Chevening Cambridge Scholarships - Malta

Subjects: All subjects.
Eligibility: The Trusts cannot admit students to the University or any of its Colleges. Applicants for awards from the Trusts must therefore also apply to the University of Cambridge and be offered a place at Cambridge in the normal way. All applicants must have a first class or high second class honours degree or equivalent and must be under 26. For students from Malta.
Level of Study: Postgraduate.
Purpose: To assist study for one year taught postgraduate courses.
Type: Scholarship.
No. of awards offered: 2.
Frequency: Annual.
Value: The scholarships will cover the University Composition Fee at the overseas rate and approved College fees.
Length of Study: 1 year.
Study Establishment: Cambridge University.
Country of Study: United Kingdom.
Application Procedure: Candidates must complete a Preliminary Application Form, which can be obtained from local universities, offices of the British Council or the main address. Completed application forms must be returned to the main address. Candidates short-listed will be sent forms for admission to the University of Cambridge and a scholarship application form. These forms must be returned to The Board of Graduate Studies.
Closing Date: September 21st, a full year in advance of the proposed entry date to Cambridge for preliminary application, January 31st for actual application.

For further information contact:

The Board of Graduate Studies
4 Mill Lane, Cambridge, CB2 1TZ, England
Contact: The Secretary

British Chevening Cambridge Scholarships - Mozambique

Subjects: All subjects.
Eligibility: The Trusts cannot admit students to the University or any of its Colleges. Applicants for awards from the Trusts must therefore also apply to the University of Cambridge and be offered a place at Cambridge in the normal way. All applicants must have a first class or high second class honours degree, or equivalent and normally be under 26. For students from Mozambique.
Level of Study: Postgraduate.
Type: Scholarship.
No. of awards offered: Up to 4.
Frequency: Annual.
Value: Scholarships will cover the University Composition Fee at the overseas rate; approved College fees; a maintenance allowance sufficient for a single student.
Length of Study: 1 year.
Study Establishment: Cambridge University.
Country of Study: United Kingdom.
Application Procedure: Candidates must complete a Preliminary Application Form, which can be obtained from local universities, offices of the British Council or the main address. Completed application forms must be returned to the main address. Candidates short-listed will be sent forms for admission to the University of Cambridge and a scholarship application form. These forms must be returned to The Board of Graduate Studies.
Closing Date: September 21st, a full year in advance of the proposed entry date to Cambridge for preliminary application, January 31st for actual application.

For further information contact:

The Board of Graduate Studies
4 Mill Lane, Cambridge, CB2 1TZ, England
Contact: The Secretary

British Chevening Cambridge Scholarships - Thailand

Subjects: All subjects.
Eligibility: The Trusts cannot admit students to the University or any of its Colleges. Applicants for awards from the Trusts must therefore also apply to the University of Cambridge and be offered a place at Cambridge in the normal way. All applicants must have a first class or high second class honours degree, or equivalent and normally be under 26. For students from Thailand.
Level of Study: Postgraduate.
Type: Scholarship.
No. of awards offered: 2.
Frequency: Annual.
Value: Scholarships will cover the University Composition Fee at the overseas rate; approved College fees; a maintenance allowance suffcient for a single student.
Length of Study: 1 year.
Study Establishment: Cambridge University.
Country of Study: United Kingdom.

Application Procedure: Candidates must complete a Preliminary Application Form, which can be obtained from local universities, offices of the British Council or the main address. Completed application forms must be returned to the main address. Candidates short-listed will be sent forms for admission to the University of Cambridge and a scholarship application form. These forms must be returned to The Board of Graduate Studies.
Closing Date: September 21st, a full year in advance of the proposed entry date to Cambridge for preliminary application, January 31st for actual application.

For further information contact:

The Board of Graduate Studies
4 Mill Lane, Cambridge, CB2 1TZ, England
Contact: The Secretary

British Chevening Cambridge Scholarships - The Philippines

Subjects: All subjects.
Eligibility: The Trusts cannot admit students to the University or any of its Colleges. Applicants for awards from the Trusts must therefore also apply to the University of Cambridge and be offered a place at Cambridge in the normal way. All applicants must have a first class or high second class honours degree or equivalent and normally be under 26. For students from the Philippines.
Level of Study: Postgraduate.
Type: Scholarship.
No. of awards offered: 3.
Frequency: Annual.
Length of Study: 1 year.
Study Establishment: Cambridge University.
Country of Study: United Kingdom.
Application Procedure: Candidates must complete a Preliminary Application Form, which can be obtained from local universities, offices of the British Council or the main address. Completed application forms must be returned to the main address. Candidates short-listed will be sent forms for admission to the University of Cambridge and a scholarship application form. These forms must be returned to The Board of Graduate Studies.
Closing Date: September 21st, a full year in advance of the proposed entry date to Cambridge for preliminary application, January 31st for actual application.

For further information contact:

The Board of Graduate Studies
4 Mill Lane, Cambridge, CB2 1TZ, England
Contact: The Secretary

British Chevening Cambridge Scholarships - Vietnam

Subjects: All subjects.
Eligibility: The Trusts cannot admit students to the University or any of its Colleges. Applicants for awards from the Trusts must therefore also apply to the University of Cambridge and be offered a place at Cambridge in the normal way. All

applicants must have a first class or high second class honours degree, or equivalent and normally be under 26. For students from Vietnam.

Level of Study: Postgraduate.

Purpose: To assist towards one year taught postgraduate courses of study.

Type: Scholarship.

No. of awards offered: 2.

Frequency: Annual.

Length of Study: 1 year.

Study Establishment: Cambridge University.

Country of Study: United Kingdom.

Application Procedure: Candidates for these scholarships should apply directly to the British Embassy, Vietnam.

Closing Date: October 1st.

For further information contact:

British Embassy
16 Ly Thuong Kiet, Hanoi, Vietnam

British Chevening Cambridge Scholarships for Postgraduate Study - Cuba

Subjects: All subjects.

Eligibility: The Trusts cannot admit students to the University or any of its Colleges. Applicants for awards from the Trusts must therefore also apply to the University of Cambridge and be offered a place at Cambridge in the normal way. All applicants must have a first class or high second class honours degree, or equivalent and normally be under 26. Applicants must be from Cuba.

Level of Study: Postgraduate.

Purpose: To assist one year taught postgraduate courses.

Type: Scholarship.

No. of awards offered: 2.

Frequency: Annual.

Study Establishment: Cambridge University.

Country of Study: United Kingdom.

Application Procedure: Candidates must complete a Preliminary Application Form, which can be obtained from local universities, offices of the British Council or the main address. Completed application forms must be returned to the main address. Candidates short-listed will be sent forms for admission to the University of Cambridge and a scholarship application form. These forms must be returned to The Board of Graduate Studies.

Closing Date: September 21st, a full year in advance of the proposed entry date to Cambridge for preliminary application, January 31st for actual application.

For further information contact:

The Board of Graduate Studies
4 Mill Lane, Cambridge, CB2 1TZ, England
Contact: The Secretary

British Chevening Cambridge Scholarships for Postgraduate Study - Mexico

Subjects: All subjects.

Eligibility: The Trusts cannot admit students to the University or any of its Colleges. Applicants for awards from the Trusts must therefore also apply to the University of Cambridge and be offered a place at Cambridge in the normal way. All applicants must have a first class or high second class honours degree, or equivalent and normally be under 26. For students from Mexico.

Level of Study: Postgraduate.

Type: Scholarship.

No. of awards offered: 1.

Frequency: Annual.

Value: Scholarships will cover the University Composition Fee at the overseas rate; approved College fees; a maintenance allowance suffcient for a single student.

Length of Study: 1 year.

Study Establishment: Cambridge University.

Country of Study: United Kingdom.

Application Procedure: All candidates for this scholarship must complete a Preliminary Application Form which can only be obtained from the British Council, Mexico City.

For further information contact:

British Council
Maestro Antonio Caso 127
Col San Rafael
Delegacion Cuauhtemoc
Apartado postal 30-588, Mexico City, 06470 DF, Mexico

British Chevening Scholarships for Postgraduate Study - Pakistan

Subjects: All subjects.

Eligibility: The Trusts cannot admit students to the University or any of its Colleges. Applicants for awards from the Trusts must therefore also apply to the University of Cambridge and be offered a place at Cambridge in the normal way. All applicants must have a first class or high second class honours degree, or equivalent and normally be under 26. For students of outstanding academic merit from Pakistan.

Level of Study: Postgraduate.

Type: Scholarship.

No. of awards offered: 5.

Frequency: Annual.

Study Establishment: Cambridge University.

Country of Study: United Kingdom.

Application Procedure: Candidates must complete a Preliminary Application Form, which can be obtained from local universities, offices of the British Council or the main address. Completed application forms must be returned to the main address. Candidates short-listed will be sent forms for admission to the University of Cambridge and a scholarship application form. These forms must be returned to The Board fof Graduate Studies.

Closing Date: September 21st, a full year in advance of the proposed entry date to Cambridge for preliminary application, January 31st for actual application.

For further information contact:

The Board of Graduate studies
4 Mill Lane, Cambridge, CB2 1TZ, England
Contact: The Secretary

British Prize Scholarships

Subjects: All subjects.
Eligibility: The Trusts cannot admit students to the University or any of its Colleges. Applicants for awards from the Trusts must therefore also apply to the University of Cambridge and be offered a place at Cambridge in the normal way. All applicants must have a first class or high second class honours degree, or equivalent and normally be under 26.
Level of Study: Postgraduate.
Purpose: To assist study for one year taught postgraduate courses.
Type: Scholarship.
No. of awards offered: 2.
Frequency: Annual.
Study Establishment: Cambridge University.
Country of Study: United Kingdom.
Application Procedure: Candidates must complete a Preliminary Application Form, which can be obtained from local universities, offices of the British Council or the main address. Completed application forms must be returned to the main address. Candidates short-listed will be sent forms for admission to the University of Cambridge and a scholarship application form. These forms must be returned to The Board of Graduate Studies.
Closing Date: September 21st, a full year in advance of the proposed entry date to Cambridge for preliminary application, January 31st for actual application.
Additional Information: One scholarship annually to a student from Barbados and one from the Eastern Caribbean (Antigua and Barbuda, Dominica, Grenada, St Kitts-Nevis, St Lucia, St Vincent and the Grenadines).

For further information contact:

The Board of Graduate Studies
4 Mill Lane, Cambridge, CB2 1TZ, England
Contact: The Secretary

Cambridge Livingstone Trust Scholarships for Postgraduate Study

Subjects: All subjects.
Eligibility: The Trusts cannot admit students to the University or any of its Colleges. Applicants for awards from the Trusts must therefore also apply to the University of Cambridge and be offered a place at Cambridge in the normal way. All applicants must have a first class or high second class honours degree, or equivalent and normally be under 26. For students from Botswana, Lesptho, Malawi, Namibia, Swaziland, Zambia and Zimbabwe.
Level of Study: Doctorate.
Purpose: To assist students with study for a one year taught postgraduate course.
Type: Scholarship.
No. of awards offered: Varies.

Frequency: Annual.
Length of Study: 1 year.
Study Establishment: Cambridge University.
Country of Study: United Kingdom.
Application Procedure: Candidates must complete a Preliminary Application Form, which can be obtained from local universities, offices of the British Council or the main address. Completed application forms must be returned to the main address. Candidates short-listed will be sent forms for admission to the University of Cambridge and a scholarship application form. These forms must be returned to The Board of Graduate Studies.
Closing Date: September 21st, a full year in advance of the proposed entry date to Cambridge for preliminary application, January 31st for actual application.

For further information contact:

The Board of Graduate Studies
4 Mill Lane, Cambridge, CB2 1TZ, England
Contact: The Secretary

Cambridge Livingstone Trust Scholarships for Study Towards a PhD

Subjects: All subjects.
Eligibility: The Trusts cannot admit students to the University or any of its Colleges. Applicants for awards from the Trusts must therefore also apply to the University of Cambridge and be offered a place at Cambridge in the normal way. All applicants must have a first class or high second class honours degree, or equivalent and normally be under 26. For students from Botswana, Lesotho, Malawi, Namibia, Swaziland, Zambia and Zimbabwe.
Level of Study: Doctorate.
Type: Scholarship.
No. of awards offered: Varies.
Frequency: Annual.
Value: The scholarships will cover the University Composition Fee at the home rate; approved college fees; a maintenance allowance sufficient for a single student; a contribution to a return economy airfare.
Length of Study: Tenable for up to 3 years.
Study Establishment: Cambridge University.
Country of Study: United Kingdom.
Application Procedure: Candidates must complete a Preliminary Application Form, which can be obtained from local universities, offices of the British Council or the main address. Completed application forms must be returned to the main address. Candidates short-listed will be sent forms for admission to the University of Cambridge and a scholarship application form. These forms must be returned to The Board of Graduate Studies.
Closing Date: September 21st, a full year in advance of the proposed entry date to Cambridge for preliminary application, January 31st for actual application.

For further information contact:

The Board of Graduate Studies
4 Mill Lane, Cambridge, CB2 1TZ, England
Contact: The Secretary

Cambridge Nehru Scholarships

Subjects: All subjects.
Eligibility: The Trusts cannot admit students to the University or any of its Colleges. Applicants for awards from the Trusts must therefore also apply to the University of Cambridge and be offered a place at Cambridge in the normal way. All applicants must have a first class or high second class honours degree, or equivalent and normally be under 26. For students from India.
Level of Study: Doctorate.
Purpose: To assist study towards a PhD.
Type: Scholarship.
No. of awards offered: 8.
Frequency: Annual.
Value: The scholarships will cover the University Composition Fee at the home rate; approved college fees; a maintenance allowance sufficient for a single student; a contribution to a return economy airfare.
Length of Study: Tenable for up to 3 years.
Study Establishment: Cambridge University.
Country of Study: United Kingdom.
Application Procedure: Candidates from India may obtain further details and a Preliminary Application Forms by writing before August 17th of the year before entry to The Joint Secretary, Nehru Trust for Cambridge University, Teen Murti House, Teen Murti Marg, New Delhi, 110011, giving details of academic qualifications. Completed forms must be returned to the same address no later than September 9th. Those candidates who are successfully short-listed will be sent forms for admission to the University of Cambridge as a graduate student which should be completed and returned to The Secretary, Board of Graduate Studies, 4 Mill Lane, Cambridge, CB2 1TZ no later than January 31st.
Closing Date: September 9th for preliminary application; January 31st for actual application.

Cambridge Raffles Scholarships

Subjects: All subjects.
Eligibility: The Trusts cannot admit students to the University or any of its Colleges. Applicants for awards from the Trusts must therefore also apply to the University of Cambridge and be offered a place at Cambridge in the normal way. All applicants must have a first class or high second class honours degree, or equivalent and normally be under 26. For students from Singapore.
Level of Study: Postgraduate.
Type: Scholarship.
No. of awards offered: 2.
Frequency: Annual.
Length of Study: 1 year.
Study Establishment: Cambridge University.
Country of Study: United Kingdom.

Application Procedure: Candidates must complete a Preliminary Application Form, which can be obtained from local universities, offices of the British Council or the main address. Completed application forms must be returned to the main address. Candidates short-listed will be sent forms for admission to the University of Cambridge and a scholarship application form. These forms must be returned to The Board of Graduate Studies.
Closing Date: September 21st, a full year in advance of the proposed entry date to Cambridge for preliminary application, January 31st for actual application.

For further information contact:

The Board of Graduate Studies
4 Mill Lane, Cambridge, CB2 1TZ, England
Contact: The Secretary

Cambridge Shared Scholarships

Subjects: All subjects.
Eligibility: The Trusts cannot admit students to the University or any of its Colleges. Applicants for awards from the Trusts must therefore also apply to the University of Cambridge and be offered a place at Cambridge in the normal way. All applicants must have a first class or high second class honours degree or equivalent (if applying for a postgraduate course), be under the age of 35 on October 1st of the year they are applying for, return to their own country to work or study after completing the course, not be employed by a government department or by a parastatal organisation, not at present be living in a developed country, and not have taken studies lasting a year or more in a developed country. Candidates wishing to pursue a course of study related to the economic and social development of their country will be given priority. Citizens from developing countries of the Commonwealth are eligible - The Falkland Islands, St Helena, Tristan de Cunha, Bangladesh, Pakistan, Sri Lanka, The Maldives, Brunei, Cameroon, Gambia, Ghana, Kenya, Sierra Leone, Tanzania, Uganda, India, Malta, Mauritius, Seychelles, Kiribati, Pitcairn, Tuvalu, Nauru, Solomon Islands, Vanuatu, Papua New Guinea, Tonga, Western Samoa, South Africa, Botswana, Namibia, Lesotho, Malawi, Swaziland and commonwealth countries of the Caribbean, Zambia, Mozambique, Zimbabwe.
Level of Study: Postgraduate, Undergraduate.
Type: Scholarship.
No. of awards offered: 50.
Frequency: Annual.
Value: Scholarships will cover up to the University Composition Fee at the overseas rate; approved College fees; a maintenance allowance sufficient for a single student; a contribution to a return economy airfare.
Length of Study: 1 year.
Study Establishment: Cambridge University.
Country of Study: United Kingdom.
Application Procedure: Please apply to the address relevant to your country. If there is no specfic address for your country then apply to the main address.

Closing Date: September 1st for preliminary form, January 31st for actual form for India; September 21st for the preliminary form, January 31st for the actual form for rest of world.

Additional Information: The shared scholarships for undergraduate study are only available when the course is not available at the student's local or regional university. Preliminary application forms should be sent to the address applicable to that particular country. The final application forms should be sent to The Secretary, Board of Graduate Studies.

For further information contact:

Board of Graduate Studies
4 Mill Lane, Cambridge, CB2 1TZ, England
Contact: The Secretary
or
Cambridge Commonwealth Trust (TPG)
c/o Nehru Trust for Cambridge University
Teen Murti House
Teen Murti Marg, New Delhi, 110011, India

Cambridge Thai Foundation Scholarships

Subjects: All subjects.

Eligibility: The Trusts cannot admit students to the University or any of its Colleges. Applicants for awards from the Trusts must therefore also apply to the University of Cambridge and be offered a place at Cambridge in the normal way. All applicants must have a first class or high second class honours degree, or equivalent and normally be under 26. For PhD study applicants must be successfully nominated for an ORS award which pays the difference between the home and overseas rate of the University Composition Fee. For students from Thailand.

Level of Study: Doctorate, Postgraduate.

Type: Scholarship.

No. of awards offered: 1 PhD, 2 postgraduate study.

Frequency: Annual.

Value: Scholarships will cover the university Composition Fee at the home rate, approved College fees, a maintenance allowance sufficient for a single student, a contribution to a return economy airfare.

Length of Study: Tenable for up to 3 years-PhD; 1 year Postgraduate study.

Study Establishment: Cambridge University.

Country of Study: United Kingdom.

Application Procedure: Candidates must complete a Preliminary Application Form, which can be obtained from local universities, offices of the British Council or the main address. Completed application forms must be returned to the main address. Candidates short-listed will be sent forms for admission to the University of Cambridge and a scholarship application form. These forms must be returned to The Board of Graduate Studies.

Closing Date: September 21st, a full year in advance of the proposed entry date to Cambridge for preliminary application, January 31st for actual application.

For further information contact:

The Board of Graduate Studies
4 Mill Lane, Cambridge, CB2 1TZ, England
Contact: The Secretary

Cambridge-Malaysia Scholarship for Study Towards the Degree Of PhD

Subjects: All subjects.

Eligibility: The Trusts cannot admit students to the University or any of its Colleges. Applicants for awards from the Trusts must therefore also apply to the University of Cambridge and be offered a place at Cambridge in the normal way. All applicants must have a first class or high second class honours degree, or equivalent and normally be under 26. For students from Malaysia.

Level of Study: Doctorate.

Purpose: To assist study towards a PhD.

Type: Scholarship.

No. of awards offered: 1.

Frequency: Annual.

Value: The scholarships will cover the university Composition Fee at the home rate, approved College fees, a maintenance allowance sufficient for a single student, a contribution to a return economy airfare.

Length of Study: Up to 3 years.

Study Establishment: Cambridge University.

Country of Study: United Kingdom.

Application Procedure: Candidates must complete a Preliminary Application Form, which can be obtained from local universities, offices of the British Council or the main address. Completed application forms must be returned to the main address. Candidates short-listed will be sent forms for admission to the University of Cambridge and a scholarship application form. These forms must be returned to The Board of Graduate Studies.

Closing Date: September 21st, a full year in advance of the proposed entry date to Cambridge for preliminary application, January 31st for actual application.

For further information contact:

The Board of Graduate Studies
4 Mill Lane, Cambridge, CB2 1TZ, England
Contact: The Secretary

Cambridge-Malaysia Scholarships for One Year Taught Postgraduate Courses of Study

Subjects: All subjects.

Eligibility: The Trusts cannot admit students to the University or any of its Colleges. Applicants for awards from the Trusts must therefore also apply to the University of Cambridge and be offered a place at Cambridge in the normal way. All applicants must have a first class or high second class honours degree, or equivalent and normally be under 26. For students from Malaysia.

Level of Study: Postgraduate.

Type: Scholarship.

No. of awards offered: 4.

Frequency: Annual.

Value: Scholarships will cover up to the University Composition Fee at the overseas rate; approved College fees; a maintenance allowance sufficient for a single student; a contribution to a return economy airfare.
Length of Study: 1 year.
Study Establishment: Cambridge University.
Country of Study: United Kingdom.
Application Procedure: Candidates must complete a Preliminary Application Form, which can be obtained from local universities, offices of the British Council or, the main address. Completed application forms must be returned to the main address. Candidates short-listed will be sent forms for admission to the University of Cambridge and a Scholarship application form. These forms must be returned to The Board of Graduate Studies.
Closing Date: September 21st, a full year in advance of the proposed entry date to Cambridge for preliminary application, January 31st for actual application.

For further information contact:

The Board of Graduate Studies
4 Mill Lane, Cambridge, CB2 1TZ, England
Contact: The Secretary

Canada Cambridge Scholarships

Subjects: All subjects.
Eligibility: The Trusts cannot admit students to the University or any of its Colleges. Applicants for awards from the Trusts must therefore also apply to the University of Cambridge and be offered a place at Cambridge in the normal way. All applicants must have a first class or high second class honours degree, or equivalent and normally be under 26. For students from Canada.
Level of Study: Doctorate.
Type: Scholarship.
No. of awards offered: 5.
Frequency: Annual.
Value: The scholarships will pay the University Composition Fee at the home rate and approved College fees.
Study Establishment: Cambridge University.
Country of Study: United Kingdom.
Application Procedure: Application form for the scholarship will be sent out to eligible candidates once the completed form for admission to the University of Cambridge has reached the Board of Graduate Studies.
Closing Date: Scholarship forms must be returned by April 30th.

For further information contact:

The Board of Graduate Studies
4 Mill Lane, Cambridge, CB2 1TZ, England
Contact: The Secretary

CEU Soros Cambridge Scholarships

Subjects: For study in the subjects relevant to the needs of Central and Eastern Europe, the former Soviet Union and Mongolia.

Eligibility: For graduates from the Central European University. Applicants must be successfully nominated for an ORS award, which covers the difference between the home and overseas rate of the University Composition Fee, pursue research in the same subject area they followed at the CEU, and pursue a course of research which requires one academic year of fieldwork away from Cambridge in Central and Eastern Europe and the former Soviet Union or at the CEU.
Level of Study: Doctorate.
Purpose: To assist study towards a PhD.
Type: Scholarship.
No. of awards offered: 3.
Frequency: Annual.
Value: Scholarships will cover the University Composition Fee at the home rate; approved College fees; a maintenance allowance sufficient for a single student; a return economy airfare; fieldwork costs in the region.
Length of Study: Tenable for up to 3 years.
Study Establishment: Cambridge University.
Country of Study: United Kingdom.
Application Procedure: Applicants for the CEU Soros Cambridge Scholarship must complete a application form for admission to the University of Cambridge as a graduate student which can be obtained from, and must be returned to, the Scholarships Office at the Central European University, no later than December 16th.
Additional Information: There are also five awards available to enable candidates pursuing a course of research leading to the degree of PhD at the Central European University to undertake short periods of study at Cambridge as part of their PhD at the CEU. Potential candidates should make application through the Scholarships Office at the CEU, in consultation with their academic advisors.

Charles Wallace Bangladesh and Pakistan Trusts Shared Scholarships

Subjects: Arts, humanities, development studies.
Eligibility: The Trusts cannot admit students to the University or any of its Colleges. Applicants for awards from the Trusts must therefore also apply to the University of Cambridge and be offered a place at Cambridge in the normal way. All applicants must have a first class or high second class honours degree, or equivalent and normally be under 26. For students from Bangladesh and Pakistan.
Level of Study: Postgraduate.
Type: Scholarship.
No. of awards offered: 5.
Frequency: Annual.
Study Establishment: Cambridge University.
Country of Study: United Kingdom.
Application Procedure: Candidates must complete a Preliminary Application Form, which can be obtained from local universities, offices of the British Council or the main address. Completed application forms must be returned to the main address. Candidates short-listed will be sent forms for admission to the University of Cambridge and a scholarship application form. These forms must be returned to The Board fof Graduate Studies.

Closing Date: September 21st, a full year in advance of the proposed entry date to Cambridge for preliminary application, January 31st for actual application.
Additional Information: Two scholarships are for students from Bangladesh and three are for students from Pakistan.

For further information contact:

The Board of Graduate Studies
4 Mill Lane, Cambridge, CB2 1TZ, England
Contact: The Secretary

Coles Myer Cambridge Scholarship

Subjects: All subjects.
Eligibility: The Trusts cannot admit students to the University or any of its Colleges. Applicants for awards from the Trusts must therefore also apply to the University of Cambridge and be offered a place at Cambridge in the normal way. All applicants must have a first class or high second class honours degree, or equivalent and normally be under 26. For students from Australia.
Level of Study: Doctorate.
Type: Scholarship.
No. of awards offered: 1.
Frequency: As available.
Study Establishment: Cambridge University.
Country of Study: United Kingdom.
Application Procedure: Application forms for the scholarship will be sent out to eligible candidates once the completed form for admission to the University of Cambridge has reached the Board of Graduate Studies.
Closing Date: Scholarship forms must be returned by April 30th.

For further information contact:

The Board of Graduate Studies
4 Mill Lane, Cambridge, CB2 1TZ, England
Contact: The Secretary

Corpus Christi ACE Scholarship

Subjects: All subjects (with preference given to candidates wishing to pursue a MPhil in Environment and Development).
Eligibility: The Trusts cannot admit students to the University or any of its Colleges. Applicants for awards from the Trusts must therefore also apply to the University of Cambridge and be offered a place at Cambridge in the normal way. All applicants must have a first class or high second class honours degree, or equivalent and normally be under 26. For students from the Developing World with preference for applicants wishing to pursue the MPhil in environment and development.
Level of Study: Postgraduate.
Type: Scholarship.
No. of awards offered: 1.
Frequency: Annual.
Length of Study: 1 year.
Study Establishment: Corpus Christi College, Cambridge.
Country of Study: United Kingdom.

Application Procedure: Candidates must complete a Preliminary Application Form, which can be obtained from local universities, offices of the British Council or the main address. Completed application forms must be returned to the main address. Candidates short-listed will be sent forms for admission to the University of Cambridge and a scholarship application form. These forms must be returned to The Board of Graduate Studies.
Closing Date: September 21st, a full year in advance of the proposed entry date to Cambridge for preliminary application, January 31st for actual application.

For further information contact:

The Board of Graduate Studies
4 Mill Lane, Cambridge, CB2 1TZ, England
Contact: The Secretary

Cyprus Cambridge Scholarships

Subjects: All subjects.
Eligibility: The Trusts cannot admit students to the University or any of its Colleges. Applicants for awards from the Trusts must therefore also apply to the University of Cambridge and be offered a place at Cambridge in the normal way. All applicants must have a first class or high second class honours degree, or equivalent and normally be under 26. For students from Cyprus. Candidates must be successfully nominated for an ORS award, which covers the difference between the home and overseas rate of the University Composition Fee.
Level of Study: Doctorate.
Purpose: To assist study towards a PhD.
Type: Scholarship.
No. of awards offered: 1.
Frequency: As available.
Value: The scholarships will take into account the financial resources of the applicant and will cover up to the University Composition Fee at the overseas rate; approved College fees; a maintenance allowance sufficient for a single student; a contribution to a return economy airfare.
Length of Study: Tenable for up to 3 years.
Study Establishment: Cambridge University.
Country of Study: United Kingdom.
Application Procedure: Candidates must complete a Preliminary Application Form, which can be obtained from local universities, offices of the British Council or the main address. Completed application forms must be returned to the main address. Candidates short-listed will be sent forms for admission to the University of Cambridge and a scholarship application form. These forms must be returned to The Board of Graduate Studies.
Closing Date: September 21st, a full year in advance of the proposed entry date to Cambridge for preliminary application, January 31st for actual application.

For further information contact:

The Board of Graduate Studies
4 Mill Lane, Cambridge, CB 2 1TZ, England
Contact: The Secretary

Developing World Education Fund Cambridge Scholarships for One Year Taught Postgraduate Courses of Study

Subjects: All subjects.
Eligibility: The Trusts cannot admit students to the University or any of its Colleges. Applicants for awards from the Trusts must therefore also apply to the University of Cambridge and be offered a place at Cambridge in the normal way. All applicants must have a first class or high second class honours degree, or equivalent and normally be under 26. For students from China.
Level of Study: Postgraduate.
Type: Scholarship.
No. of awards offered: 2.
Frequency: Annual.
Study Establishment: Cambridge University.
Country of Study: United Kingdom.
Application Procedure: Candidates must complete a Preliminary Application Form, which can be obtained from local universities, offices of the British Council or the main address. Completed application forms must be returned to the main address. Candidates short-listed will be sent forms for admission to the University of Cambridge and a scholarship application form. These forms must be returned to The Board of Graduate Studies.
Closing Date: September 21st, a full year in advance of the proposed entry date to Cambridge for preliminary application, January 31st for actual application.

For further information contact:

The Board of Graduate Studies
4 Mill Lane, Cambridge, CB2 1TZ, England
Contact: The Secretary

Developing World Education Fund Cambridge Scholarships for Study Towards the Degree of PhD

Subjects: All subjects.
Eligibility: The Trusts cannot admit students to the University or any of its Colleges. Applicants for awards from the Trusts must therefore also apply to the University of Cambridge and be offered a place at Cambridge in the normal way. All applicants must have a first class or high second class honours degree, or equivalent and normally be under 26. For students from Bangladesh, Pakistan, Sri Lanka and China. Applicants must be successfully nominated for and ORS award, which covers the difference between the home and overseas rate of the University Composition Fee.
Level of Study: Doctorate.
Purpose: To support study towards a PhD.
Type: Scholarship.
No. of awards offered: Varies.
Frequency: Annual.

Value: Scholarships will cover up to the University Composition Fee at the overseas rate; approved College fees; a maintenance allowance sufficient for a single student; a contribution to a return economy airfare.
Length of Study: Tenable for up to 3 years.
Study Establishment: Cambridge University.
Country of Study: United Kingdom.
Application Procedure: Candidates must complete a Preliminary Application Form, which can be obtained from local universities, offices of the British Council or the main address. Completed application forms must be returned to the main address. Candidates short-listed will be sent forms for admission to the University of Cambridge and a scholarship application form. These forms must be returned to The Board fof Graduate Studies.
Closing Date: September 21st, a full year in advance of the proposed entry date to Cambridge for preliminary application, January 31st for actual application.

For further information contact:

The Board of Graduate Studies
4 Mill Lane, Cambridge, CB2 1TZ, England
Contact: The Secretary

Dharam Hinduja Cambridge Scholarships

Subjects: All subjects.
Eligibility: The Trusts cannot admit students to the University or any of its Colleges. Applicants for awards from the Trusts must therefore also apply to the University of Cambridge and be offered a place at Cambridge in the normal way. All applicants must have a first class or high second class honours degree, or equivalent and normally be under 26. For students from India.
Level of Study: Doctorate.
Purpose: To assist with study towards a PhD.
Type: Scholarship.
No. of awards offered: 2.
Frequency: Annual.
Value: The scholarships will cover the University Composition Fee at the home rate; approved college fees; a maintenance allowance sufficient for a single student; a contribution to a return economy airfare.
Length of Study: Tenable for up to 3 years.
Study Establishment: Cambridge University.
Country of Study: United Kingdom.
Application Procedure: Candidates from India may obtain further details and a Preliminary Application Forms by writing before August 17th of the year before entry to The Joint Secretary, Nehru Trust for Cambridge University, Teen Murti House, Teen Murti Marg, New Delhi, 110011, giving details of academic qualifications. Completed forms must be returned to the same address no later than September 9th. Those candidates who are successfully short-listed will be sent forms for admission to the University of Cambridge as a graduate student which should be completed and returned to The Secretary, Board of Graduate Studies, 4 Mill Lane, Cambridge, CB2 1TZ no later than January 31st.
Closing Date: September 9th, preliminary application; January 31st actual application.

Dharam Hinduja Cambridge Shared Scholarships

Subjects: All subjects.
Eligibility: The Trusts cannot admit students to the University or any of its Colleges. Applicants for awards from the Trusts must therefore also apply to the University of Cambridge and be offered a place at Cambridge in the normal way. All applicants must have a first class or high second class honours degree, or equivalent and normally be under 26. For students from India.
Level of Study: Postgraduate.
Type: Scholarship.
No. of awards offered: 4.
Frequency: Annual.
Study Establishment: Cambridge University.
Country of Study: United Kingdom.
Application Procedure: Candidates from India may obtain further details and a Preliminary Application Forms by writing before August 17th of the year before entry to The Joint Secretary, Nehru Trust for Cambridge University, Teen Murti House, Teen Murti Marg, New Delhi, 110011, giving details of academic qualifications. Completed forms must be returned to the same address no later than September 9th. Those candidates who are successfully short-listed will be sent forms for admission to the University of Cambridge as a graduate student which should be completed and returned to The Secretary, Board of Graduate Studies, 4 Mill Lane, Cambridge, CB2 1TZ no later than January 31st.
Closing Date: September 9th, preliminary application; January 31st actual application.

Downing Müller Cambridge Scholarships

Subjects: All subjects.
Eligibility: The Trusts cannot admit students to the University or any of its Colleges. Applicants for awards from the Trusts must therefore also apply to the University of Cambridge and be offered a place at Cambridge in the normal way. All applicants must have a first class or high second class honours degree, or equivalent and normally be under 26. For students from a Third World country, Eastern Europe or from a German speaking country liable to pay fees at the overseas rate.
Level of Study: Doctorate.
Purpose: To assist study towards a PhD.
Type: Scholarship.
No. of awards offered: 2.
Frequency: Annual.
Value: The scholarships will cover the University Composition Fee at the home rate; approved college fees; a maintenance allowance suffiecient for a single student; a contribution to a return economy airfare.
Length of Study: Tenable for up to 3 years.
Study Establishment: Downing College, Cambridge.
Country of Study: United Kingdom.
Application Procedure: Candidates must complete a Preliminary Application Form, which can be obtained from local universities, offices of the British Council or the main address. Completed application forms must be returned to

the main address. Candidates short-listed will be sent forms for admission to the University of Cambridge and a scholarship application form. These forms must be returned to The Board of Graduate Studies.
Closing Date: September 21st, a full year in advance of the proposed entry date to Cambridge for preliminary application, January 31st for actual application.

For further information contact:

The Board of Graduate Studies
4 Mill Lane, Cambridge, CB2 1TZ, England
Contact: The Secretary

Downing Müller Cambridge Shared Scholarships

Subjects: All subjects.
Eligibility: For students from a developing country of the Commonwealth. Applicants must be under the age of 35 on October 1st of the year of entry, undertake to return to their own country to work or study after completing the course at Cambridge, not be employed by a government department or be a parastatal organisation, not be at present living or studying in a developed country, and not have undertaken studies lasting a year or more in a developed country. Priority will be given to candidates wishing to pursue a course of study related to the economic and social development of their country.
Level of Study: Postgraduate.
Type: Scholarship.
No. of awards offered: 2.
Frequency: Annual.
Value: The scholarships will cover the University Composition Fee at the home rate; approved college fees; a maintenance allowance sufficient for a single student; a contribution to a return economy airfare.
Length of Study: 1 year.
Study Establishment: Dowing College.
Country of Study: United Kingdom.
Application Procedure: Candidates must complete a Preliminary Application Form, which can be obtained from local universities, offices of the British Council or the main address. Completed application forms must be returned to the main address. Candidates short-listed will be sent forms for admission to the University of Cambridge and a scholarship application form. These forms must be returned to The Board of Graduate Studies.
Closing Date: September 21st, a full year in advance of the proposed entry date to Cambridge for preliminary application, January 31st for actual application.
Additional Information: From time to time, a Downing Müller Cambridge Scholarship will be offered to a candidate from Eastern Europe.

For further information contact:

The Board of Graduate Studies
4 Mill Lane, Cambridge, CB2 1TZ, England
Contact: The Secretary

English Speaking Union Cambridge Scholarship

Subjects: For study in the field of English and the teaching of the English language.
Eligibility: The Trusts cannot admit students to the University or any of its Colleges. Applicants for awards from the Trusts must therefore also apply to the University of Cambridge and be offered a place at Cambridge in the normal way. All applicants must have a first class or high second class honours degree, or equivalent and normally be under 26. For students from Mauritius and the Seychelles.
Level of Study: Postgraduate.
Type: Scholarship.
No. of awards offered: 1.
Frequency: As available.
Value: The scholarships will cover the University Composition Fee at the home rate; approved college fees; a maintenance allowance sufficient for a single student; a contribution to a return economy airfare.
Length of Study: 1 year.
Study Establishment: Cambridge University.
Country of Study: United Kingdom.
Application Procedure: Candidates for this scholarship must apply directly to the British High Commission, King George V Avenue, Floreal, Mauritius.
Closing Date: September 21st, a full year in advance of the proposed entry date to Cambridge for preliminary application, January 31st for actual application.

FCO-China Chevening Fellowships

Subjects: All subjects.
Eligibility: The Trusts cannot admit students to the University or any of its Colleges. Applicants for awards from the Trusts must therefore also apply to the University of Cambridge and be offered a place at Cambridge in the normal way. All applicants must have a first class or high second class honours degree, or equivalent and normally be under 26.
Level of Study: Postgraduate.
Type: Fellowship.
No. of awards offered: 3.
Frequency: Annual.
Study Establishment: Cambridge University.
Country of Study: United Kingdom.
Application Procedure: Candidates must complete a Preliminary Application Form, which can be obtained from local universities, offices of the British Council or the main address. Completed application forms must be returned to the main address. Candidates short-listed will be sent forms for admission to the University of Cambridge and a scholarship application form. These forms must be returned to The Board of Graduate Studies.
Closing Date: September 21st, a full year in advance of the proposed entry date to Cambridge for preliminary application, January 31st for actual application.

For further information contact:

The Board of Graduate Studies
4 Mill Lane, Cambridge, CB2 1TZ, England
Contact: The Secretary

Guy Clutton-Brock Scholarship

Subjects: All subjects.
Eligibility: The Trusts cannot admit students to the University or any of its Colleges. Applicants for awards from the Trusts must therefore also apply to the University of Cambridge and be offered a place at Cambridge in the normal way. All applicants must have a first class or high second class honours degree, or equivalent and normally be under 26. For a student from Zimbabwe who has been offered a place at Magdelene College, Cambridge.
Level of Study: Doctorate, Postgraduate.
Type: Scholarship.
No. of awards offered: 1 PhD, 1 postgraduate study.
Frequency: As available.
Value: Scholarships will cover the University Composition Fee at the overseas rate; approved College fees; a maintenance allowance sufficient for a single student; a contribution to a return economy airfare.
Length of Study: Up to 3 years PhD; 1year postgraduate study.
Study Establishment: Magdelene College, Cambridge.
Country of Study: United Kingdom.
Application Procedure: Candidates must complete a Preliminary Application Form, which can be obtained from local universities, offices of the British Council or the main address. Completed application forms must be returned to the main address. Candidates short-listed will be sent forms for admission to the University of Cambridge and a scholarship application form. These forms must be returned to The Board of Graduate Studies.
Closing Date: September 21st, a full year in advance of the proposed entry date to Cambridge for preliminary application, January 31st for actual application.

For further information contact:

The Board of Graduate Studies
4 Mill Lane, Cambridge, CB2 1TZ, England
Contact: The Secretary

Hamilton Cambridge Scholarship

Subjects: All subjects.
Eligibility: The Trusts cannot admit students to the University or any of its Colleges. Applicants for awards from the Trusts must therefore also apply to the University of Cambridge and be offered a place at Cambridge in the normal way. All applicants must have a first class or high second class honours degree, or equivalent and normally be under 26.
Level of Study: Doctorate.
Type: Scholarship.
No. of awards offered: 1.
Frequency: As available.

Value: Scholarships will cover the University Composition Fee at the overseas rate; approved College fees; a maintenance allowance sufficient for a single student; a contribution to a return economy airfare.
Length of Study: Tenable for up to 3 years.
Study Establishment: Selwyn College.
Country of Study: United Kingdom.
Application Procedure: Candidates must complete a Preliminary Application Form, which can be obtained from local universities, offices of the British Council or the main address. Completed application forms must be returned to the main address. Candidates short-listed will be sent forms for admission to the University of Cambridge and a scholarship application form. These forms must be returned to The Board of Graduate Studies.
Closing Date: September 21st, a full year in advance of the proposed entry date to Cambridge for preliminary application, January 31st for actual application.

For further information contact:

The Board of Graduate Studies
4 Mill Lane, Cambridge, CB2 1TZ, England
Contact: The Secretary

Hong Kong Cambridge Scholarships

Subjects: All subjects.
Eligibility: The Trusts cannot admit students to the University or any of its Colleges. Applicants for awards from the Trusts must therefore also apply to the University of Cambridge and be offered a place at Cambridge in the normal way. All applicants must have a first class or high second class honours degree, or equivalent and normally be under 26. With preference for graduates of the Chinese University of Hong Kong and the University of Hong Kong.
Level of Study: Doctorate.
Type: Scholarship.
No. of awards offered: Up to 5.
Frequency: Annual.
Length of Study: Up to 3 years.
Study Establishment: Cambridge University.
Country of Study: United Kingdom.
Application Procedure: Candidates must complete a Preliminary Application Form, which can be obtained from local universities, offices of the British Council or the main address. Completed application forms must be returned to the main address. Candidates short-listed will be sent forms for admission to the University of Cambridge and a scholarship application form. These forms must be returned to The Board of Graduate Studies.
Closing Date: September 21st, a full year in advance of the proposed entry date to Cambridge for preliminary application, January 31st for actual application.

For further information contact:

The Board of Graduate Studies
4 Mill Lane, Cambridge, CB2 1TZ, England
Contact: The Secretary

International Renaissance Foundation/FCO Scholarships

Subjects: All subjects.
Eligibility: The Trusts cannot admit students to the University or any of its Colleges. Applicants for awards from the Trusts must therefore also apply to the University of Cambridge and be offered a place at Cambridge in the normal way. All applicants must have a first class or high second class honours degree, or equivalent and normally be under 26. For students from the Ukraine.
Level of Study: Postgraduate.
Type: Scholarship.
No. of awards offered: 3.
Frequency: Annual.
Study Establishment: Cambridge University.
Country of Study: United Kingdom.
Application Procedure: Candidates must complete a Preliminary Application Form, which can be obtained from local universities, offices of the British Council or the main address. Completed application forms must be returned to the main address. Candidates short-listed will be sent forms for admission to the University of Cambridge and a scholarship application form. These forms must be returned to The Board of Graduate Studies.
Closing Date: September 21st, a full year in advance of the proposed entry date to Cambridge for preliminary application, January 31st for actual application.

For further information contact:

The Board for Graduate Studies
4 Mill Lane, Cambridge, CB2 1TZ, England
Contact: The Secretary

Jawaharlal Nehru Memorial Fund Cambridge Scholarships

Subjects: With preference for study in the broad fields of science policy, technology, global restructuring, philosophy and history of science, comparative studies in religion and culture, international relations and constitutional studies, Indian history, civilisation and culture, interface of social change and economic development, environmental ecology and sustainable development.
Eligibility: The Trusts cannot admit students to the University or any of its Colleges. Applicants for awards from the Trusts must therefore also apply to the University of Cambridge and be offered a place at Cambridge in the normal way. All applicants must have a first class or high second class honours degree, or equivalent and normally be under 26. Applicants for all scholarships for study towards the degree of PhD must be successful in winning an ORS award, which pays the difference between the home and overseas rate of the University Composition Fee. Those who have, in addition to a first class honours degree, a first class Master's degree, or its equivalent, may be given preference. This scholarship is for students from India.
Level of Study: Doctorate.
Purpose: To assist study towards a PhD.
Type: Scholarship.
No. of awards offered: 2.

Frequency: Annual.
Value: The scholarships will cover the University Composition Fee at the home rate; approved college fees; a maintenance allowance sufficient for a single student; a contribution to a return economy airfare.
Length of Study: Tenable for up to 3 years.
Study Establishment: Cambridge University.
Country of Study: United Kingdom.
Application Procedure: Candidates from India may obtain further details and a Preliminary Application Forms by writing before August 17th of the year before entry to The Joint Secretary, Nehru Trust for Cambridge University, Teen Murti House, Teen Murti Marg, New Delhi, 110011, giving details of academic qualifications. Completed forms must be returned to the same address no later than September 9th. Those candidates who are successfully short-listed will be sent forms for admission to the University of Cambridge as a graduate student which should be completed and returned to The Secretary, Board of Graduate Studies, 4 Mill Lane, Cambridge, CB2 1TZ no later than January 31st.
Closing Date: September 9th, preliminary application; January 31st actual application.

Jawaharlal Nehru Memorial Trust Cambridge Scholarships

Subjects: All subjects.
Eligibility: The Trusts cannot admit students to the University or any of its Colleges. Applicants for awards from the Trusts must therefore also apply to the University of Cambridge and be offered a place at Cambridge in the normal way. All applicants must have a first class or high second class honours degree, or equivalent and normally be under 26. Applicants for all scholarships for study towards the degree of PhD must be successful in winning an ORS award, which pays the difference between the home and overseas rate of the University Composition Fee. Those who have, in addition to a first class honours degree, a first class Master's degree, or its equivalent, may be given preference. For students from India.
Level of Study: Doctorate.
Purpose: To assist study towards a PhD.
Type: Scholarship.
No. of awards offered: 1.
Frequency: Annual.
Value: The scholarships will cover the University Composition Fee at the home rate; approved college fees; a maintenance allowance sufficient for a single student; a contribution to a return economy airfare.
Length of Study: Tenable for up to 3 years.
Study Establishment: Trinity College, Cambridge.
Country of Study: United Kingdom.
Application Procedure: Candidates from India may obtain further details and a Preliminary Application Forms by writing before August 17th of the year before entry to The Joint Secretary, Nehru Trust for Cambridge University, Teen Murti House, Teen Murti Marg, New Delhi, 110011, giving details of academic qualifications. Completed forms must be returned to the same address no later than September 9th. Those candidates who are successfully short-listed will be sent forms for admission to the University of Cambridge as a

graduate student which should be completed and returned to The Secretary, Board of Graduate Studies, 4 Mill Lane, Cambridge, CB2 1TZ no later than January 31st.
Closing Date: September 9th, preliminary application; January 31st actual application.

Jawaharlal Nehru Memorial Trust Cambridge Shared Scholarships

Subjects: All subjects.
Eligibility: The Trusts cannot admit students to the University or any of its Colleges. Applicants for awards from the Trusts must therefore also apply to the University of Cambridge and be offered a place at Cambridge in the normal way. All applicants must have a first class or high second class honours degree, or equivalent and normally be under 26. For students from India.
Level of Study: Postgraduate.
Type: Scholarship.
No. of awards offered: 2.
Frequency: Annual.
Study Establishment: Cambridge University.
Country of Study: United Kingdom.
Application Procedure: Candidates from India may obtain further details and a Preliminary Application Forms by writing before August 17th of the year before entry to The Joint Secretary, Nehru Trust for Cambridge University, Teen Murti House, Teen Murti Marg, New Delhi, 110011, giving details of academic qualifications. Completed forms must be returned to the same address no later than September 9th. Those candidates who are successfully short-listed will be sent forms for admission to the University of Cambridge as a graduate student which should be completed and returned to The Secretary, Board of Graduate Studies, 4 Mill Lane, Cambridge, CB2 1TZ no later than January 31st.
Closing Date: September 9th, preliminary application; January 31st actual application.

Kalimuzo Cambridge Scholarship

Subjects: All subjects.
Eligibility: The Trusts cannot admit students to the University or any of its Colleges. Applicants for awards from the Trusts must therefore also apply to the University of Cambridge and be offered a place at Cambridge in the normal way. All applicants must have a first class or high second class honours degree, or equivalent and normally be under 26. For a student from Uganda.
Level of Study: Doctorate.
Purpose: To support study towards a PhD.
Type: Scholarship.
No. of awards offered: 1.
Frequency: Annual.
Study Establishment: Cambridge University.
Country of Study: United Kingdom.
Application Procedure: Candidates must complete a Preliminary Application Form, which can be obtained from local universities, offices of the British Council or the main address. Completed application forms must be returned to the main address. Candidates short-listed will be sent forms for admission to the University of Cambridge and a

scholarship application form. These forms must be returned to The Board of Graduate Studies.

Closing Date: September 21st, a full year in advance of the proposed entry date to Cambridge for preliminary application, January 31st for actual application.

Additional Information: The scholarship is awarded in the memory of Professor Frank Kalimuzo former Vice-Chancellor of Makerere University.

For further information contact:

The Board of Graduate Studies
4 Mill Lane, Cambridge, CB2 1TZ, England
Contact: The Secretary

Kalimuzo Cambridge Shared Scholarships

Subjects: All subjects.
Eligibility: The Trusts cannot admit students to the University or any of its Colleges. Applicants for awards from the Trusts must therefore also apply to the University of Cambridge and be offered a place at Cambridge in the normal way. All applicants must have a first class or high second class honours degree, or equivalent and normally be under 26. For students from Uganda.
Type: Scholarship.
No. of awards offered: 3.
Frequency: Annual.
Study Establishment: Cambridge University.
Country of Study: United Kingdom.
Application Procedure: Candidates must complete a Preliminary Application Form, which can be obtained from local universities, offices of the British Council or the main address. Completed application forms must be returned to the main address. Candidates short-listed will be sent forms for admission to the University of Cambridge and a scholarship application form. These forms must be returned to The Board of Graduate Studies.
Closing Date: September 21st, a full year in advance of the proposed entry date to Cambridge for preliminary application, January 31st for actual application.
Additional Information: Scholarships offered in the memory of Professor Frank Kalimuzo former Vice-Chancellor of Makerere University.

For further information contact:

The Board of Graduate Studies
4 Mill Lane, Cambridge, CB2 1TZ, England
Contact: The Secretary

Karim Rida Said Cambridge Scholarships

Subjects: All subjects.
Eligibility: The Trusts cannot admit students to the University or any of its Colleges. Applicants for awards from the Trusts must therefore also apply to the University of Cambridge and be offered a place at Cambridge in the normal way. All applicants must have a first class or high second class honours degree, or equivalent and normally be under 26. Applicants must be successfully nominated for an ORS award which pays the difference between the home and

overseas rate of the University Composition Fee. For students from Egypt, Jordan, Lebanon, Palestine and Syria.
Level of Study: Doctorate, Postgraduate.
Type: Scholarship.
No. of awards offered: 2 PhD, 4 postgraduate study.
Frequency: Annual.
Value: Scholarships will cover the University Composition Fee at the overseas rate; approved College fees; a maintenance allowance sufficient for a single student; a contribution to a return economy airfare.
Length of Study: Tenable for up to 3 years-PhD; 1 year Postgraduate study.
Study Establishment: Cambridge University.
Country of Study: United Kingdom.
Application Procedure: Candidates must complete a Preliminary Application Form, which can be obtained from local universities, offices of the British Council or the main address. Completed application forms must be returned to the main address. Candidates short-listed will be sent forms for admission to the University of Cambridge and a scholarship application form. These forms must be returned to The Board of Graduate Studies.
Closing Date: September 21st, a full year in advance of the proposed entry date to Cambridge for preliminary application, January 31st for actual application.
Additional Information: Scholars must undertake to return to their home country, or to another member state of the Arab League, on completion of studies at Cambridge.

For further information contact:

The Board of Graduate Studies
4 Mill Lane, Cambridge, CB2 1TZ, England
Contact: The Secretary

Kater Cambridge Scholarship

Subjects: All subjects.
Eligibility: The Trusts cannot admit students to the University or any of its Colleges. Applicants for awards from the Trusts must therefore also apply to the University of Cambridge and be offered a place at Cambridge in the normal way. All applicants must have a first class or high second class honours degree, or equivalent and normally be under 26. Open to students from Australia.
Level of Study: Doctorate.
Purpose: For study towards a PhD.
Type: Scholarship.
No. of awards offered: 1.
Frequency: As available.
Value: Scholarships will cover up to the University Composition Fee at the overseas rate; approved College fees; a maintenance allowance sufficient for a single student; a contribution to a return economy airfare.
Length of Study: Tenable for up to 3 years.
Study Establishment: Cambridge University.
Country of Study: United Kingdom.
Application Procedure: Application form for the scholarship will be sent out to eligible candidates once the completed form for admission to the University of Cambridge has reached the Board of Graduate Studies.

Closing Date: Studentship forms must be returned by April 30th.

For further information contact:

The Board of Graduate Studies
4 Mill Lane, Cambridge, CB2 1TZ, England
Contact: The Secretary

Kenya Cambridge Scholarship

Subjects: All subjects.
Eligibility: The Trusts cannot admit students to the University or any of its Colleges. Applicants for awards from the Trusts must therefore also apply to the University of Cambridge and be offered a place at Cambridge in the normal way. All applicants must have a first class or high second class honours degree, or equivalent and normally be under 26. For a student from Kenya.
Level of Study: Doctorate.
Type: Scholarship.
No. of awards offered: 1.
Frequency: Annual.
Length of Study: Tenable for up to 3 years.
Study Establishment: Cambridge University.
Country of Study: United Kingdom.
Application Procedure: Candidates must complete a Preliminary Application Form, which can be obtained from local universities, offices of the British Council or the main address. Completed application forms must be returned to the main address. Candidates short-listed will be sent forms for admission to the University of Cambridge and a scholarship application form. These forms must be returned to The Board of Graduate Studies.
Closing Date: September 21st, a full year in advance of the proposed entry date to Cambridge for preliminary application, January 31st for actual application.

For further information contact:

The Board of Graduate Studies
4 Mill Lane, Cambridge, CB2 1TZ, England
Contact: The Secretary

Kenya Cambridge Shared Scholarship

Subjects: All subjects.
Eligibility: The Trusts cannot admit students to the University or any of its Colleges. Applicants for awards from the Trusts must therefore also apply to the University of Cambridge and be offered a place at Cambridge in the normal way. All applicants must have a first class or high second class honours degree, or equivalent and normally be under 26. For a student from Kenya.
Level of Study: Postgraduate.
Type: Scholarship.
No. of awards offered: 1.
Frequency: Annual.
Study Establishment: Cambridge University.
Country of Study: United Kingdom.

Application Procedure: Candidates must complete a Preliminary Application Form, which can be obtained from local universities, offices of the British Council or the main address. Completed application forms must be returned to the main address. Candidates short-listed will be sent forms for admission to the University of Cambridge and a scholarship application form. These forms must be returned to The Board of Graduate Studies.
Closing Date: September 21st, a full year in advance of the proposed entry date to Cambridge for preliminary application, January 31st for actual application.

For further information contact:

The Board of Graduate Studies
4 Mill Lane, Cambridge, CB2 1TZ, England
Contact: The Secretary

Kopke Cambridge Scholarship

Subjects: All subjects.
Eligibility: The Trusts cannot admit students to the University or any of its Colleges. Applicants for awards from the Trusts must therefore also apply to the University of Cambridge and be offered a place at Cambridge in the normal way. All applicants must have a first class or high second class honours degree, or equivalent and normally be under 26. Open to candidates from Australia.
Level of Study: Doctorate.
Purpose: To assist towards the study for a PhD.
Type: Scholarship.
No. of awards offered: 1.
Frequency: As available.
Value: Scholarships will cover up to the University Composition Fee at the overseas rate; approved College fees; a maintenance allowance sufficient for a single student; a contribution to a return economy airfare.
Length of Study: Tenable for up to 3 years.
Study Establishment: Cambridge University.
Country of Study: United Kingdom.
Application Procedure: Application form for the scholarship will be sent out to eligible candidates once the completed form for admission to the University of Cambridge has reached the Board of Graduate Studies.
Closing Date: Scholarship forms must be returned by April 30th.

For further information contact:

The Board of Graduate Studies
4 Mill Lane, Cambridge, CB2 1TZ, England
Contact: The Secretary

Lady Noon Cambridge Shared Scholarships

Subjects: All subjects.
Eligibility: The Trusts cannot admit students to the University or any of its Colleges. Applicants for awards from the Trusts must therefore also apply to the University of Cambridge and be offered a place at Cambridge in the normal way. All

applicants must have a first class or high second class honours degree, or equivalent and normally be under 26. For students from Pakistan.
Level of Study: Postgraduate.
Type: Scholarship.
No. of awards offered: 1.
Frequency: Annual.
Length of Study: 1 year.
Study Establishment: Cambridge Unibersity.
Country of Study: United Kingdom.
Application Procedure: Candidates must complete a Preliminary Application Form, which can be obtained from local universities, offices of the British Council or the main address. Completed application forms must be returned to the main address. Candidates short-listed will be sent forms for admission to the University of Cambridge and a scholarship application form. These forms must be returned to The Board fof Graduate Studies.
Closing Date: September 21st, a full year in advance of the proposed entry date to Cambridge for preliminary application, January 31st for actual application.

For further information contact:

The Board of Graduate Studies
4 Mill Lane, Cambridge, CB2 1TZ, England
Contact: The Secretary

Link Foundation/FCO Chevening Cambridge Scholarships

Subjects: All subjects.
Eligibility: The Trusts cannot admit students to the University or any of its Colleges. Applicants for awards from the Trusts must therefore also apply to the University of Cambridge and be offered a place at Cambridge in the normal way. All applicants must have a first class or high second class honours degree, or equivalent and normally be under 26. For students from New Zealand.
Level of Study: Postgraduate.
Purpose: The fund taught postgraduate courses.
Type: Scholarship.
No. of awards offered: 3.
Frequency: Annual.
Value: The scholarships will make a substantial contribution of up to £10,000 towards the costs of study and a contribution of £1,000 towards the return airfare to the UK.
Length of Study: 1 year.
Study Establishment: Cambridge University.
Country of Study: United Kingdom.
Application Procedure: Application form for the scholarship will be sent out to eligible candidates once the completed form for admission to the University of Cambridge has reached The Board of Graduate Studies.
Closing Date: Scholarship forms must be returned by April 30th.

For further information contact:

The Board of Graduate Studies
4 Mill Lane, Cambridge, CB2 1TZ, England
Contact: The Secretary

Luis López Méndez CONICIT Cambridge Scholarships

Subjects: Social sciences and humanities.
Eligibility: The Trusts cannot admit students to the University or any of its Colleges. Applicants for awards from the Trusts must therefore also apply to the University of Cambridge and be offered a place at Cambridge in the normal way. All applicants must have a first class or high second class honours degree, or equivalent and normally be under 26. For students from Venezuela.
Level of Study: Postgraduate.
Type: Scholarship.
No. of awards offered: 4.
Frequency: Annual.
Value: Scholarships will cover the University Composition Fee at the overseas rate; approved College fees; a maintenance allowance sufficient for a single student; a contribution to a return economy airfare.
Length of Study: 1 year.
Study Establishment: Cambridge University.
Country of Study: United Kingdom.
Application Procedure: Candidates must complete a Preliminary Application Form, which can be obtained from local universities, offices of the British Council or the main address. Completed application forms must be returned to the main address. Candidates short-listed will be sent forms for admission to the University of Cambridge and a scholarship application form. These forms must be returned to The Board of Graduate Studies.
Closing Date: September 21st, a full year in advance of the proposed entry date to Cambridge for preliminary application, January 31st for actual application.
Additional Information: Successful candidates will be eligible to be considered for further funding to enable them to pursue a course of research leading to the degree of PhD at Cambridge. Two such scholarships will be awarded annually, subject to the scholars applying for an ORS award.

For further information contact:

The Board of Graduate Studies
4 Mill Lane, Cambridge, CB2 1TZ, England
Contact: The Secretary

Malaysian Commonwealth Scholarships

Subjects: All subjects.
Eligibility: The Trusts cannot admit students to the University or any of its Colleges. Applicants for awards from the Trusts must therefore also apply to the University of Cambridge and be offered a place at Cambridge in the normal way. All applicants must have a first class or high second class honours degree, or equivalent and normally be under 26. For students from Commonwealth countries.
Level of Study: Doctorate, Postgraduate.
Type: Scholarship.
No. of awards offered: A number of full-cost scholarships for PhD students, a number of scholarships for postgraduate study students.
Frequency: Annual.

Value: Full-cost, PhD; postgraduate scholarships will cover the University Composition Fee at the overseas rate; approved College fees; a maintenance allowance sufficient for a single student; a contribution to a return economy airfare.
Length of Study: 3 years PhD; 1 year postgraduate study.
Study Establishment: Cambridge University.
Country of Study: United Kingdom.
Application Procedure: Candidates must complete a Preliminary Application Form, which can be obtained from local universities, offices of the British Council or the main address. Completed application forms must be returned to the main address. Candidates short-listed will be sent forms for admission to the University of Cambridge and a scholarship application form. These forms must be returned to The Board of Graduate Studies.
Closing Date: September 21st, a full year in advance of the proposed entry date to Cambridge for preliminary application, January 31st for actual application.

For further information contact:

The Board of Graduate Studies
4 Mill Lane, Cambridge, CB2 1TZ, England
Contact: The Secretary

Mandela Cambridge Scholarships

Subjects: All subjects.
Eligibility: The Trusts cannot admit students to the University or any of its Colleges. Applicants for awards from the Trusts must therefore also apply to the University of Cambridge and be offered a place at Cambridge in the normal way. All applicants must have a first class or high second class honours degree, or equivalent and normally be under 26. Applicants for study towards a PhD must be successfully nominated for an ORS award which pays the difference between the home and overseas rate of the University Composition Fee. For students from South Africa.
Level of Study: Doctorate, Postgraduate.
Purpose: To assist study towards a PhD and one year taught postgraduate courses.
Type: Scholarship.
No. of awards offered: 10 PhD, 20 Postgraduate study.
Frequency: Annual.
Value: Scholarships will cover up to the University Composition Fee at the overseas rate; approved College fees; a maintenance allowance sufficient for a single student; a contribution to a return economy airfare.
Length of Study: Up to 3 years PhD, 1year taught postgraduate courses.
Study Establishment: Cambridge University.
Country of Study: United Kingdom.
Application Procedure: Candidates must complete a Preliminary Application Form, which can be obtained from local universities, offices of the British Council or the main address. Completed application forms must be returned to the main address. Candidates short-listed will be sent forms for admission to the University of Cambridge and a scholarship application form. These forms must be returned to The Board of Graduate Studies.

Closing Date: September 21st, a full year in advance of the proposed entry date to Cambridge for preliminary application, January 31st for actual application.
Additional Information: Offered by the Malaysian Commonwealth Studies Centre, the Cambridge Local Examinations Syndicate, Trinity College, Cambridge and the Cambridge University Press in honour of President Mandela.

For further information contact:

The Board of Graduate Studies
4 Mill Lane, Cambridge, CB2 1TZ, England
Contact: The Secretary

Mandela Magdalene College Scholarships

Subjects: All subjects.
Eligibility: The Trusts cannot admit students to the University or any of its Colleges. Applicants for awards from the Trusts must therefore also apply to the University of Cambridge and be offered a place at Cambridge in the normal way. All applicants must have a first class or high second class honours degree, or equivalent and normally be under 26. For students who have been offered a place at Magdalene College, Cambridge.
Level of Study: Postgraduate.
Type: Scholarship.
No. of awards offered: Up to 3.
Frequency: Annual.
Value: Scholarships will cover the University Composition Fee at the overseas rate; approved College fees; a maintenance allowance sufficient for a single student; a contribution to a return economy airfare.
Length of Study: 1 year.
Study Establishment: Magdalene College, Cambridge.
Country of Study: United Kingdom.
Application Procedure: Candidates must complete a Preliminary Application Form, which can be obtained from local universities, offices of the British Council or the main address. Completed application forms must be returned to the main address. Candidates short-listed will be sent forms for admission to the University of Cambridge and a scholarship application form. These forms must be returned to The Board of Graduate Studies.
Closing Date: September 21st, a full year in advance of the proposed entry date to Cambridge for preliminary application, January 31st for actual application.

For further information contact:

The Board Of Graduate Studies
4 Mill Lane, Cambridge, CB2 1TZ, England
Contact: The Secretary

Ministry of Education, Malaysia, Scholarships

Subjects: All subjects.
Eligibility: The Trusts cannot admit students to the University or any of its Colleges. Applicants for awards from the Trusts must therefore also apply to the University of Cambridge and be offered a place at Cambridge in the normal way. All applicants must have a first class or high second class

honours degree, or equivalent and normally be under 26. Candidates must be nominated by the Ministry of Education.
Level of Study: Postgraduate.
Type: Scholarship.
No. of awards offered: 4.
Frequency: Annual.
Value: Scholarships will cover up to the University Composition Fee at the overseas rate; approved College fees; a maintenance allowance sufficient for a single student; a contribution to a return economy airfare.
Length of Study: 1 year.
Study Establishment: Cambridge University.
Country of Study: United Kingdom.
Application Procedure: Candidates must complete a Preliminary Application Form, which can be obtained from local universities, offices of the British Council or the main address. Completed application forms must be returned to the main address. Candidates short-listed will be sent forms for admission to the University of Cambridge and a scholarship application form. These forms must be returned to The Board of Graduate Studies.
Closing Date: September 21st, a full year in advance of the proposed entry date to Cambridge for preliminary application, January 31st for actual application.

For further information contact:

The Board of Graduate Studies
4 Mill Lane, Cambridge, CB2 1TZ, England
Contact: The Secretary

Ministry of Science, Technology and the Environment Cambridge Scholarships

Subjects: All subjects.
Eligibility: The Trusts cannot admit students to the University or any of its Colleges. Applicants for awards from the Trusts must therefore also apply to the University of Cambridge and be offered a place at Cambridge in the normal way. All applicants must have a first class or high second class honours degree, or equivalent and normally be under 26. Candidates must be nominated by the Ministry of Science, Technology and the Environment. For students from Malaysia.
Level of Study: Postgraduate.
Type: Scholarship.
No. of awards offered: 10.
Frequency: Annual.
Value: Scholarships will cover up to: the University Composition Fee at the overseas rate; approved College fees a maintenance allowance sufficient for a single student; a contribution to a return economy airfare.
Length of Study: 1 year.
Study Establishment: Cambridge University.
Country of Study: United Kingdom.
Application Procedure: Candidates must complete a Preliminary Application Form, which can be obtained from local universities, offices of the British Council or the main address. Completed application forms must be returned to the main address. Candidates short-listed will be sent forms

for admission to the University of Cambridge and a scholarship application form. These forms must be returned to The Board of Graduate Studies.
Closing Date: September 21st, a full year in advance of the proposed entry date to Cambridge for preliminary application, January 31st for actual application.

For further information contact:

The Board of Graduate Studies
4 Mill Lane, Cambridge, CB2 1TZ, England
Contact: The Secretary

Nehru Trust for the Indian Collections Vicoria and Albert Cambridge Shared Scholarship

Subjects: For the MPhil in either archaeology (archaeological heritage museums) or social anthropology (with special preference to the work of a museum).
Eligibility: The Trusts cannot admit students to the University or any of its Colleges. Applicants for awards from the Trusts must therefore also apply to the University of Cambridge and be offered a place at Cambridge in the normal way. All applicants must have a first class or high second class honours degree, or equivalent and normally be under 26. For students from India.
Level of Study: Postgraduate.
Type: Scholarship.
No. of awards offered: 1.
Frequency: Annual.
Study Establishment: Cambridge University.
Country of Study: United Kingdom.
Application Procedure: Candidates from India may obtain further details and a Preliminary Application Forms by writing before August 17th of the year before entry to The Joint Secretary, Nehru Trust for Cambridge University, Teen Murti House, Teen Murti Marg, New Delhi, 110011, giving details of academic qualifications. Completed forms must be returned to the same address no later than September 9th. Those candidates who are successfully short-listed will be sent forms for admission to the University of Cambridge as a graduate student which should be completed and returned to The Secretary, Board of Graduate Studies, 4 Mill Lane, Cambridge, CB2 1TZ no later than January 31st.
Closing Date: September 9th, preliminary application; January 31st actual application.

Nepal Cambridge Scholarships

Subjects: All subjects.
Eligibility: The Trusts cannot admit students to the University or any of its Colleges. Applicants for awards from the Trusts must therefore also apply to the University of Cambridge and be offered a place at Cambridge in the normal way. All applicants must have a first class or high second class honours degree, or equivalent and normally be under 26. For students from Nepal.
Level of Study: Postgraduate.
Type: Scholarship.
No. of awards offered: 1.
Frequency: Annual.

Value: The scholarships will cover the University Composition Fee at the overseas rate, approved College fees, a maintenance allowance sufficient for a single student, a contribution to a return economy airfare.
Length of Study: 1 year.
Study Establishment: Cambridge University.
Country of Study: United Kingdom.
Application Procedure: Candidates must complete a Preliminary Application Form, which can be obtained from local universities, offices of the British Council or the main address. Completed application forms must be returned to the main address. Candidates short-listed will be sent forms for admission to the University of Cambridge and a scholarship application form. These forms must be returned to The Board of Graduate Studies.
Closing Date: September 21st, a full year in advance of the proposed entry date to Cambridge for preliminary application, January 31st for actual application.

For further information contact:

The Board of Graduate Studies
4 Mill Lane, Cambridge, CB2 1TZ, England
Contact: The Secretary

Oxford and Cambridge Society of Bombay Cambridge Shared Scholarship

Subjects: All subjects.
Eligibility: The Trusts cannot admit students to the University or any of its Colleges. Applicants for awards from the Trusts must therefore also apply to the University of Cambridge and be offered a place at Cambridge in the normal way. All applicants must have a first class or high second class honours degree, or equivalent and normally be under 26. For a resident of Bombay City or the state of Maharashtra whose application is supported by the Oxford and Cambridge Society of Bombay.
Level of Study: Postgraduate.
Type: Scholarship.
No. of awards offered: 1.
Frequency: Annual.
Study Establishment: Cambridge University.
Country of Study: United Kingdom.
Application Procedure: Candidates from India may obtain further details and a Preliminary Application Forms by writing before August 17th of the year before entry to The Joint Secretary, Nehru Trust for Cambridge University, Teen Murti House, Teen Murti Marg, New Delhi, 110011, giving details of academic qualifications. Completed forms must be returned to the same address no later than September 9th. Those candidates who are successfully short-listed will be sent forms for admission to the University of Cambridge as a graduate student which should be completed and returned to The Secretary, Board of Graduate Studies, 4 Mill Lane, Cambridge, CB2 1TZ no later than January 31st.
Closing Date: September 9th, preliminary application; January 31st actual application.

Packer Cambridge Scholarships

Subjects: All subjects.
Eligibility: The Trusts cannot admit students to the University or any of its Colleges. Applicants for awards from the Trusts must therefore also apply to the University of Cambridge and be offered a place at Cambridge in the normal way. All applicants must have a first class or high second class honours degree, or equivalent and normally be under 26. For students from Australia.
Level of Study: Doctorate.
Purpose: To support study towards a PhD.
Type: Scholarship.
No. of awards offered: 5.
Frequency: As available.
Value: Scholarships will cover up to the University Composition Fee at the overseas rate; approved College fees; a maintenance allowance sufficient for a single student; a contribution to a return economy airfare.
Length of Study: Tenable for up to 3 years.
Study Establishment: Cambridge University.
Country of Study: United Kingdom.
Application Procedure: Application form for the scholarship will be sent out to eligible candidates once the completed form for admission to the University of Cambridge has reached The Board of Graduate Studies.
Closing Date: Scholarship forms must be returned by April 30th.

For further information contact:

The Board of Graduate Studies
4 Mill Lane, Cambridge, CB2 1TZ, England
Contact: The Secretary

Part-Cost Bursaries - India

Subjects: All subjects.
Eligibility: The Trusts cannot admit students to the University or any of its Colleges. Applicants for awards from the Trusts must therefore also apply to the University of Cambridge and be offered a place at Cambridge in the normal way. All applicants must have a first class or high second class honours degree, or equivalent and normally be under 26. For applicants who are not successful at winning a scholarship.
Level of Study: Unrestricted.
Type: Bursary.
No. of awards offered: Varies.
Value: Determined in the light of the financial circumstances of the applicant.
Study Establishment: Cambridge University.
Country of Study: United Kingdom.

Pok Rafeah Cambridge Scholarship

Subjects: All subjects.
Eligibility: The Trusts cannot admit students to the University or any of its Colleges. Applicants for awards from the Trusts must therefore also apply to the University of Cambridge and be offered a place at Cambridge in the normal way. All applicants must have a first class or high second class honours degree, or equivalent and normally be under 26.

Applicants for scholarships for study towards the degree of PhD must be successfully nominated for an ORS award, which covers the difference between the home and overseas rate of the University Composition Fee. For students from Indonesia.

Level of Study: Doctorate, Postgraduate.
Type: Scholarship.
No. of awards offered: 1 for study towards a PhD, 2 for postgraduate study.
Frequency: Annual.
Value: The scholarships will cover the University Composition Fee at the home rate, approved College fees, a maintenance allowance sufficient for a single student, a contribution to a return economy airfare.
Length of Study: Up to 3 years for PhD; 1 year for taught postgraduate course.
Study Establishment: Cambridge University.
Country of Study: United Kingdom.
Application Procedure: Candidates must complete a Preliminary Application Form, which can be obtained from local universities, offices of the British Council or the main address. Completed application forms must be returned to the main address. Candidates short-listed will be sent forms for admission to the University of Cambridge and a scholarship application form. These forms must be returned to The Board of Graduate Studies.
Closing Date: September 21st, a full year in advance of the proposed entry date to Cambridge for preliminary application, January 31st for actual application.

For further information contact:

The Board of Graduate Studies
4 Mill Lane, Cambridge, CB2 1TZ, England
Contact: The Secretary

Poynton Cambridge Scholarships

Subjects: All subjects.
Eligibility: The Trusts cannot admit students to the University or any of its Colleges. Applicants for awards from the Trusts must therefore also apply to the University of Cambridge and be offered a place at Cambridge in the normal way. All applicants must have a first class or high second class honours degree, or equivalent and normally be under 26. For students from Australia.
Level of Study: Doctorate.
Purpose: To assist study towards a PhD.
Type: Scholarship.
No. of awards offered: 5.
Frequency: Annual.
Length of Study: Tenable for up to 3 years.
Study Establishment: Cambridge University.
Country of Study: United Kingdom.
Application Procedure: Application form for the scholarship will be sent out to eligible candidates once the completed form for admission to the University of Cambridge has reached The Board of Graduate Studies.
Closing Date: Scholarship forms must be returned by April 30th.

For further information contact:

The Board of Graduate Studies
4 Mill Lane, Cambridge, CB2 1TZ, England
Contact: The Secretary

President Árpád Göncz Scholarship

Subjects: All subjects.
Eligibility: The Trusts cannot admit students to the University or any of its Colleges. Applicants for awards from the Trusts must therefore also apply to the University of Cambridge and be offered a place at Cambridge in the normal way. All applicants must have a first class or high second class honours degree, or equivalent and normally be under 26. For a student from Hungary.
Level of Study: Postgraduate.
Purpose: To assist with one year taught postgraduate courses of study. Originally set up to commemorate the visit of the President of Hungary to the University of Cambridge.
Type: Scholarship.
No. of awards offered: 1.
Frequency: Annual.
Value: Scholarships will cover the University Composition Fee at the overseas rate; approved College fees; a maintenance allowance sufficient for a single student; a contribution to a return economy airfare.
Length of Study: 1 year.
Study Establishment: Cambridge University.
Country of Study: United Kingdom.
Application Procedure: Candidates must complete a Preliminary Application Form, which can be obtained from local universities, offices of the British Council or the main address. Completed application forms must be returned to the main address. Candidates short-listed will be sent forms for admission to the University of Cambridge and a scholarship application form. These forms must be returned to The Board of Graduate Studies.
Closing Date: September 21st, a full year in advance of the proposed entry date to Cambridge for preliminary application, January 31st for actual application.

For further information contact:

The Board of Graduate Studies
4 Mill Lane, Cambridge, CB2 1TZ, England
Contact: The Secretary

President Aylwin Studentship

Subjects: All subjects.
Eligibility: The Trusts cannot admit students to the University or any of its Colleges. Applicants for awards from the Trusts must therefore also apply to the University of Cambridge and be offered a place at Cambridge in the normal way. All applicants must have a first class or high second class honours degree, or equivalent and normally be under 26. Applicants must be successfully nominated for an ORS award, which covers the difference between the home and overseas rate of the University Composition Fee. For students from Chile.
Level of Study: Doctorate.

Type: Studentship.
No. of awards offered: 1.
Frequency: Annual.
Value: These studentships will cover the University Composition Fee at the home rate, approved college fees, a maintenance allowance sufficient for a single student, a contribution to a return economy airfare.
Length of Study: Tenable for up to 3 years.
Study Establishment: Cambridge University.
Country of Study: United Kingdom.
Application Procedure: Candidates for these studentships should apply in the first instance to the Agencia de Cooperacion International (AGCI), Providencia 1017, 1er Piso, Santiago from whom Preliminary Application Forms can be obtained.
Closing Date: September 21st, a full year in advance of the proposed entry date to Cambridge for preliminary application, January 31st for actual application.

President's Cambridge Scholarships for One Year Taught Postgraduate Study

Subjects: All subjects.
Eligibility: The Trusts cannot admit students to the University or any of its Colleges. Applicants for awards from the Trusts must therefore also apply to the University of Cambridge and be offered a place at Cambridge in the normal way. All applicants must have a first class or high second class honours degree, or equivalent and normally be under 26. For students from Ghana.
Level of Study: Postgraduate.
Type: Scholarship.
No. of awards offered: Up to 5.
Frequency: Annual.
Length of Study: 1 year.
Study Establishment: Cambridge University.
Country of Study: United Kingdom.
Application Procedure: Candidates must complete a Preliminary Application Form, which can be obtained from local universities, offices of the British Council or the main address. Completed application forms must be returned to the main address. Candidates short-listed will be sent forms for admission to the University of Cambridge and a scholarship application form. These forms must be returned to The Board of Graduate Studies.
Closing Date: September 21st, a full year in advance of the proposed entry date to Cambridge for preliminary application, January 31st for actual application.

For further information contact:

The Board of Graduate Studies
4 Mill Lane, Cambridge, CB2 1TZ, England
Contact: The Secretary

President's Cambridge Scholarships for Study Towards a PhD

Subjects: All subjects.
Eligibility: The Trusts cannot admit students to the University or any of its Colleges. Applicants for awards from the Trusts must therefore also apply to the University of Cambridge and be offered a place at Cambridge in the normal way. All applicants must have a first class or high second class honours degree, or equivalent and normally be under 26. For students from Ghana.
Level of Study: Doctorate.
Type: Scholarship.
No. of awards offered: Up to 5.
Frequency: Annual.
Length of Study: Tenable for up to 3 years.
Study Establishment: Cambridge University.
Country of Study: United Kingdom.
Application Procedure: Candidates must complete a Preliminary Application Form, which can be obtained from local universities, offices of the British Council or the main address. Completed application forms must be returned to the main address. Candidates short-listed will be sent forms for admission to the University of Cambridge and a scholarship application form. These forms must be returned to The Board of Graduate Studies.
Closing Date: September 21st, a full year in advance of the proposed entry date to Cambridge for preliminary application, January 31st for actual application.

For further information contact:

The Board of Graduate Studies
4 Mill Lane, Cambridge, CB2 1TZ, England
Contact: The Secretary

Prince of Wales Scholarships

Subjects: All subjects.
Eligibility: The Trusts cannot admit students to the University or any of its Colleges. Applicants for awards from the Trusts must therefore also apply to the University of Cambridge and be offered a place at Cambridge in the normal way. All applicants must have a first class or high second class honours degree, or equivalent and normally be under 26. For students from New Zealand. All applicants must be successfully nominated for an ORS award, which covers the difference between the home and overseas rate of the University Composition Fee.
Level of Study: Doctorate.
Purpose: To support study towards a PhD.
Type: Scholarship.
No. of awards offered: 5.
Frequency: Annual.
Value: Scholarships will cover the University Composition Fee at the overseas rate; approved College fees; a maintenance allowance sufficient for a single student; a contribution to a return economy airfare.
Length of Study: Tenable for up to 3 years.
Study Establishment: Cambridge University.
Country of Study: United Kingdom.
Application Procedure: Candidates should apply directly to the Scholarships Officer at their own university. Otherwise they should apply directly to the Scholarships Officer at the New Zealand Vice Chancellor's Committee.
Closing Date: October 1st.

For further information contact:

New Zealand Vice Chancellors' Committee
PO Box 11-915
Manners Street, Wellington, New Zealand
Contact: Scholarships Officer

Prince Philip Graduate Exhibitions

Subjects: All subjects.
Eligibility: The Trusts cannot admit students to the University or any of its Colleges. Applicants for awards from the Trusts must therefore also apply to the University of Cambridge and be offered a place at Cambridge in the normal way. All applicants must have a first class or high second class honours degree, or equivalent and normally be under 26. One scholarship will go to a student who has graduated from the Chinese University of Hong Kong and one will go to a student who has graduated from the University of Hong Kong. Applicants must be successfully nominated for an ORS award.
Level of Study: Doctorate.
Type: Scholarship.
No. of awards offered: 2.
Frequency: Annual.
Value: Scholarships will cover the University Composition Fee at the overseas rate; approved College fees; a maintenance allowance sufficient for a single student; a contribution to a return economy airfare.
Length of Study: Up to 3 years.
Study Establishment: Cambridge University.
Country of Study: United Kingdom.
Application Procedure: Candidates must complete a Preliminary Application Form, which can be obtained from local universities, offices of the British Council or the main address. Completed application forms must be returned to the main address. Candidates short-listed will be sent forms for admission to the University of Cambridge and a scholarship application form. These forms must be returned to The Board of Graduate Studies.
Closing Date: September 21st, a full year in advance of the proposed entry date to Cambridge for preliminary application, January 31st for actual application.

For further information contact:

The Board of Graduate Studies
4 Mill Lane, Cambridge, CB2 1TZ, England
Contact: The Secretary

Sally Mugabe Memorial Shared Cambridge Scholarship

Subjects: Preference given to candidates studying subjects relevant to the needs of Zimbabwe, in particular the broad area of social studies relating to the welfare, education and health of women and children.
Eligibility: All applicants must be under the age of 35 on October 1st of the year they are applying for, undertake to return to their own country to work or study after completing the course, not be employed by a government department or by a parastatal organisation, not be at present living or studying in a developed country, and not have undertaken studies lasting a year or more in a developed country. Priority will be given to candidates wishing to pursue a course of study related to the economic and social development of their country. For a woman graduate from Zimbabwe.
Level of Study: Postgraduate.
Type: Scholarship.
No. of awards offered: 1.
Frequency: Annual.
Value: Scholarships will cover the University Composition Fee at the overseas rate; approved College fees; a maintenance allowance sufficient for a single student; a contribution to a return economy airfare.
Length of Study: 1 year.
Study Establishment: Cambridge University.
Country of Study: United Kingdom.
Application Procedure: Candidates must complete a Preliminary Application Form, which can be obtained from local universities, offices of the British Council or the main address. Completed application forms must be returned to the main address. Candidates short-listed will be sent forms for admission to the University of Cambridge and a scholarship application form. These forms must be returned to The Board of Graduate Studies.
Closing Date: September 21st, a full year in advance of the proposed entry date to Cambridge for preliminary application, January 31st for actual application.

For further information contact:

The Board of Graduate Studies
4 Mill Lane, Cambridge, CB2 1TZ, England
Contact: The Secretary

Schlumberger Cambridge Scholarships

Subjects: All subjects.
Eligibility: The Trusts cannot admit students to the University or any of its Colleges. Applicants for awards from the Trusts must therefore also apply to the University of Cambridge and be offered a place at Cambridge in the normal way. All applicants must have a first class or high second class honours degree or equivalent and normally be under 26. For students from a developing country.
Level of Study: Doctorate.
Type: Scholarship.
No. of awards offered: 1.
Frequency: Annual.
Value: Scholarships will cover the University Composition Fee at the overseas rate; approved College fees; a maintenance allowance sufficient for a single student; a contribution to a return economy airfare.
Length of Study: Tenable for up to 3 years.
Study Establishment: Cambridge University.
Country of Study: United Kingdom.
Application Procedure: Candidates must complete a Preliminary Application Form, which can be obtained from local universities, offices of the British Council or the main address. Completed application forms must be returned to the main address. Candidates short-listed will be sent forms

for admission to the University of Cambridge and a scholarship application form. These forms must be returned to The Board of Graduate Studies.

Closing Date: September 21st, a full year in advance of the proposed entry date to Cambridge for preliminary application, January 31st for actual application.

For further information contact:

The Board of Graduate Studies
4 Mill Lane, Cambridge, CB2 1TZ, England
Contact: The Secretary

Soros/FCO Cambridge Scholarships

Subjects: Social sciences and humanities.
Eligibility: The Trusts cannot admit students to the University or any of its Colleges. Applicants for awards from the Trusts must therefore also apply to the University of Cambridge and be offered a place at Cambridge in the normal way. All applicants must have a first class or high second class honours degree, or equivalent and normally be under 26. For students from Albania, Bosnia, Croatia, Estonia, Latvia, Lithuania, Macedonia, Slovenia and the Federal Republic of Yugoslavia.
Level of Study: Postgraduate.
Type: Scholarship.
No. of awards offered: Up to 16.
Frequency: Annual.
Value: Scholarships will cover: the University Composition Fee at the overseas rate; approved College fees; a maintenance allowance sufficient for a single student; a contribution to a return economy airfare.
Study Establishment: Cambridge University.
Country of Study: United Kingdom.
Application Procedure: Candidates must complete a Preliminary Application Form, which can be obtained from local universities, offices of the British Council or the main address. Completed application forms must be returned to the main address. Candidates short-listed will be sent forms for admission to the University of Cambridge and a scholarship application form. These forms must be returned to The Board of Graduate Studies.
Closing Date: September 21st, a full year in advance of the proposed entry date to Cambridge for preliminary application, January 31st for actual application.

For further information contact:

The Board of Graduate Studies
4 Mill Lane, Cambridge, BB2 1TZ, England
Contact: The Secretary

South African College Bursaries

Subjects: All subjects.
Eligibility: The Trusts cannot admit students to the University or any of its Colleges. Applicants for awards from the Trusts must therefore also apply to the University of Cambridge and be offered a place at Cambridge in the normal way. All

applicants must have a first class or high second class honours degree, or equivalent and normally be under 26. For students from South Africa.
Purpose: To enable citizens of South and Southern Africa to take up college places at Cambridge.
Type: Bursary.
No. of awards offered: Varies.
Study Establishment: Cambridge University.
Country of Study: United Kingdom.
Application Procedure: Candidates must complete a Preliminary Application Form, which can be obtained from local universities, offices of the British Council or the main address. Completed application forms must be returned to the main address. Candidates short-listed will be sent forms for admission to the University of Cambridge and a scholarship application form. These forms must be returned to The Board of Graduate Studies.
Closing Date: September 21st, a full year in advance of the proposed entry date to Cambridge for preliminary application, January 31st for actual application.
Additional Information: The bursaries are normally held in conjunction with other awards from Cambridge Commonwealth Trust and other sources.

For further information contact:

The Board of Graduate Studies
4 Mill Lane, Cambridge, CB2 1TZ, England
Contact: The Secretary

Tan Sri Lim Goh Tong Cambridge Bursaries

Subjects: All subjects.
Eligibility: The Trusts cannot admit students to the University or any of its Colleges. Applicants for awards from the Trusts must therefore also apply to the University of Cambridge and be offered a place at Cambridge in the normal way. All applicants must have a first class or high second class honours degree, or equivalent and normally be under 26. For students from Malaysia.
Level of Study: Unrestricted.
Type: Bursary.
Frequency: Annual.
Value: The value will normally be at a fixed rate of up to £2,000 per annum to be held in conjunction with other awards from the Cambridge Commonwealth Trust or other sources. Candidates will be means tested.
Study Establishment: Cambridge University.
Country of Study: United Kingdom.
Application Procedure: Candidates must complete a Preliminary Application Form, which can be obtained from local universities, offices of the British Council or the main address. Completed application forms must be returned to the main address. Candidates short-listed will be sent forms for admission to the University of Cambridge and a scholarship application form. These forms must be returned to The Board of Graduate Studies.
Closing Date: September 21st, a full year in advance of the proposed entry date to Cambridge for preliminary application, January 31st for actual application.

For further information contact:

The Board of Graduate Studies
4 Mill Lane, Cambridge, CB2 1TZ, England
Contact: The Secretary

Tanzania Cambridge Scholarship

Subjects: All subjects.
Eligibility: The Trusts cannot admit students to the University or any of its Colleges. Applicants for awards from the Trusts must therefore also apply to the University of Cambridge and be offered a place at Cambridge in the normal way. All applicants must have a first class or high second class honours degree, or equivalent and normally be under 26. For a student from Tanzania. Applicants must be successfully nominated for an ORS award, which covers the difference between the home and overseas rate of the University Composition Fee.
Level of Study: Doctorate.
Type: Scholarship.
No. of awards offered: 1.
Frequency: Annual.
Value: Scholarships will cover the University Composition Fee at the overseas rate; approved College fees; a maintenance allowance sufficient for a single student; a contribution to a return economy airfare.
Length of Study: Tenable for up to 3 years.
Study Establishment: Cambridge University.
Country of Study: United Kingdom.
Application Procedure: Candidates must complete a Preliminary Application Form, which can be obtained from local universities, offices of the British Council or the main address. Completed application forms must be returned to the main address. Candidates short-listed will be sent forms for admission to the University of Cambridge and a scholarship application form. These forms must be returned to The Board of Graduate Studies.
Closing Date: September 21st, a full year in advance of the proposed entry date to Cambridge for preliminary application, January 31st for actual application.

For further information contact:

The Board of Graduate Studies
4 Mill Lane, Cambridge, CB2 1TZ, England
Contact: The Secretary

Tanzania Cambridge Shared Scholarships

Subjects: All subjects.
Eligibility: The Trusts cannot admit students to the University or any of its Colleges. Applicants for awards from the Trusts must therefore also apply to the University of Cambridge and be offered a place at Cambridge in the normal way. All applicants must have a first class or high second class honours degree, or equivalent. For students from Tanzania. Applicants must be under the age of 35 on October 1st of the year they are applying for; return to their own country to work or study after completing the course at Cambridge; not be employed by a government department or by a parastatal organisation; not at present be living or studying in a developed country; not have undertaken studies lasting a year or more in a developed country. Priority will be given to candidates wishing to pursue a course of study related to the economic and social development of their country.
Level of Study: Postgraduate.
Type: Scholarship.
No. of awards offered: Up to 4.
Frequency: Annual.
Value: Scholarships will cover the University Composition Fee at the overseas rate; approved College fees; a maintenance allowance sufficient for a single student; a contribution to a return economy airfare.
Length of Study: 1 year.
Study Establishment: Cambridge University.
Country of Study: United Kingdom.
Application Procedure: Candidates must complete a Preliminary Application Form, which can be obtained from local universities, offices of the British Council or the main address. Completed application forms must be returned to the main address. Candidates short-listed will be sent forms for admission to the University of Cambridge and a scholarship application form. These forms must be returned to The Board of Graduate Studies.
Closing Date: September 21st, a full year in advance of the proposed entry date to Cambridge for preliminary application, January 31st for actual application.

For further information contact:

The Board of Graduate Studies
4 Mill Lane, Cambridge, CB2 1TZ, England
Contact: The Secretary

Tate and Lyle/FCO Cambridge Scholarships

Subjects: All subjects.
Eligibility: The Trusts cannot admit students to the University or any of its Colleges. Applicants for awards from the Trusts must therefore also apply to the University of Cambridge and be offered a place at Cambridge in the normal way. All applicants must have a first class or high second class honours degree, or equivalent and normally be under 26. Successful applicants will be expected to return to their home country at the end of the course of study at Cambridge. Open to students from Barbados, Belize, the Eastern Caribbean States, Fiji, Guyana, Jamaica and Trinidad and Tobago, Hungary, Slovakia, Ukraine, Mauritius, Mexico, Saudi Arabia, the Philippines, Swaziland, Zambia, Zimbabwe, Vietnam.
Level of Study: Postgraduate.
Purpose: To assist one year taught postgraduate courses of study.
Type: Scholarship.
No. of awards offered: Up to 10.
Frequency: Annual.
Value: Scholarships will cover the University Composition Fee at the overseas rate; approved College fees; a maintenance allowance sufficient for a single student; a contribution to a return economy airfare.
Study Establishment: Cambridge University.
Country of Study: United Kingdom.

Application Procedure: Candidates must complete a Preliminary Application Form, which can be obtained from local universities, offices of the British Council or the main address. Completed application forms must be returned to the main address. Candidates short-listed will be sent forms for admission to the University of Cambridge and a scholarship application form. These forms must be returned to The Board of Graduate Studies.

Closing Date: September 21st, a full year in advance of the proposed entry date to Cambridge for preliminary application, January 31st for actual application.

For further information contact:

The Board of Graduate Studies
4 Mill Lane, Cambridge, CB2 1TZ, England
Contact: The Secretary

Tidmarsh Cambridge Scholarship

Subjects: All subjects.
Eligibility: The Trusts cannot admit students to the University or any of its Colleges. Applicants for awards from the Trusts must therefore also apply to the University of Cambridge and be offered a place at Cambridge in the normal way. All applicants must: have a first class or high second class honours degree or equivalent and normally be under 26. For students from Canada who have been successfully nominated for an ORS award, which covers the difference between the home and overseas rate of the University Composition Fee.
Level of Study: Doctorate.
Purpose: To assist study towards a PhD.
Type: Scholarship.
No. of awards offered: 1.
Frequency: As available.
Value: The scholarship will pay the University Composition Fee at the home rate, approved College fees and a maintenance allowance sufficient for a single student.
Study Establishment: Cambridge University.
Country of Study: United Kingdom.
Application Procedure: Application form for the scholarship will be sent out to eligible candidates once the completed form for admission to the University of Cambridge has reached the Board of Graduate Studies.
Closing Date: Scholarship forms must be returned by April 30th.

For further information contact:

The Board for Graduate Studies
4 Mill Lane, Cambridge, CB2 1TZ, England
Contact: The Secretary

Zambia Cambridge Scholarships

Subjects: All subjects.
Eligibility: The Trusts cannot admit students to the University or any of its Colleges. Applicants for awards from the Trusts must therefore also apply to the University of Cambridge and be offered a place at Cambridge in the normal way. All applicants must have a first class or high second class

honours degree, or equivalent and normally be under 26. For a student from Zambia.
Level of Study: Doctorate, Postgraduate.
Type: Scholarship.
No. of awards offered: 1 PhD, 1 postgraduate study.
Frequency: As available.
Value: Scholarships will cover the University Composition Fee at the overseas rate; approved College fees; a maintenance allowance sufficient for a single student; a contribution to a return economy airfare.
Length of Study: Tenable for up to 3 years; 1 year for postgraduate study.
Study Establishment: Cambridge University.
Country of Study: United Kingdom.
Application Procedure: Candidates must complete a Preliminary Application Form, which can be obtained from local universities, offices of the British Council or the main address. Completed application forms must be returned to the main address. Candidates short-listed will be sent forms for admission to the University of Cambridge and a scholarship application form. These forms must be returned to The Board of Graduate Studies.
Closing Date: September 21st, a full year in advance of the proposed entry date to Cambridge for preliminary application, January 31st for actual application.

For further information contact:

The Board of Graduate Studies
4 Mill Lane, Cambridge, CB2 1TZ, England
Contact: The Secretary

Zimbabwe Cambridge Scholarships

Subjects: All subjects.
Eligibility: The Trusts cannot admit students to the University or any of its Colleges. Applicants for awards from the Trusts must therefore also apply to the University of Cambridge and be offered a place at Cambridge in the normal way. All applicants must have a first class or high second class honours degree, or equivalent and normally be under 26. All applicants for the PhD must be successfully nominated for an ORS award which pays the difference between home and overseas rate of the University Composition Fee. For a student from Zimbabwe.
Level of Study: Doctorate, Postgraduate.
Type: Scholarship.
No. of awards offered: 1 PhD, 1 postgraduate study.
Frequency: As available.
Value: Scholarships will cover: the University Composition Fee at the overseas rate; approved College fees; a maintenance allowance sufficient for a single student; a contribution to a return economy airfare.
Length of Study: 3 years- PhD; 1 year postgraduate study.
Study Establishment: Cambridge University.
Country of Study: United Kingdom.
Application Procedure: Candidates must complete a Preliminary Application Form, which can be obtained from local universities, offices of the British Council or the main address. Completed application forms must be returned to the main address. Candidates short-listed will be sent forms for admission to the University of Cambridge and a

scholarship application form. These forms must be returned to The Board of Graduate Studies.

Closing Date: September 21st, a full year in advance of the proposed entry date to Cambridge for preliminary application, January 31st for actual application.

For further information contact:

The Board of Graduate Studies
4 Mill Lane, Cambridge, CB2 1TZ, England
Contact: The Secretary

THE CANADA COUNCIL FOR THE ARTS

350 Albert Street
PO Box 1047, Ottawa, ON, K1P 5V8, Canada
Tel: (1) 613 566 4414 ext 5060
Fax: (1) 613 566 4390
Email: lise.rochon@canadacouncil.ca
www: http://www.canadacouncil.ca
Contact: Ms Lise Rochon

The Canada Council for the Arts is a national agency which provides grants and services to professional Canadian artists and art organisations in dance, media arts, music, theatre, writing and publishing, interdisciplinary work and performance art, and visual arts.

Killam Research Fellowships

Subjects: Humanities, social sciences, natural sciences, health sciences, engineering, and studies linking any of the disciplines within these broad fields.
Eligibility: Open to Canadian citizens or permanent residents of Canada. Killam Research Fellowships are aimed at established scholars who have demonstrated outstanding ability through substantial publications in their fields over a period of several years.
Level of Study: Postgraduate.
Purpose: To support advanced research projects undertaken by Canadian citizens and permanent residents of Canada.
Type: Fellowship.
No. of awards offered: Varies.
Frequency: Annual.
Value: Killam Research Fellowships provide partial or full salary replacement, to a maximum of C$53,000, based on actual salary for the year before tenure of the award; the Council does not object if the Research Fellow's institution supplements the award during the year of tenure to reflect any salary increase.
Length of Study: Up to 2 years.
Country of Study: Canadians may hold the award in any country; permanent residents must use the award in Canada.

Application Procedure: Requests must be submitted on the appropriate application forms which are available from the Canada Council Killam Programme Section. The Killam Programme brochure provides detailed information on the Killam Research Fellowships.
Closing Date: May 31st.

CANADA MEMORIAL FOUNDATION

The Association of Commonwealth Universities
John Foster House
36 Gordon Square, London, WC1H 0PF, England
Tel: (44) 171 387 8572
Fax: (44) 171 387 2655
Contact: Awards Division Head

Canada Memorial Foundation Scholarships

Subjects: Any subject - clinical medicine currently excluded.
Eligibility: Open to UK citizens who are permanently resident in the UK and hold, or expect to hold, an upper second class honours degree or equivalent qualification. Candidates should normally be under 30 years of age and must show convincing reasons why they wish to study in Canada.
Level of Study: Postgraduate.
Purpose: To fund a student taking a research degree (12 months) or postgraduate course at a university or other appropriate institution in Canada. Not offered for study leading to PhD.
Type: Scholarship.
No. of awards offered: 2.
Frequency: Annual.
Value: Full cost: covers fees, maintenance, air fares. Other allowances for books and study travel.
Length of Study: 12 months only. Candidates wishing to take a 2 year course will be required to show they have funding to complete the course.
Study Establishment: A university or other appropriate institution.
Country of Study: Canada.
Application Procedure: CVs are not accepted; application form must be completed. Application forms are available between June and October.
Closing Date: Last Friday in October.
Additional Information: Application forms are not sent out in the week prior to closing date.

For further information contact:

Human Capacity Development
Association of Commonwealth Universities
John Foster House
36 Gordon Square, London, WC1H 0PF, England

CANADIAN ACADEMIC INSTITUTE IN ATHENS/CANADIAN ARCHAEOLOGICAL INSTITUTE IN ATHENS

59 Queens Park Crescent, Toronto, ON, M5S 2C4, Canada
Tel: (1) 416 926 7290
Fax: (1) 416 926 7292
Email: sheilacampbell@utoronto.ca
Contact: Grants Management Officer

Thompson (Homer and Dorothy) Fellowship

Subjects: Modern Greek, classical languages and literatures, history, archaeology, history of art, and music.
Eligibility: Open to Canadian citizens or landed immigrants.
Level of Study: Postdoctorate, Postgraduate.
Purpose: To support the study of graduate or postdoctorate studies of a person who needs to work in Greece.
Type: Fellowship.
No. of awards offered: 1.
Frequency: Annual.
Value: C$3,000, plus reduced rent in the CAIA hostel for the period of the fellowship.
Length of Study: 1 year.
Study Establishment: The Canadian Archaeological Institute at Athens.
Country of Study: Greece.
Application Procedure: Write enclosing a curriculum vitae, an outline of the proposed research and have three referees send letters to the Canadian address.
Closing Date: March 15th.
Additional Information: In addition to studies the Fellow assists the director of CAIA with office work (10 hours per week). Therefore some previous experience in Greece and some modern Greek is recommended. Greek address: Odos Aiginitou 7, Athens, Greece.

CANADIAN BUREAU FOR INTERNATIONAL EDUCATION (CBIE)

220 Laurier Avenue West
Suite 1100, Ottawa, ON, K1P 5Z9, Canada
Tel: (1) 613 237 4820
Fax: (1) 613 237 1073
Email: gbeauoloirn@cbie.ca
www: http://www.cbie.ca
Contact: Grants Management Officer

The Canadian Bureau for International Education (CBIE) is a national non-profit association comprising educational institutions, organisations and individuals dedicated to internal education and intercultural training. CBIE's mission is to promote the free movement of learners and trainees across national boarders. Activities include advocacy, research and information services, training programmes, scholarship management, professional development for international educators and a host of other services for members and learners.

Celanese Canada Internationalist Fellowships

Subjects: All subjects.
Eligibility: Applications are considered in an annual competition. Application is open to Canadians and permanent residents of Canada who hold at least one university degree, or are in the final year of a degree programme. College graduates (post-secondary level) holding a recognised bachelor's degree are also eligible. The latest degree must have been awarded no longer than five years from the date of application Applicants must have achieved a high academic standing. The fellowshgips are tenable anywhere in the world outside Canada.
Type: Fellowship.
No. of awards offered: 25.
Frequency: Annual.
Value: C$10,000 non-renewable.
Length of Study: A minimum of 8 consecutive months including at least 4 taught months of study courses.
Country of Study: Any country.
Application Procedure: Application forms are available at CBIE's website. To receive printed or electronic versions please write to the main address or email flepage@cbie.ca or gbeaudoin@cbie.ca. Applicants must submit a completed application form, a letter of intent outlining the proposed study programme abroad, curriculum vitae, academic transcripts, and two letters of reference, (one academic and one personal).
Closing Date: March 1st (date subject to change so check before applying).

CANADIAN FEDERATION OF UNIVERSITY WOMEN (CFUW)

251 Bank Street
Suite 600, Ottawa, ON, K2P1X3, Canada
Tel: (1) 613 234 2732
Email: cfuw.ho@sympatico.ca
www: http://www.cfuw.ca
Contact: Ms Dorothy Howland, Chair of the Fellowships Committee

Founded in 1919, the Canadian Federation of University Women is a voluntary, non-partisan, non-profit, self-funded bilingual organisation of 10,000 women university graduates. CFUW members are active in public affairs, working to raise the social, economic, and legal status of women, as well as to improve education, the environment, peace, justice, and human rights.

Alice E Wilson Awards

Subjects: All subjects.
Eligibility: Open to women who are Canadian citizens or have held landed immigrant status for at least one year prior to submitting application. Candidates should have a Bachelor's degree or its equivalent from a recognised university, not necessarily in Canada. Special consideration is given to candidates returning to study after at least three years. Candidates must have been accepted into the proposed programme of study.
Level of Study: Postgraduate.
Purpose: To assist women's study. Special consideration is given to candidates returning to study after at least three years.
No. of awards offered: Varies.
Frequency: Annual.
Value: C$1,000.
Study Establishment: A recognised university.
Country of Study: Any country.
Application Procedure: Application forms are available from the Federation.
Closing Date: November 15th.

Beverley Jackson Fellowship

Subjects: All subjects.
Eligibility: Open to women over the age of 35 at the time of application who are enrolled in graduate work at an Ontario university. Candidates should hold at least a Bachelor's degree or equivalent from a recognised university and be Canadian citizens or have held landed immigrant status for at least one year prior to submission of application and must have been accepted into the proposed programme of study.
Level of Study: Postgraduate.
Purpose: To provide partial funding for graduate study.
Type: Fellowship.
No. of awards offered: 1.
Frequency: Annual.
Value: C$3,000.
Study Establishment: A recognised university in Ontario.
Country of Study: Canada.
Application Procedure: Please write for details.
Closing Date: November 15th.
Additional Information: The Fellowship is funded by UWC North York.

CFUW 1989 Polytechnique Commemorative Award

Subjects: Any subject, with special consideration given to study of issues related to women.
Eligibility: Open to women who hold at least a Bachelor's degree or equivalent from a recognised university, who are Canadian citizens or have held landed immigrant status for at least one year, and who are able to justify the relevance of their work to women.
Level of Study: Postgraduate.
Purpose: To provide partial funding for graduate study.
No. of awards offered: 1.
Frequency: Annual.

Value: C$2,400.
Study Establishment: A recognised university.
Country of Study: Any country.
Application Procedure: Please write for details.
Closing Date: November 15th.

CFUW Professional Fellowship

Subjects: All subjects.
Eligibility: Open to women who are Canadian citizens or who have held landed immigrant status for at least one year prior to submitting application. Candidates should hold a bachelor's degree or its equivalent from a recognised Canadian university and wish to pursue graduate work at Master's degree level.
Level of Study: Postgraduate.
Purpose: To provide partial funding for graduate study at Master's degree level.
Type: Fellowship.
No. of awards offered: 1.
Frequency: Annual.
Value: C$5,000 paid in two half-yearly instalments.
Study Establishment: A recognised university.
Country of Study: Any country.
Application Procedure: Please write for details.
Closing Date: November 15th.
Additional Information: The Fellowship is not renewable. Application forms are available from the Federation.

The Dr Marion Elder Grant Fellowship

Subjects: All subjects.
Eligibility: Open to women who have a Bachelor's degree or equivalent from a recognised university, who are Canadian citizens or have held landed immigrant status for at least one year prior to submission of application and who have been accepted into the proposed programme of study. All things being equal, preference will be given to the holder of an Acadia University degree.
Level of Study: Postgraduate.
Purpose: To provide partial funding for full-time graduate study.
Type: Fellowship.
No. of awards offered: 1.
Frequency: Annual.
Value: C$8,000.
Study Establishment: A recognised university.
Country of Study: Any country.
Application Procedure: Please write for details.
Closing Date: November 15th.

Georgette Lemoyne Award

Subjects: All subjects.
Eligibility: Open to women who have a Bachelor's degree or equivalent from a recognised university and who are Canadian citizens or have held landed immigrant status for at least one year prior to submission of application and who have been accepted into the proposed programme of study.
Level of Study: Postgraduate.
Purpose: To provide partial funding for graduate study.

No. of awards offered: 1.
Frequency: Annual.
Value: C$1,000.
Study Establishment: A Canadian university where one language of administration and instruction is French.
Country of Study: Canada.
Application Procedure: Application forms are available from the Federation.
Closing Date: November 15th.

Margaret Dale Philp Award

Subjects: The humanities or social sciences with special consideration given to candidates who wish to specialise in Canadian history.
Eligibility: Open to women who are Canadian citizens or who have held landed immigrant status for at least one year prior to submission of application. Candidates should hold a Bachelor's degree or its equivalent from a recognised university, reside in Canada, and wish to embark on, or continue, a programme leading to an advanced degree and have been accepted into the proposed programme of study.
Level of Study: Postgraduate.
Purpose: To provide partial funding for graduate study.
No. of awards offered: 1.
Frequency: Annual.
Value: C$1,000.
Study Establishment: A recognised university.
Country of Study: Canada.
Application Procedure: Please write for details.
Closing Date: November 15th.

Margaret McWilliams Predoctoral Fellowship

Subjects: All subjects.
Eligibility: Open to women who are Canadian citizens or who have held landed immigrant status for at least one year prior to submission of application. A candidate should hold a Bachelor's degree or its equivalent from a recognised university, not necessarily in Canada, and be a full-time student at an advanced stage (at least one year) in her doctoral programme.
Level of Study: Doctorate.
Purpose: To provide funding for doctoral study.
Type: Fellowship.
No. of awards offered: 1.
Frequency: Annual.
Value: C$10,000 paid in two half-yearly instalments.
Country of Study: Any country.
Application Procedure: Please write for details.
Closing Date: November 15th.
Additional Information: The Fellowship is not renewable. Application forms are available from the Federation.

CANADIAN FRIENDS OF THE HEBREW UNIVERSITY

3080 Yonge Street
Suite 5024, Toronto, ON, M4N 3P4, Canada
Tel: (1) 416 485 8000
Fax: (1) 416 485 8565
Email: admissions@cfhu.org
Contact: Academic Affairs Committee

Canadian Friends of the Hebrew University Awards

Subjects: Arts and humanities.
Eligibility: Open to Canadian citizens or landed immigrants.
Level of Study: Postgraduate, Undergraduate.
Purpose: To enable Canadian students to attend the Hebrew University of Jerusalem.
Type: Bursary.
No. of awards offered: Varies.
Frequency: Annual.
Value: Approximately C$750-C$4,000, at the discretion of the Academic Affairs Committee.
Length of Study: 1 year.
Study Establishment: Hebrew University of Jerusalem.
Country of Study: Israel.
Application Procedure: Please write for details.
Closing Date: March 31st.

CANADIAN HIGH COMMISSION

Canada House
Trafalgare Square, London, SW1Y 5BJ, England
Tel: (44) 171 258 6692
Fax: (44) 171 258 6476
www: http://www.canada.org.uk
Contact: Ms Vivien Hughes, Canadian Studies Project Officer

Canadian Department of External Affairs Faculty Enrichment Program

Subjects: Social sciences and humanities, architecture and town planning, business administration and management, education and teacher training, fine art, law, mass communication and information, transport and communication, recreation, welfare and protection.
Eligibility: Open to full-time, permanent teaching members of the academic staff of a recognised institution of higher education in the UK.
Level of Study: Full-time faculty.
Purpose: To assist in the undertaking of studies relating to Canada or comparative Canada-UK topics in order to devise a new course on Canada or to modify or extend significantly the Canadian component (minimum 50%) of an existing course.
Type: Varies.
No. of awards offered: Varies.
Frequency: Annual.

Value: Up to a maximum of C$4,000, paid in two instalments.
Length of Study: 3-5 weeks.
Country of Study: Canada.
Closing Date: October 31st.

Canadian Department of External Affairs Faculty Research Program

Subjects: Social sciences and humanities in relation to Canada and aspects of its bilateral relations with the UK. Purely scientific subjects are ineligible.
Eligibility: Open to full-time academic staff members and professors emeritus of universities, colleges of higher education or equivalent degree granting institutions of the UK. Scholars at research and policy planning institutions who undertake significant Canadian projects or Canada's bilateral relations research projects may also apply.
Level of Study: Full-time faculty.
Purpose: To promote research about Canada or aspects of Canada's bilateral relations with the UK, leading to the publication of articles in the scholarly press.
Type: Varies.
No. of awards offered: Varies.
Frequency: Annual.
Value: Up to a maximum of C$4,000, paid in two instalments.
Length of Study: 3-5 weeks.
Country of Study: Canada or United Kingdom.
Closing Date: October 31st.

Canadian Department of External Affairs Institutional Research Program

Subjects: Canadian topics within the social sciences and humanities, comparative studies, or aspects of Canada's bilateral relations with the UK.
Eligibility: Open to recognised institutions of higher education, research and policy planning institutes or other established research institutions. Minimum of three full-time British academics.
Level of Study: Full-time faculty.
Purpose: To assist institutions of higher education to undertake, under the direction of a designated principal researcher, major team research about Canada, comparative Canada-UK topics, or on aspects of Canada's bilateral relations with the UK, leading to the publication of a substantial work, e.g. book or monograph.
Type: Varies.
No. of awards offered: Varies.
Frequency: Annual.
Value: Up to C$20,000.
Country of Study: Canada or United Kingdom.
Closing Date: October 31st.

CANADIAN INSTITUTE OF UKRAINIAN STUDIES

University of Alberta
352 Athabasca Hall, Edmonton, AB, T6G 2E8, Canada
Tel: (1) 403 492 2972
Fax: (1) 403 492 4967
Email: cius@gpu.srv.ualberta.ca
Contact: Fellowship Office

The Canadian Institute of Ukrainian Studies is involved in research and publication of Ukrainian subject matter.

The Helen Darcovich Memorial Doctoral Fellowship

Subjects: Ukrainian or Ukrainian Canadian topic in education, history, law, humanities, social sciences, women's studies or library sciences.
Eligibility: Open to qualified applicants of any nationality.
Level of Study: Doctorate.
Purpose: To aid students to complete a thesis on a Ukrainian or Ukrainian Canadian topic in education, history, law, humanities, social sciences, women's studies or library sciences.
Type: Fellowship.
No. of awards offered: 1.
Frequency: Annual.
Value: Up to C$8,000.
Length of Study: 1 academic year.
Study Establishment: Any approved institution of higher learning in Canada or elsewhere; although for non-Canadian applicants, preference will be given to students enrolled at the University of Alberta.
Country of Study: Any country.
Application Procedure: Please write to the main address for details.
Closing Date: May 1st.
Additional Information: Only in exceptional circumstances may an award be held concurrently with other awards.

Marusia and Michael Dorosh Master's Fellowship

Subjects: A Ukrainian or Ukrainian Canadian topic in education, history, law, humanities, social sciences, women's studies or library sciences.
Eligibility: Open to qualified applicants of any nationality.
Level of Study: Postgraduate.
Purpose: To aid a student to complete a thesis on a Ukrainian or Ukrainian Canadian topic in education, history, law, humanities, social sciences, women's studies or library sciences.
Type: Fellowship.
No. of awards offered: 1.
Frequency: Annual.
Value: C$4,500.
Length of Study: 1 academic year.

Study Establishment: Any approved institution of higher learning in Canada or elsewhere; although for non-Canadian applicants, preference will be given to students enrolled at the University of Alberta.
Country of Study: Any country.
Application Procedure: Please write to the main address for details.
Closing Date: May 1st.
Additional Information: Only in exceptional circumstances may an award be held concurrently with other awards.

Neporany Research and Teaching Fellowship

Subjects: Ukrainian studies.
Eligibility: Applicants must hold a doctorate, or have equivalent professional achievement, in Ukrainian studies.
Level of Study: Postdoctorate.
Purpose: To support academic Ukrainian studies.
Type: Fellowship.
No. of awards offered: 1.
Frequency: Annual.
Value: C$20,000.
Length of Study: 1 term, ie. half of the academic year.
Study Establishment: Tenable at any university with research facilities at which the Fellow's academic Ukraian studies speciality may be pursued and the Fellow enabled to teach a course related to the speciality.
Country of Study: Any country.
Application Procedure: Please write for further details at the main address.
Closing Date: March 1st.

Research Grants

Subjects: A Ukrainian or Ukrainian Canadian studies in history, literature, language, education, social sciences, library sciences.
Eligibility: Please write for details.
Level of Study: Postgraduate.
Type: Research Grant.
No. of awards offered: 1.
Frequency: Annual.
Value: Up to C$8,000.
Length of Study: 12 months.
Study Establishment: Any approved institution of higher learning in Canada or elsewhere; although for non-Canadian applicants, preference will be given to students enrolled at the University of Alberta.
Country of Study: Any country.
Application Procedure: Application form and the 'Guide to Research Applications' are available from the main address.
Closing Date: May 1st.

CANADIAN-SCANDINAVIAN FOUNDATION

c/o Office of the Director of Libraries
McGill University
3459 McTavish Street, Montreal, PQ, H3A 1Y1, Canada
Tel: (1) 514 398 4740
Fax: (1) 514 398 7356
Email: moller@libi.lan.mcgill.ca
Contact: Dr Hans Moller, Vice President

The Canadian-Scandinavian Foundation was established in 1950 and offers research and study support to qualified young, talented Canadians of university age and aspiring scholars.

Brucebo Scholarship

Subjects: Fine arts, preferably painting.
Eligibility: Open to young Canadian painters.
Level of Study: Unrestricted.
Purpose: To support 2-3 months residency for a promising young Canadian painter or artist at the Brucebo studio cottage.
Type: Scholarship.
No. of awards offered: 1.
Frequency: Annual.
Value: Approximately SEK25,000 (including transport costs, a food stipend, and lodging).
Length of Study: 3 months.
Study Establishment: At Brucebo studio cottage on the Island of Gotland, Sweden.
Country of Study: Sweden.
Application Procedure: Please request an application form.
Closing Date: January 31st.
Additional Information: The facility can accommodate a family member (or equivalent).

CSF Special Purpose Grants

Subjects: All subjects.
Eligibility: Open to qualified Canadians and landed immigrants.
Level of Study: Postgraduate.
Purpose: To provide travel support for shorter study or research visit to a Scandinavian or Nordic country destination.
Type: Grant.
No. of awards offered: 2-3.
Frequency: Annual.
Value: Approx. C$600-C$1,000.
Length of Study: A short period of time.
Country of Study: Scandinavia and Finland.
Application Procedure: Application form must be completed.
Closing Date: January 31st.

W B Bruce Fine Arts European Travel Scholarship

Subjects: Fine arts, preferably painting.
Eligibility: Open to Canadian citizens and landed immigrants.

Level of Study: Unrestricted.

Purpose: To fund a European study visit, including visits to Nordic countries during the autumn or winter term (not peak season) for a talented, young Canadian painter.

Type: Scholarship.

No. of awards offered: 1.

Frequency: Annual.

Value: SEK25,000.

Study Establishment: Studios and other fine arts institutions.

Country of Study: Europe or Scandinavia.

Application Procedure: Application form must be completed.

Closing Date: January 31st.

THE CANON FOUNDATION

Rijnsburgerweg 3, Leiden, NL-2334 BA, Netherlands
Tel: (31) 71 5156555
Fax: (31) 71 5157027
Email: foundation@canon-europa.com
Contact: Executive Officer

The Canon Foundation is a non-profit, grant making philanthropic organisation founded to promote, develop and spread science, knowledge and understanding, in particular between Europe and Japan.

Canon Foundation Visiting Research Fellowships/Professorships

Subjects: All subjects.

Eligibility: Open to Japanese and European nationals only.

Level of Study: Doctorate, Postdoctorate, Postgraduate.

Purpose: To contribute to scientific knowledge and international understanding, particularly between Japan and Europe.

Type: Monetary.

No. of awards offered: 10-12.

Frequency: Annual.

Value: Maximum award of DFL60,000.

Length of Study: 1 year maximum.

Country of Study: Europeans to Japan only, and Japanese to Europe.

Application Procedure: Applications must be completed and submitted with two reference letters, CV, list of papers, two photographs, and copies of certificates of higher education.

Closing Date: October 15th.

CANTERBURY HISTORICAL ASSOCIATION

c/o History Department
University of Canterbury
Private Bag, Christchurch, New Zealand
Fax: (64) 3 364 2003
Contact: Dr G W Rice, Secretary

J M Sherrard Award

Subjects: New Zealand regional and local history writing.

Eligibility: Open to qualified applicants from New Zealand only.

Level of Study: Unrestricted.

Purpose: To foster high standards of scholarship in New Zealand regional and local history.

Type: Cash Prize.

No. of awards offered: Varies.

Frequency: Every two years.

Value: NZ$1,000.

Country of Study: New Zealand.

Application Procedure: Titles are selected from the New Zealand National Bibliography and are assessed by a panel of judges. No application is required.

Additional Information: The prize money is often divided among two or three finalists. A commendation list is also published.

CARNEGIE TRUST FOR THE UNIVERSITIES OF SCOTLAND

Cameron House
Abbey Park Place, Dunfermline, Fife, KY12 7PZ, Scotland
Tel: (44) 1383 622148
Fax: (44) 1383 622149
Email: carnegie.trust@ed.ac.uk
www: http://www.geo.ed.ac.uk/carnegie/carnegie.html
Contact: Secretary

The Carnegie Trust for the Universities of Scotland, founded in 1901, is one of the many philantrophic agencies established by Andrew Carnegie. The trust aims to offer assistance to students, to aid the expansion of the Scottish universities and to stimulate research.

Carnegie Grants

Subjects: Any subject in the university curriculum.

Eligibility: Open to graduates of a Scottish university, or full-time members of staff of a Scottish university.

Level of Study: Postgraduate, Professional development.

Purpose: To support personal research projects or aid in the publication of books in certain fields, where likely to benefit the universities of Scotland.

Type: Grant.

No. of awards offered: Varies.

Frequency: Throughout the year.

Value: Varies according to requests; candidates must provide a detailed estimate of anticipated costs, but the normal maximum is £2,000.
Length of Study: Up to 3 months.
Country of Study: Any country.
Application Procedure: Application form must be completed; these are available from the Trust office.
Closing Date: February 1st, June 1st, November 1st; prior to Executive Committee meetings in those months.

Carnegie Scholarships

Subjects: Most subjects in the university curriculum.
Eligibility: Open to persons possessing a first class honours degree from a Scottish university.
Level of Study: Postgraduate.
Purpose: To support postgraduate research.
Type: Scholarship.
No. of awards offered: 16.
Frequency: Annual.
Value: £6,788 (in 1998/99) per year, plus tuition fees and allowances.
Length of Study: A maximum of 3 years, subject to annual review.
Study Establishment: Any university in the UK.
Country of Study: United Kingdom.
Application Procedure: Candidates should be nominated by a senior member of staff of a Scottish university. Application forms are available from the Trust office.
Closing Date: March 15th.

CATHERINE MCCAIG'S TRUST

Clerk to the Governors
c/o McLeish Carswell
29 St Vincent Place, Glasgow, G1 2DT, Scotland
Tel: (44) 141 248 4134
Fax: (44) 141 226 3118
Contact: Ms Anne F Wilson

McCaig Bursaries and Postgraduate Scholarships

Subjects: Gaelic studies.
Eligibility: Bursaries are open to students enrolling in a course of Gaelic studies at any Scottish university; Postgraduate Scholarships are open to MA students of any Scottish university who have studied Gaelic among their course subjects.
Level of Study: Postgraduate.

Type: Scholarship.
Frequency: Annual.
Value: £250 per year for the entire course of study (Bursaries); £750 per year, renewable (Postgraduate Scholarships).
Length of Study: 1-3 years.
Country of Study: United Kingdom.
Application Procedure: Application forms are available from the Clerk.
Closing Date: May.

THE CATHOLIC UNIVERSITY OF LOUVAIN (UCL)

Secrétariat à la Coopération Internationale
Halles Universitaires
Place de l'Université 1, Louvain-la-Neuve, B-1348, Belgium
Tel: (32) 10 47 30 93
Fax: (32) 10 47 40 75
Email: baeyens@sco.ucl.ac.be
www: http://www.ucl.ac.be
Contact: Mr Duque Christian

The French-speaking Catholic University of Louvain (UCL) organises a yearly scholarship contest for postgraduate studies, medical specialisation and PhD.

Catholic University of Louvain Cooperation Fellowships

Subjects: Any subject relevant to third world development.
Eligibility: Open to nationals of developing countries, who hold all the requirements to be admitted at postgraduate level at UCL. Applicants should have an excellent academic background and some professional experience, they should demonstrate that their study programme is able to promote the development of their home country and they should have a good command of French (DELF). Applicants must be less than 35 years for a PhD or 40 years for a specialisation.
Level of Study: Doctorate, Postgraduate.
Purpose: To promote economic, social, cultural and political progress in the developing countries by postgraduate training of graduates from these countries.
Type: Fellowship.
No. of awards offered: Up to 20.
Frequency: Annual.
Value: Tuition, living expenses, family allowance, medical insurance, transportation costs to home country at the end of studies.
Length of Study: A maximum of 4 years.
Study Establishment: The Catholic University of Louvain.
Country of Study: Belgium.
Application Procedure: Application form must be completed; additional documentation is required (motivated letter and CV).
Closing Date: December 31st.
Additional Information: Application forms available on request.

CDS INTERNATIONAL, INC.

871 United Nations Plaza, New York, NY, 10017-1814, United States of America
Tel: (1) 212 497 3513
Fax: (1) 212 497 3535
Email: rdelfino@cdsintl.org
www: http://www.cdsintl.org
Contact: Ms Rebecca R Delfino

CDS International is a non-profit organisation which administers work exchange programmes. CDS International's goal is to further the international exchange of knowledge and technological skills, and to contribute to the development of a pool of highly trained and interculturally experienced business, academic, and government leaders.

Congress Bundestag Youth Exchange for Young Professionals

Subjects: Acceptance to the scholarship programme is based on clear career goals and related work experience, intercultural curiosity, and a sense of diplomacy. Eligible fields include business, technical, computer science, social and service fields.
Eligibility: Open to US citizens aged between 18 and 24 years who are high school graduates, have well-defined career goals and related part or full-time work experience, who are able to communicate and work well with others and have maturity enabling them to adapt to new situations.
Level of Study: Professional development.
Purpose: To foster the exchange of knowledge and culture between German and American youth while providing career-enhancing theoretical and practical work experience.
No. of awards offered: Approx. 60.
Value: International air fare and partial domestic transportation, language training and study at a German professional school, seminars (including transportation, insurance).
Length of Study: 7 months of study and a 5 month internship.
Study Establishment: A field-specific post-secondary professional school in Germany.
Country of Study: Germany.
Application Procedure: Application forms may be requested by mail or email and may also be downloaded from the website.
Closing Date: December 15th.
Additional Information: Participants must have US$300 to US$350 pocket money per month. During their year American exchangees will have the opportunity to improve their skills through formal study and work experience. The programme also includes intensive language instruction and housing with a host family or in a dormitory.

CENTER FOR ADVANCED STUDY IN THE BEHAVIORAL SCIENCES

75 Alfa Road, Stanford, CA, 94305, United States of America
Tel: (1) 650 321 2052
Fax: (1) 650 321 1192
Contact: Mr Robert A Scott, Associate Director

Center for Advanced Study in the Behavioral Sciences Postdoctoral Residential Fellowships

Subjects: Behavioural sciences, biological sciences and the humanities.
Eligibility: There are no restrictions with regard to race or nationality, but applicants must hold a PhD.
Level of Study: Postdoctorate.
Type: Fellowship.
No. of awards offered: Approx. 45.
Frequency: Annual.
Value: Equal to up to half of a nine-month university salary with an informal cap, plus travel allowance to and from the Center for recipients and their families.
Length of Study: 9-12 months.
Study Establishment: The Center.
Country of Study: USA.
Application Procedure: Please contact the Center for details.
Additional Information: Fellows should be nominated by academic officers or distinguished scholars and are expected to seek additional sources of support to share in Fellowship costs. All names submitted will be kept for reviews at two-year intervals. Persons authorised for Fellowships are invited to indicate the year which would best suit their program.

THE CENTER FOR FIELD RESEARCH

Box 9104
680 Mount Auburn Street, Watertown, MA, 02471, United States of America
Tel: (1) 617 926 8200
Fax: (1) 617 926 8532
Email: cfr@earthwatch.org
www: http://www.earthwatch.org/cfr/cfr.html
Telex: 510 600 6452
Contact: Ms Tricia Fagan, Program Co-ordinator

Center for Field Research Grants

Subjects: Disciplines include, but are not limited to, anthropology, archaeology, biology, botany, cartography, conservation, ethnology, folklore, geography, geology, hydrology, marine sciences, meteorology, musicology, nutrition, ornithology, restoration, sociology, and sustainable development.

Eligibility: There are no residency requirements or nomination processes. Preference is given to applicants who hold a PhD and have both field and teaching experience; however, support is also offered for outstanding projects by younger postdoctoral scholars and, in special cases, graduate students. Women and minority applicants are encouraged. Research teams must include qualified volunteers from the Earthwatch Institute.
Level of Study: Doctorate, Postdoctorate.
Purpose: To provide grants for field research projects that can constructively utilise teams of non-specialist field assistants in accomplishing their research goals.
Type: Grant.
No. of awards offered: Approx. 140.
Frequency: Annual.
Value: Varies; grants are awarded on a per capita basis, depending upon the number of participants. Normal range of support is US$7,000-US$130,000.
Length of Study: Terms last for 2-3 weeks, projects can go on all year.
Study Establishment: At research sites; approximately one-quarter of the research currently funded takes place within the USA. Teams are in the field for 2-3 weeks; longer-term support is available through multiple teams; renewals are encouraged.
Country of Study: Any country.
Application Procedure: Preliminary proposal must be submitted 13 months prior to field dates. Application forms may be obtained by contacting Earthwatch Headquarters or visiting the organisations' website.
Closing Date: None.

CENTER FOR HELLENIC STUDIES

3100 Whitehaven Street NW, Washington, DC, 20008, United States of America
Tel: (1) 202 234 3738
Fax: (1) 202 797 3745
Email: chs@harvard.edn
www: http://www.chs.harvard.edu
Contact: The Directors

The Center for Hellenic Studies (Trustees for Harvard University) is a residential research institute for professional scholars in Ancient Greek studies.

Center for Hellenic Studies Junior Fellowships

Subjects: Ancient Greek studies (primarily literature, language, philosophy, history, religion, archaeology and art history with restrictions).
Eligibility: Open to scholars and teachers of Ancient Greek studies with a PhD degree or equivalent qualification and some published work, in the early stages of their career.
Level of Study: Postdoctorate.**Purpose:** To provide selected classics scholars fairly early in their careers with an academic year free of other responsibilities to work on a publishable project.

Type: Fellowship.
No. of awards offered: 12.
Frequency: Annual.
Value: Up to US$22,000, plus private living quarters and a study at the Center building, limited funds for research expenses and research related travel.
Length of Study: 9 months from September to June; not renewable.
Study Establishment: Center for Hellenic Studies, in Washington DC.
Country of Study: USA.
Application Procedure: Application form, CV, description of research project, samples of publications (up to 50pp), and three letters of recommendation must be submitted. Enquiries about eligibility and early applications are encouraged.
Closing Date: October 15th.
Additional Information: Residence at the Center is required.

CENTRAL QUEENSLAND UNIVERSITY (CQU)

Research Services Office, Rockhampton, QLD, 4702, Australia
Tel: (61) 61 07 4930 9828
Fax: (61) 7 4930 9801
Email: research-enquiries@cqu.edu.au
www: http://www.cqu.edu.au
Contact: Research Higher Degrees Officer

Central Queensland University's higher degree programmes are characterised by open and flexible learning opportunities which provide a distinctive postgraduate research experience for students. With particular strengths in sustainable regional development and resource utilisation; industrially relevant engineering; contemporary communication; and innovative teaching, learning and professional practice, the focus of higher degree programmes is on the conduct of cutting edge research in areas which challenge boundaries of the traditional disciplines.

CQU International Student Scholarship

Subjects: Research higher degrees can be undertaken, dependent upon the availability of supervision, in the range of discipline areas represented in CQU's five faculties - arts, health and sciences, business and law, education and creative arts, engineering and physical systems, and informatics and communication.
Eligibility: Candidates must be eligible for admission to a research higher degree at CQU.
Level of Study: Doctorate, Postgraduate.
Purpose: To enable the scholar to proceed as a full-time candidate to a research Master's or doctorate.
Type: Scholarship.**No. of awards offered:** 1.
Frequency: Annual.
Value: Tuition fees plus A$5,000 and living allowance p.a.
Length of Study: 2-3 years.
Study Establishment: Central Queensland University.
Country of Study: Australia.

Application Procedure: Application must be made as prescribed. Certified academic transcripts and certified citizenship status are required. All enquiries from overseas should be directed to the CQU International office.
Closing Date: September 30th.

CQU University Postgraduate Research Award

Subjects: Research higher degrees can be undertaken, dependent upon the availability of supervision, in the range of discipline areas represented in CQU's five faculties - arts, health and sciences, business and law, education and creative arts, engineering and physical systems, and informatics and communication.
Eligibility: Candidates must be eligible for admission to a research higher degree at CQU.
Level of Study: Doctorate, Postgraduate, Research.
Purpose: To enable the scholar to proceed as a full-time candidate to a research Master's or doctorate.
Type: Scholarship.
No. of awards offered: 11.
Frequency: Annual.
Value: A$15,888 living allowance plus A$2,000 research support (per year).
Length of Study: 2-3 years.
Study Establishment: Central Queensland University.
Country of Study: Australia.
Application Procedure: Application must be made as prescribed. Certified academic transcripts and certified citizenship status are required. All enquiries from overseas should be directed to the CQU International office.
Closing Date: October 31st.

CENTRE FOR INTERNATIONAL MOBILITY (CIMO)

PO Box 343
Hakaniemenkatu 2, Helsinki, SF-00531, Finland
Tel: (358) 9 7 747 7033
Fax: (358) 9 7 747 7064
Email: cimoinfo@cimo.fi
www: http://www.cimo.fi
Contact: Grants Management Officer

The Centre for International Mobility, CIMO, is a service-sector organisation whose expertise is geared to the promotion of cross-cultural communication in education, training and international mobility with the focus on education and training, work and young people. CIMO gathers, processes and distributes information, and co-ordinates international education and training programmes.

CIMO Bilateral Scholarships

Subjects: Various subjects.
Eligibility: Open to applicants from: Australia, Austria, Belgium, Bulgaria, Canada, China, Cuba, Czech Republic, Denmark, Egypt, France, Germany, Great Britain, Greece, Hungary, Iceland, India, Republic of Ireland, Israel, Italy, Japan, Luxembourg, Mexico, Mongolia, the Netherlands, Norway, Poland, Portugal, Republic of Korea, Romania, Slovakia, Spain, Sweden, Switzerland, Turkey and the USA.
Level of Study: Postgraduate.
Type: Scholarship.
Frequency: Annual.
Value: The bilateral scholarships usually consist of a monthly allowance of FIM4,100. For short-term visitors there is a daily allowance, the amount of which is determined annually. Accommodation is provided for short-term visitors. There are no travel grants to or from Finland.
Length of Study: Postgraduate research of 3-9 months; study visits of 1-2 weeks.
Study Establishment: A Finnish university.
Country of Study: Finland.
Application Procedure: Applications should be made to the appropriate authority in the applicant's country, which selects the candidates to be proposed to CIMO.
Closing Date: Depends on the country.

CIMO Nordic Scholarship Scheme for the Baltic Countries and Northwest Russia

Subjects: Education and research in all fields. Priority is given to fields that promote further development in the region, as well as to fields where the special competence and experience of Nordic countries can be made use of.
Eligibility: Open to applicants from the five Nordic countries and the three Baltic Republics as well as areas in Northwest Russia.
Level of Study: Unrestricted.
Purpose: To promote collaboration between the five Nordic countries and the three Baltic Republics as well as areas in northwest Russia, within the fields of education and research.
Type: Scholarship.
Frequency: Twice a year.
Length of Study: 1-6 months.
Study Establishment: A Finnish university.
Country of Study: Finland.
Application Procedure: Application form must be completed and can be obtained by writing to the Nordic Information Offices and to CIMO.
Closing Date: October 1st, March 1st.
Additional Information: Priority will be given to applications where contact or co-operation has been established.

CIMO Scholarships for Advanced Finnish Studies and Research

Subjects: Finnish language, literature, Finno-Ugric linguistics, ethnology and folkloristics.
Eligibility: Open to nationals of all countries. The applicant should be older than 35.
Level of Study: Postgraduate, Undergraduate.
Purpose: To support postgraduate research and advanced studies of Finnish.
Type: Scholarship.
Value: Monthly allowance of FIM 4,100. No travel grants are available to or from Finland.

Length of Study: 4-9 months.
Study Establishment: A Finnish university.
Country of Study: Finland.
Application Procedure: Applications should be made, preferably in Finnish, on CIMO's application forms, which are available at Finnish embassies and consulates abroad. Applications should be sent to CIMO. For postgraduate studies the grant is applied by the Finnish receiving University.
Closing Date: Applications are accepted at any time.

CIMO Scholarships for Young Researchers and University Teaching Staff

Subjects: Education and research in all subjects.
Eligibility: Open to nationals of any county. The applicant should not be older than 35.
Level of Study: Doctorate, Postdoctorate, Postgraduate.
Purpose: To promote international co-operation in teaching and research.
Type: Scholarship.
Frequency: Every three months.
Value: FIM4,000-6,000 per month.
Length of Study: 3-12 months.
Study Establishment: University.
Country of Study: Finland.
Application Procedure: Application form must be completed. The Finnish receiving university department must apply for the grant.
Closing Date: Applications are accepted at any time.
Additional Information: Established contact with the receiving institute prior to application is required.

CENTRE FOR SCIENCE DEVELOPMENT (CSD)

Private Bag X270, Pretoria, 0001, South Africa
Tel: (27) 12 202 2742
Fax: (27) 12 202 2892
Email: fbotha@silwane.hsrc.ac.za
www: http://www.hsrc.ac.za
Contact: M F T Morolo, Manager

The Centre for Science Development (CSD) is the funding and research support division of the Human Sciences Research Council (HSRC). Its mandate is to provide funding for research grants and postgraduate scholarships in the humanities and social sciences in order to enhance their contribution to a National System of Innovation in South Africa.

CSD Grants for Attendance at International Conferences

Subjects: Humanities and social sciences.
Eligibility: Open to South African specialists, who are considered with due attention to the following: the status of the applicant in the particular field covered by the conference;

that the applicant will read a paper at the conference; and the likelihood that research in South Africa will benefit through the participation of the applicant in the conference and that her/his position is such that the knowledge acquired will be easily disseminated on her/his return to South Africa. Preference will be given to applicants invited officially by the organisers of the conference, to read personally a paper, and whose work in the relative field justifies this.
Level of Study: Professional development.
Purpose: To provide South African researchers with the opportunity to participate in international conferences abroad.
Type: Grant.
No. of awards offered: Varies.
Frequency: Every two years.
Value: Not exceeding R6,000 for Europe, the British Isles and the Mediterranean area; R8,000 for the USA, Canada, South America, Australia, New Zealand, Japan and the Far East. These amounts represent approximately 50% of the normal total cost, and are provided only when the candidate's own institution contributes at least 30% of the total costs involved. Grantees already abroad may receive 50% of the travelling expenses from their base abroad to the conference centre, and a daily allowance of R300 with a maximum of six days for the duration of the conference, provided that the university or institution contributes 30% of the total cost.
Country of Study: Outside South Africa.
Application Procedure: All applications should be accompanied by a complete list of the applicant's publications and a list of all conferences attended by her/him outside South Africa during the previous five years.
Closing Date: Four months prior to the conference date.
Additional Information: A report regarding attendance at the conference, as well as a copy of the paper read, must be submitted to the CSD who may consider it for publication in 'Bulletin'. Normally only one application for a particular conference will receive favourable consideration so as to ensure that available funds are distributed as widely as possible.

CSD Grants for Foreign Research Fellows

Subjects: Humanities and social sciences.
Eligibility: Open to distinguished researchers who are not South African citizens and are not resident in South Africa.
Level of Study: Unrestricted.
Purpose: To bring foreign researchers of indisputable scientific status in the field of the human sciences to South Africa as Research Fellows to enable them to participate actively in research.
Type: Fellowship.
No. of awards offered: Varies.
Frequency: Annual.
Value: An economy return air ticket and a subsistence fee of R400 per day.
Length of Study: Not less than 1 week and no more than 15 days.
Country of Study: South Africa.
Application Procedure: An application must be submitted on the prescribed form by the host institution and should include a detailed curriculum vitae of the prospective Research Fellow; particulars of the research programme of the host

institution and a description of the role she/he will fulfil therein and a description of the manner in which other South African researchers may be exposed to the Fellow's expertise.

Closing Date: Four months prior to the visit.

Additional Information: A detailed report (compiled by the Research Fellow) on the visit must be submitted to the CSD not later than one month after the conclusion of the visit.

CSD Prestige Scholarships for Doctoral Studies Abroad

Subjects: Humanities and social sciences.

Eligibility: Open to South African citizens who hold at least a Master's degree, and require specialised training as research workers in a field for which there are no, or inadequate, training facilities in South Africa. These scholarships are intended for oustanding achievers.

Level of Study: Doctorate.

Type: Scholarship.

No. of awards offered: 10.

Frequency: Annual.

Value: R48,000, plus a travel grant of R6,000.

Length of Study: 1 academic year; may be renewed for an additional year.

Study Establishment: Various universities.

Country of Study: United Kingdom, Europe, USA, Canada, Australia or the Far East.

Closing Date: June 30th.

Additional Information: A scholar must register for degree studies at a university abroad. The scholarship will be paid on production of proof of registration. Annual reports must be submitted through the supervisor. On completion of their research abroad, candidates must return to South Africa for at least two years.

CSD Publication Grants

Subjects: Humanities and social sciences.

Eligibility: Open to South African residents who can produce concisely and accurately presented work that is the result of original research, is of scientific value, and is mainly new material and not readily available to research workers. Short manuscripts which satisfy these requirements will receive priority.

Level of Study: Unrestricted.

Purpose: To publish work of outstanding quality which, owing to a limited sales potential or for other reasons, could not otherwise be published through the usual channels.

Type: Grant.

No. of awards offered: Varies.

Frequency: As required.

Value: Partial or full cost of publication up to R9,000.

Country of Study: South Africa.

Application Procedure: Applications for the publication of dissertations and doctoral theses will not normally be considered. Two copies of the manuscript must be presented

o the Centre for Science Development in an edited form. The applicant must submit three quotations from well-known publishers with the condition of publication, format, type of paper, cost of illustrations and labour, etc., the guarantee required by the publisher, and the proposed selling price. Once notified that her or his application has been successful, the applicant must take steps to ensure, if possible, that publication takes place during the financial year in which the grant is made. Further information may be obtained from the registrars of any South African university as well as from the Centre itself.

Closing Date: Specialised publications publishing first-time applications considered throughout the year; professional journals September 30th.

CSD Research Grants

Subjects: Humanities and social sciences.

Eligibility: Open to applicants who have already achieved recognition for academic achievements and earned a reputation as research leaders in the area concerned and hold a PhD degree.

Level of Study: Postdoctorate.

Purpose: To allow researchers of indisputable scientific status to undertake a demarcated and advanced research project locally or abroad.

Type: Grant.

No. of awards offered: Varies.

Frequency: Annual.

Value: Varies, according to budget.

Length of Study: 2-4 months; not renewable, local research has no time limit.

Study Establishment: A centre of high academic status outside South Africa, or locally.

Country of Study: Any country.

Application Procedure: Applications must be submitted on the prescribed form obtainable at the university.

Closing Date: June 30th.

Additional Information: A grant for overseas trips will be considered if the applicants have exhausted the research sources in the particular field in South Africa and have already determined that there are inadequate facilities in South Africa for the specific research. A grant will not be considered if the research is to be undertaken for obtaining a further qualification.

CSD Scholarships for Doctoral/D-Tech Studies at Universities and Technikons in South Africa

Subjects: Humanities and social sciences.

Eligibility: Open to South African citizens who are registered at a South African university for doctoral/D-Tech studies.

Level of Study: Doctorate.

Type: Scholarship.

No. of awards offered: Varies.

Frequency: Annual.

Value: R13,000.
Length of Study: 1 year; may be renewed for an additional year.
Study Establishment: An appropriate institution.
Country of Study: South Africa.
Application Procedure: Applications should be submitted to the university on the prescribed form obtainable at the university.
Closing Date: June 30th.
Additional Information: Scholarships for part-time study are also available at the rate of R6,000.

CSD Scholarships for Honours Degree Studies at Universities in South Africa

Subjects: Humanities and social sciences.
Eligibility: Open to South African citizens with at least a 65% pass in the Bachelor's degree examination or in the subject in which they wish to specialise and wish to study full-time at a South African university for a Bachelor honours degree or the equivalent advanced course in the field of humanities and social sciences.
Level of Study: Postgraduate.
Type: Scholarship.
No. of awards offered: Varies.
Frequency: Annual.
Value: R6,000.
Length of Study: 1 year.
Study Establishment: An appropriate university.
Country of Study: South Africa.
Application Procedure: Applications should be submitted to the university on the prescribed form obtainable at the university.
Closing Date: January 15th.
Additional Information: A scholarship holder must pass the honours degree examination within the prescribed time for which the scholarship is awarded, otherwise the scholarship must be refunded or the course repeated and successfully completed at the expense of the scholarship holder.

CSD Scholarships for Master's Degree Studies/Studies for Master's Degree in Technology in South Africa

Subjects: Humanities and social sciences.
Eligibility: Open to South African citizens who have passed their previous degree examination with at least 65%.
Level of Study: Postgraduate.
Type: Scholarship.
No. of awards offered: Varies.
Frequency: Annual.
Value: R9,000.
Length of Study: 1 year.
Study Establishment: An appropriate institution.
Country of Study: South Africa.
Application Procedure: Applications should be submitted to the university on the prescribed form obtainable at the university.
Closing Date: February 28th.

Additional Information: Scholarships for part-time study are also available at the rate of R5,000.

CENTRO DE ESTUDIOS POLITICOS Y CONSTITUTIONALES

Plaza de la Marina Espanola 9, Madrid, E-28071, Spain
Tel: (34) 915 40 19 50
Fax: (34) 915 47 85 49
Email: formac@ceps.es
www: http://www.ceps.es
Contact: Subdirreccion General

Centro de Estudios Politicos Y Constitutionales Grant

Subjects: Political science and constitutional law, theory of the study of law, contemporary history, public and European law.
Eligibility: Open to nationals of all countries with appropriate qualifications and a sound knowledge of Spanish.
Level of Study: Postgraduate.
Purpose: To provide financial assistance for promising students specialising in constitutional law and politics.
Type: Grant.
No. of awards offered: 1.
Frequency: Annual.
Value: 50,000 pesetas.
Length of Study: 1 academic year.
Country of Study: Spain.
Application Procedure: Please submit certificates of educational qualifications.
Closing Date: Please write for details.
Additional Information: The current course programme will be sent by post to anyone who expresses an interest over the telephone or in writing.

THE CHARLES A AND ANNE MORROW LINDBERGH FOUNDATION

708 South 3rd Street
Suite 110, Minneapolis, MN, 55415-1141, United States of America
Tel: (1) 612 338 1703
Fax: (1) 612 338 6826
Email: lindfdtn@mtn.org
www: http://www.mtn.org/lindfdtn
Contact: Ms Marlene White, Grants Administrator

The Foundation is dedicated to furthering a balance between technological advancement and environmental preservation which was the Lindbergh's shared vision.

Lindbergh Grants

Subjects: Adaptive technology, waste minimisation and management, agriculture, aviation/aerospace, conservation of natural resources, humanities/education, arts, intercultural communication, exploration, biomedical research, health and population sciences.
Eligibility: Open to nationals of any country.
Level of Study: Unrestricted.
Purpose: To provide grants to individuals whose initiative in a wide spectrum of disciplines seeks to actively further a better balance between technology and the natural environment.
Type: Research Grant.
No. of awards offered: Approx. 10.
Frequency: Annual.
Value: Maximum of US$10,580.
Country of Study: Any country.
Application Procedure: Application form must be completed.
Closing Date: Second Tuesday in June.

CHARLES AND JULIA HENRY FUND

University Registry
The Old Schools, Cambridge, CB2 1TN, England
Tel: (44) 122 333 2317
Fax: (44) 122 333 2332
Email: mrf25@admin.cam.ac.uk
www: http://www.admin.cam.ac.uk
Contact: Ms Melanie Foster, Scholarships Clerk

Henry Fellowships (Harvard and Yale)

Subjects: Unrestricted, but subject to approval and feasibility.
Eligibility: Open to unmarried citizens, under 26 years of age, of the UK and Commonwealth. They should be undergraduates of a UK university who have completed six terms of residence by January 1st preceding the fellowship, or graduates of a UK university who are in their first year of postgraduate study at a UK university.
Level of Study: Postgraduate.
Purpose: To strengthen bonds between Britain and the USA.
Type: Fellowship.
No. of awards offered: 2.
Frequency: Annual.
Value: US$16,300 plus a travel grant of £1,250,(reviewed annually), tuition fees and health insurance.
Length of Study: 1 year.
Study Establishment: Harvard University, Cambridge, Massachusetts, or Yale University, New Haven, Connecticut.
Country of Study: USA.
Application Procedure: Application form must be completed and referee's reports submitted.
Closing Date: Early December.

Additional Information: Applicants must produce evidence of intellectual ability and must also submit a scheme of study or research not consisting of a degree course. The Fellowships are awarded in conjunction with other awards to finance a continuing course of study and are not tenable for degree courses. Fellows must undertake to return to the British Isles or some other part of the Commonwealth on the expiration of their term of tenure. The Fellowship must be vacated if the Fellow marries.

CHARLES BABBAGE INSTITUTE

University of Minnesota
103 Walter Library
117 Pleasant Street SE, Minneapolis, MN, 55455, United States of America
Tel: (1) 612 624 5050
Fax: (1) 612 625 8054
Email: cbi@tc.umn.edu
www: http://www.cbi.umn.edu
Contact: Ms Colleen Christensen, Secretary

The Charles Babbage Institute is a research centre dedicated to promoting the study of the history of computing and its impact on society, and preserving relevant documentation. CBI fosters research and writing in the history of computing by providing fellowship support, archival resources, and information to scholars, computer scientists and the general public.

Adelle and Erwin Tomash Fellowship in the History of Information Processing

Subjects: History of information processing.
Eligibility: Open to graduate students whose dissertation deals with a historical aspect of information processing.
Level of Study: Doctorate.
Purpose: To advance the professional development of historians of information processing.
Type: Fellowship.
No. of awards offered: 1.
Frequency: Annual.
Value: US$10,000 stipend, plus up to US$2,000 to be used for tuition, fees, travel and other research expenses.
Length of Study: 1 year.
Country of Study: Any country.
Application Procedure: Applicants should send their curriclum vitae and a five-page statement and justification of the research problem, a discussion of methods, research materials, and evidence of faculty support for the project. Applicants should also arrange for three letters of reference and certified transcripts of graduate school credits to be sent directly to Charles Babbage Institute.
Closing Date: January 15th.

CHAUTAUQUA INSTITUTION

Box 1098
Dept 6
Schools Office, Chautauqua, NY, 14722, United States of America
Tel: (1) 716 357 6233
Fax: (1) 716 357 9014
www: http://www.chautauque-inst.org
Contact: Mr Richard R Redington, Vice President

The Chautauqua Institution was founded in 1874. It is a is a non-profit organisation which offers nine week summer schools for, the arts, education, religion and recreation.

Chautauqua Institution Awards

Subjects: Instrumental and vocal music, theatre, art and dance.
Eligibility: Open to candidates of any sex, nationality and age.
Level of Study: Postgraduate, Undergraduate.
Purpose: To assist talented advanced students enrolled in the Chautauqua summer programme of fine and performing arts.
Type: Award.
No. of awards offered: Varies.
Frequency: Annual.
Value: US$200-US$2,000.
Length of Study: 7-8 weeks.
Study Establishment: The Chautauqua Institution.
Country of Study: USA.
Closing Date: Ten days before live audition (walk-ins accepted); March 1st for taped auditions; April 1st for art portfolio of slides.
Additional Information: Most scholarships are given in music. No travel grants are provided.

THE CHICAGO TRIBUNE

Tribune Books
435 North Michigan Avenue, Chicago, IL, 60611, United States of America
Tel: (1) 312 222 4540
Fax: (1) 312 222 3751
www: http://www.chicagotribune.com
Contact: Ms Marcy Keno, Nelson Algren Awards

Heartland Prizes

Subjects: A novel and a book of nonfiction embodying the spirit of the nations heartland.
Eligibility: The awards are not limited to Midwestern writers or regional subjects.
Level of Study: Professional development.

Purpose: To recognise works that reinforce and perpetuate the values of heartland America.
Type: Prize.
No. of awards offered: 2.
Frequency: Annual.
Value: $5,000.
Country of Study: USA.
Application Procedure: Please write for details.
Closing Date: Publishers may submit books between August 1st and July 31st.

Nelson Algren Awards

Subjects: Short fiction.
Eligibility: Submissions must be written by an American and be unpublished.
Level of Study: Unrestricted.
Purpose: To award writers of short fiction.
Type: Award.
No. of awards offered: 4.
Frequency: Annual.
Value: US$5,000 (1 award); US$1,000 (3 runner-up awards).
Country of Study: Any country.
Application Procedure: Please send a self-addressed, postage paid envelope, with a request for written guidelines. The competition will begin accepting entries November 1st.
Closing Date: February 1st.
Additional Information: The work must be unpublished and 2,500-10,000 words in length.

CHILDREN'S LITERATURE ASSOCIATION (CHLA)

PO Box 138, Battle Creek, MI, 49016 - 0138, United States of America
Tel: (1) 616 965 8180
Fax: (1) 616 965 3568
Email: chla@mlc.lib.mi.us
www: http://ebbs.english.vt.edu/chla
Contact: Ms Kathryn Kiessling, Administrator

The Children's Literature Association is a non-profit organisation devoted to promoting serious scholarship and criticism in children's literature.

ChLA Research Fellowships and Scholarships

Subjects: Children's literature.
Eligibility: Applicants must be members of the Children's Literature Association.
Level of Study: Unrestricted.
Purpose: To award proposals dealing with criticism or original scholarship with the expectation that the undertaking will lead to publication and make a significant contribution to the field of children's literature in the area of scholarship or criticism.

Type: Fellowships and scholarships.
No. of awards offered: Varies.
Frequency: Annual.
Value: Up to US$1,000 - individual awards may range from US$250-US$1,000 and are may be used only for research related expenses such as travel to special collections or materials and supplies. Funds are not intended for work leading to the completion of a professional degree.
Country of Study: Any country.
Application Procedure: Send five copies of the application in English.
Closing Date: February 1st.
Additional Information: In honour of the achievement and dedication of Dr Margaret P Esmonde, proposals that deal with critical or original work in the areas of science fantasy or science fiction for children or adolescents will be awarded the Margaret P Esmonde Memorial Scholarship.

CLARA HASKIL ASSOCIATION

rue du Conseil 31, Vevey 1, CH-1800, Switzerland
Tel: (41) 21 922 67 04
Fax: (41) 21 922 67 34
Email: clara.haskil@smile.ch
www: http://www.regart.ch/clara-haskil/
Contact: Mr Patrick Peikert, Director

The Clara Haskil Association exists to recognise and help a young pianist whose approach to piano interpretation is of the same spirit that constantly inspired Clara Haskil, and that she illustrated so perfectly.

Clara Haskil Competition

Subjects: Piano performance.
Eligibility: Open to pianists of any nationality and either sex, who are no more than 27 years of age.
Level of Study: Postgraduate.
Purpose: To recognise and help a young pianist whose approach to piano interpretation is of the same spirit that constantly inspired Clara Haskil and that she illustrated so perfectly.
Type: Prize.
No. of awards offered: 1.
Frequency: Every two years.
Value: CHF20,000.
Country of Study: Any country.
Closing Date: July of the Competition year.
Additional Information: The Competition is usually held during the last weeks of August. There is an entry fee of SwFr250.

COLOMBO PLAN

The Colombo Plan Bureau
12 Melbourne Avenue
PO Box 596, Colombo, 4, Sri Lanka
Tel: (94) 1 581813
Fax: (94) 1 580754
Email: cplan@slt.lk

Colombo Plan Scholarships, Fellowships and Training Awards

Subjects: Colombo Plan awards are usually, but not necessarily, restricted to areas of study that are of significant interest to developing countries.
Eligibility: A request for an award usually originates from a recipient developing country on the basis of its priority needs, and the donor country to which the request is directed may grant it if training facilities and resources in the requested field are available. In some cases, however, offers of training originate from the donor countries themselves. Individuals wishing to apply for Colombo Plan Scholarships must be sponsored by their own governments.
Level of Study: Postgraduate.
No. of awards offered: Varies.
Frequency: Annual.
Value: Varies.
Country of Study: Colombo Plan member countries.
Application Procedure: Candidates should apply to the Ministry in their home country. The Colombo Plan office does not handle applications.
Additional Information: Please contact the Colombo Plan office for further details on the application procedure.

COMMISSION OF THE EUROPEAN COMMUNITIES - DG XXII/A/2

Rue De La Loi 200, Brussels, B-1040, Belgium
Fax: (32) 2 299 4153
www: http://europa.eu.int/en/com/dg22/socrates/erasinf.html
Telex: comeu b 21877
Contact: Mr Massimo Gaudina, Administrator

This unit deals with the ERASMUS chapter of the Socrates programme. Its objectives are the development of the European dimension of higher education and the improvement of quality.

ERASMUS Grants

Subjects: Any field of studies.
Eligibility: Condition: Agreement between home and host university.
Level of Study: Postgraduate.
Purpose: The encourage the mobility of university and postgraduate students in Europe.
Type: Partial Fellowship.

No. of awards offered: Approx. 100,000.
Frequency: Annual.
Value: Varies.
Length of Study: 3-12 months.
Country of Study: European countries.
Application Procedure: Through the Home University (International Relation Office).
Closing Date: Varies.

COMMONWEALTH SCHOLARSHIP AND FELLOWSHIP PLAN

Commonwealth Scholarship Commission in the United Kingdom
c/o Association of Commonwealth Universities
John Foster House
36 Gordon Square, London, WC1H 0PF, England
Tel: (44) 171 387 8572
Fax: (44) 171 387 2655
Contact: Executive Secretary

Commonwealth Scholarships, Fellowships and Academic Staff Scholarships

Subjects: In general arts, social studies, pure science, technology, medicine (largely tenable in the UK), dentistry, agriculture, forestry and veterinary science.
Eligibility: Commonwealth Scholarships are open to Commonwealth citizens under 35 years of age who are normally resident in some part of the Commonwealth other than the particular awarding country. Scholarships are intended for young graduates of high intellectual promise who may be expected to make a significant contribution to their own countries on their return from postgraduate study overseas. Commonwealth Fellowships are intended for a few senior scholars of established reputation and achievement. The main emphasis is on awards to scholars in the academic (including technological) fields who play important roles in the life of their country.
Level of Study: Postgraduate.
Purpose: To enable Commonwealth students of high intellectual promise to pursue studies in Commonwealth countries other than their own so that on their return home they can make a distinctive contribution to life in their own countries and to mutual understanding in the Commonwealth.
Type: Scholarship, Fellowship.
No. of awards offered: 1,000+.
Frequency: Annual.
Value: Determined by each awarding country (ie. the country in which the award is tenable). Generally, the emoluments for scholarships include fares to and from the awarding country, payment of tuition fees, allowances for books, special clothing and local travel, and a personal maintenance allowance. In some countries a dependant's allowance is

paid. Visiting Fellows will receive fares to and from the awarding country, a per diem expenses allowance, medical and hospital services and an allowance for travel within the awarding country.
Length of Study: 1-3 academic years (scholarships), or from 3 months to 1 academic year (fellowships).
Study Establishment: Universities, colleges, other educational institutions.
Country of Study: Commonwealth countries.
Application Procedure: Applications for scholarships should be made to the appropriate scholarship agency in the candidate's country of normal residence. These agencies distribute prospectuses and application forms for the various awards and will, generally speaking, be the best local centres for information about the Plan. Academic Staff Scholarships and other awards for senior scholars are usually awarded by invitation only or through nomination by an individual's own university.
Closing Date: Varies according to the country in which the candidate applies; usually some 12-18 months before the period of study.
Additional Information: Award holders must undertake to return to their own countries on completion of their studies overseas.

For further information contact:

The Executive Director
IDP Education Australia
GPO Box 2006, Canberra, ACT, 2601, Australia
Tel: (61) 6 285 8200
Fax: (61) 6 285 3036
Contact: Contact for developed countries
or
Secretary
Australian International Development Assistance Bureau
GPO Box 887, Canberra, ACT, 2601, Australia
Contact: Contact for developing countries
or
Ministry of Education and Culture
PO Box N3913, Nassau, Bahamas
Tel: (1 809) 322 8140
Fax: (1 809) 322 84912
Contact: Permanent Secretary
or
Ministry of Education
Building No 6
17th and 18th Floors
Bangladesh Secretariat, Dhaka, 2, Bangladesh
Tel: (880) 2 232 356
Contact: Secretary
or
Ministry of Education
Jemmotts Lane, St Michael, Barbados
Tel: (1 809) 427 3272
Fax: (1 809) 436 2411
Contact: Permanent Secretary
or
Ministry of the Public Service, Belmopan, Belize
Tel: (501) 8 22204
Fax: (501) 8 22206
Contact: Permanent Secretary

or
Ministry of Education
PO Box HM1185, Hamilton, HM EX, Bermuda
Tel: (1 809) 236 6904
Fax: (1 809) 236 4006
Contact: Chief Education Officer

or
Bursaries Department
Ministry of Education
Private Bag 005, Gaborone, Botswana
Tel: (267) 312706
Fax: (267) 312891
Contact: First Secretary

or
Ministry of Health, Education and Welfare
Government of the British Virgin Islands, Road Town, Tortola
Island, British Virgin Islands
Tel: (1 809 49) 43701
Contact: Permanent Secretary

or
Ministry of Education
Bandar Seri Bagawan 1170, Brunei
Tel: (673) 2 44233
Fax: (673) 2 40250
Contact: Permanent Secretary

or
Cameroon Commonwealth Scholarship Agency
Ministry of Higher Education
Department of Student Assistance Academic and
Professional Guidance
PO Box 1457, Yaounde, Cameroon
Tel: (237) 23 10 01
Fax: (237) 23 97 241569

or
International Council for Canadian Studies
Commonwealth Scholarship Section
325 Dalhousie Street
Suite 800, Ottawa, ON, K1N 7G2, Canada
Tel: (1) 613 789 7828
Fax: (1) 613 789 7830
Contact: Grants Management Officer

or
Ministry of Foreign Affairs, Nicosia, Cyprus
Contact: The Permanent Secretary

or
Office of the Prime Minister
Establishment and Personnel Department
Government Headquarters
Kennedy Avenue, Roseau, Dominica
Tel: (1 767) 448 2401 ext 3274
Fax: (1 767) 448 5044
Contact: The Chief Establishment Officer

or
Commonwealth Scholarship Commission in the United
Kingdom
c/o Association of Commonwealth Universities
John Foster House
36 Gordon Square, London, WC1H 0PF, England
Tel: (44) 171 387 8572
Fax: (44) 171 387 2655
Contact: Executive Secretary

or
Falkland Islands Government Secretariat, Stanley, Falkland
Islands
Tel: (500) 27289
Fax: (500) 27292
Contact: The Government Secretary

or
Education
Science and Technology, Fiji
Tel: (679) 314477
Fax: (679) 303511
Contact: The Permanent Secretary

or
Ministry of Education
No 1 Bedford Place Building, Banjul, Gambia
Contact: Permanent Secretary

or
Scholarships Secretariat
PO Box M75, Accra, Ghana
Tel: (233) 21 662681
Contact: Registrar of Scholarships

or
Department of Education
40 Town Range, Gibraltar
Tel: (350) 71430
Fax: (350) 71564
Contact: Director

or
Department of Personnel and Management Services (DPMS)
Prime Minister's Ministry
Botanical Gardens, St George's, Grenada
Tel: (1 809) 440 3767
Fax: (1 809) 440 6609
Contact: Permanent Secretary

or
Public Service Ministry (Scholarships Administration Division)
Vlissengen Road and Durban Street, Kingston, Georgetown,
Guyana
Tel: (592) 68732
Fax: (592) 57899
Contact: Permanent Secretary

or
Ministry of Human Resource Development (Department of
Education)
External Scholarships Division
A1 W3
Curzon Road Barracks
Kasturba Gandhi Marg, New Delhi, 110001, India
Tel: (91) 11 384501
Fax: (91) 11 381355
Contact: Deputy Secretary

or
Cabinet Office
Efficiency and Reform Directorate
8th Floor Citibank Building
63-67 Knutsford Boulevard, Kingston, 5, Jamaica
Tel: (1 809) 929 8871
Fax: (1 809) 920 1291
Contact: Divisional Director

or
Ministry of Education
Jogoo House
Harambee Avenue
PO Box 30040, Nairobi, Kenya
Tel: (254) 334411
Fax: (254) 214287
Contact: Permanent Secretary
or
Ministry of Education, Science and Technology
PO Box 263, Bikenibeu Tarawa, Kiribati Islands
Tel: (686) 28091
Fax: (686) 28222
Contact: Secretary
or
National Manpower Development Secretariat
PO Box 517, Maseru, 100, Lesotho
Tel: (266) 323842
Contact: Director
or
Department of Human Resource Management
PO Box 30227, Lilongwe, 3, Malawi
Tel: (265) 782122
Fax: (265) 782230
Contact: Secretary for Personnel Management and Training
or
Public Services Department
Training and Career Development Division
2nd Level
Block B
JPA Complex
Tun Ismail Road, Kuala Lumpur, 50510, Malaysia
Contact: Director-General of Public Service
or
External Resources Section
Ministry of Foreign Affairs, Male, Maldives
Tel: (960) 317583
Fax: (960) 317592
Contact: Director of External Resources
or
Ministry of Education and Human Resources, Floriana, Malta
Tel: (356) 235489
Fax: (356) 221634
Contact: Assistant Director of Education
or
Ministry of Education and Science
2nd Floor
Sun Trust Building
Edith Cavell Street, Port Louis, Mauritius
Tel: (230) 208 7716
Fax: (230) 212 3783
Contact: Permanent Secretary
or
Ministry of Education and Culture
Bursaries and Scholarships Division
Private Bag 133391, Windhoek, Namibia
Tel: (264) 61 491 3314
Contact: The Permanent Secretary

or
Department of Education, Aiwo District, Nauru
Tel: (674) 44 43130
Fax: (674) 44 43718
Contact: Secretary for Health and Education
or
New Zealand Vice-Chancellors' Committee
PO Box 11-915
Manners Street, Wellington, New Zealand
Tel: (64) 802 5923
Fax: (64) 801 5089
Contact: Scholarships Officer
or
International Cooperation Wing
Ministry of Education, Islamabad, Pakistan
Tel: (92) 51920 1717
Contact: Deputy Educational Adviser (Scholarships)
or
Department of Personnel Management
PO Wards Strip, Waigani, National Capital District, Papua New Guinea
Contact: Secretary
or
Ministry of Foreign Affairs
PO Box L1861, Apia, Samoa (Western)
Tel: (685) 21500
Fax: (685) 21504
Contact: Secretary
or
Ministry od Education
Mont Fleuri
PO Box 48
Victoria, Mahé, Seychelles
Tel: (248) 24777
Fax: (248) 24859
Contact: The Principal's Secretary
or
Ministry of Education, Youth and Sports
New England, Freetown, Sierra Leone
Contact: The Chief Education Officer
or
Prime Minister's Office
Public Services Division
100 High Street
#07-01
The Treasury, 170434, Singapore
Tel: (65) 323 23900
Fax: (65) 323 23900
Contact: Permanent Secretary
or
The National Training Unit
Ministry of Education Human Resources Development
PO Box G28, Honiara, Solomon Islands
Fax: (677) 20485
Contact: The Chief Administrative Officer
or
International Relations
Department of Education
123 Schoeman Street, Pretoria, 0002, South Africa
Contact: Director

or
Ministry of Higher Education
18 Ward Place, Colombo, 7, Sri Lanka
Tel: (94) 1685 268
Contact: Secretary
or
Education Department, Jamestown, St Helena
Tel: (290) 290 2710
Fax: (290) 290 2461
Contact: Chief Education Officer
or
Ministry of Planning, Personnel, Establishment and Training
PO Box 974, Castries, St Lucia
Tel: (1 758) 452 1882
Fax: (1 758) 31305
Contact: Permanent Secretary
or
Ministry of Labour and Public Service
PO Box 170, Mbabane, Swaziland
Tel: (268) 43521
Fax: (268) 43380
Contact: Principal Secretary
or
Ministry of Science Technology and Higher Education
PO Box 2645, Dar-es-Salaam, Tanzania
Tel: (255) 51 112 805
Fax: (255) 51 44 244
Contact: Principal Secretary
or
Ministry of Education
PO Box 161, Nuku'alofa, Tonga
Tel: (676) 24 122
Fax: (676) 24 105
Contact: The Hon Minister
or
Scholarships and Advanced Training Section
ABMA Building
55-57 St Vincent Street, Port-of-Spain, Trinidad & Tobago
Tel: (1 809) 625 9964
Fax: (1 809) 624 2640
Contact: Chief Personnel Officer
or
Ministry of Social Services
Funafuti Island, Tuvalu
Contact: Education Division
or
The Central Scholarships Committee (CSC)
Ministry of Education and Sports
PO Box 7063, Kampala, Uganda
Tel: (256) 41 234440
Fax: (256) 41 230437
Contact: Permanent Secretary
or
Training and Scholarships Coordination Unit
Public Service Department
Private Mail Bag 059, Port Vila, Vanuatu
Tel: (678) 23708
Fax: (678) 25936
Contact: Principal Training and Scholarships Officer

or
Ministry of Education and Welfare
Grand Turk, Turks & Caicos Islands, West Indies
Tel: (1 809) 946 2580
Fax: (1 809) 946 2577
Contact: The Permanent Secretary
or
Training Division
The Secretariat
The Valley, Anguilla, West Indies
Tel: (1 809) 497 3522
Fax: (1 809) 497 5873
Contact: The Director
or
Establishment Division
Government Headquarters
Church Street, Basseterre, St Kitts & Nevis, West Indies
Tel: (1 809) 465 2521
Fax: (1 809) 465 5202
Contact: Permanent Secretary
or
Department of Education
PO Box 910
George Town, Grand Cayman, Cayman Islands, West Indies
Tel: (1 809) 945 1199
Fax: (1 809) 945 1457
Contact: Chief Education Officer
or
Services Commissions Department
Hlifax Street, Kingstown, St Vincent & The Grenadines, West Indies
Tel: (1 809) 456 1690
Fax: (1 809) 457 2638
Contact: Chief Personnel Officer
or
Department of Administration
Government Headquarters
PO Box 292, Plymouth, Montserrat, West Indies
Tel: (1 809) 491 3314
Fax: (1 809) 491 6234
Contact: Permanent Secretary
or
Ministry of Education, Culture and Youth Affairs
PO Box 1264
Church Street, St John's, Antigua & Barbuda, West Indies
Tel: (1 809) 462 4959
Fax: (1 809) 462 4970
Contact: The Permanent Secretary
or
Bursaries Committee
Ministry of Higher Education
PO Box 50093, Lusaka, Zambia
Tel: (260) 1 250726
Fax: (260) 1 254242
Contact: Secretary

or
Office of the President and Cabinet
Department of National Scholarships
PO Box UA 275
Union Avenue, Harare, Zimbabwe
Contact: Secretary

COMMONWEALTH SCHOLARSHIP COMMISSION IN THE UNITED KINGDOM

c/o Association of Commonwealth Universities
John Foster House
36 Gordon Square, London, WC1H 0PF, England
Tel: (44) 171 387 8572
Fax: (44) 171 387 2655
Contact: Ms Mary C Denyer, Awards Administrator

Commonwealth Academic Staff Scholarships

Subjects: All subjects.
Eligibility: Open to Commonwealth citizens or British protected persons permanently resident in a developing country of the Commonwealth, who should hold, or be about to obtain, a degree or an equivalent qualification, and should already hold a teaching appointment in a university or similar institution or have the assurance of such an appointment on his or her return. Candidates should be under 42 years of age at the time the award is taken up. All candidates must have sufficient competence in English to profit from the proposed study. These awards are not given to Indian nationals.
Level of Study: Postgraduate.
Purpose: To help universities in the developing countries of the Commonwealth build up the numbers and enhance the experience of their locally born staff. The scholarships are intended to enable promising staff members from universities and similar institutions in the developing Commonwealth to obtain experience in a university or other appropriate institution in the UK.
Type: Scholarship.
No. of awards offered: 45-50.
Frequency: Annual.
Value: To cover cost of return air fare to the UK, approved tuition, laboratory and examination fees, personal maintenance allowance at the rate of £493 per month or £592 a month for those studying at institutions in the London Metropolitan area, grant for books and equipment, and grant towards the expense of preparing a thesis or dissertation, where applicable, grant for approved travel within the UK, an initial clothing allowance in special cases, and in certain circumstances a marriage and child allowance. The emoluments are not subject to UK income tax.
Length of Study: 1-3 years.
Study Establishment: A university or comparable institution.
Country of Study: United Kingdom.

Application Procedure: Candidates must be nominated by one of the following: the vice-chancellor of a UK university, the vice-chancellor of the university on whose permanent staff the applicant serves or is to serve, (heads of Bangladeshi universities should send their nominations to the University Grants Commission in Dhaka); the Commonwealth Scholarship agency in the candidate's own country (for addresses, see the entry for the Commonwealth Scholarship and Fellowship Plan); in special cases, the head of an autonomous non-university institution in the Commonwealth, or the vice-chancellor of a UK university.
Closing Date: December 31st.
Additional Information: Scholars are required to sign an undertaking to return to resume their academic post in their own country on completion of the scholarships.

Commonwealth Fellowships

Subjects: All subjects.
Eligibility: Open to Commonwealth citizens and to British protected persons permanently resident in a developing Commonwealth country. Preference is given to candidates between 28 and 50 years of age. Candidates must have completed a Doctoral degree more than five but not more than ten years ago, and should have had at least two years' experience as a staff member of a university or similar institution in their own country.
Level of Study: Postdoctorate.
Purpose: To help universities in the developing countries of the Commonwealth build up the numbers and enhance the experience of their locally born staff. The fellowships are intended to enable promising staff members from universities and similar institutions in the developing Commonwealth to obtain experience in a university or other appropriate institution in the UK.
Type: Fellowship.
No. of awards offered: Approx. 50.
Frequency: Annual.
Value: £705 per month or £846 for those studying at institutions in the London Metropolitan area (reviewed annually) plus approved air fares to and from the UK and in certain circumstances a marriage and child allowance. A grant for approved travel within the UK and a book grant are also paid and, where recommended, an initial clothing allowance is offered. The emoluments are not subject to UK income tax.
Length of Study: 6 or 12 months.
Study Establishment: A university or comparable institution.
Country of Study: United Kingdom.
Closing Date: December 31st.
Additional Information: Fellows are required to sign an undertaking to return to resume their academic post in their country on completion of the Fellowships. Candidates must be nominated by one of the following: the vice-chancellor of a UK university, the vice-chancellor of the university on whose permanent staff the applicant serves or is to serve (heads of Indian universities should send their nominations to the University Grants Commission in New Delhi and heads of Bangladeshi universities to the University Grants Commission in Dhaka); the Commonwealth Scholarship agency in the candidate's own country (for addresses, see the entry for the

Commonwealth Scholarship and Fellowship Plan); in special cases, the head of an autonomous non-university institution in the Commonwealth, or the vice-chancellor of a UK university. The Fellowship may not be held concurrently with other awards or with paid employment.

CONCORDIA UNIVERSITY

1455 de Maisonneuve Boulevard West, Montreal, PQ, H3G 1M8, Canada
Tel: (1) 514 848 3801
Fax: (1) 514 848 2812
Email: awardsgs@vax2.concordia.ca
www: http://www.concordia.ca/
Contact: Graduate Studies Office

Concordia University is the result of the 1974 merger between Sir George Williams University and Loyola College. The University incorporates superior teaching methods with an inter-disciplinary approach to learning and is dedicated to offering the best possible scholarship to the student body and to promoting research beneficial to society.

Concordia University Graduate Fellowships

Subjects: All subjects.
Eligibility: Open to graduates of any nationality.
Level of Study: Doctorate, Postgraduate.
Type: Fellowship.
No. of awards offered: Varies.
Frequency: Annual.
Value: C$2,900 per term for Master's level; C$3,600 per term for doctoral level.
Length of Study: A maximum of 4 terms at the Master's level and 9 terms at the doctoral level, calculated from the date of entry in the program.
Study Establishment: Concordia University.
Country of Study: Canada.
Application Procedure: Completed application form, three letters of recommendation and official transcripts of all university studies must be received by the closing date.
Closing Date: February 1st.
Additional Information: Academic merit is the prime consideration in the granting of the award. Awarded for full-time graduate studies.

David J Azrieli Graduate Fellowship

Subjects: Any subject.
Eligibility: Open to Master's or doctoral students of any nationality. Candidates must not have completed more than two terms of their Master's programme or four terms of their Doctoral programmes at Concordia at the time of the application.
Level of Study: Doctorate, Postgraduate.
Type: Fellowship.
No. of awards offered: 1.
Frequency: Annual.
Value: C$15,000 per year.

Length of Study: 1 year; not renewable.
Study Establishment: Concordia University.
Country of Study: Canada.
Application Procedure: Completed application form, three letters of recommendation and official transcripts of all university studies must be received by the closing date.
Closing Date: February 1st.
Additional Information: Academic merit is the prime consideration in the granting of the award which is for full-time study in a graduate programme leading to a Master's or doctoral degree.

J W McConnell Memorial Fellowships

Subjects: All subjects.
Eligibility: Open to Canadian citizens and permanent residents. Financial need is one of the criteria. Academic excellence is of prime consideration.
Level of Study: Doctorate, Postgraduate.
Type: Fellowship.
No. of awards offered: Varies.
Frequency: Annual.
Value: C$2,900 per term at the Master's level; C$3,600 per term at the doctoral level.
Length of Study: A maximum of 4 terms at the Master's level and 9 terms at the doctoral level, calculated from the date of entry in the programme.
Study Establishment: Concordia University.
Country of Study: Canada.
Application Procedure: Application form, three letters of recommendation and official transcripts of all university studies must be submitted by the closing date.
Closing Date: February 1st.
Additional Information: Academic merit is the prime consideration in the granting of the awards.

John W O'Brien Graduate Fellowship

Subjects: Arts and humanities, business administration and management, education and teacher training, engineering, fine and applied arts, mass communication and information, mathematics and computer science, natural sciences, religion and theology.
Eligibility: Open to full-time graduate students of any nationality. Candidates must not have completed more than two terms of Master's study or four terms of doctoral study at Concordia, at the time of application.
Level of Study: Doctorate, Postgraduate.
Purpose: Awarded to applicants in full-time study towards a Master's or doctoral degree.
Type: Fellowship.
No. of awards offered: 1.
Frequency: Annual.
Value: C$3,300 per term at the Master's level and C$4,000 per term at the doctoral level.
Length of Study: A maximum of 3 terms.
Study Establishment: Concordia University.

Country of Study: Canada.
Application Procedure: Application form, three letters of recommendation and official transcripts of all university studies must be submitted by the closing date.
Closing Date: February 1st.
Additional Information: Academic merit is the prime consideration in the granting of awards which are for full-time study in a graduate programme leading to a Master's or doctoral degree.

Stanley G French Graduate Fellowship

Subjects: All subjects.
Eligibility: Open to graduates of any nationality. Candidates must not have completed more than two terms of a Master's programme or four terms of a doctoral programme at Concordia, at the time of application.
Level of Study: Doctorate, Postgraduate.
Type: Fellowship.
No. of awards offered: 1.
Frequency: Annual.
Value: C$3,300 per term for Master's level; C$4,000 per term for doctoral level.
Length of Study: A maximum of 3 terms.
Study Establishment: Concordia University.
Country of Study: Canada.
Application Procedure: Completed application form, three letters of recommendation and official transcripts of all university studies must be submitted by the closing date.
Closing Date: February 1st.
Additional Information: Academic merit is the prime consideration in the granting of awards, which are for full-time study in a graduate programme leading to a Master's or doctoral degree.

CONCOURS INTERNATIONAL DE CHANT DE PARIS

8 rue du Dome, Paris, F-75116, France
Tel: (33) 1 47 04 76 38
Fax: (33) 1 47 27 35 03
Email: ufam@wanadoo.fr
www: http://www.infoservice.fr/ufam
Contact: Ms Christiane de Bayser, Presidente

Grand Prix Opera and Grand Prix Paul Derenne

Subjects: Music.
Level of Study: Postgraduate.
Type: Competition.
No. of awards offered: 8.
Frequency: Every two years.
Country of Study: Any country.
Application Procedure: A brochure is available on request.
Closing Date: May.

COOPER-HEWITT NATIONAL DESIGN MUSEUM

2 E 91st Street, New York, NY, 10128-9990, United States of America
Tel: (1) 212 849 8404
Fax: (1) 212 849 8401
www: http://www.si.edu/ndm/
Contact: Ms Catherine Sylte, Administration Assistant

Cooper-Hewitt National Design Museum seeks to enrich the lives of all people by exploring the creation and consequences of the designed environment.

Peter Krueger-Christie's Fellowship

Subjects: Drawing and prints, textiles, Western European & American decorative arts & design, wallcoverings, contemporary design, architecture.
Eligibility: Applicants must hold a Master's degree in a field related to decorative arts and design or art history. It is not required that he or she be a doctoral candidate.
Level of Study: Postgraduate, Professional development.
Purpose: To provide a young scholar with the opportunity to pursue in-depth research in historic or contemporary design or various related fields that complement the interests and resources of the Cooper-Hewitt National Design Museum.
Type: Fellowship.
No. of awards offered: 1.
Frequency: Annual.
Value: US$18,000 for the academic year and an allowance of 2,000 for research-related travel.
Length of Study: 1 year.
Study Establishment: Cooper-Hewitt National Design Museum.
Country of Study: USA.
Application Procedure: Application form must be completed and submitted with a detailed work plan, official transcripts, résumé, synopsis of the Master's thesis, and three letters of reference.
Closing Date: April 30th.

CORNELL UNIVERSITY

Center for the Humanities
Andrew D White House
27 East Avenue, Ithaca, NY, 14853-1101, United States of America
Tel: (1) 607 255 9274
Email: homctr-mailbox@cornell.edu
www: http://www.arts.cornell.edu/sochum/
Contact: Ms Lisa Patti, Program Administrator

Cornell is a learning community that seeks to serve society by educating the leaders of the future and extending the frontiers of knowledge. The University aims to pursue understanding beyond the limitations of existing knowledge, ideology and disciplinary structure and to affirm the value of the cultivation and enrichment of the human mind to individuals and society.

Mellon Postdoctoral Fellowships

Subjects: Arts and humanities.
Eligibility: Open to US and Canadian citizens and permanent residents who have completed requirements for the PhD within the last four or five years and before application deadline.
Level of Study: Postdoctorate.
Type: Fellowship.
No. of awards offered: 3-4.
Frequency: Annual.
Value: US$30,000.
Length of Study: 9 months (1 academic year).
Study Establishment: Cornell University.
Country of Study: USA.
Closing Date: Postmark January 4th.
Additional Information: While in residence at Cornell, postdoctoral fellows have department affiliation, limited teaching duties, and the opportunity for scholarly work. Areas of specialisation change each year.

Society for the Humanities Postdoctoral Fellowships

Subjects: Humanities.
Eligibility: Open to holders of the PhD degree who have at least one or two years of teaching experience at the college level. Applicants should be scholars with interests that are not confined to a narrow humanistic speciality and whose research coincides with the focal theme for the year. Fellows of the Society devote most of their time to research writing, but they are encouraged to offer a weekly seminar related to their special projects.
Level of Study: Postdoctorate.
Type: Fellowship.
No. of awards offered: 8-10.
Frequency: Annual.
Value: US$32,000.
Length of Study: 1 academic year.
Study Establishment: Cornell University.
Country of Study: USA.
Application Procedure: Applicants must contact this office to receive information on the theme and application materials.
Closing Date: Postmark on or before October 21st.
Additional Information: Information about this year's theme is available upon request.

THE CORPORATION OF YADDO

Box 395, Saratoga Springs, NY, 12866, United States of America
Tel: (1) 518 584 0746
Fax: (1) 518 584 1312
Email: yaddo@yaddo.org
Contact: Ms Lesley M Leduc, Program Co-ordinator

Yaddo is an artists' community located on a 400-estate in Saratoga Springs, New York. Its mission is to nurture the creative process by providing an opportunity for artists to work without interruption in a supportive environment. Yaddo awards approximately 200 residences per year of two weeks to two months.

Yaddo Residency

Subjects: Writing, photography, drawing, sculpture, music and drama, choreography, film, painting, performance art, printmaking and video.
Eligibility: Open to all who have achieved some professional standing by having work published, exhibited, or performed. Applications are welcomed from artists from the USA and abroad. Open to visual artists, writers, composers, and artists working in film/video, choreography, performance art.
Level of Study: Professional development.
Purpose: To provide uninterrupted time and space for creative artists to think, experiment and create.
Type: Residency.
No. of awards offered: Approx. 200.
Frequency: Annual.
Value: Room, board and studio space. No stipend.
Length of Study: From 2 weeks to 2 months.
Study Establishment: Yaddo.
Country of Study: USA.
Application Procedure: Send a SASE (US55 cents) to Corporation of Yaddo, Admissions Department. Requirements include: completed application form, letters from two sponsors, copies of professional résumé, work samples, and US$20 application fee.
Closing Date: January 15th, August 1st.

THE COSTUME SOCIETY OF AMERICA (CSA)

55 Edgewater Drive
PO Box 73, Earleville, MD, 21919, United States of America
Tel: (1) 410 275 1619
Fax: (1) 410 275 8936
Email: kboyer@dmv.net
www: http://www.costumesocietyamerica.com
Contact: Grants Management Officer

The Costume Society of America advances the global understanding of all aspects of dress and appearance. The Society seeks as members those who are involved in the study, education, collection, preservation, presentation and interpretation of dress and appearance in past, present, and future societies.

Adele Filene Travel Award

Subjects: Cultural heritage, museum studies and related areas.
Eligibility: Open to currently enrolled students with CSA membership who have been accepted for presentation of a juried paper or poster at the national symposium.
Level of Study: Unrestricted.

Purpose: To assist CSA members currently enrolled as students in their travel to CSA national symposia to present either a juried paper or a poster.
Type: Travel Grant.
No. of awards offered: 1-3.
Frequency: Annual.
Value: Up to US$500.
Country of Study: USA.
Application Procedure: Please send three letters of support with the following: a copy of the juried abstract and a one-page letter of application.
Closing Date: Applications are accepted at any time.

CSA Travel Research Grant

Subjects: Textile and fashion design, museum studies, and related areas.
Eligibility: Applicants must be current CSA members, and have held membership for two years or more. They must give proof of work in progress, and indicate why the particular collection is important to the project.
Level of Study: Professional development.
Purpose: To aid any individual non-student CSA member in travelling to collections for research purposes.
Type: Research Grant.
No. of awards offered: Varies.
Frequency: Annual.
Value: US$500.
Country of Study: Any country.
Application Procedure: Please send a letter of application (two page limit) and include: name of collection and projected date of visit; a description of the project underway; evidence of work accomplished to date; reasons for visiting the designated collection; projected completion date of project; what audience the project will be directed to; and current CV.
Closing Date: September 1st.

Stella Blum Research Grant

Subjects: North American costume.
Eligibility: Open to students who are matriculating in a degree programme at an accredited institution and who are members of the Society.
Level of Study: Unrestricted.
Purpose: To assist students with research expenses.
Type: Grant.
No. of awards offered: 1.
Frequency: Annual.
Value: Up to US$3,000. Allowable costs include: transportation to and from the research site; living expenses at the research site; supplies such as film, photographic reproductions, books, paper, computer disks; postage and telephone; services such as typing, computer searches, graphics.
Study Establishment: An accredited institution.
Country of Study: USA.
Application Procedure: Applicants must complete an application form; these are available upon request.
Closing Date: February 1st.
Additional Information: The award will be given based on merit rather than need. Judging criteria will include: creativity

and innovation, specific awareness of and attention to costume matters, impact on the broad field of costume, awareness of interdisciplinarity of the field, ability to successfully implement the proposed project in a timely manner, and faculty advisor recommendation.

COUNCIL FOR BRITISH ARCHAEOLOGY (CBA)

Bowes Morrell House
111 Walmgate, York, YO1 9WA, England
Tel: (44) 1904 671417
Fax: (44) 1904 671384
Email: 100271.456@compuserve.com
www: http://www.britarch.ac.uk
Contact: Finance Officer

The Council for British Archaeology has been campaigning for the better care of Britain's archaeology for over fifty years. It works to improve awareness and enjoyment of archaeology for the benefit of all. It is the leading point of contact for information about the UK's historic environment.

British Archaeological Research Trust Grants

Subjects: Archaeology.
Eligibility: Open to UK residents; academic qualifications are not required.
Level of Study: Unrestricted.
Purpose: To support personal archaeological research, particularly that which is innovative and extends the range of techniques available to archaeologists.
Type: Research Grant.
No. of awards offered: 2-6.
Frequency: Annual.
Value: Up to £1,000.
Study Establishment: An approved location.
Country of Study: United Kingdom.
Closing Date: June 30th.
Additional Information: Grants may be held concurrently with other income.

CBA Grant for Publication

Subjects: British archaeology.
Eligibility: Open to all institutional or individual members of the council, except those already in receipt of a direct government grant.
Level of Study: Unrestricted.
Purpose: To finance archaeological publication which contributes significantly to research on problems of national or special regional significance.
Type: Grant.
No. of awards offered: 10-15.
Frequency: Three times each year.
Value: Usually no more than £1,000 (average £400).
Country of Study: United Kingdom.
Application Procedure: Please write for application form.

Closing Date: April 1st, July 1st, December 1st.
Additional Information: No grant will be made for the publication of records or of publications based exclusively on records, or for the publication of excavation reports where the excavation has been financed by government agencies. Grants will not normally be given to finance other than final excavation reports.

Council for British Archaeology Challenge Funding

Subjects: Archaeology.
Eligibility: Open to UK residents; academic qualifications are not required.
Level of Study: Unrestricted.
Purpose: To encourage voluntary effort in making original contributions to the study and care of Britain's historic environment.
Type: Research Grant.
No. of awards offered: Varies.
Frequency: Varies.
Value: Varies.
Country of Study: United Kingdom.
Application Procedure: Applicants are required to submit a project outline.
Closing Date: Varies.

THE COUNCIL FOR BRITISH RESEARCH IN THE LEVANT

29 The Walk, Southport, Lancashire, PR8 4BG, England
Tel: (44) 1704 569664
Fax: (44) 1704 569664
Email: cm@biaahuk.demon.co.uk
www: http://www.edesign.demon.co.uk/cbrl.htm
Contact: Ms Caroline Middleton, The Secretary

The Council for British Research in the Levant is the new body for humanities research in Cyprus, Israel, Jordan, Lebanon, Palestine and Syria.

Research Grant

Subjects: Archaeology and other social sciences subjects, for example, economics, geography, historical studies, legal studies, languages and literature, linguistics, music, philosophy, politics, social anthropology, sociology and theology/religious studies.
Eligibility: No restrictions.
Level of Study: Unrestricted.
Purpose: To support research projects from initial exploratory work through to publication.
Type: Research Grant.
No. of awards offered: Varies.
Frequency: Annual.
Value: Up to £16,000.
Study Establishment: Council for British research in the Levant.

Country of Study: Cyprus, Israel, Jordan, Lebanon, Palestine and Syria.
Application Procedure: An application form must be completed. It is available from the UK Secretary at the main address.
Closing Date: November 1st.

Travel Grant

Subjects: Subjects covered include archaeology and other social sciences subjects, for example, economics, geography, historical studies, legal studies, languages and literature, linguistics, music, philosophy, politics, social anthropology, sociology and theology/religious studies.
Eligibility: No restrictions.
Level of Study: Unrestricted.
Purpose: To cover the travel and subsistence costs of students and academics and researchers undertaking reconnaissance tours or smaller research projects in the countries of the Levant.
Type: Travel Grant.
No. of awards offered: Varies.
Frequency: Annual.
Value: Usually under £800.
Study Establishment: Council for British Research in the Levant.
Country of Study: Cyprus, Israel, Jordan, Lebanon, Palestine and Syria.
Application Procedure: Application form available from the UK Secretary at the main address.
Closing Date: November 1st.

COUNCIL FOR INTERNATIONAL EXCHANGE OF SCHOLARS (CIES)

3007 Tilden Street NW
Suite 5L, Washington, DC, 20008-3009, United States of America
Tel: (1) 202 686 8664
Fax: (1) 202 362 3442
Email: appreguest@cies.iie.org
www: http://www.cies.org/
Contact: Mr Janel Showalter, Publications Officer

The Council for International Exchange of Scholars (CIES) is a private, non-profit organisation that facilitates international exchanges in higher education. Under a co-operative agreement with the US information agency, it assists in the administration of the Fulbright Scholar Program. CIES is affiliated with the institute of international education.

Fulbright Scholar Awards for Research and Lecturing Abroad

Subjects: All academic disciplines and some professional fields.
Eligibility: Open to US citizens with a PhD or comparable professional qualifications. University or college teaching

experience is normally expected for lecturing awards. For selected assignments, proficiency in a foreign language may be required.

Level of Study: Postdoctorate.

Purpose: To increase mutual understanding between the people of the USA and the people of other nations, strengthen the ties that unite the USA with other nations, and promote international co-operation for educational and cultural advancement.

Type: Research and/or lecturing.

No. of awards offered: 700+.

Frequency: Annual.

Value: Varies by country.

Length of Study: From 2 months to 1 academic year.

Country of Study: Any country.

Application Procedure: Applications are available from CIES.

Closing Date: August 1st.

Additional Information: Individual countries' programs are described in the Council's publication.

THE COUNTESS OF MUNSTER MUSICAL TRUST

Wormley Hill, Godalming, Surrey, GU8 5SG, England
Tel: (44) 1428 685427
Fax: (44) 1428 685064
Email: munstertrust@compuserve.com
Contact: The Secretary

The Trust provides financial assistance towards the cost of studies or maintenance of outstanding postgraduate students who merit further training at home or abroad. Each year the Trust is able to offer a small number of interest-free loans for instrument purchase.

The Countess of Munster Musical Trust Awards

Subjects: Musical studies.

Eligibility: Open to UK or British Commonwealth citizens, who are over 18 years of age and under 25 years of age for instrumentalists and composers, or under 27 years of age for female singers and under 28 for male singers, who show outstanding musical ability and potential. Conductors are not considered.

Level of Study: Doctorate, Postgraduate, Professional development.

Purpose: To enable students, selected after interview and audition, to pursue a course of specialist or advanced studies.

Type: Grant.

No. of awards offered: Unlimited, but normally no more than 100 each year.

Frequency: Annual.

Value: By individual assessment to meet tuition fees and maintenance according to need (£500-£5,000).

Length of Study: 1 year, with the possibility of renewal.

Country of Study: Any country.

Application Procedure: Application form must be completed and submitted between November 1st and January 31st for awards to be applied for from the following September.

Closing Date: January 31st.

Additional Information: Awards are made to selected applicants following audition and interview.

THE CROSS TRUST

PO Box 17
25 South Methven Street, Perth, PH1 5ES, Scotland
Tel: (44) 1738 620451
Fax: (44) 1738 631155
Contact: Mrs Barbara Anderson, Assistant Secretary

The Cross Trust

Subjects: Any approved subject.

Eligibility: Open to graduates or undergraduates of Scottish universities or of Central Institutions in Scotland and to Scottish secondary school pupils. Applicants must be of Scottish birth or parentage.

Level of Study: Postgraduate, Undergraduate.

Purpose: To enable young Scottish people to extend the boundaries of human life and to allow travel to extend experience, or encourage performance and participation in drama or opera. The Trust may support the pursuit of studies or research.

No. of awards offered: Varies.

Frequency: Varies.

Value: Varies.

Study Establishment: Anywhere as approved.

Country of Study: Any country.

Application Procedure: Application form must be completed.

Closing Date: No closing date.

Additional Information: Awards will only be considered from postgraduate students who have part funding in place from another organisation.

DATATEL SCHOLARS FOUNDATION

4375 Fair Lakes Court, Fairfax, VA, 22033, United States of America
Tel: (1) 703 968 9000
Fax: (1) 703 968 4573
Email: scholars@datatel.com
Contact: The Awards Committee

Datatel Scholars Foundation Scholarship

Subjects: All subjects.

Eligibility: Open to students attending a higher learning institution selected from Datatel, Inc.'s more than 450 college, university and non-profit client sites. USA or Canadian citizenship is not required.

Level of Study: Doctorate, Postgraduate, Undergraduate.

Purpose: To award scholarships to eligible students to attend a higher learning institution selected from Datatel's college and client sites.

Type: Scholarship.

No. of awards offered: Determined annually.

Frequency: Annual.

Value: US$700 to US$2,000 depending on tuition amount.

Length of Study: 1 year.

Study Establishment: Datatel client site institution.

Country of Study: USA or Canada.

Application Procedure: Applications must be completed and forwarded by the institution's Office of Financial Aid. The Foundation does not accept applications directly from students.

Closing Date: February 15th.

Additional Information: If requesting applications from the Foundation, please mention the name of your college or university so it can determine if the institution qualifies.

THE DENMARK-AMERICA FOUNDATION

Fiolstraede 24
3rd Floor, Copenhagen, DK-1171, Denmark
Tel: (45) 33 12 83 23
Fax: (45) 33325323
Email: fulbdk@unidhp.uni-c.dk
Contact: Ms Marie Monsted, Executive Director

The Denmark-America Foundation was founded in 1914 as a private Foundation, and today its work remains based on donations from Danish firms, foundations and individuals. The Foundation offers scholarships for studies in the USA at the graduate and postgraduate university level and has a trainee programme.

Denmark-America Foundation Grants

Subjects: All subjects.

Eligibility: Open to Danes only.

Level of Study: Doctorate, Postdoctorate, Postgraduate, Professional development.

Purpose: To further understanding between Denmark and the USA.

Type: Bursary.

No. of awards offered: Varies.

Frequency: Twice a year.

Value: Varies.

Length of Study: Between 3 months and 1 year.

Country of Study: USA.

Application Procedure: Special application form must be completed - please contact the Secretariat.

Closing Date: To be announced.

DEPARTMENT OF EDUCATION & SCIENCE (IRELAND)

Floor 1J
Block 4
Irish Life Centre
Talbot Street, Dublin, 1, Ireland
Tel: (353) 1 873 4700
Fax: (353) 1 872 9293
Contact: Ms Rita Frawley

Department of Education and Science (Ireland) Exchange Scholarships and Postgraduate Scholarships Exchange Scheme

Subjects: All subjects.

Eligibility: Open to Australian, Austrian, Belgian, Chinese, Finnish, German, Greek, Italian, Japanese, Netherlands, Norwegian, Russian Federation, Spanish and Swiss nationals, who are university graduates or advanced undergraduates who have completed at least three years of academic study. A good knowledge of English and/or Irish is necessary, depending on the course taken.

Level of Study: Postgraduate.

Purpose: To assist students to pursue study or research in Ireland.

Type: Scholarship.

No. of awards offered: 30.

Frequency: Annual.

Value: IR£3,144.

Length of Study: 8 months.

Study Establishment: An Irish university: University College Dublin, University College Cork, University College Galway, Trinity College Dublin, Dublin City University, University of Limerick, St Patrick's College Maynooth, or other similar institution of higher learning.

Country of Study: Ireland.

Application Procedure: Candidates should apply to the appropriate institution in their home country, as follows: Austria - the Federal Ministry for Science and Research, Vienna; Australia - the Ministry of Education, Canberra; Belgium - the Ministry of Education for the Flemish Community, Brussels; China - the Ministries of Foreign Affairs and Education, Beijing; Finland - Finnish Centre for International Mobility (CIMO), Helsinki; France - the Foreign Ministry, Paris; Germany - the German Academic Exchange Board (Deutscher Akademischer Austauschdienst-DAAD), Bonn; Greece - the Ministries of Foreign Affairs and Education, Athens; Italy - the Ministry of Foreign Affairs, Rome; Japan - the Ministries of Foreign Affairs and Education, Tokyo; Netherlands - Netherlands Organisation for International Co-operation in Higher Education (NUFFIC), The Hague; Norway - the Ministry of Foreign Affairs, Office of Cultural Relations, Oslo; Russian Federation - the Ministry of Education of the Russian Federation; Spain - the Ministry of Foreign Affairs, Madrid; Switzerland - Swiss University

Authorities, Berne. Five scholarships are offered to students from the United Kingdom to pursue postgraduate studies in Ireland. The value of each scholarship is £6,000. Applications should be made to the Irish Embassy, London.
Closing Date: April 30th.

DoE (Ireland) Summer School Exchange Scholarships

Subjects: All subjects.
Eligibility: Open to Belgian, French, Finnish, German, Hungarian, Italian, Netherlands, Russian Federation and Spanish nationals who are university graduates or advanced undergraduates. A good knowledge of English and/or Irish is necessary, depending on the course taken.
Level of Study: Postgraduate.
Purpose: To assist European students to attend a summer school in Ireland.
Type: Scholarship.
No. of awards offered: 33.
Frequency: Annual.
Value: IR£720 Exception - IR£950 for Hungarian and Russian Federation nationals.
Length of Study: From 2 weeks to 1 month.
Study Establishment: Summer schools at University College Dublin, University College Galway or University College Cork.
Country of Study: Ireland.
Application Procedure: Candidates should apply to the appropriate institution in their home country, as follows: Belgium - the Ministry of Education for the Flemish Community, Brussels; France - the Foreign Ministry, Paris; Finland - Finnish Centre for International Mobility (CIMO), Helsinki; Germany - the German Academic Exchange Board (Deutscher Akademischer Austauschdienst-DAAD), Bonn; Hungary - the Ministry of Culture and Education, Budapest; Italy - the Ministry of Foreign Affairs, Rome; Netherlands - Netherlands Organisation for International Co-operation in Higher Education (NUFFIC), The Hague; Russian Federation - the Ministry of Education of the Russian Federation; Spain - the Ministry of Foreign Affairs, Madrid.
Closing Date: April 30th.

Irish Government Scholarship

Subjects: All subjects.
Eligibility: Open to Australian postgraduate students. The scholar is required to return to Australia on the completion of the scholarship programme or on the completion of further studies leading on from the initial scholarship programme.
Level of Study: Postgraduate.
Type: Scholarship.
No. of awards offered: 1.
Frequency: Annual.
Value: IR£3,144 payable in 8 monthly instalments, plus university or college registration and tuition fees.
Length of Study: 1 academic year.
Study Establishment: University or institute of higher learning.

Country of Study: Ireland.
Application Procedure: Please write to the Grants Management Officer at the Embassy for details.
Closing Date: March.

For further information contact:

Embassy of Ireland
20 Arkana Street, Yarralumla, ACT, 2600, Australia
Tel: (61) 6 273 3022
Fax: (61) 6 273 3741

DEPARTMENT OF EDUCATION FOR NORTHERN IRELAND (DENI)

Student Support Branch
Rathgael House
Balloo Road, Bangor, Co Down, BT19 7PR, Northern Ireland
Tel: (44) 1247 279 414
Fax: (44) 1247 279 100
Contact: Mrs Margaret Cardwell

DENI offers research and advanced course studentships to provide for the payment of approved fees and the maintenance of students whilst being trained in methods of research and undertaking approved postgraduate courses of instruction.

DENI Postgraduate Studentships and Bursaries for Study in Northern Ireland

Subjects: Science and technology, social sciences and humanities.
Eligibility: Studentships and bursaries in universities in Northern Ireland are open to UK and EU residents only. Applicants for studentships must have at least an upper second class degree. Bursaries are open to UK residents who must be ordinarily resident in Northern Ireland on the date of the application for an award and hold a university degree or qualification regarded by the department as equivalent to a degree.
Level of Study: Postgraduate.
Purpose: To provide students ordinarily resident in the United Kindgom with assistance for bursaries similar to those given by the British Academy, the Engineering and Physical Sciences Council, the Economic and Social Research Council and the Natural Environment Research Council for attendance at courses in Northern Ireland.
Type: Studentships and Bursaries.
No. of awards offered: Varies, but is proportional to the number available in the rest of the UK.
Frequency: Annual.
Value: In line with the other UK awarding bodies.
Length of Study: Varies.

Study Establishment: Appropriate institutions in Northern Ireland.

Country of Study: Northern Ireland.

Application Procedure: Application form must be completed and can be obtained from universities in Northern Ireland.

Closing Date: determined by the institution concerned.

Additional Information: Please contact Mrs Cardwell for further details.

DEPARTMENT OF EMPLOYMENT, EDUCATION, TRAINING & YOUTH AFFAIRS

Research Grants & Training Section
Loc 731
GPO Box 9880, Canberra, ACT, 2601, Australia
Tel: (61) 6 240 8653
Fax: (61) 6 240 9781
Email: rbfellow@deetya.gov.au
www:
http://www.deetya.gov.au/divisions/hed/research/research.htm
Contact: The Director

The Department of Employment, Education, Training and Youth Affairs is a Ministry within the Australian Government, which works together with the Australian Research Council, and other agencies such as the Higher Education Contribution Scheme and the National Board of Employment, Education and Training on providing employment and training schemes.

Overseas Postgraduate Research Scholarships (OPRS)

Subjects: All subjects.

Eligibility: Applicants cannot be considered if they have commenced a course of study at any university at the same level for which the scholarship is oughjt.

Level of Study: Doctorate, Postgraduate.

Purpose: To assist study leading to the dehree of PhD or to a masters research degree.

Type: Scholarship.

No. of awards offered: Varies.

Value: The scholarship covers the course fee and is awarded.

Length of Study: 3 years in the first instance.

Country of Study: Australia.

Application Procedure: Please write for details.

Closing Date: August 30th.

Additional Information: Awarded to varying organisations, The Australian National University being one of them.

DEPARTMENT OF INDIAN AND NORTHERN AFFAIRS

Room 1902
North Tower
Les Terrasses de la Chaudière, Ottawa, ON, K1A 0H4, Canada
Tel: (1) 819 997 8396
Fax: (1) 819 994 0443
www: http://www.inac.gc.ca
Contact: Indian Programming & Funding Allocations Director

Inuit Cultural Grants Program

Subjects: Inuit literature, music and art, cross-cultural crafts and cultural exchange.

Eligibility: Open to Canadian Inuit whose application meets the purpose of the programme. Grants are made to Inuit individuals and organisations only. Applicants, wherever possible, should have the support of a community organisation. Applicants are encouraged to seek financing for their projects from other appropriate sources in addition to the Cultural Grants Program. Grants are made available on a one time basis only and are not intended to provide direct on going support to projects or activities of a regular nature such as annually occurring festivities, workshops or conferences.

Level of Study: Unrestricted.

Purpose: To assist Inuit groups to develop their culture and contribute to modern Canadian society; to enable Inuit to share their cultural heritage with other Canadians; to promote awareness of Canada's cultural diversity; to assist Inuit to become full participants in Canadian society.

No. of awards offered: Approx. 15.

Frequency: Annual, if funds are available.

Value: Averaging C$2,000, and not to exceed C$5,000 per award.

Country of Study: Canada.

Application Procedure: No application forms are required. Applicants are asked to describe their projects in full, mentioning how they intend to carry out the project, and the contribution the completed project will make to the promotion of Inuit culture. A detailed budget, listing the costs of carrying out the project is also required. Finally, the approaches made to other possible funding sources should also be mentioned.

Closing Date: Applications are accepted at any time.

For further information contact:

Inuit Cultural Grants Program
Department of Indian and Northern Affairs
10 Wellington Street, Hull, QC, KIA OH4, Canada
Contact: Mr Steve Peach, Chairperson

DEPARTMENT OF THE NAVY (USA)

c/o Washington Navy Yard
Building 57, Washington, DC, 20374-0571, United States of America
www: http://www.navy.mil
Contact: Naval Historical Center

The Rear Admiral John D Hayes Pre-doctoral Fellowship in US Naval History

Subjects: United States naval history.
Eligibility: Applicants must be citizens of the United States; enrolled in a recognised graduate school; have completed requirements for the PhD except the dissertation by June 30th 1999; and have an approved dissertation topic in the field of US naval history.
Level of Study: Doctorate, Postdoctorate.
Purpose: To provide financial and scholarly aid for dissertation research and writing.
Type: Fellowship.
No. of awards offered: 1.
Frequency: Annual.
Value: $8,000 for the fellowship year (September-June) provided in two payments. The award of the grant will depend on continuing avaiability of funds.
Length of Study: 1 year.
Study Establishment: The Naval Historical Center.
Country of Study: USA.
Application Procedure: Applicants must submit a completed and signed application with supporting data attached, including a copy of approved dissertation outline. Additionally, candidates must arrange for submission of official transcripts of undergraduate and graduate coursework, and letters of recommendation as specified on the application form. Allow sufficient time for all supporting documents to be received by the Naval Historical Center In advance of the deadline date.
Closing Date: February 28th.

For further information contact:

Naval Historical Center
Washington Navy Yard
901 M Street SE, Washingtom, DC, 20374-5060, United States of America
Contact: Senior Historian

The Vice Admiral Edwin B Hopper Research Grants

Subjects: United States naval history.
Eligibility: Applicant must be citizens of the United States and hold a PhD degree from accredited university.
Level of Study: Doctorate, Postdoctorate.
Purpose: To assist scholars in the research or writing of books or articles by helping to defray the cost of travel, living expenses and document duplication, related to the research process.
Type: Grant.

No. of awards offered: 2.
Frequency: Annual.
Value: $2,500.
Length of Study: 1 year.
Study Establishment: Naval Historical Center.
Country of Study: USA.
Application Procedure: Applicants should send a letter stating the purpose and scope of research project, including a proposed budget, and a complete application to the Senior Historian at the Naval Historical Centre. It is expected that the applicant will include evidence of professional qualifications, and awards of honours received. In addition, two letters of recommendation from individuals familiar with the applicant's field of study will be required.
Closing Date: January 31st.

For further information contact:

Naval Historical Center
Washington Navy Yard
901 M Street SE, Washington, DC, 20374-5060, United States of America

DEUTSCHE FORSCHUNGSGEMEINSCHAFT (DFG)

Kennedyallee 40, Bonn, 53175, Germany
Tel: (49) 228 885 1
Fax: (49) 228 885 2777
Email: postmaster@dfg.d400.de
www: http://www.dfg.de

The Deutsche Forschungsgemeinschaft is the central public funding organisation for academic research in Germany. The DFG's mandate is to serve science and the arts in all fields by supporting research projects carried out in universities and research institutions in Germany, to promote co-operations between scientists, and to forge and support links between German academic science and industry, and with partners in foreign countries. In doing this, the DFG gives special attention to the education and support of young scientists and scholars. Foreign scientists and scholars who wish to obtain a fellowship to work in Germany may turn to the DAAD or to the Alexander von Humboldt Stiftung.

Collaborative Research Grants

Subjects: All subjects.
Eligibility: Promising groups of German nationals and permanent residents in Germany.
Level of Study: Postdoctorate, Research.
Purpose: To promote long term co-operative research in universtites and academic research.
Type: A variable number of Grants.
No. of awards offered: Varies.
Value: Dependent on the requirements of the project.
Length of Study: 3-15 years.

Study Establishment: Universities and academic institutions in Germany.
Country of Study: Germany.
Application Procedure: Applications must be formally filed by the universities. For further information please write or visit the website.
Closing Date: Please write for details.
Additional Information: A list of Collaborative Research Centres is available (in German only) from the DFG.

Emmy Noethen-Programme

Subjects: All subjects.
Eligibility: Promising young postdoctoral scientists up to the age of approximately 30, who are German nationals, or permanent residents of Germany.
Level of Study: Postdoctorate.
Purpose: To give outstanding young scholars the opportunity to obtain the scientific qualifications needed to be appointed as a lecturer within a period of five years after receiving their PhD.
Type: Project Grant.
No. of awards offered: 100.
Frequency: Annual.
Value: For the two years of research spent abroad the candidate is to receive a project grant in keeping with the requirements of the project, including an allowance, for subsistence and travel. For the three years of research spent at a German university or research institution the candidate is to receive a project grant of up to DM 400,000 per annum.
Length of Study: 5 years.
Study Establishment: Universities or research institutions worldwide.
Country of Study: Any country.
Application Procedure: For an application form and further information please contact Dr Bruno Zimmerman, or visit the website.
Closing Date: Please write for details.

For further information contact:

Germany
Tel: (49) 288 855 2254
Fax: (49) 288 885 2180
Contact: Dr Bruno Zimmermann

Eugen and Ilse Seibold Prize

Subjects: Arts and humanities.
Eligibility: Outstanding young German or Japanese scholars.
Level of Study: Postdoctorate.
Purpose: To promote outstanding young scientists and scholars who have made significant contributions to the scientific interchange between Japan and Germany.
Type: Award.
No. of awards offered: 2.
Frequency: Every two years (1999, 2001, 2003).
Value: Approx. DM 20,000 per prize.
Length of Study: Varies.
Study Establishment: Universities or research institutions.
Country of Study: Germany or Japan.

Application Procedure: Applications are by nomination. For further information please write or visit the website.
Closing Date: Please write for details.

Fellowships

Subjects: All subjects.
Eligibility: Promising young scientists or scholars who are German nationals or permanent residents of Germany.
Level of Study: Postdoctorate.
Purpose: To promote young scientists and scholars qualified with an outstanding PhD degree.
Type: A variable number of Fellowships.
No. of awards offered: Up to 1000.
Frequency: Annual.
Value: Varies.
Length of Study: Varies.
Study Establishment: Universities worldwide.
Country of Study: Any country.
Application Procedure: Please write for details, or visit the website.
Closing Date: Applications accepted at any time.

Gerhard Hess Awards

Subjects: All subjects.
Eligibility: Promising young scientists and scholars, who are German nationals, or permanent residents of Germany.
Level of Study: Postdoctorate, Predoctorate, Research.
Purpose: To promote young scientists and scholars up to the age of 35 years, who show exceptional promise and achievement and are seeking to establish an independent research group in a qualified research environment.
Type: Award.
No. of awards offered: 10.
Frequency: Annual.
Value: Up to DM 200,000 per award.
Length of Study: 2 - 5 years.
Study Establishment: German universities and research institutions.
Application Procedure: Application is by nomination.
Closing Date: Please write for details.

Gottfried Wilhelm Leibnitz Research Prize

Subjects: All subjects.
Eligibility: Outstanding scholars in German universities.
Level of Study: Predoctorate, Research.
Purpose: To promote outstanding scientists and scholars in German universities and research institutions.
Type: Research Grant.
No. of awards offered: Varies.
Frequency: Annual.
Value: DM 1.5 - 3million per Prize for 5 years study.
Length of Study: 5 years.
Study Establishment: German universities or research institutions.
Country of Study: Germany.
Application Procedure: Application is by nomination. Nominations are restricted to selected institutions (DFG member organisations) or individuals (former prize winners,

chairpersons of DFG review committees). For further information please write or visit the website.
Closing Date: Please write for details.
Additional Information: A list of prize winners is available (in German only) from the DFG.

Graduate Colleges

Subjects: All subjects.
Eligibility: Highly qualified graduate and doctoral students of any nationality.
Level of Study: Postgraduate, Predoctorate.
Purpose: To promote high quality graduate studies at doctoral level through participation of graduate students recruited through country wide calls in research programmes.
Type: A variable number of Fellowships.
No. of awards offered: Varies.
Length of Study: Up to 9 years.
Study Establishment: German universities.
Country of Study: Germany.
Application Procedure: Applications should be submitted in response to calls. For further information please visit the website.
Closing Date: Please write for details.
Additional Information: A list of Graduate Colleges presently funded is available (in Germany only) from the DFG.

Guest Professorships

Subjects: All subjects.
Eligibility: Foreign scientists, whose individual research is of special interest to research and teaching in Germany.
Level of Study: Postdoctorate.
Purpose: To support stays of foreign scientists at German universities, if the stay is of special interest to research and teaching in Germany.
Type: A variable number of Fellowships.
No. of awards offered: Varies.
Frequency: Annual.
Value: Dependent on the duration of the stay.
Length of Study: 3 months - 1 year.
Study Establishment: German universities.
Country of Study: Germany.
Application Procedure: Submission of a proposal by the university intending to host the guest Professor.

Hans Maier-Leibnitz Prize

Subjects: All subjects.
Eligibility: Promising young scholars up to the age of 33, who are German nationals or permanent residents of Germany.
Level of Study: Doctorate, Postdoctorate.
Purpose: To promote outstanding young scientists at doctorate level.
Type: Award.
No. of awards offered: 6.
Frequency: Annual.
Value: DM 30,000 per prize.
Length of Study: Varies.
Study Establishment: German universities or research institutions.

Country of Study: Germany.
Application Procedure: Application is by nomination. Please write for details or visit the website.
Closing Date: Please write for details.

Heisenberg Programme

Subjects: All subjects.
Eligibility: High calibre young scientists up to the age of 35 years of age, who are German nationals or permanent residents of Germany.
Level of Study: Postdoctorate.
Purpose: To promote outstanding young scientists up to the age of 35 years of age, who are German nationals, or permanent residents of Germany.
Type: Scholarship.
No. of awards offered: Varies.
Frequency: Annual.
Value: Varies.
Length of Study: 5 years.
Study Establishment: German universities or research institutions.
Country of Study: Germany.
Application Procedure: Applicants must submit a research proposal, a detailed curriculum vitae, copies of degree certificates, a copy of the thesis, a letter explaining the choice of host institution, a list of all the candidates previously published material, and a letter outlining the candidates financial requirements in duplicate. For further information please contact DFG.
Closing Date: Applications are accepted at any time.

Individual Grants

Subjects: All subjects.
Eligibility: Promising researchers and scholars, who are German nationals or permanent residents of Germany.
Level of Study: Postdoctorate, Postgraduate, Predoctorate, Research.
Purpose: To foster the proposed research projects of promising academic scientists or scholars.
Type: A variable number of Grants.
No. of awards offered: Varies.
Frequency: Throughout the year.
Value: Dependent on the requirement of the project.
Length of Study: 2 to 3 years initially, with the option of applying for a renewal.
Study Establishment: Universities worldwide.
Country of Study: Any country.
Application Procedure: Submission of a proposal for a research project. Please write for more details or visit the website: http://www.dfg.de/english/internat-coop.html.
Closing Date: Applications accepted at any time.

Joint Research Projects

Subjects: All subjects.
Eligibility: German scholars and scholars from any participating Eastern European country.
Level of Study: Postdoctorate, Research.

Purpose: To foster co-operation between German scientists and scientists in Middle and Eastern European countries and countries of the former Soviet Union.
Type: A variable number of Grants.
No. of awards offered: Varies.
Frequency: Annual.
Value: Dependent on the length of the research project and the number of participants.
Length of Study: Varies.
Study Establishment: Universities in any participating country.
Country of Study: Any country.
Application Procedure: Applications for sponsorship must be submitted by researchers from German research institutes. Please write for details or visit the website http://dfg.de/english/internat_coop.html.
Closing Date: Please write for details.

Priority Programs

Subjects: All subjects.
Eligibility: Interested groups of scientists from Germany or any country participating in the scheme.
Level of Study: Postdoctorate, Research.
Purpose: To promote proposals made by interested groups of scientists in selected fields.
Type: A variable number of Grants.
No. of awards offered: Varies.
Value: The Senate decides on the financial ceiling for each programme.
Length of Study: Up to 6 years.
Study Establishment: Universities or academic establishments in the countries participating in the scheme.
Country of Study: Any country.
Application Procedure: Priority Programmes are operated through calls for proposals, with all applications subject to open panel review, usually after discussion with the applicants. For further information please write or visit the website.
Closing Date: Please write for details.

Research Groups

Subjects: All subjects.
Eligibility: Interested groups of German nationals and permanent residents of Germany.
Level of Study: Postdoctorate, Research.
Purpose: To promote intensive co-operation between highly qualified researches in one or several institutions in fields of high scientific promise.
Type: Research Grant.
No. of awards offered: Varies.
Frequency: Annual.
Value: Dependent on the requirements of the project.
Length of Study: Up to 6 years.
Study Establishment: German universities.
Country of Study: Germany.
Application Procedure: Please submit proposals to the Senate of the DFG. For further information please write or visit the website.
Closing Date: Please write for details.

Additional Information: A list of currently operating Research Groups is available (in German only) from the DFG.

DONATELLA FLICK ASSOCIAZIONE

47 Brunswick Gardens, London, W8 4AW, England
Tel: (44) 171 792 2885
Fax: (44) 171 792 2574
Contact: Ms Judy Strang, Administrator

Donatella Flick Conducting Competition

Subjects: Conducting.
Eligibility: Open to conductors who are citizens of member states of the EC and aged under 35.
Level of Study: Professional development.
Purpose: To assist a young conductor to establish an international conducting career.
Type: Prize.
No. of awards offered: 1.
Frequency: Every two years (2000/2002).
Value: £15,000.
Length of Study: 1 year.
Study Establishment: London Symphony Orchestra.
Country of Study: Any country.
Application Procedure: Application form must be submitted with references specific to competition, video and other supporting documentation (other prizes, reviews, CV etc).
Closing Date: Please write for details c/o the administrator.
Additional Information: Entry is by recommendation, documentation and supporting video; finalists are selected for audition. Three finalists conduct a public concert. The course of study of entrants must be approved by the organising committee.

DR M AYLWIN COTTON FOUNDATION

c/o Albany Trustee Company Ltd
PO Box 232
Pollet House, St Peter Port, GY1 4LA, Guernsey
Tel: (44) 1481 724136
Fax: (44) 1481 710478
Contact: Grants Management Officer

Cotton Research Fellowships

Subjects: Archaeology, architecture, history, language and the arts of the Mediterranean.
Eligibility: Open to senior scholars.
Level of Study: Professional development.

Type: Fellowship.
No. of awards offered: Varies.
Frequency: Annual.
Value: Up to £10,000.
Country of Study: Any country.
Application Procedure: Application forms are available on request.
Closing Date: February 28th.
Additional Information: The Foundation also provides grants annually to finance the publication costs of a completed work or a work due for publication in the immediate future.

DR WILLIAMS'S TRUST

14 Gordon Square, London, WC1H 0AG, England
Tel: (44) 171 387 3727
Fax: (44) 171 388 1142
Contact: Secretary

The Trust gives further education grants to Protestant Dissenting Ministers in the UK. It also owns the Dr Williams Library in London.

Glasgow Bursary

Subjects: Religious studies - theology, Christian history, etc.
Eligibility: Open to Protestant Dissenting ministers wishing to take refresher courses; graduate Protestant Dissenting ministers for a course leading to the degree of MTh; and mature students intending to enter the Protestant Dissenting ministry after training. Applicants must be from England or Wales.
Level of Study: Postgraduate.
Purpose: To support an educated nonconformist ministry.
Type: Bursary.
No. of awards offered: 1.
Frequency: Annual, if funds are available.
Value: Normally £14,500 per year, plus fees, paid each term.
Length of Study: 1 year; renewable for a second year.
Study Establishment: University of Glasgow Faculty of Divinity.
Country of Study: United Kingdom.
Application Procedure: Please contact the Director of the Trust for details.
Closing Date: March 31st.

DUMBARTON OAKS: TRUSTEES FOR HARVARD UNIVERSITY

1703 32nd Street NW, Washington, DC, 20007, United States of America
Tel: (1) 202 339 6410
www: http://www.doaks.org
Contact: Associate Director

Dumbarton Oaks houses important research and study collections in the areas of Byzantine and Medieval Studies, Landscape Architecture Studies and Pre-Colombian Studies. While the gallery holds exhibitions and the gardens are open to the public, the research facilities exist primarily to serve scholars who hold appointments at Dumbarton Oaks.

Dumbarton Oaks Fellowships and Junior Fellowships

Subjects: Byzantine civilization in all its aspects, including the late Roman and Early Christian period, and the Middle Ages generally, studies of Byzantine cultural exchanges with the Latin West, Slavic and Near Eastern Countries, pre-Columbian studies, studies in landscape architecture.
Eligibility: Junior Fellowships are open to persons of any nationality who have passed all preliminary examinations for a higher degree and are writing a dissertation. Candidates must have a working knowledge of any languages required for research. Fellowships are open to scholars of any nationality holding a PhD or relevant advanced degree and wishing to pursue research on a project of their own at Dumbarton Oaks.
Level of Study: Doctorate, Postdoctorate.
Purpose: To promote study and research or to support writing of doctoral dissertations in Byzantine studies, Pre-Columbian studies and studies in landscape architecture.
Type: Fellowship.
No. of awards offered: 10-11 Fellowships in Byzantine studies; 3-4 in each of the other fields.
Frequency: Annual.
Value: US$13,200 per year (Junior Fellowships); US$24,000 per year (Fellowships). Both Junior and Regular Fellows receive furnished accommodation or a housing allowance of US$1,800, if needed, to assist with the cost of bringing and maintaining dependants in Washington, and an expense account of US$800 for approved research expenditure during the academic year. Fellows are also provided with travel assistance.
Length of Study: Up to 1 academic year full-time study; non-renewable.
Study Establishment: Full-time resident work at Dumbarton Oaks.
Country of Study: USA.
Application Procedure: Please contact Dumbarton Oaks for current application brochure.
Closing Date: November 1st of the academic year preceding that for which the Fellowship is required.
Additional Information: Dumbarton Oaks also awards a limited number of Summer Fellowships.

DUQUESNE UNIVERSITY

Department of Philosophy
Duquesne University, Pittsburgh, PA, 15282, United States of America
Tel: (1) 412 396 6500
Fax: (1) 412 396 5197
Email: thompson@duq2.cc.duq.edu
www: http://www.dug.edu
Contact: Ms Joan Thompson, Senior Secretary

The PhD Programme in the Department of Philosophy at Duquesne University emphasises continental philosophy, ie. phenomenology and 20th century French and German philosophy, as well as the history of philosophy.

Duquesne University Graduate Assistantship

Subjects: Philosophy.
Eligibility: Open to holders of a BA in philosophy, or its equivalent, who have a QPA of at least 3.7 and an excellent GRE. Candidates should have knowledge of a second language.
Level of Study: Doctorate.
Purpose: To provide a stipend to enable students to obtain a PhD in philosophy.
Type: Graduate Assistantship.
No. of awards offered: 13 each year, 2 for first-year students.
Frequency: Annual.
Value: A stipend of approximately US$9,000, plus all tuition for coursework.
Length of Study: 5-6 years.
Study Establishment: McAnulty College and Graduate School of Liberal Arts.
Country of Study: USA.
Application Procedure: Applications should include a statement of intent and three letters of recommendation, GREs and application form and fee, plus TOEFL scores.
Closing Date: February 15th before the Autumn term.

EARTHWATCH INSTITUTE

680 Mount Auburn Street
Box 9104, Watertown, MA, 02272, United States of America
Tel: (1) 617 828 8200 ext 119
Fax: (1) 617 926 1973
Email: info@earthwatch.org
www: http://www.earthwatch.org
Contact: Mr Matt Craig, Education Awards Manager

Earthwatch Institute is a non-profit organisation formed in 1972 which supports scientific field research by placing paying volunteers in two week expeditions worldwide. Earthwatch's mission is to promote sustainable conservation of the world's natural resources and cultural heritage by creating partnerships between scientists, educators, and the general public.

Earthwatch Teacher Advancement Awards

Subjects: Science education; historical and cultural education.
Eligibility: Open to full-time teachers (K-12) who are US citizens.
Level of Study: Unrestricted.
Purpose: Professional development; hands-on environmental education; participation in scientific research.
Type: Participation Grant.
No. of awards offered: 265.
Frequency: Annual.
Value: US$1,100-US$2,100.
Length of Study: 2-3 weeks.
Country of Study: Any country.
Application Procedure: Please complete an application form. Please contact the Earthwatch Institute, USA for applications, if not applying from Europe.
Closing Date: February 15th.
Additional Information: Teacher Advancement Awards are funded by over 40 corporations, foundations, and individuals nationwide. Some grants have particular stipulations, for example: through a grant from The Klingenstein Fund, independent school educators are eligible to receive funding for participation on Earthwatch expeditions.

For further information contact:

Earthwatch Europe
57 Woodstock Road, Oxford, OX2 6HJ, England
Tel: (44) 1865 311 600
Fax: (44) 1865 311 383

EAST-WEST CENTER

Award Services
1601 East-West Road, Honolulu, HI, 96848-1601, United States of America
Tel: (1) 808 944 7735
Fax: (1) 808 944 7730
Contact: Fellowships Office

The East-West Center promotes understanding among the governments and peoples of Asia, the Pacific, and the United States of America; through collaborative research and training and through dialogue and cultural interchange. The Center supports degree Fellows from the region in various educational activities, including study at the University of Hawaii.

Graduate Degree Fellowship

Subjects: Agriculture, forestry and fishery, architecture and town planning, arts and humanities, business administration and management, education and teacher training, engineering, fine and applied arts, law, mass communications and information science, mathematics and computer science, medical sciences, natural sciences, recreation, welfare and protective services, and social and behavioural sciences.

Eligibility: Applicants must have obtained a 4 year bachelor's degree or its equivalent, must be a citizen or permanent resident of the United States of America or a citizen of a country in Asia or the Pacific, and must come to the Center on the Exchange Visitor (J-1) Visa.
Level of Study: Doctorate, Postgraduate.
Purpose: To enable degree study at the University of Hawaii and participation in the educational activities of the Center.
Type: Fellowship.
No. of awards offered: Varies.
Frequency: Annual.
Value: May apply for funding for housing, stipend, tuition, health insurance, books, materials, and supplies.
Length of Study: Initially 12 months, with possible renewal.
Study Establishment: University of Hawaii.
Country of Study: USA.
Application Procedure: Applicants must send the completed East-West Center and University of Hawaii application forms to the East-West Center. Applicants must include test information, curriculum vitae, essay and other documents. Applicants must also arrange for the required test scores, official transcripts, and letters of reference to be submitted to the East-West Center.
Closing Date: October 15th.

EASTMAN SCHOOL OF MUSIC OF THE UNIVERSITY OF ROCHESTER

26 Gibbs Street, Rochester, NY, 14604, United States of America
Tel: (1) 716 274 1060
Fax: (1) 716 232 8601
Email: esmadmit@uhura.cc.rochester.edu
www: http://www.rochester.edu/eastman
Contact: Mr Bob Borden, Financial Aid

In its sixteen year history Eastman School of Music has remained faithful to its founding mission to grow articulate and literate musicians. The breadth and depth of the accomplishments of its graduates is testimony to the strength and value of an Eastman education.

Eastman School of Music Graduate Awards

Subjects: Music.
Eligibility: Open to nationals of all countries. Candidates should have the qualifications necessary for admission to the Eastman School of Music. Non-US citizens are usually offered service scholarships in ensemble work at graduate level.
Level of Study: Doctorate, Postgraduate.
Purpose: To support the School's academic programmes.
Type: Tuition scholarships and stipends.
No. of awards offered: Approx. 200.
Frequency: Annual.
Value: Up to US$25,685.
Length of Study: 1 academic year; renewable.

Study Establishment: At the School.
Country of Study: USA.
Application Procedure: An application form must be completed. In addition, most awards require an interview in Rochester.
Closing Date: January 1st.

ECONOMIC AND SOCIAL RESEARCH COUNCIL (ESRC)

Polaris House
North Star Avenue, Swindon, Wiltshire, SN2 1UJ, England
Tel: (44) 1793 413000
Fax: (44) 1793 413001
Email: ptd@esrc.ac.uk
www: http://www.esrc.ac.uk/postgrad.html
Contact: Ms Zoë Grimwood, Divisional Administrator

The Economic and Social Research Council is an independent, government funded body set up by Royal Charter. The Mission ESRC is to promote and support, by any means, high-quality basic, strategic and applied research and related postgraduate training in the Social Sciences; to advance knowledge and provide trained social scientists which meet the needs of users and beneficiaries, thereby contributing to the economic competitiveness of the United Kingdom, the effectiveness of public services and policy, and the quality of life; and to provide advice on, and disseminate knowledge and promote public understanding of social sciences.

ESRC Research and Advanced Course Studentships

Subjects: Social sciences.
Eligibility: Open to UK or EC nationals with a first or upper second class honours degree in any subject from a UK university or the CNAA; a Master's degree from a UK university or the CNAA; a degree from a UK university or the CNAA, or a UK professional qualification acceptable to the ESRC as of degree standard plus at least one academic year, having been satisfactorily completed of full-time study, or its part-time equivalent, towards a UK higher degree; or a UK professional qualification acceptable to the ESRC as of degree standard plus three years' subsequent full-time relevant professional work experience. Candidates must have been ordinarily resident in Great Britain throughout the three year period preceding the date of application and not have been so resident during any part of that three year period wholly or mainly for the purpose of receiving full-time education.
Level of Study: Postgraduate.
Purpose: The ESRC's mission is to promote social science research and postgraduate training. The ESRC aims to provide funding for high quality postgraduate training and research on issues of importance to business, the public sector and government.

Type: Standard Research Studentship, Standard Advanced Course Studentship, CASE Research Studentship.
No. of awards offered: Varies.
Frequency: Annual.
Value: ESRC studentship awards can cover fees and maintenance, depending on the student's situation, circumstances, and the type of award.
Length of Study: Up to 3 years.
Study Establishment: Institutional outlets and courses which have been given recognition by ESRC.
Country of Study: United Kingdom.
Application Procedure: Application forms and information sheets are available each year from February and should be collected from the social science departments of any university or Institute of Higher Education at that time.
Closing Date: May 1st (competition applications), June 1st (quota nominations).
Additional Information: Guidance notes are available from social science departments, course organisers, and university careers services from the middle of February each year.

EDUCATIONAL TESTING SERVICE

Mail Stop 16-T, Princeton, NJ, 08541-0001, United States of America
Tel: (1) 609 734 1806
Fax: (1) 609 734 5420
Email: ldelauro@ets.org
www: http://www.ets.org
Contact: Ms Linda J DeLauro

ETS Postdoctoral Fellowships

Subjects: Psychology, education, sociology of education, psychometrics, statistics, computer science, linguistics.
Eligibility: Open to any individuals with a doctorate in a relevant discipline, who can provide evidence of prior research.
Level of Study: Postdoctorate.
Purpose: To provide research opportunities to individuals, and to increase the number of women and minority professionals in educational measurement and related fields.
Type: Fellowship.
No. of awards offered: Up to 3.
Frequency: Annual.
Value: US$35,000 for the 12 month period. In addition, limited relocation expenses may be available.
Length of Study: 12 months beginning in June, including 1 month vacation.
Country of Study: USA.
Application Procedure: There is no formal application form. However applicants are encouraged to discuss research plans with an ETS scientist prior to applying. Applicants should submit: a résumé, research proposal, official

transcripts of previous studies and three letters of recommendation from people who are familiar with the applicant's work.
Closing Date: All application materials must arrive at ETS by February 1st.
Additional Information: Affirmative action goals will also be considered in the selection process. Applicants will be notified by April 1st.

EDWARD F ALBEE FOUNDATION, INC.

14 Harrison Street, New York, NY, 10013, United States of America
Tel: (1) 212 226 2020
Contact: Foundation Secretary

William Flanagan Memorial Creative Persons Center

Subjects: Writing, painting.
Eligibility: Open to artists and writers in need who have displayed talent.
Level of Study: Unrestricted.
Purpose: To provide accommodation.
Type: Accommodation only.
No. of awards offered: 20 places.
Frequency: Annual.
Value: No financial aid or grants; accommodation only.
Length of Study: 4 months between June 1st and October 1st.
Study Establishment: The Center in Montauk, Long Island.
Country of Study: USA.
Application Procedure: Application form must be completed. Forms are available upon request, and should be accompanied by a pre-paid return envelope. Other materials are also required - please write for further details.
Closing Date: January 1st to April 1st.
Additional Information: The environment is communal and residents are expected to do their share in maintaining the conditions of the Center.

ELIZABETH GREENSHIELDS FOUNDATION

1814 Sherbrooke Ouest/West
Suite 1, Montreal, PQ, H3H 1E4, Canada
Tel: (1) 514 937 9225
Fax: (1) 514 937 0141
Email: egreen@total.net
Contact: Ms Micheline Leduc, Administrator

The purpose of the Foundation is to aid artists in the early stages of their careers. Awards are limited to candidates working in the areas of painting, drawing, printmaking, and sculpture. Work must be figurative or representational - abstract art is precluded by the terms of the Foundation's charter.

The Elizabeth Greenshields Grant

Subjects: Painting, drawing, printmaking, sculpture.
Eligibility: Open to nationals of any country, there is no age limit.
Level of Study: Unrestricted.
Purpose: To assist talented young artists in the early stages of their career.
Type: Grant.
No. of awards offered: 45-55.
Frequency: Throughout the year.
Value: C$10,000.
Country of Study: Any country.
Application Procedure: Requests for application are made in writing (return postage paid), by phone, fax, or email. Applications are submitted along with six slides (12 for sculptors).
Closing Date: Grants are awarded throughout the year, there is no deadline.
Additional Information: Applicant's work must be representational (the Foundation's charter precludes abstract art). Application forms are sent upon request to individuals only. The Foundation is not a school.

EMILY ENGLISH TRUST

16 Ogle Street, London, W1P 7LG, England
Tel: (44) 171 636 4481
Fax: (44) 171 637 4307
Contact: Mrs Susan Dolton

Emily English Award

Subjects: Musical performance - violin.
Eligibility: Open to violinists under the age of 24 years of any nationality, who have been resident in the UK for three years. The award may be used for postgraduate study only.
Level of Study: Postgraduate.
Purpose: To assist the studies of talented young violinists.
No. of awards offered: 1.
Frequency: Annual.
Value: £10,000.
Country of Study: Any country.
Application Procedure: Applicants must complete an application form and provide two references.
Closing Date: March.
Additional Information: Selected students will be asked to audition.

ENGLISH-SPEAKING UNION (ESU)

Dartmouth House
37 Charles Street, London, W1X 8AB, England
Tel: (44) 171 493 3328
Fax: (44) 171 495 6108
Contact: Ms Andrea Wathern, Cultural Affairs

English-Speaking Union Chautauqua Scholarships

Subjects: Art (painting, ceramics and sculpture), music education, literature and international relations, drama.
Eligibility: Open to British teachers, between 25 and 35 years of age, with particular interest in the arts.
Level of Study: Professional development.
Purpose: To enable British teachers to study at the Chautauqua Summer School organized by the University of Syracuse.
Type: Scholarship.
No. of awards offered: 2.
Frequency: Annual.
Value: £850 plus board, room, tuition and lecture sessions at the Summer School.
Length of Study: 6 weeks.
Study Establishment: Chautauqua Institution's Summer School, Chautauqua, New York.
Country of Study: USA.
Application Procedure: Please write for details.
Closing Date: November 30th.

ESU Music Scholarships

Subjects: Music.
Eligibility: Candidates must be aged 28 or under, from Britain or the Commonwealth and be students or graduates from music colleges and other equivalent institutions.
Level of Study: Professional development.
Purpose: To enable musicians of outstanding ability to study at summer schools in North America, Canada, France and the UK.
Type: Scholarship.
No. of awards offered: 9.
Frequency: Annual.
Value: Covers the cost of tuition, board and lodging and relevant flight costs.
Length of Study: 3-9 weeks, depending on particular scholarship.
Study Establishment: Summer school.
Country of Study: United States of America, Canada or France.
Application Procedure: Candidates must be nominated by the relevant college heads of department and supported by a teacher's reference.
Closing Date: November.

EPISCOPAL CHURCH FOUNDATION

815 Second Avenue
Room 400, New York, NY, 10017, United States of America
Tel: (1) 212 697 2858
Fax: (1) 212 297 0142
Email: ditz@episcopalfoundation.org
www: http://www.episcopalfoundation.org
Contact: Ms Anne E Ditzler, Program Associate

The Episcopal Church Foundation is an independent, lay-led organisation which offers innovative programs in leadership development, education, and philanthropy for the clergy and laity of the Episcopal Church.

Episcopal Church Foundation Graduate Fellowship Program

Subjects: Religious studies.
Eligibility: Open to seniors and graduates of an accredited seminary of the Episcopal Church, Harvard Divinity School or Union Theological Seminary as an Episcopal candidate. Applicants must be recommended by the Dean of their theological seminary. If not a graduate of one of these seminaries, the applicant must have endorsement by the Dean of one of the eleven accredited Episcopal seminaries.
Level of Study: Doctorate.
Purpose: To support doctoral students whose career objective is to teach at an Episcopal seminary in the USA.
Type: Fellowship.
No. of awards offered: 3.
Frequency: Annual.
Value: Dependent on individual circumstances.
Length of Study: 1 year; renewable for up to 2 additional years.
Study Establishment: At accredited institutions in the USA and abroad.
Country of Study: Any country.
Application Procedure: Application materials are available from the Dean's office at any of the eleven accredited Episcopal seminaries as well as Harvard Divinity School and Union Theological Seminary.
Closing Date: November 1st.

THE ERIC THOMPSON TRUST

c/o The Royal Philharmonic Society
10 Stratford Place, London, W1N 9AE, England
Tel: (44) 171 491 8110
Fax: (44) 171 493 7463
Contact: Clerk to The Trustees

The Eric Thompson Trust offers aspiring professional organists financial assistance with special studies such as summer schools, travel and subsistence for audition or performance, or other incidental costs incurred in their work.

Eric Thompson Trust Grants-in-Aid

Subjects: Organ.
Eligibility: No restriction as to nationality, but normally UK in practice. Some professional training as an organist is required.
Level of Study: Professional development.
Purpose: To provide aspiring professional organists with financial assistance with special studies such as summer schools, travel and subsistence for auditions or performance, or other incidental costs incurred in their work.
Type: Grant-in-Aid.
No. of awards offered: Varies.
Frequency: Annual.
Value: Determined by Trustees, but normally limited to a contribution towards costs.
Country of Study: Any, but probably largely United Kingdom in practice.
Application Procedure: Applicants (usually young professional organists) should send full details of their needs, together with information on their training and career and, where available, references and other relevant material, to the Clerk to the Trustees.
Closing Date: December 31st and June 30th, for consideration in January and July respectively.

EUROPEAN UNIVERSITY INSTITUTE (EUI)

Via dei Roccettini 9
50016 San Domenico di Fiesole, Florence, Italy
Tel: (390) 55 46851
Fax: (390) 55 4685 444
Email: applyres@datacomm.iue.it
www: http://www.iue.it/
Contact: Dr Andreas Frydal, Head of Academic Service

The EUI's main aim is to make a contribution to the intellectual life of Europe. Created by the EU member states, it is a postgraduate research institution, pursuing interdisciplinary research programmes on the main issues confronting European society and on the construction of Europe.

European University Institute Postgraduate Scholarships

Subjects: History and civilisation, economics, law or political and social sciences.
Eligibility: Open to nationals of the 15 EU member states. Candidates must possess a good honours degree or its equivalent, and have full written and spoken command of at least two of the Institute's official languages. Under certain conditions, nationals of countries other than the EU may also be admitted to the Institute and be eligible for a Scholarship.
Level of Study: Doctorate, Postgraduate.
Purpose: To provide the opportunity for study leading to the doctorate degree from the Institute.
Type: Scholarship.

No. of awards offered: Approx. 120.

Frequency: Annual.

Value: Varies.

Length of Study: 12 months; renewable for up to an additional 2 years.

Study Establishment: The Institute, in Florence.

Country of Study: Italy.

Application Procedure: Application forms are available from the Institute and from the Institute's website.

Closing Date: January 31st.

Additional Information: The Scholarships are granted over two academic years, by the governments of the 15 EU member states to nationals of their own countries, currently distributed over two academic years as follows: Federal Republic of Germany 29; France 26; Italy 29; UK 26; Spain 25; Netherlands 15; Denmark 8; Belgium 10; Republic of Ireland 8; Greece 10; Luxembourg 3; Portugal 13; Austria 10; Finland 4; and Sweden 8.

Jean Monnet Fellowships

Subjects: Humanities and social sciences, with special attention to problems related to the European Community and to the development of Europe's cultural and academic heritage.

Eligibility: Open mainly to candidates with a doctoral degree at an early stage of their academic career. Established academics on leave are also eligible.

Level of Study: Postdoctorate.

Purpose: To encourage postdoctoral research.

Type: Fellowship.

No. of awards offered: 20-30.

Frequency: Annual.

Value: 24,000,000-42,000,000 lire per year, depending on age, plus allowances for dependants, travel and medical insurance. Flat-rate basis of 2,000,000 lire per month for academics with paid sabbatical.

Length of Study: 1 year, possibly renewable for a further year.

Study Establishment: European University Institute, Florence.

Country of Study: Italy.

Application Procedure: Application forms can be obtained by contacting the office at the EUI via the Internet or by contacting the Jean Monnet Fellowships Officer at the general EUI address.

Closing Date: November (the date may be modified- contact the EUI for verification).

Additional Information: Web page: http://www.iue.it/jmf/welcome.html.

EVANGELICAL LUTHERAN CHURCH IN AMERICA (ELCA)

Division for Ministry
8765 West Higgins Road, Chicago, IL, 60631-4195, United States of America
Tel: (1) 773 380 2885
Fax: (1) 773 380 2829
www: http://www.elca.org
Contact: Dr Jonathan Strandjord

ELCA Educational Grant Program

Subjects: Theological studies.

Eligibility: Restricted to members of the Evangelical Lutheran Church in America who are pursuing advanced degree programs (PhD/ThD) in theological education and intend to teach in that field.

Level of Study: Doctorate.

Purpose: To provide funding for students in advanced degree track in theological education, who intend to teach.

Type: Grant.

No. of awards offered: Approx. 40.

Frequency: Annual.

Value: US$500-US$3,000.

Length of Study: 4 years.

Country of Study: USA.

Application Procedure: Application forms are available through the Department for Theological Education in the Division for Ministry. Forms are available in January, and must be returned by March 15th with two references.

Closing Date: March 15th.

EXETER COLLEGE

Oxford, OX1 3DP, England
Tel: (44) 1865 279 660
Fax: (44) 1865 279 630
www: http://www.exeter.ox.ac.uk
Contact: Tutor for Graduates

Exeter College Senior Scholarship in Theology

Subjects: Theology, or theology and philosophy.

Eligibility: Applicants must hold by the time of admission at least a second class honours degree in a subject other than theology.

Level of Study: Undergraduate.

Purpose: To support a graduate who wishes to read for the Final Honour School of Theology or of Philosophy and Theology.

Type: Scholarship.

No. of awards offered: 1.

Frequency: Every two years.

Value: Minimum value £200 may be supplemented up to a maximum of all college fees, university fees to the amount charged to home and EU students, and maintenance to the current maximum Local Education Authority maintenance grant.
Length of Study: 1-2 years.
Study Establishment: Exeter College, University of Oxford.
Country of Study: United Kingdom.
Application Procedure: Apply in writing to the Tutor for Graduates, with CV and names of three academic references.

Queen Sofia Research Fellowship

Subjects: Spanish literature.
Eligibility: Applicants should be close to completing doctoral work, or postdoctoral, and must be under 31 at the time of taking up the fellowship. Must be fluent in Spanish.
Level of Study: Doctorate, Postdoctorate.
Purpose: To support research into peninsular Spanish literature.
Type: Fellowship.
No. of awards offered: 1.
Frequency: Every 2-3 years.
Value: Entitled to free lunch and dinner, free rooms in college if unmarried, and housing allowance if not resident in the college.
Length of Study: 2-3 years.
Study Establishment: Exeter College, University of Oxford.
Country of Study: United Kingdom.
Application Procedure: Enquiries may be addressed to the the College Secretary.

F BUSONI INTERNATIONAL PIANO COMPETITION

Concorso Pianistico Internazionale
'F Busoni'
Conservatorio Statale di Musica 'C Monteverdi'
Piazza Domenicani 19, Bolzano, I-39100, Italy
Tel: (390) 471 976568
Fax: (390) 471 973579
www: http://www.tqs.iunet.it/asteria/busoni.htm
Contact: La Segretaria

The annual Busoni International Piano Competition was first held in 1949 to commemorate the 25th anniversary of the death of composer Ferruccio Busoni. The aim of the competition is to create a forum for Busoni's music as well as for promising young pianists.

F Busoni International Piano Competition

Subjects: Piano performance.
Eligibility: Open to pianists of any nationality under 32 years of age.
Level of Study: Unrestricted.
Purpose: To award excellence in piano performance.
Type: Prize.

No. of awards offered: 8.
Frequency: Annual.
Value: 1st prize 20,000,000 lire plus 60 important concert contracts; 2nd prize 12,000,000 lire; 3rd prize 8,000,000 lire; 4th prize 6,000,000 lire; 5th prize 5,000,000 lire; 6th prize 4,000,000 lire.
Country of Study: Italy.
Application Procedure: Application form should be accompanied by birth certificate, reports or certificates of study, brief CV and documentation of any artistic activity, three recent photographs, entrance fee, and written evidence of prizes at international competitions, if any.
Closing Date: May 31st.
Additional Information: The competition is held in August and September each year.

FEDERAL COMMISSION FOR SCHOLARSHIPS FOR FOREIGN STUDENTS

Route du Jura 1, Fribourg, CH-1700, Switzerland
Tel: (41) 37 26 74 24
Fax: (41) 37 26 74 04
Contact: Grants Management Officer

Swiss Scholarships for Students from Developing Countries

Subjects: All courses or research work offered at Swiss institutions of higher education.
Eligibility: Open to persons who can satisfy the eligibility requirements of the Swiss educational institution. A good knowledge of French or German is essential and a preliminary language examination is given at the Swiss Embassy in the candidate's country (some scholars may be required to take the language course at Fribourg prior to their proposed course of study). Scholarships for basic academic courses will only be granted to candidates coming from countries which have no university (yet) or where the university education system is in the process of being developed.
Level of Study: Postgraduate, Undergraduate.
Purpose: To enable students from developing countries to further their studies or begin research work at a Swiss institution of higher education.
Type: Scholarship.
No. of awards offered: Varies.
Frequency: Annual.
Value: Students not having obtained a university degree (the BA and BSc degrees are not necessarily recognised as university degrees) SF1,450 per month; postgraduates SF1,650 per month; students attending the language course at Fribourg SF4,050 total for the duration of the course (three months).
Length of Study: 1 academic year.

Study Establishment: At institutions of higher education. Scholarships for postgraduate students may, in principle, be renewed for a second academic year. Only in exceptional cases will candidates be allowed to continue their studies towards a doctorate by means of the Scholarship.
Country of Study: Switzerland.
Application Procedure: Application forms must be completed and submitted along with: copies of secondary school certificates; copies of certificates, diplomas and university degrees with marks; two academic references; plan outlining the programme of study whilst in Switzerland; curriculum vitae; writeen comfirmation from a professor at the chosen instiution that the applicants project is feasible at the institution; medical certificate. The documents must be written in German, French, Italian or English or translated into one of these languages. Art students must submit Photographs of 3 pieces of their work, rough drafts (with indication of the date) for fine arts; very good quality cassette tapes of 3 different styles of music, composers must submit scores, for music.
Closing Date: Usually end of October of the previous year.
Additional Information: The Commission is part of the Federal Department of Home Affairs. The scholarships are offered to foreign governments and only candidates recommended by their home authorities are eligible. Candidates must apply to the international scholarship agency in their own country.

Swiss Scholarships for Students from Industrial Countries

Subjects: All courses or research work offered at Swiss institutions of higher education.
Eligibility: Open to persons who can satisfy the eligibility requirements of the Swiss educational institution. A good knowledge of French or German is essential and a preliminary language examination is given at the Swiss embassy in the candidate's country (some scholars may be required to take the language course at Fribourg prior to their proposed course of study).
Level of Study: Postgraduate.
Purpose: To enable foreign students to further their studies or begin research work at a Swiss institution of higher education.
Type: Scholarship.
No. of awards offered: Varies.
Frequency: Annual.
Value: Scholars are exempt from tuition fees and insured against illness and accidents. The Scholar pays the fare to Switzerland and the Swiss government pays the return fare only for overseas students (Canada, US, Japan, China, Australia, New Zealand, etc.) Monthly allowances are offered as follows: SF1,450 for students who have not obtained a university degree (foreign BA and BSc degrees are not always recognised); SF1,650 for postgraduates; SF1,650 for fine arts and music students; SF4,050 for the whole of the language course.
Length of Study: 1 academic year.
Study Establishment: At institutions of higher education. Scholarships for postgraduate students can only exceptionally be renewed for a second academic year.

Country of Study: Switzerland.
Application Procedure: Application forms must be completed and submitted along with: copies of secondary school certificates; copies of certificates, diplomas and university degrees with marks; two academic references; plan outlining the programme of study whilst in Switzerland; curriculum vitae; writen comfirmation from a professor at the chosen instiution that the applicants project is feasible at the institution; medical certificate. The documents must be written in German, French, Italian or English or translated into one of these languages. Art students must submit Photographs of 3 pieces of their work, rough drafts (with indication of the date) for fine arts; very good quality cassette tapes of 3 different styles of music, composers must submit scores, for music.
Closing Date: Usually end of October of the previous year.
Additional Information: The Commission is part of the Federal Department of Home Affairs. The Scholarships are offered to foreign governments and only candidates recommended by their home authorities are eligible. Candidates must apply to the international scholarship agency in their own country (US students: Institution of International Education, 809 United Nations Plaza, New York, New York 10017. Canadian students: Association of Universities and Colleges of Canada, 151 Slater Street, Ottawa, Ontario K1P 5N1. UK students: The British Council, 10 Spring Gardens, London SW1A 2BN). The Commission also administers the Postgraduate Scholarships for Nationals of the Council for Cultured Co-operation, Council of Europe. Those who wish to obtain general information on the courses offered at Swiss universities may consult the brochure 'The Swiss Universities' available at Swiss embassies and consulates.

FINE ARTS WORK CENTER IN PROVINCETOWN, INC.

24 Pearl Street, Provincetown, MA, 02657, United States of America
Tel: (1) 508 487 9960
Fax: (1) 508 487 8873
Email: fawc@capecod.net
www: http://www.capecodaccess.com/fineartsworkcenter
Contact: Mr Hunter O'Hanian, Executive Director

Established in 1968, The Fine Arts Work Center offers seven month fellowships to emerging visual artists and creative writers. Housing studios and monthly stipends are provided to create a community of peers as a catalyst for artistic growth.

Fine Arts Work Center in Provincetown Fellowships

Subjects: Visual arts and creative writing (fiction and poetry).
Eligibility: Open to all, but preference is given to emerging artists of outstanding promise. Applicants are accepted on the basis of work submitted.

Level of Study: Unrestricted.
Purpose: To give artists the opportunity to work at the Center in a congenial and stimulating environment and to devote most of their time to their art and writing.
Type: Fellowship.
No. of awards offered: 20 (10 for the visual arts, 10 for writing).
Frequency: Annual.
Value: US$375-US$450 per month, plus housing and studio space.
Length of Study: 7 months.
Study Establishment: Provincetown, Massachusetts.
Country of Study: USA.
Application Procedure: Send SASE for application, fee US$35.
Closing Date: February 1st for visual artists; December 1st for writers.
Additional Information: The Center is a working community, not a school.

FLEMISH COMMUNITY

c/o Embassy of Belgium
3330 Garfied Street NW, Washington, DC, 20008, United States of America
Tel: (1) 202 625 5850
Fax: (1) 202 342 8346
Contact: Flemish Community Fellowships Office

Fellowship of the Flemish Community

Subjects: Art, music, humanities, social and political sciences, law, economics, sciences and medicine.
Eligibility: Open to US citizens of no more than 35 years of age, who hold a Bachelor's or Master's degree, and who have no other Belgian sources of income.
Level of Study: Postgraduate.
Purpose: To assist American college students who wish to continue their postgraduate education in Flanders, Belgium.
Type: Fellowship.
No. of awards offered: 5.
Frequency: Annual.
Value: A monthly stipend of 26,200 Belgian Francs; tuition fees at a Flemish institution up to 18,500 Belgian Francs; health insurance and public liability insurance in accordance with Belgian law. There is no reimbursement of travel expenses.
Length of Study: 10 months.
Study Establishment: Universities, conservatories of music, or art academies affiliated with the Flemish Community.
Country of Study: Belgium.
Application Procedure: Application form must be completed and submitted typed, in triplicate with a certified true copy of the applicant's birth certificate; copy of diplomas; summary of the thesis; official transcripts; two recommendations from current teachers or employers; and latest GPA where applicable.
Closing Date: January 15th.

Additional Information: Applicants will be notified of the result of applications no later than the end of July, and the academic year for most institutes of higher learning in Flanders starts at the end of September.

FONDATION PHILIPPE WIENER-MAURICE ANSPACH

39 avenue Franklin D Roosevelt, Brussels, B-1050, Belgium
Contact: Mr M Philippe de Bruycker, Executive Secretary

Postdoctorate Grants

Subjects: All subjects.
Eligibility: Eligible candidates must have done the doctorate at the Universite Libre de Bruxelles having passed with a minimum of grand distinction.
Level of Study: Postdoctorate.
Purpose: For doctors of all disciplines who completed their thesis at the Universite Libre de Bruxelles and want to continue at Oxford or Cambridge.
Type: Grant.
Value: 100,000 Belgium Francs per month. Fees and lab costs are paid by the Foundation.
Length of Study: A maximum of 1 year.
Study Establishment: Oxford or Cambridge University.
Country of Study: United Kingdom.
Application Procedure: Applicants must: complete an application form which must be obtained from the secretariat; include a full CV and photocopies of certificates; give information on the research planned- a timetable and someone who will supervise the research in the UK; provide a letter of recommendation from an English sponsor; letters of recommendation from 2 members of university staff.
Closing Date: March 25th.

Predoctorate Grants

Subjects: All subjects.
Eligibility: Open to students who have finished the second stage of their predoctoral course at the Universite Libre de Bruxelles and who want to develop their studies or research during an academic year at Oxford or Cambridge. Access to the grants is dependent on their having completed the first stages of study at the Universite Libre de Bruxelles; having passed with a minimum of grand distinction.
Level of Study: Predoctorate.
Purpose: For student at Universite Libre de Bruxelles who want to continue their studies at Oxford or Cambridge.
Type: Grant.
Value: Between £9,250 and £13,758 with the college fees being paid by the foundation.
Study Establishment: Oxford or Cambridge University.
Country of Study: United Kingdom.
Application Procedure: The following information must be submitted: an application form must be completed which can be obtained from the secretariat; a CV and photocopies of certificates; university grades and details of specific project

completed so far; information on the type of study or research the applicant wants to do; two letters of academic reference.
Closing Date: December 1st.

FOREST ROBERTS THEATRE

Panowski Playwriting Competition
Northern Michigan University
1401 Presque Isle, Marquette, MI, 49855-5364, United States of America
Tel: (1) 906 227 2082
Fax: (1) 906 227 2567
Contact: Ms Erica A Milkovich, Award Co-ordinator

Mildred and Albert Panowski Playwriting Award

Subjects: Playwriting.
Eligibility: Open to amateur, pre-professional, and professional playwrights. Plays must be written in English.
Level of Study: Unrestricted.
Purpose: To encourage and stimulate artistic growth among educational and professional playwrights and to provide the students and faculty of Northern Michigan University the unique opportunity to mount and produce an original work on the university stage.
No. of awards offered: 1.
Frequency: Annual.
Value: US$2,000 cash award and production of the winning script.
Country of Study: USA.
Application Procedure: Applicants should send SASE for rules and application form.
Closing Date: Plays must be received by the Friday before Thanksgiving.
Additional Information: There is no restriction as to theme or genre. Entries must be original, full-length plays. Musicals, one-act plays, and previously submitted works are unacceptable. Submissions must not have been previously produced or published. Please write for a complete copy of the rules.

FORT COLLINS SYMPHONY ASSOCIATION

PO Box 1963, Fort Collins, CO, 80522, United States of America
Tel: (1) 970 482 4823
Fax: (1) 970 482 4858
Email: leehill@fcsymphony.org
www: http://www.fcsymphony.org
Contact: Mr Lee Hill, Executive Director

Adeline Rosenberg Memorial Prize Competition

Subjects: Music performance.
Eligibility: The senior division is open to musicians 25 years

of age or under. The junior division is open to all musicians between 12 and 18 years of age on the day of competition.
Level of Study: Unrestricted.
Purpose: To foster excellence in young performers of classical music.
No. of awards offered: Senior division 3 prizes, Junior division 4 prizes.
Frequency: Annual.
Value: Senior division: 1st prize US$3,000, 2nd prize US$2,000, 3rd prize US$1,000; Junior division: 1st prize US$250, 2nd prize US$100.
Country of Study: Any country.
Application Procedure: Application form, plus application fee: seniors-US$35, juniors-US$25. Tape is required for senior division. Applications available after October 1st 1999, send self addressed stamped envelopes.
Closing Date: January 20th.
Additional Information: The Senior Division alternates between orchestral instruments (odd years) and piano (even years) and winning contestants are expected to perform with the Fort Collins Symphony Orchestra. Junior Division encompasses both instrumental and piano categories every year and 1st prize Junior winners may be offered a performance with the Symphony (depending on available concert), 2000-SR division-piano only.

FOUNDATION FOR EUROPEAN LANGUAGE AND EDUCATIONAL CENTRES (EUROCENTRES)

Seestrasse 247, Zurich, CH-8038, Switzerland
Tel: (41) 1 485 50 40
Fax: (41) 1 481 61 24
Email: 100632.136@compuserve.com
www: http://www.clark.net/pub/eurocent/home.html
Contact: Mr Eric Steenbergen

Eurocentres Scholarship

Subjects: Languages - English, French, Italian, Spanish and German.
Eligibility: Open to applicants between 18 and 30 years of age who are able to submit proof of satisfactory scholastic and professional (practical experience) records and who have good previous knowledge of the language to be studied.
Level of Study: Unrestricted.
Purpose: To assist people to attend a language course or learn a language.
Type: Scholarship.
No. of awards offered: Varies.
Frequency: Varies.
Value: Between US$250 and US$750 per grant; to cover part of the tuition fees but not the cost of travel accommodation, personal expenses, etc.
Study Establishment: On one of the various courses organised by the Foundation.
Country of Study: Europe or USA.

Closing Date: October 15th for courses beginning in January; January 15th for courses beginning in April; March 31st for courses beginning in July; June 15th for courses beginning in September/October.

Additional Information: The Scholarships should assist those people with a special aptitude for learning. Candidates must also show that further language study is an essential element of their work career.

FOUNDATION FOR THE ADVANCEMENT OF MESOAMERICAN STUDIES, INC (FAMSI)

268 S Suncoast Blvd, Crystal River, FL, 34429-5498, United States of America
Tel: (1) 352 795 5990
Fax: (1) 352 795 1970
Email: famsi@famsi.org
www: http://www.famsi.org
Contact: Dr Sandra Noble, Director

The Foundation was created in 1993 to foster increased understanding of ancient Mesoamerican cultures. The Foundation aims to assist and promote qualified scholars who might otherwise be unable to undertake or complete their programs of research and synthesis.

FAMSI Research Grant

Subjects: Mesoamerican studies.
Eligibility: Preference is for recent graduates, degree candidates, or active professionals who are involved in fully-developed programmes of Mesoamerican study. FAMSI does not provide funds for equipment, salary or stipends.
Level of Study: Doctorate, Postdoctorate, Postgraduate, Professional development.
Purpose: To support scholarly works with the potential for significant contributions to the understanding of ancient Mesoamerican cultures.
Type: Research Grant.
No. of awards offered: 10-20.
Frequency: Annual.
Value: General Research Grants - up to US$10,000; Contingency Grants - up to US$5,000; Special Project Grants - please write for details.
Length of Study: 1 year.
Study Establishment: Unrestricted.
Country of Study: Pre Columbian Mesoamerica: Mexico, Guatemala, Belize, Honduras or El Salvador.
Application Procedure: Please write for a brochure and an application form. The form must be submitted with three letters of reference, CV, budget, statement of purpose, and an abstract in English.
Closing Date: September 30th.

FOUNDATION PRAEMIUM ERASMIANUM

Jan van Goyenkade 5, Amsterdam, NL-1075 HN, Netherlands
Tel: (31) 20 676 02 22
Fax: (31) 20 675 22 31
Email: spe@erasmusprijs.org
www: http://www.erasmusprijs.org
Contact: Y C Goester, Secretary

The Foundation Praemium Erasmianum operates internationally in the fields of social studies, and the arts and humanities, as well as through the awarding of the Erasmus Prize and other activities.

ERASMUS Prize

Subjects: Arts, humanities, social studies.
Eligibility: There are no eligibility restrictions.
Level of Study: Unrestricted.
Purpose: To honour persons who have made an exceptional contribution to European culture.
No. of awards offered: 1.
Frequency: Annual.
Value: NLG300,000.
Country of Study: Any country.
Application Procedure: Please write for details.

Foundation Praemium Erasmianum Study Prize

Subjects: Humanities, social sciences.
Eligibility: Open to students at Dutch universities.
Level of Study: Postdoctorate.
Purpose: To honour young academicians who have written an excellent thesis in the field of humanities or social sciences.
No. of awards offered: 5.
Frequency: Annual.
Value: NLG7,500.
Country of Study: Any country.
Application Procedure: Please send applications to the relevant faculties or universities.
Closing Date: July 15th.

FRANCIS CHAGRIN FUND

c/o Society for the Promotion of New Music
Francis House
Francis Street, London, SW1P 1DE, England
Tel: (44) 171 828 9696
Fax: (44) 171 931 9928
Email: spnm@spnm.org.uk
www: http://www.spnm.org.uk
Contact: Mr Peter Craik, Adminstrator

From contemporary jazz, classical and popular music to that written for film, dance and other creative media; the Francis Chagrin Fund is on of the main advocates of new music in Britain today.

Francis Chagrin Award

Subjects: Music therapy and composition.
Eligibility: Applicants must be British composers, or composers resident in the United Kingdom. Their works must be unpublished.
Level of Study: Unrestricted.
Purpose: To help cover the costs incurred by composers in reproducing performance materials for unpublished works awaiting their first performance.
Type: Grant.
No. of awards offered: Unlimited.
Frequency: Dependent on funds available.
Value: £250 maximum.
Application Procedure: An application form must be completed and to submitted to SPNM, with receipts. Application forms are available from SPNM.

Francis Chagrin Fund Awards

Subjects: Subjects relevant to musical compositions/electronic tapes awaiting their first performance.
Eligibility: Open to British nationals and those living in the UK.
Level of Study: Unrestricted.
Purpose: To cover the costs of reproducing performance materials for works awaiting their first performance.
Type: Grant.
No. of awards offered: Varies.
Frequency: Awards are considered once a month by committee.
Value: Reimbursement of expenses, £3,000 per year maximum.
Country of Study: United Kingdom.
Application Procedure: Application form is required plus CV, two references and relevant invoices.
Closing Date: Applications are accepted at any time; the committee meets once a month.

FRANK KNOX MEMORIAL FELLOWSHIPS

48 Westminster Palace Gardens
Artillery Row, London, SW1P 1RR, England
Tel: (44) 171 222 1151
Fax: (44) 171 222 5355
Contact: Ms Anna Mason, Secretary

The Frank Knox Memorial Fellowships were established at Harvard University in 1945 by a gift from Mrs Anna Reid Knox, widow of the late Col Frank Knox, to allow students from the United States, Australia, Canada, New Zealand and the United Kingdom to participate in an educational exchange programme.

Frank Knox Fellowships at Harvard University

Subjects: Arts, sciences (including engineering and medical sciences), business administration, design, divinity, education, law, public administration, public health.
Eligibility: Open to UK citizens normally resident in the UK who, at the time of application, have spent at least two of the last four years at a UK university or university college and will have graduated by the start of tenure.
Level of Study: Postgraduate.
Type: Fellowship.
No. of awards offered: 4.
Frequency: Annual.
Value: US$16,000 plus tuition fees. Unmarried Fellows may be accommodated in one of the university dormitories or halls.
Length of Study: 1 academic year. Depending on the availability of sufficient funds the fellowships may be renewed for Fellows registered for a degree programme of more than 1 year's duration.
Study Establishment: Harvard University, Cambridge, Massachusetts.
Country of Study: USA.
Application Procedure: Harvard University will try to arrange a suitable course for each individual. Fellowships are not awarded for postdoctoral study, and no application will be considered from persons already in the USA. Candidates must file an 'Admissions Application' directly with the graduate school of their choice at an early date; admission to a school is a prior condition of the award of a Fellowship. Candidates wishing to study business administration should apply by November 9th. A period of full-time work since graduation is necessary prior to embarking on the MBA programme. Travel grants are not awarded, although in cases of extreme hardship applications can be made to Harvard University for travel cost assistance.
Closing Date: November 1st.

FRANKLIN AND ELEANOR ROOSEVELT INSTITUTE

Franklin D Roosevelt Library
511 Albany Post Road, Hyde Park, NY, 12538, United States of America
Tel: (1) 914 229 5321
Fax: (1) 914 229 9046
Email: emurphy@idsi.net
www: http://newdeal.feri.org/feri/
Contact: Chairman, Grants Committee

The Franklin and Eleanor Roosevelt Institute is a private non-profit corporation dedicated to preserving the legacy and promoting the ideals of Franklin and Eleanor Roosevelt.

Roosevelt Institute Grant-in-Aid

Subjects: The Roosevelt years and clearly related subjects.
Eligibility: Open to qualified researchers of any nationality with a viable plan of work. Proposals are recommended for

funding by an independent panel of scholars which reports to the Institute Board.

Level of Study: Doctorate, Postdoctorate.
Purpose: To encourage younger scholars to expand our knowledge and understanding of the Roosevelt period and to give continued support to more experienced researchers who have already made a mark in the field.
Type: Grant.
No. of awards offered: 15-20.
Frequency: Twice a year.
Value: Up to US$2,500.
Study Establishment: Franklin D. Roosevelt Library.
Country of Study: USA.
Application Procedure: Two copies - application face sheet, research proposal, relevance of holdings, travel plans, time estimate, CV and budget.
Closing Date: February 15th and September 15th.
Additional Information: Application form and guidelines are available on-line or by emailing, faxing, or writing to the Roosevelt Institute.

FRIEDRICH NAUMANN FOUNDATION

Institut fur Forschung und Begabtenforderung
Konigswinterer Strasse 407, Konigswinter, D-53639, Germany
Tel: (49) 2223 701 410
Fax: (49) 2223 701 222
Contact: Ms Marie Louise Wohlleben

The Friedrich Naumann Foundation is the foundation for liberal policy in Germany. Its purpose is to provide political education and establish domestic and foreign meeting places where current political problems, economics, sociology and science can be taught; and to support talented young people by providing scholarships.

Friedrich Naumann Foundation Scholarships

Subjects: Subjects related to liberal philosophies.
Eligibility: Open to German students and graduates. Foreign applicants have to come from one of the countries where the Foundation has a project, and must be planning to take a doctorate or postgraduate course.
Level of Study: Doctorate, Postgraduate.
Purpose: To support the new liberal minded academics.
Type: Scholarship.
No. of awards offered: Varies.
Frequency: Twice a year.
Value: Up to DM 1,390 per month, plus health insurance.
Length of Study: For the duration of studies after BA or German equivalent (up to 3 years for graduates).
Country of Study: Germany.
Application Procedure: Application forms and information about the Friedrich Naumann Foundation Scholarship Programme are available on request.
Closing Date: May 31st and November 30th.

Additional Information: Applicants should have received an acceptance from a German university for doctorate or postgraduate studies. Fluency in German is required. Once a student has received a doctorate, no scholarship can be awarded for further studies. Students in the final stage of their doctorate do not qualify for a grant.

FRIENDS OF AMERICAN WRITERS

c/o Mrs Jane C Larson
400 East Randolph Street
Apt 2123, Chicago, IL, 60601, United States of America
Tel: (1) 312 856 1147
Contact: Mrs Jane C Larson

Adult Literature Award, Juvenile Literary Award

Subjects: Fiction and non-fiction.
Eligibility: Open to residents of, or those who have lived for at least five years in, Arkansas, Illinois, Indiana, Iowa, Kansas, Michigan, Minnesota, Missouri, North Dakota, South Dakota, Nebraska, Ohio or Wisconsin, and to books set in those regions. Candidates may not have published more than three books.
Level of Study: Unrestricted.
Purpose: To encourage the study of American literature and to encourage emerging American writers.
Type: Prize.
No. of awards offered: 2 Adult Literature Awards, 2 Juvenile Literary Awards.
Frequency: Annual.
Value: Adult Literature Awards: first prize US$1,600; second prize US$1,000. Juvenile Literary Awards: first prize US$1,000; second prize US$600.
Country of Study: Any country.
Application Procedure: No applications are necessary, but candidates should send two copies of each book as early as possible along with biographical material regarding the author.
Closing Date: December 1st for notification in April.

FRIENDS OF FRENCH ART

100 Vanderlip Drive
Villa Narcissa, Rancho Palos Verdes, CA, 90275, United States of America
Tel: (1) 310 377 4444
Fax: (1) 310 377 4584
Contact: Ms Elin Vanderlip, President

Friends of French Art restore art in peril, both in France and the United States.

Summer Art Restoration Program

Subjects: We are a non-profit organisation dedicated to restoring art-in-peril.
Eligibility: Open to graduate students in the field of Art Restoration.
Level of Study: Postgraduate.
Purpose: To give graduate students in the field of art-conservation the opportunity to work the summer in France.
Type: Air fare to France, and a place to stay while working on a specific art restoration project.
No. of awards offered: Varies.
Frequency: Annual.
Value: Approx. $5,000.
Length of Study: Summer programme.
Country of Study: France.
Application Procedure: We have been sending students from the University of Delaware, Winterthur Art Conservation Department.

For further information contact:

University of Delaware
Winterthur Art Conservation Department, Winterthur, DE, 19735, United States of America

FRIENDS OF ISRAEL EDUCATIONAL TRUST

Academic Study Group
PO Box 7545, London, NW2 2OZ, England
Tel: (44) 171 435 6803
Fax: (44) 171 794 0291
Email: foi_asg@msn.com
Contact: Mr John Levy

The Friends of Israel Educational Trust aim to encourage a critical understanding of developments, and to forge new collaborative links between Israel and the Arab world.

Friends of Israel Educational Trust Academic Study Bursary

Subjects: All subjects.
Eligibility: Open to research or teaching postgraduates. The Academic Study Group will only consider proposals from British academics who have already linked up with professional counterparts in Israel and agreed terms of reference for an initial visit.
Level of Study: Postdoctorate.
Purpose: To provide funding for British academics planning to pay a first research/study visit to Israel.
Type: Bursary.
No. of awards offered: 15.
Frequency: Annual.
Value: £300 per person.
Country of Study: Israel.
Application Procedure: There is no application form.
Closing Date: November 15th and March 15th.

Friends of Israel Educational Trust Young Artist Award

Subjects: Fine arts.
Eligibility: Open to promising young British painters and illustrators.
Level of Study: Postgraduate, Professional development.
Purpose: To enable a promising British painter to pay a working visit to Israel and prepare work for an exhibition on Israeli themes, in the UK.
No. of awards offered: 1-2.
Frequency: Annual.
Value: To cover air fare, accommodation and keep.
Length of Study: A minimum of 2 months.
Study Establishment: A kibbutz.
Country of Study: Israel.
Closing Date: Mid-April.

FROMM MUSIC FOUNDATION

c/o Department of Music
Harvard University, Cambridge, MA, 02138, United States of America
Tel: (1) 617 495 2791
Fax: (1) 617 496 8081
Contact: Ms Ann Stevernagel

Fromm Foundation Commission

Subjects: Music (composition only).
Eligibility: There are no eligibility restrictions.
Level of Study: Unrestricted.
Purpose: To support composition by young and lesser well known composers. Includes a stipend for premiere performance of commissioned work.
No. of awards offered: Up to 10.
Frequency: Annual.
Country of Study: Any country.
Application Procedure: Please obtain guidelines from Fromm Music Foundation.
Closing Date: June 1st.

FULBRIGHT COMMISSION (ARGENTINA)

Viamonte 1653
2 Piso, Buenos Aires, Capital Federal, 1055, Argentina
Tel: (54) 11 4814 3561
Fax: (54) 11 4814 1377
Email: gc@fulb-ba.satlink.net
Contact: Ms M Graciela Abarca, Program Officer/ Educational Advisor

The Fulbright Programme is an educational exchange programme which sponsors awards for individuals approved by the J William Fulbright Board. The programme's major aim is to promote international co-operation and contribute to the development of friendly, sympathetic and peaceful relations between the United States and other countries in the world.

Fulbright Commission (Argentina) Awards for US Lecturers and Researchers

Subjects: All subjects except medical science.
Eligibility: Open to US researchers and lecturers. Applicants must be proficient in spoken Spanish.
Level of Study: Professional development.
Purpose: To enable US lecturers to teach at an Argentine university for one semester, and to enable US researchers to conduct research at an Argentine institution for three months.
No. of awards offered: 10-12.
Frequency: Annual.
Value: Varies, according to professional experience.
Length of Study: 3 months.
Country of Study: Argentina.
Application Procedure: For further details please contact Ralph Blessing at CIES, Washington DC (la3@ciesnet.cies.org).
Closing Date: August 1st.

Fulbright Commission (Argentina) Master's Program

Subjects: All subjects except medical sciences.
Eligibility: Open to Argentines only.
Level of Study: Postgraduate.
Purpose: To support Argentines pursuing Master's degree in the USA.
No. of awards offered: 80.
Frequency: Annual.
Value: US$12,000 - US$15,000 per year.
Length of Study: 2 years.
Country of Study: USA.
Application Procedure: Please contact the Fulbright Commission in Argentina between February 1st and April 30th.
Closing Date: April 30th.

Fulbright Commission (Argentina) US Students Research Grant

Subjects: All subjects except medical science.
Eligibility: Open to US citizens who hold a bachelor's degree, are writing a Master's thesis or PhD dissertation and are proficient in Spanish.
Level of Study: Doctorate, Graduate, Postgraduate.
Purpose: To enable US students to study in Argentina.
Type: Research Grant.
No. of awards offered: 10-12.
Frequency: Annual.
Value: Approximately US$17,350 for eight months.
Length of Study: 8 months.

Country of Study: Argentina.
Application Procedure: Application form must be completed - for further details please contact Rachel Goldberg at IIE, New York (rgoldeberg@iie.org).

FULBRIGHT SCHOLAR PROGRAM

Suite 5M
3007 Tilden Street NW, Washington, DC, 20008-3009, United States of America
Tel: (1) 202 686 8664
Fax: (1) 202 362 3442
Email: apprequest@cies.iie.org
www: http://www.cies.org/
Contact: Grants Management Officer

Fulbright Postdoctoral Research and Lecturing Awards for Non-US Citizens

Subjects: All subjects.
Eligibility: Open to nationals of countries and territories having US diplomatic or consular posts, who have a doctoral degree or equivalent qualification. Preference is given to those persons who have not had extensive previous experience in the USA.
Level of Study: Postdoctorate.
Type: Grant.
No. of awards offered: Varies, approx. 700.
Frequency: Annual.
Value: A maintenance allowance and international travel expenses.
Length of Study: From 3 months to 1 academic year.
Country of Study: USA.
Application Procedure: Applications must be made to the binational educational commission or the US embassy or consulate in the candidate's home country.
Closing Date: Varies by country.

GENERAL BOARD OF HIGHER EDUCATION AND MINISTRY

PO Box 871, Nashville, TN, 37202-0871, United States of America
Tel: (1) 615 340 7388
Fax: (1) 615 340 7395
Contact: Dr John E Harnish

Dempster Fellowship

Subjects: Theology.
Eligibility: Open to members of the United Methodist Church who are teaching or plan to teach in seminaries, or to teach religion or related subjects in universities or colleges.

Applicants must have received a MDiv from one of the member seminaries at the Association of United Methodist Schools.
Level of Study: Doctorate.
Purpose: To support research in the field of theology.
Type: Fellowship.
No. of awards offered: 5.
Frequency: Annual.
Value: US$10,000 per year.
Country of Study: Any country.
Application Procedure: Please write for details.
Closing Date: February 1st.

GEOLOGICAL SOCIETY OF AMERICA (GSA)

3300 Penrose Place
PO Box 9140, Boulder, CO, 80301-9140, United States of America
Tel: (1) 303 447 2020 ext 137
Fax: (1) 303 447 1133
Email: lcarter@geosociety.org
www: http://www.geosociety.org
Contact: Ms Leah J Carter, Research Grants Administrator

Established in 1888, the Geological Society of America is a non-profit organisation dedicated to the advancement of the science of geology. GSA membership is for the generalist and the specialist in the field of geology; it offers something for everyone.

The Archchaeology Geology Division - Claude C Albritton, Jr Scholarships

Subjects: Earth sciences and archaeology.
Eligibility: Applicants must be graduate students at universities in the United States, Canada, Mexico or Central America.
Purpose: To award outstanding student research within archaeology and geology.
Type: Grant.
Application Procedure: Applications must on on current GSA forms available in geology departments in the United States and Canada, or directly from the GSA. Application forms and information will also be available on the web page.

For further information contact:

Institute for Applied Sciences
Box 310559
University of North Texas, Denton, Texas, 76203, United States of America
Contact: Mr Reid Ferring

GEORGE A AND ELIZA GARDNER HOWARD FOUNDATION

Brown University
Box 1867
42 Charlesfield Street, Providence, RI, 02912, United States of America
Tel: (1) 401 863 2640
Fax: (1) 401 863 7341
Email: howard-foundation@brown.edu
www: http://www.stg.brown.edu/projects/gradschool/howard
Contact: Ms Susan M Clifford, Co-ordinator

Howard Foundation Fellowships

Subjects: The Foundation awards a limited number of fellowships each year for independent projects in fields selected on a rotational basis.
Eligibility: Nominees should normally have the rank of assistant or associate professor or their non-academic equivalents. Support is intended to augment paid sabbatical leaves, making it financially possible for grantees to have an entire year in which to pursue their projects, free of any other professional responsibilities. Accepted nominees should therefore be eligible for sabbaticals or other leave with guaranteed additional support. Candidates regardless of their country of citizenship, must be professionally based in the USA either by affiliation with an institution or by residence.
Level of Study: Postgraduate.
Purpose: To assist individuals in the middle stages of their careers.
Type: Fellowship.
No. of awards offered: 10.
Frequency: Annual.
Value: US$20,000.
Length of Study: 1 year.
Country of Study: Any country.
Application Procedure: Applications are accepted only upon nomination. Details of the nomination procedure are available from the Foundation. Fellowships are not available for work leading to any academic degree.
Closing Date: October 15th for nominations; November 30th for completed applications. Fellowships will be announced May 1st, for commencement of tenure July 1st.
Additional Information: 2000-2001 philosophy, sociology, anthropology.

GERMAN ACADEMIC EXCHANGE SERVICE (DAAD)

950 Third Avenue
19th Floor, New York, NY, 10022, United States of America
Tel: (1) 212 758 3223
Fax: (1) 212 755 5780
Email: daadny@daad.org
www: http://www.daad.org
Contact: Grants Management Officer

The DAAD is a private, publicly funded, self-governing organisation of higher education institutes in Germany. DAAD promotes international academic relations and co-operation, especially through exchange programmes for students and faculty. The head office of DAAD is in Bonn and there are branch offices in Berlin, Beijing, Cairo, Jakarta, London, Moscow, Nairobi, New Delhi, New York, Paris, Rio de Janeiro, San Jose and Tokyo. The addresses of the branch offices are available on the DAAD website, or from the Bonn office.

Alexander von Humboldt 'Bundeskanzler' Scholarships

Subjects: Unrestricted, but a background in the humanities, social sciences, law or economics is preferred.
Eligibility: Candidates with demonstrated leadership qualities and excellence in their field should be nominated by US university presidents. Nominees must be US citizens and no more than 40 years of age.
Level of Study: Postgraduate.
Purpose: To enable highly qualified young Americans in academia, business or politics to gain substantial insight into German political, economic, social and cultural life in the course of an extended, self-structured stay.
Type: Scholarship.
No. of awards offered: Up to 10.
Frequency: Annual.
Value: Varies.
Study Establishment: German universities or research institutions.
Country of Study: Germany.
Application Procedure: For details and application material please write to the Alexander Von Humboldt Foundation, email: humboldt@umail.umd.edu or refer to the DAAD website.

For further information contact:

Alexander von Humboldt Foundation
 US Liason
1055 Thomas Jefferson Street
NW
Suite 2030, Washington, DC, 20007, United States of America
Tel: (1) 202 296 2990
Fax: (1) 202 833 8514
Contact: Grants Management Officer

Alexander von Humboldt Research Fellowships

Subjects: All subjects.
Eligibility: Open to highly qualified scholars and scientists of any nationality, who hold a PhD or equivalent and are not yet 40 years of age.
Level of Study: Postdoctorate.
Purpose: To promote promising young scholars and scientists of any nationality.
Type: Fellowship.
No. of awards offered: Varies.
Frequency: Annual.
Value: Varies.
Study Establishment: German universities or research institutions.
Country of Study: Germany.
Application Procedure: Please write for details.

For further information contact:

Alexander von Humboldt Foundation US Liason
1055 Thomas Jefferson Street N W
Suite 2030, Washington, DC, 20007, United States of America
Tel: (1) 202 296 2990
Fax: (1) 202 833 8514

DAAD Canadian Government Grants

Subjects: All subjects.
Eligibility: Open to Canadian citizens between 18 and 32 years of age who have a good command of German.
Level of Study: Postgraduate.
Purpose: To promote young scholars from Quebec who wish to pursue research in German studies.
Type: Grant.
No. of awards offered: Varies.
Frequency: Annual.
Value: Varies.
Length of Study: 1 academic year.
Study Establishment: German universities or research institutions.
Country of Study: Germany.
Application Procedure: Forms to be obtained from Canadian universities or directly from the DAAD office in New York.
Closing Date: Please write for details.

For further information contact:

(Residents from Québec only)
Direction de la générale de l'enseignement et de la recherche universitaires

Ministére de l'Enseignement supéet de la Science
1035 rue de la Chevrotière, Québec, G1R 5A5, Canada
Tel: (1) 418 643 2955
Fax: (1) 418 643 0622

DAAD Center for Contemporary German Literature Grant

Subjects: Research in contemporary German literature.
Eligibility: Open to suitably qualified scholars of any nationality.
Level of Study: Postgraduate.
Purpose: A summer research grant of up to $3,000 for faculty planning to work in the field of contemporary German literature at the Center for Contemporary German Literature at Washington University in St Louis will be awarded annually. The Center is administered by the German Department in conjunction with the Olin Library at Washington University.
Type: Grant.
No. of awards offered: 1.
Frequency: Annual.
Value: US$3,000.
Length of Study: 3 months.
Study Establishment: The Center for Contemporary German Literature.
Country of Study: USA.
Application Procedure: Please write for details.
Closing Date: March 1st.

For further information contact:

Center for Contemporary German Literature
Campus Box 1104
Washington University, St Louis, MO, 63130, United States of America
Tel: (1) 314 935 4784
Fax: (1) 314 935 7255
Contact: Professor Paul Michael Luetzeler, Director

DAAD Fulbright Grants

Subjects: All subjects.
Eligibility: Open to US citizens between 18 and 32 years of age who have a good command of German. Applicants must have been enrolled at a US university for at least one year at the time of application.
Level of Study: Postgraduate.
Purpose: This scholarship provides funds for graduate study and/ or research in Germany for one academic year.
Type: Grant.
No. of awards offered: Varies.
Frequency: Annual.
Value: Varies.
Length of Study: 1 academic year.
Country of Study: Germany.
Application Procedure: Forms may be obtained from campus Fulbright advisor.
Closing Date: Please write for details.

For further information contact:

Institute of International Education (IIE)
809 United Nations Plaza, New York, NY, 10017, United States of America
Tel: (1) 212 984 5330
Fax: (1) 212 984 5325
Contact: Grants Management Officer

DAAD Information Visits

Subjects: All subjects.
Eligibility: Applicants must have been enrolled at a US university for at least one year at time of application.
Level of Study: Graduate.
Purpose: To increase knowledge of specific German subjects and institutions within the framework of an academic study tour homogenous group of 15-25 students.
Frequency: Annual.
Length of Study: 7-21 days.
Country of Study: Germany.
Application Procedure: Forms may be obtained from the DAAD New York office or they can be downloaded from the internet.
Closing Date: At least six months before the intended visit.

DAAD Leo Baeck Institute Grants

Subjects: The social, communal and intellectual history of German-speaking Jewry.
Eligibility: Open to doctoral students and recent PhDs.
Level of Study: Doctorate, Postdoctorate.
Purpose: Fellowships are available to assist doctoral students and recent PhDs in their research on the social, communal and intellectual history of German speaking Jewry. The fellowships provide funds for research at the Leo Baeck Institute in New York or for research in Germany.
Type: Fellowship.
No. of awards offered: 6.
Frequency: Annual.
Value: Varies.
Study Establishment: The Leo Baeck Institute in New York or in Germany.
Country of Study: USA or Germany.
Application Procedure: Please write for details.
Closing Date: November 1st.

For further information contact:

The Leo Baeck Institute
129 East 73rd Street, New York, NY, 10021, United States of America
Tel: (1) 212 744 6400
Fax: (1) 212 988 1305
Contact: Ms Carol Kahn Strauss

DAAD Research Grants for Recent PhDs and PhD Candidates

Subjects: All subjects.
Eligibility: Open to recent PhDs (up to two years after the degree) of no more than 35 years of age and PhD candidates

of no more than 32 years of age. Applicants must have been enrolled at a US university for at least one year at the time of application.
Level of Study: Doctorate, Postdoctorate.
Purpose: The purpose of this grant is to enable PhD candidates and recent PhDs to carry out dissertation or post-doctoral research at libraries, archives, institutes or laboratories in Germany for a period of one to six months during the calender year.
Type: Grant.
No. of awards offered: Varies.
Frequency: Annual.
Value: A monthly maintenance allowance, international travel subsidy, and health insurance.
Length of Study: 2-6 months.
Country of Study: Germany.
Application Procedure: Request forms from the DAAD or download from the internet.
Closing Date: August 1st for visits during the first half of the year; February 1st for visits during the second half of the year.

DAAD Study Visit Research Grants for Faculty

Subjects: All subjects.
Eligibility: Open to individuals with at least two years of teaching and/or research experience after the PhD or equivalent and a research record in the proposed field.
Level of Study: Faculty.
Purpose: To allow scholars to pursue research at universities and other institutions in Germany for one to three months during the calendar year.
Type: Grant.
No. of awards offered: Varies.
Frequency: Annual.
Value: A monthly maintenance allowance.
Length of Study: 1-3 months.
Country of Study: Germany.
Application Procedure: Forms may be obtained from the New York office or downloaded from the internet.
Closing Date: August 1st for visits during the first half of the year; February 1st for visits during the second half of the year.

DAAD/AICGS Grant

Subjects: Topics dealing with postwar Germany.
Eligibility: Open to PhD candidates, recent PhDs and junior faculty members.
Level of Study: Doctorate, Postdoctorate.
Purpose: This fellowship is available to assist doctoral candidates, recent PhDs and junior faculty working on topics dealing with postwar Germany. The grant provides funds for summer residency at the American Institute for Contemporary German Studies (AICGS).
Type: Fellowship.
No. of awards offered: 1.
Frequency: Annual.
Study Establishment: The American Institute for Contemporary German Studies (AICGS).
Country of Study: USA.
Application Procedure: Please write for details.
Closing Date: April 15th.

For further information contact:

AICGS
1400 16th Street NW
Suite 420, Washington, DC, 20036-2217, United States of America
Tel: (1) 202 332 9312
Fax: (1) 202 265 9531

Hochschulsommersprachkurse at German Universities

Subjects: German studies and language courses.
Eligibility: Applicants must have been enrolled for at least one year in a US or Canadian university.
Level of Study: Graduate, Postgraduate, Undergraduate.
Purpose: To provide language courses with an integrated thematic focus on literary, cultural, political and economic aspects of modern and contemporary Germany.
Frequency: Annual.
Length of Study: 3-4 weeks.
Study Establishment: German universities.
Country of Study: Germany.
Application Procedure: Forms may be obtained from the DAAD office New York or they can be downloaded from the internet.
Closing Date: January 31st.
Additional Information: Please contact Ms Barbara Motyka.

Learn 'German in Germany' for Faculty

Subjects: All fields but in English and German.
Eligibility: Open to faculty of US universities.
Level of Study: Faculty.
Purpose: To enable recipients to attend intensive language courses at the Goethe Institutes.
Frequency: Annual.
Length of Study: 4 and 8 weeks.
Study Establishment: Goethe Institutes.
Country of Study: Germany.
Application Procedure: Forms may be obtained from the DAAD office in New York or they can be downloaded from the internet.
Closing Date: January 31st.

Summer Language Course at the University of Leipzig

Subjects: All fields, but students in the fields of English, German or any other modern language are not eligible.
Eligibility: Applicants must have been enrolled at a US university for at least one year at time of application.
Level of Study: Graduate, Postgraduate, Undergraduate.
Purpose: To support intensive language course, lectures, discussions on contemporary issues, independent project work, and excursions.
Frequency: Annual.
Length of Study: 8 weeks.
Study Establishment: University of Leipzig.
Country of Study: Germany.

Application Procedure: Forms may be obtained from the DAAD New York office or they can be downloaded from the internet.
Closing Date: January 31st.

Summer Language Courses at Goethe Institutes

Subjects: All fields, but students in the fields of English and German are not eligible.
Eligibility: Applicants must be enrolled at a US university at time of application.
Level of Study: Postgraduate.
Purpose: To offer intensive eight week language courses.
Frequency: Annual.
Length of Study: 8 weeks.
Study Establishment: Goethe Institutes.
Country of Study: Germany.
Application Procedure: Forms may be obtained from the New York office or they can be downloaded from the internet.
Closing Date: January 31st.

GERMAN HISTORICAL INSTITUTE

1607 New Hampshire Avenue NW, Washington, DC, 20009, United States of America
Tel: (1) 202 387 3355
Fax: (1) 202 483 3430
Email: info@ghi-dc.org
www: http://www.ghi-dc.org
Contact: The Awards Committee

The German Historical Institute is an independent research institute dedicated to the promotion of historical research in the Federal Republic of Germany and the United States. The Institute supports and advises German and American historians and political scientists and encourages the co-operation between them.

German Historical Institute Collaborative Research Programme for Postdoctoral Scholars

Subjects: German and American post-World War II history, transatlantic studies, comparative studies in social, cultural, and political history.
Eligibility: Open to German and American doctoral students. Applications from women and minorities are especially encouraged.
Level of Study: Postdoctorate.
Purpose: To support a research programme for postdoctoral scholars on the topic of continuity, change, and glogalisation in postwar Germany and America.
Type: Scholarship.
Frequency: Annual, if funds are available.
Value: Depending on length of study.
Length of Study: 6-12 months.
Country of Study: USA.

Application Procedure: Please contact the Scholarships Office for details.

German Historical Institute Courses in German Handwriting and Archives

Subjects: German handwriting, German archives, German, history, transatlantic studies.
Eligibility: Open to German and American doctoral students. Applications from women and minorities are especially encouraged.
Level of Study: Doctorate.
Purpose: To introduce students to German handwriting of previous centuries by exposing them to a variety of German archives, familiarising them with major research topics in German culture and history, and encouraging the exchange of ideas among the next generation of American scholars.
Type: Scholarship.
Frequency: Annual, if funds are available.
Value: US$2,500.
Length of Study: 2 weeks.
Country of Study: Germany.
Application Procedure: Please write for details.
Closing Date: December 31st.

German Historical Institute Dissertation Scholarships

Subjects: Humanities and social sciences - comparative studies in social, cultural and political history, studies of German-American relations, transatlantic studies.
Eligibility: Open to German and American doctoral students. Applications from women and minorities are especially encouraged.
Level of Study: Doctorate.
Purpose: To give support to German and American doctoral students working on topics related to the Institute's general scope of interest.
Type: Scholarship.
No. of awards offered: 12.
Frequency: Annual, if funds are available.
Value: US$1,100 per month.
Length of Study: Up to 6 months.
Country of Study: USA.
Application Procedure: Please contact the Scholarships Office for details.
Closing Date: May 31st.
Additional Information: The American candidates are expected to evaluate source material in the United States which is important for their research on German history. At the end of the scholarship they are required to report on their findings.

German Historical Institute Transatlantic Doctoral Seminar in German History

Subjects: German history, transatlantic studies.
Eligibility: Open to German and American doctoral students. Applications from women and minorities are especially encouraged.

Level of Study: Doctorate.
Purpose: To bring together young scholars from Germany and North America who are nearing completion of thie doctoral degrees. It provides an opprtunity to debate doctoral projects in a transatlantic setting.
Type: Scholarship.
Frequency: Annual, if funds are available.
Value: US$2,000.
Length of Study: 4 days.
Country of Study: USA or Germany.
Application Procedure: Please contact the scholarship office for details.
Closing Date: December 1st.

GERMANISTIC SOCIETY OF AMERICA

Institute of International Education
809 United Nations Plaza, New York, NY, 10017, United States of America
Tel: (1) 212 984 5330
www: http://www.iie.org
Contact: US Student Programs

Germanistic Society of America Fellowships

Subjects: Primarily in the fields of German language, literature, philosophy, history, art history, political science, economics and banking, international law and public affairs.
Eligibility: Open to US citizens who have a good academic record and capacity for independent study. Preference is given to candidates with a Master's degree.
Level of Study: Postgraduate.
Type: Fellowship.
No. of awards offered: 6.
Frequency: Annual.
Value: US$11,000 per academic year. Candidates selected will be considered for Fulbright Travel Grants.
Length of Study: 1 academic year (9 months).
Country of Study: Germany.
Closing Date: October 23rd.

THE GETTY GRANT PROGRAM, J PAUL GETTY TRUST

1200 Getty Center Drive
Suite 800, Los Angeles, CA, 90049-1685, United States of America
Tel: (1) 310 440 7320
Fax: (1) 310 440 7703
www: http://www.getty.edu/grant
Contact: Ms Joan Weinstein, Program Officer

The Getty Grant Programme is part of the J Paul Getty Trust, a private operating foundation dedicated to the visual arts and the humanities. The Getty Grant Programme supports a wide range of projects that promote research in the history of art and related fields, advancement of the understanding of art, and the conservation of cultural heritage.

The J Paul Getty Postdoctoral Fellowships in the History of Art and Humanities

Subjects: History of art and related fields.
Eligibility: Fellowships are open to scholars of all nationalities who have earned a doctoral degree within the past six years.
Level of Study: Postdoctorate.
Purpose: To provide support for outstanding scholars in the early stages of their careers to pursue interpretative research projects that make a substantial and original contribution to the understanding of art and its history.
Type: Fellowship.
No. of awards offered: 15.
Frequency: Annual.
Value: US$35,000.
Length of Study: 12 months.
Country of Study: Any country.
Application Procedure: Application forms, detailed instructions, and additional information are available from the Getty Grant Programme Office.
Closing Date: November 1st.

Senior Research Grants

Subjects: History of art and related fields.
Eligibility: Senior Research Grant teams may consist of two or more art historians, or of an art historian and one or more scholars from other disciplines. Each team must have no fewer than two scholars who are at least six years beyond the postdoctoral level.
Level of Study: Postdoctorate.
Purpose: To provide opportunities for teams of scholars to collaborate on interpretative research projects that offer new explanations of art and its history.
Type: Research Grant.
No. of awards offered: Varies.
Frequency: Annual.
Value: Varies according to the needs of the project.
Length of Study: 1-2 years.
Country of Study: Any country.
Application Procedure: Application forms, detailed instructions, and additional information are available from the Getty Grant Programme Office.
Closing Date: November 1st.

GÉZA ANDA FOUNDATION

Bleicherweg 18, Zurich, CH-8002, Switzerland
Tel: (41) 1 205 14 23
Fax: (41) 1 205 14 29
Email: gezaanda@bluewin.ch
www: http://www.gezaanda.org
Contact: Ms Ruth Bossart

The Géza Anda Foundation was established in 1977 in memory of the pianist, Géza Anda. It holds an international piano competition, every three years, awarding three prize winners some special prizes, and the opportunity for the laureates to appear as soloists in concerts and recitals.

International Géza Anda Piano Competition

Subjects: Piano.
Eligibility: Open to young pianists who are no more than 32 years of age.
Level of Study: Unrestricted.
Purpose: To sponsor young pianists in the musical spirit of Géza Anda.
Type: Prize.
No. of awards offered: 3.
Frequency: Every three years, next in 2000.
Value: Cash prizes of CHF60,000 and other benefits such as free concert management services for three years.
Country of Study: Switzerland.
Application Procedure: There are four rounds in the competition: audition, recital, Mozart, and final concert with orchestra.
Closing Date: March 1st.

GILCHRIST EDUCATIONAL TRUST

Mary Trevelyan Hall
10 York Terrace East, London, NW1 4PT, England
Tel: (44) 171 631 8300 ext 773
Contact: Mrs Everidge, Secretary

GET Grants

Subjects: All subjects.
Eligibility: Open to students in the UK who are within sight of the end of a course and are facing unexpected financial difficulties which may prevent completion of their studies; students in the UK who are required to spend a short period studying abroad as part of their course; recognised British university expeditions; and pioneer educational establishments.
Level of Study: Doctorate, Postgraduate.
Purpose: To promote the advancement of education and learning in every part of the world.
Type: Grant.
No. of awards offered: Varies.
Frequency: Dependent on funds available.

Value: Modest.
Country of Study: United Kingdom, or students studying at a United Kingdom university who are required to spend a short period abroad.
Application Procedure: University expeditions are required to complete an application form. Eligible individuals are sent a list of information required.
Closing Date: For University Expeditions: February 28th. All other categories: at any time.
Additional Information: Individuals entitled to a mandatory grant/loan are not eligible.

GLADYS KRIEBLE DELMAS FOUNDATION

521 Fifth Avenue
Suite 1612, New York, NY, 10175-1699, United States of America
Tel: (1) 212 687 0011
Fax: (1) 212 687 8877
Email: delmasfdtn@aol.com
www: http://www.delmas.org
Contact: Ms Kate Rushing

The Gladys Krieble Delmas Foundation promotes the advancement and perpetuation of humanistic enquiry and artistic creativity by encouraging excellence in scholarship and in the performing arts, and by supporting research libraries and other institutions that preserve the resources which transmit this cultural heritage.

Gladys Krieble Delmas Foundation Grants

Subjects: The history of Venice and the former Venetian empire, and for study of contemporary Venetian society and culture. Disciplines of the humanities and social sciences are eligible areas of study, including but not limited to - art, architecture, archaeology, theatre, music, literature, political science, economics and law.
Eligibility: The US programme is open to US citizens and permanent residents of the USA who have some experience in advanced research. Graduate students must have fulfilled all doctoral requirements except for completion of the dissertation, but including acceptance of the dissertation proposal, at the time of application. There is also a programme for scholars from Commonwealth countries.
Level of Study: Postdoctorate.
Purpose: To promote research in Venice and the Veneto.
Type: Grant.
No. of awards offered: Usually 15-25.
Frequency: Annual.
Value: From US$500 up to a maximum of US$12,500 for a full academic year. At the discretion of the trustees and advisory board of the Foundation, funds may be made available for aid in publication of results.
Length of Study: Up to 1 academic year.
Country of Study: Italy.

Application Procedure: Candidates should obtain the Foundation's instruction sheet and application forms for application.
Closing Date: December 15th.

GRADUATE INSTITUTE OF INTERNATIONAL STUDIES, GENEVA

Institut Universitaire de Hautes Études Internationales
Case Postale 36
132 rue de Lausanne, Geneva, CH-1211, Switzerland
Tel: (41) 22 731 17 30
Fax: (41) 738 43 06
Email: info@hei.unige.ch
www: http://heiwww.unige.ch
Telex: 412 151 Pax Ch
Contact: Secretary General

The Institute is a teaching and research establishment devoted to the scientific study of contemporary international relations. The international character of the Institute is emphasised by the use of both English and French as working languages. Its plural approach, which draws upon the method of history and political science, of law and of economics, reflects its aim to promote a broad approach and in-depth understanding of international relations.

Graduate Institute of International Studies (Geneva) Scholarships

Subjects: History and international politics, international economics, international law, political science.
Eligibility: Open to any person who can give evidence of a sound knowledge of the French language and of sufficient prior study in political science, economics, law or modern history, by the presentation of a college or university degree.
Level of Study: Doctorate, Postgraduate, Professional development.
Type: Scholarship.
No. of awards offered: 12.
Frequency: Annual.
Value: CHF1,000 per month.
Length of Study: 1 year; possibly renewable.
Study Establishment: Intensive research and study towards a doctorate at the Graduate Institute of International Studies, Geneva.
Country of Study: Switzerland.
Application Procedure: Please contact the Institute for details.
Closing Date: March 1st.
Additional Information: Scholarships are normally awarded to more advanced students of the Institute. As a general rule, they are not granted during the first year of studies. Scholars are exempt from Institute fees, but not from the obligatory fees of the University of Geneva which confers the doctorate (doctorat en relations internationales).

GRAHAM FOUNDATION FOR ADVANCED STUDIES IN THE FINE ARTS

4 West Burton Place, Chicago, IL, 60610, United States of America
Tel: (1) 312 787 4071
Email: info@grahamfoundation.org
www: http://www.grahamfoundation.org
Contact: Ms Patricia M Snyder, Administrator

The Graham Foundation is broadly interested in educational areas directly concerned with architecture - primarily at an advanced level - and with other arts and academic disciplines that are immediately contributive to architecture. The Foundation offers financial support to individuals and institutions undertaking work in the areas of its concerns. The Foundation does not offer scholarship aid.

Graham Foundation Grants

Subjects: Architecture and fine arts only as they relate to architecture.
Eligibility: There are no restrictions on eligibility.
Level of Study: Postdoctorate, Professional development.
Purpose: To assist individuals in projects related to architecture and the built environment.
Type: Grant.
No. of awards offered: 50-60.
Frequency: Semi-annually.
Value: Up to US$10,000.
Country of Study: Any country.
Application Procedure: No special application forms are required. A proposal describing the project, the people involved, and the amount sought, must be submitted. A supporting budget is required. No direct scholarship aid is offered.
Closing Date: January 15th and July 15th.

GRAND PRIX INTERNATIONAL DU SALON DE LA RECHERCHE PHOTOGRAPHIQUE

SIRP-Animation Royan
Palais des Congres
BP 102, Royan Cedex, F-17201, France
Tel: (33) 5 46 239 591
Fax: (33) 5 46 385 201
Email: lemaigre@club-internet.fr
www: http://www.altern.org/sirp
Contact: Mr Frédéric Lemaigre, Grants Management Officer

Grand Prix International du Salon de la Recherche Photographique

Subjects: Photography.
Eligibility: Open to amateurs and professionals from all over

the world.

Level of Study: Unrestricted.

Purpose: To award both amateur and professional photographers from all over the world.

Type: Competition.

No. of awards offered: 2.

Frequency: Annual.

Value: 1st prize FF20,000; 2nd prize FF10,000.

Country of Study: Any country.

Application Procedure: Please write for details.

Closing Date: May 17th.

GREEK MINISTRY OF EDUCATION

Embassy of Greece
Cultural Department
1a Holland Park, London, W1H 3TP, England
Tel: (44) 171 229 3850
Fax: (44) 171 229 7221
Contact: Dr V Solomonidis, Cultural Attaché

Greek Ministry of Education Scholarships for British Students

Subjects: All subjects.

Eligibility: Open to UK nationals who hold at least a Bachelor's degree. Candidates graduating during the year of application will be considered. Some knowledge of Modern Greek is advisable.

Level of Study: Doctorate, Postdoctorate, Postgraduate, Professional development.

Purpose: To support postgraduate research in any subject.

Type: Scholarship.

No. of awards offered: 10.

Frequency: Annual.

Value: 100,000 drachmas monthly plus 20,000 drachmas to meet expenses on first arrival (or 30,000 for those who will settle out of Athens), plus 30,000 drachmas for scholars requiring to travel within Greece for their research.

Length of Study: 4-10 months.

Study Establishment: At any university or institution of higher education in Greece.

Country of Study: Greece.

Application Procedure: Application forms may be requested from January. These must be submitted with references.

Closing Date: March 15th.

GREEK STATE SCHOLARSHIPS FOUNDATION

Embassy of Greece
1A Holland Park, London, W1H 3TP, England
Tel: (44) 171 229 3850
Fax: (44) 171 229 7221
Contact: Dr Victoria Solomonidis, Cultural Attaché

Greek State Scholarships Foundation Grants

Subjects: Greek language, literature, philosophy, history and art.

Eligibility: Open to nationals of USA, Canada, Latin America, Australia, Japan, and Western Europe. Applicants must hold a graduate degree from a foreign university and a first postgraduate degree. For postdoctoral studies, applicants must hold a doctorate degree from a foreign university. Applicants must have an excellent knowledge of English or French. Various age restrictions apply: applicants must not exceed 35 years of age, except for postdoctoral applicants who must not exceed 40 years of age, and applicants for futher education studies who must not exceed 50 years of age.

Level of Study: Doctorate, Postdoctorate, Postgraduate.

Purpose: To enable nationals from America, Japan and Western Europe to study in Greece.

Type: Scholarship.

No. of awards offered: Up to 40.

Frequency: Annual.

Value: 150,000 drachmas for initial expenses, stay permit dues, exemption from tuition or registration fees, free medical care in case of emergency. The amount of support varies from award to award; please write for exact details.

Length of Study: Varies; from a few months to 3 years.

Study Establishment: Greek university.

Country of Study: Greece.

Application Procedure: Application form must be completed and submitted with CV; transcripts of previous university studies; health certificate, confirming the good health of the applicant; three letters of recommendation; a validated photocopy of the identification card; and a recent photograph.

Closing Date: March 31st.

Additional Information: Applications may also be made by applying to Mrs M Mikedaki-Drakaki, State Scholarships Foundation, 14 Lysicrates Street, Athens, 105 58, Greece.

GRIFFITH UNIVERSITY

Office for Research and International Projects, Nathan, QLD,
4111, Australia
Tel: (61) 7 3875 6596
Fax: (61) 7 3875 7994
Email: m.brown@or.gu.edu.au
www: http://www.gu.edu.au
Contact: Ms Maxine Brown, Postgraduate Scholarships
Officer

Griffith University Postgraduate Research Scholarships

Subjects: All subjects.
Eligibility: Open to any person, irrespective of nationality,
holding or expecting to hold an upper second class honours
degree or equivalent from a recognised institution.
Level of Study: Postgraduate.
Purpose: To provide financial support for candidates
undertaking full-time research leading to the award of the
degree of Doctor of Philosophy or Master of Philosophy.
Type: Scholarship.
No. of awards offered: Varies.
Frequency: Annual.
Value: A$16,135 per year (tax exempt), plus a dependant
child allowance of A$1,500 per year (tax exempt) for some
overseas students, limited travel allowance and a thesis
production allowance.
Length of Study: Up to 2 years for Research Master's, and
up to 3 years for PhD (with possible extension of up to 6
months for PhD), subject to satisfactory progress.
Study Establishment: Griffith University.
Country of Study: Australia.
Application Procedure: Application form to be received by
October 30th in the year preceding the commencement of
study.
Closing Date: October 30th for commencement by March
30th the following year.
Additional Information: The Scholarship does not cover the
cost of tuition fees which range between A$12,000 and
A$15,000 per annum. Applicants must demonstrate
proficiency in the English language by scoring an overall
score of 6.5 in an International English Language Testing
System (IELTS) test, or test score of 580 on the Test of
English as a Foreign Language (TOEFL) including the Test of
Written English score of no less than 5.0.

The Sir Allan Sewell Visiting Fellowship

Subjects: Available for all faculties of Griffith University.
Eligibility: Open to researchers of any nationality.
Level of Study: Professional development.

Purpose: To commemorate the distinguished service of Sir
Allan Sewell to Griffith University by offering awards to enable
visits by distinguished scholars engaged in academic work
who can contribute to the research and teaching in one or
more areas of interest to a faculty or college of the university.
Type: Fellowship.
No. of awards offered: 4.
Frequency: Annual.
Value: Up to A$6,000.
Length of Study: A minimum of 8 weeks.
Study Establishment: University.
Country of Study: Australia.
Application Procedure: Fellows must be invited by
faculties/colleges of the University to apply.

GRIMSBY INTERNATIONAL SINGERS COMPETITION

23 Enfield Avenue
New Waltham, Grimsby, DN36 5RD, England
Tel: (44) 1472 812 113
Contact: Dr Anne Holmes, Co-Chair

Alec Redshaw Memorial Awards

Subjects: Vocal performance - oratorio, concert and operatic
repertoire, Lieder and early music, contemporary and French
melody.
Eligibility: Open to males and females of any nationality,
between the ages of 20 and 30 years (singers), 20 and 27
years (accompanists).
Level of Study: Unrestricted.
Purpose: To give young professional singers a platform, and
possibly engagements. All rounds are open to the public.
Music society secretaries are invited, also agents.
Type: Competition.
No. of awards offered: 17 prizes: 16 for singers and 1 for an
accompanist.
Frequency: Every three years.
Value: 4 Prizes of £2,500; 4 Prizes of £1,250; 4 Prizes of
£750; prizes of £250 each for best Italian aria, German Lied,
French melody, English song; and £750 for accompanist.
Country of Study: Any country.
Application Procedure: Please submit completed
application form plus two references; entry fee of £45,
accompanist entry fee of £25, copy of birth certificate, and
two passport size photographs.
Closing Date: March 31st.
Additional Information: The competition is held in the Town
Hall, Grimsby.

HAGLEY MUSEUM AND LIBRARY

PO Box 3630, Wilmington, DE, 19807, United States of America
Tel: (1) 302 658 2400 ext 243
Fax: (1) 302 655 3188
Email: cvl@udel.edu
www: http://hagley.lib.de.us
Contact: Dr Philip B Scranton

Hagley Museum and Library Grants-in-Aid of Research

Subjects: American economic and technological history, and French eighteenth-century history.
Eligibility: Open to degree candidates and advanced scholars of any nationality. Research must be relevant to Hagley's collections.
Level of Study: Doctorate, Postdoctorate.
Purpose: To support travel to the Hagley Library for scholarly research in the collections.
Type: Research Grant.
No. of awards offered: 25 grants-in-aid each year.
Frequency: Quarterly.
Value: Up to US$1,200 per month.
Length of Study: 2-8 weeks.
Study Establishment: The Hagley Library.
Country of Study: USA.
Application Procedure: Application and five pages of proposal.
Closing Date: March 31st, June 30th, October 30th.
Additional Information: Candidates may apply for research in the imprint, manuscript, pictorial and artefact collections of the Hagley Museum and Library. In addition the resources of the 125 libraries in the greater Philadelphia area will be at the disposal of the visiting Scholar. The research fellowship is to be used only in the Hagley Library.

Hagley/Winterthur Arts and Industries Fellowship

Subjects: Business and economics, design, architecture, crafts, fine arts, technology and industrial history.
Eligibility: Open to advanced scholars, graduate students and independent researchers.
Level of Study: Doctorate, Postdoctorate.
Purpose: To support scholarly research at Hagley and Winterthur Libraries on historical and cultural relationships between economic life and the arts.
Type: Fellowship.
No. of awards offered: 6.
Frequency: Annual.
Value: US$1,200 per month.
Length of Study: A maximum of 3 months.
Country of Study: USA.
Application Procedure: Please submit application and proposal (five pages), and two recommendations.
Closing Date: December 1st.
Additional Information: The award is a residential travel grant; the scholar must travel to Delaware to use the Collections at both the Hagley and Winterthur libraries.

Henry Bellin du Pont Fellowship

Subjects: Areas of study relevant to the Library's archival and artefact collections.
Eligibility: Open to persons who have already completed their formal professional training. Consequently, degree candidates and persons seeking support for degree work are not eligible to apply. Applicants must be from out of state and preference will be given to those whose travel costs to Hagley will be higher. Research must be relevant to Hagley's collections.
Level of Study: Doctorate, Postdoctorate.
Purpose: To support access to and use of Hagley's research collections; to enable individual out-of-state scholars to pursue their own research and to participate in the interchange of ideas among the Center's scholars.
Type: Fellowship.
No. of awards offered: Varies.
Frequency: Annual.
Value: A stipend of US$1,500 per month.
Length of Study: 2-6 months.
Study Establishment: The Library.
Country of Study: USA.
Application Procedure: Application and proposal of five pages.
Closing Date: March 31st, June 30th, October 30th.
Additional Information: Fellows must devote their full time to their studies and may not accept teaching assignments or undertake any other major activities during the tenure of their fellowships. Tenure must be continuous and last from two to six months. At the end of their tenure, Fellows must submit a final report on their activities and accomplishments. As a centre for advanced study in the humanities, Hagley is a focal point of a community of scholars. Fellows are expected to participate in seminars which meet periodically, as well as attend noon-time colloquia, lectures, concerts, exhibits, and other public programs offered during their tenure. Research fellowships are to be used in the Hagley Library only, not as scholarships for college.

THE HAMBIDGE CENTER

PO Box 339, Rabun Gap, GA, 30568, United States of America
Tel: (1) 706 746 5718
Fax: (1) 706 746 9933
Email: hambidge@acme-brain.com
www: http://www.acme-brain.com/~hambidge
Contact: Mr Bob Thomas, Assistant to the Director and Residecy Manager

The Hambidge Center's primary function is an Artist Residency Programme with a mission to provide artists with time and space to pursue their work, enable artists to enhance their communities' art environment, provide public accessibility through a gallery and nature trails, and to protect and sustain natural environment, land and endangered species.

Hambidge Center Residency Program

Subjects: Any field or discipline of creative work.
Eligibility: Open to qualified applicants in all disciplines who can demonstrate seriousness, dedication and professionalism. International residents are welcome.
Level of Study: Unrestricted.
Purpose: To provide an environment for creative work.
Type: Residency.
No. of awards offered: 70-80.
Frequency: Dependent on space available.
Value: Cost to residents is US$125 per week and includes all linens plus evening meals Monday to Friday for the May to October season. No meals are available November to April.
Length of Study: From 2 weeks to 2 months.
Study Establishment: The Hambidge Center.
Country of Study: USA.
Application Procedure: Application form provided with SASE sent to Center for the attention of the Residency Program.
Closing Date: Applications are accepted and reviewed periodically throughout the year. November 1st is the deadline for March through until August, and May 1st is the deadline for September through until February.
Additional Information: The Hambidge Center, located in Northeast Georgia, is set in 600 acres of mountain/valley terrain, with waterfalls and nature trails.

THE HARRY S TRUMAN LIBRARY INSTITUTE

500 West US Hwy 24, Independence, MO, 64050, United States of America
Tel: (1) 816 833 0425
Fax: (1) 816 833 2715
Email: library@truman.nara.gov
www: http://www.trumanlibrary.org
Contact: The Secretary

Harry S Truman Library Institute Dissertation Year Fellowships

Subjects: The public career of Harry S Truman and the history of the Truman administration.
Eligibility: Open to individuals who have completed their dissertation research and are ready to begin writing.
Level of Study: Postgraduate.
Purpose: To encourage historical scholarship in the Truman era.
Type: Fellowship.
No. of awards offered: 1.
Frequency: Annual.

Value: US$16,000, payable in two instalments.
Country of Study: USA.
Application Procedure: Please write for an application form.
Closing Date: February 1st for notification in April.
Additional Information: Recipients will not be required to come to the Truman Library but will be expected to furnish the Library with a copy of their dissertation.

Harry S Truman Library Institute Research Grants

Subjects: The public career of Harry S Truman and the history of the Truman administration.
Eligibility: Open to graduate students and postdoctoral scholars who are working on a project pertaining to Truman's public career or to some facet of his administration.
Level of Study: Postdoctorate, Postgraduate.
Purpose: To enable graduate students and postdoctoral scholars to come to the library for one to three weeks to use its archival facilities.
Type: Research Grant.
No. of awards offered: Varies.
Frequency: Twice a year.
Value: Up to US$2,500, to cover round-trip air fare between the applicant's home and Independence, and a modest sum to cover living expenses while working at the Library.
Length of Study: 1-3 weeks.
Study Establishment: The Library.
Country of Study: USA.
Application Procedure: Please write for details.
Closing Date: April 1st, October 1st.

Harry S Truman Library Institute Scholar's Award

Subjects: The public career of Harry S Truman or some aspect of the history of the Truman administration or of the USA during that administration.
Eligibility: Open to established scholars and scholars about to embark on their careers.
Level of Study: Postgraduate.
No. of awards offered: 1.
Frequency: Every two years.
Value: Based primarily on a proposed budget submitted by the applicant and may amount to as much as one-half the applicant's academic-year salary.
Study Establishment: Recipients will be expected to spend a major portion of their research time utilising the resources of the Truman Library.
Country of Study: USA.
Application Procedure: Please write for details.
Closing Date: December 15th.
Additional Information: The research should result in a book-length manuscript intended for publication; one copy of the publication resulting from work done under the award is to be provided by the author to the Library.

HARVARD BUSINESS SCHOOL

Morgan 295
Soldiers Field, Boston, MA, 02163, United States of America
Tel: (1) 617 495 6008
Fax: (1) 617 496 5994
Email: esampson@hbs.edu
www: http://www.hbs.edu
Contact: Professor Nancy F Koehn

Alfred D Chandler Jr Traveling Fellowships in Business History and Institutional Economic History

Subjects: Business history, institutional economic history, topics such as labour relations and government regulation will also be considered if the approach is primarily institutional.
Eligibility: Open to Harvard University graduate students in history, economics, business administration, or a related discipline such as sociology, government, or law, whose research requires travel to distant archives or repositories; graduate students or non-tenured faculty in those fields from other North American universities, whose research requires travel to the Boston-Cambridge area (to study, for example, in the collections at the Baker, Widener, McKay, Law, Kress, or Houghton libraries); and Harvard College undergraduates writing senior theses in those fields, whose research requires similar travel.
Level of Study: Postgraduate.
Purpose: To facilitate library and archival research in business history or institutional economic history, broadly defined.
Type: Fellowship.
No. of awards offered: Varies.
Frequency: Annual.
Value: US$1,000-US$3,000 from a total of approximately US$15,000.
Country of Study: Any country.
Application Procedure: Application forms are available on request.
Closing Date: December 1st.

Harvard-Newcomen Fellowship in Business History

Subjects: Any research project connected with economic and business history.
Eligibility: Open to applicants who have received a PhD within the ten years preceding the start of the fellowship (July 1st or September 1st). Harvard University is an equal opportunity, affirmative action employer.
Level of Study: Postdoctorate.
Purpose: To assist young scholars in improving their professional acquaintance with business and economic history and to engage in research that will benefit from the resources of the Harvard Business School and the Boston-Cambridge scholarly community.
Type: Fellowship.
No. of awards offered: 1.
Frequency: Annual.
Value: US$46,000.

Length of Study: 12 months.
Study Establishment: Harvard Business School for one year, including participation in the business history course and seminar (one semester each) plus other courses the applicant wishes to audit.
Country of Study: USA.
Application Procedure: Application forms are available on request.
Closing Date: November 1st.

HARVARD UNIVERSITY, CENTER FOR THE STUDY OF WORLD RELIGIONS

42 Francis Avenue, Cambridge, MA, 02138, United States of America
Tel: (1) 617 495 4476
Fax: (1) 617 496 5411
Email: mhedderick@hds.harvard.edu
www: http://divweb.harvard.edu/cswr/
Contact: Ms Malgorzata Radziszewska-Hedderick, Educative Planning Co-ordinator

Harvard Center for the Study of World Religions fosters excellence in the study of religions of the world. Two characteristics mark the Center: the international scope of its subject matter and constituency, and the encouragement of multiple disciplinary approches toward the study of religion. The Center offers no scheduled courses of instruction but rather is distiguished by the quality of scholars in residence - Senior Fellows and others, affiliated faculty, and visiting lecturers.

Harvard University, Center for the Study of World Religions, Senior Fellowship

Subjects: Religious studies - historical and comparative study of religions.
Eligibility: Open to postdoctoral scholars whose research proposal is in the area of historical or comparative religion.
Level of Study: Postdoctorate.
Purpose: Senior fellowship at the Centre provides individual scholars, from many nations, time for investigation and access to the resources of Harvard University. It also facilitates the exchange of ideas growing out of such research.
Type: Fellowship.
No. of awards offered: Varies.
Frequency: Annual.
Value: Opportunity to reside at the Center, admission to the Director's seminar and University library access, $4,000 stipend.
Length of Study: 1 academic year.
Study Establishment: Harvard University Center for the Study of World Religions, in Cambridge, Massachusetts.
Country of Study: USA.

Application Procedure: Applicants are asked to complete an application form, arrange for two letters of recommendation (using forms provided by the Center) and provide a research proposal and curriculum vitae.

Closing Date: January 15th.

Additional Information: Funds are limited and the $4,000 fellowship stipend awarded to Fellows covers only a small fraction of the expenses facing visiting Center Fellows. Therefore, scholars admitted as fellows need to seek the bulk of their financial support from sources other than the Center.

HATTORI FOUNDATION

Norfolk Lodge
72E Leopold Road, London, SW19 7JQ, England
Tel: (44) 181 944 5319
Fax: (44) 181 946 6970
Contact: Ms Kim Gaynor, Administrator

The chief aim of the Foundation is to encourage and assist exceptionally talented young instrumental soloists or chamber ensembles who are British nationals or resident in the United Kingdom, and whose talent and achievement give promise of an international career.

Hattori Foundation Awards

Subjects: Solo performance (instrumental), chamber music.

Eligibility: Open to British or foreign nationals, between 21 and 27 years of age, studying full-time in the UK. Foreign applicants must have won a major prize in an international competition or won a national competition. Candidates should be of postgraduate performance status.

Level of Study: Postgraduate, Professional development.

Purpose: To assist young instrumentalists of exceptional talent in establishing a soloist (or chamber music) career at international level.

Type: Individual project assistance.

No. of awards offered: Up to 20.

Frequency: Annual.

Value: No pre-determined amounts. The grant is based on the requirements of the approved project.

Length of Study: Varies, but 1 year maximum.

Country of Study: British nationals: any country; foreign nationals: resident in the United Kingdom only.

Application Procedure: Please submit application and reference forms, plus 30 minute performance (recital) on cassette tape.

Closing Date: April 30th.

Additional Information: Grants may be made for study, concert experience, and international competitions. Projects must be submitted for approval and discussion with the Director of Music and the trustees. Auditions take place in June and are in two stages.

HAYSTACK MOUNTAIN SCHOOL OF CRAFTS

PO Box 518, Deer Isle, ME, 04627, United States of America
Tel: (1) 207 348 2306
Fax: (1) 207 348 2307
Email: haystack@haystack-mtn.org
www: http://www.haystack-mtn.org
Contact: Ms Jacqueline Michaud, Development Director

The Haystack Mountain School of Crafts studio programme in the arts offers two and three week workshops in a variety of craft and visual mediums including clay, wood, glass, metals, fibres, blacksmithing, and graphics.

Haystack Scholarship

Subjects: Handicrafts, instruction in fine crafts.

Eligibility: Open to nationals of any country.

Level of Study: Unrestricted.

Purpose: To allow craftspeople of all skill levels to study at Haystack sessions for two or three week periods. Technical Assistant and Work Study positions as well as minority scholarships.

Type: Scholarship.

No. of awards offered: 90.

Frequency: Annual.

Value: US$500 to US$1,000.

Length of Study: 2-3 weeks.

Country of Study: Any country.

Application Procedure: Application including references and supporting materials are required.

Closing Date: March 25th.

HEBREW IMMIGRANT AID SOCIETY (HIAS)

333 Seventh Avenue, New York, NY, 10001, United States of America
Tel: (1) 212 613 1351
Email: mbellow@hias.org
Contact: Ms Marina Belotserkousky, Associate Director

HIAS is the international migration agency of the organised Jewish community.

HIAS Scholarship Awards

Subjects: All subjects.

Eligibility: Open to HIAS-assisted refugees and their children who arrived in the USA in 1985 or later. Applicants must have completed one year (two semesters) at a USA high school, college, or graduate school.

Level of Study: Doctorate, Postgraduate, Undergraduate.

Purpose: To assist HIAS-assisted refugees and their children.

Type: One-time grant.

No. of awards offered: 150.

Frequency: Annual.
Value: Average award: US$1,000.
Length of Study: 1 year must be completed.
Country of Study: USA.
Application Procedure: Requests for applications must be in writing and must include a self-addressed stamped envelope. Applications are judged on financial need, academic scholarship and community service. Applications are available starting in February each year.
Closing Date: April 15th.

HERBERT HOOVER PRESIDENTIAL LIBRARY ASSOCIATION

PO Box 696, West Branch, IA, 52358, United States of America
Tel: (1) 319 643 5327
Fax: (1) 319 643 2391
Email: info@hooverassoc.org
www: http://www.hooverassoc.org
Contact: Ms Patricia A Hand

The Herbert Hoover Presidential Library Association is a private non-profit support group for the Herbert Hoover Presidential Library Museum and National Historic Site in West Branch, Iowa.

Herbert Hoover Presidential Library Association Travel Grants

Subjects: American history, journalism, political science, economic history.
Eligibility: Open to current graduate students, postdoctoral students, and qualified non-academic researchers. Priority is given to well-developed proposals that utilise the resources of the Hoover Presidential Library and which have the greatest likelihood of publication and subsequent use by educators, students and policy makers.
Level of Study: Doctorate, Postdoctorate, Postgraduate, Professional development, Undergraduate.
Purpose: To encourage scholarly use of the holdings, and to promote the study of subjects of interest and concern to Herbert Hoover, Lou Henry Hoover and other public figures.
Type: Travel Grant.
No. of awards offered: Varies.
Frequency: Annual.
Value: Usually US$500-US$1,200 to cover the cost of a trip to the Library, but requests will be considered for longer research stays.

Study Establishment: Herbert Hoover Presidential Library in West Branch, IA.
Country of Study: USA.
Application Procedure: Please submit application form, project proposal of not more than 1200 words, and three letters of reference mailed separately.
Closing Date: March 1st.
Additional Information: For archival holdings information, call (1) 319 643 5301.

HILDA MARTINDALE EDUCATIONAL TRUST

c/o Registry
Royal Holloway University of London, Egham, Surrey, TW20 0EX, England
Tel: (44) 1784 434 455
Fax: (44) 1784 437 520
Contact: Miss J L Hurn, Secretary to the Trustees

The Trust was set up by Mrs Hilda Martindale in order to help women of the British Isles with the costs of vocational training for any profession or career likely to be of use or value to the community. Applications are considered annually by six women Trustees.

Hilda Martindale Exhibitions

Subjects: Any vocational training for a profession or career likely to be of value to the community.
Eligibility: Open to women of the British Isles.
Level of Study: Postgraduate, Professional development.
Purpose: To assist with the costs of vocational training.
Type: Grant.
No. of awards offered: 25-35.
Frequency: Annual.
Value: Varies, normally £200-£1,000.
Length of Study: 1 year.
Study Establishment: Any establishment in the UK approved by the trustees.
Country of Study: United Kingdom.
Application Procedure: Application form (two copies) to be obtained from and returned to the Secretary to the Trustees.
Closing Date: March 1st, for the following academic year. Late or retrospective applications will not be considered.
Additional Information: Assistance is not given for short courses, courses abroad, elective studies, intercalated BSc years, access courses, or academic research. Awards are not given to those who are eligible for grants from LEAs, research councils, British Academy or other public sources.

THE HINRICHSEN FOUNDATION

10-12 Baches Street, London, N1 6DN, England
Contact: The Secretary

Hinrichsen Foundation Awards

Subjects: Contemporary music composition, performance and research.
Eligibility: Preference will be given to UK applicants and/or projects taking place in the UK.
Purpose: To promote the written areas of music by assisting contemporary composition and its performance, and musical research.
No. of awards offered: Varies.
Frequency: Dependent on funds available.
Value: Varies.
Country of Study: Any country.
Application Procedure: Application form and two references are required.
Closing Date: Applications are accepted at any time.
Additional Information: Grants are not given for recordings, for the funding of commissions, for degree or other study courses or for the purchase of instruments or equipment.

HISTORIC NEW ORLEANS COLLECTION

533 Royal Street, New Orleans, LA, 70130, United States of America
Tel: (1) 504 523 4662
Fax: (1) 504 598 7108
Email: hnoinfo@hnoc.org
www: http://www.hnoc.org
Contact: Dr John Lawrence

L Kemper Williams Prizes

Subjects: History.
Eligibility: There are no eligibility restrictions.
Level of Study: Unrestricted.
Purpose: To honour the best contribution to historical work about Louisiana.
Type: Cash and Plaque.
No. of awards offered: 1.
Frequency: Annual.
Value: US$1,500 published work.
Country of Study: Any country.
Application Procedure: Please submit four copies of work and four copies of the application form.
Closing Date: January 15th for works published from the previous calendar year.
Additional Information: The administration of these prizes is determined by a committee of scholars chosen by the Louisiana Historical Association. Funding is provided by the Historic New Orleans Collection.

HOSEI UNIVERSITY

17-1 Fujimi 2 chome
Chiyoda-ku, Tokyo, 102, Japan
Tel: (81) 3 3264 9662
Fax: (81) 3 3239 9873
Email: ic@l.hosei.ac.jp
www: http://www.hosei.ac.jp/ic/

Hosei International Fund Foreign Scholars Fellowship

Subjects: Humanities, social and natural sciences, and engineering.
Eligibility: Open to foreign citizens (including stateless persons), who have sufficient knowledge and fluency in either English or Japanese, hold advanced academic degree(s) (Master's or Doctorate) or the equivalent, and are not more than 35 years of age as of April 1st the year they begin their research.
Level of Study: Doctorate.
Purpose: To enable young foreign scholars to undertake non-degree research through a specific research project.
Type: Fellowship.
No. of awards offered: 3.
Frequency: Annual.
Value: Y210,000 per month, Y150,000 maximum for one-way travelling expenses.
Length of Study: 6-12 months.
Study Establishment: Hosei University.
Country of Study: Japan.
Application Procedure: The application must include: the application form, sealed letters of recommendation, a photocopied certificate from the school which the applicant last attended, and a copy of a book, article or thesis written by the applicant in either Japanese (around 2,000 characters) or English (around 1,000 words). All application documents should be sent to International Center at Hosei University.
Closing Date: May 31st every year.
Additional Information: The study undertaken at the University on this programme is non-degree; the participants will receive no course credits.

HOUSE OF HUMOUR AND SATIRE

PO Box 104, Gabrovo, BG-5300, Bulgaria
Tel: (359) 66 27229
Fax: (359) 66 26989
Email: humorhouse@usa.net
www: http://www.humorhouse.org/
Telex: 67413
Contact: Ms Tatyana Tsankova, Director

House of Humour and Satire Prizes

Subjects: Drawing and painting. The prize is for the best achievement which combines a smart humorous idea and exquisite execution.

Eligibility: Open to nationals of any country.

Level of Study: Unrestricted.

Purpose: To stimulate the creation of humour art.

Type: Cash Prize.

No. of awards offered: Approx. 6-10.

Frequency: Every two years.

Value: From US$300 to US$1,000.

Country of Study: Any country.

Application Procedure: Please write for an application form which will be sent out in autumn 2000.

Closing Date: March 1st, every odd year.

Additional Information: Prizes are awarded in a number of different categories. Conditions for entry and competition categories for the year 2001 will be made available in autumn 2000.

HUMANITARIAN TRUST

36-38 Westbourne Grove, London, W2 5SH, England
Contact: Mrs M Myers, Secretary of Trustees

Humanitarian Trust Awards

Subjects: Unrestricted, subject to the discretion of the Trustees. Awards are not made for journalism, theatre, music or any arts subjects. All aspects of medical sciences are eligible apart from nursing, medical auxiliaries, midwifery, radiology, treatment techniques, and medical technology. Candidates are only considered when studying academic subjects.

Eligibility: Open to persons already holding an original grant.

Level of Study: Graduate, Postgraduate, Undergraduate.

Purpose: General charitable purposes beneficial to the community.

Type: Award.

No. of awards offered: Approx.15.

Frequency: Twice a year.

Value: Approximately £200.

Length of Study: 1 year; not renewable.

Study Establishment: Any approved institution.

Country of Study: United Kingdom.

Application Procedure: Please write in. Submit two references, preferably from tutors or heads of department, and a breakdown of anticipated income and expenditure.

Additional Information: Awards are not made for travel or overseas courses. They are intended only as supplementary assistance and are to be held concurrently with other awards.

HUNGARIAN TELEVISION, INTERART FESTIVALCENTER

PO Box 80
1051 Vörösmarty Tér 1, Budapest, H-1366, Hungary
Tel: (36) 1 317 9838
Fax: (36) 1 317 9910
Contact: Grants Management Officer

The Hungarian Television Interart Festivalcenter has organised the International Conductors' Competition every third year, since 1974. The goal of the competition is to discover gifted young conductors from Hungary and abroad, to introduce them to the possible audience and to stimulate public interest in musical performance, musical values and modes and possibilities of interpretation.

Hungarian Television/Interart Festivalcenter International Conductors' Competition

Subjects: Conducting.

Eligibility: Open to conductors of all nationalities.

Level of Study: Professional development.

Purpose: To hold a competition in memory of Jànos Ferencsik.

Type: Competition.

No. of awards offered: 3.

Frequency: Every three years.

Value: First prize: US$5,000; Second prize: US$3,000; Third prize: US$2,000.

Country of Study: Any country.

Application Procedure: Application form must be completed and submitted with study documents, two photos and a video-recording.

Closing Date: December 1st.

THE HUNTINGTON

Committee on Awards
1151 Oxford Road, San Marino, CA, 91108, United States of America
Tel: (1) 626 405 2194
Fax: (1) 626 449 5703
Email: cpowell@huntington.org
www: http://www.huntington.org
Contact: Mr Robert C Ritchie, Chairman

Barbara Thom Postdoctoral Fellowship

Subjects: British and American history, literature, art, and history of science.

Eligibility: Preference will be given to scholars who are four or five years beyond the award of PhD.

Level of Study: Postdoctorate.

Purpose: To support a non-tenured faculty member while revising a manuscript for publication.

Type: Fellowship.

No. of awards offered: 2.

Frequency: Annual.
Value: US$30,000.
Length of Study: 1 year.
Study Establishment: The Huntington.
Country of Study: USA.
Application Procedure: For application information please contact the Chair, Committee on Awards, at the address given.
Closing Date: Applications are accepted between October 1st and December 15th.

Huntington Short-Term Fellowships

Subjects: British and American history, literature, history of science and art.
Eligibility: Open to nationals of any country who have demonstrated, to a degree commensurate with their age and experience, unusual abilities as scholars through publications of a high order of merit. Attention is paid to the value of the candidate's project and the degree to which the special strengths of the Library and Art Gallery will be used.
Level of Study: Postdoctorate, Postgraduate.
Purpose: To enable outstanding scholars to carry out significant research in the collections of the Library and Art Gallery by assisting in balancing budgets of such persons on leave at reduced pay and living away from home.
Type: Fellowship.
No. of awards offered: Approx. 100 Fellowships, depending on funds available.
Frequency: Annual.
Value: US$1,800 per month.
Length of Study: 1-5 months.
Study Establishment: The Huntington.
Country of Study: USA.
Application Procedure: For an application form please contact the Chair, Committee on Awards, at the address given.
Closing Date: Applications are accepted between October 1st and December 15th.
Additional Information: Fellowships are available for work towards doctoral dissertations.

Mellon Postdoctoral Research Fellowships

Subjects: British and American history, literature, art, and history of science.
Eligibility: Preference will be given to scholars who have not held a major award in the three years preceding the year of this award.
Level of Study: Postdoctorate.
Purpose: To support scholarship in a field appropriate to the Huntington's collections.
Type: Fellowship.
No. of awards offered: 2.

Frequency: Annual.
Value: US$30,000.
Length of Study: 1 year.
Study Establishment: The Huntington.
Country of Study: USA.
Closing Date: Applications are accepted between October 1st and December 15th.

National Endowment for the Humanities Fellowships

Subjects: British and American history, literature, art, and history of science.
Eligibility: Preference will be given to scholars who have not held a major award in the 3 years preceding the year of this award.
Level of Study: Postdoctorate.
Purpose: To support scholarship in a field appropriate to the Huntington's collections.
Type: Fellowship.
No. of awards offered: 3.
Frequency: Annual.
Value: Up to US$30,000.
Length of Study: 4 to 12 months.
Application Procedure: For application information please contact the Chair, Committee on Awards, at the address given.
Closing Date: Applications are accepted between October 1st and December 15th.

The W M Keck Foundation Fellowship for Young Scholars

Subjects: British and American history, literature and art, history of science.
Eligibility: There are no restrictions on age, nationality, or citizenship.
Level of Study: Postgraduate.
Purpose: To encourage outstanding young scholars to pursue their own lines of enquiry (completing dissertation research or beginning a new project) in the fields of British and American history, literature, art, and history of science.
Type: Fellowship.
No. of awards offered: Varies.
Frequency: Annual.
Value: US$2,300 per month.
Length of Study: 1-3 months.
Study Establishment: The Huntington.
Country of Study: USA.
Application Procedure: For application information please contact the Chair, Committee on Awards, at the address given.
Closing Date: Applications are accepted between October 1st and December 15th.

IAN FLEMING CHARITABLE TRUST

Fleming Awards
16 Ogle Street, London, W1P 7LG, England
Tel: (44) 171 636 4481
Fax: (44) 171 637 4307
Contact: Mrs Susan Dolton

Ian Fleming Charitable Trust Music Education Awards

Subjects: Musical performance.
Eligibility: Open to singers and instrumentalists possessing the potential to become first-class performers, who have been resident in the UK for three years and are no more than 26 years of age (30 years for singers).
Level of Study: Postgraduate, Professional development, Unrestricted.
Purpose: To help exceptionally talented young musicians.
No. of awards offered: Approx. 20.
Frequency: Annual.
Value: Varies; to cover tuition, maintenance and the purchase of instruments. Award will not exceed £4,000 per applicant (£40,000 available).
Country of Study: Any country.
Application Procedure: Application forms must be completed and two references provided; selected applicants will be invited to auditions.
Closing Date: Early February.
Additional Information: Selected applicants will be asked to audition in March/April.

IAN KARTEN CHARITABLE TRUST

The Mill House
Newark Lane, Ripley, Surrey, GU23 6DP, England
Fax: (44) 1483 222420
Contact: Mr Ian H Karten, Trustee and Administrator

Ian Karten Scholarship

Subjects: Most subjects, with varying levels of priority.
Eligibility: Open to British students of any religion or ethnic background. Jewish students of any nationality, under 30 years of age on October 1st of year for which grant is sought, are also eligible.
Level of Study: Doctorate, Postgraduate.
Purpose: To assist eligible students with the costs of postgraduate programmes of research at universities in the United Kingdom.
Type: Scholarship.
No. of awards offered: 100.
Frequency: Annual.
Value: Varies.
Study Establishment: UK university or conservatoire.

Country of Study: United Kingdom.
Application Procedure: Applicants should apply in writing in February for details of application procedure, giving brief details about themselves and their course, enclosing a SAE.
Closing Date: May 31st.

THE INCORPORATED EDWIN AUSTIN ABBEY MEMORIAL SCHOLARSHIPS

PO Box 5, Rhayader, Powys, LD6 5WA, Wales
Tel: (44) 1597 810 704
Email: faithclark@netmatters.co.uk
Contact: Ms Faith Clark

Abbey Awards in Painting

Subjects: Painting.
Eligibility: There are no age restrictions.
Level of Study: Professional development.
Purpose: To allow mid-career painters to pursue their artistic studies and mural decoration.
No. of awards offered: Varies.
Frequency: Annual, if funds are available.
Value: Varies.
Length of Study: 2-3 months.
Study Establishment: British School at Rome.
Country of Study: Italy.
Application Procedure: Awards are advertised. Application forms will be sent in response to letters enclosing stamped self addressed envelopes.
Closing Date: January 31st.
Additional Information: Awards are for painters only.

Abbey Scholarship in Painting

Subjects: Painting.
Level of Study: Postgraduate.
Purpose: To spend one academic year at the British School at Rome in order to pursue artistic studies and mural decoration.
Type: Scholarship.
No. of awards offered: 1.
Frequency: Annual.
Value: Varies.
Length of Study: 1 academic year.
Study Establishment: British School at Rome.
Country of Study: Italy.
Application Procedure: The scholarship is advertised and administered through the British School at Rome.
Closing Date: Applications are accepted at any time.

For further information contact:

The British School at Rome
Via Gramsci, Rome, 00197, Italy
Tel: (390) 6 32 64 939
Fax: (390) 6 32 21 201

INDIANA UNIVERSITY CENTER ON PHILANTHROPY

550 W North Street
Ste 301, Indianapolis, IN, 46202-3162, United States of
America
Tel: (1) 317 274 4200
Fax: (1) 317 684 8900
Email: jafellow@iupui.edu
www: http://www.philanthropy.iupui.edu
Contact: Mr Robert Payton

The Indiana University Center on Philanthropy is dedicated to
education, research and public service in philanthropy. An
academic unit of Indiana University, the Center is located on
the Indiana University Purdue University at Indianapolis
(IUPUI) campus.

Jane Addams/Andrew Carnegie Fellowships in Philanthropy

Subjects: The theory and practice of the philanthropic
tradition, its history and societal role, its ethics and values, its
opportunities and limitations, and its responsibilities. Fellows
spend a portion of their time working under appropriate
supervision at a local non-profit organisation in their field of
interest.
Eligibility: Open to recent graduates with a bachelor's degree
(or equivalent degree from another country). The programme
is not intended for students who already have committed to a
graduate programme, or who have received a graduate
degree.
Level of Study: Postgraduate.
Purpose: To advance and renew interest in public service by
engaging recent college graduates in intensive study and
voluntary action.
Type: Fellowship.
No. of awards offered: 6.
Frequency: Annual.
Value: US$15,000 plus all tuition and mandatory fees will be
waived.
Length of Study: 10 months.
Study Establishment: Indiana University Center on
Philanthropy.
Country of Study: USA.
Application Procedure: Please write for details.
Closing Date: February 2nd.
Additional Information: Candidates should have a special
interest in some aspect of the non-profit community. Fellows
must be able to spend the full programme period in
Indianapolis.

INSTITUT FRANÇAIS DE WASHINGTON

234 Dey Hall
CB#3170
UNC-CH, Chapel Hill, NC, 27599-3170, United States of
America
Tel: (1) 919 962 0154
Fax: (1) 919 962 5457
Email: cmaley@email.unc.edu
Contact: Dr Catherine A Maley, President

Edouard Morot-Sir Fellowship in Literature

Subjects: French studies in the areas of - art, economics,
history, history of science, linguistics, literature and social
sciences.
Eligibility: Final stage PhD dissertation, or PhD held no longer
than six years before application deadline.
Level of Study: Doctorate, Postdoctorate.
Type: Fellowship.
Frequency: Annual.
Value: US$1,000.
Length of Study: At least 2 months.
Country of Study: France.
Application Procedure: No application form; applicants write
two pages maximum describing research project and planned
trip and giving curriculum vitae. A letter of recommendation
from the dissertation director is also required.
Closing Date: January 15th.
Additional Information: Awards are for maintenance (not
travel) during research in France.

Gilbert Chinard Fellowships

Subjects: French studies in the areas of - art, economics,
history, history of science, linguistics, literature and social
sciences.
Eligibility: Final stage PhD dissertation, or PhD held no longer
than six years before application deadline.
Level of Study: Doctorate, Postdoctorate.
Type: Fellowship.
No. of awards offered: 3.
Frequency: Annual.
Value: US$1,000.
Length of Study: At least 2 months.
Country of Study: France.
Application Procedure: No application form; applicants write
two pages maximum describing research project and planned
trip and giving curriculum vitae. A letter of recommendation
from the dissertation director is also required for PhD
candidates.
Closing Date: January 15th.
Additional Information: Awards are for maintenance (not
travel) during research in France.

INSTITUTE FOR ADVANCED STUDIES IN THE HUMANITIES

University of Edinburgh
Hope Park Square, Edinburgh, EH8 9NW, Scotland
Tel: (44) 131 650 4671
Fax: (44) 131 668 2252
Email: iash@ed.ac.uk
www: http://www.ed.ac.uk/~iash/homepage.html
Contact: A M Taylor, Assistant to Director

The Institute aims to promote scholarship in the Humanities, and wherever possible to foster inter-disciplinary enquiries. This is achieved by means of fellowships awarded for the pursuit of relevant research; and by the public dissemination of findings in seminars, lectures, conferences, exhibitions, cultural events, and publications.

Andrew W Mellon Foundation Fellowships in the Humanities

Subjects: Humanities.
Eligibility: Restricted to Bulgarian, Czech, Hungarian, Polish Romanian and Slovak scholars. Fellows must be able to speak English.
Level of Study: Postdoctorate.
Purpose: To promote advanced research within the field of humanities, broadly understood, and to sponsor inter-disciplinary research.
Type: Grant.
No. of awards offered: 3.
Frequency: Annual.
Length of Study: 3 months.
Study Establishment: The Institute for Advanced Studies in the Humanities.
Country of Study: Scotland.
Application Procedure: Application forms are available from the Institute.
Closing Date: March 31st.

European Enlightenment Project Fellowships

Subjects: All disciplines concerned with the European Enlightenment.
Eligibility: Open to postdoctoral scholars; degree candidates are not eligible. Fellows must be able to speak English.
Level of Study: Postdoctorate.
Purpose: To support leading scholars, from any discipline, whose work concerns the European Enlightenment (1720-1800), to take part in the Institute's five-year project on the Enlightenment.
Type: Fellowship.
No. of awards offered: 100 over 5 years.
Frequency: Annual.
Length of Study: 3-6 months.
Study Establishment: The Institute for Advanced Studies in the Humanities.
Country of Study: Scotland.

Application Procedure: Application forms are available from the Institute.
Closing Date: December 1st.

Institute for Advanced Studies in the Humanities Visiting Research Fellowships

Subjects: Archaeology, history of art, classics, English literature, history, European and oriental languages and literature, linguistics, philosophy, Scottish studies, history of science, law, divinity, music and the social sciences.
Eligibility: Open to scholars of any nationality holding a doctorate or offering equivalent evidence of aptitude for advanced studies. Degree candidates are ineligible.
Level of Study: Postdoctorate.
Purpose: To promote advanced research within the field of the humanities, broadly understood, and also to sponsor inter-disciplinary research.
Type: Fellowship.
No. of awards offered: 15.
Frequency: Annual.
Value: Most fellowships are honorary, but limited support towards expenses is available to a small number of candidates.
Length of Study: 2-6 months.
Study Establishment: The Institute for Advanced Studies in the Humanities.
Country of Study: United Kingdom.
Application Procedure: Application forms are available from the Institute.
Closing Date: December 1st.
Additional Information: Fellows have the use of study-rooms at the Institute, near the university library and within easy reach of the National Library of Scotland, the Central City Library, the National Galleries and Museums, the Library of the Society of Antiquaries in Scotland, and the Scottish Record Office. Candidates should advise their referees to write on their behalf direct to the Institute and to ensure that references are received in Edinburgh before January 7th.

INSTITUTE FOR ADVANCED STUDY

Olden Lane, Princeton, NJ, 08540, United States of America
Tel: (1) 609 734 8000
Fax: (1) 609 924 8399
Email: gwhidden@ias.edu
www: http://www.ias.edu
Contact: Ms Georgia Whidden

The Institute is an independent, private institution whose mission is to support advanced scholarship and fundamental research in historical studies, mathematics, natural sciences, and social science. It is a community of scholars where theoretical research and intellectual enquiry are carried out.

Institute for Advanced Study Postdoctoral Residential Fellowships

Subjects: Social science, history, astronomy, theoretical physics, mathematics, and theoretical biology.
Eligibility: There are no restrictions on eligibility.
Level of Study: Postdoctorate.
Purpose: To support advanced study.
Type: Stipend.
No. of awards offered: 180.
Frequency: Annual.
Value: US$25,000-US$35,000.
Length of Study: Average: 1 year.
Country of Study: USA.
Application Procedure: Application materials are available from the School administrative officers.
Closing Date: Varies: November 15th - December 15th.

INSTITUTE FOR ECUMENICAL AND CULTURAL RESEARCH

PO Box 6188, Collegeville, MN, 53621-6188, United States of America
Tel: (1) 320 363 3366
Fax: (1) 320 363 3313
Email: iecr@csbsju.edu
www: http://www.csbsju.edu/iecr
Contact: Mr Patrick Henry, Executive Director

The Institute seeks to discern the meaning of Christian identity and unity in a religiously and culturally diverse nation and world, and to communicate that meaning for the mission of the church and the renewal of human community. The Institute is committed to research, study, prayer, reflection and dialogue, in a place shaped by the Benedictine tradition of worship and work.

Bishop Thomas Hoyt Jr Fellowship

Subjects: Ecumenical and cultural research.
Eligibility: Open to a North American, Canadian, or Mexican, person of colour writing a doctoral dissertation within the general area of the Institute's concern.
Level of Study: Postgraduate.
Purpose: To provide the Institute's residency fee to a North American person of colour writing a doctoral dissertation, in order to help the churches to increase the number of persons of colour working in ecumenical and cultural research.
Type: Residency fee.
No. of awards offered: 1 each year (or 2 if for semesters).
Frequency: Annual.
Value: US$3,000; this figure is slated to rise gradually in future years; check the web page for projections.
Length of Study: 1 academic year or semester.
Study Establishment: The Institute.
Country of Study: USA.
Application Procedure: A candidate will apply in the usual way to the Resident Scholars Programme (see separate listing). If invited by the admissions committee to be a

Resident Scholar, the person will then be eligible for consideration for the Hoyt Fellowship.
Closing Date: January 15th prior to intended period of stay.

Institute for Ecumenical and Cultural Research Resident Scholars Program

Subjects: Religious studies.
Eligibility: The normal prerequisite is possession of the academic doctorate, but the admission committee will on occasion consider candidates with some other preparation, or those writing a dissertation.
Level of Study: Postdoctorate.
Purpose: To encourage constructive and creative thought, in a community setting, not only in theology and religious studies, but also more generally in scholarly research as it relates to the Christian tradition, including the interplay of Christianity and culture.
No. of awards offered: 9-18.
Frequency: Annual.
Value: The Institute charges a residency fee (US$3,000 per year; US$1,700 spring; these figures are slated to rise gradually in future years), considerably less than the value of the housing (incl. utilities), library study, and Institute programme provided.
Length of Study: 1 academic year or semester.
Study Establishment: The Institute.
Country of Study: USA.
Application Procedure: Applications on the form provided.
Closing Date: January 15th prior to intended period of stay.

INSTITUTE FOR HOUSING AND URBAN DEVELOPMENT STUDIES

PO Box 1935, Rotterdam, NL-3000 BX, Netherlands
Tel: (31) 10 402 1544
Fax: (31) 10 404 5671
Email: ihs@ihs.nl
www: http://www.ihs@ihs.nl
Contact: Mr F Van Wilgenburg, Head P&M Bureu

The Institute for Housing and Urban Development Studies (IHS), is an international educational institute offering postgraduate education in the field of urban management, housing and urban environmental management. Established in 1958, IHS has long worked in the training of urban professionals from developing countries and Central and Eastern Europe.

Institute for Housing and Urban Development Studies Fellowships for Courses

Subjects: Housing planning and building.
Eligibility: Open to participants from any country who have relevant professional experience and are engaged in work related to urban management, housing or urban environment, are proficient in English (the language of the course) and have

an undergraduate level degree from a university or similar institution.

Level of Study: Postgraduate.
Type: Fellowship and HIS Study Loan Scheme.
No. of awards offered: Varies.
Frequency: Four times per year.
Value: Varies.
Length of Study: 3 month postgraduate courses; 17 months Master's degree.
Study Establishment: IHS.
Country of Study: Netherlands.
Application Procedure: Applicants must apply through IHS application forms which are available from the Institute.
Closing Date: Varies depending on the course.
Additional Information: Technical assistance agencies include: the Fellowships Programme of the Netherlands Government - application forms can be obtained from the Dutch Embassy in the applicant's home country, and should be submitted to the Fellowships Programme through the national governments; the European Union candidates from countries associated with the EU through the Lomé Convention may apply for a fellowship through their national government to the EU Resident Representative in their own country; the United Nations - details of fellowships and procedures to be followed are obtainable from the Resident Representative, UN Development Programme in the applicant's home country. In addition, international financing agencies, such as World Bank, may award fellowships to local personnel involved in their project activities.

INSTITUTE FOR HUMANE STUDIES (IHS)

4084 University Drive
Suite 101, Fairfax, VA, 22030, United States of America
Tel: (1) 703 934 6920
Fax: (1) 703 352 7535
Email: ihs@gmu.edu
www: http://www.osf1.gmu.edu/~ihs
Contact: Grants Management Officer

Humane Studies Fellowships

Subjects: Social sciences, law, humanities, literature, communications or journalism.
Eligibility: Open to graduate students and undergraduates with junior or senior standing in the next academic year at accredited colleges and universities.
Level of Study: Postgraduate.
Purpose: To support outstanding students with a demonstrated interest in the classical liberal tradition intent on pursuing an intellectual/scholarly career.
Type: Fellowship.
Frequency: Annual.
Value: Up to US$12,000.
Country of Study: Any country.

Application Procedure: Application form must be completed and submitted with three completed evaluations, three essays, official test scores, official transcripts and term paper/writing sample.
Closing Date: December 31st.

IHS Summer Graduate Research Fellowship

Subjects: Research within the humane sciences - history, political and moral philosophy, political economy, economic history, legal and social theory.
Eligibility: Open to graduate students in the humanities, social sciences and law, who intend academic careers and are pursuing research in the classical liberal tradition.
Level of Study: Postgraduate.
Purpose: To encourage interdisciplinary studies in classical liberal and libertarian thought.
Type: Fellowship.
No. of awards offered: 8-10.
Frequency: Annual.
Value: US$5,000.
Study Establishment: George Mason University.
Country of Study: USA.
Application Procedure: Please submit proposal, current CV, a copy of GRE or LSAT scores and transcripts, a writing sample, and reference details.
Closing Date: February 15th.

IHS Young Communicators Fellowship

Subjects: Journalism, film, writing (fiction or non-fiction), publishing or free-market-oriented public policy.
Eligibility: Open to advanced students and recent graduates who have a clearly demonstrated interest in the classical liberal tradition of individual rights and market economies.
Level of Study: Professional development.
Purpose: To help place Fellows in strategic positions that can enhance their abilities and credentials to pursue targeted careers.
Type: Fellowship.
No. of awards offered: Varies.
Frequency: Annual.
Value: US$5,000, to include stipend, housing and travel.
Country of Study: Any country.
Application Procedure: Candidates should submit a proposal of 500-1,000 words explaining what specific summer position, similar short-term position, or training programme could be pursued if supported by a fellowship; how the proposed opportunity would enhance the applicant's career prospects; and how the proposed opportunity could contribute to the applicant's understanding of classical liberal principles and their application to today's issues; as well as a current résumé listing educational background, including major field and any academic honors received; current educational status; work experience, including summer positions and internships; and citations of any publications. Candidates should also submit a writing sample or other sample of work appropriate to the intended career and provide the name, address, and phone number of an academic and/or professional reference.

Closing Date: March 15th for summer positions; ten weeks prior to the start of other positions.

INSTITUTE OF ELECTRICAL AND ELECTRONICS ENGINEERS, INC.

445 Hoes Lane, Piscataway, NJ, 08855-1331, United States of America
Tel: (1) 732 562 3840
Fax: (1) 732 981 9019
Email: awards@ieee.org
www: http://www.ieee.org
Contact: Director

IEEE Fellowship in Electrical History

Subjects: History of electrical engineering and technology.
Eligibility: Open to suitably qualified graduate students.
Level of Study: Postgraduate.
Purpose: To support graduate work in the history of electrical engineering.
Type: Fellowship.
No. of awards offered: 1.
Frequency: Annual.
Value: US$15,000.
Length of Study: 1 year.
Study Establishment: A college or university of recognised standing.
Country of Study: Any country.
Application Procedure: Completed application, transcripts, three letters of recommendation and research proposal must be submitted for consideration.
Closing Date: February 1st.
Additional Information: The Fellowship is made possible by a grant from the IEEE Life Member Fund and is awarded by the IEEE History Committee. Application materials become available in October. Materials may be requested from the Center directly.

For further information contact:

IEEE Center for the History of Electrical Engineering
Rutgers - The State University of New Jersey
39 Union Street
PO Box 5062, New Brunswick, NJ, 08903-5062, United States of America
Tel: (1) 908 932 1066
Fax: (1) 908 932 1193
Contact: Director

INSTITUTE OF EUROPEAN HISTORY

Institut für Europäische Geschichte
Alte Universitätsstrasse 19, Mainz, D-55116, Germany
Tel: (49) 6131 399 340
Fax: (49) 613 1 237 539
Email: ieg2@inst-euro-history.uni-mainz.de
www: http://www.inst-euro-history.uni-mainz.de
Contact: Dr Andreas Kunz, Department Director

The Institute of European History in Mainz, founded in 1950, is an institution of higher learning dedicated to the promotion of historical research. Its Abteilung für Religionsgeschichte specialises in the history of occidental religion and has developed into a centre for ecumenical research on the Reformation. The Abteilung für Universalgeschichte concentrates its research activities on the history of Europe from the 16th to the 20th centuries. To promote research in these fields, the Institute annually awards 20 fellowships to young historians from Europe and overseas.

Institute of European History Fellowships

Subjects: Scientific research on Western religious history and on modern and contemporary European history generally.
Eligibility: Open to holders of a Master's degree, and to Fellows in the advanced stages of graduate work, at least two years after admission to doctoral candidacy, and who have successfully completed their comprehensive oral examinations.
Level of Study: Doctorate, Postdoctorate.
Type: Fellowship.
Frequency: Three times each year.
Value: In line with the guidelines of the German Academic Exchange Service (DAAD): a monthly stipend, a family allowance, health insurance and a travel allowance.
Study Establishment: The Institute of European History.
Country of Study: Germany.
Application Procedure: Contact the Director of the Institute of World History or of the History of Occidental Religion.
Closing Date: February, June, October.

INSTITUTE OF HISTORICAL RESEARCH (IHR)

Senate House
Malet Street, London, WC1E 7HU, England
Tel: (44) 171 636 0272
Fax: (44) 171 436 2183
Email: ihrdir@sas.ac.uk
www: http://www.ihr.sas.ac.uk:8080/
Contact: The Director

The Institute of Historical Research is the University of London's centre for advanced study in history. It is an important meeting place for scholars from all over the world and has an open-access library, common room and computer training room, publishes works of reference, administers several research projects and runs courses, conferences and seminars.

Isobel Thornley Research Fellowship

Subjects: Arts and humanities, medieval history, modern history, contemporary history.
Eligibility: Open to candidates without regard to nationality, but only to those registered for a PhD at London University.
Level of Study: Doctorate.
Purpose: To help candidates at an advanced stage of a PhD to complete their doctorate.
Type: Fellowship.
No. of awards offered: 1.
Frequency: Dependent on funds available.
Value: £6,200.
Length of Study: 1 year.
Study Establishment: IHR.
Country of Study: United Kingdom.
Application Procedure: Application forms are available from the Assistant Secretary in early January.
Closing Date: Around mid-February.

Past and Present Postdoctoral Fellowships in History

Subjects: History.
Eligibility: Applicants may be of any nationality and their PhD may have been awarded in any country. Those who have previously held another postdoctoral fellowship will not normally be eligible. The fellowship may not be held in conjunction with any other award. Fellowships will begin on October 1st each year and it is a strict condition of these awards that the PhD thesis should have been submitted by that date.
Level of Study: Postdoctorate.
Purpose: To provide one year's postdoctoral study in history.
Type: Fellowship.
No. of awards offered: 1.
Frequency: Dependent on funds available.
Value: £12,600.
Length of Study: 1 year.
Study Establishment: IHR.
Country of Study: England.
Application Procedure: Application forms are available from the Assistant Secretary in early January.
Closing Date: Around end of February.

Royal History Society Fellowship

Subjects: Arts and humanities - medieval history, modern history, contemporary history.
Eligibility: Open to nationals of any country.

Level of Study: Doctorate.
Purpose: To help candidates at an advanced stage of a PhD to complete their doctorates.
Type: Fellowship.
No. of awards offered: 1.
Frequency: Annual.
Value: Approx. .£6,200.
Length of Study: 1 year.
Study Establishment: IHR.
Country of Study: United Kingdom.
Application Procedure: Application forms are available from the Assistant Secretary in early January.
Closing Date: Around mid-February.

Scouloudi Fellowships

Subjects: Arts and humanities, medieval history, modern history, contemporary history.
Eligibility: Only open to UK citizens or to candidates with a first degree from a UK university.
Level of Study: Doctorate.
Purpose: To help candidates at an advanced stage of a PhD to complete their doctorates.
Type: Fellowship.
No. of awards offered: 7.
Frequency: Annual.
Value: Approx. £6,200.
Length of Study: 1 year.
Study Establishment: IHR.
Country of Study: United Kingdom.
Application Procedure: Application forms are available from the Assistant Secretary in early January.
Closing Date: Around mid-February.

Yorkist History Trust Fellowship

Subjects: Arts and humanities, medieval history.
Eligibility: Open to candidates without regard to nationality, but only to those researching British history or topics relevant to British history from the late 14th Century to the early 16th Century.
Level of Study: Doctorate.
Purpose: To help candidates at an advanced stage of a PhD to complete their doctorates.
Type: Fellowship.
No. of awards offered: 1.
Frequency: Dependent on funds available.
Value: Approx. £6,200.
Length of Study: 1 year.
Study Establishment: IHR.
Country of Study: United Kingdom.
Application Procedure: Application forms are available from the Assistant Secretary in early January.
Closing Date: Around mid-February.

INSTITUTE OF HORTICULTURE

14/15 Belgrave Square, London, SW1X 8PS, England
Tel: (44) 171 245 6943
Fax: (44) 171 245 6943
Email: ioh@horticulture.org.uk
www: http://www.horticulture.demon.co.uk/
Contact: Grants Management Officer

The Institute of Horticulture is the professional institute for horticulturists of all disciplines in the industry.

Martin McLaren Horticultural Scholarship

Subjects: Horticulture, botany or landscape architecture.
Eligibility: Applicants should have gained a botany, horticulture or landscape architecture degree, and be in the early stages of their career. The age limit is 27 years of age.
Level of Study: Postgraduate.
Purpose: To fund one year of an MSc course at an American university for a graduate of horticulture, botany, landscape architecture or similar.
Type: Scholarship.
No. of awards offered: 1.
Frequency: Annual.
Length of Study: 1 year.
Study Establishment: University.
Country of Study: USA.
Application Procedure: Application form must be completed: please contact the IOH.
Closing Date: November 10th.
Additional Information: The Martin Mclaren Horticultural Scholarship/Garden Club of America Interchange Fellowship is one year spent in UK/US university.

INSTITUTE OF IRISH STUDIES

Queen's University
8 Fitzwilliam Street, Belfast, BT9 6AW, Northern Ireland
Tel: (44) 1232 273386
Fax: (44) 1232 439238
Email: irish.studies@qub.ac.uk
Contact: Dr B M Walker, Director

The Institute of Irish Studies was established in 1965 to promote and co-ordinate research in those fields of study which have a particular Irish interest. The Institute's primary role is to promote research and to communicate the results of this research through seminars, conferences and publications.

Institute of Irish Studies Research Fellowships

Subjects: Any academic discipline relating to Ireland.
Eligibility: Candidates must hold at least a second class honours degree, have research experience, and have a viable research proposal.
Level of Study: Postdoctorate.
Purpose: To promote research.

Type: Fellowship.
No. of awards offered: Up to 3.
Frequency: Annual.
Value: £12,500.
Length of Study: 1 year.
Study Establishment: The Institute of Irish Studies.
Country of Study: Northern Ireland.
Application Procedure: Applicants mus apply for an application form in writing in November. Awards are usually advertised in December.
Closing Date: January 21st.

Institute of Irish Studies Senior Visiting Research Fellowship

Subjects: Any academic discipline relating to Ireland.
Eligibility: Open to established scholars of senior standing with a strong publication record.
Level of Study: Postdoctorate.
Purpose: To promote research.
Type: Fellowship.
No. of awards offered: Up to 2.
Frequency: Annual.
Value: £16,500.
Length of Study: 1 year.
Study Establishment: The Institute of Irish Studies.
Country of Study: Northern Ireland.
Application Procedure: Applicants must apply for an application form in writing in November. Awards are usually advertised in December.
Closing Date: January 21st.

INTERNATIONAL BEETHOVEN PIANO COMPETITION

Lothringerstrasse 18, Vienna, A-1030, Austria
Tel: (43) 1 58 806 190
Fax: (43) 1 58 806 107
Contact: Ms Elga Ponzer, Secretary General

International Beethoven Piano Competition

Subjects: Piano.
Eligibility: Open to pianists of all nationalities born between January 1st 1969 and December 31st 1984.
Level of Study: Unrestricted.
Purpose: To encourage the artistic development of young pianists.
No. of awards offered: 6.
Frequency: Every four years.
Value: 1st prize: AS98,000 and a Bosendorfer Model 200 piano; 2nd Prize: AS70,000; 3rd Prize: AS56,000; plus three further prizes of AS20,000.
Country of Study: Austria.
Application Procedure: Please write for details.
Closing Date: September 30th, 2000.

Additional Information: The eleventh International Beethoven Piano Competition in Vienna will take place in 2001.

For further information contact:

Universität für Musik und darstellende Kunst Wien Lothringer straße 18, Wien, A-1030, Austria
Tel: (43) 58 806 190
Fax: (43) 58 806 107

INTERNATIONAL CELLO FESTIVAL

Paulo Foundation
Mikonkatu 3 B, Helsinki, FIN-00100, Finland
Fax: (358) 9 6220 4633
Email: toimisto@paulo.fi
www: http://www.paulo.fi
Contact: Ms Kirsti Nygård

International Paulo Cello Competition

Subjects: Cello performance.
Eligibility: Open to cellists born between 1968 and 1985 inclusive.
Level of Study: Unrestricted.
Type: Competition/Prize.
No. of awards offered: 6.
Frequency: Every five years (next in 2001).
Value: Prizes as follows: 1st) 70,000 FIM, 2nd) 40,000 FIM, 3rd) 25,000 FIM, 4th) 10,000 FIM, 5th) 10,000 FIM, 6th) 10,000 FIM.
Country of Study: Finland.
Application Procedure: Send for brochure containing details of application and audition pieces.
Closing Date: May 2001.
Additional Information: For further information please contact the Foundation.

INTERNATIONAL CHAMBER MUSIC COMPETITION

UFAM
10 rue du Dome, Paris, F-75116, France
Tel: (33) 1 47 04 76 38
Fax: (33) 1 47 27 35 03
Email: ufam@wanadoo.fr
www: http://www.infoservice.fr/ufam
Contact: Ms C de Bayser, Presidente

International Chamber Music Competition

Subjects: Groups of wind and string instruments, with or without piano, harp, guitar or percussion instruments. String instruments accompanying wind instruments are also

permitted.
Eligibility: Open to groups of musicians of any nationality, who are no more than 36 years of age. The average age of the group should not exceed 34 years.
Level of Study: Postgraduate.
Purpose: To enable musicians to play engagements across the world.
Type: Competition.
No. of awards offered: Varies.
Frequency: Every two years.
Value: From a total fund of FF110,000. Winners are also offered important performance engagements.
Country of Study: Any country.
Application Procedure: A brochure is available on request.
Closing Date: September 20th in the year of the Competition.
Additional Information: The Competition includes various sections for groups of various sizes, who may perform with or without piano accompaniment.

Paris International Singing Competition

Subjects: Singing.
Eligibility: Open to female singers of no more than 32 years of age and to male singers of no more than 34 years of age. The competition is open to singers of all nationalities.
Level of Study: Unrestricted.
Purpose: To help young singers to start their career.
Type: Prize.
Frequency: Every two years (even-numbered years).
Value: From a total fund of FF150,000, with a Grand Prix of FF50,000, plus free accommodation for competitors. Winners are also offered important singing engagements.
Country of Study: France.
Application Procedure: A brochure is available on request.
Closing Date: May.

INTERNATIONAL COUNCIL FOR CANADIAN STUDIES (ICCS)

325 Dalhousie S 800, Ottawa, ON, K1N 7G2, Canada
Tel: (1) 613 789 7828
Fax: (1) 613 7897830
Email: general@iccs-ciec.ca
www: http://www.iccs-ciec.ca
Contact: Program Officer

Canadian Commonwealth Scholarship Program

Subjects: Any subjects except medicine, and introduction to languages.
Eligibility: Open to members of the British Commonwealth.
Level of Study: Doctorate, Graduate, Postgraduate, Research.
Purpose: To provide opportunities for students of other Commonwealth countries to pursue advanced studies in Canada. The scholarships are intended for men and women

of high intellectual promise who may be expected to make a significant contribution to their own countries on their return from study in Canada.
Type: Scholarship.
No. of awards offered: Varies.
Frequency: Annual.
Length of Study: A maximum of 3 years.
Country of Study: Canada.
Application Procedure: Application forms should be sent directly to the appropriate Commonwealth Agency at the students home country.
Closing Date: Varies.

Commonwealth Scholarship Plan

Subjects: All subjects.
Eligibility: Open to Canadian citizens, or those permanent residents who are graduates of a Canadian university, who have completed a university degree or expect to graduate prior to the tenure of the award. No age restriction pertains, but reference will be given to applicants who have obtained a university degree within the last five years.
Level of Study: Doctorate, Graduate, Postgraduate, Research.
Type: Scholarship.
No. of awards offered: Varies.
Frequency: Annual.
Value: Varies.
Country of Study: India, New Zealand, Sri Lanka, Tobago, Uganda or United Kingdom.
Application Procedure: Please write for details or visit our website at http://www.iccs-cies.ca.
Closing Date: Applications for New Zealand, December 31st; Applications for other countries, October 31st.
Additional Information: The Canadian Commonwealth and Fellowship Committee will select nominations to be forwarded to the awarding country. The number of nominations varies, but will be approximately double the number of awards expected to be made. The decision of the Canadian Committee is final and not open to appeal. The actual offer of a Scholarship will be made by the Commonwealth Scholarship Agency in the awarding country. In general, the Agency tries to place selected candidates in the institutions of their choice; however, where this is not possible, an alternative institution offering opportunities for the proposed course of study will be chosen.

Foreign Government Awards

Subjects: Any subject, except medicine or introduction to language.
Eligibility: Open to Canadian citizens with a working knowledge of the host country's language and a Bachelor's degree (or PhD for postdoctoral fellowships), completed before the beginning of the award term.
Level of Study: Doctorate, Graduate, Postdoctorate, Postgraduate, Research.
Purpose: To assist Canadians to study or conduct research abroad at the Master's, doctoral or postdoctoral level.
Type: Scholarship.
No. of awards offered: Varies.

Frequency: Annual.
Value: Generally to cover tuition fees, books, a living allowance, transportation and miscellaneous expenses.
Country of Study: Colombia, Finland, France, or Mexico.
Application Procedure: Applications are initially evaluated by a 'preselection committee' of Canadian academics. The committee submits a list of recommended candidates and alternates to each host country, where award recipients are chosen. A list of participating countries is available on request.
Closing Date: October 30th or January 20th for Colombia.

INTERNATIONAL COUNCIL FOR RESEARCH AND INNOVATION IN BUILDING AND CONSTRUCTION

CIB
PO Box 1837, Rotterdam, NL-3000 BV, Netherlands
Tel: (31) 10 411 0240
Fax: (31) 10 433 4372
Email: secretariat@cibworld.nl
www: http://www.cibworld.nll
Contact: The Secretary General

CIB was established in 1953 as an association whose purpose is to provide a global network for international exchange and co-operation in research and innovation in building and construction.

CIB Developing Countries Fund

Subjects: All aspects of building and construction research and innovation.
Eligibility: Candidates must be a staff member of a CIB member institute in a developing country and must themselves be nationals of developing countries.
Level of Study: Professional development.
Purpose: To enable staff members of CIB member institutes in developing countries to participate in events of professional benefit.
Type: Fellowship.
Frequency: No limit on frequency, but dependent on funds available.
Value: Total or partial reimbursement of fees, travel and subsistence costs.
Length of Study: 3-5 days at conferences, seminars, workshops, etc.
Country of Study: Any country.
Application Procedure: Please contact CIB Secretary General.
Closing Date: No closing date but at least two months before date of commencement of event.
Additional Information: Each application is assessed on its merits.

INTERNATIONAL FEDERATION OF UNIVERSITY WOMEN (IFUW)

8 rue de l'Ancien-Port, Geneva, CH-1201, Switzerland
Tel: (41) 22 731 23 80
Fax: (41) 22 738 04 40
Email: ifuw@iprolink.ch
www: http://www.ifuw.org
Contact: Grants Management Officer

A non-profit, non-governmental organisation comprising of graduate women working locally, nationally and internationally to advocate for the improvement of the status of women and girls at the international level; to promote lifelong education; and to enable graduate women to use their expertise to effect change.

The British Federation Crosby Hall Fellowship

Subjects: All subjects.
Eligibility: Women applicants for all awards must be either a member of one of IFUW's national federations or associations or, in the case of women graduates living in countries where there is not yet a national affiliate, an independent member of IFUW.
Level of Study: Doctorate, Postdoctorate, Postgraduate, Research.
Purpose: To encourage advance scholarship and original research.
Type: Fellowship.
No. of awards offered: 1.
Frequency: Every two years, next one offered for 2000-2001.
Value: £2,500.
Study Establishment: An approved institution of higher education.
Country of Study: United Kingdom.
Application Procedure: Applicants should write for details enclosing a stamped addressed envelope. Applicants must apply through their respective Federation or Association. A list of IFUW national federations can be sent upon request or obtained through the internet.
Closing Date: Early September in the year preceding the competition.
Additional Information: Applicants in the US and the UK should write to the addresses shown for these countries; all others should write to the main address.

For further information contact:

BFWG
4 Mandeville Courtyard
142 Battersea Park Road, London, SW11 4NB, England
Tel: (44) 171 498 8037
Fax: (44) 171 498 8037

or
AAUW/IFUW Liason
1111 Sixteenth Street
NW, Washington, DC, 28036, United States of America
Fax: (1) 202 872 1425

Ida Smedley Maclean, CFUW/A Vibert Douglas, IFUW and Action Fellowship

Subjects: All subjects.
Eligibility: Women applicants for all awards must be either a member of one of IFUW's national federations or associations or, in the case of women graduates living in countries where there is not yet a national affiliate, an independent member of IFUW. Applicants should be well started on a research programme and should have completed at least one year of graduate work.
Level of Study: Doctorate, Postdoctorate, Postgraduate.
Purpose: To encourage advanced scholarship and original research.
Type: Fellowship.
No. of awards offered: 1 of each fellowship.
Frequency: Every two years. Next competition will offer awards for 2000-2001.
Value: Maclean Fellowship: CHF8,000-10,000; Douglas Fellowship: C$6,000; SAAP Fellowship: CHF8,000-10,000.
Length of Study: At least 8 months.
Study Establishment: An approved institution of higher education other than that in which the applicant received her education or habitually resides.
Country of Study: Any country.
Application Procedure: Applicants should write for details enclosing a stamped addressed envelope. Applicants must apply through their respective federation or association. A list of IFUW national federations can be sent upon request or be obtained from the internet.
Closing Date: Early September in the year preceding the competition.
Additional Information: Applicants in the US and the UK should write to the addresses shown for these countries; all others should write to the main address.

For further information contact:

BFWG
4 Mandeville Courtyard
142 Battersea Park Road, London, SW11 4NB, England
Tel: (44) 171 498 8037
Fax: (44) 171 498 8037
or
AAUW/IFUW
1111 Sixteenth Street NW, Washington, DC, 28036, United States of America
Fax: (1) 202 872 1425

Winifred Cullis and Dorothy Leet Grants, NZFUW Grants

Subjects: All subjects.
Eligibility: Women applicants for all awards must be either a member of one of the IFUW's national federations or

associations or, in the case of women graduates living in countries where there is not yet a national affiliate, an independent member of IFUW.

Level of Study: Doctorate, Graduate, Postdoctorate, Postgraduate.

Purpose: To enable recipients to carry out research, obtain specialised training essential to research, or training in new techniques.

Type: Grant.

No. of awards offered: Varies.

Frequency: Every two years. Next competition will offer awards for 2000-2001.

Value: Varies;CHF3,000-CHF6,000.

Length of Study: Minimum of 2 months.

Country of Study: Any country.

Application Procedure: Applicants should write for details enclosing a stamped addressed envelope. Applicants must apply through their respective federation or association. A list of IFUW national federations can be sent upon request or obtained from the internet.

Closing Date: Early September in the year preceding the competition.

Additional Information: Applicants in the US and the UK should write to the addresses shown for these countries; all others should write to the main address.

For further information contact:

BFWG
4 Mandeville Courtyard
142 Battersea Park Road, London, SW11 4NB, England
Tel: (44) 171 498 8037
Fax: (44) 171 498 8037
or
AAUW/IFUW Liason
1111 Sixteenth Street
NW, Washington, DC, 28036, United States of America
Fax: (1) 202 872 1425

INTERNATIONAL FREDERIC CHOPIN COMPETITION

Frederic Chopin Society in Warsaw
Ostrogski Castle
ul Okólnik 1, Warsaw, PL-00-368, Poland
Tel: (48) 827 54 71
Fax: (48) 827 95 99
www: http://www.chopin/pl
Contact: The Jury

The Society organises The International Chopin Piano Competition; Scholarly Piano Competition for Polish Pianists; Grand Prix du Disque Frederic Chopin; courses in Chopin's music interpretation; Chopin music recitals, and a museum and collection.

International Frederic Chopin Piano Competition

Subjects: Piano performance of Chopin music.

Eligibility: Open to pianists of any nationality, between 17 and 28 years of age.

Level of Study: Unrestricted.

Purpose: To recognise the best artistic interpretation of Chopin's music and to encourage professional development.

Type: Prize.

No. of awards offered: 6.

Frequency: Every five years (next in 2000).

Value: First prize US$25,000 and a gold medal; second prize US$20,000 and a silver medal; third prize US$15,000 and a bronze medal; fourth prize US$11,000; fifth prize US$8,000; sixth prize US$6,000.

Country of Study: Any country.

Closing Date: March 1st.

Additional Information: Apart from the prizes specified above, the following special awards shall be granted by: the Frederic Chopin Society for the best performance of a polonaise US$5,000; the Polish Radio for the best performance of mazurkas US$5,000; the National Philharmonic for the best performance of a concerto US$5,000.

INTERNATIONAL HARP CONTEST IN ISRAEL

4 Aharonowitz Street, Tel Aviv, 63566, Israel
Tel: (972) 3 5280233
Fax: (972) 3 6299524
Email: harzimco@netvision.net.il
Contact: Ms Esther Herlitz, Director

The International Harp Contest takes place in Israel every three years and is judged by jury of internationally known musicians.

International Harp Contest

Subjects: Harp playing.

Eligibility: Open to harpists of any nationality who are no more than 35 years of age.

Level of Study: Professional development.

Purpose: To encourage excellence in harp playing.

Type: Harp and Cash.

No. of awards offered: 5.

Frequency: Every three years.

Value: 1st prize: a grand concert harp from the House of Lyon and Healy, Chicago; 2nd prize: US$5,000; 3rd prize: US$3,000; Gulbenkian Prize: US$2,500; Propes Prize: US$1,500.

Country of Study: Any country.

Application Procedure: Application form needs to be completed and submitted with recommendations and record of concert experience, CV and birth certificate.

Closing Date: May 1st.

Additional Information: Board and lodging is provided by the Contest Committee. There is a registration fee of US$150.

INTERNATIONAL M LONG-J THIBAUD COMPETITION

32 Avenue Matignon, Paris, F-75008, France
Tel: (33) 1 42 66 66 80
Fax: (33) 1 42 66 06 43
Email: longthi@club-internet.fr
Contact: Mrs Claude Perin, General Secretary

Premier Grand Prix Marguerite Long, Premier Grand Prix Jacques Thibaud

Subjects: Piano (Prix Marguerite Long) and violin (Prix Jacques Thibaud).
Eligibility: Open to musicians under 30 years of age, of all nationalities.
Level of Study: Professional development.
No. of awards offered: 6.
Frequency: Every three years.
Value: FF150,000, plus 30 concert engagements and a tour of Asia and America South and North.
Country of Study: France.
Application Procedure: Registration form to be completed and copies of Diplomas submitted.
Closing Date: September 1st.
Additional Information: Full particulars are given on the application form which is available on request. There is a registration fee of FF500.

INTERNATIONAL ORGAN COMPETITION 'GRAND PRIX DE CHARTRES'

Grand Prix de Chartres
Concours international d'orgue
75 rue de Grenelle, Paris, F-75007, France
Tel: (33) 1 45 48 31 74
Fax: (33) 1 45 49 14 34
www: http://www.concertartists.com/Chartres.html
Contact: Secretariat

International Organ Competition 'Grand Prix de Chartres'

Subjects: Organ performance, in two categories - interpretation and improvisation.
Eligibility: Open to organists of any nationality who are 35 years of age or under in the year of the Competition.

Level of Study: Unrestricted.
Type: Prize plus concerts in France and other countries.
No. of awards offered: 2.
Frequency: Every two years.
Value: First prize FF30,000; second prize FF20,000; public prize FF10,000.
Country of Study: France.
Application Procedure: Please write for details.
Closing Date: April 15th.

INTERNATIONAL PEACE SCHOLARSHIP FUND

c/o PEO
3700 Grand Avenue, Des Moines, IA, 50312, United States of America
Tel: (1) 515 255 3153
Fax: (1) 515 255 3820
Contact: Ms Carolyn J Larson, Project Supervisor

PEO International Peace Scholarship

Subjects: All subjects.
Eligibility: Any nationality may apply apart from candidates from USA or Canada. Eligiblility is based on financial need, nationality, degree, full time status and residence the entire term of study.
Level of Study: Doctorate, Postgraduate.
Purpose: Grant-in-Aid for international women studying graduate degrees (Master's, PhD) in the US or Canada.
Type: Grant-in Aid.
No. of awards offered: Approx. 150.
Frequency: Annual.
Value: US$5,000 maximum per year.
Length of Study: Maximum 3 years.
Country of Study: USA or Canada.
Application Procedure: Eligibility must be established before application material is sent. Write to IPS Office and request eligibility form. If eligibile an application form is sent.
Closing Date: December 15th for receipt of eligibility form, January 31st for receipt of application form.
Additional Information: Scholarships cannot be used for travel, research dissertations, internships or practical training. An applicant must have a contact person who is a citizen of the United States or Canada, and who will act as a non-academic adviser. Applicant must have round trip return travel expense guaranteed at the time of the application. Applicants must return to their own country on completion of their studies.

INTERNATIONAL READING ASSOCIATION

800 Barksdale Road
PO Box 8139, Newark, DE, 19714-8139, United States of America
Tel: (1) 302 731 1600 ext 226
Fax: (1) 302 731 1057
Email: research@reading.org
www: http://www.reading.org
Contact: Ms Gail Keating, Projects Manager, Research

Nila Banton Smith Research Dissemination Support Grant

Subjects: Reading/literacy research.
Eligibility: Open to all members worldwide. All applicants must be members of the International Reading association.
Level of Study: Professional development.
Purpose: To facilitate the dissemination of literacy research to the education community.
Type: Reading and/or literacy research dissemination grant.
No. of awards offered: 1.
Frequency: Annual.
Value: US$5,000.
Application Procedure: Obtain guidelines with specific information from the main address.
Closing Date: October 15th.

INTERNATIONAL RESEARCH AND EXCHANGES BOARD (IREX)

1616 H Street NW, Washington, DC, 20006, United States of America
Tel: (1) 202 628 8188
Fax: (1) 202 628 8189
Email: irex@info.irex.org
www: http://www.irex.org/
Contact: Ms Joyce Warner, Director of Academic Exchanges and Research Div

Since 1958, IREX and its predecessor organisation, the Inter-University Committee on Travel Grants, have administered advanced field research and professional training exchanges between the United States and countries in Europe, Asia and the Near East. Committed to international education in its broadest sense, IREX's efforts encompass academic research, professional training, institution building, technical assistance and policy programmes with universities and other organisational partners in the region.

IREX Grant Opportunities for US Scholars

Subjects: Arts and Humanities, Social Sciences.
Eligibility: Open to US citizens and permanent residents. Applicants must have a good command of the host country language.
Level of Study: Doctorate, Professional development.
Purpose: To provide field access for US specialists to scholars, policymakers and research resources of Central and Eastern Europe, Eurasia and Mongolia.
Type: Grant.
No. of awards offered: Varies.
Frequency: Annual.
Value: up to US$10,000.
Length of Study: Varies, depending on the programme.
Country of Study: Countries of Central and Eastern Europe, Eurasia and Mongolia.
Application Procedure: Please contact IREX for application forms and booklets on current programmes.
Closing Date: Applications are accepted at any time.
Additional Information: Grant opportunities for international scholars may also be available. Please contact IREX for details.

INTERNATIONALER ROBERT-SCHUMANN-WETTBEWERB ZWICKAU

Organisationsbüro
Münzstrasse 12, Zwickau, D-08056, Germany
Tel: (49) 375 212 636
Fax: (49) 375 834 130
Contact: Mr Hanelore Heil

International Robert Schumann Competition

Subjects: Piano performance, individual singing, and choral singing.
Eligibility: Open to pianists up to the age of 30 and to individual singers up to the age of 32.
Level of Study: Professional development.
Purpose: To support the interpretation of the work of Robert Schumann.
Type: Competition.
No. of awards offered: 10.
Frequency: Every four years.
Value: First prize: 10,000DM; second prize: 5,000DM; third prize: 3,500DM.
Country of Study: Germany.
Application Procedure: Please write for further information.

IRISH-AMERICAN CULTURAL INSTITUTE (IACI)

1 Lackawanna Place, Morristown, NJ, 07960, United States of America
Tel: (1) 973 605 1991
Fax: (1) 973 605 8875
Email: irishwaynj@aol.com
www: http://www.irishaci.org
Contact: Ms Katie Finn

Founded in 1962, the IACI is the sole US organisation with the distinction of having the Irish President as patron. A non-profit membership organisation, the IACI take no political or sectarian position.

Irish Research Funds

Subjects: Any subject. Historical research has predominated, but other areas of research will be considered equally.
Eligibility: Open to individuals of any nationality. Media production costs and journal subventions will not be considered for funding.
Level of Study: Postgraduate.
Purpose: To promote scholarly enquiry and publication regarding the Irish-American experience.
Type: Grant.
No. of awards offered: Varies.
Frequency: Annual.
Value: US$1,000-US$5,000.
Country of Study: Any country.
Application Procedure: Write for details. Applications must have an Irish and American aspect. An application form must be completed.
Closing Date: October 1st.
Additional Information: Enquiries for this award should be directed to Katie Finn.

Irish-American Cultural Institute Visiting Fellowship in Irish Studies at National University of Ireland, Galway

Subjects: Irish studies.
Eligibility: Open to scholars normally resident in the USA whose work relates to any aspect of Irish studies.
Level of Study: Postgraduate.
Purpose: For scholars normally residents in the US who wish to spend a semester at Nui-Galway and whose work relates to any aspect of Irish studies.
Type: Fellowship.
No. of awards offered: 1.
Frequency: Annual.
Value: Stipend of US$13,000, plus transatlantic transportation.
Length of Study: A period of not less than 4 months.
Country of Study: Ireland.
Closing Date: December 31st for the forthcoming academic year.

Additional Information: The holder of the fellowship will be provided with services appropriate to a visiting faculty member during his or her time at UCG. There are certain relatively minor departmental responsibilities expected of the holder during his or her time at UCG, and certain other expectations regarding publication, upon completion of the fellowship. The application form is brief, and requests a current CV and list of publications. Applications must be received on a form which is available on request. The fellowship is jointly funded with University College Galway.

ITALIAN INSTITUTE FOR HISTORICAL STUDIES

Via Benedetto Croce 12, Naples, I-80134, Italy
Tel: (390) 81 5517159
Fax: (390) 81 5512390
Contact: Ms Marta Herling, Secretary

Postgraduate Institute for the study of history and philosphy. The study of history is seen in connection with the disciplines of philosophy, the arts, economics and literature. The Institute offers two annual scholarships for non-Italian postgraduates specialising in humanities and social sciences.

Adolfo Omodeo Scholarship

Subjects: History and philosophy. The study of history is seen in connection with the disciplines of philosophy, the arts, economics and literature.
Eligibility: Open to nationals of all countries; applicants must possess a BA degree.
Level of Study: Postgraduate.
Purpose: To allow students to participate in life at the Institute while completing a personal research project with the assistance of its staff.
Type: Scholarship.
No. of awards offered: 1.
Frequency: Annual.
Value: 12,000,000 lire.
Length of Study: 8 months.
Study Establishment: Italian Institute for Historical Studies.
Country of Study: Italy.
Application Procedure: Application must include: birth certificate, proof of citizenship, university diploma, scholarly work, curriculum, programme of research, letters of reference, and copies of publications.
Closing Date: September 30th.

Frederico Chabod Scholarship

Subjects: History and philosophy. The study of history is seen in connection with the disciplines of philosophy, the arts, economics and literature.
Eligibility: Open to nationals of all countries; applicants must possess a BA degree.
Level of Study: Postgraduate.

Purpose: To allow students to participate in life at the Institute, while completing a personal research project with the assistance of its staff.
Type: Scholarship.
No. of awards offered: 1.
Frequency: Annual.
Value: 12,000,000 lire.
Length of Study: 8 months.
Study Establishment: Italian Institute for Historical Studies.
Country of Study: Italy.
Application Procedure: Applications must include birth certificate, proof of citizenship, university diploma, scholarly work, curriculum, programme of research, letters of reference, and copies of publications.
Closing Date: September 30th.

THE J B HARLEY RESEARCH FELLOWSHIPS TRUST

c/o British Library Map Library
96 Euston Road, London, NW1 2DBG, England
Tel: (44) 171 412 7525
Fax: (44) 171 412 7780
Email: tony.campbell@bl.uk
Contact: Mr Tony Campbell

The J B Harley Research Fellowships in the History of Cartography

Subjects: History of cartography.
Eligibility: Doctorate or postdoctoral (or equivalent) research level; applications must be in English; London commuters are ineligible.
Level of Study: Doctorate, Postdoctorate.
Purpose: To promote the use of the great wealth of historical cartographical material available in London.
Type: Grant.
No. of awards offered: 3.
Frequency: Annual.
Value: £250 per week.
Length of Study: 2-4 weeks.
Study Establishment: London libraries.
Country of Study: United Kingdom.
Application Procedure: Outline research proposal and CV must be submitted. Details in leaflet are available upon request.
Closing Date: November 1st.
Additional Information: Further details, about previous winners and numbers of applicants can be found at http://ihr.sas.ac.uk/maps/harley.html.

JACOB'S PILLOW DANCE FESTIVAL, INC.

Box 287, Lee, MA, 01238, United States of America
Tel: (1) 413 637 1322
Fax: (1) 413 243 4744
www: http://www.jacobspillow.org
Contact: Mr J R Glover, Education Director

Jacob's Pillow's mission is two-fold: to nurture and sustain artistic creation, presentation, education, and preservation; and to engage and deepen public appreciation and support for dance. Founded in 1932 by modern dance pioneer Ted Shawn, the school at Jacob's Pillow provides rigorous dance training and education for some 100 pre-professionals and artists and teachers seeking professional development in a residential artist community.

Jacob's Pillow Dance Festival Dance Scholarships

Subjects: Dance traditions, techniques, repertory and theory. Classes are offered in all forms of dance, and the workshops vary from year to year.
Eligibility: Open to US and foreign nationals who are over 16 years of age, have experience in the field of dance, and complete applications requirements for the workshop you wish to attend.
Level of Study: Unrestricted.
Purpose: To allow high-level dancers an opportunity to participate in summer dance workshops with world renowned faculty and artists.
Type: Scholarship.
No. of awards offered: 40-50.
Frequency: Annual.
Value: Room, board, tuition, and performance tickets. There is no travel allowance for foreign nationals.
Length of Study: Varies.
Study Establishment: Jacob's Pillow Dance Festival School.
Country of Study: USA.
Application Procedure: Information on audition requirements is available from the school each year after December 1st for the upcoming summer programme. This can be obtained by either by writing, phoning or visiting the website.
Closing Date: March/April.
Additional Information: Scholarships are only offered to enable dancers to attend the summer school; no academic or general scholarships are available.

JAMES COOK UNIVERSITY OF NORTH QUEENSLAND

Research Students Office, Townsville, QLD, 4811, Australia
Tel: (61) 77 81 4575
Fax: (61) 77 81 6204
www: http://www.jcu.edu.au
Contact: Research Students Officer

James Cook University Postgraduate Research Scholarship

Subjects: Most subjects offered at the University.
Eligibility: Open to any student who has attained at least a Bachelor's degree at honours level (Class 2A).
Level of Study: Postgraduate.
Purpose: To encourage full-time postgraduate research leading to a Master's or PhD degree.
Type: Scholarship.
No. of awards offered: Up to 4.
Frequency: Annual.
Value: A$15,888 per year. The award does not cover annual tuition fees for overseas students.
Length of Study: 3 years with a possible additional 6 months in exceptional circumstances (PhD); or for 2 years (Master's program).
Study Establishment: James Cook University.
Country of Study: Australia.
Closing Date: October 31st.

JAMES MADISON MEMORIAL FELLOWSHIP FOUNDATION

2201 North Dodge Street
PO Box 4030, Iowa City, IA, 52243-4030, United States of America
Tel: (1) 800 525 6928
Fax: (1) 319 337 1204
Email: recogprog@act.org
www: http://www.jamesmadison.com
Contact: Fellowships Office

The mission of the James Madison Memorial Fellowship Foundation is to strengthen secondary school teaching of the principles, framing and development of the US constitution.

James Madison Senior Fellowship Program

Subjects: History, political science, and the arts.
Eligibility: Applicants must be US citizens.
Level of Study: Postgraduate.
Purpose: For graduate study leading to a Master's degree.
Type: Fellowship.
No. of awards offered: Up to 60.
Frequency: Annual.
Value: Up to US$24,000.
Length of Study: Up to 5 years.
Country of Study: USA.

Application Procedure: Please write for details or call the toll free number to request application materials. Also more information is available on the website.
Closing Date: March 1st.

JANSON JOHAN HELMICH OG MARCIA JANSONS LEGAT

Blommeseter
Norderhov, Hönefoss, N-3500, Norway
Tel: (47) 32 13 54 65
Fax: (47) 32 13 56 26
Contact: Mr Reidun Haugen

Janson Johan Helmich Scholarships and Travel Grants

Subjects: All subjects.
Eligibility: Open to qualified Norwegian postgraduate students with practical experience, for advanced study abroad.
Level of Study: Doctorate, Postgraduate, Professional development.
Purpose: To support practical or academic training.
Type: Scholarship.
No. of awards offered: 30.
Frequency: Annual.
Value: Maximum NOK75,000.
Country of Study: Any country.
Application Procedure: Application form must be completed.
Closing Date: March 15th.

JAPAN SOCIETY FOR THE PROMOTION OF SCIENCE (JSPS)

Jochi Kioizaka Bldg
6-26-3 Kioi-cho
Chiyoda-ku, Tokyo, 102, Japan
Tel: (81) 3 3263 1721
Fax: (81) 3 3263 1854
Contact: Mr Nagahide Onozawa

JSPS Invitation Fellowship Programme for Research in Japan

Subjects: All fields of the humanities, social sciences and natural sciences.
Eligibility: Open to university professors and associate/assistant professors, senior scientists, and other persons with substantial professional experience.
Level of Study: Professional development.
Purpose: To promote international co-operation and mutual understanding in scientific research.
Type: Fellowship.

No. of awards offered: Varies.
Frequency: Annual.
Value: A round-trip airfare will be provided, with a monthly maintenance allowance of Y300,000 or Y270,000 according to the professional status of the awardee. Domestic travel expenses of Y100,000, research expenses of Y40,000, a monthly housing allowance not to exceed Y100,000 and accident and sickness insurance cover.
Length of Study: 6-10 months.
Study Establishment: Japanese research institutions.
Country of Study: Japan.
Application Procedure: Please write for details.
Closing Date: September.
Additional Information: A short term programme is also available, with a fellowship period of 14 to 60 days, and a reduced award amount.

JSPS Postdoctoral Fellowships for Foreign Researchers

Subjects: Humanities, social sciences, natural sciences, engineering and medicine.
Eligibility: Open to citizens of countries which have diplomatic relations with Japan. Applicants must have a doctorate degree.
Level of Study: Postdoctorate.
Purpose: To assist promising and highly-qualified young foreign researchers wishing to conduct research in Japan.
Type: Fellowship.
No. of awards offered: Varies.
Frequency: Annual.
Value: A round-trip airfare is provided with a monthly maintenance allowance of Y270,000, a settling-in allowance of Y200,000, a monthly housing allowance not to exceed Y100,000, a monthly family allowance of 50,000 Yen if accompanied by dependants, and accident/sickness insurance coverage for the Fellow only.
Length of Study: 2 years (12 month tenure may be considered).
Study Establishment: Japanese universities and similar institutions.
Country of Study: Japan.
Application Procedure: Please write for details.

JAPANESE GOVERNMENT

Embassy of Japan
112 Empire Circuit, Yarralumla, ACT, 2600, Australia
Tel: (61) 6 273 3244
Fax: (61) 6 273 1848
www: http://www.jwindow.net/GOV/gov.html
Contact: Ms E Prior

Japanese Government (Monbusho) Scholarships Research Category

Subjects: Humanities and social sciences - literature, history, aesthetics, law, politics, economics, commerce, pedagogy,

psychology, sociology, music and fine arts. Natural sciences - pure science, engineering, agriculture, fisheries, pharmacology, medicine, dentistry, and home economics.
Eligibility: Open to Australian graduates under 35 years of age and likewise nationals of any country which has diplomatic relations with Japan.
Level of Study: Doctorate, Postgraduate.
Type: Scholarship.
No. of awards offered: Approx. 20.
Frequency: Annual.
Value: Return air fare, plus Y185,500 per month.
Length of Study: 18-24 months.
Study Establishment: A Japanese university.
Country of Study: Japan.
Application Procedure: Application form available.
Closing Date: June.
Additional Information: Applicants must be willing to study the Japanese language.

JEAN SIBELIUS INTERNATIONAL VIOLIN COMPETITION

PB 31, Helsinki, SF-00101, Finland
Tel: (358) 9 4114 3443
Fax: (358) 9 2 200 2680
Contact: Ms Harri Pohjolainen, Competition Secretary

The International Jean Sibelius Violin Competition is organised by the Sibelius Society. The first competition was held in 1965 to mark the 100th anniversary of the maestro's birth.

Jean Sibelius International Violin Competition

Subjects: Musical performance - violin.
Eligibility: Open to violinists of any nationality born in 1970 or later.
Level of Study: Unrestricted.
Purpose: To recognise and reward exceptional young violinists.
Type: Prize.
No. of awards offered: 9.
Frequency: Every five years (next in 2000).
Value: First prize US$16,000; second prize US$12,500; third prize US$9,000; plus five prizes of US$1,800. A further prize of US$1,800 is given by the Finnish Broadcasting Company for the best performance of Sibelius' Violin Concerto.
Country of Study: Any country.
Application Procedure: The competition brochure with rules, application forms and programme is published in March 1999. The brochure will be sent to schools around the world, it can also be sent directly on request. Please contact the Competition Secretary.
Closing Date: August 18th 2000.
Additional Information: The next competition will be held on November 18th to December 2nd 2000. For further information please contact the Competition Secretary.

JENNY MOORE FUND FOR WRITERS

George Washington University
English Department, Washington, DC, 20052, United States
of America
Tel: (1) 202 994 6180
Fax: (1) 202 994 7915
Email: ckibler@gwis2.circ.gwu.edu
Contact: Mr David McAleavey

The Fund, together with the George Washington English
Department, sponsors the Jenny Moore Writer-in-Washington
programme and a reading series.

Jenny Moore Writer-in-Washington

Subjects: Authorship - genre alternates between fiction and
poetry with the occasional year for creative non-fiction or
playwriting.
Eligibility: There are no eligibility restrictions, although
significant publications are necessary.
Level of Study: Professional development.
Purpose: To offer a free writing workshop and teach one
writing course to GW students.
Type: Residency.
No. of awards offered: 1.
Frequency: Annual.
Country of Study: Any country.
Application Procedure: Please submit 25-page writing
sample, CV and letters of recommendation.
Closing Date: November 15th.
Additional Information: The 2000-2001 programme will be
for a poet.

JEUNESSES MUSICALES OF SERBIA

Terazije 26/11, Belgrade, 11000, Yugoslavia
Tel: (381) 11 686 380
Fax: (381) 11 235 1517
Email: ijmebyc@music-competition.co.yu
www: http://www.music-competition.co.yu
Contact: Mrs Biljana Zdravkovic, Executive Secretary

The International Jeunesses Musicales Competition was
created in Belgrade in 1969. It is dedicated to the most
promising young musicians at the beginning of their
international careers. The categories - instruments solo,
chamber ensembles, composers - are repeated each five or
six years so that each generation will have an equal chance.

International Jeunesses Musicales Competition

Subjects: Musical performance.
Eligibility: Open to young musicians ready for international
appearances.
Level of Study: Professional development.

Purpose: To award the most promising young musicians at
the beginning of their international careers.
Type: Competition.
Frequency: Annual.
Value: Cash prizes in YU Dinars, special prizes, concert
engagements.
Country of Study: Any country.
Application Procedure: Please submit application form,
recommendations, photo, and curriculum vitae.
Closing Date: December 31st.
Additional Information: March 20th - April 2nd 1999 - Piano
and Piano Duo; March 20th - April 2nd 2000 - Violincello and
Composition; March 20th - April 2nd 2001 - Violin and String
Quartet. Three in each category with several prizes. This
competition has been organised for 28 years.

JEWISH FOUNDATION FOR EDUCATION OF WOMEN

330 West 58th Street
Suite 509, New York, NY, 10019, United States of America
Tel: (1) 212 265 2565
Fax: (1) 212 765 2675
Email: fdnscholar@aol.com
www: http://www.jfew.org
Contact: Ms Marge Goldwater, Executive Director

The Jewish Foundation for Education of Women is a private,
non-sectarian organisation. It provides scholarship assistance
for higher education to women with financial need within a
50-mile radius of New York City through several specific
programmes.

Fellowship Programme for Émigrés Pursuing Careers in Jewish Education

Subjects: Religious education, Jewish.
Eligibility: Women must be residents of New York City or a
50-mile radius thereof. Students entering or enrolled in full-
time rabbinical and catorial programmes, or Master's and
doctoral programmes in Jewish education or Jewish studies
are eligible.
Level of Study: Doctorate, Graduate, Professional
development.
Purpose: To provide fellowships for graduate work to women
from the former Soviet Union who are interested in pursuing
careers in Jewish education.
Type: Fellowship.
No. of awards offered: 5-10.
Frequency: Annual.
Value: US$10,000 to US$20,000 per year.
Length of Study: 2 years for Master's degree; 4 years for
Rabbinical and Cantorial programmes; 4 years for PhD.
Study Establishment: Study must take place in New York
City, USA.
Country of Study: USA.

Application Procedure: To request application please write, or send and email. In the application request please be sure to indicate current educational status and the programme for which financial aid is required.
Closing Date: February 15th.
Additional Information: The foundation also provides recipients with the opportunity to meet with the programme supervisor for enriched learning on a monthly basis and to productively share experiences as a means of learning how to teach more effectively.

JOHN CARTER BROWN LIBRARY AT BROWN UNIVERSITY

Box 1894, Providence, RI, 02912, United States of America
Contact: Fellowship Co-ordinator

The John Carter Brown Library, an independently funded and administered institution for advanced research in history and the humanities, is located on the campus of Brown University.

Alexander O Vietor Memorial Fellowship

Subjects: Research in European and American maritime history between 1450 and 1800.
Eligibility: Open to Americans and foreign nationals who are engaged in predoctoral, postdoctoral, or independent, research. Graduate students must have passed their preliminary or general examinations at the time of application.
Level of Study: Doctorate, Postdoctorate.
Purpose: To assist students in research of early maritime history.
Type: Fellowship.
No. of awards offered: 1.
Frequency: Annual.
Value: A stipend of US$1,100 monthly.
Length of Study: 2-4 months.
Country of Study: USA.
Application Procedure: To request an application form please write to the Director at the main address, or email fellowships@brown.edu.
Closing Date: January 15th.

Barbara S Mosbacher Fellowship

Subjects: All aspects of discovery, exploration, settlement, and development of the New World.
Eligibility: Open to Americans and foreign nationals who are engaged in pre or postdoctoral, or independent, research. Graduate students must have passed their preliminary or general examinations at the time of application.
Level of Study: Postdoctorate, Predoctorate, Research.
Purpose: To assist scholars in any area of research related to the Library's holdings.
Type: Fellowship.
No. of awards offered: Varies.
Value: US$1,100 per month.
Length of Study: 2-4 months.

Country of Study: USA.
Application Procedure: To request an application form please write to the Director at the main address, or email fellowships@brown.edu.
Closing Date: January 15th.

Center for New World Comparative Studies Fellowship

Subjects: Early history of the Americas from the late 15th-Century to 1830 - research relating to materials at the Library regarding all aspects of the discovery, exploration, settlements and development of the New World.
Eligibility: Open to Americans and foreign nationals who are engaged in predoctoral, postdoctoral, or independent, research. Graduate students must have passed their preliminary or general examinations at the time of application.
Level of Study: Doctorate, Postdoctorate.
Purpose: To enable research with a definite comparative dimension relating to the history of the Americas before C.1825.
Type: Fellowship.
No. of awards offered: 2.
Frequency: Annual.
Value: A stipend of US$1,100 monthly.
Length of Study: 2-4 months.
Country of Study: USA.
Application Procedure: To request an application form please write to the Director at the main address, or email fellowships@brown.edu.
Closing Date: January 15th.

Charles H Watts Memorial Fellowship

Subjects: All aspects of discovery, exploration, settlement, and development of the New World.
Eligibility: Open to Americans and foreign nationals who are engaged in pre or postdoctoral, or independent, research. Graduate students must have passed their preliminary or general examinations at the time of application.
Level of Study: Postdoctorate, Predoctorate, Research.
Purpose: To assist scholars in any area of research related to the Library's holdings.
Type: Fellowship.
No. of awards offered: Varies.
Value: US$1,100 per month.
Length of Study: 2-4 months.
Country of Study: USA.
Application Procedure: To request an application form please write to the Director at the main address, or email fellowships@brown.edu.
Closing Date: January 15th.

Helen Watson Buckner Memorial Fellowship

Subjects: All aspects of discovery, exploration, settlement, and development of the New World.
Eligibility: Open to Americans and foreign nationals who are engaged in pre or postdoctoral, or independent, research. Graduate students must have passed their preliminary or

general examinations at the time of application.
Level of Study: Postdoctorate, Predoctorate, Research.
Purpose: To assist scholars in any area of research related to the Library's holdings.
Type: Fellowship.
No. of awards offered: Varies.
Value: US$1,100 per month.
Length of Study: 2-4 months.
Country of Study: USA.
Application Procedure: To request an application form please write to the Director at the main address, or email fellowships@brown.edu.
Closing Date: January 15th.

Jeannette D Black Memorial Fellowship

Subjects: Early history of the Americas from the late 15th-Century to 1830 - research relating to materials at the Library regarding all aspects of the discovery, exploration, settlements and development of the New World.
Eligibility: Open to Americans and foreign nationals who are engaged in predoctoral, postdoctoral, or independent, research. Graduate students must have passed their preliminary or general examinations at the time of application.
Level of Study: Doctorate, Postdoctorate.
Purpose: To enable research into the history of cartography or a closely related area.
Type: Fellowship.
No. of awards offered: 1.
Frequency: Annual.
Value: A stipend of US$1,100 monthly.
Length of Study: 2-4 months.
Country of Study: USA.
Application Procedure: To request an application form please write to the Director at the main address, or email fellowships@brown.edu.
Closing Date: January 15th.

The Lampadia Foundation Fellowship

Subjects: History.
Eligibility: Restricted to senior scholars from Argentina, Brazil or Chile.
Type: Fellowship.
No. of awards offered: Varies.
Value: US$35,000.
Length of Study: 10 months.
Country of Study: USA.
Application Procedure: To request an application form please write to the Director at the main address, or email fellowships@brown.edu.
Closing Date: January 15th.

Library Associates Fellowship

Subjects: All aspects of discovery, exploration, settlement, and development of the New World.
Eligibility: Open to Americans and foreign nationals who are engaged in pre or postdoctoral, or independent, research. Graduate students must have passed their preliminary or general examinations at the time of application.

Level of Study: Postdoctorate, Predoctorate, Research.
Purpose: To assist scholars in any area of research related to the Library's holdings.
Type: Fellowship.
No. of awards offered: Varies.
Value: US$1,100 per month.
Length of Study: 2-4 months.
Country of Study: USA.
Application Procedure: To request an application form please write to the Director at the main address, or email fellowships@brown.edu.
Closing Date: January 15th.

Long Term Fellowships

Subjects: All aspects of discovery, exploration, settlement, and development of the New World.
Eligibility: Applicants must be American citizens or have been resident in the US for three years immediately preceding the term of the Fellowship.
Purpose: To assist scholars in any area of research related to the Library's holdings.
Type: Fellowship.
No. of awards offered: Varies.
Value: US$2,800 per month.
Length of Study: 5-10 months.
Application Procedure: To request an application form please write to the Director at the main address, or email fellowships@brown.edu.
Closing Date: January 15th.
Additional Information: Recipients are expected to relocate to Providence and be in continuous residence at the John Carter Brown Library for the entire term of the award and to participate in the intellectual life of Brown University. Those living within commuting distance of the library (approximately 50 miles distance) are ordinarily not eligible for JCB fellowships.

Maria Elena Cassiet Fellowships

Subjects: History.
Eligibility: Restricted to scholars who are permanent residents of countries in Spanish America. Open to Americans and foreign nationals who are engaged in pre or postdoctoral, or independent, research. Graduate students must have passed their preliminary or general examinations at the time of application.
Level of Study: Postdoctorate, Predoctorate, Research.
Purpose: To assist with historical research.
Type: Fellowship.
No. of awards offered: Varies.
Value: US$1,100.
Length of Study: 2-4 months.
Application Procedure: To request an application form please write to the Director at the main address, or email fellowships@brown.edu.
Closing Date: January 15th.

Paul W McQuillen Memorial Fellowship

Subjects: All aspects of discovery, exploration, settlement, and development of the New World.
Eligibility: Open to Americans and foreign nationals who are engaged in pre or postdoctoral, or independent, research. Graduate students must have passed their preliminary or general examinations at the time of application.
Level of Study: Postdoctorate, Predoctorate, Research.
Purpose: To assist scholars in any area of research related to the Library's holdings.
Type: Fellowship.
No. of awards offered: Varies.
Value: US$1,100 per month.
Length of Study: 2 to 4 months.
Country of Study: USA.
Application Procedure: To request an application form please write to the Director at the main address, or email fellowships@brown.edu.
Closing Date: January 15th.

Ruth and Lincoln Ekstrom Fellowship

Subjects: Research on the history of women and the family in the Americas prior to 1825, including the question of cultural influences on gender formation.
Eligibility: Open to Americans and foreign nationals who are engaged in pre or postdoctoral, or independent, research. Graduate students must have passed their preliminary or general examinations at the time of application.
Level of Study: Postdoctorate, Predoctorate, Research.
Purpose: To assist candidates with research.
Type: Fellowship.
No. of awards offered: Varies.
Value: US$1,100.
Length of Study: 2-4 months.
Country of Study: USA.
Application Procedure: To request an application form please write to the Director at the main address, or email fellowships@brown.edu.
Closing Date: January 15th.

JOHN F AND ANNA LEE STACEY SCHOLARSHIP FUND

c/o National Cowboy Hall of Fame
1700 North East 63rd Street, Oklahoma City, OK, 73111, United States of America
Tel: (1) 405 478 2250
Contact: Mr Ed Muno

In accordance with the will of the late Anna Lee Stacey, a trust fund has been created for the education of young men and women who aim to make art their profession.

John F and Anna Lee Stacey Scholarships

Subjects: Painting and drawing in the classical tradition of western culture.

Eligibility: Open to US citizens of 18-35 years of age who are skilled in and devoted to the classical or conservative tradition of western culture.
Level of Study: Postgraduate.
Purpose: To foster a high standard in the study of form, colour, drawing, painting, design, and technique, as these are expressed in modes showing patent affinity with the classical tradition of western culture.
Type: Scholarship.
No. of awards offered: 1-3.
Frequency: Annual.
Value: A total of approximately US$5,000.
Length of Study: 1 year.
Country of Study: Any country.
Application Procedure: Application form must be completed and submitted with 35mm slides of the applicant's work. Send slides and completed application blank by US mail not rail or air express.
Closing Date: February 1st.
Additional Information: Do not send slides or any materials before October 1st, as the Committee does not maintain storage facilities.

JOHN SIMON GUGGENHEIM MEMORIAL FOUNDATION

90 Park Avenue, New York, NY, 10016, United States of America
Tel: (1) 212 687 4470
Fax: (1) 212 697 3248
Email: fellowships@gf.org
www: http://www.gf.org
Contact: Ms Patricia E O'Sullivan, Assistant Secretary

The John Simon Guggenheim Memorial Foundation is concerned with encouraging and supporting scholars and artists to engage in research in any field of knowledge and creation within the arts.

Guggenheim Fellowships to Assist Research and Artistic Creation (Latin America and the Caribbean)

Subjects: Sciences, humanities, social sciences, creative arts.
Eligibility: Open to citizens and permanent residents of countries of Latin America and the Caribbean who have demonstrated an exceptional capacity for productive scholarship or exceptional creative ability in the arts.
Level of Study: Postdoctorate, Professional development.
Purpose: To further the development of scholars and artists by assisting them to engage in research in any field of knowledge and creation in any of the arts, under the freest possible conditions and irrespective of race, colour or creed.
Type: Fellowship.
No. of awards offered: Approx. 35.
Frequency: Annual.

Value: Grants will be adjusted to the needs of Fellows, considering their other resources and the purpose and scope of their plans. (Average grant in 1998 was US$30,118).
Length of Study: Ordinarily for 1 year, but in no instance for a period shorter than 6 consecutive months.
Country of Study: Any country.
Application Procedure: Application form must be completed. Further information is available on the Foundation's website.
Closing Date: December 1st.
Additional Information: Members of the teaching profession receiving sabbatical leave on full or part salary are eligible for appointment, as are holders of other Fellowships and of appointments at research centers. The fellowships are awarded by the Trustees upon nominations made by a committee of selection.

Guggenheim Fellowships to Assist Research and Artistic Creation (US and Canada)

Subjects: Sciences, humanities, social sciences, creative arts.
Eligibility: Open to citizens and permanent residents of the USA and Canada who have demonstrated an exceptional capacity for productive scholarship or exceptional creative ability in the arts.
Level of Study: Postdoctorate, Professional development.
Purpose: To further the development of scholars and artists by assisting them to engage in research in any field of knowledge and creation in any of the arts, under the freest possible conditions and irrespective of race, colour or creed.
Type: Fellowship.
No. of awards offered: Approx. 165.
Frequency: Annual.
Value: Grants will be adjusted to the needs of Fellows, considering their other resources and the purpose and scope of their plans. (Average grant in 1998 was US$32,000).
Length of Study: Ordinarily for 1 year, but in no instance for a period shorter than 6 consecutive months.
Country of Study: Any country.
Application Procedure: Application form must be completed. Further information is available on the Foundation's website.
Closing Date: October 1st.
Additional Information: Members of the teaching profession receiving sabbatical leave on full or part salary are eligible for appointment, as are holders of other Fellowships and of appointments at research centers. Fellowships are awarded by the Trustees upon nominations made by a committee of selection.

KEELE UNIVERSITY

Staffordshire, ST5 5BG, England
Tel: (44) 1782 584002
Fax: (44) 1782 632343
Email: aab01@admin.keele.ac.uk
www: http://www.keele.ac.uk
Contact: Director of Academic Affairs

Keele University Graduate Teaching Assistantships

Subjects: Various subjects from the fields of arts and humanities, business administration and management, education and teacher training, fine and applied arts, law, mathematics and computer science, medical sciences, natural sciences, social and behavioural sciences.
Eligibility: Candidates should hold a good honours degree and are required to register as full-time candidates for a higher degree at the University of Keele.
Level of Study: Postgraduate.
Purpose: To assist research and give teaching experience.
Type: Studentship.
No. of awards offered: 2-3.
Frequency: Annual.
Value: £6,455 per year.
Length of Study: 1 year; may be extended for an unspecified additional period.
Study Establishment: Keele University.
Country of Study: United Kingdom.
Application Procedure: Please contact the admissions office for details.
Closing Date: February 1st.

KENNAN INSTITUTE FOR ADVANCED RUSSIAN STUDIES

Woodrow Wilson International Center for Scholars
One Woodrow Wison Plaza
1300 Pennsylvania Avenue NW, Washington, DC, 20523,
United States of America
Tel: (1) 202 287 3400
Fax: (1) 202 287 3772
Email: kiars@wwic.si.edu
www:
http://wwics.si.edu/programs/region/kennan/kenmain.htm
Contact: Fellowships/Grants Office

The Institute sponsors advanced research on the successor states to the USSR, and encourages Eurasian studies with its public lecture and publication programs, maintaining contact with scholars and research centres abroad. The Institute seeks to function as a forum where the community can interact with public policymakers.

Kennan Institute Research Scholarship

Subjects: Research proposals examining topics in Eurasian studies are eligible, with those topics relating to regional Russia, the NIS, and contemporary issues especially welcome.

Eligibility: Research Scholarships are available to academic participants in the early stages of their career before tenure, or scholars whose careers have been interrupted or delayed. For non-academics, an equivalent degree or professional achievement is expected.

Level of Study: Postdoctorate.

Purpose: To offer support to young scholars studying the former Soviet Union, allowing them time and resources in the Washington DC area to work on their first published work, or to continue their research.

Type: Scholarship.

No. of awards offered: 5-6.

Frequency: Dependent on funds available.

Value: US$3,000 per month plus research facilities, word processing support, and some research assistance.

Length of Study: 3-6 months.

Study Establishment: The Kennan Institute.

Country of Study: Former Soviet Union: Russia; Ukraine; Belarus; Moldova; Georgia; Armenia; Azerbaijan; Kazakhstan; Kirgizia; Uzbekistan; Turkmenistan; Tajikistan.

Application Procedure: An application form must be completed. The application must include project proposals; biographical data; and three letters of recommendation specifically in support of the research to be conducted at the Institute. Applications received by fax or e-mail will not be accepted.

Closing Date: All materials must be received by October 1st.

Kennan Institute Short Term Grants

Subjects: Eurasian studies in the social sciences and humanities.

Eligibility: Short-term grants are available to academic participants with a doctoral degree or those who have nearly completed their dissertations. For non-academic participants, an equivalent level of professional development is required. Applicants can be citizens of any country, but must note their citizenship when applying.

Level of Study: Doctorate.

Purpose: To support scholars in need of the academic and archival resources of the Washington DC area in order to complete their research.

Type: Scholarship.

No. of awards offered: In each competition round 4 to non-US citizens, 4 to US citizens.

Frequency: Dependent on funds available.

Value: US$100 per day.

Length of Study: Up to 31 days.

Study Establishment: The Kennan Institute.

Country of Study: Former Soviet Union: Russia; Ukraine; Belarus; Moldova; Georgia; Armenia; Azerbaijan; Kazakhstan; Kirgizia; Uzbekistan; Turkmenistan; Tajikistan.

Application Procedure: There is no application form required for short-term grants. Four rounds of competition are held each year. Each applicant should submit a concise

description of his or her research project (700-800) words; a curriculum vitae; a statement on preferred dates of residence in Washington DC; and two letters of recommendation specifically in support of the research to be conducted at the institute. All materials must be received by the deadline date.

Closing Date: March 1st, June 1st, September 1st, December 1st.

KENNEDY MEMORIAL TRUST

48 Westminster Palace Gardens
Artillery Row, London, SW1P 1RR, England
Tel: (44) 171 222 1151
Fax: (44) 171 222 5355
Contact: Ms Anna Mason, Secretary

As part of the British National Memorial to President Kennedy, the Trust awards scholarships to British postgraduate students for study at Harvard University or the Massachusetts Institute of Technology. -The awards, which are offered annually following a national competition, cover tuition costs and a stipend to meet living expenses.

Kennedy Scholarships

Subjects: All fields of arts, science, social science and political studies.

Eligibility: Open to UK citizens who are resident in the UK, and who have been wholly or mainly educated in the UK. At the time of application, candidates must have spent at least two of the last five years at a UK university or university college, and must have graduated by the start of tenure in the following year, or have graduated not more than three years prior to the commencement of studies.

Level of Study: Postgraduate.

Purpose: As part of the British National Memorial to President Kennedy to enable students to undertake a course of postgraduate study in the United States.

Type: Scholarship.

No. of awards offered: 12.

Frequency: Annual.

Value: US$16,000 to cover support costs, special equipment and some travel in the USA, plus tuition fees and travelling expenses to and from the USA.

Length of Study: 1 year. In certain circumstances, students who are applying for PhD or 2-year Master's programmes may be considered for extra funding to help support a second year of study.

Study Establishment: Harvard University and the Massachusetts Institute of Technology, Cambridge.

Country of Study: USA.

Application Procedure: Please submit a form, statement of purpose, references, and letter of endorsement from applicant's British university. Applications should come via the applicant's UK university.

Closing Date: November 7th.

Additional Information: No application will be considered from persons already in the USA. Scholarships for the study of business administration and management will only be granted in exceptional circumstances, and candidates must have completed two years' employment in business or public service since graduation. An independent application to Harvard or MIT is necessary. Scholars are not required to study for a degree in the USA but are encouraged to do so if they are eligible and able to complete the requirements for it.

KING EDWARD VII BRITISH-GERMAN FOUNDATION

10 Langton Street, London, SW10 0JH, England
Contact: Secretary

The Foundation provides scholarships to postgraduate students of British nationality under the age of 30 to study in Germany and promote Anglo-German relations and understanding.

King Edward VII Scholarships

Subjects: All subjects.
Eligibility: Open to British nationals who are graduates of British universities, are under 30 years of age, and who wish to study further in Germany.
Level of Study: Postgraduate.
Purpose: To promote Anglo-German relations.
Type: Scholarship.
No. of awards offered: Up to 3.
Frequency: Annual.
Value: DM1200 per month, a book grant of DM150, exemption from tuition fees, plus travelling expenses between a Scholar's home in the UK and his/her place of study in Germany.
Length of Study: 10 months.
Study Establishment: A university or other institution of higher education.
Country of Study: Germany.
Application Procedure: Write for application form, enclosing A5 SAE.
Closing Date: December 31st.

KING FAISAL FOUNDATION

PO Box 22476, Riyadh, 11495, Saudi Arabia
Tel: (966) 1 465 2255
Fax: (966) 1 465 8685
Email: info@kff.com
www: http://www.kff.org
Telex: 401180 FAISAL SJ
Contact: Dr Abd Allah S Al-Uthaimin, Secretary General

King Faisal International Award for Arabic Literature

Subjects: Arabic Literature.
Eligibility: There are no restrictions except that applications from political parties will not be accepted.
Level of Study: Unrestricted.
Purpose: To show appreciation to scholars who have made significant breakthrough and advance in Arabic Literature.
Type: Prize.
No. of awards offered: 1.
Frequency: Annual.
Value: US$200,000.
Country of Study: Any country.
Application Procedure: Universities, international institutes and scientific organisations are invited to submit nominations each year.
Closing Date: May 31st for the following year.
Additional Information: In the year 2000 the award will be given in the field of studies pertaining to early Arab literary critique.

King Faisal International Award for Islamic Studies

Subjects: Islamic Studies.
Eligibility: There are no restrictions on eligibility except that applications from political parties will not be accepted.
Level of Study: Unrestricted.
Purpose: To show appreciation for scholars who have made significant breakthrough and advances in Islamic Studies.
Type: Prize.
No. of awards offered: 1.
Frequency: Annual.
Value: US$200,000.
Country of Study: Any country.
Application Procedure: Universities, international institutes and scientific organisations are invited to nominate candidates each year.
Closing Date: May 31st for the following year.
Additional Information: In the year 2000 the award will be given in the field of studies dealing with the spread and cultural impact of Islam outside the Arab world.

KOREA FOUNDATION

Diplomatic Center Building
1376-1
Seocho 2-dong
Seocho-gu, Seoul, 137-072, Korea, Republic (South)
Tel: (82) 2 3463 5600
Fax: (82) 2 3463 6075
Email: fellow@kofo.or.kr
Contact: Mr Hyeon Seon Choi, Vice President

The Korea Foundation seeks to improve awareness and understanding of Korea worldwide as well as to foster co-operative relationships between Korea and foreign countries through a variety of exchange programmes.

Korea Foundation Fellowship for Korean Language Training

Subjects: Korean studies related to the humanities, culture and arts, social sciences, or comparative research.
Eligibility: Candidates must have a basic knowledge of and an ability to communicate in the Korean language. In the case of Korean nationals, only those with foreign residency status are eligible to apply. Candidates who are receiving support from other organisations or programmes administered by the Korea Foundation are not eligible to receive this fellowship at the same time.
Level of Study: Graduate, Postgraduate, Undergraduate.
Purpose: To provide foreign scholars and graduate students, who need systematic Korean language education, the opportunity to enrol in a Korean-language programme at a language institute affiliated with a Korean university.
Type: Fellowship.
No. of awards offered: Varies.
Frequency: Annual.
Value: There is a monthly stipend: the grant amount will be determined by the Foundation according to the Fellow's academic experience and current position. Awards range between US$1,000 to US$1,250. The tuition for language training will be paid by the Foundation directly to the Korean language institute that the Foundation designates. Travellers' Insurance is also provided. Please note that the cost of an international round-trip airline ticket is not covered under this fellowship.
Length of Study: 6 months, 9 months or 12 months.
Study Establishment: A language institute affiliated with a Korean university.
Country of Study: Korea.
Application Procedure: For application forms and guidelines, candidates should contact the Korean studies center at their institution, or the Korea Foundation.
Closing Date: May 31st.

Korea Foundation Fellowship for Korean Studies

Subjects: Korea-related research in the humanities and social sciences, culture and arts, and comparative research related to Korea.
Eligibility: Open to university professors and instructors, doctoral candidates, researchers and other professionals. Candidates must be proficient in Korean or English. In the case of Korean nationals, only those with foreign residency status or regular faculty positions at foreign universities are eligible to apply. Fellows in this programme must concentrate on their research and may not enrol in any language courses or other university courses during the fellowship period. Candidates who are receiving support from other organisations or programmes administered by the Korea Foundation are not eligible to receive this fellowship at the same time.
Level of Study: Doctorate, Professional development, Research.
Purpose: To promote Korean studies and support professional researchers in Korean studies by facilitating their research activities in Korea.
Type: Fellowship.

No. of awards offered: Varies.
Frequency: Annual.
Value: There is a monthly stipend: the grant amount will be determined by the Foundation according to the Fellow's research experience and current position. Awards range between US$1,250 to US$1,600. The Foundation will also provide an international airline ticket (economy class) for round-trip transportation between the airport nearest to the Fellow's residence and Korea. Travellers' Insurance is also provided.
Length of Study: 3-12 months.
Country of Study: Korea.
Application Procedure: For application forms and guidelines, candidates should contact the Korean studies center at their institution, or the Korea Foundation.
Closing Date: May 31st.

KOSCIUSZKO FOUNDATION

15 East 65th Street, New York, NY, 10021-6595, United States of America
Tel: (1) 212 734 2130
Fax: (1) 212 628 4552
Email: thekf@pegasusnet.com
www: http://www.kosciuszkofoundation.org/
Contact: Mr Thomas J Pniewski, Director Cultural Affairs

The Kosciuszko Foundation founded in 1925, is dedicated to promoting educational and cultural relations between the United States and Poland, and to increasing American awareness of Polish culture and history. In addition to its grants and scholarships, which total more than $1 million annually, the Foundation presents cultural programmes including lectures, concerts and exhibitions, promoting Polish culture in the United States, and nurturing the spirit of multicultural co-operation.

Chopin Piano Competition

Subjects: Piano performance of Chopin.
Eligibility: Open to citizens and permanent residents of the USA, and to international full-time students with valid student visas. Applicants must be between 16 and 22 years of age as of the opening date of the Competition.
Level of Study: Unrestricted.
Purpose: To encourage highly talented students of piano to study and play works of Chopin.
Type: Prize.
No. of awards offered: 3.
Frequency: Annual.
Value: 1st prize of US$2,500; 2nd prize of US$1,500; 3rd prize of US$1,000. Scholarships may be awarded in the form of shared prizes.
Country of Study: USA.
Application Procedure: Write for application form and listing of other requirements.
Closing Date: April 15th.

Additional Information: The Competition is held on three consecutive days in mid-April. Applications should be marked Chopin Piano Competition.

Kosciuszko Foundation Graduate and Postgraduate Studies and Research in Poland Program

Subjects: All subjects.
Eligibility: Open to US graduate and postgraduate students who wish to pursue a course of graduate or postgraduate study and/or research at institutions of higher learning in Poland. Also eligible are university faculty who wish to spend a sabbatical pursuing research in Poland.
Level of Study: Graduate, Postgraduate.
Purpose: To enable Americans to continue their graduate and postgraduate studies in Poland.
Type: Grant.
No. of awards offered: Varies.
Frequency: Annual.
Value: Tuition and housing, plus a monthly stipend in Polish currency for living expenses.
Country of Study: Poland.
Application Procedure: Please write for details.
Closing Date: January 16th.
Additional Information: Applicants must have a working knowledge of the Polish language and are reviewed based on academic background, motivation for pursuing graduate studies and/or research in Poland, and a proposal of studies and research in Poland.

Marcella Sembrich Voice Competition

Subjects: Polish song.
Eligibility: Open to all singers preparing for their professional careers, who are US citizens or international full-time students with valid student visas, at least 18 years old and born after October 1, 1963.
Level of Study: Unrestricted.
Purpose: To encourage young singers to study the repertoire of Polish composers, and to honour the Polish soprano, Marcella Sembrich.
No. of awards offered: 3.
Frequency: Dependent on funds available.
Value: First prize: US$1,000 cash scholarship and round-trip air fare from New York City to the International Moniuszko Competition in Warsaw, recital at the Moniuszko Festival, and an invitation to perform at the Sembrich Memorial Association (Lake George, NY). Second and third prizes are US$750 and US$500 respectively.
Country of Study: Any country.
Application Procedure: Applicants should submit: competition application form and non-refundable fee of US$35, with supporting documents; suggested program; and an audio cassette recording (two) copies of approximately ten minutes.
Closing Date: December 15th.

Year Abroad Programme at the Jagiellonian University in Krakow

Subjects: Polish language.
Eligibility: Open to US citizens of Polish background. Students may participate in this programme during their junior or senior year of college. Although it is an undergraduate programme, students in a MA or PhD programme (but not at the dissertation level) can also apply.
Level of Study: Doctorate, Postgraduate, Undergraduate.
Purpose: To enable American students to study in Poland.
Type: Travel Grant.
No. of awards offered: Varies.
Frequency: Annual.
Value: Tuition and housing, plus a monthly stipend in Polish currency for living expenses.
Length of Study: 1 year.
Country of Study: Poland.
Application Procedure: Please write for details.
Closing Date: January 16th.

KPMG/MARTIN MUSICAL SCHOLARSHIP FUND

Lawn Cottage
23a Brackley Road, Beckenham, Kent, BR3 1RB, England
Tel: (44) 181 658 9432
Fax: (44) 181 658 9432
Contact: Mr Martin Jones, Administrator

Gillian Sinclair Music Trust

Subjects: Musical performance (all Instruments).
Level of Study: Postgraduate.
Frequency: Twice a year.
Value: Two recitals and two £500 awards.
Country of Study: Any country.
Application Procedure: Application form must be completed, and returned with a stamped addressed envelope and registration fee of £10. This is non-returnable.
Closing Date: December 1st.

John E Mortimer Foundation Awards

Subjects: Musical performance (all instruments).
Level of Study: Postgraduate.
Frequency: Annual.
Value: Prizes are of varying value.
Country of Study: Any country.
Application Procedure: Application form must be completed, and returned with a stamped addressed envelope and registration fee of £10. This is non-returnable.
Closing Date: December 1st.

The June Allison Award

Subjects: Musical performance (woodwind only).
Level of Study: Postgraduate.

Purpose: To assist exceptional musical talent with specialist and advanced study and to help in bridging the gap between study and fully professional status.
Type: Award.
Frequency: Annual.
Value: £500 plus recital.
Country of Study: Any country.
Application Procedure: Application form must be completed, and returned with a stamped addressed envelope and registration fee of £10. This is non-returnable.
Closing Date: December 1st.

KPMG Scholarship

Subjects: Musical performance.
Eligibility: Open to nationals of any country.
Level of Study: Unrestricted.
Purpose: To assist with tuition fees and maintenance whilst studying.
Type: Scholarship.
No. of awards offered: 1.
Frequency: Annual.
Value: £2,000.
Country of Study: Any country.
Application Procedure: Application form must be completed.
Closing Date: October 1st.

Martin Musical Scholarships

Subjects: Music performance.
Eligibility: Open to practising musicians as well as students who are instrumental performers (including pianists) preparing for a career on the concert platform either as a soloist or orchestral player, and no more than 25 years of age. Preference is given to UK citizens.
Level of Study: Postgraduate.
Purpose: To assist exceptional musical talent with specialist and advanced study and to help in bridging the gap between study and fully professional status.
Type: Scholarship.
No. of awards offered: Varies.
Frequency: Annual.
Value: Varies.
Length of Study: 2 years; renewable.
Country of Study: United Kingdom, Europe or USA.
Application Procedure: Application form must be completed.
Closing Date: October 1st.
Additional Information: It is not the present policy of the Fund to support organists, singers, conductors, composers, academic students or piano accompanists.

Sidney Perry Scholarship

Subjects: Musical performance.
Eligibility: Open to nationals of any country.
Level of Study: Postgraduate.
Purpose: To support postgraduate study.
Type: Scholarship.
No. of awards offered: Varies.

Frequency: Annual.
Value: Varies.
Length of Study: Up to 2 years.
Country of Study: Any country.
Application Procedure: Application form must be completed.
Closing Date: October 1st.

The LDF Casbolt Memorial Award

Subjects: Musical performance (violin only).
Level of Study: Postgraduate.
Type: Award.
Frequency: Annual.
Value: £500.
Country of Study: Any country.
Application Procedure: Application form must be completed, and returned with a stamped addressed envelope and registration fee of £10. This is non-returnable.

Trevor Snoad Memorial Trust

Subjects: Music performance (viola).
Eligibility: Open to outstanding viola players.
Level of Study: Postgraduate.
No. of awards offered: 1.
Frequency: Annual.
Value: £500.
Country of Study: Any country.
Application Procedure: Application form must be completed.
Closing Date: October 1st.
Additional Information: An award is valid for two years and must be taken up within that time. There is no limit to the number of times an unsuccessful candidate may apply. Each candidate is eligible to apply for two awards. Selection of candidates is by audition. Preliminary auditions are held in the autumn with final auditions in the spring.

THE KURT WEILL FOUNDATION FOR MUSIC

7 East 20 Street
3rd Floor, New York, NY, 10003, United States of America
Tel: (1) 212 505 5240
Fax: (1) 212 353 9663
Email: kwfinfo@kwf.org
www: http://www.kwf.org
Contact: Ms Joanna C Lee, Associate Director for Business Affairs

The Kurt Weill Foundation for Music, Inc, is a non-profit, private foundation chartered to preserve and perpetuate the legacies of the composer Kurt Weill (1900-1950) and his wife, singer-actress Lotte Kenya (1891-1981). In pursuit of this goal, the Foundation awards grants and prizes to support excellence in research and performance, sponsors a broad range of print and on-line publications, maintains the Weill-Lenya Research Center, and administers Weill's copyrights.

Kurt Weill Foundation Music Grant

Subjects: Any subject related to the perpetuation of Kurt Weill's artistic legacy.
Eligibility: There are no eligibility restrictions.
Level of Study: Doctorate, Postdoctorate, Postgraduate, Professional development.
Purpose: The Kurt Weill Foundation for Music is a non-profit corporation which promotes public understanding and appreciation of the musical works of Kurt Weill. To this end, the Foundation solicits proposals from individuals and non-profit organisations for funding of projects related to the perpetuation of Kurt Weill's artistic legacy.
No. of awards offered: Varies.
Frequency: Annual.
Value: For college and university production and performances, caps of US$5,000. Otherwise, no restrictions on requested amounts.
Country of Study: Any country.
Application Procedure: Application forms must be completed for all but performances over US$5,000.
Closing Date: November 1st (no date for professional proposals over US$5,000).

Kurt Weill Prize

Subjects: American Music Theater (20th Century).
Eligibility: Open to nationals of any country.
Level of Study: Unrestricted.
Purpose: To encourage scholarship relating to the musical theatre in the 20th century.
Type: Cash Prize.
No. of awards offered: 1.
Frequency: Every two years.
Value: US$2,500 for books, US$500 for articles.
Country of Study: Any country.
Application Procedure: Applicants must submit five copies of their published work, only if published in 1997 or 1998.
Closing Date: April 30th.
Additional Information: Works must have been published within the period 1997-1998, for the 1999 Prize.

LA TROBE UNIVERSITY

Bundoora Campus, Melbourne, VIC, 3083, Australia
Tel: (61) 3 9479 2971
Fax: (61) 3 9479 1464
Email: c.cocks@latrobe.edu.au
www: http://www.latrobe.edu.au/www/rgso
Contact: Scholarships and Candidature Co-ordinator

La Trobe University is one of the leading research universities in Australia. The University has internationally regarded strengths across a diverse range of disciplines. It offers a detailed and broad research training programme and provides unique access to technology transfer and collaboration with end users of its research and training via its Research and Development Park.

Australian Postgraduate Awards

Subjects: Health sciences, humanities and social sciences, science technology and engineering, law and management.
Eligibility: Applicants must have completed at least 4 years of tertiary education studies at a high level of achievement (for example, first class honours degree or equivalent) at an Australian university. Applicants must be Australian citizens or have permanent resident status and have lived in Australia continuously for the twelve months prior to the closing date for application. Applicants who have previously held an Australian Government Award (APA, APRA or CPRA) for more than 3 months are not eligible for an APA. Applicants who have previously held an Australian Postgraduate Course Award (APCA) may apply only for an APA to support PhD research.
Level of Study: Doctorate, Postgraduate.
Purpose: To support research leading to Masters or Doctoral degrees.
Type: Award.
No. of awards offered: Varies.
Value: A$16,135 per annum full-time (tax exempt plus allowances; A$8,734 per annum part-time (taxable) plus allowances.
Length of Study: Master's candidates 2 years, PhD candidates 3 years. Periods of study already undertaken towards the degree will be deducted from the tenure of the award.
Study Establishment: Bundoora Campus, La Trobe University.
Country of Study: Australia.
Application Procedure: Application kits are available from the school in which the candidate wishes to study. Applications must be submitted in duplicate, to the Research and Graduate Studies Office, La Trobe University, Bundoora Campus, Bundoora, Victoria, Australia 3083.
Closing Date: October 31st.
Additional Information: APA holders are required to pay the annual General Service Fee- A$320 (Bundoora Campus), A$276 (Bendigo Campus). The awards may be held concurrently with other nonAustralian government awards. Paid work may be permitted to a maximum of 8 hours per week (full time award) or 4 hours per week (part time award).

International Postgraduate Research Scholarships (IPRS)

Subjects: Health sciences, humanities and social sciences, science, technology and engineering, law and management.
Eligibility: IPRS are awarded on the basis of academic merit and research capacity to suitably qualified overseas graduates eligible to commence a higher degree (doctoral or Masters) by research. The IPRS may be held concurrently with a university research scholarship and applicants for an IPRS are advised to apply for La Trobe University Postgraduate Research Scholarship (LTUPRS). The scheme is open to citizens of all overseas countries (excluding New

Zealand). Successful applicants will research specialisation and, in most instances, will become members of a research team working under the direction of senior researchers. Applicants who have already commenced a Masters or PhD candidature are not eligible to apply for and IPRS to support the degree course for which they have already enrolled. Applicants for Masters Candidature by coursework and minor thesis are not eligible to apply for the IPRS.
Level of Study: Doctorate, Postgraduate.
Purpose: To attract top quqality overseas postgraduate students to areas of research strength in higher education institutions and to support Austrlia's research effort.
Type: Scholarship.
No. of awards offered: Varies.
Value: Tuition fess, basic health care cover.
Length of Study: Masters 2 years, PhD 3 years.
Study Establishment: Bundoora Campus, La Trobe University.
Country of Study: Australia.
Application Procedure: Application forms should be submitted on the application form for international candidates available from the International Programmes Office email: international@latrobe.edu.au.
Additional Information: APA holders are required to pay the annual General Service Fee- A$320 (Bundoora Campus), A$276 (Bendigo Campus).

La Trobe University Postdoctoral Research Fellowship

Subjects: All subjects.
Eligibility: Open to students who have been awarded their doctorates within the last five years. Applicants must hold a doctoral degree or equivalent at the date of appointment. The university may also take into account the proposed area of research having regard to the university's research promotion and management strategy policies.
Level of Study: Postdoctorate.
Purpose: To advance research activities on the various campuses of the university by bringing to or retaining in Australia promising scholars.
Type: Fellowship.
No. of awards offered: 1.
Frequency: Annual.
Value: A$33,200-A$45,055 per year, plus air fares and a resettlement allowance.
Length of Study: 2 years.
Country of Study: Australia.
Application Procedure: An application form and guidelines will be available either upon request in writing or via email, or they can be downloaded from the University's website. Administrative contact: Ms Jennie Somerville, Grants Administrator, Research & Graduate Studies Office, tel: (61) 3 9479 2049, fax: (61) 3 9479 1464; email: j.somerville@latrobe.edu.au.
Closing Date: September.
Additional Information: A project must be proposed by the applicant in collaboration with a La Trobe University research worker or team. The approved project will be designated in the letter of offer and the major objectives of a Fellow's

project shall not be altered without the written approval of the university.

La Trobe University Postgraduate Research Scholarships (LTUPRS)

Subjects: Health sciences, humanities and social sciences, science, technology and engineering, law and management.
Eligibility: Open to citizens of all countries including Australia and New Zealand. Applicants must have completed four years of tertiary education studies at a very high level of achievement (first class honours degree or equivalent at an Australian university or recognised overseas university. Applicants who have previously held an LTUPRS for more than 3 months are not eligible to apply.
Level of Study: Postgraduate.
Purpose: To support research leading to Masters of Doctoral degrees.
Type: Scholarship.
No. of awards offered: Vaies.
Value: A$15,800 per annum full-time (tax exempt plus allowances; A$8,500 per annum part-time (taxable) plus allowances.
Length of Study: Masters 2 years, PhD 3 years. Periods of study already undertaken towards the degree will be deducted from the tenure of the award.
Study Establishment: Bundoora Campus, La Trobe University.
Country of Study: Australia.
Application Procedure: Application kits are available from the school in which the candidate wishes to study. Applications must be submitted in duplicate, to the Research and Graduate Studies Office, La Trobe University, Bundoora Campus, Bundoora, Victoria, Australia 3083.
Additional Information: Paid work may be permitted to a maximum of 8 hours per week.

LANCASTER UNIVERSITY

Student Support Office
University House
Bailrigg, Lancaster, LA1 4YW, England
Tel: (44) 1524 65201
Fax: (44) 1524 594294
www: http://www.lancs.ac.uk
Contact: Ms Lorna M Mullett

Cartmel College Scholarship Fund

Subjects: Any subject offered by the University.
Eligibility: Open to candidates of any nationality, who must have a place at Lancaster University. Priority is given to members of Cartmel College and to new students.
Level of Study: Postgraduate.
Purpose: To assist students unable to obtain adequate grants from other bodies.
Type: Scholarship.
No. of awards offered: Varies.
Frequency: Annual.

Value: £300-£500 not including fees.
Study Establishment: Lancaster University.
Country of Study: United Kingdom.
Application Procedure: Please write to Lorna M Mullet at the Student Support Office for details.
Closing Date: June 1st.

Lancaster University County College Awards

Subjects: Any subject offered by the University.
Eligibility: Open to candidates of any nationality, who must have place at Lancaster University. Candidates must be former members of the County College and must be prepared to reside in the College.
Level of Study: Postgraduate.
Purpose: To assist students whose course of study will lead to financial hardship.
No. of awards offered: Varies.
Frequency: Annual.
Value: Free residence.
Study Establishment: Lancaster University; recipients must reside in County College, and be former members of the College.
Country of Study: United Kingdom.
Application Procedure: Please write to Lorna M Mullett at the Student Support Office.
Closing Date: June 1st.

Lancaster University International Bursaries

Subjects: All subjects.
Eligibility: Open to nationals of India and the People's Republic of China, who have not previously studied at Lancaster University.
Level of Study: Postgraduate.
Purpose: To offer financial support.
Type: Bursary.
No. of awards offered: 6.
Frequency: Annual.
Value: £2,000.
Length of Study: 1 year minimum.
Study Establishment: Lancaster University.
Country of Study: United Kingdom.
Application Procedure: Applications are available on request; please contact the International Office.
Closing Date: June 30th.

Peel Awards

Subjects: Any subject offered by the University.
Eligibility: Open to candidates of any nationality, who must have a place at Lancaster University and must be over 21 years of age.
Level of Study: Postgraduate, Undergraduate.
Purpose: To enable students who are unable to secure finance from other sources to study at Lancaster University.
No. of awards offered: Varies.
Frequency: Annual.
Value: Varies. Awards do not cover fees.
Study Establishment: Lancaster University.
Country of Study: United Kingdom.

Application Procedure: Application form available on request from Lorna M Mullett in the Student Support Office.
Closing Date: June 1st.

LANDSCAPE ARCHITECTURE FOUNDATION

c/o American Society of Landscape Architects
636 Eye Street NW, Washington, DC, 20001/3736, United States of America
Tel: (1) 202 898 2444
Fax: (1) 202 898 1185
Email: msippel@asla.org
www: http://www.asla.org
Contact: Ms Melinda Sippel, Scholarship Co-ordinator

AILA/Yamagani/Hope Fellowship

Subjects: Landscape architecture.
Eligibility: The applicant must have a Bachelor's or Master's degree in landscape architecture.
Level of Study: Postgraduate, Professional development.
Purpose: The fellowship may be used to support credit or non credit courses, seminars or workshops; for travel or related expenses in support of an independent research project; or for development of post-secondary educational materials or curriculum plans.
Type: Fellowship.
No. of awards offered: 1.
Frequency: Annual.
Value: US$1,000.
Country of Study: Any country.
Application Procedure: Applicants should submit a 500 word essay, a 100 word statement of intent, two letters of recommendation, and a completed application form.
Closing Date: August 2nd.

Edith H Henderson Scholarship

Subjects: Landscape architecture.
Eligibility: Applicants must be participating in a class in public speaking or creative writing.
Level of Study: Postgraduate.
Purpose: To assist students with skills in public presentation.
Type: Scholarship.
No. of awards offered: 1.
Frequency: Annual.
Value: US$1,000.
Country of Study: USA.
Application Procedure: Three copies each of a completed application form and a typewritten essay (200-400 words maximum), plus a review of Mrs Henderson's book entitled Edith Henderson's Home Landscape Companion; must be submitted.
Closing Date: Applications should be postmarked no later than March 31st.

Hawaii Chapter/David T Woolsey Scholarship

Subjects: Landscape architecture.
Eligibility: Open to students from Hawaii.
Level of Study: Postgraduate, Undergraduate.
Purpose: The award provides funds for a third, fourth, or fifth year or graduate student of landscape architecture from Hawaii.
Type: Scholarship.
No. of awards offered: 1.
Frequency: Annual.
Value: US$1,000.
Country of Study: Any country.
Application Procedure: Applicants should submit: a typed autobiography and personal statement of 500 words maximum, three photographic samples of their work, two letters of recommendation, completed application forms, and a financial aid form.
Closing Date: March 31st.
Additional Information: LAF/CLASS Fund scholarships and Internships are also available for architecture students from UCLA and CaL Poly. These include the University Programme, six scholarships at US$1,500; Landscape Architecture Programme, five scholarships at US$500; Internship Programme, two scholarships for US$2,000; Ornamental Horticulture Programme, three scholarships at US$1,000. Enquiries should be directed to the LAF/CLASS Fund Programme Administrator at the given address.

JJR Research Grant

Subjects: Land use policies; regulatory systems; regional and town planning; community development; ecotourism; computer modeling; construction materials; energy, land, water, and transport management.
Eligibility: Application is open to any landscape architect or allied professional who has at least five years' experience in professional practice.
Level of Study: Postgraduate.
Purpose: In order for landscape architecture to make its full contribution as a profession and a discipline, the knowledge base on which it rests must be continually refined and expanded through applied research.
Type: Research Grant.
No. of awards offered: 1.
Frequency: Annual.
Value: Minimum of US$2,000.
Country of Study: USA.
Application Procedure: Applicants must submit an application form and a typed 1000 word abstract describing the planned research effort and how this research will be implemented. Also include a description of the final product.
Closing Date: Postmarked no later than August 2nd.
Additional Information: Completed applications will be forwarded to the Landscape Architecture Foundation's Education and Research Vice President and Committee for initial review and recommendation. Final selection will be made by the Committee Chairperson and the Johnson Johnson & Roy, Inc representative.

Ralph Hudson Environmental Fellowship

Subjects: Landscape architecture.
Eligibility: Application is open to a full-time individual professor in landscape architecture. Must be a resident of the USA, Canada or Mexico.
Level of Study: Professional development.
Purpose: In order for landscape architecture to make its full contribution as a profession and a discipline, the knowledge base on which it rests must be systematically examined, tested, refined and extended through providing a high level of university education. This award is intended to advance the educational profession and academic community through research in areas relating to open space, parks and recreation.
Type: Fellowship.
No. of awards offered: 1.
Frequency: Annual.
Value: US$3,500.
Country of Study: Any country.
Application Procedure: Application form must be completed.
Closing Date: August 2nd.

Raymond E Page Scholarship

Subjects: Landscape architecture.
Eligibility: Open to students of landscape architecture.
Level of Study: Undergraduate.
Purpose: To further the profession through the development of parks and other public facilities.
Type: Scholarship.
No. of awards offered: 2.
Frequency: Annual.
Value: US$500.
Country of Study: Any country.
Application Procedure: Applicants should submit a two page essay, describing how the award is to be used, a letter of recommendation from a previous professor, and a completed application form.
Closing Date: March 31st.

Thomas P Papandrew Scholarship

Subjects: Landscape architecture.
Eligibility: Applicants must be a member of an under-represented ethnic goup.
Level of Study: Postgraduate.
Purpose: To assist meritorious minority students in pursuing their career.
Type: Scholarship.
No. of awards offered: 1.
Frequency: Annual.
Study Establishment: The College of Architecture and Environmental Design.
Country of Study: USA.
Application Procedure: Apply to the Department of Planning.
Closing Date: Applications should be postmarked no later than March 31st.

Toro Industry Advancement Award

Subjects: Landscape architecture.
Eligibility: Open to qualified applicants of any nationality.
Level of Study: Postgraduate.
Purpose: To recognise exemplary design projects that display effective use of irrigation techniques in creating quality environments.
Type: Grant.
No. of awards offered: 1.
Frequency: Annual.
Value: US$2,000.
Country of Study: USA.
Application Procedure: A brief statement outlining the project, photographs of the project use, and a completed application form, must be submitted.
Closing Date: August 2nd.

William J Locklin Scholarship

Subjects: Landscape architecture.
Eligibility: Open to students pursuing a programme in lighting design, or landscape architectural students focusing on lighting design in studio projects.
Level of Study: Postgraduate.
Purpose: To emphasise the importance of 24-hour lighting in landscape designs.
Type: Scholarship.
No. of awards offered: 1.
Frequency: Annual.
Value: US$1,000.
Country of Study: USA.
Application Procedure: A typed 300 word essay highlighting the design project, visual samples, a letter of recommendation from a current professor, and a completed application form, must be submitted.
Closing Date: Postmarked no later than March 31st.

LATVIAN CULTURE FUND

Basteja 12, Riga, 1050, Latvia
Tel: (371) 7 227230
Fax: (371) 7 212545
Email: peterisb@parks.lv
Contact: Mr Petreris Bankouskis, Chairman of the Board

The Latvian Culture Fund provides direct individually aimed support to all cultural activities, regardless of their location, in the form of grants and scholarships.

Spidola Award and Scholarships

Subjects: Arts, social sciences, humanities.
Eligibility: There are no restrictions.
Level of Study: Postgraduate, Professional development.
Purpose: To award achievement in research in the fields of arts, humanities, and social sciences.
Type: Prize and Scholarship.
No. of awards offered: 3 awards, 12 scholarships.
Frequency: Annual.

Value: Scholarship US$2,100; award US$8,800.
Length of Study: 12 months.
Country of Study: Baltic Region: Lativia, Lithuania, Estonia, Sweden, Finland, Norway, Denmark.
Application Procedure: Application form to be completed.
Closing Date: December 15th.

LEEDS INTERNATIONAL PIANOFORTE COMPETITION

Piano Competition Office
The University of Leeds, Leeds, West Yorkshire, LS2 9JT, England
Tel: (44) 113 244 6586
Fax: (44) 113 244 6586
Email: info@leedspiano.bdx.co.uk
www: http://www.leedspiano.com
Contact: Mrs Paul Holloway, Hon Administrator

The aim of the Leeds International Pianoforte Competition is to offer talented young professional pianists of all nationalities the chance to be recognised by the musical world and the media and to help them build their professional careers.

Leeds International Pianoforte Competition

Subjects: Piano performance.
Eligibility: Open to professional pianists who were born on or after September 1st 1968.
Level of Study: Professional development.
Purpose: To promote the careers of talented professional pianists.
Type: Prize.
No. of awards offered: 36.
Frequency: Every three years.
Value: Total prizes in excess of £55,000 and a number of national and international engagements for all six finalists.
Country of Study: Any country.
Application Procedure: Application forms by not later than March 15th 2000.
Closing Date: March 15th.
Additional Information: The competition is to be held during 6-23 September 2000.

LEMMERMANN FOUNDATION

c/o Studio Associato Romanelli
via Cosseria, Rome, 5-00192, Italy
Tel: (390) 6 324 30 23
Fax: (390) 6 321 26 46
Email: lemmermann@mail.nexus.it
www: http://www.nexus.it/lemmermann
Contact: Ms Valentina Nardo, Scholarships Secretary

Lemmermann Foundation Scholarship

Subjects: Literature, archaeology, history of art - Pre-Roman to present day.

Eligibility: Applicants must not be more than 30 years of age, must be attending a recognised university course, and must have a basic knowledge of the Italian language.
Level of Study: Doctorate, Postgraduate.
Purpose: To assist students who need to study in Rome to carry out research and prepare their thesis concerning Rome and Roman culture from the period Pre-Roman to present day.
Type: Scholarship.
Frequency: Twice a year.
Value: 1,500,000 Italian Lira each month.
Length of Study: From 2-6 months.
Country of Study: Italy.
Application Procedure: Applicants must send a description of the area of study and thesis, two letters of reference, a curriculum vitae, and a photocopy of their passport. For further information contact Fonazione Lemmermann at the main address.
Closing Date: March 15th, September 30th.

LEO BAECK INSTITUTE

129 E 73rd Street, New York, NY, 10021, United States of America
Tel: (1) 212 744 6400
Fax: (1) 212 988 1305
Email: lbi1@interport.net
Contact: Ms Carol Kahn Strauss, Executive Director

This Institute is a research, study and lecture centre, and a library and repository for archival and art materials. It is devoted to the preservation of original materials pertaining to history and culture of German-speaking Jewry.

David Baumgardt Memorial Fellowship

Subjects: Modern intellectual history of German-speaking Jewry.
Level of Study: Doctorate, Postdoctorate, Postgraduate.
Purpose: The fellowship provides financial support to scholars whose research projects are connected with the writings of Professor David Baumgardt or his scholarly interests.
Type: Fellowship.
No. of awards offered: 1.
Frequency: Annual.
Value: US$3,000.
Length of Study: 1 year.
Country of Study: New York.
Application Procedure: An application consists of, completed application form, curriculum vitae, full description of the research project, a financial plan, evidence of highest degree obtained and evidence of enrolment in a PhD programme. For doctoral candidates, all the above plus official transcript two recommendation letters. For postdoctoral candidates all the above plus two letters of recommendation from scholars in the field. Applications and guidelines available on request.
Closing Date: November 1st.

Fritz Halbers Fellowship

Subjects: Culture and history of German-speaking Jewry.
Level of Study: Doctorate, Graduate, Postgraduate.
Purpose: To provide financial assistance to scholars whose projects are connected with the culture and history of the German speaking Jewry.
Type: Fellowship.
No. of awards offered: 1 or more.
Frequency: Annual.
Value: US$3,000.
Length of Study: 1 Year.
Country of Study: New York.
Application Procedure: An application consists of, completed application form, curriculum vitae, full description of the research project, a financial plan, evidence of highest degree obtained and evidence of enrolment in a PhD programme. For doctoral candidates, all the above plus official transcript and two recommendation letters. For postdoctoral candidates all the above plus two letters of recommendation from scholars in the field. Application form and guidelines on request.
Closing Date: November 1st.

LBI /DAAD Fellowships

Subjects: German and German-Jewish history.
Eligibility: Applicants must have US citizenship, a knowledge of German and an affiliation with an American institution of higher education.
Level of Study: Doctorate, Postgraduate.
Purpose: To assist research into German and German-Jewish history.
Type: Fellowship.
No. of awards offered: 5.
Frequency: Annual.
Value: Depending on requirement of project.
Length of Study: 2 months at LBI New York or 3-6 months at research institutions in Germany.
Study Establishment: LBI New York or research institutions in Germany.
Country of Study: USA or Germany.
Application Procedure: Please write for an application form.
Closing Date: November 1st.
Additional Information: These awards are in conjunction with awards offered by the German Academic Exchange Service (DAAD) in New York, USA.

LBI/DAAD Fellowhips for Research in the Federal Republic of Germany

Subjects: Social, communal and intellectual history of German-speaking Jewry.
Eligibility: Applicants must be US citizens, and PhD candidates or recent PhDs who have received their degrees within the preceding two years.

Level of Study: Doctorate, Postdoctorate.
Purpose: To provide financial assistance to doctoral students doing research for their dissertation and to academics in the preparation of a scholarly essay or book.
Type: Fellowship.
No. of awards offered: 1-2.
Frequency: Annual.
Value: DM 1700.
Length of Study: 1 year.
Country of Study: Germany.
Application Procedure: An application consists of the application form, a curriculum vitae, a full description of the research project, and for doctoral students: official transcripts (graduate and undergraduate work); written evidence that they are enrolled in PhD programme; and two letters of recommendation, one by their doctoral advisor, one by another scholar familiar with the work. For postdoctoral candidates: evidence of their degree (transcripts not required); and two letters of recommendations from two colleagues familiar with their research.
Closing Date: November 1st.
Additional Information: The fellowship holders agree to submit a brief report on their research activities upon conclusion of their fellowship. These awards are in conjunction with awards offered by the German Academic Exchange Service (DAAD) in New York, USA.

LBI/DAAD Fellowship for Research at the Leo Baeck Institute

Subjects: Social, communal and intellectual history of German-speaking Jewry.
Level of Study: Doctorate, Graduate, Postdoctorate, Undergraduate.
Type: Fellowship.
No. of awards offered: 2.
Frequency: Annual.
Value: US$2000.
Length of Study: 1 year.
Country of Study: USA
Application Procedure: An application consists of the application form, a curriculum vitae, a full description of the research project, and for doctoral students: official transcripts (graduate and undergraduate work); written evidence that they are enrolled in PhD programme; and two letters of recommendation, one by their doctoral advisor, one by another scholar familiar with the work. For postdoctoral candidates: evidence of their degree (transcripts not required); and two letters of recommendations from two colleagues familiar with their research.
Closing Date: November 1st.
Additional Information: The fellowship holders agree to submit a brief report on their research activities after the period for which the fellowship was granted.

LEWIS WALPOLE LIBRARY

154 Main Street, Farmington, CT, 06032-2958, United States of America
Tel: (1) 203 432 2822
Fax: (1) 203 432 4538
Email: walpole@yale.edu
Contact: The Librarian

The Lewis Walpole Library is a research centre for the study of all aspects of English 18th century studies and is a prime centre for the study of Horace Walpole and Strawberry Hill.

Lewis Walpole Library Fellowship

Subjects: 18th century British studies (history, literature, theatre, drama, art, architecture, politics, philosophy and social history).
Eligibility: Applicants should normally be pursuing an advanced degree or must be engaged in postdoctoral research or equivalent research.
Level of Study: Doctorate, Postdoctorate, Postgraduate, Research.
Purpose: To enable one month of study in any aspect of British 18th century studies in the Library's collection of 18th century British prints, paintings, books and manuscripts.
Type: Fellowship.
No. of awards offered: At least 2.
Frequency: Annual.
Value: US$1,500 plus modest travel allowance.
Study Establishment: Lewis Walpole Library.
Country of Study: USA.
Application Procedure: Please submit CV, brief outline of research proposal (no more than three pages) and two confidential letters of recommendation.
Closing Date: January 15th.

LIBRARY COMPANY OF PHILADELPHIA

1314 Locust Street, Philadelphia, PA, 19107, United States of America
Tel: (1) 215 546 3181
Fax: (1) 215 546 5167
Email: jgreen@library company.org
www: http://www.librarycompany.org
Contact: Fellowships Office

Founded in 1731, the Library Company was the largest public library in America until the 1850's, and contains printed materials on aspects of American culture and society in that period. It is a research library of 450,000 books, pamphlets, newspapers, and periodicals; 75,000 prints, maps, and photographs, and 150,000 manuscripts.

Library Company of Philadelphia Research Fellowships in American History and Culture

Subjects: 18th and 19th Century American social and cultural history, African American history, literary history, history of the book in America.

Eligibility: The fellowship supports both postdoctoral and dissertation research. The project proposal should demonstrate that the Library Company has primary source central to the research topic. Candidates are encouraged to enquire about the appropriateness of a proposed topic before applying.

Level of Study: Doctorate, Postdoctorate.

Purpose: To offer short-term fellowships for research in residence in its collections.

Type: Fellowship.

No. of awards offered; Usually 12-15.

Frequency: Annual.

Value: US$1,500.

Length of Study: 1 month.

Study Establishment: Independent research library.

Country of Study: USA.

Application Procedure: There are no application forms. To apply, please send four copies each of a curriculum vitae, a 2-4 page description of the proposed project, and a single letter of reference.

Closing Date: February 1st. Fellows may take up residence at any time from the following June through May of the next year.

Additional Information: Fellows will be assisted in finding reasonably priced accommodation. International applications are especially encouraged since one fellowship (jointly sponsored with the Historical Society of Pennsylvania) is reserved for scholars whose residence is outside the USA. A partial catalogue of the Library's holdings is available through the website.

LIGHT WORK

316 Waverly Avenue, Syracuse, NY, 13244, United States of America
Tel: (1) 315 443 1300
Fax: (1) 315 443 9516
Email: jjhoone@syr.edu
Contact: Mr Jeffrey Hoone, Director

Light Work is an artist-run space which focuses on providing direct support for artists working in photography through its Artist-in-Residence Program, exhibitions and publications.

Light Work Artist-in-Residence Program

Subjects: Photography.

Eligibility: Open to artists of any nationality working in photography with a demonstrated, serious intent and experience in the field. Students are not eligible.

Level of Study: Professional development.

Purpose: To support and encourage the production of new work by emerging and mid-career artists.

Type: Residency.

No. of awards offered: 15.

Frequency: Annual.

Value: US$1,200 stipend plus darkroom and apartment for one month.

Length of Study: 1 month; not renewable.

Country of Study: USA.

Application Procedure: Write for guidelines: there are no application forms. Submit a cover letter, résumé, 20 slides, other support materials and an SASE.

Closing Date: Applications are accepted at any time.

Additional Information: The Residencies are non-academic. Artists will be asked to give one informal lecture about their work and to contribute work produced in Syracuse to the Light Work collection. Work by participating artists is published in the Contact Sheet. Light Work also curates two photography galleries at Syracuse University and accepts exhibition proposals.

LONDON ARTS BOARD

Elme House
133 Long Acre, London, WC2E 9AF, England
Tel: (44) 171 240 1313
Fax: (44) 171 670 2400
Contact: Ms Hazel Taylor, Public Affairs Administrator

London Arts Board (LAB) is the Arts Funding and Regional Development Agency for the Capital City. It is one of 10 English Arts Boards.

London Arts Board Awards and Schemes for Artists

Subjects: The arts.

Eligibility: Open to individual writers, artists, composers and photographers, who wish to undertake an arts project in London.

Level of Study: Professional development.

Purpose: To help artists in the Capital to reach a new and wider audience, London Arts Board administers 23 different funding programmmes.

Type: A variety of commissions, bursaries, fellowships and residencies.

No. of awards offered: Varies.

Value: Varies.

Length of Study: Varies.

Study Establishment: London.

Country of Study: United Kingdom.

Application Procedure: Application forms are available from the Information Officer, London Arts Board, Elme House, 133 Long Acre, London WC2E 9AF.

Closing Date: Please write for details.

Additional Information: For information on the Awards and Schemes administered by the other Regional Arts Boards, please contact one of the following the listed addresses.

For further information contact:

West Midlands Arts
82 Granville Street, Birmingham, West Midlands, B1 2LH, England
Tel: (44) 121 631 3121
Fax: (44) 121 643 7239
Contact: Grant Management Officer
or
Eastern Arts
Cherry Hinton Hall
Cherry Hinton Road, Cambridge, CB1 4DW, England
Tel: (44) 1223 215355
Fax: (44) 1223 248075
Contact: Grants Management Officer
or
Yorkshire Arts
21 Bond Street, Dewsbury, West Yorkshire, WF13 1AX, England
Tel: (44) 1924 455555
Fax: (44) 1924 466522
Contact: Grants Management Officer
or
South West Arts
Bradninch Place
Gandy Street, Exeter, Devon, EX4 3LS, England
Tel: (44) 1392 218188
Fax: (44) 1392 413554
Contact: Grants Management Officer
or
East Midlands Arts
Mountfields House
Forest Road, Loughborough, Leicestershire, LE11 3HU, England
Tel: (44) 1509 218292
Fax: (44) 1509 262214
Contact: Grants Management Officer
or
Arts Board: North West
12 Harter Street, Manchester, M1 6HY, England
Tel: (44) 161 228 3062
Fax: (44) 161 236 1257
Contact: Grants Management Officer
or
Northern Arts
(Arts North Limited)
10 Osborne Terrace, Newcastle upon Tyne, NE2 1NZ, England
Tel: (44) 191 281 6334
Fax: (44) 191 281 3276
Contact: Grants Management Officer
or
South East Arts
10 Mount Ephraim, Tunbridge Wells, Kent, TN4 8AS, England
Tel: (44) 1892 515210
Fax: (44) 1892 549383
Contact: Grants Management Officer
or
Southern Arts
13 St Clement Street, Winchester, Hampshire, SO23 9DQ, England

Tel: (44) 1962 855099
Fax: (44) 1962 861186
Contact: Grants Management Officer

LONDON STRING QUARTET FOUNDATION

62 High Street, Fareham, Hampshire, PO16 7BG, England
Tel: (44) 1329 283603
Fax: (44) 1329 281969
Email: lsqf@compuserve.com
www: http://www.lsqf.com
Contact: Mr Dennis Sayer, Administrator

The London String Quartet Foundation is a registered charity whose purpose is to promote the London International String Quartet Competition every three years.

London International String Quartet Competition

Subjects: Musical performance.
Eligibility: There are no restrictions except age. Quartets must not exceed an aggregate age of 120 years.
Level of Study: Unrestricted.
Purpose: To encourage young string quartets to participate in an international competition.
No. of awards offered: 6 major monetary prizes with concerts organized for the 1st prizewinner.
Frequency: Every three years (next in 2000).
Value: 1st £8,000 plus The Amadeus Trophy; 2nd £5,600; 3rd £4,000; 4th £2,800; 5th £2,000; Menuhin Prize £1,000; Audience Prize £1,000; Sidney Griller Award: £1,000 plus trophy.
Country of Study: Any country.
Application Procedure: Application form must be completed.
Closing Date: December 1st in the year preceding the award.

THE LONDON SYMPHONY ORCHESTRA

Barbican Centre
Barbican, London, EC2Y 8DS, England
Tel: (44) 171 588 1116
Fax: (44) 171 374 0127
www: http://www.lso.co.uk
Contact: Ms Helen Smith, Administrator

Shell LSO Music Scholarship

Subjects: Musical training. Candidates take part in auditions, master classes and workshops with principals of the LSO. Four finalists perform with the LSO and the scholarship is awarded to the winner.

Eligibility: The Scholarship is open to British nationals, or persons normally resident in the UK for at least the past three years aged between 14 and 22 years.
Level of Study: Unrestricted.
Purpose: The Scholarship is to be used in the best interests of the winner's development, and to facilitate his or her entry into the musical profession.
Type: Scholarship.
No. of awards offered: 1 Scholarship, 4 cash prizes.
Frequency: Annually, in a 4-year cycle covering each section of the orchestra.
Value: Scholarship £6,000, gold medal; 2nd Prize, £3,000, silver medal; 2 x 3rd Prizes, each £1,500, bronze medal; 4th Prize and Gerald McDonald Prize £750.
Country of Study: Any country.
Application Procedure: Application forms plus two references must be submitted.
Closing Date: December.

LOREN L ZACHARY SOCIETY FOR THE PERFORMING ARTS

2250 Gloaming Way, Beverly Hills, CA, 90210, United States of America
Tel: (1) 310 276 2731
Fax: (1) 310 275 8245
Contact: Mr Nedra Zachary, National Vocal Competition Director

Loren L Zachary National Vocal Competition for Young Opera Singers

Subjects: Operatic singing.
Eligibility: Open to female singers between 21 and 33 years of age and male singers between 21 and 35 years of age who have completed operatic training and are fully prepared to pursue professional stage careers.
Level of Study: Professional development.
Purpose: To assist in the careers of young opera singers through competitive auditions and monetary awards.
Type: Competition.
No. of awards offered: 10.
Frequency: Annual.
Value: US$10,000 for the top winner. A round trip flight to Europe for opera auditioning purposes is also awarded to a finalist. US$34,950 was distributed amongst the finalists (1998).
Country of Study: Any country.
Application Procedure: Application forms need to be completed and accompanied by proof of age and application fee of US$35.
Closing Date: New York auditions: February. Los Angeles auditions: March.

Additional Information: Applicants must be present at all phases of the auditions. Tapes are not acceptable. Auditions take place in New York and in Los Angeles, March to June. For application forms and exact dates, interested singers should send a stamped business-size envelope to the Society in November. No fax requests.

THE MACDOWELL COLONY

100 High Street, Peterborough, NH, 03458, United States of America
Tel: (1) 603 924 3886
Fax: (1) 603 924 9142
www: http://www.macdowellcolony.org
Contact: Ms Pat Dodge, Admissions Co-ordinator

Founded in 1907 to provide creative artists with uninterrupted tome and seclusion to work and enjoy the experience of living in a community with gifted artists. Residences of up to eight weeks for writers, composers, film and video makers, visual artists, architects, and interdisciplinary artists. Artists in residence receive room, board and exclusive use of a studio.

MacDowell Colony Residencies

Subjects: Creative writing, visual arts, musical composition, film/video making, architecture.
Eligibility: Open to established and emerging artists in the fields specified.
Level of Study: Unrestricted.
Purpose: To provide a place where creative artists can take advantage of uninterrupted work time and seclusion in which to work and enjoy the experience of living in a community of gifted artists.
Type: Residency.
No. of awards offered: A total of 31 studios are available each application period for individual residencies.
Frequency: Three application reviews each year.
Value: Accepted applicants are asked to contribute toward residency costs.
Length of Study: Up to 8 weeks.
Study Establishment: The Colony, for one of three seasons: summer, autumn to winter, and winter to spring.
Country of Study: USA.
Application Procedure: Please write for call for details.
Closing Date: January 15th, April 15th and September 15th for residencies to become tenable in summer, autumn to winter, and winter to spring respectively.
Additional Information: The studios are offered for the independent pursuit of the applicants' art. No workshops or courses are given. There are no stipends. Requests for information should be accompanied by an SASE.

MANHATTAN SCHOOL OF MUSIC

120 Claremont Avenue, New York, NY, 10027, United States
of America
Tel: (1) 212 749 2802 ext 449
Fax: (1) 212 749 3025
Contact: Ms Amy A Anderson

Manhattan School of Music is a major national and
international force in the education of professional musicians.
It is the largest private conservatory in the nation offering both
classical and jazz training.

Manhattan School of Music Scholarships

Subjects: Professional music study at the Bachelor's,
Master's and doctoral levels as well as Professional Studies
Certificate.
Eligibility: Open to all students who demonstrate through
performance that they have attained excellence in the field of
music and have the capacity for further development.
Level of Study: Doctorate, Postgraduate, Undergraduate.
Purpose: To recognise outstanding talent, achievements and
performance.
Type: Scholarship.
No. of awards offered: 400.
Frequency: Annual.
Value: Tuition expenses only; awards range from US$1,000 to
full tuition costs, payable in equal instalments by semester.
Length of Study: 1 academic year; renewable for a total of 4
years (undergraduates) or 2 years (graduates).
Study Establishment: At the School.
Country of Study: USA.
Application Procedure: For US/permanent residents,
PROFILE form and FAFSA. For international students
International Application for MSM Scholarship in house form.
Closing Date: March 15th for March auditions, April 15th for
May auditions.
Additional Information: Students must demonstrate financial
need and provide the necessary income documents in order
to qualify.

MANIPUR UNIVERSITY

Canchipur, Imphal, Manipur, 795003, India
Tel: (91) 385 220529
Fax: (91) 385 221429
Email: manipur@shakti.ncst.ernet.in
Contact: Mr Joychandra Singh, Registrar

Besides 22 postgraduate departments of the University on
the campus, and 59 colleges affiliated to it; there are two
other affiliated colleges teaching MBBS, MD, MS and
LLB/LLM.

Manipur University Scholarship

Subjects: Arts and humanities, home economics, natural
sciences, physics, geography, political science and geology.

Eligibility: The scholar should not be in receipt of any other
award, scholarship or fellowship, from any other source.
Level of Study: Doctorate.
Purpose: For research under the MPhil/PhD programmes.
Type: Scholarship.
No. of awards offered: 1 in each department.
Frequency: Annual.
Value: Rs500 (Rupees) per month.
Length of Study: A maximum of 1 years.
Study Establishment: Manipur University faculty.
Country of Study: India.
Application Procedure: After expiry of the tenure of
scholarship offered to the previous awardee, the university
calls for applications in plain paper from MPhil/PhD students
during any month of the year.
Closing Date: Generally about one month from the date of
notice of award applications.
Additional Information: Information can be obtained from
the Information Officer at the university.

MANOUG PARIKIAN TRUST

16 Ogle Street, London, W1P 7LG, England
Tel: (44) 171 636 4481
Fax: (44) 171 637 4307
Contact: Mrs Susan Dolton

Manoug Parikian Award

Subjects: Musical performance - violin.
Eligibility: Open to violinists under the age of 21 years of any
nationality who have been resident in the UK for three years.
Level of Study: Professional development.
Purpose: To assist the studies of a talented young violinist.
No. of awards offered: 1.
Frequency: Annual.
Value: £3,500.
Country of Study: Any country.
Application Procedure: An application form must be
completed and two references provided.
Closing Date: March.
Additional Information: Selected students will be asked to
audition.

MARCEL HICTER FOUNDATION

14 rue Cornet de Grez, Brussels, B-1210, Belgium
Tel: (32) 2 219 9886
Fax: (32) 2 217 3572
Email: fond.hicter@glo.be
Contact: Mr Jean-Pierre Deru, Director

Marcel Hicter Foundation Travel Bursary Scheme

Subjects: Arts and culture administration and management.
Eligibility: Open to candidates from countries which have
signed the European Cultural Convention.

Level of Study: Unrestricted.

Purpose: To facilitate and enhance the mobility of European experts and trainees taking part in cultural administration or arts management training programmes.

Type: Travel Bursary.

No. of awards offered: Dependent on funds available.

Frequency: 8 times a year.

Value: The bursary covers travel expenses (by shortest route and cheapest fare possible).

Length of Study: A minimum of 5 days for trainees, and 6 hours for experts.

Country of Study: European countries which have signed the European Cultural Convention.

Application Procedure: Application form must be completed and signed by the applicant and the host organisation.

Closing Date: Applications must be sent to the Foundation to meet one of the following deadlines: January 15th; March 1st; April 15th; June 1st; July 15th; September 1st; October 15th; December 1st.

MARINE CORPS HISTORICAL CENTER

History and Museums Division
Building 58
901 M Street SE
Washington Navy Yard, Washington, DC, 20374-5040, United States of America
Tel: (1) 202 433 4244
Fax: (1) 202 433 7265
Contact: Grants and Fellowships Co-ordinator

The Marine Corps Historical Center is the focal point of history related activities within the US Marine Corps. The Historical Center is the building housing the History and Museums Division of Headquarters, US Marine Corps. The Historical Branch provides reference services to the public and government agencies, maintains the Marine Corps' archives and oral history collection, and produces the official histories of Marine activities, units and bases. The Museums Branch maintains the artefact and personal papers collections, and operates the Marine Corps Museum, and the Air-Ground Museum.

Beeler-Raider Fellowship

Subjects: Topics in US military and naval history, as well as history and history-based studies in the social and behavioural sciences, with a direct relationship to the US Marine Corps.

Eligibility: The competition is limited to citizens or nationals of the USA. While the programme concentrates on graduate students, fellowships are available to other qualified persons.

Level of Study: Postgraduate.

Purpose: To encourage graduate level and advanced study of the combat contributions of enlisted Marines.

Type: Fellowship.

No. of awards offered: 1.

Frequency: Annual.

Value: US$2,500.

Study Establishment: Fellowship recipients are expected to do a portion of their research in Washington, DC. Fellows will also receive access to the Historical Center's facilities and collections.

Application Procedure: Preliminary application for a grant involves writing to the Director of Marine Corps History and Museums outlining the qualifications, and should either propose a specific topic or request a suggested topic based on the applicant's interests and qualifications. If the evaluation of the preliminary application is favourable, the applicant will be asked to make formal application on a form provided by the Historical Center. Application forms may be obtained from the Co-ordinator, Grants and Fellowships, Marine Corps Historical Center. The applicant is responsible for insuring that all required documentation is mailed before the closing date. The Director of Marine Corps History and Museums will notify all applicants individually of their decision not later than mid-July.

Closing Date: May 1st.

College Internships

Subjects: History.

Eligibility: Applicants must be registered students at a college or university which will grant academic credit for work experience as interns in subject areas related to the students' course of study. While there are no restrictions on individuals applying for intern positions, it has been found that mature and academically superior students are most successful. The agreement of the academic institution to the internship for credit is essential.

Level of Study: Professional development.

Purpose: To offer opportunities for college students to participate on a professional level in its many historical and museum activities. The intent of the programme is to give promising and talented student interns a chance to earn college credit while gaining meaningful experience in fields in which they might choose to seek employment after school or pursue a vocational interest.

Type: Internship.

No. of awards offered: Varies.

Value: A small grant of daily expense money is provided. Any other costs of the internship must be made by the student.

Study Establishment: Internships are served either at the Marine Corps Historical Center, Washington DC, or the Marine Corps Air Ground Museum, Marine Corps Development and Education Command, Quantico, Virginia.

Country of Study: USA.

Application Procedure: Please contact the Chief Historian, Marine Corps Historical Center for further details.

Dissertation Fellowships

Subjects: Topics in US military and naval history, as well as history and history-based studies in the social and behavioural sciences, with a direct relationship to the US Marine Corps.

Eligibility: Applicants must be citizens of the United States, enrolled in a recognised graduate school, have completed by September all requirements for the doctoral degree except the dissertation and have an approved, pertinent dissertation topic. A fellowship will not be awarded to an applicant who has held or accepted an equivalent fellowship from any other Department of Defence agency, however recipients of the Marine Corps' Master's thesis fellowships may apply.

Level of Study: Doctorate.

Purpose: To award a qualified graduate student working on a doctoral dissertation relevant to Marine Corps history.

Type: Fellowship.

No. of awards offered: 1.

Frequency: Annual.

Value: A stipend of US$7,500.

Study Establishment: Fellows are expected to do a portion of their research in Washington, DC. Fellows will also receive access to the Historical Center's facilities and collections.

Application Procedure: Application forms are available from the Chairman of the History Department of the applicant's university, or by writing to the Director of the Marine Corps History and Museums, Marine Corps Historical Center. The applicant is responsible for insuring that all required documentation is mailed before the closing date. The Director of Marine Corps History and Museums will notify all applicants individually of their decision not later than mid-July.

Closing Date: May 1st.

Additional Information: Evaluation of applicants is on the basis of academic achievements, faculty recommendations, demonstrated research and writing ability, and the nature of the topic is of proposed benefit to the study and understanding of Marine Corps history. All awards will be based on merit, without regard to race, creed, colour, or sex.

Master's Thesis Fellowships

Subjects: Topics in US military and naval history, as well as history and history-based studies in the social and behavioural sciences, with a direct relationship to the US Marine Corps. This programme gives preference to projects covering the pre-1975 period where records are declassified or can be most readily declassified and made available to scholars.

Eligibility: Applicants must be actively enrolled in an accredited Master's degree programme which requires a Master's thesis. The competition is limited to citizens or nationals of the USA. A fellowship will not be awarded to anyone who has held or accepted an equivalent fellowship from any other Department of Defense agency.

Level of Study: Postgraduate.

Purpose: To award a number of fellowships to qualified graduate students working on topics pertinent to Marine Corps history.

Type: Fellowship.

No. of awards offered: Varies.

Frequency: Annual.

Value: A stipend of US$2,500.

Study Establishment: Fellowship recipients are expected to do a portion of their research in Washington, DC. Fellows will also receive access to the Historical Center's facilities and collections.

Application Procedure: Application forms are available from the Chairman of the History Department of the applicant's

university, or by writing to the Director of the Marine Corps History and Museums, Marine Corps Historical Center. The applicant is responsible for insuring that all required documentation is mailed before the closing date. The Director of Marine Corps History and Museums will notify all applicants individually of their decision not later than mid-July.

Closing Date: May 1st.

Research Grants

Subjects: Topics in US military and naval history, as well as history and history-based studies in the social and behavioural sciences, with a direct relationship to the US Marine Corps. This programme gives preference to projects covering the pre-1975 period where records are declassified or can be most readily declassified and made available to scholars.

Eligibility: While the programme concentrates on graduate students, grants are available to other qualified persons. Applicants for grants should have the ability to conduct advanced study in those aspects of American military history and museum activities related to the US Marine Corps.

Level of Study: Research.

Purpose: To encourage graduate level and advanced study in Marine Corps history and related fields.

Type: Grant.

Frequency: Annual.

Value: Varies, from US$400 to US$2,000.

Study Establishment: Recipients are expected to do a portion of their research in Washington, DC. Recipients will also receive access to the Historical Centre's facilities and collections.

Application Procedure: Preliminary application for a grant involves writing to the Director of Marine Corps History and Museums outlining the qualifications, and should either propose a specific topic or request a suggested topic based on the applicant's interests and qualifications. If the evaluation of the preliminary application is favourable, the applicant will be asked to make formal application on a form provided by the Historical Center.

MARY ROBERTS RINEHART FUND

MSN 3E4
English Department
George Mason University, Fairfax, VA, 22030-4444, United States of America
Tel: (1) 703 993 1180
Contact: Grants Management Officer

The Foundation is housed within a public university and was established to support and encourage unpublished writers.

Mary Roberts Rinehart Grants

Subjects: Literary composition - fiction and poetry, or non-fiction and drama. Only works in English will be read.
Eligibility: Open to new and relatively unknown writers, without regard to citizenship, sex, colour or creed. Published writers are ineligible.
Level of Study: Unrestricted.
Purpose: To encourage young writers who need financial assistance - not otherwise available - to complete works-in-progress.
Type: Grant.
No. of awards offered: 2.
Frequency: Annual.
Value: Varies; approximately US$1,000.
Country of Study: Any country.
Application Procedure: There are no formal application forms. The only way to have a work considered is to have it submitted, in manuscript form, by a sponsoring writer, agent, writing teacher or editor who is familiar with the author.
Closing Date: November 30th for announcement the following March.

MARYLAND INSTITUTE COLLEGE OF ART (MICA)

1300 W Mt Royal Ave, Baltimore, MD, 21217, United States of America
Tel: (1) 410 225 2306
Fax: (1) 410 669 2408
www: http://www.mica.edu
Contact: Dr Leslie King-Hammond, Dean of Graduate Studies

Coca-Cola National Fellows Programme for the MFA in Studio for Art Educators

Subjects: Painting, printmaking, photography, drawing.
Eligibility: Open to art educators committed to teaching in urban public schools and districts with populations of large numbers of people of colour.
Level of Study: Graduate.
Purpose: Tuition scholarship.
Type: Fellowship.
No. of awards offered: 4.
Frequency: Annual.
Value: To cover the cost of tuition.
Length of Study: A 4-summer, 6-week residency, plus winter seminar/critique.
Study Establishment: Maryland Institute College of Art.
Country of Study: USA.
Closing Date: April 15th.

MICA Fellowship

Subjects: Arts.
Eligibility: Applicants must have a TOFBC score of 500. One international fellowship is also available.

Level of Study: Graduate.
Purpose: To serve as a tuition scholarship.
Type: Fellowship.
No. of awards offered: 6.
Frequency: Annual.
Value: US$10,000.
Length of Study: 2 years.
Study Establishment: Maryland Institute College of Art.
Country of Study: USA.
Closing Date: March 1st.

MICA International Fellowship Award

Subjects: Fine and applied arts.
Eligibility: Open to qualified applicants of any nationality.
Level of Study: Postgraduate.
Purpose: To serve as a tuition scholarship.
Type: Fellowship.
No. of awards offered: 1.
Frequency: Annual.
Value: US$10,000.
Study Establishment: Maryland Institute College of Art.
Country of Study: Any country.
Application Procedure: Write for application details.
Closing Date: March 1st.

MASSEY UNIVERSITY

Academic Section
Private Bag 11-222, Palmerston North, New Zealand
Tel: (64) 6 350 5549
Fax: (64) 6 350 5603
Email: m.e.gilbert@massey.ac.nz
www: http://www.massey.ac.nz
Contact: Ms Margaret E Gilbert, Scholarships Adminstrative Assistant

Massey University has over 30,000 students, 12,000 studying on campus with the remaining 18,000 studying by correspondence. The four colleges - Business, Education, Humanities and Social Sciences, and Sciences - provide a comprehensive range of undergraduate and graduate degrees and diplomas all geared to meeting national and international needs.

Massey Doctoral Scholarship

Subjects: Agriculture, forestry, town planning, arts and humanities, business administration and management, education and teacher training, engineering, commercial law, media studies, mathematics and computer science, nursing, midwifery, natural sciences, social welfare and social work, environmental studies, religious studies, tourism, social and behavioural studies, air transport.
Eligibility: Minimum qualification of a first class honours degree.
Level of Study: Doctorate.
Purpose: For research towards a PhD degree.
Type: Scholarship.

No. of awards offered: 20-30.
Frequency: Annual.
Value: NZ$12,000 per year.
Length of Study: 3 years.
Study Establishment: University.
Country of Study: New Zealand.
Application Procedure: Application form must be completed.
Closing Date: October 1st, July 1st.

MEET THE COMPOSER, INC.

2112 Broadway
Suite 505, New York, NY, 10023, United States of America
Tel: (1) 212 787 3601
Fax: (1) 212 787 3745
Email: mtc@meetthecomposer.org
www: http://www.meetthecomposer.org
Contact: Mr Fard Johnson, Senior Program Manager

Meet The Composer's mission is to increase artistic and financial opportunities for American composers by fostering the creation, performance, dissemination, and appreciation of their music.

Commissioning Music/USA

Subjects: Music commissioning.
Eligibility: Open to US citizens only.
Level of Study: Unrestricted.
Purpose: To support the commissioning of new works by American composers in orchestral, chamber, opera, music theatre, choral, jazz, experimental and avant garde music.
Country of Study: USA.
Application Procedure: Call or write to Meet The Composer for programme deadlines and application materials.
Closing Date: June 1st.

Meet The Composer Fund

Subjects: Music.
Eligibility: Open to US citizens only.
Level of Study: Professional development.
Purpose: To enable composers to participate actively in performances of their work. Participation may include performing, conducting, speaking with the audience, presenting workshops, giving interviews and coaching performances.
Frequency: Varies.
Value: Varies.
Country of Study: USA.
Application Procedure: Please write, phone or visit our website for details.

Meet the Composer New Residencies

Subjects: Composer writes work to celebrate local culture.
Eligibility: Open to US citizens only.
Level of Study: Professional development.

Purpose: To place composers in service to communities by creating residencies based in partnerships between arts organisations and community community based organisations.
Type: Residency.
Length of Study: 3 years.
Country of Study: USA.
Application Procedure: Call or write to Meet The Composer for programme deadlines and application materials.
Additional Information: Applications to all Meet The Composer programs are submitted by non-profit organisations sponsoring individual composers.

New Music For Schools

Subjects: For professional composers to work with teachers, students and their families, nurturing creativity in the classroom while writing works for students to play and sing.
Eligibility: Open to US citizens only.
Level of Study: Professional development.
Purpose: The programme supports composer residencies in primary and secondary schools throughout the mid-Atlantic and midwest and commissions new work for student ensembles.
Type: Residency.
Value: Varies.
Length of Study: 2 week-6 month residencies.
Country of Study: USA.
Application Procedure: Please write, phone or visit our website for details.

MEMORIAL FOUNDATION FOR JEWISH CULTURE

Room 1703
15 East 26th Street, New York, NY, 10010, United States of America
Tel: (1) 212 679 4074
Fax: (1) 212 889 9080
Contact: Dr Jerry Hochbaum, Executive Vice President

The Memorial Foundation for Jewish Culture was established in 1965 to help assure a creative future for Jewish life throughout the world. The Foundation encourages Jewish scholarship, Jewish cultural creativity, and makes possible the training of professionals to serve in Jewishly deprived communities.

International Fellowships in Jewish Studies

Subjects: A field of Jewish specialisation which will make a significant contribution to the understanding, preservation, enhancement or transmission of Jewish culture.
Eligibility: Open to recognised and/or qualified scholars, researchers or artists of any nationality who possess the knowledge and experience to formulate and implement a project in a field of Jewish specialisation.
Level of Study: Unrestricted.

Purpose: To assist well-qualified individuals to carry out independent scholarly, literary or artistic projects.
Type: Fellowship.
No. of awards offered: Varies.
Frequency: Annual.
Value: Variable, depending on the country in which the project is undertaken; usually US$1,000-US$4,000.
Length of Study: 1 academic year; renewable for 1 additional year in exceptional cases.
Country of Study: Any country.
Application Procedure: Applicants must write requesting an application.
Closing Date: October 31st.

International Scholarship Programme for Community Service

Subjects: The rabbinate, Jewish education, communal service or religious functionaries, for example, shohatim, mohalim.
Eligibility: Open to any individual, regardless of country of origin, who is presently receiving, or plans to undertake training in his or her chosen field in a recognised Yeshiva, teacher training seminary, school of social work, university or other educational institution.
Level of Study: Unrestricted.
Purpose: To assist well-qualified individuals for career training.
Type: Scholarship.
No. of awards offered: Varies.
Frequency: Annual.
Value: Varies, depending on the country in which the recipient is trained and other considerations; usually US$1,000-US$4,000.
Length of Study: 1 year; renewable.
Study Establishment: In Diaspora Jewish communities in need of such personnel.
Country of Study: Any except USA, Canada or Israel.
Application Procedure: Please write for details.
Closing Date: November 30th.
Additional Information: Recipients must commit themselves to serve a community of need. They should also be knowledgeable in the language and culture of that country or be prepared to learn it.

Memorial Foundation for Jewish Culture International Doctoral Scholarships

Subjects: Jewish studies.
Eligibility: Open to graduate students of any nationality who are specialising in a Jewish field and are officially enrolled or registered in a doctoral programme at a recognised university.
Level of Study: Doctorate.
Purpose: To assist in the training of future Jewish scholars for careers in Jewish scholarship and research, and to enable religious, educational and other Jewish communal workers, to obtain advanced training for leadership positions.
Type: Scholarship.
No. of awards offered: Varies.
Frequency: Annual.

Value: Varies, depending on the country where study is undertaken; usually between US$2,000 and US$5,000 per year.
Length of Study: 1 academic year; renewable for a maximum of 4 years.
Study Establishment: A recognised university.
Country of Study: Any country.
Application Procedure: Applicants must write requesting an application.
Closing Date: October 31st.

Scholarships for Post-Rabbinical Students

Subjects: Jewish studies.
Eligibility: Open to a recently ordained rabbi engaged in full-time studies at a Yeshiva, Kollel or rabbinical seminary.
Level of Study: Unrestricted.
Purpose: To assist in the training of future Jewish religious scholars and leaders, and to help newly ordained rabbis obtain advanced training for careers as head of Yeshivot, as Dayanim, and in other leadership positions.
Type: Scholarship.
No. of awards offered: Varies.
Frequency: Annual.
Value: US$1,000-US$4,000.
Length of Study: 1 year.
Country of Study: Any country.
Application Procedure: Please write for details.
Closing Date: November 30th.
Additional Information: The following Institutional Support Programmes are also available: Grants for Jewish Research and Publication: Grants are awarded to universities and recognized scholarly bodies for research and publication in Jewish fields; to universities and Jewish educational organisations for the preparation of textbooks and educational literature for children and youth. The Foundation also provides grants to bolster Jewish educational programmes in areas of need. Grants are awarded on the understanding that the recipient institution will assume responsibility for the programme following the initial limited period of Foundation support. Grants are made only for team or collaborative projects.

MENDELSSOHN SCHOLARSHIP FOUNDATION

c/o Royal Academy of Music
Marylebone Road, London, NW1 5HT, England
Contact: Ms Jean Shannon, Honorary Secretary

Mendelssohn Scholarship

Subjects: Musical composition.
Eligibility: Open to music students of any nationality under 30 years of age who are resident in the UK or Republic of Ireland.
Level of Study: Postgraduate.

Purpose: To enable postgraduate students to pursue their study.
Type: Scholarship.
No. of awards offered: 1.
Frequency: Every two years.
Value: £5,000.
Country of Study: Any country.
Application Procedure: Application form must be completed and submitted with photocopy of applicant's birth certificate.
Closing Date: Usually first half of March in the scholarship year.
Additional Information: Candidates compete for the scholarship by submitting up to three compositions, which are assessed by independent judges. There is a small entrance fee for the competition. All enquiries in writing only please. The next scholarship will be awarded in 2000.

METROPOLITAN MUSEUM OF ART

1000 Fifth Avenue, New York, NY, 10028-0198, United States of America
Tel: (1) 212 650 2763
Fax: (1) 212 570 3972
Contact: Internship Programmes/Education

The Metropolitan Museum of Art is one of the world's largest and finest art museums. Its collections include more than two million works of art spanning 5,000 years of world culture, from prehistory to the present, and from every part of the world.

Lifchez/Stronach Curatorial Internship

Subjects: Art history.
Eligibility: The student should come from a background of financial need or other disadvantage that might jeopardise his or her pursuing such a career without this support. The museum may not be able to assist foreign nationals to obtain a visa.
Level of Study: Postgraduate.
Purpose: To support a student from a disadvantaged background interested in a curatorial career.
Type: Internship.
No. of awards offered: Varies.
Frequency: Annual.
Value: US$15,000.
Length of Study: 9 months from September to June.
Study Establishment: Metropolitan Museum of Art.
Country of Study: USA.
Application Procedure: There are no application forms. A typed application should include: name and address; full résumé; two academic recommendations; official transcripts; list of art-history or other relevant courses taken; an essay or letter of not more than 500 words describing the applicant's career goals, interest in museum work, and reasons for applying.
Closing Date: Please check with the museum.

Additional Information: This award is made possible by Mr Raymond Lifchez and Mrs Judith L. Stronach.

Metropolitan Museum of Art Six-Month Internship

Subjects: Art history or related fields.
Eligibility: Open to candidates of any nationality, although it is not always possible to obtain a visa for foreign nationals.
Level of Study: Postgraduate.
Purpose: To support studies in art history and related fields.
Type: Internship.
No. of awards offered: Varies.
Frequency: Annual.
Value: US$8,000.
Length of Study: 6 months from June to December.
Study Establishment: Metropolitan Museum of Art.
Country of Study: USA.
Application Procedure: There are no application forms. A typed application should include: name and address; full résumé; two academic recommendations; official transcripts; list of art-history or other relevant courses taken; an essay or letter of not more than 500 words describing the applicant's career goals, interest in museum work, and reasons for applying.
Closing Date: Please check with the museum.
Additional Information: This programme intends to promote greater diversity in the national pool of future museum professionals. This award is made possible by the Altman Foundation.

Metropolitan Museum of Art Summer Internships for College Students

Subjects: Art history or related fields.
Eligibility: Open to college juniors, seniors and recent graduates who have not yet entered graduate school. Candidates should have a strong background in art history and intend to pursue careers in art museums. It is not always possible to obtain a visa for foreign nationals.
Level of Study: Postgraduate.
Purpose: To support students showing an interest in museum careers.
Type: Internship.
No. of awards offered: Varies.
Frequency: Annual.
Value: US$2,500.
Length of Study: 10 weeks from June to August.
Study Establishment: Metropolitan Museum of Art.
Country of Study: USA.
Application Procedure: There are no application forms. A typed application should include: name and address; full résumé; two academic recommendations; official transcripts; list of art-history or other relevant courses taken; an essay or letter of not more than 500 words describing the applicant's career goals, interest in museum work, and reasons for applying.
Closing Date: Please check with the museum.

Additional Information: This award is made possible by the Altman Foundation, Francine Lefrak Friedburg, and the Ittleson Foundation, Inc.

Metropolitan Museum of Art Summer Internships for Graduate Students

Subjects: Art history or an allied field.
Eligibility: Open to individuals who have completed at least one year of graduate work in art history or an allied field and who intend to pursue careers in art museums. It is not always possible to obtain a visa for foreign nationals.
Level of Study: Postgraduate.
Purpose: To support students showing an interest in museum careers.
Type: Internship.
No. of awards offered: Varies.
Frequency: Annual.
Value: US$2,750.
Length of Study: Ten weeks from June to August.
Study Establishment: Metropolitan Museum of Art.
Country of Study: USA.
Application Procedure: There are no application forms. A typed application should include: name and address; full résumé; two academic recommendations; official transcripts; list of art-history or other relevant courses taken; an essay or letter of not more than 500 words describing the applicant's career goals, interest in museum work, and reasons for applying.
Closing Date: Please check with the museum.
Additional Information: The award is funded, in part, by the Solow Art and Architecture Foundation.

MICHIGAN SOCIETY OF FELLOWS

University of Michigan
3030 Rackham Building
915 E Washington Street, Ann Arbor, MI, 48109-1070, United States of America
Tel: (1) 734 763 1259
Fax: (1) 734 763 2447
Email: society.of.fellows@umich.edu
www: http://www.rackham.umich.edu/faculty/society.htm
Contact: Ms Luan McCarthy Briefer, Administration Assistant

The Michigan Society of Fellows provides financial and intellectual support to individuals selected for outstanding achievement, professional promise, and interdisciplinary interests. The Society invite applications from qualified candidates for three year postdoctoral fellowships at the University of Michigan.

Michigan Society of Fellows Postdoctoral Fellowships

Subjects: All subject fields offered by the University of Michigan.

Eligibility: Applicants must have completed the PhD or comparable professional or artistic degree within three years of appointment.
Level of Study: Postdoctorate.
Purpose: To provide financial and intellectual support for individuals selected for outstanding achievement, professional promise, and interdisciplinary interests.
Type: Fellowship.
No. of awards offered: 4.
Frequency: Annual.
Value: Stipend of US$36,000 per year.
Length of Study: 3 years.
Study Establishment: University of Michigan.
Country of Study: USA.
Application Procedure: Application form must be completed; please write to request application materials.
Closing Date: Early October - this date will vary from year to year.

THE MILLAY COLONY FOR THE ARTS, INC (MCA)

East Hill Road
PO Box 3, Austerlitz, NY, 12017-0003, United States of America
Tel: (1) 518 392 3103
Fax: (1) 518 392 7664
Email: application@millaycolony.org
www: http://www.millaycolony.org
Contact: Executive Director

MCA Residencies

Subjects: Visual arts; musical composition; creative writing.
Eligibility: Open to professional visual artists, composers and writers.
Level of Study: Unrestricted.
Type: Residency.
No. of awards offered: 6 residencies per month (72 annually).
Frequency: Monthly.
Value: Room, board and studio space for one month. No fees. The Millay Colony does not provide financial assistance of any kind. However, as the Colony depends on gifts for its existence, contributions are welcomed.
Length of Study: 1 month.
Study Establishment: The Millay Colony.
Country of Study: USA.
Application Procedure: SASE is required for application form or the form can be accessed by email.
Closing Date: February 1st, May 1st, September 1st.
Additional Information: Decisions are made by committees of professional artists. The Millay Colony is set in the 600-acre Steepletop estate, a National Historic landmark which was the home of Edna St Vincent Millay in upstate New York.

MINISTÈRE DES AFFAIRES ÉTRANGÈRES

Bureau des Boursiers Français a l'Etranger
244 boulevard Saint-Germain, Paris, F-75303, France
Tel: (33) 1 43 17 72 22
Fax: (33) 1 43 17 97 57
Email: boursiers-francais@diplomatie.fr
Contact: Mr Serge François

Lavoisier Award

Subjects: All subjects.
Eligibility: Applicants must be French and under 40 years of age.
Level of Study: Doctorate, Postdoctorate, Postgraduate.
Purpose: To encourage scientific co-operation abroad.
Type: Scholarship.
No. of awards offered: 350.
Frequency: Dependent on funds available.
Value: Between FF40,000 and FF80,000 per year, depending on the cost of living in the host country.
Length of Study: 1 year.
Study Establishment: Unrestricted.
Country of Study: Any country.
Application Procedure: Please write for application forms between October and February.
Closing Date: March 1st.

MINISTRY OF EDUCATION, SCIENCE AND CULTURE (ICELAND)

Sölvhólsgata 4, Reykjavik, IS-150, Iceland
Tel: (354) 560 9500
Fax: (354) 562 3068
Email: postur@mrn.stjr.is
www: http://www.mrn.stjr.is
Contact: Mr Pórunn Bragadóttir, Division for Higher Education, Science & Research

Scholarships in Icelandic Studies

Subjects: Icelandic language, literature and history.
Eligibility: The Ministry decides each year in which countries these scholarships are to be made available, and requests the Ministry of Education in each of the recipient countries to select a candidate for the award.
Level of Study: Unrestricted.
Purpose: To support study of Icelandic language, Icelandic history and Icelandic literature; at the University of Iceland.
Type: Scholarship.
No. of awards offered: 25.
Frequency: Annual.
Value: 440,000 kronur, plus tuition.
Length of Study: 8 months.
Study Establishment: University of Iceland, Reykjavik.

Country of Study: Iceland.
Application Procedure: Candidates should apply to the relevant government department in their own country. US candidates should apply to the Institute of International Education, 809 United Nations Plaza, New York, New York 10017. UK candidates should apply to the Icelandic Embassy, 1 Eaton Terrace, London SW1. Candidates of Icelandic origin from Canada or the US should apply to the Icelandic National League, 62-2nd Avenue, Box 99 Gimli, Manitoba, ROC 1BO, Canada.
Closing Date: Nomination of candidates must reach the Ministry of Culture and Education, Iceland, before May 15th.

MINISTRY OF FOREIGN AFFAIRS (FRANCE)

French Embassy
6 Perth Avenue, Yarralumla, ACT, 2600, Australia
Tel: (61) 2 6216 0100
Fax: (61) 2 6216 0156
Email: cst@france.net.au
www: http://www.france.net.au
Contact: Linguistic Service

BCLE Assistantships in Australia

Subjects: French language studies.
Eligibility: Open to French citizens only.
Level of Study: Postgraduate.
Purpose: To enable French assistants to take up positions supporting the teaching of French in Australian schools.
Type: Assistantship.
No. of awards offered: Approx. 28.
Frequency: Annual.
Value: A living allowance of approximately FF5,000 and medical cover is provided.
Length of Study: 1 year; not renewable.
Study Establishment: Australian schools.
Country of Study: Australia.
Application Procedure: Please apply to the French Ministry of Education.
Additional Information: These awards are organised by the Bureau de Coopération Linguistique et Educative (BCLE).

BCLE Assistantships in France and New Caledonia

Subjects: French language studies.
Eligibility: Open to young Australian graduates only.
Level of Study: Postgraduate.
Purpose: To enable young Australian graduates who intend to teach French to improve their language skills.
Type: Assistantship.
No. of awards offered: Approx. 28.
Frequency: Annual.
Value: A living allowance of approximately FF5,000 and medical cover is provided.
Length of Study: 9 months.

Study Establishment: High school in France or New Caledonia.
Country of Study: France or New Caledonia.
Application Procedure: Please write for details.
Closing Date: September 1st.
Additional Information: These awards are organised by the Bureau de Coopération Linguistique et Educative (BCLE).

French Government Postgraduate Scholarships

Subjects: French language, literature and civilisation.
Eligibility: Open to Australian citizens, who hold a BA and have completed three years of university French.
Level of Study: Postgraduate.
Type: Scholarship.
No. of awards offered: 2.
Frequency: Annual.
Value: A monthly maintenance allowance of approximately FF4,700 plus medical cover.
Length of Study: 1 year.
Study Establishment: An approved French university.
Country of Study: France.
Application Procedure: Applications should be lodged after the student's admission to the postgraduate programme of a French university. Application forms are available from the French departments of universities.
Closing Date: December 31st.

MINNESOTA HISTORICAL SOCIETY

Research Department
345 Kellogg Boulevard West, St Paul, MN, 55102, United States of America
Tel: (1) 651 297 4464
Fax: (1) 651 297 1345
Email: debbie.miller@mnhs.org
www: http://www.mnhs.org
Contact: Ms Deborah L Miller

Minnesota Historical Society Research Grant

Subjects: The history of Minnesota and its region, which includes the bordering Canadian provinces as well as the American Midwest.
Eligibility: Open to applicants of any nationality with English reading and writing ability.
Level of Study: Unrestricted.
Purpose: To support original research and interpretative writing on the history of Minnesota by academicians, independent scholars and professional and non professional writers.
Type: Research Support.
No. of awards offered: Varies.
Frequency: Annual.

Value: Varies, up to US$1,500 for research that will result in an article, or up to US$5,000 for research that will result in a book, or up to US$500 for mini grants, or up to US$1,000 for visiting scholar grants.
Length of Study: Varies.
Country of Study: Any country.
Application Procedure: Application form must be completed; other documentation is also required. Guidelines and applications are available by writing to the given address or by sending an email message to Debbie Miller.
Closing Date: January 2nd, April 1st, September 1st.

MIRIAM LICETTE TRUST

16 Ogle Street, London, W1P 7LG, England
Tel: (44) 171 636 4481
Fax: (44) 171 637 4307
Contact: Mrs Susan Dolton

Miriam Licette Scholarship

Subjects: Musical performance, song.
Eligibility: Open to soprano, mezzo-soprano or contralto singers for advanced study in France. Applicants should be under 30 years of age and British or have been resident in the UK for three years. Applicants mother tongue must not be French.
Level of Study: Postgraduate, Professional development.
Purpose: To assist a female student of French song.
Type: Scholarship.
No. of awards offered: 1.
Frequency: Every two years.
Value: £5,000.
Country of Study: France.
Application Procedure: Selected students will be asked to audition. An application form must be completed and two references provided.
Closing Date: Mid-February.

MODERN LANGUAGE ASSOCIATION OF AMERICA

10 Astor Place, New York, NY, 10003-6981, United States of America
Tel: (1) 212 614 6406
Fax: (1) 212 533 0680
www: http://www.mla.org
Contact: Office of Special Projects

Aldo and Jeane Scaglione Prize for Comparative Literary Studies

Subjects: Comparative literary studies involving at least two literatures.
Eligibility: Books published in the year before the award is given. Authors must be members of the MLA.

Level of Study: Professional development.
Purpose: To recognise outstanding scholarly work in comparative literary studies involving at least two literatures.
Type: Prize.
Frequency: Annual.
Application Procedure: Four copies of the book must be sent, please write for details.
Closing Date: May 1st.

Aldo and Jeane Scaglione Prize for Studies in Slavic Languages and Literatures

Subjects: Writing.
Eligibility: Books published in the year or two before the prize is given. Authors need not be members of the MLA.
Level of Study: Professional development.
Purpose: To recognise an oustanding scholarly work on the linguistics or literatures of the Slavic languages.
Type: Prize.
Frequency: Every two years.
Application Procedure: Four copies of the book are required, please write for details.
Closing Date: May 1st.

Aldo and Jeane Scaglione Prize for Translation of a Scholarly Study of Literature

Subjects: Translation.
Eligibility: Books published in the year or two before the prize is given. Authors need not be members of the MLA.
Level of Study: Professional development.
Purpose: To recognise an outstanding translation into English of a book-length work of literary history, literary criticism, philology, or literary theory.
Type: Prize.
Frequency: Every two years (even-numbered years).
Application Procedure: Four copies of the book are required, please write for details.
Closing Date: May 1st.

Aldo and Jeanne Scaglione Prize for French and Francophone Literary Studies

Subjects: French Francophone linguistic or literary studies.
Eligibility: Books published in the year before the prize is given. Authors must be members of the MLA.
Level of Study: Professional development.
Purpose: To recognise outstanding scholarly work in French Francophone linguistic or literary studies.
Type: Prize.
Frequency: Annual.
Application Procedure: Four copies of the book must be sent, please write for details.
Closing Date: May 1st.

James Russell Lowell Prize

Subjects: Open to studies dealing with literary theory, media, cultural history, or interdisciplinary topics.

Eligibility: Books published the year before the award is due to be given. Authors must be current members of the MLA.
Level of Study: Professional development.
Purpose: To recognise an outstanding literary or linguistic study, a critical edition of an important work, or a critical biography.
Type: Prize.
Frequency: Annual.
Application Procedure: Six copies of the book must be sent, please write for details.
Closing Date: March 1st.

Katherine Singer Kovacs Prize

Subjects: Latin American and Spanish literatures and cultures.
Eligibility: Books published in the year before the prize is given. Competing books should be broadly interpretative works that enhance understanding of the interrelations among literature, the arts and society.
Level of Study: Professional development.
Purpose: To recognise an outstanding book published in English in the field of Latin American and Spanish literatures and cultures.
Type: Prize.
Frequency: Annual.
Application Procedure: Six copies of the book must be sent, please write for details.
Closing Date: May 1st.

Kenneth W Mildenberger Prize

Subjects: A research article in the field of teaching foreign languages and literatures.
Eligibility: Articles published in refereed journals in the two years prior to the prize being given. Authors need not be members of the MLA.
Level of Study: Professional development.
Purpose: To support a research article in the field of teaching foreign languages and literatures.
Type: Prize.
Frequency: Annual.
Application Procedure: Four copies of the book are required, please write for details.
Closing Date: May 1st.

Lois Roth Award for a Translation of Literary Work

Subjects: Translation.
Eligibility: Translations published in the year before the prize is given. Translators need not be members of the MLA.
Level of Study: Professional development.
Purpose: To recognise an oustanding translation into English of a book-length literary work.
Type: Prize.
Frequency: Every two years (odd numbered).
Application Procedure: Five copies are required, please write for details.
Closing Date: April 1st.

Mina P Shaughnessy Prize

Subjects: Writing.
Eligibility: Books published in the year prior to the prize being given. Authors need not be members of the MLA.
Level of Study: Professional development.
Purpose: To recognise a research publication in the field of teaching English language, literature, rhetoric and composition.
Type: Prize.
Frequency: Annual.
Application Procedure: Four copies of the book are required, please write for details.
Closing Date: May 1st.

MLA Prize for a Distinguished Scholarly Edition

Subjects: Writing.
Eligibility: At least one volume must have been published in the year or two prior to the award being given. Editors need not be members of the MLA.
Level of Study: Professional development.
Purpose: To recognise an outstanding scholarly edition. Editions may be single or multiple volumes.
Type: Prize.
Frequency: Every two years.
Application Procedure: Four copies of the editions are required, please write for details.
Closing Date: May 1st.

MLA Prize for a First Book

Subjects: Open to studies dealing with literary theory, media, cultural history, or interdisciplinary topics.
Eligibility: The book must have been published in the year before the prize is given as the first book-length publication of a current MLA member.
Level of Study: Professional development.
Purpose: To recognise an outstanding literary or linguistic study, a critical edition of an important work, or a critical biography.
Type: Prize.
Frequency: Annual.
Application Procedure: Six copies of the book must be sent, please write for details.
Closing Date: April 1st.

MLA Prize for Independent Scholars

Subjects: English or other modern languages and literatures.
Eligibility: Books published the year before the prize is given. At the time of publication of the book the author must not be enrolled in a programme leading to an academic degree or hold a tenured, tenure-accruing, or tenure track position in postsecondary education. Authors or publishers must request an application form from the MLA. Authors need not be members of the MLA.
Level of Study: Professional development.
Purpose: To award a scholarly book in the field of English or other modern languages and literatures.
Type: Prize.

Frequency: Annual.
Application Procedure: Six copies of the application must be sent, please write for details.
Closing Date: May 1st.

Morton N Cohen Award for Distinguished Edition of Letter

Subjects: Writing.
Eligibility: At least one volume must have been published in the year or two prior to the award being given. Editors need not be members of the MLA.
Level of Study: Professional development.
Purpose: To recognise an outstanding edition of letters. Editions may be single or multiple volumes.
Type: Award.
Frequency: Every two years.
Application Procedure: Four copies of the editions are required, please wrote for details.
Closing Date: May 1st.

MONASH UNIVERSITY

Wellington Road, Clayton, VIC, 3168, Australia
Tel: (61) 3 9905 2009
Fax: (61) 3 9905 5042
Email: research.training.support@adm.monash.edu.au
www: http://www.monash.edu.au
Contact: Manager, Research, Training and Support Branch

Logan Research Fellowships

Subjects: All subjects.
Eligibility: There are no restrictions, other than applicants must hold a PhD and have 2-6 years' postdoctoral research experience.
Level of Study: Postdoctorate.
Purpose: To attract outstanding researchers with 2-6 years' postdoctoral research experience.
Type: Fellowship.
No. of awards offered: 5.
Frequency: Annual.
Value: Salary of research fellowship level B (A$46,269) per year or above, plus research support grants of between A$5,000 and A$20,000 per year depending on the nature of the research. Return air fare provided.
Length of Study: 3 years with the possibility of an additional 3 years.
Study Establishment: Monash University.
Country of Study: Australia.
Application Procedure: Application forms and referees report forms must be submitted.
Closing Date: April 30th.
Additional Information: Electronic lodgement of application is preferred.

Monash Graduate Scholarships

Subjects: All subjects.
Eligibility: Open to graduates or graduands of any Australian or overseas university, who should hold at least a first class honours Bachelor's degree or the equivalent, or should be completing the final year of a course leading to such a degree.
Level of Study: Doctorate, Research.
Purpose: To provide support for supervised full-time research at Master's and doctorate level.
Type: Scholarship.
No. of awards offered: 110.
Frequency: Annual.
Value: A$16,135 stipend plus thesis preparation and other allowances.
Length of Study: Up to 2 years for the Master's degree; up to 3 years with the possibility of an additional 6 month extension for the doctoral degree.
Study Establishment: Monash University.
Country of Study: Australia.
Application Procedure: Application kit available four months before closing date.
Closing Date: October 31st.
Additional Information: International students must meet English language proficiency requirements.

Monash University Partial Tuition Postgraduate Research Scholarship Scheme

Subjects: All subjects.
Eligibility: Open to graduates or graduands of any Australian or overseas university, who should hold at least a first class honours Bachelor's degree or the equivalent, or should be completing the final year of a course leading to such a degree.
Level of Study: Doctorate, Research.
Purpose: To provide support for supervised full-time research at Master's and doctoral level.
Type: Scholarship.
No. of awards offered: 9.
Frequency: Annual.
Value: The award meets two thirds of the tuition fee for international students.
Length of Study: Up to 2 years for the Master's degree; up to 3 years with the possibility of an additional 6 month extension for the doctoral degree.
Study Establishment: Monash University.
Country of Study: Australia.
Application Procedure: Application kit available four months before closing date.
Closing Date: October 31st.

Monash University Silver Jubilee Postgraduate Scholarship

Subjects: 2000 science, 2001 arts and art design, 2002 law or education, or business and economics, 2003 engineering and computing and information technology.
Eligibility: Open to graduates or graduands of any Australian or overseas university, who should hold at least a first class honours Bachelor's degree or the equivalent, or should be completing the final year of a course leading to such a degree.
Level of Study: Doctorate, Research.
Purpose: To provide supervised full-time research at Master's and doctorate level.
Type: Scholarship.
No. of awards offered: 1.
Frequency: Annual.
Value: Stipend: A$20,822 per year plus establishment, relocation, incidentals and thesis allowance.
Length of Study: Up to 2 years for the Master's degree; up to 3 years with the possibility of an additional 6 month extension for the doctoral degree.
Study Establishment: Monash University.
Country of Study: Australia.
Application Procedure: Application kit is available four months before the closing date.
Closing Date: October 31st.
Additional Information: International students must meet English proficiency requirements.

Sir James McNeill Foundation Postgraduate Scholarship

Subjects: Engineering, medicine, music or science.
Eligibility: Open to graduates or graduands of any Australian or overseas university, who should hold a first class honours Bachelor's degree or the equivalent, or should be completing the final year of a course leading to such a degree.
Level of Study: Doctorate.
Purpose: To enable a PhD scholar to pursue a full-time programme of research which is both environmentally responsible and socially beneficial to the community.
Type: Scholarship.
No. of awards offered: 1.
Frequency: Annual.
Value: A$21,322 per year, plus allowances.
Length of Study: Up to 4 years.
Study Establishment: Monash University.
Country of Study: Australia.
Application Procedure: Application kit is available four months before the closing date.
Closing Date: October 31st.
Additional Information: International students must meet English proficiency requirements.

MONTREAL SYMPHONY ORCHESTRA

260 de Maisoneurve Blvd West
Montreal, Québec, PQ, H2X 1Y9, Canada
Tel: (1) 514 842 34 02
Fax: (1) 514 842 07 28
www: http://www.osm.ca
Contact: Ms Judith De Repentigny, Educational Programmes Co-ordinator

Montreal Symphony Orchestra Competitions

Subjects: Piano, singing, string and wind performance.
Eligibility: Open to Canadian citizens and landed immigrants only.
Level of Study: Unrestricted.
Purpose: To award best performances in piano, singing, strings and winds.
Type: Scholarship.
No. of awards offered: 10.
Frequency: Every two years.
Country of Study: Any country.
Application Procedure: Applicants must complete a registration form showing proof of eligibility, and submit résumé and registration fee.
Closing Date: November 1st.

MRS GILES WHITING FOUNDATION

Writers' Program
1133 Avenue of the Americas, New York, NY, 10036-6710, United States of America
Tel: (1) 212 336 2138
Contact: Ms Kellye Rosenheim, Assistant Director

Whiting Fellowships in the Humanities

Subjects: Humanities.
Eligibility: Open to students selected by their participating institutions: Bryn Mawr, University of Chicago, Columbia, Harvard, Princeton, Stanford, and Yale. Direct applications are not accepted by the Foundation.
Level of Study: Doctorate.
Purpose: To recognise and award outstanding doctoral candidates in the humanities during the final year of dissertation-writing.
Type: Fellowship.
No. of awards offered: Varies.
Frequency: Annual.
Value: Varies; the amount of the stipend is set by each school (normal range US$13,500-US$15,000).
Country of Study: Any country.

Whiting Writers' Awards

Subjects: Writing.
Eligibility: Nominated candidates may be writers of fiction, poetry or non-fiction; they may be essayists, literary scholars, playwrights, novelists, poets or critics. Selections are based on the quality of nominee writing accomplishment and the likelihood of outstanding future work. The programme places special emphasis on promising emerging talent; to qualify, writers need not be young, given that new talent may emerge at any age.
Level of Study: Unrestricted.
Purpose: To identify and support emerging writers of exceptional promise.
No. of awards offered: 10.
Frequency: Annual.
Value: US$30,000.
Country of Study: Any country.
Application Procedure: Direct applications and informal nominations are not accepted by the Foundation. Recipients are nominated by writers, educators and editors from communities across the USA whose experience and vocations bring them into contact with individuals of unusual talent. The nominators and selectors are appointed by the Foundation and serve anonymously and nominees are not informed of their candidacies.

MRS SUSAN DOLTON

16 Ogle Street, London, W1P 7LG, England
Tel: (44) 171 636 4481
Fax: (44) 171 637 4307
Contact: Administrator

Myra Hess Awards Trust

Subjects: Musical performance.
Eligibility: Open to outstanding young instrumentalists between 18 and 30 years of age; preference is given to those entering a professional career. Singers, organists, harpists, harpsichordists and those playing percussion, brass or baroque instruments are ineligible.
Level of Study: Postgraduate, Professional development.
Purpose: To give assistance for the purchase of instruments, for tuition and maintenance, and towards the cost of first recitals.
No. of awards offered: 5-10.
Frequency: Annual.
Value: Up to £3,000 each.
Country of Study: Any country.
Application Procedure: Selected applicants are asked to audition in January or June/July. An application form must be completed and two references provided.
Closing Date: December.

MURIEL TAYLOR SCHOLARSHIP FUND FOR CELLISTS

2 Davis Place
Sparrows Green, Wadhurst, East Sussex, TN5 6TE, England
Tel: (44) 1892 782 082
Contact: Ms Kate Beresford, The Hon Competition Secretary

The trustees committee organises adjudication of usually four finalists chosen from cassette presentation for preliminary adjudication by two first time adjudicators. The four finalists are invited to play to the competition adjudicator in London. The prize is awarded on the day of the competition, the adjudicator speaking individually to each entrant.

Muriel Taylor Cello Scholarship

Subjects: Cello.
Eligibility: Open to candidates of any nationality and qualifications who are between 17 and 23 years of age on March 31st in the year of competition.
Level of Study: Unrestricted.
Purpose: To help talented young cellists continue their studies, usually following study at a recognised tertiary college of music, RAM or RCM.
Type: Scholarship.
No. of awards offered: 1.
Frequency: Annual.
Value: £2,000 for tuition fees.
Study Establishment: A recognised tertiary college of music.
Country of Study: Any country.
Application Procedure: Please write to the Competition Secretary for details.
Closing Date: January 31st.
Additional Information: The competition is held annually, usually mid-April.

For further information contact:

The Warehouse
13 Theed Street, London, SE1 8ST, England

NANSEN FUND

77 Saddlebrook Lane, Houston, TX, 77024, United States of America
Tel: (1) 713 686 3963
Fax: (1) 713 680 8255
Contact: Fellowships Office

John Dana Archbold Fellowship

Subjects: All subjects.
Eligibility: Eligibility is limited to those aged between 20 and 35, in good health, of good character, and citizens of the USA, who are not recent immigrants from Norway.
Level of Study: Postdoctorate, Postgraduate, Professional development.

Purpose: To support educational exchange between the United States and Norway.
Type: Fellowship.
No. of awards offered: 1-2.
Frequency: Every two years.
Value: Grants vary, depending on costs and rates of exchange. The University of Oslo will charge no tuition and the Nansen Fund will pay up to US$10,000 for supplies, maintenance and travel. The maintenance stipend is sufficient to meet expenses in Norway for a single person. Air fare from the US to Norway is covered.
Length of Study: 1 year.
Study Establishment: University of Oslo.
Country of Study: Norway.
Application Procedure: Application form must be completed and submitted with references and transcripts.
Closing Date: January 31st.
Additional Information: Every other year the Norway-America Association, the sister organisation of the Nansen Fund, offers fellowships for Norwegian citizens wishing to study at a university in the USA. For further information please contact: The Norway - America Association, Drammensveien 20c, Oslo, N0 255, Norway, Tel: +47 224 477 16.

NATIONAL ACADEMY OF DESIGN

1083 Fifth Avenue, New York, NY, 10128, United States of America
Tel: (1) 212 369 4880
Fax: (1) 212 360 6795
www: http://www.greatcollegetown.com/nad.html
Contact: Grants Management Officer

Founded in 1825, the National Academy fosters the awareness, appreciation, teaching, and professional practice of art in America. The National Academy Museum collects and exhibits historic and contemporary American art. The National Academy School teaches painting, sculpture, drawing and printmaking. The National Academy members elect notable American artists and architects to membership in honorary association of their peers, whose work is collected and displayed at the Museum. Academy members govern all programmes of these three branches of the National Academy, which is the only institution of its kind in America.

National Academy of Design Prizes for Painting in their Annual Exhibition

Subjects: Painting.
Eligibility: Open to US artists only.
Level of Study: Unrestricted.
Type: Prize.
No. of awards offered: 22.
Frequency: Every two years.
Value: Varies; US$200-US$5,000.
Country of Study: USA.

Application Procedure: Further details may be obtained from the Academy. The prospectus for the annual exhibition is available in early autumn in odd numbered years.

National Academy of Design Prizes for Prints, Drawings and Pastels in their Annual Exhibition

Subjects: Prints, drawings and pastels.
Eligibility: Open to artists from the USA.
Level of Study: Unrestricted.
Type: Prize.
No. of awards offered: 6.
Frequency: Annual.
Value: Varies; US$200-US$400.
Country of Study: Any country.
Application Procedure: Further details may be obtained from the Academy. The prospectus for the annual exhibition is available in early autumn in odd numbered years.

National Academy of Design Prizes for Sculpture in their Annual Exhibition Competition

Subjects: Sculpture.
Eligibility: Open to sculptors from the USA.
Level of Study: Unrestricted.
Type: Prize.
No. of awards offered: 7-10.
Frequency: Every two years.
Value: Varies; US$200-US$15,000.
Country of Study: USA.
Application Procedure: Further details may be obtained from the Academy.
Closing Date: December in odd numbered years, January in even numbered years.

National Academy of Design Prizes for Watercolour in their Annual Exhibition Competition

Subjects: Watercolour painting.
Eligibility: Open to US artists only.
Level of Study: Unrestricted.
Type: Prize.
No. of awards offered: 7.
Frequency: Every two years.
Value: Varies; US$200-US$3,500.
Country of Study: USA.
Application Procedure: Further details may be obtained from the Academy.
Closing Date: Please write for details.

NATIONAL ASSOCIATION OF COMPOSERS

PO Box 49256
Barrington Station, Los Angeles, CA, 90049, United States of America
Tel: (1) 541 8213
Fax: (1) 373 3244
www: http://www.thebook.com/nacusa
Contact: Mr Marshall Bialosky, President

The National Association of Composers presents concerts of the members' music throughout the United States, mainly the West Coast (Los Angeles and San Francisco), and the East Coast (mainly New York, Philadelphia, and Boston).

National Association of Composers Young Composers' Competition

Subjects: Music composition.
Eligibility: Open to nationals of any country between the ages of 18-30.
Level of Study: Postdoctorate, Postgraduate.
Purpose: To foster the creation of new American concert hall music.
Type: Cash and musical performance.
No. of awards offered: 2.
Frequency: Annual.
Value: US$200 first place; US$50 second place.
Country of Study: Any country.
Application Procedure: There are no application forms; contestants simply send in their music. Applicants must be members of NACUSA.
Closing Date: October 30th.

NATIONAL ASSOCIATION OF SCHOLARS (NAS)

575 Ewing Street, Princeton, NJ, 08540-2741, United States of America
Tel: (1) 609 683 7878
Fax: (1) 609 683 0316
Email: nas@nas.org
www: http://www.nas.org
Contact: Fellowships Office

The National Association of Scholars (NAS) is an organisation of professors, graduate students, college administrators, and independent scholars committed to rational discourse as the foundation of academic life in a free democratic society. The NAS works to enrich the substance and strengthen the integrity of scholarship and teaching, convinced that only through an informed understanding of the Western intellectual heritage and the realities of the contemporary world, can citizen and scholar be equipped to sustain our civilisation's achievements.

The Peter Shaw Memorial Award

Subjects: Writing on issues pertaining to higher education and American intellectual culture.
Eligibility: NAS nominated.
Purpose: Established to honour the memory of Peter Shaw, this award is given to recognise exemplary writing on issues pertaining to higher education and American intellectual culture.
Type: Award.
Frequency: Memorial/Honorary service recognition. Every 18 months.
Value: US$1,000, a plaque, and travel expenses to attend the national conference and present a speech.
Application Procedure: N/A.

NATIONAL BLACK MBA ASSOCIATION

180 North Michigan
Suite 1515, Chicago, IL, 60601, United States of America
Tel: (1) 312 236 2622
Fax: (1) 312 236 4131
www: http://www.nbmbaa.org
Contact: Ms Lisa Collins, Program Manager

National Black MBA Association Scholarships

Subjects: An essay topic is selected annually by the Scholarship Committee.
Eligibility: Open to minority full-time students enrolled in an accredited US business programme pursuing an MBA degree.
Level of Study: Doctorate, Postgraduate.
Type: Scholarship, Fellowship.
No. of awards offered: 25 for MBA, 2 for PhD.
Frequency: Annual.
Value: MBA - US$3,000 average; PhD - US$10,000 and US$5,000.
Country of Study: USA.
Application Procedure: Application form must be completed and submitted with official transcripts.
Closing Date: March 31st.

THE NATIONAL CHAPTER OF CANADA IODE

Suite 254
40 Orchard View Boulevard, Toronto, ON, M4R 1B9, Canada
Tel: (1) 416 487 4416
Fax: (1) 416 487 4417
Contact: Grants Management Officer

The mission of IODE, a Canadian women's charitable organisation, is to improve the quality of life for children, youth and those in need, through educational, social service and citizenship programs.

IODE War Memorial Doctoral Scholarship

Subjects: All subjects.
Eligibility: Open to Canadian citizens who hold a first degree from a recognised Canadian university. At the time of applying a candidate must be enrolled in a programme at the doctoral level or equivalent.
Level of Study: Doctorate.
Purpose: To honour the memory of the men and women who gave their lives for Canada in World Wars I and II, this memorial was established to provide scholarships for study at the doctoral level.
Type: Scholarship.
No. of awards offered: 9.
Frequency: Annual.
Value: C$12,000 for study in Canada; C$15,000 for study overseas within the Commonwealth.
Country of Study: Canada or other Commonwealth countries.
Application Procedure: Applications and supporting documents are available in September and must be submitted by December 1st.
Closing Date: December 1st.

THE NATIONAL COLLEGIATE ATHLETIC ASSOCIATION

6201 College Boulevard, Overland Park, KS, 66211-2422, United States of America
Tel: (1) 913 339 1906
Fax: (1) 913 339 0035
www: http://www.ncaa.org
Contact: Ms Julie M Quickel, Committee and Scholarship Co-ordinator

NCAA Postgraduate Scholarship

Subjects: All subjects.
Eligibility: Minimum GPA of 3.000 on a 4.000 scale or its equivalent; student athlete enrolled at an NCAA member institution must be in last year of intercollegiate competition.
Level of Study: Postgraduate.
Purpose: To honour outstanding student athletes from NCAA member institutions who are also outstanding scholars.
Type: Grant.
No. of awards offered: 174.
Frequency: Annual.
Value: Award (one time grant of US$5,000) is not earmarked for a specific area of postgraduate study but awardee must use as a full time graduate student in a graduate or professional school of an academically accredited institution.
Country of Study: Any country.
Application Procedure: Candidates are nominated by their Faculty Athletics Representative or Director of Athletics.
Closing Date: Three deadlines - may vary slightly each year.

NATIONAL ENDOWMENT FOR THE HUMANITIES (NEH)

Division of Research and Education
Room 318
1100 Pennsylvania Avenue NW, Washington, DC, 20506,
United States of America
Tel: (1) 202 606 8200
Fax: (1) 202 606 8204
Email: researcg@neh.gov
www: http://www.neh.gov
Contact: Mr Russell M Wyland, Operations Officer

Through grants to educational institutions, fellowships to scholars and teachers, and through the support of significant research this division is designed to strengthen sustained, thoughtful study of the humanities at all levels of education and promote original research in the humanities.

Graduate Study Fellowships for Faculty at Historically Black Colleges and Universities

Subjects: The humanities.
Eligibility: Open to faculty members of historically Black US colleges and universities.
Level of Study: Doctorate.
Purpose: To strengthen teaching at historically Black colleges and universities in the US.
Type: Fellowship.
No. of awards offered: Varies.
Frequency: Annual.
Value: Up to US$30,000.
Length of Study: 9-12 months.
Country of Study: USA.
Application Procedure: Application materials are available from the NEH or by visiting the NEH website.
Closing Date: March 15th.

Humanities Focus Grants

Subjects: Arts and humanities.
Eligibility: Open to citizens from the USA.
Level of Study: Unrestricted.
Purpose: To support curriculum and materials development efforts, faculty study programmes within and among educational institutions, and dissemination of significant development in humanities and education.
Type: Grant.
No. of awards offered: Approx. 30.
Frequency: Annual.
Value: Varies depending upon the project.
Length of Study: Varies depending upon the project.
Country of Study: Any country.
Application Procedure: An NEH application form is required in addition to project materials. Forms are available from NEH or from the Endowment's website.
Closing Date: April 15th.

National Education Projects

Subjects: Art and humanities.
Eligibility: Open to citizens from the USA.
Level of Study: Unrestricted.
Purpose: To support curriculum and materials development efforts, faculty study programmes within and among educational institutions, and dissemination of significant developments in humanities education. Projects should be national in scope and utilise, when appropriate, new technologies.
Type: Grant.
No. of awards offered: Approx. 20.
Frequency: Annual.
Value: Varies depending upon the project.
Length of Study: Varies depending upon the project.
Country of Study: Any country.
Application Procedure: An NEH application form is required in addition to project materials. Forms are available from NEH or from the Endowment's website.
Closing Date: October 15th.

NEH Centers for Advanced Study Grants

Subjects: The humanities.
Eligibility: Open to independent research libraries and museums, American research centres overseas, and centres for advanced study.
Level of Study: Postgraduate.
Purpose: To support coordinated research in well-defined subject areas at centres for advanced study through block fellowship grants.
Type: Grant.
No. of awards offered: Varies.
Frequency: Annual.
Value: Varies.
Country of Study: Any country.
Closing Date: October 1st.
Additional Information: Individuals should apply directly to the centres, a list of which is available from the Division of Research and Education.

NEH Collaborative Research

Subjects: Arts and humanities.
Level of Study: Postdoctorate.
Purpose: Provides up to three years support for collaborative research. These grants support original research undertaken by two or more scholars, which because of their scope, complexity or duration, cannot be sponsored through one year fellowships.
Type: Research Grant.
No. of awards offered: Varies.
Frequency: Annual.
Value: Varies depending on the project.
Length of Study: Up to 3 years.
Country of Study: Any country.
Application Procedure: An NEH application form is required in addition to project material.
Closing Date: September 1st.

Additional Information: People seeking further information on the full range of programs in the Division should contact NEH.

NEH Fellowships for College Teachers and Independent Scholars

Subjects: Projects which may contribute to scholarly knowledge, to the conception and substance of individual courses in the humanities, or to the general public's understanding of the humanities. Projects may address broad topics or consist of study and research in a specialized field.
Eligibility: Open to teachers in two year, four year and five year colleges and universities, faculty members of university departments and programmes that do not grant the PhD, individuals affiliated with institutions other than colleges and universities, and scholars and writers working independently. Applicants need not have advanced degrees, but candidates for degrees and persons seeking support for work leading toward degrees are not eligible. Applicants should be US citizens or foreign nationals who have resided in the USA for at least three years.
Level of Study: Postdoctorate.
Purpose: To encourage and support full-time independent advanced study and research by people of diverse interests, backgrounds and circumstances.
Type: Fellowship.
No. of awards offered: Approx. 86.
Frequency: Annual.
Value: The maximum stipend is US$30,000.
Length of Study: 6-12 consecutive months.
Country of Study: Any country.
Application Procedure: Application form must be completed.
Closing Date: May 1st.
Additional Information: Application guidelines are available from the Division of Research and Education, room 318 (Tel: 202 606 8467), or by visiting the NEH website.

NEH Fellowships for University Teachers

Subjects: Projects which may contribute to scholarly knowledge, to the conception and substance of individual courses in the humanities, or to the general public's understanding of the humanities. Projects may address broad topics or consist of study and research in a specialised field.
Eligibility: Open to faculty members of departments and programmes in universities that grant the PhD and faculty members of postgraduate professional US schools. Applicants need not have advanced degrees, but candidates for degrees and persons seeking support for work leading toward degrees are not eligible. Applicants should be US citizens or foreign nationals who have resided in the USA for at least three years.
Level of Study: Postdoctorate.
Purpose: To encourage and support full-time independent advanced study and research by people of diverse interests, backgrounds and circumstances.
Type: Fellowship.
No. of awards offered: Approx. 86.
Frequency: Annual.

Value: The maximum stipend is US$30,000.
Length of Study: Periods of 6-12 consecutive months.
Country of Study: Any country.
Application Procedure: Application form must be completed.
Closing Date: May 1st.
Additional Information: Application guidelines are available from the NEH Public Affairs Office, Room 318 (Tel: 202 606 8446) or by visiting the NEH website. Enquiries should be directed to Jane A Rosenberg, Division of Research and Education.

NEH Preservation and Access Grants

Subjects: Arts and humanities.
Eligibility: Open to individuals, non-profit institutions, cultural organisations, state agencies and institutional consortia.
Level of Study: Postgraduate.
Purpose: To support projects that will describe, organise, preserve and increase the availability of resources supporting research, education and public programming in the humanities.
Type: Grant.
Frequency: Annual.
Value: Varies.
Country of Study: Any country.
Application Procedure: Application guidelines and instructions are available upon request.
Closing Date: July 1st.

NEH Reference Materials Program

Subjects: The creation of dictionaries, historical/linguistic atlases, encyclopedias, concordances, catalogues/raisonnés, linguistic grammars, descriptive catalogues, databases, and other materials that serve to codify information essential to research in the humanities. Grants are also given to projects that provide access to materials that are national or international in scope.
Eligibility: Open to institutions of higher education, non-profit professional associations and scholarly societies, and individuals.
Level of Study: Postgraduate.
Purpose: To provide support for projects that promise to facilitate research in the humanities by organising essential resources for scholarship and by preparing reference works that can improve scholarly access to information and collections.
Type: Grant.
No. of awards offered: Varies.
Frequency: As required.
Value: Dependent upon proposal.
Country of Study: USA.
Closing Date: July 1st.
Additional Information: For information, write or call the Division of Preservation and Access, Room 411.

NEH Seminars and Institutes for College Teachers

Subjects: All disciplines of the humanities and the humanistic social sciences.
Eligibility: Open to individuals who primarily teach undergraduates and have not recently had the opportunity to use the resources of a major library. Independent scholars are also eligible. Applicants must have completed their professional training by March 1st. Candidates for degrees and persons seeking support for work leading towards a degree are ineligible. Applications from members of PhD-granting departments are not normally accepted. Applicants should be US citizens or foreign nationals who have resided in the USA for at least three years.
Level of Study: Postgraduate, Professional development.
Type: Summer seminar and institute.
No. of awards offered: Approx. 25 seminars, each with 15 members and 10 institutes, each with 25 members.
Frequency: Annual.
Value: Varies, to cover travel expenses to and from the seminar center, books, and other research expenses and living expenses.
Length of Study: 4-8 weeks.
Study Establishment: Various institutions under the direction of distinguished scholars and teachers.
Country of Study: Any country.
Application Procedure: Applications are available from individual seminar directors. A list of directors and programme description are available from NEH.
Closing Date: March 1st.

NEH Seminars and Institutes for School Teachers

Subjects: The humanities.
Eligibility: Open to US citizens who are full-time teachers at US public, private or parochial schools, of grades K through to 12. Other school personnel may also apply.
Level of Study: Professional development.
Purpose: To provide opportunities for US teachers of grades K through to 12 to work with master teachers and distinguished scholars, studying important works in a systematic and thorough way.
No. of awards offered: Approx. 25 seminars, each with 15 members, approximately 10 institutes, each with 25 members.
Frequency: Annual.
Value: Varies depending on the length of the seminar or institute; to cover travel expenses to and from the host institution, books, other research expenses and living expenses.
Length of Study: 4-8 weeks.
Country of Study: Any country.
Application Procedure: Application forms and essays are required.
Closing Date: March 1st.
Additional Information: A list of the seminars and institutes is distributed widely in late fall and is also available from the

Research and Education division. Interested school teachers should write directly to the Division of Research and Education. Applications are then submitted to the seminar or institute director, and not to the NEH.

NEH Summer Stipends

Subjects: The humanities; the work proposed may be within the applicant's special areas of interest, or in some field that will enable them to understand their own fields better and enlarge their competence.
Eligibility: Each college and university in the USA and its territorial possessions may nominate two members of its faculty and staff. One nominee should be in the early stages of his/her career (junior scholar). For the purposes of the programme, instructors and assistant professors will be considered junior nominees and associate professors and professors will be considered senior nominees. Writers and independent scholars may apply without nomination. All applicants should be US citizens or foreign nationals who have resided in the USA for at least three years.
Level of Study: Unrestricted.
Purpose: To allow college and university staff to pursue two consecutive months of full-time study and research.
Type: Stipends.
No. of awards offered: Approx. 130.
Frequency: Annual.
Value: US$4,000.
Length of Study: Full-time study or research, for 2 consecutive months.
Country of Study: USA.
Application Procedure: Application guidelines are available from the Division of Research and Education, Room 318 (Tel: 202 606 8551), or by visiting the NEH website. Enquiries should be directed to Leon Bramson.
Closing Date: October 1st.

Schools for a New Millenium Implementation Grants

Subjects: Arts and humanities.
Eligibility: Open to citizens from the USA.
Level of Study: Unrestricted.
Purpose: To support whole schools, in partnership with colleges and communities, to implement professional development activities that integrate digital technology into the humanities classroom.
Type: Grant.
No. of awards offered: Approx. 20.
Frequency: Annual.
Value: Varies depending upon the project.
Length of Study: Varies depending upon the project.
Country of Study: Any country.
Application Procedure: An NEH application form is required in addition to project materials. Forms are available from NEH or from the Endowment's website.
Closing Date: October 1st.

NATIONAL FEDERATION OF MUSIC SOCIETIES

Francis House
Francis Street, London, SW1P 1DE, England
Tel: (44) 171 828 7320
Fax: (44) 171 828 5504
Email: postmaster@nfms.demon.co.uk
Contact: Ms Kate Fearnley, Award Administrator

The National Federation of Music Societies represents and supports ameteur choirs, orchestras and music promoters of all kinds throughout the United Kingdom. The 1,750 member societies represent over 135,000 musicians and music lovers; they present 7,500 concerts each year to an audience of 1.7 million; and spend in excess of £16.5 million each year.

NFMS Award for Young Concert Artists

Subjects: Mens' voices, womens' voices, strings, wind and bass, piano.
Eligibility: Open to singers under 30 years of age, instrumentalists under 28 years of age. All applicants must be UK citizens normally resident in the UK.
Level of Study: Professional development.
Purpose: To support young musicians at the start of their professional careers.
No. of awards offered: 3-4.
Frequency: Annual.
Value: 70 engagements with affiliated societies.
Country of Study: Any country.
Application Procedure: Please complete application form and submit with CV.
Closing Date: As advertised in the national press.

NATIONAL FEDERATION OF STATE POETRY SOCIETIES, INC.

4242 Stevens, Minneapolis, MN, 55409, United States of America
Tel: (1) 612 824 1964
Fax: (1) 612 872 3200
Email: pjdoyle@crossnet.org
Contact: Mr P J Doyle

A national coalition of state poetry societies which promotes creation and appreciation of poetry.

Edna Meudt Memorial Scholarships

Subjects: Poetry.
Eligibility: Open to juniors or seniors of accredited universities or colleges who write poetry.
Level of Study: Unrestricted.
Purpose: To encourage the study and writing of poetry.
Type: Scholarship.
No. of awards offered: 2.
Frequency: Annual.

Value: US$500, plus publication and travel stipend for awards ceremony.
Country of Study: Any country.
Application Procedure: Candidates must complete and submit a ten-poem manuscript (titled) plus application form.
Closing Date: February 1st.
Additional Information: Committee members will evaluate, judge and select scholarship winners on or before March 1st.

NATIONAL HISTORICAL PUBLICATIONS & RECORDS COMMISSION (NHPRC)

Room 607
National Archives Building (Archives 1)
7th & Pennsylvania Avenue NW, Washington, DC, 20408, United States of America
Tel: (1) 202 501 5610
Fax: (1) 202 501 5601
Email: nhprc@archl.nara.gov
www: http://www.nara.gov/nara/nhprc/nhprc.html
Contact: Ms Laurie A Baty, Program Officer

NHPRC Documentary Editing and Archival and Records Management Grants

Subjects: History.
Eligibility: Open to a state, tribal, local government, individual, not-for-profit organisation. Federal agencies are excluded.
Level of Study: Unrestricted.
Purpose: To make accessible for use those records that further an understanding and appreciation of American History.
Type: Grant.
No. of awards offered: Varies.
Frequency: Two times each year, depending on available funds.
Country of Study: USA.
Application Procedure: Contact the agency for current guidelines and application materials. These details are also available via our website at http://www.nara.gov/nara/nhprc/.
Closing Date: June 1st, October 1st, depending on the category under which applying.

NHPRC Fellowship in Documentary Editing

Subjects: Documentary editing.
Eligibility: Individuals must have completed coursework and examinations leading to the doctorate. Applicants may be working on their dissertation. Official transcripts must be submitted. Applicants must be US citizens.
Level of Study: Doctorate, Postdoctorate.
Purpose: To provide individuals with training in the field of documentary editing.
Type: Fellowship.
No. of awards offered: Varies.

Frequency: Annual.
Value: Currently US$33,000 (+US$8,250 benefits).
Length of Study: 9-12 months.
Country of Study: USA.
Application Procedure: Potential applicants should contact the Commission for guidelines and host institution information. This information is available by December of the preceding year.
Closing Date: March 1st (Postmarked).

NATIONAL HUMANITIES CENTER (NHC)

PO Box 12256, Research Triangle Park, NC, 27709-2256,
United States of America
Tel: (1) 919 549 0661
Fax: (1) 919 990 8535
Email: nhc@ga.unc.edu
www: http://www.nhc.rtp.nc.us:8080
Contact: Fellowship Program

The National Humanities Center is a residential institute for advanced study in history, languages and literature, philosophy, and other fields of the humanities. Each year it awards approximately thirty-five to forty fellowships to scholars of demonstrated achievement and to promising younger scholars.

NHC Fellowships in the Humanities

Subjects: History, philosophy, languages and literature, classics, religion, history of the arts, and other fields in the liberal arts.
Eligibility: Open to scholars of any nationality. Social scientists, natural scientists, or professionals whose work has a humanistic dimension may also apply. Applicants must hold a doctorate or have equivalent professional accomplishments. Fellowships are awarded to senior scholars of recognised accomplishment and to promising young scholars engaged in research beyond the revision of their dissertations.
Level of Study: Postdoctorate.
Purpose: To support advanced postdoctoral scholarship in the humanities.
Type: Fellowship.
No. of awards offered: 35-40.
Frequency: Annual.
Value: Fellowship stipends are individually determined in accordance with the needs of each Fellow and the Center's ability to meet them. As the Center cannot in most instances replace full salaries, applicants are urged to seek partial funding in the form of sabbatical salaries or grants from other sources. In addition to stipends, the Center provides round-trip travel expenses for Fellows and their immediate families to and from North Carolina.

Length of Study: 1 academic year, although a few Fellowships may be awarded for a single semester.
Study Establishment: The Center.
Country of Study: USA.
Application Procedure: Applicants must submit the Center's form supported by their CV, a 1000 word project proposal, and three letters of recommendation.
Closing Date: October 15th.
Additional Information: Fellowships are supported by grants from the Andrew W Mellon Foundation, the National Endowment for the Humanities, the Research Triangle Foundation, The Lilly Endowment, Delta Delta Delta, the Rockefeller Foundation and the Center's own endowment funds.

NATIONAL LEAGUE OF AMERICAN PEN WOMEN, INC.

1300 17th Street NW, Washington, DC, 20036, United States
of America
Tel: (1) 202 785 1997
Fax: (1) 202 452 6868
Email: nlapw1@juno.com
www: http://www.
Contact: Ms Mary Jane Hillery, National Scholarship Chairperson

National League of American Pen Women Grants for Mature Women

Subjects: Art, letters and music.
Eligibility: Open to non Pen Women and those who have never been a Pen Woman, over 35 years of age who wish to pursue special work in their field of art, letters, and music. Applicants must be US citizens.
Level of Study: Unrestricted.
Purpose: To further creative purpose.
Type: Grant.
No. of awards offered: 1 in each category.
Frequency: Every two years (even-numbered years).
Value: US$1,000. The award may be used for college, framing, research.
Country of Study: USA.
Application Procedure: There are no application forms. Applicants should send a letter stating their age, background and creative purpose and include proof of their citizenship.
Closing Date: January 15th of even numbered years.
Additional Information: Send a self addressed envelope by Septembert 1st of the odd-numbered year to receive current information. Information can also be obtained from 66 Willow Road, Sudbury, MA 01776 - 2165, USA.

NATIONAL LIBRARY OF AUSTRALIA

Canberra, ACT, 2600, Australia
Tel: (61) 2 62 62 1258
Fax: (61) 2 62 73 5763
Email: g.powell@nla.gov.au
Contact: Mr Graeme Powell, Manuscript Librarian

The National Library of Australia is responsible for developing and maintaining a comprehensive collection of Australian library materials, and a strong collection of non-Australian publications, and for administering and co-ordinating a range of national bibliographical activities.

Harold White Fellowships

Subjects: Few subject limitations, but most fellowships fall within the categories of - arts and humanities, fine and applied arts, and social sciences.
Eligibility: Open to established scholars, writers and librarians from any country. Fellowships are not normally offered to candidates working for a higher degree.
Level of Study: Unrestricted.
Purpose: To promote the Library as a centre of scholarly activity and research; to encourage scholarly and literary use of the collection and the production of publications based on them; to publicise the Library's collections.
Type: Fellowship.
No. of awards offered: 3-5.
Frequency: Annual.
Value: A$470 per week.
Length of Study: 3-6 months.
Study Establishment: The Library.
Country of Study: Australia.
Application Procedure: Application forms are available from the Library.
Closing Date: April 30th.
Additional Information: Normally Fellows will be expected to give a public lecture and at least one seminar during their tenure on the subject of their research. At least three-quarters of the Fellowship time should be spent in Canberra.

NATIONAL POETRY SERIES

PO Box G, Hopewell, NJ, 08525, United States of America
Tel: (1) 609 466 9712
Fax: (1) 609 466 4706
Contact: Ms Stephanie Stio, Co-ordinator

The National Poetry Series was established in 1978 to ensure publication of five books of poetry each year. Winning manuscripts are selected by means of an annual open competition, judged by five distinguished poets.

National Poetry Series

Subjects: Authorship.
Eligibility: NPS accepts entries from American citizens who have an unpublished book length manuscript in English to submit.
Level of Study: Unrestricted.
Purpose: To promote America's awareness of poetry and to ensure the trade publication of five new books of poetry in America each year.
Type: Book Publication.
No. of awards offered: 5.
Frequency: Annual.
Value: Each winner receives US$1,000 plus book publication.
Country of Study: USA.
Application Procedure: Interested poets should send an SASE by January of the year of the contest to receive submission guidelines. Manuscripts should be submitted with a US$25 entrance fee.
Closing Date: Poetry manuscript are accepted between January 1st and February 15th.

NATIONAL RESEARCH COUNCIL OF CANADA

Recruitment Unit
Montreal Road
M58, Ottawa, ON, K1A 0R6, Canada
Tel: (1) 613 998 4126
Fax: (1) 613 990 7669
Email: ra.coordinator@nrc.ca
www: http://www.nrc.ca
Contact: Research Associates Co-ordinator

NRC is a dynamic, nationwide R&D organisation committed to helping Canada realize its potential as an innovative and competitive nation.

Industrial Research Assistance Program

Subjects: All subjects.
Eligibility: Recent college and university graduates who are unemployed or under employed.
Purpose: To help small and medium sized Canadian firms (SMEs) create and adopt innovative technologies that yield new products, create high quality jobs, and make industry more competitive. Another aim is to give recent university and college graduates who are unemployed or underemployed a chance to develop their work skills with SMEs in Canada.
Type: Internship.
No. of awards offered: Up to 1000 internships.
Study Establishment: Small and medium sized businesses in Canada.
Country of Study: Canada.
Application Procedure: Contact the Industrial Research Assistance Programme (IRAP) on the internet: http://pub.irap.nrc.ca/IRAP/web/IRAPcomm.nsf/Home or write to the National Research Council of Canada, Montreal Road, M58, Ottawa, Ontario, K1A OR6.

Additional Information: The programme administers two internship programmes : the Science and Technology Internships Programme and the Science Collaborative Research Internships Programme. Please write for more details or visit the website:http://pub.irap.nrc.ca/IRAP/web/IRAPcomm.nsf/home.

NATIONAL UNIVERSITY OF SINGAPORE

Registrar's Office
10 Kent Ridge Crescent, 119074, Singapore
Tel: (65) 874 6576
Fax: (65) 773 1462
Email: reggen42@nus.edu.sg
www: http://www.nus.edu.sg
Contact: Grants Management Officer

ASEAN Graduate Scholarships

Subjects: Graduate studies by coursework leading to the following degrees - MA in English studies, Chinese studies, Southeast Asian studies, urban design, Master of social sciences in economics, applied psychology, social work, applied sociology, Master in public policy, Master of architecture, Master of business administration (English and Chinese medium), Master of dental surgery in oral and maxillofacial surgery, endodontics, orthodontics and prosthodonics, Master of laws, Master of comparative law, Master of clinical embryology, Master of medicine in anaesthesiology, diagnostic radiology, internal medicine, obstetrics & gynaecology, occupational medicine, ophthalmology, paediatric, public health, psychiatry, surgery, Master of science in project management, building science, real estate, management of technology, chemical engineering, civil engineering, electrical engineering, environmental engineering, industrial & systems engineering, material science & engineering, mechanical engineering, safety, health & environmental technology, transportation systems & management, computer & information sciences, Asia-Pacific human resource management, mathematics.
Eligibility: Open to citizens of ASEAN member countries (except Singapore).
Level of Study: Postgraduate.
Purpose: To provide outstanding candidates, from member countries of the Association of Southeast Asian Nations (ASEAN), an opportunity to pursue postgraduate studies at the National University of Singapore.
Type: Scholarship.
No. of awards offered: 10.
Frequency: Annual.
Value: Stipend of S$1,350 each month, a once-only book allowance of S$500, approved fees and expenses, etc.
Study Establishment: National University of Singapore.
Country of Study: Singapore.

Application Procedure: Application forms for the designated degrees must be completed and submitted with supporting documents to the respective Faculties/Graduate Schools.
Closing Date: Concurrent with the closing date of graduate courses of the respective Faculties/Graduate Schools.
Additional Information: ASEAN is the abbreviation for the Association of South East Asian Nation and it comprises the following 9 nations in South East Asia- Brunei, Indonesia, Laos, Malaysia, Myanmar, Philippines, Singapore, Thailand and Vietnam, as on November 1998.

National University of Singapore Postgraduate Research Scholarship

Subjects: Science, humanities, business.
Eligibility: Open to graduates with at least an Honours Class II Upper Bachelor's degree, or equivalent.
Level of Study: Doctorate, Postgraduate.
Purpose: To encourage qualified candidates to pursue postgraduate research in their fields of interest in NUS.
Type: Scholarship.
No. of awards offered: 410.
Frequency: Annual.
Value: S$1,200 - S$1,400 plus full fee subsidy over 2-3 years.
Length of Study: 2 or 3 years.
Study Establishment: NUS.
Country of Study: Singapore.
Application Procedure: Application form must be completed.
Closing Date: Usually mid-May and mid-December.

NATIVE AMERICAN SCHOLARSHIP FUND, INC.

8200 Mountain Road NE
Suite 203, Albuquerque, NM, 87110, United States of America
Tel: (1) 505 262 2351
Fax: (1) 505 262 0534
Email: nasf@nasf.com
www: http://nasf.com/
Contact: Ms Lucille Kelley, Director of Recruitment

NASF offers 2 scholarship programmes. The math, education, science, business, engineering and computer science (MESBEC) provides scholarships to native Americans studying in these fields. The Native American Leadership in Education (NALE) is for Native Americans who are para-professionals in the schools. It helps them to complete their college degrees and earn teaching credentials, administrative certification, and counsellor certification. NASF fund Indian students in other fields such as humanities, fine arts, and social science. Students must be a quarter or more American Indian and enrolled with their tribe.

Native American Scholarship Program

Subjects: All subjects.
Eligibility: Restricted to US citizens of Native American Indian and Alaskan Native ancestry.
Level of Study: Unrestricted.
Purpose: To provide scholarships to high-potential Native American students in the fields that are critical for the political, economic, social and business development of American Indian tribes.
Type: Scholarship.
No. of awards offered: 190.
Frequency: Annual.
Value: US$500 - US$2,500 per academic year.
Length of Study: 4 years.
Study Establishment: An accredited college or university.
Country of Study: USA.
Application Procedure: Please write to reques for application forms.
Closing Date: September 15th for spring, April 15th for fall, and March 15th for summer.

NETHERLANDS GOVERNMENT

Royal Netherlands Embassy
120 Empire Circuit, Yarralumla, ACT, 2600, Australia
Tel: (61) 6 273 3111
Fax: (61) 6 273 3206
Email: nlgovcan@ozemail.com.au
Contact: Grants Management Officer

Huygens Programme

Subjects: All subjects.
Eligibility: Students who have completed or are near completion of a higher education programme, and who hold or are about to be awarded a higher education degree or diploma. Applicants must be no older than 35; have a good command of Dutch or English; have graduated no longer than two years previously, unless the application is for PhD research; be able to stay in the Netherlands for at least three months; have an admission letter of the host institute indicating how prospective study falls within the framework of institutional co-operation; and be an Australian citizen.
Level of Study: Postgraduate.
Purpose: The Huygens Programme aims to promote the influx of talented foreign students from countries with which the Netherlands has concluded a cultural agreement; and from countries which the Dutch Ministry of Education, Culture and Science has concluded agreements on the award of the scholarships.
Type: Scholarship.
No. of awards offered: 500 worldwide.
Frequency: Annual.
Value: The scholarship includes: a monthly allowance of f1545 for board, lodging and books. This allowance is sufficient for one person only; travel costs from and to your country (up to f500 for EU countries, f1000 for Central and Eastern European countries and f2,500 for other countries);

reimbursement of necessary travel expenses in the Netherlands (second-class rail); exemtion from the statutory tuition fees at Dutch institutes of higher education; medical insurance (not including dental treatment); costs of application for permission to stay in the Netherlands.
Length of Study: 3-12 months.
Study Establishment: A university, art academy, school of music or other institute of tertiary education.
Country of Study: Netherlands.
Application Procedure: Applicants are required to submit the following documents in fourfold: a completed application form, with annexes; photocopies of degrees diplomas and academic records; results of English language tests (TOEFL/IELTS) (if English is not their native language); curriculum vitate; motivation for applying for scholarship; two refernce letters from academic supervisors; admisssion letter from the Dutch host institution; a copy of their passport (only for countries where authorization is required for temorary stay); if necessary, a letter stating that, if the institution fee is higher than the statuatory fee for the academic year for which they are applying, they are willing to pay the extra fee themselves. All the documents have to be in English or Dutch (original or translation). Artists are required to include some photographs of their work, and musicians a tape of their performance.
Closing Date: Febrary 1st.

NETHERLANDS ORGANIZATION FOR INTERNATIONAL CO-OPERATION IN HIGHER EDUCATION

NUFFIC
PO Box 29777, The Hague, NL-2502 LT, Netherlands
Tel: (31) 70 4260 260
Fax: (31) 70 4260 229
Email: nuffic@nuffics.nl
www: http://www.nufficcs.nl
Contact: Information Department

Since its founding in 1952, NUFFIC has been an independent non-profit organisation. Its mission is to foster international co-operation in higher education. Special attention is given to development co-operation.

European Development Fund Awards for Citizens of ACP Countries

Subjects: All subjects.
Eligibility: Open to citizens of the African, Caribbean and Pacific countries associated with the European Union.
Level of Study: Unrestricted.
No. of awards offered: Varies.
Value: Course fees, books and field trips, international travel expenses, insurance, monthly allowance and stipend to cover the initial expenseof getting established.
Length of Study: For the duration of the course.

Country of Study: Countries associated with the European Union, ACP countries.
Application Procedure: Information and application forms can be obtained from the Netherlands Embassy in the candidate's country and the EU Delegations and offices of the Commission. The application is submitted through the candidate's employer and government. Delegations of the Commission can be found (Usually in the capital cities) in the following countries: Angola, Barbados and the Eastern Caribbean, Benin, Botswana, Burkina Faso, Burundi, Cameroon, Cape Verde, Central African Republic, Chad, Congo (Democratic Republic), Congo (Republic), Cote d'Ivoire, Djibouti, Dominican Republic, Eritrea, Ethiopia, Gabon, Gambia, Ghana, Guinea,Guinea Bissau, Guyana, Haiti, Jamaica, Kenya, Lesotho, Liberia, Madagascar, Malawi, Mali, Mauritania, Mauritius, Mozambique, Namibia, Niger, Nigeria, Papua New Guinea, Rwanda, Senegal, Sierra Leone, Solomon Islands, Somalia, Sudan, Suriname, Swaziland, Tanzania, Togo, Trinidad and Tobago, Uganda, Zambia and Zimbabwe. Offices of the Commission can be found in the following countries: Antigua and Barbuda, Bahamas, Belize, Comoros, Equatorial Guinea, Netherlands Antilles and Aruba, New Caledonia, Samoa, Sao Tome and Principe, Seychelles, Tonga and Vanuatu.
Closing Date: Please contact the Commission for details.
Additional Information: NUFFIC does not administer these awards and will not accept applications.

NFP Netherlands Fellowships Programme of Development Co-operation

Subjects: Most of the courses offered by the Institutes for International Education in the Netherlands.
Eligibility: Open to candidates who have the education and work experience required for the course, as well as an adequate command of the language in which it is conducted (usually English, sometimes French). The age limit is 40 for men and 45 for women. It is intended that candidates, upon completion of training, return to their home countries and resume their jobs. When several candidates with comparable qualifications apply, priority will be given to women. Candidates for a fellowship must be nominated by their employer, and formal employment should be continued during the fellowship period. As a rule the candidate's government is required to state its formal support, except in the case of certain development-oriented non-government organisations.
Level of Study: Postgraduate.
Purpose: To develop human potential through education and training mainly in the Netherlands with a view to diminish qualitative and quantitative deficiencies in the availability of trained manpower in developing countries.
Type: Fellowship.
No. of awards offered: Varies.
Value: Normal living expenses, fees and health insurances. International travel expenses are provided only when the course lasts three months or longer.
Length of Study: For the duration of the course in question.
Country of Study: NFP fellowships are used mainly in the Netherlands.

Application Procedure: For information on the nationality eligibility for these fellowships and on the application procedure, candidates should contact the Netherlands Embassy in their own country. Information on the courses for which the Scholarships are available can be obtained from NUFFIC.
Closing Date: Please write for details.

NETHERLANDS-SOUTH AFRICA ASSOCIATION

Studiefonds voor Zuidafrikanse Studenten NZAV
Keizersgradet 141, Amsterdam, 1015 CK, Netherlands
Tel: (31) 20 624 9318
Fax: (31) 20 638 2596
Email: nzav@pi.net
Contact: Dr S B I Veltanys-Visser, Secretary

Netherlands-South Africa Study Fund

Subjects: All subjects.
Eligibility: Open to nationals of South Africa.
Level of Study: Postgraduate.
Purpose: To support postgraduate study in Holland.
No. of awards offered: 5-10.
Frequency: Twice a year.
Value: 1,100 Dutch Guilders per month.
Length of Study: Up to 1 year.
Country of Study: Netherlands.
Application Procedure: Please write for details.
Closing Date: May 15th and December 15th.

NEW DRAMATISTS

424 West 44th Street, New York, NY, 10036, United States of America
Tel: (1) 212 757 6960
Fax: (1) 212 265 4738
Email: newdram@aol.com
www: http://www.itp.tsoq.nyu.edu/~diana/ndintro.html
Contact: Ms Karen Noyes, Development Assistant

New Dramatists Inc is a non-profit organisation dedicated to finding gifted playwrights and giving them the time, the space, and the tools to develop their craft so that they may fulfill their full potential and make lasting contributions to the theatre.

L Arnold Weissberger Award

Subjects: Playwriting arts and humanities, writing.
Eligibility: Open to candidates of any nationality.
Level of Study: Professional development.
Purpose: To recognise outstanding achievement.
Type: Grants (plus a public staged reading in New York City and publication by Samuel French, Inc).

No. of awards offered: 1.
Frequency: Annual.
Value: US$5,000.
Country of Study: Any country.
Application Procedure: Please submit script and letter of nomination..
Additional Information: Plays must be full length, unpublished and unproduced. Children's plays and musicals are not eligible. Plays must be nominated by an industry professional (ie. agent, literary manager, artistic director, or chairperson of accredited university, theater or playwriters' programs). Nominations will be limited to ONE per nominator. Nomination letters accompanying script submissions are recommended, but not required. All submitted scripts must include the name, address, phone number and letter of application of the nominator.

NEW ENGLAND THEATER CONFERENCE (NETC)

c/o Department of Theater
Northeastern University
360 Huntington Avenue, Boston, MA, 02115, United States of America
Tel: (1) 617 424 9275
Fax: (1) 617 424 1057
Email: netc@world.std.com
Contact: C E Boniface, Manger of Operations

The New England Theater Conference works to develop, expand and assist theater activity at community, educational and professional levels. Script competitions have a national and international reach.

Aurand Harris Memorial Playwriting Award

Subjects: Playwriting for young audiences.
Eligibility: Open to all playwrights in New England, who wish to submit a full length play for young audiences which is both commercially unpublished and unproduced.
Level of Study: Unrestricted.
Purpose: To support new full-length plays for young audiences.
Type: Prize.
No. of awards offered: 2.
Frequency: Annual.
Value: First prize US$1,000; second prize US$500.
Country of Study: Any country.
Application Procedure: Send SASE for current guidelines. There is a processsing fee of US$10.00.
Closing Date: April 15th. Winners will be announced in September.
Additional Information: This is a competition and not a financial aid program.

John Gassner Memorial Playwriting Award

Subjects: Playwriting (new full-length plays).
Eligibility: Open to all playwrights in New England, or NETC members, who wish to submit a full-length play which is both commercially unpublished and unproduced.
Level of Study: Unrestricted.
Type: Prize.
No. of awards offered: 2.
Frequency: Annual.
Value: First prize US$1,000; second prize US$500.
Country of Study: Any country.
Application Procedure: Send SASE for current guidelines. There is a processing fee of US$10.
Closing Date: April 15th.
Additional Information: Portions of winning plays are given staged readings. This is a competition and not a financial aid program.

NEW JERSEY STATE OPERA

50 Park Place
10th Floor
Robert Treat Center, Newark, NJ, 07102, United States of America
Tel: (1) 973 623 5757
Fax: (1) 973 623 5761
Contact: Ms Wanda Anderton

The New Jersey State Opera has as its purpose the production of fully-conceived and staged productions of grand opera. The Company is interested in developing the careers of talented young artists. Opportunities for competition winners include cash prizes and performance possibilities in upcoming productions.

New Jersey State Opera Vocal Competition

Subjects: Opera.
Eligibility: Open to singers aged 22-34, without restrictions on nationality, who have a serious commitment to an operatic career.
Level of Study: Unrestricted.
Purpose: To assist artists in furthering their career and to promote the recognition of young talent.
Type: Prize.
No. of awards offered: 4.
Frequency: Annual.
Value: US$1,000-US$5,000; plus performance possibilities in upcoming productions.
Country of Study: Any country.
Application Procedure: Completed application, two recommendations, proof of age, and photo must be submitted. If over 27, proof of operatic experience must be presented.
Closing Date: February 27th.
Additional Information: There is a registration fee.

NEW YORK STATE HISTORICAL ASSOCIATION

PO Box 800
Lake Road, Cooperstown, NY, 13326-0800, United States of
America
Tel: (1) 607 547 1481
Fax: (1) 607 547 1405
www: http://www.nysha.org
Contact: Mr Wendell Tripp, Editor

Dixon Ryan Fox Manuscript Prize of the New York State Historical Association

Subjects: History.
Eligibility: Open to nationals of any country.
Level of Study: Doctorate, Postdoctorate, Postgraduate,
Professional development, Unrestricted.
Purpose: To honour the best unpublished book-length
monograph dealing with the history of New York State.
Type: Financial support.
No. of awards offered: 1.
Frequency: Annual.
Value: US$3,000 plus assistance in publishing.
Length of Study: Book length.
Country of Study: USA (New York State).
Application Procedure: Two copies of the manuscript are to
be submitted, typed, double-spaced with at least 1″ margins.
Ribbon/photocopies on bond paper (no carbons).
Closing Date: January 20th.

NEW ZEALAND COMMONWEALTH SCHOLARSHIPS AND FELLOWSHIPS COMMITTEE

PO Box 11-915, Wellington, New Zealand
Tel: (64) 4 381 8510
Fax: (64) 4 381 8501
Email: schols@nzvcc.ac.nz
www: http://www.nzvcc.ac.nz
Contact: The Scholarships Officer

The New Zealand Commonwealth Scholarships and
Fellowships Committee is a secretariat which provides
administrative policy services to the seven vice-chancellors of
the New Zealand Universities.

New Zealand Commonwealth Scholarships

Subjects: All subjects.
Eligibility: Open to graduates who are citizens of a
Commonwealth country and who have graduated within the
last five years.
Level of Study: Postgraduate.

Purpose: To enable persons of high intellectual promise to
study in New Zealand in the expectation that they will make a
significant contribution to life in their own countries on their
return.
Type: Scholarship.
No. of awards offered: Approx. 10.
Frequency: Annual.
Value: NZ$1,000 per month, plus travel and allowances.
Length of Study: Up to 3 years.
Country of Study: New Zealand.
Application Procedure: Nominations should be sent to the
appropriate agency in the home country.
Closing Date: Differs from country to country. Applications
close in New Zealand on August 1st.
Additional Information: Scholarships are provided by the
New Zealand government and fall within the framework of the
Commonwealth Scholarship and Fellowship Plan.

NEW ZEALAND VICE-CHANCELLORS COMMITTEE

PO Box 11-915, Wellington, New Zealand
Tel: (64) 4 801 5091
Fax: (64) 4 801 5089
www: http://www.nzvcc.ac.nz
Contact: The Scholarships Officer

Claude McCarthy Fellowships

Subjects: Literature, science, medicine.
Eligibility: Open to any graduate of a New Zealand university.
Level of Study: Postgraduate.
Purpose: To enable graduates of New Zealand universities to
undertake original work or research.
Type: Fellowship.
No. of awards offered: Varies, depending upon funds
available, usually 12-15.
Frequency: Annual.
Value: Varies, according to country of residence during
tenure, and the project itself. Assistance for expenses
incurred in travel, employment of technical staff, special
equipment, etc. may be provided.
Length of Study: Normally for not more than 1 year.
Country of Study: Any country.
Closing Date: August 1st.

L B Wood Travelling Scholarship

Subjects: All subjects.
Eligibility: Open to all holders of postgraduate scholarships
from any faculty of any university in New Zealand, provided
that application is made within three years of the date of
graduation.
Level of Study: Doctorate.
Purpose: To assist graduates of New Zealand universities to
undertake doctoral studies in the UK.
Type: Scholarship.
No. of awards offered: 2.

Frequency: Annual.
Value: NZ$3,000 per year, as a supplement to another postgraduate scholarship.
Length of Study: Up to 3 years.
Study Establishment: University or institution of university rank.
Country of Study: United Kingdom.
Closing Date: October 1st.

Shirtcliffe Fellowship

Subjects: Arts, science, law, commerce, agriculture.
Eligibility: Open to graduates of New Zealand universities.
Level of Study: Doctorate.
Purpose: To provide further aid for New Zealand doctoral students.
Type: Fellowship.
No. of awards offered: 3.
Frequency: Annual.
Value: NZ$2,000 as a supplement to the postgraduate scholarship emolument.
Length of Study: Up to 3 years.
Study Establishment: A suitable education institution.
Country of Study: New Zealand or a Commonwealth country overseas.
Closing Date: October 1st.

William Georgetti Scholarships

Subjects: All subjects.
Eligibility: Candidates must be New Zealand citizens or permanent residents. Open to graduates who have been resident in New Zealand for five years immediately before application and who are aged between 21 and 28 years of age.
Level of Study: Postgraduate.
Purpose: To encourage postgraduate study and research in a field which is important to the social, cultural or economic development of New Zealand.
Type: Scholarship.
No. of awards offered: Varies.
Frequency: Annual.
Value: Up to NZ$5,100 for study in New Zealand; up to NZ$10,000 for study overseas.
Study Establishment: Universities in New Zealand or overseas.
Country of Study: Any country.
Closing Date: October 1st.
Additional Information: Age eligibility is recently undergoing a change. Application is currently being made to the New Zealand High Court to make the age restriction open.

THE NEWBERRY LIBRARY

60 West Walton Street, Chicago, IL, 60610, United States of America
Tel: (1) 312 255 3666
Fax: (1) 312 255 3513
Email: research@newberry.org
www: http://www.newberry.org
Contact: Committee on Awards

The Newberry Library, open to the public without charge, is an independent research library and educational institution dedicated to the expansion and dissemination of knowledge in the humanities. With a broad range of books and manuscripts relating to the civilisations of Western Europe and the Americas, the Library's mission is to acquire and preserve research collections of such material, and to provide for and promote their effective use by a diverse community of users.

American Society for Eighteenth-Century Studies

Subjects: Arts and humanities.
Eligibility: Applicants must be a member of the Society.
Level of Study: Postdoctorate, Postgraduate.
Purpose: To support scholars wanting to use the Newberry's collections to study the period 1660-1815.
Type: Fellowship.
No. of awards offered: Varies.
Frequency: Annual.
Value: US$800 per month, pro-rata.
Length of Study: From 1 to 3 months.
Study Establishment: The Newberry Library.
Country of Study: USA.
Application Procedure: Please submit completed application form, description of project, and three letters of reference.
Closing Date: March 1st.

Arthur Weinberg Fellowship for Independent Scholars

Subjects: Humanities.
Eligibility: Independent scholars who have demonstrated excellence through publications. For scholars working outside the academy in a field appropriate to the Newberry's collections. Preference is given to scholars working on historical issues related to social justice and/or reform.
Type: Fellowship.
No. of awards offered: Varies.
Frequency: Annual.
Value: $800.
Length of Study: 1 month.
Application Procedure: Please write for details. Application forms may also be downloaded from the website.
Closing Date: March 1st.

Audrey Lumsden-Kouvel Fellowship

Subjects: Late medieval or renaissance studies.
Eligibility: Open to postdoctoral scholars wishing to carry on extended research in late medieval or renaissance studies. Applicants must plan to be in continuous residence for at least three months. Preference will be given to those who plan longer stays during the academic year or who wish to use the fellowship to extend a sabbatical.
Level of Study: Postdoctorate.
Purpose: To enable scholars to use the Newberry's extensive holdings in late medieval and renaissance history and literature.
Type: Fellowship.
No. of awards offered: 1.
Frequency: Annual.
Value: A stipend of up to US$3,000.
Length of Study: At least 3 months.
Study Establishment: The Newberry Library.
Country of Study: USA.
Application Procedure: Please write for details. Application forms may also be downloaded from the website.
Closing Date: March 1st.

Center for Renaissance Studies Fellowships

Subjects: Renaissance studies.
Eligibility: Open to faculty members and graduate students of the 32 member institutions of the Center.
Level of Study: Postgraduate.
Type: Fellowship.
No. of awards offered: Varies.
Frequency: Annual.
Value: Varies.
Study Establishment: Participation in seminars either at the Library or at the Folger Institute of Renaissance and Eighteenth-Century Studies.
Country of Study: USA.
Application Procedure: Requests for information should be addressed to the Center or to the applicant's faculty representative.
Additional Information: Funds are also available from the Folger Institute. Information and application for all of the fellowships can be found at the website.

Center for Renaissance Studies Seminar and Summer Institute Fellowships

Subjects: Renaissance studies.
Eligibility: Open to postdoctoral scholars teaching in US colleges and universities.
Level of Study: Postdoctorate.
Purpose: To enable participation in a summer institute.
Type: Fellowship.
No. of awards offered: 10.
Frequency: Annual.
Value: A stipend of US$3,000.
Length of Study: 6 weeks.
Study Establishment: The Center.
Country of Study: USA.

D'Arcy McNickle Center Frances C Allen Fellowships

Subjects: Humanities and social sciences.
Eligibility: Open to women of American Indian heritage who are pursuing an academic programme at any stage beyond the undergraduate degree.
Level of Study: Postgraduate.
Type: Fellowship.
No. of awards offered: Varies.
Frequency: Annual.
Value: Varies according to need.
Length of Study: Length of tenure varies according to need but Fellows are expected to spend a significant amount of their Fellowship term in residence at the Center.
Study Establishment: The Newberry Library.
Country of Study: USA.
Closing Date: March 1st.

Hermon Dunlap Smith Center for the History of Cartography Fellowships

Subjects: The history of cartography.
Eligibility: Open to established scholars of any nationality.
Level of Study: Postgraduate.
Type: A variable number of Fellowships.
Value: US$800 per month (maximum stipend of US$30,000).
Study Establishment: In residence, for periods not exceeding 3 months (short-term); or for 6-12 months (long-term).
Country of Study: USA.
Closing Date: March 1st, October 15th (short-term); March 1st (long-term).

For further information contact:

60 West Walton Street, Chicago, IL, 60610, United States of America
Tel: (1) 312 943 9090
Contact: Committee on Awards

Herzog August Bibliothek Wolfenbüttel Fellowship

Subjects: Art history and related areas.
Eligibility: Applicants for long and short term fellowships at the Newberry may ask to also be considered for this joint fellowship which provides a period of residence in Wolfenbüttel, Germany. The proposed project should link the collections of both libraries. Applicants should plan to hold both fellowships sequentially to ensure continuity of research.
Level of Study: Postdoctorate.
Purpose: To enable a period of residence in Wolfenbüttel, Germany for study of the collections housed in the Herzog August Bibliothek.
Type: Fellowship.
Frequency: Annual.
Value: DM2,000 per month, plus up to DM1,200 travel expenses.
Length of Study: 3 months.
Study Establishment: The Newberry Library.

Application Procedure: Please write for details. Application forms may also be downloaded from the website.

Lloyd Lewis Fellowships in American History

Subjects: Any field of American history appropriate to the collections of the Newberry Library.
Eligibility: Open to established scholars, holding the PhD, who have demonstrated, through publications, excellence in the field. Foreign nationals may apply if they have resided in the US for three or more years.
Level of Study: Postdoctorate.
Purpose: To pursue projects in any area of American history appropriate to the Newberry's collection.
Type: Fellowship.
No. of awards offered: 2-3.
Frequency: Annual.
Value: Up to US$40,000.
Length of Study: 6-11 months.
Study Establishment: In residence at the Library with participation in the Library's scholarly community.
Country of Study: USA.
Application Procedure: Please write for details. Application forms may also be downloaded from the website.
Closing Date: January 20th.
Additional Information: Lewis Fellows participate in the Library's scholarly community through regular participation in seminars, colloquia, and other events. Lewis Fellowships may be combined with sabbaticals or other stipendiary support. Applicants may ask to be considered for NEH and Mellon Fellowships at the time of their application.

Mellon Postdoctoral Fellowships

Subjects: The humanities.
Eligibility: Applications are invited from postdoctoral scholars in any field of relevant to the Library's collection for awards to support their research and writing.
Level of Study: Postdoctorate.
Purpose: To support residential postdoctoral research and writing.
Type: Fellowship.
No. of awards offered: Varies.
Frequency: Annual.
Value: Up to US$30,800.
Length of Study: 6-10 months.
Study Establishment: The Newberry Library.
Country of Study: USA.
Application Procedure: Please write for details. Application forms may also be downloaded from the website. Completed applications must include three letters of recommendation.
Closing Date: January 20th.
Additional Information: Fellows will become part of the Newberry's community of scholars, participating in biweekly Fellows seminars, colloquia, and other events. Applicants may combine this award with sabbatical or other stipendiary support. Individuals applying for National Endowment for the Humanities and Lloyd Lewis Fellowships at the Newberry Library will also be considered for the Mellon Research Fellowships.

Monticello College Foundation Fellowship for Women

Subjects: Any field appropriate to the Library's collections.
Eligibility: Open to women who hold the PhD who are in the early stages of their academic careers. This academic award is designed for a woman at the early stage of her career whose work gives clear promise of scholarly productivity and who would benefit significantly from six months of research, writing and participation in the intellectual life of the library.
Level of Study: Postdoctorate.
Purpose: To offer young women the opportunity to undertake work in residence at the Library and to significantly enhance their careers through research and writing.
Type: Fellowship.
No. of awards offered: 1.
Frequency: Annual.
Value: US$12,500.
Length of Study: 6 months.
Study Establishment: The Newberry Library.
Country of Study: USA.
Application Procedure: Please write for details. Application forms may also be downloaded from the website.
Closing Date: January 20th.
Additional Information: Other things being equal, preference is given to the applicant whose proposed study is concerned with the study of women.

National Endowment for the Humanities Fellowships

Subjects: Any field appropriate to the Library's collections.
Eligibility: Open to US citizens or foreign nationals with three years US residence, who are established scholars at the postdoctoral level or its equivalent. Preference is given to applicants who have not held major fellowships for three years preceding the proposed period of residency.
Level of Study: Postdoctorate.
Purpose: To encourage scholarly research, and to deepen and enrich the opportunities for serious intellectual exchange through the active participation of Fellows in the Library community.
Type: Fellowship.
No. of awards offered: Varies.
Frequency: Annual.
Value: Up to US$30,000 (for 11 months' residency).
Length of Study: 6-11 months.
Study Establishment: The Newberry Library.
Country of Study: USA.
Application Procedure: Please write for application form. Completed application form must include all letters of reference. Application forms may also be downloaded from the website.
Closing Date: January 20th.
Additional Information: Applicants may combine this award with sabbatical or other stipendary support. Scholars conducting research in American history may also ask to be considered for the Lloyd Lewis Fellowship at the time of their application.

Newberry Library - American Antiquarian Society Short-Term Resident Fellowships for Individual Research

Subjects: Art history and related areas.
Eligibility: Eligibility for this fellowship is the same as the Newberry Library Fellowships, but fellows in this joint programme are awarded stipends by both institutions. Applicants should explain their need for both collections.
Level of Study: Postdoctorate.
Purpose: To enable individual research.
Type: Fellowship.
Frequency: Annual.
Value: US$800 per month, pro-rata.
Length of Study: 2 weeks-2 months; 3 months for those travelling from a foreign country.
Study Establishment: The Newberry Library.
Country of Study: USA.
Closing Date: January 20th.

Newberry Library - British Academy Fellowship for Study in Great Britain

Subjects: The humanities.
Eligibility: Open to established scholars at the postdoctoral level or equivalent. Preference is given to readers and staff of the Newberry Library and to established scholars who have previously used the Newberry Library.
Level of Study: Postdoctorate.
Purpose: In co-operation with the British Academy the Newberry Library offers an exchange fellowship for three months study in Great Britain in any field in which the Newberry's collections are strong.
Type: Fellowship.
No. of awards offered: 1.
Frequency: Annual.
Value: A stipend of £30 per day while in Great Britain.
Length of Study: 3 months.
Country of Study: United Kingdom.
Application Procedure: Please write for details. Application forms may also be downloaded from the website.
Closing Date: January 20th.
Additional Information: The home institution is expected to continue to pay the Fellow's salary.

Newberry Library - Ecole des Chartes Exchange Fellowship

Subjects: Renaissance studies.
Eligibility: Preference is given to graduate students at institutions in the Renaissance Center Consortium.
Level of Study: Doctorate.
Purpose: To enable a graduate student to study at the Ecole des Chartes in Paris.
Type: Fellowship.
No. of awards offered: Varies.
Frequency: Annual.

Value: Varies - provides a monthly stipend and free tuition for an American graduate student at the École Nationale des Chartes in Paris.
Length of Study: 3 months to 1 year.
Study Establishment: Ecole des Chartes.
Country of Study: France.
Application Procedure: Please request an application form from the Center.
Closing Date: December 15th.
Additional Information: The École des Chartes is the oldest institution in Europe specialising in the archival sciences, including paleography, bibliography, textual editing, and the history of the book.

Newberry Library Short-Term Resident Fellowships for Individual Research

Subjects: Any field appropriate to the Library's collections.
Eligibility: Open to nationals of any country who hold a PhD degree or have completed all requirements for the degree except the dissertation.
Level of Study: Doctorate, Postdoctorate.
Purpose: Short term Fellowships provide access to Newberry's collections for those who live beyond commuting distance from Chicago.
Type: Fellowship.
No. of awards offered: Varies.
Frequency: Annual.
Value: US$800 per month, pro-rata.
Length of Study: Up to 2 months; 3 months for foreign applicants.
Study Establishment: The Newberry Library.
Country of Study: USA.
Application Procedure: Please write for details. Application forms may also be downloaded from the website.
Closing Date: March 1st.
Additional Information: Preference is given to those who particularly need the facilities of the Library and live outside Chicago.

Rockefeller Foundation Residential Fellowships in Gender Studies in Early Modern Europe

Subjects: The humanities.
Eligibility: Administered by the Newberry's Center for Renaissance Studies, Rockefeller Fellowships are reserved for postdoctoral scholars in literature, history and other humanities fields who are exploring a topic related to issues of gender in European cultures from the late middle ages through to the 17th century.
Level of Study: Postdoctorate.
Purpose: To support postdoctoral research in late medieval and early modern gender studies using the Newberry Library's collections.
Type: Fellowship.

No. of awards offered: 2.
Frequency: Annual.
Value: US$30,000.
Length of Study: 11 months.
Study Establishment: The Newberry Library.
Country of Study: USA.
Application Procedure: Please write for details. Application forms may also be downloaded from the website.
Closing Date: January 20th.
Additional Information: Fellows will participate in Library seminars and activities, as well as programmes of the Center for Renaissance Studies.

Spencer Foundation Fellowships in the History of Education

Subjects: The humanities, education. Topics may range from the history of instruction, to educational philosophy, to the history of literacy, and beyond.
Eligibility: Both established scholars and holders of PhD degree at the early stages of their careers may apply for support for projects in the history of education apporopriate to the Newberry's collection..
Level of Study: Postgraduate.
Purpose: To support individual research and opportunities to pursue projects in an interdisciplinary setting.
Type: Fellowship.
No. of awards offered: 2.
Frequency: Annual.
Value: Junior Fellowship US$25,000; Senior Fellowship US$35,000.
Length of Study: 6-11 months.
Study Establishment: The Newberry Library.
Country of Study: USA.
Application Procedure: Please write for details. Application forms may also be downloaded from the website.
Closing Date: January 20th.

Weiss/Brown Publication Subvention Award

Subjects: Humanities.
Eligibility: Authors of scholarly books already accepted for publication. Subject matter must cover European civilisation before 1700 in the areas of music, theatre, French or Italian literature or cultural studies.
Purpose: To subsidise the publication of a scholarly book or books on French or Italian music, theatre, literature or cultural studies before 1700.
Type: Award.
Frequency: Annual.
Value: Variable, up to US$15,000.
Application Procedure: Please write for details. Application forms may also be downloaded from the website. Applicants will be asked to provide detailed information regarding the publication and the subvention request.
Closing Date: January 20th.

NEWBY TRUST LTD

Hill Farm
Froxfield, Petersfield, Hampshire, GU32 1BQ, England
Tel: (44) 1730 827557
Fax: (44) 1730 827557
Contact: Miss W Gillam, Company Secretary

Newby Trust Awards

Subjects: All subjects.
Eligibility: Open to students of any nationality. Students not already in the UK are rarely considered. Foreign students must already be studying in the UK.
Level of Study: Doctorate, Postgraduate, Professional development.
Purpose: General educational purposes among others.
Type: Grant.
No. of awards offered: Varies.
Frequency: Annual.
Value: Up to £1,000 for fees or maintenance.
Study Establishment: University.
Country of Study: United Kingdom, unless there are strong reasons for studying elsewhere.
Application Procedure: Personal letter with CV, two letters of reference, statement of income and expenditure (including fees), and self stamped addressed must be submitted. Application forms are not supplied..
Closing Date: None, but applications in September/October are rarely considered.
Additional Information: Funding is not available for the following- CPS law exam; BSC intercalculated with a medical degree; postgraduate medical/veterinary degrees in the first or second years.

NICOLO PAGANINI INTERNATIONAL VIOLIN COMPETITION

Casella Postale 586
c/o Officio Postele GE Centre, Genoa, 16100, Italy
Tel: (390) 10 5574215
Fax: (390) 10 2469272
Contact: Secretariat

Nicolo Paganini International Violin Competition

Subjects: Violin.
Eligibility: Open to violinists of any nationality born after June 30th 1966 and before June 30th 1983.
Level of Study: Unrestricted.
Type: Prize.
No. of awards offered: 6.
Frequency: Annual.
Value: Paganini Prize: 20,000,000 lire; 2nd Prize: 12,000,000 lire; 3rd Prize: 8,000,000 lire; 4th Prize: 4,000,000 lire; 5th Prize: 4,000,000 lire; 6th Prize: 3,000,000 lire.

Country of Study: Any country.
Application Procedure: Please write for application and registration form. A registration fee must be paid.
Closing Date: May 31st.
Additional Information: The Competition is held from late September to early October.

NAI Travel Grant

Subjects: Studies relating to Africa.
Eligibility: Applicants must hold a BA or MA degree and must be students or researchers from the Nordic countries.
Level of Study: Postgraduate.
Purpose: To provide opportunities for researchers in the Nordic countries (Denmark, Finland, Iceland, Norway and Sweden) to conduct field-work in Africa.
Type: Travel Grant.
No. of awards offered: Approx. 40.
Frequency: Annual.
Value: US$3,000 on average.
Length of Study: Varies.
Country of Study: Africa.
Application Procedure: Application forms are available from NAI or on our website.
Closing Date: September 16th.
Additional Information: Direct enquiries for this award should be directed to Ingrid Anderson.

NORTH DAKOTA UNIVERSITY SYSTEM

600 East Boulevard, Bismarck, ND, 58505, United States of America
Tel: (1) 701 328 2960
www: http://www.ndus.nodak.edu
Contact: Ms Rhonda Shaver

North Dakota Indian Scholarship

Subjects: All subjects.
Eligibility: Must be a resident of North Dakota with 1/4 degree Indian Blood. Must be accepted for admission at an institute of higher learning or state vocational programme. Recipients must be enrolled full-time and have a grade point average above 2.00.
Level of Study: Doctorate, Postgraduate.
Purpose: To assist Native American students in obtaining a basic college education.
Type: Scholarship.
No. of awards offered: 140.
Frequency: Annual.
Value: US$700.
Country of Study: USA.
Application Procedure: Send completed forms to: North Dakota Indian Scholarship Program, North Dakota University System, 10th Floor State Capitol, 600 E Boulevard Avenue, Bismarck, ND 58505-0230.
Closing Date: July 15th.

NORWEGIAN INFORMATION SERVICE IN THE UNITED STATES

825 Third Avenue
38th Floor, New York, NY, 10022-7584, United States of America
Tel: (1) 212 421 7333
Fax: (1) 212 754 0583
Email: norcons@interport.net
www: http://www.norway.org
Contact: Grants & Scholarships Department

America-Norway Heritage Fund

Subjects: All subjects.
Eligibility: Candidates must be American of Norwegian descent who have made significant contributions to American culture.
Level of Study: Professional development.
Purpose: To award special grants to Americans of Norwegian descent who have made significant contributions to American culture, enabling them to visit Norway to share the results of their work with the people of Norway.
Type: Travel Grant.
No. of awards offered: Varies.
Frequency: Annual.
Value: Recipients will recieve a grant covering travel expenses as well as an honorarium.
Length of Study: 1-2 weeks. Activities should be planned between October - April.
Country of Study: Norway.
Application Procedure: Applications for the grant are no longer accepted. Candidates will be selected by the Board of Directors of the fund in co-operation with its connections in the United States. However, the Board of Directors of the Fund will appreciate receiving proposals for the possible candidates. Suggestions may be sent to: Nordmanns-Forbundet, Rådhusgt. 23B, N-0158 Oslo, Norway, or Norge-Amerika Foreningen, Drammensveien 20 C, N-0255 Oslo, Norway. For further information please contact these addresses.

American-Scandinavian Foundation

Subjects: All subjects.
Eligibility: Awards are open to US citizens or permanent residents who will have complete their undergraduate education at the the time their overseas programme begins. Proposals from all fields are accepted.
Level of Study: Postgraduate.
Purpose: To encourage advanced study and research in the Scandinavian countries.
Type: Fellowship.
No. of awards offered: Varies.
Frequency: Annual.
Value: Grants normally US$2,500; Fellowships up to US$15,000, not both.
Country of Study: Scandinavian countries.

Application Procedure: All applications must be on ASF application forms, available on request from the ASF.
Closing Date: November 1st.
Additional Information: For further information please contact the ASF.

For further information contact:

15 E 65 Street, New York, NY, 10021, United States of America
Tel: (1) 212 879 9779
Fax: (1) 212 249 3444
Contact: Grants Management Officer

John Dana Archbold Fellowship Program

Subjects: All subjects.
Eligibility: Eligibility is restricted to persons 20 to 35 years old, in good health and good character and citizens of Norway or the USA. Qualified applicants must show evidence of real ability in their chosen field, indicate seriousness of purpose, and have a record of social adaptability. There is ordinarily no language requirement. Undergraduate applicants must have a BA or BSc degree (or equivalent) before their departure date.
Level of Study: Postgraduate.
Purpose: To increase understanding between scholars from one country and their colleagues in the other. Americans go to Norway in even numbered years and Norwegians go to the USA in odd numbered years.
Type: Fellowship.
No. of awards offered: Varies.
Frequency: Annual.
Value: Individual grants vary, depending on projected costs, but generally do not exceed US$10,000. The maintenance stipend is sufficient to meet expenses for a single person. The travel allowance covers return air fare to Oslo.
Study Establishment: Institutions in Norway (not the University of Oslo).
Country of Study: Norway or USA.
Application Procedure: Please write to the Nansen Fund, Inc. for an application form.
Closing Date: January 15th.
Additional Information: The University of Oslo International Summer School offers orientation and Norwegian languages courses six weeks before the start of the regular academic year. For Americans, tuition is paid. Attendance is required. For further information please contact the Nansen Fund, Inc.

For further information contact:

The Nansen Fund, Inc.
77 Saddlebrook Lane, Houston, TX, United States of America
Tel: (1) 713 680 8255
Fax: (1) 713 686 3963

Norwegian Emigration Fund of 1975

Subjects: Subjects dealing with emigration history and relations between the United States and Norway.
Eligibility: Scholarships can be awarded to citizens and residents of the USA. The fund may also give grants to

institutions in the USA whose activities are primarily centred on the subjects mentioned.
Level of Study: Postgraduate.
Purpose: The purpose of the fund is to award scholarships to Americans for advanced or specialised study in Norway of subjects dealing with emigration history and relations between the United States and Norway.
Type: Travel Grant.
No. of awards offered: Varies.
Frequency: Annual.
Value: NOK 50,000-60,000.
Country of Study: Norway.
Application Procedure: Please complete an application form and return it clearly marked 'Emigration Fund'. Applications and well as enclosures will not be returned.
Closing Date: February 1st.

For further information contact:

Nordmanns-Forbundet
Rådhusgt 23B
N-0158, Oslo, Norway
Fax: (47) 22 42 51 63

Norwegian Information Service Travel Grants

Subjects: Norwegian language and culture.
Eligibility: Citizens and residents of the United States who are members of NORTANA are eligible. They must be university or college teachers of Norwegian or other courses in Norwegian culture or society, or graduate students who have passed their preliminary examinations in these fields.
Level of Study: Postgraduate.
Purpose: To provide financial assistance for teachers and students visiting Norway for study and research purposes.
Type: Travel Grant.
No. of awards offered: Varies.
Frequency: Annual.
Value: US$750 - US$1,500.
Country of Study: Norway.
Application Procedure: There is no application form. Please write giving details of subject to be studied in Norway, suggested amount, description of professional position and education, length of NORTANA membership, and details of any other grants previously received from the Norwegian government.
Closing Date: February 1st.

Norwegian Marshall Fund

Subjects: Science and humanities.
Eligibility: Open to American citizens and in special cases Norwegian citizens. The Fund seeks primarily to support research projects at Norwegian universities and institutions of higher learning where participation of American researchers is desirable.
Level of Study: Postgraduate.
Purpose: To promote research in Norway by Americans, which would be of importance to both countries.
Type: Research Grant.
No. of awards offered: Varies.

Frequency: Annual.
Value: Up to US$5,000. The award granted will depend upon the nature of the project and length of stay in Norway.
Length of Study: Varies.
Study Establishment: Norwegian universities.
Country of Study: Norway.
Application Procedure: Applications forms can be obtained from the Norway-America Association, and completed form should also be sent to the Association. Applications must be in duplicate and must contain a description of the proposed research, and a letter of support from the institution where the research will be based.
Closing Date: March 15th.
Additional Information: The annual grants are announced by the Fund in November directly to Norwegian institutions of higher learning. Awards will be granted in June.

For further information contact:

The Norway-America Association
Drammensveien 20 C, Oslo, 0255, Norway
Fax: (47) 22 44 78 31

NORWICH JUBILEE ESPERANTO FOUNDATION

37 Granville Court
Cheney Lane, Oxford, OX3 0HS, England
Tel: (44) 1865 245509
Contact: Dr Kathleen M Hall, Secretary

A registered charitable trust established in 1967 (reg No 313190) founded for the advancement of education in the study and practice of Esperanto. It can pay travelling expenses to enable young persons (under 26) who have shown efficiency in the study of Esperanto to visit foreign countries; award prizes; and encourage research.

Norwich Jubilee Esperanto Foundation Grants-in-Aid

Subjects: Esperanto.
Eligibility: Open to citizens of any country who are not more than 26 years of age, who require financial assistance and have a high standard of competence in Esperanto. An efficiency test may be required. There are no set academic or age requirements for research grants.
Level of Study: Unrestricted.
Purpose: To encourage the thorough study of Esperanto by enabling young students to travel abroad, and to promote research into the teaching of Esperanto.
Type: Travel Grant.
No. of awards offered: Varies, depending on funds available.
Frequency: Dependent on funds available.

Value: Normally £50-£200; maximum £1,000.
Length of Study: From 1 week to several months.
Country of Study: Outside United Kingdom (for UK applicants); United Kingdom (for other applicants).
Application Procedure: A letter of application in Esperanto is necessary; an application form may be completed later.
Closing Date: Applications are accepted at any time provided an adequate margin is left for processing.
Additional Information: Visitors to the UK will be expected to speak in Esperanto to schools or clubs. Applications showing no knowledge of Esperanto and no interest in it are not normally acknowledged.

OMAHA SYMPHONY GUILD

1605 Howard Street, Omaha, NE, 68102, United States of America
Tel: (1) 402 342 3836
Fax: (1) 402 342 3819
Email: bravo@omahasymphony.org
www: http://www.omahasymphony.org
Contact: Ms Kimberly Mettenbrink, Volunteer Co-ordinator

The purpose of the Omaha Symphony Guild is to promote the growth and development of the Omaha Symphony Orchestra.

Omaha Symphony Guild International New Music Competition

Subjects: Music theory and composition.
Eligibility: Open to composers no younger than 25 years of age.
Level of Study: Postgraduate.
Purpose: To award composers with unpublished compositions which have never been performed by a professional orchestra.
Type: Competition.
No. of awards offered: 1.
Frequency: Annual.
Value: US$3,000 award and premiere performance.
Country of Study: USA.
Application Procedure: Write for application form. Two copies of composition score must be submitted. Photocopies are acceptable. No tapes are accepted. The entry fee is US$30.00. Make cheque payable to the Omaha Symphony Guild. Application forms can also be downloaded from the website.
Closing Date: April 15th.
Additional Information: Composition must be no longer than 20 minutes. If you require the score to be returned please include US$10 postage.

OMOHUNDRO INSTITUTE OF EARLY AMERICAN HISTORY AND CULTURE

PO Box 8781, Williamsburg, VA, 23187-8781, United States of America
Tel: (1) 757 221 1110
Fax: (1) 757 221 1047
Email: ieahc1@facstaff.wm.edu
www: http://www.wm.edu/oieahc/cont.html
Contact: Director

The Omohundro Institute of Early American History and Culture publishes books in its field of interest, the William and Mary Quarterly, and a biannual newsletter, Uncommon Sense. It also sponsors conferences and colloquia, and annually awards a two year NEH postdoctoral fellowship and a one year Andrew W Mellon postdoctoral research fellowship.

NEH Institute Postdoctoral Fellowship

Subjects: The Institute's field of interest encompasses all aspects of the lives of North America's indigenous and immigrant peoples during the Colonial, Revolutionary, and early national periods of the United States and the related histories of Canada, the Caribbean, Latin America, the British Isles, Europe and Africa from the 16th century to approximately 1815.
Eligibility: Applicants must have been US citizens for three years prior to applying.
Level of Study: Predoctorate.
Purpose: To revise a dissertation into a first book that will make a major contribution to the field of early American history and culture, for publication by the Institute.
Type: Fellowship.
No. of awards offered: 1.
Frequency: Annual.
Length of Study: 2 year residential study.
Study Establishment: The Omohundro Institute of Early American History and Culture.
Country of Study: USA.
Application Procedure: Applications are sent on request, please write for details. Applications can also be downloaded from the website.
Closing Date: November 1st.

ONTARIO ARTS COUNCIL

151 Bloor Street West
6th Floor, Toronto, ON, M5S 1T6, Canada
Tel: (1) 416 961 1660
Fax: (1) 416 961 7796
Email: info@arts.om.ca
www: http://www.arts.on.ca
Contact: Grants Co-ordinator

The Ontario Arts Council (Canada) provides support to Ontario's arts community. The council is funded through the provincial government's Ministry of Citizenship, Culture and Recreation.

Emerging Artists Awards

Subjects: The awards rotate among the disciplines of visual arts, crafts, design, and dance, media arts and literature, and theatre and music.
Eligibility: Recipients are chosen from a selection of grant applications recommended by Ontario Arts Council juries.
Purpose: To support projects that advance an individual's career.
Type: Award.
No. of awards offered: Varies.
Frequency: Annual.
Value: Individual projects in theatre (C$7,500) and music (C$7,500)..
Application Procedure: Please write for details.

Heinz Unger Award

Subjects: Conducting.
Eligibility: The Ontario Arts Council manages the selection process. A winner is chosen every two years by peer assessment from among nominations put forward by the Association of Canadian Orchestras.
Level of Study: Professional development.
Purpose: The award, established by the York Concert Society to honour the memory of their music director Heinz Unger, recognises the accomplishments of young to mid-career conductors.
Type: Award.
No. of awards offered: Varies.
Frequency: Every two years.
Application Procedure: Please write for details.

The John Hirsch Memorial Fund for the John Hirsch Director's Award

Subjects: Theatre direction.
Eligibility: The Ontario Arts Council manages the selection process. The winner is chosen through nomination and peer assessment.
Level of Study: Professional development.
Purpose: Established by a bequest to the Ontario Arts Council from the late John Hirsch, one of Canada's most distinguished directors, the award is presented to the most promising theatre director in Ontario.
Type: Award.
No. of awards offered: Varies.
Frequency: Every three years.
Application Procedure: Please write for details.

The Leslie Bell Scholarship Fund for Choral Conducting

Subjects: Conducting.
Eligibility: Open to Ontario choral conductors. The selection process is administered by the Ontario Choral Federation.
Level of Study: Professional development.
Purpose: Awarded to an Ontario choral conductor.
Type: Scholarship.
No. of awards offered: 1.

Frequency: Every two years.
Application Procedure: Please write for details.

The Orford String Quartet Scholarship

Subjects: Chamber music.
Eligibility: Open to a Canadian citizen or landed immigrant and resident of Ontario, or an Ontario-based arts organisation. Residents are generally defined as persons who have been living in Ontario for at least eight months. The Ontario Arts Council manages the selection process. The recipient is chosen by peer assessment from nominations submitted by fourteen Canadian universities and conservatories.
Level of Study: Professional development.
Purpose: To assist a Canadian string musician with studies, commissions or performances related to work in chamber music.
Type: Scholarship.
No. of awards offered: Varies.
Frequency: Every two years.
Value: C$2,000.
Application Procedure: Please write for details.

The Paul de Hueck and Norman Walford Career Achievement Awards

Subjects: Keybard artistry, singing, art photography.
Eligibility: The Ontario Arts Council will manage the selection process. In general, if you are an individual artist who is a Canadian citizen or landed immigrant and resident of Ontario, or an Ontario-based arts organisation, you can apply for an OAC grant. Residents are generally defined as persons who have been living in Ontario for at least eight months. If you are unsure about your eligibility for an OAC grant, contact OAC. If you are an individual applying for an OAC grant, you must be recognised as a professional practising artist by other artists working in the same field, have completed basic training (formal or informal) in your field(s), spend a significant amount of time practising your art and seek payment for your work.
Level of Study: Professional development.
Purpose: To recognise the achievement of outstanding Canadian artists in keyboard artistry, singing and art photography.
Type: Award.
No. of awards offered: Varies.
Application Procedure: Please write for details.

The Ruth Schartz Children's Book Award

Subjects: Writing (children's books).
Eligibility: The short list of books is selected by the Canadian Booksellers Association, and the winners are chosen by juries of school children, from a school selected by the Ontario Arts Council.
Level of Study: Professional development.
Purpose: Awarded for excellence in children's books.
Type: Award.
No. of awards offered: 2.
Frequency: Annual.

Value: Picture books (C$3,000); young adult/middle readers (C$2,000).
Application Procedure: Please write for details.

Tim Sims Encouragement Fund

Subjects: Comedy.
Eligibility: The winner is selected by a jury composed of members of the comedy community, from nominations..
Level of Study: Professional development.
Purpose: To support promising comedic performers in the early stages of their comedy careers.
Type: Award.
Frequency: Annual.
Application Procedure: Please write for details.

ONTARIO MINISTRY OF EDUCATION AND TRAINING

PO Box 4500
189 Red River Road
4th Floor, Thunder Bay, ON, P7B 6G9, Canada
Tel: (1) 800 465 3957
Fax: (1) 807 343 7278
www: http://edu.gov.on.ca
Contact: G Vibert, OGS Officer

Ontario Graduate Scholarship Programme

Subjects: All subjects.
Eligibility: Open to Canadian residents with an overall A average or equivalent during the previous two years of study. Sixty awards may be allocated to students holding a student authorisation.
Level of Study: Doctorate, Postgraduate.
Purpose: To encourage excellence in graduate studies.
Type: Scholarship.
No. of awards offered: 1,300.
Frequency: Annual.
Value: Approximately C$3,953 per term.
Length of Study: 2 or 3 consecutive terms of full-time graduate study; students must reapply each year and may receive a maximum of 4 awards.
Study Establishment: An Ontario university.
Country of Study: Canada.
Application Procedure: Candidates currently registered in a university in Ontario must submit their applications and supporting documentation through that institution.
Closing Date: November 15th.
Additional Information: Students may hold another award up to C$5,000 and may accept research assistantships or part-time teaching or demonstrating appointments, providing that the total amount paid to the Scholars within the period of the award shall not interfere with their status as full-time graduate students. The total time spent by the student in connection with such an appointment, including preparation, marking examinations, etc., must not exceed an average of ten hours per week.

OPEN SOCIETY FOUNDATION - SOFIA

1 Balsha Street
Block 9, Sofia, 1408, Bulgaria
Tel: (359) 2 919 329
Fax: (359) 2 951 6348
Email: osfinfo@osf.bg
www: http://www.osf.bg
Contact: Ms Illiana Gyulcheva, Education Consultant

Open Society Sofia Central European University Scholarship

Subjects: Economics, environmental sciences and policy, gender and culture, history, international relations and European studies, human rights, comparative constitutional law, instiutional business law, medieval studies, nationalism, political science, southeast European studies, sociology.
Eligibility: Open to nationals from countries of Central and Eastern Europe and the former Soviet Union.
Level of Study: Doctorate, Graduate, Postgraduate, Research.
Purpose: Contributes to the development of open societies of Central and Eastern Europe and the former Soviet Union by promoting a system of education in which ideas are creatively, critically and comparatively exhausted.
Type: Scholarship.
No. of awards offered: Varies.
Frequency: Annual.
Value: Approximately US$11,000. Covers tuition fees living expenses and travel to and from the teaching site.
Length of Study: 1 year.
Study Establishment: Central European University.
Country of Study: Hungary or Poland.
Application Procedure: Applicants should submit a completed application form, CV, two recommendations, and language proficiency test results by the deadline which is always mid-january preceding the academic year for which they are applying for.
Closing Date: Mid-January.

Open Society Sofia Long-term Grants

Subjects: Arts and humanities, education and teacher training, fine and applied arts, law, information science.
Eligibility: Open to Bulgarian nationals only.
Level of Study: Postdoctorate, Postgraduate, Professional development.
Purpose: To enable attendance and participation in specialised courses abroad for up to 10 months.
Type: Grant.
No. of awards offered: Varies.
Frequency: Rolling basis.
Value: Up to US$3,000.
Length of Study: Up to 10 months.
Country of Study: Any country.

Application Procedure: Please submit a completed application form, CV, list of publications, official invitation from the host institution, description of the programme of study, two references, and a description of the project.
Closing Date: Applications should be submitted no later than 45 days before the beginning of the project.

Open Society Sofia Scholarships for Foreign Scholars

Subjects: Bulgarian history, language, literature, folklore, history of Bulgarian art.
Eligibility: Open to foreign nationals only.
Level of Study: Doctorate, Postdoctorate, Postgraduate.
Purpose: To enable foreign scholars to study in Bulgaria.
Type: Scholarship.
No. of awards offered: Varies.
Frequency: Annual.
Length of Study: 1 academic year.
Country of Study: Bulgaria.
Application Procedure: Applicants must submit a CV, list of publications, a description of the proposed project (up to 3 pages), and a description of the host institution in Bulgaria.

Open Society Sofia Scholarships for Postgraduate Study Abroad

Subjects: Humanities and social sciences.
Eligibility: Open to Bulgarian nationals, who have a university degree, who are under 40 years of age, and who have been accepted to continue their education at a university abroad.
Level of Study: Doctorate, Postdoctorate, Postgraduate.
Purpose: To support Bulgarian nationals who wish to study abroad.
Type: Scholarship.
No. of awards offered: Varies.
Frequency: Annual.
Value: Up to US$7,000 each year.
Length of Study: 1 academic year.
Country of Study: Any country except Eastern Europe.
Application Procedure: Applicants should submit a completed application form, copy of official diploma, two letters of recommendation, a statement of intent, a list of publications, a letter of invitation from a prestigious institution abroad, and proof of financial funds available.
Closing Date: June.

Open Society Sofia Short-term Grants

Subjects: Arts and humanities, education and teacher training, fine and applied arts, law, information science.
Eligibility: Open to Bulgarian nationals only.
Level of Study: Postdoctorate, Postgraduate, Professional development.
Purpose: To enable attendance and participation in specialisation courses abroad.
Type: Grant.
No. of awards offered: Varies.
Frequency: Rolling basis.
Value: Up to US$1,000.

Length of Study: 1-3 months.
Country of Study: Any country.
Application Procedure: Applicants should submit a completed application form, CV, list of publications, official invitation from the host institution, description of the programme of study, two references, and a description of the project.
Closing Date: Applications should be submitted no later than 45 days before the beginning of the project.

Oxford Colleges Hospitality Scheme for East European Scholars

Subjects: All subjects offered by the University of Oxford.
Eligibility: Open to scholars from eastern and central Europe, who have a good knowledge of English and who are in the process of completing work for an advanced degree, or who are working on a book, or a new course of lectures.
Level of Study: Professional development.
Purpose: To enable scholars from eastern and central Europe to work in Oxford libraries or consult Oxford specialists in their subjects.
Type: Scholarship.
No. of awards offered: Up to 6.
Frequency: Annual.
Length of Study: 1-3 months.
Study Establishment: University of Oxford.
Country of Study: United Kingdom.
Application Procedure: Applicants must submit a completed application form, CV, list of publications, and two recommendation letters.
Closing Date: December.

SAFE Competiton for the Écoles Normales Superieures

Subjects: Humanities and social sciences.
Eligibility: Open to Bulgarian nationals only. Applicants must have an excellent knowledge of French, and be under 25 years of age.
Level of Study: Postgraduate.
Purpose: To support graduate and postgraduate study in the, humanities, and social sciences.
Type: Scholarship.
No. of awards offered: 2.
Frequency: Annual.
Length of Study: 2 academic years.
Study Establishment: ENS.
Country of Study: France.
Application Procedure: Applicants should submit a CV, transcripts, statement of intent, three letters of recommendation, a birth certificate, and a list of books to be discussed with the Selecting Committee.
Closing Date: March.

Soros Suplementary Grants Programme (SSGP)

Subjects: Social sciences, humanities, fine and performing arts.
Level of Study: Doctorate, Undergraduate.

Purpose: Assistance of citizens of the countries of central and eastern Europe who are pursuing advanced study within the region but outside of their home countries.
Type: Grant.
No. of awards offered: Varies.
Frequency: Annual.
Country of Study: East European countries, fomer Soviet Union, Mongolia.
Application Procedure: An application form must be completed.
Closing Date: April 15th.

For further information contact:

Open Society Institute-Budapest
Network Scholarships Programs
Soros Supplementary Grants Program
99-2000
Nador utca 11, Budapest, 1051, Hungary

Soros/FCO Chevening Scholarships

Subjects: All subjects offered at Oxford University.
Eligibility: Open to Bulgarian nationals, who have completed five years of university study, who are not older than 28, and who have an excellent knowledge of English.
Level of Study: Postgraduate, Professional development.
Purpose: To support young scholars who wish to use the experience gained from studying in Britain to benefit higher education, research, or public life in their home country.
Type: Scholarship.
No. of awards offered: Up to 6.
Frequency: Annual.
Length of Study: 1 academic year.
Study Establishment: Oxford University.
Country of Study: United Kingdom.
Application Procedure: Applicants must submit a completed application form, a copy of their official diploma, a summary of their dissertation, two confidential evaluation forms, proof of English proficiency, and a list of publications (if any).
Closing Date: January.

University of Warwick Scholarships for East Europe

Subjects: All subjects offered by the University of Warwick.
Eligibility: Open to Bulgarian nationals who have already completed an undergraduate degree. Applicants must have a good command of English and must be under 35 years of age.
Level of Study: Postgraduate.
Purpose: To support postgraduate study.
Type: Scholarship.
No. of awards offered: Up to 4.
Frequency: Annual.
Length of Study: 1 year.
Study Establishment: University of Warwick.
Country of Study: United Kingdom.

Application Procedure: Application form must be completed and submitted with two letters of recommendation, and evidence of English proficiency.
Closing Date: February.

ORGANIZATION OF AMERICAN HISTORIANS (OAH)

112 N Bryan Street, Bloomington, IN, 47408-4199, United States of America
Tel: (1) 812 855 9852
Fax: (1) 812 855 0696
Email: kara@oah.org
Contact: Ms Kara Hamm, Award and Prize Committee Co-ordinator

The Organization of American Historians was founded in 1907 as the Mississippi Valley Historical Association and originally focused on the history of the Mississippi Valley. Now national in scope and, with approximately 12,000 members, it is the largest professional organization created and sustained for the investigation, study and teaching of American history.

ABC-Clio America: History and Life Award

Subjects: American History.
Purpose: To recognise and encourage scholarship in American history in the journal literature advancing new perspectives on accepted interpretations or previously unconsidered topics.
Type: Award.
No. of awards offered: 1.
Frequency: Every two years.
Value: US$750.
Application Procedure: Individuals as well as editors are encouraged to submit nominations. Each entry must be published during the year before the award is given. One copy of each entry must be received by each member of the award committee by the deadline.
Closing Date: November 15th.

For further information contact:

Department of History
CB #3195
Hamilton Hall
University of North Carolina at Chapel Hill, Chapel Hill, NC, 27599, United States of America
Contact: Dr Harry Watson
or
Department of History
University of Oregon, Eugene, OR, 97403-1288, United States of America
Contact: Professor Louise C Wade
or
Amreican Studies/ Industrial and Labor Relations
290 Ives Hall
Cornell University, Ithaca, NY, 14853, United States of America

Contact: Professor Nick Salvatore, Committee Chair
or
Department of History
219 O'Shaughnessy
University of Notre Dame, Notre Dame, IN, 46556, United States of America
Contact: Professor John T McGreevy
or
ABC-Clio Inc
Box 1911, Santa Barbara, CA, 93116-1911, United States of America
Contact: Ms Angela Sturgeon
or
Department of History
309 Gregory Hall
University of Illinois at Urbana-Champaign
810 South Wright Street, Urbana, IL, 61801, United States of America
Contact: Professor Vernon Burton

Avery O Craven Award

Subjects: The Civil War.
Purpose: Awarded for the most original book on the coming of the Civil War, the Civil War years, or the Era of Reconstruction, with the exception of works of purely military history. The exception recognises and reflects the Quaker convictions of Craven, President of the Organisation of American Historians 1963-64.
Type: Award.
No. of awards offered: 1.
Frequency: Annual.
Value: US$500.
Application Procedure: Publishers are urged to enter one or more books in the competition. Each entry must be published during the period January 1st through to December 31st of the year before the award is given. One copy of each entry must be received by each member of the prize committee by October 1st of the year the entry must be published. Final page proof is submitted, a bound copy of the entry must be submitted no later than January 7th.
Closing Date: October 1st.

For further information contact:

Department of History
Emory University, Atlanta, GA, 30322, United States of America
Contact: Professor James L Roark, Committee Chair
or
Department of History
Boston University
226 Bay State Road, Boston, MA, 02215, United States of America
Contact: Professor Nina Silber
or
Department of History
Hamilton Hall
CS #3195

University of North Carolina, Chapel Hill, NC, 27599, United States of America
Contact: Professor William L Barney

Elliot Rudwick Prize

Subjects: History.
Purpose: To award a book on the experience of racial and ethnic minorities in the United States.
Type: Prize.
No. of awards offered: 1.
Frequency: Every two years.
Value: US$2000 and a certificate.
Application Procedure: Each entry must be published during the two year period January 1st through to December 31st of the following year. One copy of each entry must be received by each member of the prize committee by September 1st of the year the entry must be published. Final page proofs may be used for books to be published after September 1st and before January 1st. If a final page proof is submitted, a bound copy of the entry must be submitted no later than January 7th.
Closing Date: September 1st.
Additional Information: Next award will be given in 2001.

For further information contact:

Department of History
Social Sciences Building 256
University of Southern California, Los Angeles, CA, 90089-0034, United States of America
Contact: Professor George J Sanchez, Committee Chair
or
Department of History
Stanford University, Stanford, CA, 94305, United States of America
Contact: Professor Gordon H Chang
or
Department of History
Stetson Hall
Williams College, Williamstown, MA, 01267, United States of America
Contact: Professor Charles B Dew

Ellis W Hawley prize

Subjects: Political economy, politics, or institutions of the United States in its domestic or international affairs, from the Civil War to the present.
Eligibility: Eligible works shall include book length historical studies, written in English published during a given calendar year.
Purpose: To award the best book-length historical study of political economy, politics, or institutions of the United States in its domestic or international affairs, from the Civil War to the present.
Type: Prize.
No. of awards offered: 1.
Frequency: Annual.
Value: US$500, with a certificate of merit.

Application Procedure: One copy of each entry must be received by each member of the award committee by October 1st.
Closing Date: October 1st.

For further information contact:

H-Net Humanities OnLine
Michigan State University
310 Auditorium Building, East Lansing, MI, 48824-1120, United States of America
Contact: Dr Mark L Kornbluh
or
Department of History
University of California, Santa Barbara, CA, 93106, United States of America
Contact: Professor Laura Kalman
or
Department of History
University of Northern Carolina
Wilmington
403 South College Road, Wilmington, NC, 28403, United States of America
Contact: Professor Otis L Graham, Committee Chair

The Erik Barnouw Award

Subjects: American History.
Purpose: To recognise outstanding reporting or programming on network or cable television, or in documentary film, concerned with American history, the study of American history, or the promotion of history.
Type: Award.
No. of awards offered: 1 or 2.
Frequency: Annual.
Application Procedure: Each entry must be submitted on half inch video cassette. One copy of each entry must be received by each committee member by December 1st. Instructions regarding the prferred medium in which you would like the film shown, should it win, must be included with the copy of the film sent to the chair of the committee; otherwise, the half inch video cassette sent to the chair will be used for the screening at the annual meeting.
Closing Date: December 1st.

For further information contact:

2013 Woodtrail Drive, Columbia, SC, 29210, United States of America
Contact: Dr Barbara A Woods
or
Department of History
219 Mclever Building
PO Box 26170
University of North Carolina- Greensboro, Greensboro, NC, 27402-6170, United States of America
Contact: Professor Steven Lawson

or
Department of History
University of North Carolina at Wilmington, Wilmington, NC,
28403-3297, United States of America
Contact: Dr Robert Brent Toplin, Committee Chair

Foreign-Language Article Prize

Subjects: Concerned with past, issues of continuity and
change, also with events or processes that began, developed
or ended in what is now the United States.
Eligibility: The article should be concerned with the past
(recent or distant) or with issues of continuity and change. It
should be concerned with events or processes that began,
developed, or ended in what is now the United States.
Comparative and international studies that fall within these
guidelines are welcomed. This prize is not open to articles
whose manuscripts were originally submitted for publication
in English or by other people for whom English is their first
language.
Purpose: A prize for the best article on American History
published in a foreign language.
Type: Prize.
No. of awards offered: 1.
Frequency: Annual.
Value: us$750.
Application Procedure: Authors of eligible articles are invited
to nominate their work. Scholars who know of eligible
publications written by others are urged to inform others of
the prize. Please write a one to two page essay in English
explaining why the article is a significant and original
contribution to our understanding of American history. Send
five copies of the article by May 1st to Professor David
Thelen. The application should include the following
information: name, mailing address, institutional affiliation, fax
number and internet address if available, and language of
submitted article.
Closing Date: May 1st.

For further information contact:

Journal of American History
1215 East Atwater, Bloomington, IN, 47401, United States of
America
Contact: Professor David Thelen, Chair, Foreign-Language
Article Prize Committee

Foreign-Language Book Prize

Subjects: Concerned with the past, or with issues of
continuity and change, also concerned with events or
processes that began, developed, or ended in what is now
the United States.
Eligibility: This prize is not open to books whose manuscripts
were originally submitted for publication in English or by
people for whom English is their first language.
Purpose: To award the best book on American history
published in a foreign language.
Type: Prize.
No. of awards offered: 1.
Frequency: Annual.

Value: US$1000.
Application Procedure: Authors of eligible books are invited
to nominate their work. Scholars who know of eligible
publications written by others are urged to inform those
authors of the prizes. Please write a two page essay in
English explaining why the book is a significant and original
contribution to our understanding of American history. Send it
and four copies of the book by May 1st to Foreign-Language
Book Prize Committee at the main address.
Closing Date: May 1st.

Frederick Jackson Turner Award

Subjects: History.
Eligibility: The work must be the first book-length study of
history published by the author; if the author has a PhD,
he/she must have received it no earlier than seven years prior
to submission of the manuscript for publication; the work
must be published in the calendar year before the award is
given; the work must deal with some signifacant phase of
American history.
Purpose: To award an author's first book on some significant
phase of American history and also to the press that
publishes it.
Type: Award.
No. of awards offered: 1.
Frequency: Annual.
Value: A medal, a certificate and US$1000.
Application Procedure: Publishers are urged to enter one or
more books to the competition. Each entry must be published
in the period January through to December of the year before
the award is given. One copy of each entry must be received
by each member of the award committee by September 1st
of the same year the book is published. Final page proofs
may be used for books to be published after September 1st
and before January 1st. If the final page proof is submitted, a
bound copy of the entry must be submitted no later than
January 7th.
Closing Date: September 1st.

For further information contact:

Queen's College
High Street, Oxford, OX1 4AW, England
Contact: Professor Alan Brinkley
or
Department of History
New York University
53 Washington Square South, New York, NY, 10012-1098,
United States of America
Contact: Professor Karen Ordahl Kupperman
or
Department of history
Stanford University, Stanford, CA, 94305-2024, United States
of America
Contact: Professor George M Frederickson, Committee Chair

Horace Samuel and Marion Galbraith Merrill Travel Grants in Twentieth Century American Political History

Subjects: History, American political history.
Purpose: To promote access of younger scholars to the Washington region's rich primary source collections in late 19th and 20th century American political history.
Type: Grant.
Value: US$500-US$3,000.
Application Procedure: There is no standard application form. The complete application should not exceed ten pages: Include name, address, phone numbers, social security number, institutional affiliation when appropriate, project title, a project abstract not to exceed one hundred words, and total amount requested; in one thousand words or less describe the project's goals, methods and intended results. Submit a standard résumé of academic experience and achievements; indicate how the requested funds will be spent and the extent of matching funds avaiable; graduate students must include two letters of reference from people familiar with their academic work.
Closing Date: January 8th.

Huggins-Quarles Awards

Subjects: History.
Eligibility: Minority graduate students at the dissertation resarch stage of their PhD.
Level of Study: Postgraduate.
Purpose: To encourage minority graduate students at the dissertation research stage of their PhD programmes.
Type: Award.
Frequency: Annual.
Value: The amount requested should not exceed US$1,000.
Application Procedure: Students should submit a brief two page abstract of the dissertation project, along with a one page budget explaining the travel and research plans for the funds requested. Each application must be accompanied by a letter from the dissertation adviser attesting to the student's status and the ways in which the Huggins Quarles Award will facilitate the completion of the dissertation project.
Closing Date: January 8th.

Indiana Univeristy - OAH Minority Fellowships

Subjects: American history.
Eligibility: Applicants must be planning to work towards a PhD. In return for the tuition and support recipients will serve two years as interns with an OAH publication or committee and a third as an associate instructor in Indiana University's history department. Interviews for finalists will be scheduled at Indiana University and the OAH Business Office.
Level of Study: Graduate.
Purpose: To enable beginning, minority graduate students in American history to undertake fellowships.
Type: Fellowship.
Frequency: Annual.
Value: Tuition and support for five years.
Length of Study: 5 years.
Application Procedure: Please contact the OAH for details.

James A Rawley Prize

Subjects: History.
Purpose: To award a book dealing with the history of race relations in the United States.
Type: Prize.
No. of awards offered: 1.
Frequency: Annual.
Value: The author of the winning book will receive US$750 and a certificate.
Application Procedure: Each entry must be published in the period January 1st through to December 31st in the year before the award is given. One copy of each entry must be received by each member of the prize committee by October 1st of the year the entry must be published. Final page proofs may be used for books to be published after October 1st and before January 1st. If a final page proof is submitted, a bound copy of the entry must be submitted, a bound copy of the entry must be submitted no later than January 7th.
Closing Date: October 1st.

For further information contact:

School of English and American Studies
University of East Anglia, Norwich, NR4 7TJ, England
Contact: Mr Adam Fairclough, Committee Chair
or
Department of history
Depauw University, Greencastle, IN, 46135, United States of America
Contact: Mr John Dittmer
or
6924 Pineway, Hyattsville, MD, 20782, United States of America
Contact: Mr Louis R Harlan

Japanese Residencies for US Historians

Subjects: US history.
Level of Study: Research.
Purpose: To strengthen international comparative work, to enrich opportunities to engage significant research and to strengthen the study of US history in Japanese universities.
Type: Residency.
No. of awards offered: 3.
Frequency: Annual.
Value: The award covers round trip airfare to Japan, housing, and modest daily expenses.
Country of Study: Japan.
Application Procedure: Please contact John Dichtl, Assistant Executive Director, Organization of American Historians. Tel: 1 812 855 7345; email john@oah.org.
Additional Information: These short term fellowships are contingent on funding. Historians in residency are expected to enter into the life of their host university during the course of their brief visit by offering lectures or other public presentations, participating in symposia where appropriate, and consulting with faculty and students.

Lerner-Scott Prize

Subjects: US women's history.
Purpose: To award the best doctoral dissertation in US women's history.
Type: Prize.
No. of awards offered: 1.
Frequency: Annual.
Value: US$1000 and a certificate.
Application Procedure: A dissertation must be completed between July and June and be received by November 1st. Each application must contain a letter of support from a faculty member at the degree granting institution, along with an abstract, table of contents and sample chapter from the dissertation. Please also include email addresses for the applicants and the adviser if available. One complete copy of each entry must be received by each member of the prize committee by November 1st.
Closing Date: November 1st.

For further information contact:

Sclesinger Library
Radcliffe College
10 Garden Street, Cambridge, MA, 02138, United States of America
Contact: Ms Susan Ware
or
401 Bowling Avenue Suite 77, Nashville, TN, 37205, United States of America
Contact: Ms Elisabeth I Perry, Committee Chair
or
Department of History
Washington state University, Pullman, WA, 99164-4030, United States of America
Contact: Ms Susan Armitage

Louis Pelzer Memorial Award

Subjects: History.
Purpose: To invite candidates for graduate degrees to submit essays for the Award competition.
Type: Award.
Frequency: Annual.
Value: The winning essay will be published in the 'Journal of American History'. The organisation offers US$500 award, certificate and a medal to the winner.
Application Procedure: Essays should be submitted in quintuplicate and should not exceeds 7,000 words in length. The footnotes which should be assembled at the end of the text should be triple-spaced. Because the manuscrits are judged anonymously, the author's name and gradute programme should appear only on a separate cover page. Manuscripts should be addressed to Professor David Thelen.
Closing Date: November 30th.

For further information contact:

Loius Pelzer Memorial Awrd Committee
Journal of American History
1215 East Atwater Avenue, Bloomington, IN, 47401, United States of America
Contact: Professor David Thelen

Mary K Bonsteel Tachau Pre-Collegiate Teaching Award

Subjects: History.
Eligibility: Pre-collegiate teachers engaged at least half time in history teaching, whether in history or social studies, are eligible. Successful candidates shall demonstrate exceptional ability in one or more of the following kinds of activities: initiating or participating in projects which involve students in historical research, writing, or other means of representing their knowledge of history; initiating or participating in school, district, regional, state, or national projects which enhance the professional development of history teachers; initiating or participating in projects which aim to build bridges between pre-collegiate and collegiate history or social studies researchers; working with museums, historical preservation societies or other public history associations to enhance the place of public history in pre-collegiate and schools; developing innovative history criteria which foster a spirit of enquiry and emphasise critical skills; publishing or otherwise publicly presenting scholarship that advances history education or historical knowledge.
Purpose: To recognise the contributions made by pre-collegiate teachers to improve history education.
Type: Award.
No. of awards offered: 1.
Frequency: Annual.
Value: A certifcate, a cash award of US$750, a one-year OAH membership and one year subscription to the OAH Magazine of History. If the winner is an OAH member, the award will include a one-year renewal of membership in the awardee's usual membership category. Finally, the winner's school will receive a plaque suitable for permanent public display.
Application Procedure: Candidate's may be nominated by any person familiar with the nominee's professional accomplishments or standing. If candidates nominate themselves, one professional reference must submit a two-page letter indicating why the teacher merits the Tachau Pre-Collegiate Teaching Award. Applicants should submit one application packet (no more than 25 double-spaced pages) that includes copies of the following in the order given: a cover letter written by a colleague indicating why the teacher merits the Tachau Pre-Collegiate Teaching Award (no more than two pages); curriculum vitae (no more than five pages); samples of the nominee's written work. These submissions should include article reprints, reports by classroom observers, course outlines, research proposals, and/or other evidence of excellence in some or all the areas mentioned in the eligibility (no more than fifteen pages); a narrative, prepared by the nominee, describing the goals and effects of the candidate's work in the classroom and elsewhere for history education (no more than three pages); names addresses and telephone numbers of at least three professional references, including the writer of the cover letter, at least one of whom must be a colleague or supervisor (one page). One copy of each entry must be mailed directly to each committee member.
Closing Date: December 1st.

For further information contact:

603 Fayerweather Hall
MC 2538
Columbia University, New York, NY, 10027, United States of
America
Contact: Professor Kenneth T Jackson
or
Faifax High School
3500 Old Lee Highway, Fairfax, VA, 22030, United States of
America
Contact: Dr Linda Karen Miller
or
32 Donellan Road, Scarsdale, NY, 10583, United States of
America
Contact: Mr Eric Rothschild, Committee

Merle Curti Award in American Intellectual History

Subjects: History.
Purpose: To recognise books in the field of American
intellectual history.
Type: Award.
No. of awards offered: 1.
Frequency: Every two years next 2001.
Value: US$1000, a certificate and a medal.
Application Procedure: Publishers are urged to enter one or
more books in the competition. A copy of each entry must be
mailed directly to the committee members.
Closing Date: October 1st.

For further information contact:

16 Linden Lane, Old Westbury, NY, 11568, United States of
America
Contact: Professor David S Reynolds
or
Department of History
364 Rush Rhees Library
University of Rochester, Rochester, NY, 14627, United States
of America
Contact: Professor Robert Westbrook
or
Department of History
MS 036
Brandeis University, Waltham, MA, 02254, United States of
America
Contact: Professor James T Kloppenberg, Committee Chair

Merle Curti Award in American Social History

Subjects: History.
Purpose: To recognise books in the field of American social
history.
Type: Award.
No. of awards offered: 1.
Frequency: Every two years (even-numbered years).
Value: US$1000, a certificate and a medal.

Application Procedure: Publishers are urged to enter one or
more books in the competition. Each entry must be published
during the two year period January 1st through to December
31st in the year before the award is given. One copy of each
entry must be mailed directly to the committee members
Professor Leon Fink and Professor Judith Sealander.
Closing Date: October 1st.

For further information contact:

Department of History
Bowling Green State University, Bowling Green, OH, 43403,
United States of America
Contact: Professor Judith Sealander
or
Charles Warren Center
Robinson Hall
Harvard University, Cambridge, MA, 02138-6529, United
States of America
Contact: Professor Leon Fink

OAH Awards and Prizes

Subjects: American history.
Eligibility: Open to applicants of any nationality.
Level of Study: Unrestricted.
Purpose: To recognise scholarly and professional
achievement in the field of American history.
Frequency: Varies, depending on award, some are annual
whilst others are biennial.
Value: Varies, depending on award.
Application Procedure: Fliers for each award may be
obtained from the OAH office. The names and addresses of
committee members are listed and submissions are sent
directly to these members. There are no application forms to
fill out and no application fees.
Closing Date: Deadlines vary.

Ray Allen Billington Prize

Subjects: American Frontier History.
Purpose: To award the best book in American frontier history,
defined broadly so as to include the pioneer periods of all
geographical areas and comparisons between American
frontiers and others.
Type: Award.
No. of awards offered: 1.
Frequency: Every two years.
Value: US$1000, a certificate and a medal.
Application Procedure: Each entry must be published during
the two year period before the award is given. One copy of
each entry must be received by each member of the prize
committee by October 1st of the second year of the two-year
period. Final page proofs may be used for books to be
published after October 1st and before January 1st. If a final
page proof is submitted , a bound copy of the entry must be
submitted no later than January 7th.
Closing Date: October 1st.
Additional Information: Next awarded in 2001.

For further information contact:

Department of History
Northwestern University
1881 Sheridan Road, Evanston, IL, 60208, United States of America
Contact: Professor James H Merrel
or
Mountain West Center
UMC 0735
Utah State University, Logan, UT, 84322-0735, United States of America
Contact: Dr Clyde A Milner II, Director
or
Department of History
Stanford University, Stanford, CA, 94305, United States of America
Contact: Professor Richard White

Richard W Leopold Prize

Subjects: Foreign policy, military affairs broadly construed, the historical activities of the federal government or biography in one of the foregoing areas.
Eligibility: The winner must have been employed in a government position for the last five years. If the author has accepted an academic position, the book must have been published within two years from the time of the change.
Purpose: To improve contacts and interrelationships within the historical profession, where an increasing number of history-trained scholars hold distinguished positions in governmental agencies. It is awarded to the best book written by a historian connected with federal, state or municipal government.
Type: Prize.
No. of awards offered: 1.
Frequency: Every two years.
Value: US$1500 and a certificate.
Application Procedure: Each entry must be published during the two year period before the award is given. One copy of each entry must be received by each member of the prize committee by September 1st of the second year of the two-year period in which the entry must be published.
Closing Date: September 1st.

For further information contact:

108 West 41st Street, Austin, Texas, 78751, United States of America
Contact: Professor Penny M Von Eschen
or
Academic and International Affairs
212 Allen Building
Duke University, Durham, NC, 27708, United States of America
Contact: Professor Bruce R Kuniholm, Vice Provost

or
Department of History
450 McGraw Hall
Cornell University, Ithaca, NY, 14853-4601, United States of America
Contact: Professor Tim Borstelmann, Committee Chair

ORGANIZATION OF AMERICAN STATES (OAS)

1889 'F' Street NW, Washington, DC, 20006-3897, United States of America
Tel: (1) 202 458 3446
Fax: (1) 202 458 3897
www: http://www.oas.org
Contact: Mr Colin E Martinez, Information Officer

PRA Fellowships

Subjects: All fields except medicine and related fields and languages.
Eligibility: Candidates must be a citizen or permanent resident of an OAS member state, and hold a university degree or have demonstrated ability to pursue advanced studies in the chosen field.
Level of Study: Postgraduate.
Purpose: To promote the economic, social scientific and cultural development of the member states in order to acheive a stronger bond and better understanding among the peoples of the Americas.
Type: Fellowship.
No. of awards offered: Varies.
Frequency: Annual.
Length of Study: From 3 months to 2 years.
Study Establishment: The candidate must choose the university or study centre in their chosen country of study and make the necessary contacts to secure acceptance.
Country of Study: Any member country of the OAS.
Application Procedure: The fellowship form must be presented to the General Secretariat of the OAS through the official channels established by each government. US citizens can send applications directly to OAS headquarters in Washington, DC.
Closing Date: March 1st.

ORIENTAL CERAMIC SOCIETY

30B Torrington Square, London, WC1E 7JL, England
Tel: (44) 171 636 7985
Fax: (44) 171 580 6749
Contact: Ms Jean Martin

The Oriental Ceramic Society was established in 1921 and aims to increase the knowledge and appreciation of Asian ceramics and other arts. The Society is open to anyone interested in the arts of Asia. Membership is worldwide, and meetings, lectures and exhibitions are held regularly.

George De Menasce Memorial Trust Bursary

Subjects: Any aspect of oriental art.
Eligibility: There are no restrictions, but funds are limited.
Level of Study: Unrestricted.
Purpose: To promote research.
Type: Bursary.
No. of awards offered: 1.
Frequency: Dependent on funds available.
Value: £1,500.
Country of Study: Any country.
Application Procedure: Please write for details.
Additional Information: The recipient is required to read a paper on the research undertaken. Applicants are required to complete a form giving complete academic qualifications. Research connected with a PhD degree is not normally considered adequate for the Bursary.

PACIFIC CULTURAL FOUNDATION

38 Chungking South Road
Section 3, Taipei, Taiwan
Tel: (886) 2 3377155
Fax: (886) 2 3377167
www: http://ats.edu/faculty/spons/P0000307.HTM
Contact: Academic Section

Pacific Cultural Foundation Grants in Chinese Studies

Subjects: Chinese culture, history and contemporary Chinese problems.
Eligibility: Open to candidates who hold at least a Master's degree and who are citizens from any country except the Republic of China. Applicants for Writing Grants must have previously written in English at least one work of 30,000 words or more which has been published in book form or in a journal.
Level of Study: Postgraduate.
Purpose: To encourage foreign scholars in the free world to pursue further research.
Type: Grant.
No. of awards offered: Approx. 80.
Frequency: Annual.
Value: Up to US$10,000.
Length of Study: 1 year; not renewable, though an extension may be given.
Country of Study: Any country.
Application Procedure: Application form must be completed.
Closing Date: March 1st, September 1st.

PALOMA O'SHEA SANTANDER INTERNATIONAL PIANO COMPETITION

Calle Hernán Cortés 3, Santander, E-39003, Spain
Tel: (34) 942 31 14 51
Fax: (34) 942 31 48 16
Email: ccpianoak@mundivia.es
Contact: Secretariat General

Paloma O'Shea Santander International Piano Competition

Subjects: Piano performance.
Eligibility: Open to pianists of any nationality. The age limit is 29 years.
Level of Study: Unrestricted.
Type: Competition.
No. of awards offered: 7.
Frequency: Every three years.
Value: First Prize and Gold Medal: 6,000,000 Pesetas, a Kawai piano, recordings and concerts on various continents with presentations in important music capitals; Second Prize and Silver Medal: 2,500,000 Pesetas, concerts in Spain and other European countries; Finalist Prize and Bronze Medal: 1,000,000 Pesetas and concerts in Spain; 3 Semi-finalist Prizes: 500,000 Pesetas each; Audience Prize: Sony equipment valued at 2,000,000 Pesetas.
Length of Study: July 27th to August 7th, 2001.
Study Establishment: The preselections take place in London, Paris, Berlin, New York and Madrid. The semi finals and the finals take place in Santander.
Country of Study: Spain, England, France, Germany and the US.
Application Procedure: Please contact the Secretariat General for details.
Closing Date: December 15th 2000.
Additional Information: Representation in America: Mrs Brookes McIntyre, 1401 Brickell Avenue, Suite 1200, Miami, FL 33131, USA. Tel: (1) 305 530 29 10; Fax: (1) 305 530 29 05. In general 20 applicants are chosen to take part in the preselections, which are recorded and filmed on video. Out of them 6 participants are chosen for the semi-finals, and later 3 participants go through to the finals.

PAUL LOWIN TRUST

Perpetual Trustee Company Limited
39 Hunter Street, Sydney, NSW, 2000, Australia
Tel: (61) 2 9229 9000
Fax: (61) 2 9229 1957
Email: foundations@perpetual.com.au
www: http://www.perpetual.com.au
Contact: Administration Charitable Planning Services

Perpetual Trustee Company Limited is a member of the listed perpetual Group, the largest trustee company in Australia. We Currently manage over 240 charitable trusts and foundations with a combined value of over A$450 million.

Paul Lowin Awards

Subjects: Music composition - orchestral works; song cycles.
Eligibility: Open to Australian citizens over 18 years of age.
Level of Study: Unrestricted.
Purpose: To recognise original composition.
Type: Prize.
No. of awards offered: 2.
Frequency: Every two years.
Value: Orchestral prize A$25,000; song cycle prize A$15,000.
Country of Study: Any country.
Application Procedure: Please write for details.

PAUL MELLON CENTRE FOR STUDIES IN BRITISH ART, LONDON

16 Bedford Square, London, WC1B 3JA, England
Tel: (44) 171 580 0311
Fax: (44) 171 636 6730
www: http://www.cis.yale.edu/yups/bac/entrance.html
Contact: Director

The Paul Mellon Centre for Studies in British Art is an art and architectural research institution, based in London but part of Yale University.

Paul Mellon Centre Grants

Subjects: Any aspect of British art or architecture before 1960.
Eligibility: Open to candidates of any nationality.
Level of Study: Postdoctorate, Professional development.
Purpose: To support scholarship in British art or architecture and to disseminate knowledge through publications, exhibitions and educational programmes.
Type: Grant.
No. of awards offered: Varies, usually 15-20.
Frequency: Annual.
Value: £5,00 to £20,000 curatorial research, publication and educational grants.
Length of Study: Maximum 1 academic year.
Country of Study: United Kingdom.
Application Procedure: Candidates should submit: name, address and telephone number; outline proposal of not more than 3 pages; detailed breakdown of estimated costs and proposed completion and/or publication date, where appropriate; CV; and three letters of recommendation sent directly to the PMC in London.
Closing Date: September 15th.

PEN AMERICAN CENTER

568 Broadway, New York, NY, 10012, United States of America
Tel: (1) 212 334 1660
Fax: (1) 212 334 2181
Contact: Ms Victoria Vinton

PEN American Center is a fellowship of writers dedicated to defending free expression and advancing the cause of literature and literacy. The American Center is the largest of 130 international PEN Centers worldwide.

PEN Writers Fund

Subjects: Writing.
Eligibility: Open to US citizens and writers with US publications who are US residents.
Level of Study: Unrestricted.
Purpose: To assist professional published writers facing emergency situations. Grants are not available for any sort of professional development.
Frequency: Every two months.
Value: Grants of up to US$1,000.
Country of Study: Any country.
Application Procedure: Application consists of a two-page form, published writing samples, documentation of financial emergency (bills etc.), and professional resumé.
Additional Information: Approximately 100 writers are assisted each year, and aid is extended within eight weeks of application. A separate fund exists for writers and editors with AIDS in need of emergency assistance. The funds are not for research purposes, to enable writers to complete unfinished projects, or to fund writing publications or organisations; grants and loans are for unexpected emergencies only, and not for the support of working writers. PEN also offers numerous annual awards to recognise distinguished writing, editing and translation.

PETER WHITTINGHAM TRUST

16 Ogle Street, London, W1P 7LG, England
Tel: (44) 171 636 4481
Fax: (44) 171 637 4307
Contact: Administrator

Whittingham Award

Subjects: Popular music or jazz, applications should bear in mind the chosen idiom of such artists as Gershwin, Cole Porter, Jerome Kern, Bernstein, Hamlisch, Sondheim, George Shearing, Art Tatum and Oscar Peterson.
Eligibility: Open to individuals, ordinarily resident in the UK, of any age group, for work independently or with a project-group of any size. The project should be in creation, performance, teaching or research in the field of quality popular music or jazz. Money is not given for course fees.

Level of Study: Postgraduate.
Purpose: To promote both composition and performance in the field of popular music or jazz.
No. of awards offered: 1+.
Frequency: Annual.
Value: From £1,000-£4,000.
Application Procedure: Selected applicants are asked to attend an interview. A written description of the project must be provided together with a budget and a reference.
Closing Date: October.

PETERHOUSE

Peterhouse, Cambridge, CB2 1RD, England
Tel: (44) 1223 338200
Fax: (44) 1223 337578
Contact: The Senior Tutor

Friends of Peterhouse Bursary

Subjects: All subjects except clinical medicine.
Eligibility: Open to those who are required to pay university fees at the overseas rate. Applicants should be under 25 years of age on December 1st in the year in which they hope to come into residence.
Level of Study: Postgraduate.
Purpose: For study for a postgraduate one or two-year taught course as a registered graduate student at Peterhouse.
Type: Bursary.
No. of awards offered: 1.
Frequency: Annual.
Value: University fees only.
Length of Study: 1 year.
Study Establishment: For study at Peterhouse only.
Country of Study: United Kingdom.
Application Procedure: Application form, CV and two references must be submitted.
Closing Date: April 1st.

Peterhouse Research Fellowship

Subjects: All subjects.
Eligibility: Applicants must hold, or be studying for, a degree from Cambridge or Oxford universities.
Level of Study: Postdoctorate.
Purpose: To support a young scholar in postdoctoral research at Peterhouse.
Type: Fellowship.
No. of awards offered: 2-3.
Frequency: Annual.
Value: Maintenance and allowances.
Length of Study: 3 years.
Study Establishment: For study at Peterhouse only.
Country of Study: United Kingdom.
Application Procedure: Application form must be completed.
Closing Date: Early February.

Peterhouse Research Studentship

Subjects: All subjects.
Eligibility: Applicants should be under 25 years of age on December 1st in the year in which they hope to come into residence.
Level of Study: Postgraduate.
Purpose: To study for a PhD at Peterhouse.
Type: Studentship.
No. of awards offered: 2-3.
Frequency: Annual.
Value: Full fees and maintenance subject to deduction of the emoluments.
Length of Study: 3 years.
Study Establishment: For study at Peterhouse only.
Country of Study: United Kingdom.
Application Procedure: Application form, CV and references must be submitted.
Closing Date: April 1st.

PHI BETA KAPPA SOCIETY

1785 Massachusetts Avenue NW
Fourth Floor, Washington, DC, 20036, United States of America
Tel: (1) 202 265 3808
Fax: (1) 202 986 1601
Email: lsurles@pbk.org
www: http://www.pbk.org
Contact: Ms Linda Surles

Mary Isabel Sibley Fellowship

Subjects: French language or literature (even years), Greek language, literature, history, or archaeology (odd years).
Eligibility: Open to unmarried women between the ages of 25 and 35 (inclusive) who have demonstrated their ability to carry out original research. Candidates must hold the doctorate or have fulfilled all the requirements for the doctorate except the dissertation. There are no restrictions as to nationality. Not restricted to members of Phi Beta Kappa.
Level of Study: Doctorate, Postdoctorate, Postgraduate.
Purpose: To recognise women scholars who have demonstrated their ability to carry out original research.
Type: Fellowship.
No. of awards offered: 1.
Frequency: Annual.
Value: US$20,000.
Length of Study: 1 year; not renewable.
Country of Study: Any country.
Application Procedure: Application, transcripts, and references must be submitted. Applications are available from Phi Beta Kappa.
Closing Date: January 15th.

PHILLIPS EXETER ACADEMY

20 Main Street, Exeter, NH, 03833-2460, United States of America
Contact: Mr John O'Herney, Dean of Faculty

Philips Exeter Academy is a private secondary school with over 1,000 students.

George Bennett Fellowship

Subjects: Creative writing.
Eligibility: Preference is given to writers who have not published a book with a major commercial publisher. Work must be in English.
Level of Study: Unrestricted.
Purpose: To allow a person commencing a career as a writer the time and freedom from material considerations to complete a manuscript in progress.
Type: Fellowship.
No. of awards offered: 1.
Frequency: Annual.
Value: US$6,000 per year.
Study Establishment: Phillips Exeter Academy in Exeter, New Hampshire.
Country of Study: USA.
Application Procedure: Send a manuscript, together with an application form, personal statement and US$5.
Closing Date: December 1st for the following academic year.
Additional Information: Duties include being in residence for one academic year while working on the manuscript, and informal availability to student writers. Requests for further information should be accompanied by an SASE.

PITT RIVERS MUSEUM

University of Oxford
South Parks Road, Oxford, OX1 3PP, England
Tel: (44) 1865 284651
Fax: (44) 1865 270943
Email: peter.mitchell@prm.ox.ac.uk
www: http://www.prm.ox.ac.uk
Contact: Dr Peter Mitchell, Secretary of the Swan Fund

James A Swan Fund

Subjects: The Later Stone Age prehistory of Southern Africa and the study of the contemporary Bushman and Pygmy peoples of Africa.
Eligibility: There are no set rules. Most of the successful applicants are graduates but all applications are considered. Two academic references are required.
Level of Study: Doctorate, Graduate, Research.
Purpose: To provide support for research sponsored by the Pitt Rivers Museum on the archaeological, historical, physical and cultural nature of the Bushmen, Pygmies and other 'small peoples' of Africa (primarily field-work).
Type: Research Grant.
No. of awards offered: Varies.
Frequency: Varies.
Value: Varies, but usually in the £500-£2,000 range.
Length of Study: Varies.
Country of Study: Any country.
Application Procedure: There are no application forms. However, each application must consist of three copies of the following: a statement of the proposed research (no more than 2000 words); an itemised budget, indicating which items are for funding from the Swan Fund and details of all other Grant applications; a full CV, including publications; the names and addresses (including email where possible) of two referees. Application should be addressed to the Secretary of the Swan Fund at the Pitt Rivers Museum, South Parks Road, Oxford, OX1 3PP, UK. References should be sent independently to the Secretary at the Swan, by the closing date.
Closing Date: March 1st.
Additional Information: Successful Applicants must acknowledge the Swan Fund in all publication arising from their grant, submit a report of their work to the Secretary of the Fund and provide the Balfour Library of the Pitt Rivers Museum with one copy of all publication, including theses and dissertations.

PITTSBURGH NEW MUSIC ENSEMBLE

School of Music
Duquesne University, Pittsburgh, PA, 15282, United States of America
Tel: (1) 412 261 0554
Fax: (1) 412 396 5479
Contact: Mr David Stock, Conductor

Harvey Garl Composition Contest

Subjects: Music composition.
Eligibility: Open to US citizens only.
Level of Study: Unrestricted.
Purpose: To award a commission for The Pittsburgh New Music Ensemble.
Type: Commission.
No. of awards offered: 1.
Frequency: Every two years.
Value: US$3,000.
Country of Study: USA.
Application Procedure: Please write for an application form.
Closing Date: April 1st.
Additional Information: There is a US$20 application fee.

PLAYMARKET

Independent Newspapers Ltd/Playmarket
PO Box 9767, Wellington, New Zealand
Tel: (64) 4 382 8462
Fax: (64) 4 382 8461
Email: plymkt@clear.net.nz
www: http://www.playmarket.org.nz
Contact: Ms Susan Wilson

Playmarket was founded in 1973 to assist New Zealand playwrights with professional production of their scripts. For twenty-five years Playmarket have offered script assessment, development and agency services. Playmarket are at the heart of New Zealand theatre and its focus is playwrights.

The Sunday Star Times/Bruce Mason Playwriting Award

Subjects: Playwriting.
Eligibility: Open to New Zealand playwrights.
Level of Study: Unrestricted.
Purpose: To recognise achievement at the beginning of a career.
No. of awards offered: 1.
Frequency: Annual.
Value: NZ$5,000.
Length of Study: 1 year.
Country of Study: New Zealand.
Application Procedure: Name, address, plus two references must be submitted. No scripts need to be submitted.
Closing Date: Varies annually.
Additional Information: It is expected that the award will be used to write or complete a work for the theatre.

POLISH EMBASSY

47 Portland Place, London, W1N 3AG, England
Tel: (44) 171 636 6032
Fax: (44) 171 637 2190
Email: pci-lond@pcidir.demon.co.uk
Contact: Ms Marian Dabrouski, Councillor, Science and Education

The Polish Embassy offers grants within the framework of the British-Polish Joint Research Collaboration Programme 1999, which is designed to support joint scientific research.

Polish Embassy Short-Term Bursaries

Subjects: All subjects.
Eligibility: Candidates must be British citizens with a university degree or equivalent qualification, who have some postgraduate research or lecturing experience; preference is given to those undertaking doctoral or postdoctoral work. Married candidates must indicate whether they are prepared to go unaccompanied. Candidates wishing to study Polish philology, Slavonic languages and the history and the geography of Poland must be conversant with Polish or the appropriate Slavonic language.
Level of Study: Doctorate, Postdoctorate, Postgraduate, Professional development.
Purpose: To provide financial support for British students wishing to study in Poland.
Type: Bursary.
No. of awards offered: 40.
Frequency: Annual.
Value: A monthly allowance, free accommodation in student hostels (or possibly in hotels) or a monthly allowance towards accommodation found privately, free meals in a student canteen or a monthly allowance in lieu, a modest book grant, exemption from tuition fees, and free medical care. The Polish authorities will pay for necessary travel expenses within Poland from one academic centre to another; recipients will be required to pay their own fares to and from Poland.
Length of Study: 3-9 months.
Study Establishment: Universities and other institutions of higher education and research.
Country of Study: Poland.
Application Procedure: Please submit completed application form, CV, copy of diploma, research proposal, medical statement, and two letters of recommendation.
Closing Date: March 15th.
Additional Information: The scheme is new under agreement between Poland and the UK on exchanges in the fields of science, humanities and arts. Bursaries cannot normally be taken up during the university summer, except for the summer vacation courses 'Polonicum' and 'Polish Language'.

Polish Government Postgraduate Scholarships Scheme

Subjects: Unrestricted. The following subjects in particular are taught to a high standard in Polish universities - sociology, mathematics, geography and geology, history of Polish architecture, music (performance and composition), the arts and scientific topics.
Eligibility: Candidates must be British citizens with a university degree or equivalent qualification; priority is given to candidates who hold an honours degree and have had some experience of research, laboratory techniques or teaching since graduation. Married candidates must indicate whether they are prepared to go unaccompanied. Candidates wishing to study Polish philology, Slavonic languages and the history and the geography of Poland must be conversant with Polish or the appropriate Slavonic language. Applicants should be under 35 years of age.
Level of Study: Postgraduate, Professional development.
Purpose: To provide financial support for British students wishing to study in Poland.
Type: Scholarship.
Frequency: Annual.
Value: A monthly allowance, free accommodation in student hostels or a monthly allowance towards accommodation found privately, free meals in a student canteen or a monthly allowance in lieu, a modest book grant, exemption from tuition fees, and free medical care.

Length of Study: Periods of up to 10 months. Though applications for shorter periods of study may be considered, preference will be given to those wishing to study for periods of more than 6 months.
Study Establishment: Universities and other institutions of higher education and research.
Country of Study: Poland.
Application Procedure: Completed application form, CV, copy of diploma, research proposal, medical statement, and two letters of recommendation must be submitted. Application forms are obtainable from the Education Officer and should be returned to the Embassy by March 15th.
Closing Date: March 15th.
Additional Information: The scheme is run under agreement between Poland and the UK on exchange in the fields of science, humanities and arts.

Scholarship for Polonicum

Subjects: Polish language course.
Eligibility: Priority in the scholarship allocation will be given to applicants studying either Central European or the Polish language, history and literature.
Type: Scholarship.
No. of awards offered: 5.
Frequency: Annual.
Value: Students provided with accomodation. They will have to pay for their return travel tickets to Poland themselves.
Length of Study: 4 weeks during the summer.
Study Establishment: University of Warsaw, Jagiellonian University in Cracow and the Maria Curie-Skodowska University in Lublin.
Application Procedure: Application forms are available from the Polish Embassy. The completed ˝Polonicum˝ application form(s) of the above mentioned universities participating in the scheme, a covering letter and one letter of reference, should be sent to the Polish Embassy. For further details please contact the Polish Embassy.

PONTIFICAL INSTITUTE OF MEDIEVAL STUDIES

59 Queen's Park Crescent East, Toronto, ON, M5S 2C4, Canada
Tel: (1) 416 926 7290
Fax: (1) 416 926 7276
Email: sheila.campbell@utoronto.ca
Contact: Secretary

Council of the Institute Awards

Subjects: Medieval studies.
Eligibility: Open to scholars engaged in medieval studies.
Level of Study: Postdoctorate.

Purpose: Medieval Studies Licentiate.
Type: Bursary, Scholarship.
No. of awards offered: Varies.
Frequency: Annual.
Value: Varies, dependent on funds available.
Length of Study: 1 year.
Study Establishment: The Institute.
Country of Study: Canada.
Closing Date: March 31st.
Additional Information: The Institute also offers a small number of Research Associateships (without stipend) annually to postdoctoral students and senior scholars who wish to use the Institute library for their research. Applications must be received by January 15th.

PRAGUE SPRING INTERNATIONAL MUSIC COMPETITION

Hellichova 18, Prague, CS-118 00, Czech Republic
Tel: (42) 2 53 34 74
Fax: (42) 2 53 60 40
Email: festival@login.cz
Contact: Mr J Nedvedová

Prague Spring International Music Competition

Subjects: Music - competition categories - 1999 - organ, harpsichord, 2000 - violin, cello, conducting, 2001 - flute, oboe, 2002 - clarinet, bassoon, 2003 - brass instruments.
Eligibility: Open to musicians of any nationality who do not exceed the main age limit of 30 (Age limits: harpsichord 35 years, string quartet 120 years combined, conducting 32 years).
Level of Study: Unrestricted.
Purpose: To encourage and assist outstanding young musicians.
No. of awards offered: 3 main prizes.
Frequency: Annual.
Value: Prizes range from 10,000-120,000 Czech Crowns. Accommodation is paid for those who qualify for the second round and final.
Country of Study: Czech Republic.
Application Procedure: The applicants should enclose an audio tape with a recording of the setting compositions.
Closing Date: December 13th of the year preceding the award.
Additional Information: There is an application fee of US$100.

PREHISTORIC SOCIETY

University College London
Institute of Archaeology
31-34 Gordon Square, London, WC1H 0PY, England
Fax: (44) 171 383 2572
Contact: Administrative Assistant

The Prehistoric Society is open to professionals and amateurs alike and has over 2,000 members worldwide. Its main activities are lectures, study tours and conferences and it publishes an annual journal (PPS) and a triannual newsletter (PAST).

Prehistoric Society Conference Fund

Subjects: Archaeology, especially prehistoric.
Eligibility: Preference is given first to scholars from developing countries, whether they are members of the Society or not, then to Members of the Society not qualified to apply for conference funds available to University staff. Other members of the Society are also eligible.
Level of Study: Postgraduate.
Purpose: To finance attendance at international conferences.
Type: Travel Grant.
No. of awards offered: 2.
Frequency: Annual.
Value: Up to £250.
Length of Study: 1 year; renewals are considered.
Country of Study: Any country.
Closing Date: December 31st.
Additional Information: Recipients are required to submit a short report on the conference to PAST, the Society's newsletter, and their papers for the Society's proceedings if these are not to be included in a conference volume. Forms are available from the Honorary Secretary.

Prehistoric Society Research Fund Grant

Subjects: Prehistoric archaeology.
Eligibility: Open to all members of the Society. The Society may make specific conditions relating to individual applications.
Level of Study: Unrestricted.
Purpose: To further research in prehistory by excavation or other means.
Type: Grant.
No. of awards offered: Varies.
Frequency: Annual.
Value: At the discretion of the Society.
Length of Study: 1 year; reapplications are considered.
Country of Study: Any country.
Application Procedure: Applications should include the names of two referees.
Closing Date: December 31st.
Additional Information: Awards are made on the understanding that a detailed report will be made to the Society as to how the grant was spent.

Research Grant Conference Award

Subjects: Prehistoric archaeology.
Eligibility: There are no restrictions.
Level of Study: Unrestricted.
Purpose: To fund initial projects and visits to conferences.
Frequency: Annual.
Value: Variable (usually under £500).
Application Procedure: Application forms from registered address.
Closing Date: January 1st.

PRINCETON UNIVERSITY

c/o University Registry
The Old Schools, Cambridge, CB2 1TN, England
Tel: (44) 1223 332 317
Fax: (44) 1223 332 332
Email: mrf25@admin.cam.ac.uk
www: http://www.admin.cam.ac.uk
Contact: Ms Melanie Foster, Scholarship Clerk

Procter Visiting Fellowships

Subjects: Fellows will be required to devote themselves to advanced study and investigation in a branch of subjects of one of the liberal arts and sciences, exclusive of professional, technical or commercial subjects.
Eligibility: Open to Commonwealth citizens who hold a first class honours BA or equivalent from a UK university and are able to prove exceptional scholarly power. Preference is normally given to candidates who would be in their second or third year of postgraduate research when, if elected, they take up tenure of the award.
Level of Study: Postgraduate.
Purpose: To support study in the liberal arts and sciences.
Type: Fellowship.
No. of awards offered: 2.
Frequency: Annual.
Value: US$11,600 plus full tuition fees and medical insurance.
Length of Study: 1 year.
Study Establishment: Princeton University, New Jersey.
Country of Study: USA.
Application Procedure: Application forms available on request.
Closing Date: Early December.
Additional Information: The fellowship is normally tenable for one year as a visiting award, but provision also exists exceptionally for a fellow to be nominated for admission to a PhD programme at Princeton. Candidates who wish to be considered for nomination for the PhD programme should state so on the application form.

PROFESSOR CHARLES LEGGETT TRUST

Leggett Awards
16 Ogle Street, London, W1P 7LG, England
Tel: (44) 171 636 4481
Fax: (44) 171 637 4307
Contact: Mrs Susan Dolton

Leggett Awards

Subjects: Musical performance - 1999 trombone and clarinet, 2000 tuba and bassoon.
Eligibility: Open to players of any nationality who have been resident in the UK for three years and are aged 18 to 24 years inclusive on closing date. The award is open to individual instrumentalists. Awards are intended for those in financial need.
Level of Study: Postgraduate, Professional development.
Purpose: To provide annual awards for talented young brass and wind players.
No. of awards offered: 1+.
Frequency: Annual.
Value: From a total of £4,000.
Country of Study: Any country.
Application Procedure: An application form must be completed and two references provided.
Closing Date: November/December.
Additional Information: Selected applicants are asked to audition in January and to play a specially commissioned piece.

QUEEN ELISABETH INTERNATIONAL MUSIC COMPETITION OF BELGIUM

Concours Musical International Reine Elisabeth de Belgique
20 rue aux Laines, Brussels, B-1000, Belgium
Tel: (32) 2 513 00 99
Fax: (32) 2 514 32 97
Email: info@concours-reine-elisabeth.be
www: http://www.art-events.be/elisabeth
Contact: Secretariat

The Queen Elizabeth International Music Competition of Belgium is a non-profit association, located in Brussels, whose principal aim is to organise major international competitions for music virtuosos. In this regard, the competition participates in the Belgian and international music world, and gives its support to young musicians.

Queen Elisabeth International Music Competition of Belgium

Subjects: Piano in 1999, singing in 2000, violin in 2001.
Eligibility: Open to musicians of any nationality who are at least 17 years of age and not older than 30 (violin and piano)

or 31 (singing) years of age.
Level of Study: Unrestricted.
Type: Prize.
No. of awards offered: 6.
Frequency: A competition for each category is held at four-yearly intervals.
Value: From a total amounting to more than BF3,200,000.
Country of Study: Any country.
Application Procedure: Application form may be obtained from the Secretariat of the Competition.
Closing Date: January 15th.
Additional Information: Also master classes with jury members.

QUEEN MARIE JOSÉ INTERNATIONAL PRIZE FOR MUSICAL COMPOSITION

Prix de Composition Musicale Reine Marie-José
Case Postale 19
Meinier, Geneva, CH 1525, Switzerland
www: http://mhs.unige.ch/prixrunj
Contact: Mr Jean Némy Berthoud

Queen Marie José Prize International Prize for Musical Composition

Subjects: Musical composition.
Eligibility: Open to composers of all nationalities and of any age.
Level of Study: Unrestricted.
Type: Prize.
No. of awards offered: 1.
Frequency: Every two years (even-numbered years).
Value: CHF10,000.
Country of Study: Any country.
Application Procedure: All works submitted must be accompanied by a tape recording. The award-winning work remains its author's exclusive property, but, if possible, is performed as part of the Merlinge concerts.
Closing Date: May 31st.

THE QUEEN'S UNIVERSITY OF BELFAST

Belfast, BT7 1NN, Northern Ireland
Tel: (44) 1232 245133
Fax: (44) 1232 313537
Email: academic.council@qub.ac.uk
www: http://www.qub.ac.uk
Contact: Secretary to Academic Council

Queen's University is over 150 years old and offers degree programmes in all major subject areas, organised for teaching and research purposes into five colleges. The University is located just south of Belfast City Centre, although it has opened an outreach campus in Armagh. Queen's employs over 1,000 academic staff, and 20,000 students attend full and part-time courses.

Queen's University of Belfast Research and Senior Visiting Research Fellowships

Subjects: Irish studies.
Eligibility: Research fellowships normally go to postdoctoral applicants, but strictly speaking need just an upper second class honours degree, and research experience for senior posts. Senior academics must have held a university post for at least ten years.
Level of Study: Postdoctorate.
Purpose: For personal research at the Institute of Irish Studies.
Type: Fellowship.
No. of awards offered: 3 research fellowships, 1- 2 senior visiting research fellowships.
Frequency: Annual.
Value: £12,500 (research); £16,500 (senior visiting research).
Length of Study: 1 year.
Study Establishment: Queen's University of Belfast.
Country of Study: United Kingdom.
Application Procedure: Completion of application form required.
Closing Date: February 7th but this varies.

Queen's University of Belfast Visiting Fellowships

Subjects: Arts and sciences. These fellowships are alternated on an annual basis between the arts-based and science-based areas (before 1997, they were offered on a university-wide basis). This alternating policy will be reviewed but it is likely to continue.
Eligibility: Candidates should be of doctoral degree standing or have undertaken research to an equivalent standard.
Level of Study: Postdoctorate, Professional development.
Purpose: Awarded for personal research.
Type: Fellowship.
No. of awards offered: 2.
Frequency: Annual.
Value: Salary within the first 5 points on the Lecturer's scale.
Length of Study: 1 year.
Study Establishment: Queen's University of Belfast.
Country of Study: United Kingdom.
Application Procedure: Application form must be completed.
Closing Date: December 1st.
Additional Information: Two references are also required at a later stage in the application. We would expect a research proposal which would mean some sort of realistic achievement/results within a one year period.

Queen's University of Belfast Visiting Studentships

Subjects: Arts and sciences. The studentships are currently alternated annually between the arts-based and science-

based areas. This policy will be reviewed but will probably continue for the next competition (1999-2000), when visiting studentships will be offered in the science-based areas.
Eligibility: Open only to persons holding at least an upper second class honours degree or equivalent from another university. Candidates must show aptitude for research or other original work.
Level of Study: Doctorate.
Purpose: For original research.
Type: Studentship.
No. of awards offered: 3.
Frequency: Annual.
Value: Currently £5,295 plus fees.
Length of Study: 2 years; renewable for 1 further year.
Study Establishment: Queen's University of Belfast.
Country of Study: United Kingdom.
Application Procedure: Application form must be completed and two references submitted.
Closing Date: December 1st.
Additional Information: Two independent references must be submitted to arrive separately by the closing date.

QUEENSLAND UNIVERSITY OF TECHNOLOGY (QUT)

Office of Research
GPO Box 2434, Brisbane, QLD, 4001, Australia
Tel: (61) 7 3864 1844
Fax: (61) 7 3864 1304
www: http://www.qut.edu.au/draa/or/
Contact: Grants Management Officer

Queensland University of Technology Postdoctoral Research Fellowship

Subjects: All disciplines supported by research centres at QUT.
Eligibility: Open to holders of the PhD who have less than five years' full-time postdoctoral experience and have submitted their thesis for examination prior to closing date.
Level of Study: Postdoctorate.
Purpose: The fellowships serve both as a mechanism for fostering effective and productive interdisciplinary group research and for encouraging excellence in individual research.
Type: Fellowship.
No. of awards offered: Minimum of 2.
Frequency: Annual.
Value: A$38,000-A$41,000.
Length of Study: Up to 2 years.
Study Establishment: Queensland University of Technology in a specified centre or area of research concentration.
Country of Study: Australia.
Application Procedure: Information and application forms are available from the QUT website http://www.qut.edu.au/draa/or/fellow.html.
Closing Date: August 30th.

Additional Information: Referee reports will be called only for applicants supported by QUT research centres.

RAGDALE FOUNDATION

1260 North Green Bay Road, Lake Forest, IL, 60045, United States of America
Tel: (1) 847 234 1063
Fax: (1) 847 234 1075
Email: ragdale1@aol/com
Contact: Ms Sylvia Brown, Marketing & Programming Director

The Ragdale Foundation is an independent, non-profit organisation whose mission is to provide a peaceful place for artists of all disciplines to work. Residences offered range from two weeks to two months.

Frances Shaw Fellowship

Subjects: Writing (authorship).
Eligibility: Open to women over the age of 55 only. Applicants must be US citizens.
Level of Study: Unrestricted.
Purpose: To support women, over the age of 55, beginning to write seriously.
Type: Residency.
No. of awards offered: 1.
Frequency: Annual.
Length of Study: 2 months.
Country of Study: USA.
Application Procedure: Please write for guidelines, enclosing SASE.
Closing Date: February 1st.

Ragdale Foundation Residencies

Subjects: Creative writing, musical composition, film-making, visual arts.
Eligibility: Open to all creative writers, scholars, composers, film-makers, and visual artists. Professional recognition is helpful for admission, but it is not essential. Selections are based on the peer panel's rankings of work samples.
Level of Study: Unrestricted.
Purpose: To provide a peaceful place and uninterrupted time for writers, artists, and composers to do their work.
Type: Residency.
No. of awards offered: Up to 12 places at any one time, approx. 160 per year.
Frequency: Throughout the year, except May and December 15th to January 1st.
Value: A charge of US$105 per day is made, although information regarding financial assistance is available on request. The charge covers the cost of all meals, use of linen and laundry facilities, a convenient, private work space and sleeping accommodation.
Length of Study: Periods of 2 weeks to 2 months.
Study Establishment: Ragdale House and Barnhouse; Friend's Studio.

Country of Study: USA.
Application Procedure: Applicants are required to submit slides, tapes or samples of writing and three references.
Closing Date: January 15th for June to December; June 1st for January to April.
Additional Information: Couples are not accepted unless each qualifies independently. Ragdale is in Lake Forest, 30 miles north of Chicago on Lake Michigan. The Ragdale House and Barnhouse were designed by Howard Van Doren Shaw. Much of his landscaping also remains intact: a garden, lanes through meadow and prairie, a wide lawn and large trees. Ragdale is on the National Register of Historic Places and the property overlooks a large nature preserve. A new studio building was constructed in 1991.

THE REID TRUST FOR THE HIGHER EDUCATION OF WOMEN

53 Thornton Hill, Exeter, Devon, EX4 4NR, England
Contact: Mrs H M Harvey, Honorary Treasurer

The Reid Trust was founded in 1868 in connection with Bedford College for Women, for the promotion and improvement of women's education. It is administered by a small committee of voluntary trustees.

Reid Trust Awards

Subjects: All subjects.
Eligibility: Open to women educated in the UK who have appropriate academic qualifications and who wish to undertake further training or research.
Level of Study: Unrestricted.
Purpose: To assist in the higher education of women.
No. of awards offered: Usually 6-10.
Frequency: Annual.
Value: £50-£750.
Country of Study: United Kingdom.
Application Procedure: Requests for application forms must be accompanied by an SAE.
Closing Date: May 31st.
Additional Information: This award is for women only.

The Reid Trust For the Higher Education of Women

Subjects: All subjects.
Eligibility: Open to women educated in Britain who have the appropriate academic qualifications, and who wish to undertake further study or research.
Level of Study: Unrestricted.
Purpose: To promote the education of women.
Type: Grant.
No. of awards offered: Usually 10 - 12.
Frequency: Annual.
Value: £50 - £750 each.
Length of Study: Unrestricted.

Country of Study: United Kingdom.
Application Procedure: Please send a stamped self-addressed envelope for an application form.
Closing Date: May 31st.

RHODES UNIVERSITY

PO Box 94, Grahamstown, 6140, South Africa
Tel: (27) 46 603 8111
Fax: (27) 46 622 5049
Email: registrar@ru.ac.za
www: http://www.ru.ac.za
Contact: Ms Helen Pienaar, Registrar's Division

Hugh Le May Fellowship

Subjects: Philosophy; theology; classics; ancient, modern or medieval history; classical, biblical, medieval or modern languages; political theory; law.
Eligibility: Open to any postdoctoral scholars of standing with research publications to their credit. Applicants must be English speakers.
Level of Study: Postdoctorate.
Purpose: To enable scholars to devote themselves to advanced (postdoctoral) work.
Type: Fellowship.
No. of awards offered: 1.
Frequency: Every two years (even-numbered years).
Value: Return economy air ticket, furnished accommodation, and small monthly cash stipend.
Length of Study: 3-4 months. May be extended by mutual agreement, subject to availability of funds.
Study Establishment: Rhodes University.
Country of Study: South Africa.
Application Procedure: Please write for details.
Closing Date: July 31st of the year before the award.
Additional Information: Fellows are not expected to undertake teaching duties.

RICHARD III SOCIETY, AMERICAN BRANCH

1915 Euclid Avenue, Charlotte, NC, 28203-4707, United States of America
Email: r3award@aol.com
www: http://www.r3.org
Contact: Ms Nancy Northcott, Schallek Fellowships Co-ordinator

William B Schallek Memorial Graduate Fellowship Award

Subjects: Medieval history.
Eligibility: Applicants must be US citizens.
Level of Study: Doctorate.

Purpose: To support graduate study of 15th century English history and culture.
Type: Fellowship.
No. of awards offered: Varies.
Frequency: Annual.
Value: In multiples of US$500 to a maximum of US$2,000.
Length of Study: 1 year.
Study Establishment: Recognised and accredited degree granting institutions.
Country of Study: Any country.
Application Procedure: Guidelines, lists of past awards and their topics, and a downloadable application form may be found at the Society's World Wide Website.
Closing Date: February 28th for the following academic year.

RICHARD TUCKER MUSIC FOUNDATION

1790 Broadway
Suite 715, New York, NY, 10019, United States of America
Tel: (1) 212 757 2218
Fax: (1) 212 757 2347
www: http://www.rtucker.com
Contact: Ms Ellen C Moran, Executive Director

Richard Tucker Award

Subjects: Operatic singing.
Eligibility: Open to American-born male and female opera singers who are recommended to the Foundation by a person other than the artist or the artist's manager. Awarded by a conferral not a competition.
Level of Study: Professional development.
Purpose: To further career development of an artist on the brink of international acclaim.
Type: Award.
No. of awards offered: 1.
Frequency: Annual.
Value: US$30,000.
Length of Study: 1 year, not renewable.
Country of Study: Any country.
Application Procedure: By recommendation only.
Closing Date: November 30th of the year preceding the award.

Richard Tucker Music Foundation Carrer Grant

Subjects: Operatic singing.
Eligibility: Open to American-born male and female opera singers. Candidates must be recommended by a professional in the operatic field with whom they have worked.
Level of Study: Professional development.
Purpose: To further the career of young American artists.
Type: Grant.
No. of awards offered: 4.
Frequency: Annual.
Value: At least US$7,500.
Length of Study: 1 year; renewable.

Country of Study: Any country.
Application Procedure: By recommendation only.
Closing Date: November 30th of the year preceding the award.

Sara Tucker Study Grant

Subjects: Operatic singing.
Eligibility: Open to American-born opera singers who are at an early level of their career. Candidates must be recommended for the grant and should be completing an apprentice programme, or have recently graduated from a conservatory.
Level of Study: Postgraduate.
Purpose: To help an artist at the earliest stage of his or her career.
Type: Grant.
No. of awards offered: 4.
Frequency: Annual.
Value: US$5,000.
Length of Study: 1 year; not renewable.
Country of Study: Any country.
Application Procedure: By recommendation only.
Closing Date: November 30th of the year preceding the award.

ROBERTO LONGHI FOUNDATION

Via Benedetto Fortini 30, Florence, I-50125, Italy
Tel: (390) 055 658 0794
Fax: (390) 055 658 0794
www: http://www.firenze.it
Contact: Secretariat

Roberto Longhi Foundation Fellowships

Subjects: Art history.
Eligibility: Open to Italian citizens who possess a degree from an Italian university with a thesis in the history of art; and to non-Italian citizens who have fulfilled the preliminary requirements for a doctoral degree in the history of art at an accredited university or an institution of equal standing. Students who have reached their 30th birthday before the application deadline are not eligible.
Level of Study: Doctorate, Postgraduate.
Purpose: The fellowships are designed for those who want to seriously dedicate themselves to research in the history of art.
Type: Fellowship.
No. of awards offered: Several.
Frequency: Annual.
Value: The monthly rate is 800,000 lire, and for residents of the city and provinces of Florence 400,000 lire.
Length of Study: 9 months.
Study Establishment: The Institute.
Country of Study: Italy.

Application Procedure: Applications should contain the candidate's biographical data (place and date of birth, domicile, citizenship); a transcript of the candidate's undergraduate and graduate records; a copy of the degree thesis (if available) and of other original works, published or unpublished; a curriculum studiorum, also indicating the knowledge of foreign languages, spoken and written; letters of reference from at least two persons of academic standing who are acquainted with the candidate's work; the subject of the research which the candidate is interested in pursuing within the range of the history of art; two passport photographs. For further information please contact the Secretariat of the Foundation.
Closing Date: Usually May 15th; please write for details.
Additional Information: Successful candidates must give the assurance that they can dedicate their full time to the research for which the fellowship is assigned. They may not enter into any connection with other institutions; they must live in Florence for the duration of the fellowship, excepting travels required for their research. They may not exceed the periods of vacations fixed by the Institute. They are required to attend seminars, lectures and other activities arranged by the Institute. The Fellows must in addition submit a written report at the end of their stay in Florence, relating the findings of their individual research undertaken at the Longhi Foundation. The non-observance of the above conditions will be considered sufficient grounds for the cancellation of a fellowship.

ROCK ISLAND ARSENAL MUSEUM

Attn: SIORI-CFS-M
Rock Island Arsenal Historical Society
R Maguire Scholarship Committee
Rock Island Arsenal, Rock Island, IL, 61299-5000, United States of America
Tel: (1) 309 782 5021

Richard C Maguire Scholarship

Subjects: History (US, world, military, religion), or related fields such as archaeology and museum study.
Eligibility: Applicants must be US citizens. Grants will be awarded on an objective and non-discriminatory basis without regard to age, sex, race, religion or affiliation.
Level of Study: Postdoctorate, Postgraduate.
Purpose: The Richard C Maguire Scholarship is awarded annually to a student working on a Master's or Doctorate degree.
Type: Scholarship.
No. of awards offered: 1.
Frequency: Annual.
Value: US$1,000.
Length of Study: 1 year only.
Study Establishment: A US College of the candidate's choice.
Country of Study: USA.

Application Procedure: For an application forms please write to the Rock Island Arsenal Museum, enclosing a stamped self-addressed envelope. Completed applications must include: proof of citizenship; a letter of acceptance into a postgraduate programme in an accredited college or university; and complete transcript of college grades.
Closing Date: March 31st.

ROCKEFELLER ARCHIVE CENTER

15 Dayton Avenue, Sleepy Hollow, NY, 10591-1598, United States of America
Tel: (1) 914 631 4505
Fax: (1) 914 631 6017
Email: archive@rockvax.rockefeller.edu
www: http://www.rockefeller.edu/archive.ctr/
Contact: Mr Darwin H Stapleton, Director

The Rockefeller Archive Center holds the archives of the Rockefeller family and its philanthropies, and assists scholarly researchers who visit the Center to examine documents in the archives.

Rockefeller Archive Center Research Grant Program

Subjects: Developments and issues of the 20th-Century in the USA and throughout the world.
Eligibility: Open to applicants of any discipline, usually graduate students or postdoctoral scholars, who are engaged in projects which require substantial use of the collections.
Level of Study: Unrestricted.
Purpose: To foster research in the records of the Rockefeller Foundation, Rockefeller University, the Rockefeller Brothers Fund, the Rockefeller family, and in collections of other institutions and individuals deposited at the Rockefeller Archive Center.
Type: Grant.
No. of awards offered: 35-40.
Frequency: Annual.
Value: Up to US$2,500 for applicants within the USA; US$3,000 for applicants from outside the USA; depending upon travel, lodging and research expenses of the applicant.
Length of Study: 1 year; renewable through application.
Study Establishment: The Rockefeller Archive Center.
Country of Study: USA.
Application Procedure: Application form must be completed.
Closing Date: November 30th for notification in March.

ROCKEFELLER FOUNDATION

420 Fifth Avenue, New York, NY, 10018, United States of America
Tel: (1) 212 852 8373
Fax: (1) 212 852 8439
Email: adia@rockfound.org
www: http://www.rockfound.org
Contact: Ms Ann R Trotter, Programme Co-ordinator

The Rockefeller Foundation is a philanthropic organisation endowed by John D Rockefeller and chartered in 1913 for the well-being of people throughout the world. It is one of America's oldest private foundations and one of the few with strong international interests. From its beginning, the Foundation has sought to identify, and address at their source, the causes of human suffering and need.

African Dissertation Internship Awards

Subjects: Agriculture, environment and health research, education, humanities, life sciences and population studies.
Eligibility: Open to citizens of Sub-Saharan African nations, who are enrolled in doctoral programmes for a degree from a United States or Canadian University.
Level of Study: Doctorate.
Purpose: To enable African doctoral candidates enrolled in universities in the United States and Canada, to return to Africa to conduct dissertation research.
Type: Grant.
No. of awards offered: 25-30.
Frequency: Twice a year.
Value: US$20,000 maximum.
Length of Study: 12 months minimum strongly preferred.
Study Establishment: A local university or research institution in Africa.
Country of Study: Sub-Saharan African countries.
Application Procedure: Application form must be completed and submitted with supporting documentation.
Closing Date: March 1st, October 1st.

ROSWELL MUSEUM AND ART CENTER FOUNDATION (USA)

PO Box 1, Roswell, NM, 88202, United States of America
Tel: (1) 505 622 6037
Fax: (1) 505 623 5603
Email: roswellair@aol.com
www: http://www.astepabove.com/rair
Contact: Mr Stephen Fleming, Program Director

Known as the 'Gift of time', the Roswell Artist-in-residence programme was established to provide Artists of merit an extended period of time to focus on their work.

Roswell Artist-in-Residence Program

Subjects: Drawing, painting, sculpture, photography, printmaking, and other fine art media.
Eligibility: There are no eligibility restrictions.
Level of Study: Postgraduate, Professional development.
Purpose: To provide time for artists to focus on their work, without distractions or interruptions.
Type: Residency.
No. of awards offered: Approx. 5.
Frequency: Annual.
Value: US$500 per month, plus housing, studio and utilities and $100.00 per dependent.
Length of Study: 6-12 months.
Country of Study: USA.
Application Procedure: Applicants must complete current application. Please send a self-addressed and stamped envelope for application materials.
Closing Date: Varies each year.
Additional Information: No dogs allowed; families welcome. For further information please contact Grant Application Requests, at the Museum.

For further information contact:

Grant Application Request
PO Box #1, Roswell, NM, 88202, United States of America
Tel: (1) 505 623 5600
Contact: Ms Marina Mahan

ROTARY FOUNDATION

One Rotary Center
1560 Sherman Avenue, Evanston, IL, 60201-3698, United States of America
Tel: (1) 847 866 3320
Fax: (1) 847 328 8554
www: http://www.rotary.org
Contact: Resource Development Supervisor/Scholarships

Through the Ambassadorial Scholarships Programme of the Rotary Foundation, Rotarians worldwide strive to promote international understanding and relations between peoples of different nations.

Rotary Foundation Academic Year Ambassadorial Scholarships

Subjects: All subjects.
Eligibility: Open to undergraduates, graduates and those wishing to undertake vocational study. Applicants must have completed two years of university work or appropriate professional experience before starting scholarship studies. Scholarships are available to individuals of all ages. Spouses or descendants of Rotarians may not apply. Applicants must be citizens of countries in which there are Rotary clubs. Must be proficient in the language of the proposed host country.
Level of Study: Unrestricted.

Purpose: To further international understanding and friendly relations among people of different countries.
Type: Scholarship.
No. of awards offered: Varies.
Frequency: Annually, dependent on funds available.
Value: Funding to cover tuition, fees, room and board, and round-trip transportation, and some educational supplies not to exceed a maximum amount of US$23,000. Funding covers these specific expenses only.
Length of Study: 1 academic year.
Study Establishment: A study institution assigned by the Trustees of the Rotary Foundation.
Country of Study: Any country other than that in which the Scholar resides, providing there are Rotary clubs there.
Application Procedure: Applicants must submit a completed application form, two recommendations, college transcripts, an autobiographical essay, statement of purpose, and a language ability form verifying applicant's background in the language of the proposed host country, if different from his/her native language.
Closing Date: Varies according to local Rotary club, but between March and July, (applicants must apply over a year in advance). Contact a local Rotary club for details.
Additional Information: Scholars will not be assigned to study in areas of a country where they have previously lived or studied for more than six months. During the study year, scholars are expected to be outstanding ambassadors of goodwill through appearances before Rotary clubs, schools, civic organisations and other forums. Upon completion of the scholarship, scholars are expected to share the experiences of understanding acquired during the study year with the people of their home countries. Candidates should contact local Rotary clubs for information on the availability of particular scholarships. Not all Rotary districts are able to offer scholarships. Further details are available from the website.

Rotary Foundation Cultural Ambassadorial Scholarships

Subjects: For cultural immersion and intensive language study.
Eligibility: Applications will be considered for candidates interested in studying Arabic, English, French, German, Hebrew, Italian, Japanese, Korean, Mandarin Chinese, Polish, Portuguese, Russian, Spanish, Swahili, and Swedish. Open to students who have completed two years of university work or appropriate professional experience before starting scholarship studies, and who have studied the proposed language for at least one year at the college level.
Scholarships are available to individuals of all ages. Spouses or descendants of Rotarians may not apply. Applicants must be citizens of countries in which there are Rotary clubs.
Level of Study: Unrestricted.
Purpose: To further international understanding and friendly relations among people of different countries.

Type: Scholarship.
No. of awards offered: Varies.
Frequency: Annually, dependent on funds available.
Value: Provide funds to cover round-trip transportation, language training expenses, and homestay living arrangements, up to US$10,000 maximum for 3-month awards and US$17,000 maximum for 6-month awards. All other expenses are the responsibility of the scholars. Funding is for these specific expenses only.
Length of Study: 3 or 6 months.
Study Establishment: A language school assigned by the Trustees of the Rotary Foundation.
Country of Study: Determined by the Rotary Foundation, according to the language of study.
Application Procedure: Applicants must apply through a Rotary club in their legal or permanent residence (or place of full-time study or employment). Applicants must submit a completed application form, two recommendations, college transcripts, an autobiographical essay and statement of purpose.
Closing Date: Varies according to local Rotary club, but between March and July (applicants must apply over a year in advance). Contact a local Rotary club for details.
Additional Information: Wherever possible, Scholars will reside with host families. During the study year, scholars are expected to be outstanding ambassadors of goodwill through appearances before Rotary clubs, schools, civic organisations and other forums. Candidates should contact local Rotary clubs for information on the availability of particular scholarships. Not all Rotary districts are able to offer scholarships. Further details are available from the website.

Rotary Foundation Multi-Year Ambassadorial Scholarships

Subjects: All subjects.
Eligibility: Open to undergraduates and graduates who have completed two years of university work or appropriate professional experience before starting scholarship studies. Scholarships are available to individuals of all ages. Spouses or descendants of Rotarians may not apply. Applicants must be citizens of countries in which there are Rotary clubs.
Level of Study: Unrestricted.
Purpose: To further international understanding and friendly relations among people of different countries and help defray the cost of pursuing a degree.
Type: Scholarship.
No. of awards offered: Varies.
Frequency: Annually, dependent on funds available.
Value: The award provides a flat grant of US$11,000 per year to be applied towards the cost of a degree programme. All additional costs must be absorbed by scholars.
Length of Study: 2 or 3 years.
Study Establishment: A foreign study institution approved by the trustees of The Rotary Foundation.
Country of Study: Any country other than that in which the Scholar resides, providing there are Rotary clubs there.

Application Procedure: Applicants must submit a completed application form, two recommendations, college transcripts, an autobiographical essay and a statement of purpose.
Closing Date: Varies according to local Rotary club, but between March and July (applicants must apply over a year in advance). Contact a local Rotary club for details.
Additional Information: Scholars will not be assigned to study in areas of a country where they have previously lived or studied for more than six months. During the study year, scholars are expected to be outstanding ambassadors of goodwill through appearances before Rotary clubs, schools, civic organisations and other forums. Upon completion of the scholarship, scholars are expected to share the experiences of understanding acquired during the study year with the people of their home countries. Candidates should contact local Rotary clubs for information on the availability of particular scholarships. Not all Rotary districts are able to offer scholarships. Further details are available from the website.

Rotary Grants for University Teachers to Serve in Developing Countries

Subjects: Fields taught must have practical use to the host country.
Eligibility: Applicants must hold a college or university appointment for three or more years, and must be proficient in the language of their prospective host country.
Level of Study: Professional development.
Purpose: To build international understanding while strengthening higher education in low-income countries.
Type: Grant.
No. of awards offered: Set.
Frequency: Dependent on funds available.
Value: Grants are available for a period of either three to five months (receiving US$10,000) or six to ten months (receiving US$20,000), to subsidise expenses of higher education faculty to teach at a college or university in a low-income country.
Length of Study: 3-10 months.
Country of Study: Countries with a per capita GNP of US$6,000 or less in which there are Rotary clubs.
Application Procedure: Teachers must apply through a local Rotary club. Applications should include a completed application form, current CV, statement of intent and two letters of recommendation. Prospective candidates must contact a local Rotary club to confirm the availability of awards, to obtain application materials, and to enquire about the local deadline.
Closing Date: Varies according to local Rotary club, but between March and July (applicants must apply over a year in advance). Please contact a local Rotary club for details.
Additional Information: Grant recipients are expected to be outstanding ambassadors of goodwill to the people of their host and home countries through appearances to Rotary clubs. Not all Rotary districts are able to offer scholarships. Further details are available from the website.

ROYAL ACADEMY OF MUSIC

Marylebone Road, London, NW1 5HT, England
Tel: (44) 171 873 7393
Fax: (44) 171 873 7394
www: http://www.ram.ac.uk
Contact: Mr Philip White, Registrar

Royal Academy of Music General Bursary Awards

Subjects: All relevant branches of music education and training.
Eligibility: Open to any student offered a place at the Academy, irrespective of race, creed and gender.
Level of Study: Postgraduate.
Purpose: To assist towards tuition fees and general living expenses for study at the Royal Academy of Music.
Type: Bursary.
No. of awards offered: Varies.
Frequency: Annually, funds often available on continuing basis.
Value: According to need and availability of funds.
Length of Study: Normally for a complete academic year. Individual requirements may be imposed.
Study Establishment: Royal Academy of Music.
Country of Study: United Kingdom.
Application Procedure: Application forms are sent automatically to all postgraduate students who are offered places.
Closing Date: January 31st for the following academic year.

ROYAL ANTHROPOLOGICAL INSTITUTE

50 Fitzroy Street, London, W1P 5HS, England
Tel: (44) 171 387 0455
Fax: (44) 171 383 4235
www: http://lucy.ukc.ac.uk/rai
Contact: Director of Grants

Emslie Horniman Anthropological Scholarship Fund

Subjects: Anthropology.
Eligibility: Open to citizens of the UK, Commonwealth or Irish Republic who are university graduates or who can satisfy the Trustees of their suitability for the study proposed. Preference is given to applicants whose proposals include field work outside the UK. Graduates who already hold a doctorate in anthropology are not eligible. Open to individuals only, no grants are given to expeditions or teams.
Level of Study: Postgraduate.
Purpose: Pre-doctoral grants for fieldwork in anthropology with preference for research outside the United Kingdom.
Type: Scholarship.
No. of awards offered: Approx. 10.
Frequency: Annual.
Value: £500 to £4,000.

Country of Study: Any country.
Application Procedure: Ask for application form.
Closing Date: March 31st.
Additional Information: No grants for library research, university fees, or subsistence in the UK.

ROYAL COLLEGE OF MUSIC

Prince Consort Road, London, SW7 2BS, England
Tel: (44) 171 591 4377
Fax: (44) 171 589 7740
Email: efleet@rcm.ac.uk
www: http://www.rcm.ac.uk
Contact: Ms Emma Fleet, International and Awards Officer

The Royal College of Music provides specialised musical education and professional training at the highest international level for performers and composers. This enables talented students to develop the musical skills, knowledge, understanding and resourcefulness which will equip them to contribute significantly to musical life in this country and internationally.

Royal College of Music Exhibitions

Subjects: Music performance, composition or conducting.
Eligibility: Unrestricted, but only for study at the College.
Level of Study: Unrestricted.
Purpose: To recognise merit in music performance, composition or conducting.
Type: Exhibition.
No. of awards offered: Approx. 50.
Frequency: Annual.
Value: Up to £11,400 (up to full fees).
Length of Study: 1-4 years.
Study Establishment: Music conservatoire.
Country of Study: United Kingdom.
Application Procedure: Application only by application for place of study.
Closing Date: October 1st.

Royal College of Music Scholarships

Subjects: Music performance, composition or conducting.
Eligibility: Unrestricted, but only for study at the College.
Level of Study: Unrestricted.
Purpose: To recognise merit in music performance, composition or conducting.
Type: Scholarship.
No. of awards offered: Approx. 50.
Frequency: Annual.
Value: Up to £11,000 (up to full fees).
Length of Study: 1-4 years.
Study Establishment: Music conservatoire.
Country of Study: United Kingdom.
Application Procedure: Application only by application for place of study.
Closing Date: October 1st.

ROYAL COLLEGE OF ORGANISTS (RCO)

7 St Andrew Street
Holborn, London, EC4A 3LQ, England
Tel: (44) 171 936 3606
Fax: (44) 171 353 8244
Contact: Mr Alan Dear, Senior Executive

RCO Grants and Travel Scholarships

Subjects: Organ playing.
Eligibility: Open to promising pupils of any nationality who are training to be organists. Some of the grants are restricted to applicants under 20 years of age.
Level of Study: Unrestricted.
Type: Grant, Travel Scholarship.
No. of awards offered: Varies.
Frequency: Annual.
Value: Not less than £50.
Length of Study: 1 year, renewable.
Country of Study: Any country.
Application Procedure: Please write for applications.
Closing Date: May 1st.

RCO Scholarships and Awards

Subjects: Organ playing.
Eligibility: Open to members of the College (only in exceptional circumstances will awards be made to non-members). Membership is open to all upon payment of an annual subscription.
Level of Study: Unrestricted.
Purpose: To assist organists with professional playing.
Type: Grant.
No. of awards offered: Varies.
Frequency: Annual.
Value: Not less than £50.
Length of Study: 1 year; renewable.
Study Establishment: Varies.
Country of Study: Any country.
Application Procedure: Please write for an application form.
Closing Date: April.

ROYAL HOLLOWAY, UNIVERSITY OF LONDON

Egham Hill, Surrey, TW20 0EX, England
Tel: (44) 1784 434 455
Fax: (44) 1784 473 662
Email: graduateoffice@rhbnc.ac.uk
www: http://www.rhbnc.ac.uk
Contact: Academic Registrar

Caroline Spurgeon Research Fellowship

Subjects: English literature.

Eligibility: Open to candidates who have obtained a higher degree or completed at least two years of research towards a higher degree. There are no restrictions but a good standard in English language is essential.
Level of Study: Postdoctorate, Postgraduate.
Purpose: To enable either a postdoctoral student to undertake research in english or a postgraduate student to complete his/her research.
Type: Fellowship.
No. of awards offered: 1.
Frequency: Dependent on funds available.
Value: Equal to a British Academy Major Studentship.
Length of Study: 1 year.
Study Establishment: Royal Holloway College.
Country of Study: United Kingdom.
Application Procedure: Details may be obtained from the Academic Registrar.
Closing Date: As advertised.
Additional Information: The College is part of the University of London.

Jubilee Research Fellowship

Subjects: Arts and music - classics, drama and theatre studies, economics, English, French, German, history, Italian, management studies, social policy and social sciences, Sciences, biology, biochemistry, chemistry, computer science, geography, geology, mathematics, physics and psychology.
Eligibility: Open to suitably qualified candidates who hold a PhD degree or equivalent. There are no restrictions, but a good standard in the English language is essential.
Level of Study: Postdoctorate.
Purpose: To promote research in subjects within the scope of the Faculty of Arts and Music or the Faculty of Science.
Type: Fellowship.
No. of awards offered: 1.
Frequency: Dependent on funds available.
Value: Normally equivalent to the lower end of the lecturer scale.
Length of Study: 3 years.
Study Establishment: Royal Holloway College.
Country of Study: United Kingdom.
Application Procedure: Details may be obtained from the Academic Registrar.
Closing Date: As advertised.
Additional Information: The College is part of the University of London.

Royal Holloway History/Classics Studentship

Subjects: Classics and historical studies, alternately.
Eligibility: Open to graduates with at least a good second class honours degree in the Classics, Greek, Latin, or in History.
Level of Study: Postgraduate.
Purpose: To enable a graduate in classics or historical studies to complete research for a higher degree.
Type: Studentship.
No. of awards offered: 1.
Frequency: Dependent on funds available.
Value: Equal to a British Academy Major Studentship.

Length of Study: 1 year.
Study Establishment: Royal Holloway College.
Country of Study: United Kingdom.
Application Procedure: Details may be obtained from the Academic Registrar.
Closing Date: As advertised.
Additional Information: The College is part of the University of London.

ROYAL INCORPORATION OF ARCHITECTS IN SCOTLAND (RIAS)

15 Rutland Square, Edinburgh, EH1 2BE, Scotland
Tel: (44) 131 229 7545
Fax: (44) 131 228 2188
Contact: Ms Linda Connolly, Awards Administrator

The Martin Jones Memorial Scholarship and Award

Subjects: Architecture.
Eligibility: Open to students and graduates of the School of Architecture in Duncan of Jordanstone College of Art, Dundee University.
Level of Study: Postgraduate.
Purpose: To support an outstanding student in pursuing a personal line of creative investigation and research.
Type: Scholarship.
No. of awards offered: 1.
Frequency: Annual.
Value: £7,500.
Country of Study: Any country.
Application Procedure: Invitations are issued in autumn each year.
Closing Date: End of January.
Additional Information: Applications should be forwarded to: Martin Jones Award, c/o School of Architecture, Duncan of Jordanstone, Perth Road, Dundee DD1 4HT.

RIAS Award for Measured Drawing

Subjects: Architecture - measured drawing.
Eligibility: Open to student members and members of the RIAS.
Level of Study: Postgraduate.
Purpose: To encourage and recognise original hand-measured drawing as essential to an architect's training.
No. of awards offered: 1.
Frequency: Annual.
Value: Premier Award for student members £200; Prize for full members £100.
Country of Study: Any country.
Closing Date: End of January.
Additional Information: The Committee will judge competitors on the following points: the choice of architectural fabric for the measured study, such as buildings

under threat (the building need not be old); the clarity of understanding and accuracy revealed by the drawing; and the elegance with which the analysis is presented. Adjudication will normally take place in March; if confirmed by the RIAS council, the result of the competition will be notified to the competitors. The presentation of the award will be made at the RIAS Annual Convention; the winning drawing will form part of a travelling exhibition of RIAS Awards and Prizes, and may at the Incorporation's discretion form part of the RIAS Archive subsequently.

RIAS John Maclaren Travelling Fellowship

Subjects: Architecture.
Eligibility: Applicants must be on the Register of Registered Architects, and be Corporate Members of the Royal Incorporation.
Level of Study: Postgraduate.
Purpose: To assist study at a School of Architecture or Engineering, or in taking up a paid position in practice in the country chosen for study, or to reward work which has involved study overseas.
Type: Fellowship.
No. of awards offered: 1.
Frequency: Every two years.
Value: £600 and a certificate.
Country of Study: Outside United Kingdom.
Closing Date: End of January.
Additional Information: It is the preference of the RIAS that the outcome of the Fellowship should be a presentation at the RIAS Convention of the results of the study with a lodgement in the RIAS Library of such manuscript and slides or photographs as may be appropriate. The Fellowship requires both scholarship and analysis, and submission to the RIAS of evidence of lasting value. Applicants, both in their proposal and in the subsequent presentation, are expected to have adopted an investigative and critical attitude towards their proposed subject of study in the manner of a learned society dissertation. The option of presenting the results orally at the Convention (with the deposit of the material in the Library), or the simple deposit of written material in the Library, will be a matter for determination between the Fellow and the RIAS Awards Committee.

RIAS/Whitehouse Studios Award for Architectural Photography

Subjects: Architectural photography - 'A building and its people'.
Eligibility: Open to student members and members of the RIAS.
Level of Study: Postgraduate.
Purpose: To recognise that architectural photography is a distinct art, and to encourage its appreciation and development.
No. of awards offered: 1.
Frequency: Annual.
Value: Certificate and £250.
Country of Study: Any country.
Closing Date: January 31st.

Additional Information: At the Incorporation's discretion, the winning photograph may also form part of the RIAS Archives.

The Sir John Burnet Memorial Award

Subjects: Architecture.
Eligibility: Competitors must be student members of the RIAS, and should be first year full-time post Part I.
Level of Study: Postgraduate.
Purpose: To test a student's skill in architectural design in communicating by drawings, prepared within a predetermined time limit, their proposals in response to a client's brief.
No. of awards offered: 1.
Frequency: Annual.
Value: £150 and a certificate.
Country of Study: Any country.
Additional Information: Submissions will be judged by the RIAS Awards Committee. The Committee may be assisted by distinguished critics, co-opted by the Committee. The judges will consider: skills in interpreting a brief within a time deadline; flair in architectural design; and skill in methods of communication and presentation. The drawings will remain the property of the Royal Incorporation.

The Sir Robert Lorimer Memorial Award

Subjects: Architecture.
Eligibility: Open to student members, and members of the RIAS under the age of 29.
Level of Study: Postgraduate.
Purpose: To encourage students to keep sketch books or notebooks, as in Lorimer's time.
No. of awards offered: 1.
Frequency: Annual.
Value: A book voucher to the value of £125, and a certificate.
Country of Study: Any country.
Closing Date: End of January.
Additional Information: The assessors prefer working sketch book(s), which are a record of study and travel, and will look for careful observation and sensitive draughtsmanship. Adjudication will normally take place in March; if confirmed by the RIAS Council, the result of the competition will be notified to the competitors. The presentation of the award will be made at the RIAS Annual Convention.

The Sir Rowand Anderson Silver Medal

Subjects: Architecture.
Eligibility: Open to student members of the RIAS within a year of passing Part II.
Level of Study: Postgraduate.
Purpose: To recognise the best student member in Scotland.
No. of awards offered: 1.
Frequency: Annual.
Value: A silver medal and a certificate.
Country of Study: Scotland.
Closing Date: October 31st.
Additional Information: The RIAS Awards Committee may require to interview candidates before making their selection. The Award and Presentation will be made at the RIAS Annual

Convention, for which the winner may be asked to make available a selection of his or her portfolio for exhibition.

The Thomas Ross Award

Subjects: Architecture pertaining particularly to Scotland, Scottish architecture and/or environment, or the study of ancient Scottish buildings or monuments.
Eligibility: Candidates must be members of the RIAS, be otherwise of graduate status or possess and produce evidence of such other qualifications as may satisfy the requirements of the RIAS.
Level of Study: Postgraduate.
Purpose: To recognise post-qualification research into architecture and/or the environment.
No. of awards offered: 1.
Frequency: Every two years.
Value: £600, a certificate, and the possibility of additional help towards publication.
Country of Study: Any country.
Closing Date: End of January.
Additional Information: The Committee will judge applicants upon the clarity of the proposal or completed work, upon the candidates' ability to write and to present material, and upon the extent to which the study covers ground not covered by existing material. The Committee may require applicants to attend an interview. The Committee, at its discretion, may make more than one Award, provided that the total number of Awards in a six-year period does not exceed three.

ROYAL INSTITUTION OF CHARTERED SURVEYORS (RICS)

12 Great George Street, London, SW1P 3AD, England
Tel: (44) 171 222 7000
Fax: (44) 171 222 9430
Email: sbrown@rics.org.uk
www: http://www.rics.org.uk/research/appform.html
Contact: Mr Stephen Brown

The Royal Institution of Chartered Surveyors is the professional institution for the surveying profession.

RICS Education Trust Award

Subjects: The theory and practice of surveying in any of its disciplines (general practice, quantity surveying, building surveying, rural practice, planning and development, land surveying and minerals surveying).
Eligibility: Open to chartered surveyors and others carrying out research studies in relevant subjects.
Level of Study: Unrestricted.
Frequency: Twice a year.
Value: Normally up to £5,000.
Country of Study: Any country.
Application Procedure: Application form to be completed.
Closing Date: September 30th, February 28th.

ROYAL IRISH ACADEMY

19 Dawson Street, Dublin, 2, Ireland
Tel: (353) 1 676 2570
Fax: (353) 1 676 2346
Email: admin@ria.ie
www: http://www.ria.ie
Contact: Ms Veronica Barker, Assistant Executive Secretary

The Royal Irish Academy was established in 1875 and is the senior learned institution in Ireland for both the sciences and humanities. It publishes a number of learned journals and monographs. It is Ireland's national representative to a large number of international unions, and through its national committees, runs conferences, lectures and workshops. It also manages a number of scholarly, long-term research projects.

Eoin O'Mahony Bursary

Subjects: Social and behavioural sciences, history.
Eligibility: Open to Irish nationals only.
Level of Study: Unrestricted.
Purpose: To assist Irish scholars undertaking overseas research on historical subjects of Irish interest.
Type: Bursary.
No. of awards offered: 1.
Frequency: Annual.
Value: IR£500.
Length of Study: Varies.
Country of Study: Any country.
Application Procedure: Application form must be completed.
Closing Date: End of January.
Additional Information: Preference will be given to projects concerning family history, in particular those which are associated with the 'Wild Geese' (genealogy). Special consideration will be given to those who have been active in local learned societies.

Royal Irish Academy European Exchange Fellowship

Subjects: Humanities, social sciences and natural sciences.
Eligibility: Irish applications must come from applicants who are resident in the Republic of Ireland. Researchers from other countries must apply to their own Academy or Learned Society.
Level of Study: Postdoctorate, Professional development.
Purpose: To promote academic exchange between Ireland and Austria, Great Britain, Hungary, France and Poland, for the humanities, social sciences and natural sciences.
Type: Fellowship.
Frequency: Annual.
Value: Varies.
Length of Study: Varies.
Country of Study: United Kingdom, France, Hungary, Poland or Austria.
Application Procedure: Application form must be completed.
Closing Date: October 15th.

ROYAL OVER-SEAS LEAGUE

Department of Cultural Affairs
Over-Seas House
Park Place
St James's Street, London, SW1A 1LR, England
Tel: (44) 171 408 0214 ext 219
Fax: (44) 171 499 6738
Email: culture@rosl.org.uk
www: http://www.rosl.org.uk
Contact: Mr Dominic Gregory, Promotions Officer

The League was founded in 1910 to encourage international friendship and understanding. The League's Royal Charter states that it must encourage the arts, particularly amongst the young people of the Commonwealth. This is fulfilled by staging an annual music competition, an annual open exhibition, and a literary lecture programme.

Royal Over-Seas League Music Competition

Subjects: Musical performance, in four solo classes - strings (including harp and guitar), woodwind/brass, keyboard, singers, and an ensemble class.
Eligibility: Open to citizens of Commonwealth (including the UK) and former Commonwealth countries, who are no more than 28 years of age (instrumentalists) or 30 years of age (singers).
Level of Study: Professional development.
Purpose: To support and promote young Commonwealth musicians.
Type: Competition.
No. of awards offered: Varies.
Frequency: Annual.
Value: Over £24,000 in prizes, including a £4,000 first prize.
Country of Study: Any country.
Application Procedure: Please write for application forms.
Closing Date: January 14th.

ROYAL PHILHARMONIC SOCIETY

10 Stratford Place, London, W1N 9AE, England
Tel: (44) 171 491 8110
Fax: (44) 171 493 7463
Email: admin@rps-uk.demon.co.uk
Contact: Ms Rosemary Johnson, General Administrator

The Royal Philharmonic Society is the second oldest concert giving society in the world. It provides a varied programme of musical activities and assists young musicians through the awards it administers, in addition to presenting the annual RPS Music Awards for outstanding achievement in British musical life.

Julius Isserlis Scholarship

Subjects: Musical performance in varying instrumental categories, awarded every two years.

Eligibility: Open to students of any nationality domiciled (permanently resident) in the UK, who are 15-25 years of age.
Level of Study: Unrestricted.
Purpose: To facilitate musical study abroad, starting within sixteen months of the award being made.
Type: Scholarship.
No. of awards offered: 1.
Frequency: Every two years (next 1999).
Value: £20,000.
Length of Study: 2 years.
Country of Study: Outside United Kingdom.
Application Procedure: Application form must be completed. There is a £20 entry fee.
Closing Date: To be announced.
Additional Information: Winner must take up residence for period of study in country designated on the application.

Royal Philharmonic Society Composition Prize

Subjects: Musical composition.
Eligibility: Open to past and present registered students of any conservatoire or university within the UK, of any nationality, under the age of 29. Former winners are not eligible.
Level of Study: Postgraduate, Undergraduate.
Purpose: To encourage young composers.
Type: Prize.
No. of awards offered: 1.
Frequency: Annual.
Value: £5,000 plus a guaranteed performance of new work.
Country of Study: Any country.
Application Procedure: Application form must be completed. There is a £20 entry fee.
Closing Date: As announced, usually in November.

THE ROYAL SCOTTISH ACADEMY

The Mound, Edinburgh, EH2 2EL, Scotland
Tel: (44) 131 225 6671
Fax: (44) 131 225 2349
Contact: The Secretary

Founded in 1826, The Royal Scottish Academy, Scotland's foremost body of artists, has promoted the works of leading contemporary painters, sculptors, printmakers and architects. It also gives practical and financial help to young artists through scholarships as well as the annual Student's Exhibition.

The John Kinross Memorial Fund Student Scholarships

Subjects: Painting, sculpture, architecture and printmaking.
Eligibility: The painting, printmaking and sculpture scholarship is open to students in final or postgraduate years of study at one of the Scottish Colleges of Art. The architecture scholarship is open to senior students at one of the six Scottish Schools of Architecture presenting work which would normally be related to the requirements of RIBA Part 1 or Part 2 Syllabus. Group work is not acceptable. Students at Scottish Colleges studying painting, sculpture, printmaking and architecture, are eligible to apply for a three month scholarship to Florence in memory of the late John Kinross.
Level of Study: Postgraduate.
Purpose: To assist young artists from the established training centres in Scotland; within the disciplines of painting, sculpture and architecture; to spend three months in Italy.
Type: Scholarship.
No. of awards offered: Varies, usually 10-15.
Frequency: Annual.
Value: Varies.
Length of Study: 3 months.
Study Establishment: In Florence (or in that area of Italy).
Country of Study: Italy.
Closing Date: Late April.

Royal Scottish Academy Annual Student Competition

Subjects: Painting, sculpture, architecture and printmaking.
Eligibility: Candidates should be residents of Scotland. Painting, printmaking and sculpture students should be in their final or postgraduate years of study at a college of art in Scotland. Applicants should submit one work. Architecture students should be in their final year and present work normally related to the requirements of the RIBA Part II syllabus.
Level of Study: Postgraduate.
Type: Competition.
No. of awards offered: Varies.
Frequency: Annual.
Value: Varies: The Macallan Award of £1,000; Royal Scottish Academy Awards £400 for printmaking, painting, sculpture, architecture; Carnegie Travelling Scholarship of £200.
Study Establishment: All Scottish colleges of Art and Architecture.
Country of Study: Scotland.
Application Procedure: Applications must be submitted via applicant's college and countersigned by the tutor.
Closing Date: February.
Additional Information: The Academy also sponsors an Annual Exhibition of painting (oil, water-colour, pastel, black and white), sculpture, architectural drawings and prints. Various monetary awards are made. (May 2nd - July 5th).

ROYAL SOCIETY FOR THE ENCOURAGEMENT OF ARTS, MANUFACTURES AND COMMERCE (RSA)

8 John Adam Street, London, WC2N 6EZ, England
Tel: (44) 171 930 5115
Fax: (44) 171 839 5805
Email: rsa@rsa.ftech.co.uk
www: http://www.cs.mdx.ac.uk/rsa/
Contact: Ms Gayle Markovitz, Project Administrator

RSA Art for Architecture Award

Subjects: Art and architecture.
Eligibility: Open to visual artists who are to be employed at the earliest stage of a building project as part of the design team. Restricted to projects within the British Isles, but open to individuals of any nationality if attached to a project.
Level of Study: Unrestricted.
Purpose: To encourage collaboration between artists and architects or other design professionals, by giving grants to support the artist's place in a design team in the early stage of a development.
Type: Varies.
No. of awards offered: 2.
Frequency: Four times per year.
Value: £2,000-£15,000. Awards are in the form of payment towards the design fees of artists appointed.
Country of Study: United Kingdom.
Application Procedure: Application form needs to be completed. Other documentation such as slides, plans, and letters of support should be submitted with all applications to Jes Fernie.
Closing Date: Quarterly through the year: March 19th, June 18th, September 17th, December 17th.
Additional Information: There is also a Publication Award, intended to help fund publications that focus on issues and practice relating to collaboration.

RSA Student Design Awards

Subjects: Design.
Eligibility: Open to students who have studied for at least one term at a recognised college of design within the UK, and some in other EC countries.
Level of Study: Postgraduate.
Purpose: Annual competition offering winning students the opportunity to undertake research or study abroad, or to undertake periods of attachment in industry.
No. of awards offered: Varies.
Frequency: Annual.
Value: £250 to £5,000.

Study Establishment: An appropriate institution or in industry.
Country of Study: Travel awards may be used to fund study tours abroad.
Application Procedure: Project briefs and details for application are published each year in the 'SDA Projects Book' available from September.
Closing Date: November.
Additional Information: The Student Design Awards Scheme is not a grant giving body, but an annual competition open to design students. The majority of periods of attachment are with companies in the UK but some are with companies abroad. Our website address is: http://www.rsa.org.uk.

ROYAL SOCIETY OF CANADA

225 Metcalfe Street
Suite 308, Ottawa, ON, K2P 1P9, Canada
Tel: (1) 613 991 6990
Fax: (1) 613 991 6996
Email: adminrsc@rsc.ca
www: http://www.rsc.ca
Contact: Grants Management Officer

The primary objective of The Royal Society of Canada is to promote learning and research in the arts and sciences. It draws on the breadth of knowledge and expertise of its members from all disciplines to recognise and honour distinguished accomplishments; to advise on the state of scholarship and culture across the country; and to inform the public of newsworthy social, scientific, and ethical questions of the day.

Sir Arthur Sims Scholarship

Subjects: Humanities, social sciences or natural sciences.
Eligibility: Open to graduates of Canadian universities who have completed one year of postgraduate study at a British institution and display outstanding merit and promise in their field of study.
Level of Study: Postgraduate.
Purpose: To encourage Canadian students to undertake postgraduate work in Great Britain.
Type: Scholarship.
No. of awards offered: 2.
Frequency: Every two years.
Value: £700 per year.
Length of Study: 2 years.
Study Establishment: Approved institutions.
Country of Study: United Kingdom.
Application Procedure: Please contact the Awards Co-ordinator for details.
Closing Date: February 15th 1999.

THE ROYAL SOCIETY OF EDINBURGH

22-26 George Street, Edinburgh, EH2 2PQ, Scotland
Tel: (44) 131 225 5000
Fax: (44) 131 220 5024
Email: resfells@rse.org.uk
www: http://www.ma.hw.ac.uk/rse/
Contact: The Research Fellowships Secretary

The Royal Society of Edinburgh is Scotland's National Academy. It is an independent body, founded in 1783 by Royal Charter for 'The Advancement of Learning and Useful Knowledge' and governed by an elected council of Fellows.

Auber Bequest

Subjects: All subjects.
Eligibility: Open to naturalised British citizens or individuals wishing to acquire British nationality who are over 60 years of age, resident in Scotland or England and are bona fide scholars engaged in academic (but not industrial) research.
Level of Study: Unrestricted.
Purpose: To provide assistance for the furtherance of academic research in any of its branches.
No. of awards offered: Varies.
Frequency: Every two years.
Value: Varies; not normally exceeding £3,000.
Length of Study: Up to 2 years.
Country of Study: Scotland or England.
Application Procedure: Application forms are available from the Research Fellowships Secretary.
Closing Date: October 31st.
Additional Information: Applicants should not at birth have been British nationals nor held dual British nationality. Applicants must have acquired British nationality.

CRF/RSE European Visiting Research Fellowships

Subjects: Within one of the following arts and letters subjects - archaeology, art and architecture, economics and economic history, geography, history, jurisprudence, linguistics, literature and philology, philosophy, religious studies.
Eligibility: Applicants must be aged 60 or under on date of appointment, which is variable, but must be within sixteen months of date of award. Applicants from continental Europe must be nominated by members of staff from a Scottish Higher Education Institution. Applicants must be a member of academic staff of a Scottish Higher Education Institution or equivalent continental European institution.
Level of Study: Professional development.
Purpose: To create a two-way flow of visiting scholars in arts and letters between Scotland and continental Europe.
Type: Fellowship.
No. of awards offered: 6-8.
Frequency: Annual.

Value: Up to £5,000 for visits of six months (reduced pro-rata for shorter visits) to cover actual costs of travel, subsistence and relevant study costs.
Length of Study: Up to 6 months.
Study Establishment: A Scottish Higher Education Institution or a recognised centre of higher education in a continental European country.
Country of Study: European countries.
Application Procedure: Application forms are available from the Research Fellowships Secretary in August/September each year.
Closing Date: Early November.
Additional Information: Successful applicants will be required to submit a report within two months of the end of the visit.

SOEID Personal Research Fellowships

Subjects: All subjects. A proportion of the Fellowships are awarded in fields likely to enhance the development of industry and encourage better uses of resources in Scotland.
Eligibility: Open to persons of all nationalities who have a PhD or equivalent qualification. Candidates must be aged 32 or under on the date of appointment (October 1st) or have between 2-6 years' postdoctoral experience, and must show they have a capacity for innovative research and have a substantial volume of published work relevant to their proposed field of study.
Level of Study: Postdoctorate.
Purpose: To encourage independent research in any discipline.
Type: Fellowship.
No. of awards offered: 2.
Frequency: Annual.
Value: Annual stipends are within the scales RGIA-2 for reseach and analogous staff in Higher Education Institutions (£16,366-£25,092 as at April 1st 1998) with annual increments and superannuation benefits. Expenses to a maximum of £2,500 in year one; £1,000 in years two and three, for travel and attendance at meetings or incidentals may be reimbursed. No support payments are available to the institution but Fellows may seek support for their research from other sources.
Length of Study: Up to 3 years full-time research.
Study Establishment: Any Higher Education Institution, research institution or industrial laboratory approved for the purpose by the Council of the Society.
Country of Study: Scotland.
Application Procedure: Candidates should negotiate directly with the proposed host institution. The Fellowships are offered with the support of the Scottish Office Education and Industry Department (SOEID). Application forms are available from the Research Fellowships Secretary.
Closing Date: Mid-March.
Additional Information: Fellows may not hold other paid appointments without the express permission of the Council, but teaching or seminar work appropriate to their special knowledge may be acceptable.

SOEID/RSE Support Research Fellowships

Subjects: All subjects. A proportion of the fellowships are awarded in fields of research likely to enhance the development of industry and encourage better use of resources in Scotland.
Eligibility: Candidates must be existing members of staff who have held a permanent appointment for not less than five years in any Higher Education Institution in Scotland. Applicants should normally be aged under 40 on the date of appointment (October 1st) and employed on the lecturer (or equivalent) grade.
Level of Study: Professional development.
Purpose: To enable support fellows to take study leave, either in their own institution or elsewhere, whilst remaining in continuous employment with their present employer.
Type: Fellowship.
No. of awards offered: 2.
Frequency: Annual.
Value: The actual cost of replacement staff will be reimbursed according to the Lecturer A scale (maximum RGI-3) with the placement determined by the employer. Superannuation costs and employer's NI contributions will also be reimbursed.
Length of Study: Up to 12 months full-time research.
Study Establishment: Any Higher Education Institution, research institution or industrial laboratory in Scotland approved for the purpose by the Council of the Society.
Country of Study: Scotland.
Application Procedure: Application forms are available from the Research Fellowships Secretary. Candidates should negotiate directly with the proposed host institution. The Fellowships are offered with the support of the Scottish Office Education and Industry Department (SOEID).
Closing Date: Mid-March.
Additional Information: Awards will take the form of funding for the appointment of a temporary replacement to enable fellows to take study leave. There is provision for reimbursement of approved expenses for support fellows to a maximum of £500 per annum, in respect of actual expenses associated with the research, including travel and attendance at meetings.

ROYAL TOWN PLANNING INSTITUTE

26 Portland Place, London, W1N 4BE, England
Tel: (44) 171 636 9107
Fax: (44) 171 323 1582
Contact: Ms Judy Woollett

The Royal Town Planning Institute was founded in 1914 and is a registered charity. Its aim is to advance the science and art of town planning in all its aspects, including local, regional and national planning for the benefit of the public. The Institute is primarily concerned with maintaining high standards of competence and conduct within the profession, promoting the role of planning within the country's social, economic and political structures, and presenting the profession's views on current planning issues.

George Pepler International Award

Subjects: Town and country planning, or some particular aspect of planning theory and practice.
Eligibility: Open to persons under 30 years of age of any nationality.
Level of Study: Professional development.
Purpose: To enable young people of any nationality to visit another country for a short period to study the theory and practice of town and country planning.
No. of awards offered: 1.
Frequency: Every two years (even-numbered years).
Value: Up to £1500.
Length of Study: Short-term travel outside the UK (for UK residents) or for visits to the UK (for applicants from abroad).
Country of Study: Any country.
Application Procedure: Applicants are required to submit a statement showing the nature of the study visit proposed, together with an itinerary. Application forms are available from the RTPI.
Closing Date: March 31st.
Additional Information: At the conclusion of the visit the recipient must submit a report. Application forms are available on request.

RYAN DAVIES MEMORIAL FUND

1 Squire Court
The Marina, Swansea, SA1 3XB, Wales
Tel: (44) 1792 301500
Fax: (44) 1792 301500
Contact: Mr Michael D Evans, Secretary

The fund honours the memory of a great Welsh performer and gives awards in the performing arts to postgraduate students of Welsh extraction.

Ryan Davies Memorial Fund Scholarship Grants

Subjects: Music and drama, performing arts.
Eligibility: Open to Welsh artists or artists of Welsh extraction only.
Level of Study: Undergraduate, up to postgraduate.
Purpose: To enable Welsh artists to continue studies following their formal training.
Type: Grant.
No. of awards offered: Up to 8.
Frequency: Annual.
Value: Up to £2,500 each.
Length of Study: Up to 1 year.
Study Establishment: Unrestricted.
Country of Study: Any country.

Application Procedure: Applications are made by forwarding all relevant information (reason for application, qualifications, referees and any further background information) to the Secretary.

Closing Date: May 30th for notification by July 31st.

Additional Information: The Fund was set up in memory of Ryan Davies, Wales' most versatile entertainer.

SAMRO ENDOWMENT FOR THE NATIONAL ARTS

PO Box 31609, Braamfontein, 2017, South Africa
Tel: (27) 11 403 6635
Fax: (27) 11 403 1934
Telex: 4 24653 SAMROSA
Contact: J Lotto, Liason Officer

SAMRO is Southern Africa's Society of Composers and Lyricists, with special reference to the performing and broadcasting rights in their music. Through the SAMRO Endowment for the National Arts, it supports music study at home and abroad for citizens of South Africa, Botswana, Lesotho, and Swaziland.

SAMRO Bursaries Undergraduate for General Music Study In Southern Africa

Subjects: Music as a major study subject in any general branch of either the serious or contemporary popular genres.

Eligibility: Open to citizens of South Africa, Botswana, Lesotho, and Swaziland, who have met the requirements for entering the first year or for proceeding to the second year of study at a tertiary institute. The age limit is 25 years. Older students considered in special circumstances.

Level of Study: Undergraduate.

Purpose: To encourage music study at tertiary level.

Type: Bursary.

No. of awards offered: 30.

Frequency: Annual.

Value: R5,000 per year.

Length of Study: 1 or 2 years.

Study Establishment: An appproved recognised statutory institute of tertiary education approved by the Trustees and situated in SAMRO's territory of operation.

Country of Study: South Africa, Botswana, Lesotho or Swaziland.

Application Procedure: Applicants must produce an official letter of acceptance into the first year or entering the second year for degree or an equivalent diploma in music. Application form must be completed.

Closing Date: February 15th.

SAMRO Intermediate Bursaries for Composition Study In Southern Africa

Subjects: Music.

Eligibility: Open to citizens of South Africa, Botswana, Lesotho and Swaziland, who have met the requirements for proceeding to the third, fourth or honours of a senior undergraduate degree or equivalent diploma course. Applicants must have been born after January 31 1969. For entering any year of a Master's or Doctorate degree, the age limit is 30. Older students are considered in special circumstances.

Level of Study: Postgraduate, Undergraduate.

Purpose: To support composition study in either the serious or contemporary popular genres of music.

Type: Bursary.

No. of awards offered: 7.

Frequency: Annual.

Value: R6,000 for senior undergraduate study, R5,000 for postgraduate study.

Length of Study: 1 year.

Study Establishment: An approved recognised statutory institute of tertiary education, and situated in SAMRO's territory of operation.

Country of Study: South Africa, Botswana, Lesotho or Swaziland.

Application Procedure: Application form must be completed.

Closing Date: February 15th.

Additional Information: Applicants must produce official letter of acceptance for proceeding to the third, fourth or honours of an undergraduate degree or equivalent diploma course. Applicants must produce an official letter of acceptance for entering any year of Master's or doctoral degrees.

SAMRO Overseas Scholarship

Subjects: Music.

Eligibility: Open to postgraduate students who are citizens of South Africa, Botswana, Lesotho, and Swaziland. The age limit is 30 years.

Level of Study: Undergraduate.

Purpose: To encourage music study at postgraduate level in the 'serious' and 'contemporary popular' music genres.

Type: Scholarship.

No. of awards offered: 2.

Frequency: Annual.

Value: R35,000 for two years, plus travel allowance of R5,000.

Length of Study: 2 years.

Study Establishment: An institute or educational entity approved by the SAMRO Endowment for the National Arts.

Country of Study: Europe or North America.

Closing Date: April 30th.

Additional Information: These awards rotate on a quadrennial basis as follows 2000: instrumentalists, 2001: pianists, 2002: composers; 2003: singers.

SAMRO Undergraduate Bursaries for School Music Teaching

Subjects: Class music teaching and/or music education as a major subject.

Eligibility: Open to citizens of South Africa, Botswana, Lesotho, and Swaziland, who have been accepted, entering their first year or for proceeding to the second year of study of an undergraduate degree or equivalent diploma course. Age limit is 40 years. Older students are considered in special circumstances.
Level of Study: Undergraduate.
Purpose: To encourage the study of school music teaching and music education at tertiary level.
Type: Bursary.
No. of awards offered: 15.
Frequency: Annual.
Value: R5,000.
Length of Study: 1 or 2 years.
Study Establishment: At a university, college of education or other approved recognised statutory institute of tertiary education approved by the Trustees and situated in SAMRO's territory of operation.
Country of Study: South Africa, Botswana, Lesotho or Swaziland.
Application Procedure: Applicants must produce an official letter of acceptance into the first year or entering the second year for an undergraduate degree or equivalent diploma in subject areas specified.
Closing Date: February 15th.

SAMUEL H KRESS FOUNDATION

174 East 80th Street, New York, NY, 10021, United States of America
Tel: (1) 212 861 4993
Fax: (1) 212 628 3146
www: http://www.shkf.org
Contact: Ms Lisa Ackerman

Kress Fellowships for Advanced Training in Fine Arts Conservation

Subjects: Specific areas of fine arts conservation.
Eligibility: Open to US nationals, or students matriculated at US institutions, who have completed their initial training in conservation.
Level of Study: Postgraduate.
Purpose: To enable young American conservators to undertake post-MA advanced internships.
Type: Fellowship.
No. of awards offered: 10.
Frequency: Annual.
Value: US$25,000.
Study Establishment: Appropriate institutions.
Country of Study: USA.
Application Procedure: Please write for details.
Closing Date: February 28th.
Additional Information: Emphasis is on hands-on training. These grants are not for completion of degree programs. Enquiries should be directed to Lisa M Ackerman.

Samuel H Kress Foundation Travel Fellowships

Subjects: Art history.
Eligibility: Open to predoctoral candidates at American universities.
Level of Study: Doctorate.
Purpose: To facilitate travel for PhD candidates in the history of art to view materials essential for the completion of dissertation research.
Type: Fellowship.
No. of awards offered: 10-15.
Frequency: Annual.
Value: Varies (US$1,000-US$10,000).
Country of Study: Any country.
Application Procedure: Applicants must be nominated by their art history department. Limit of two applicants per department.
Closing Date: November 30th.

Samuel H Kress Foundation Two-Year Research Fellowships at Foreign Institutions

Subjects: Art history.
Eligibility: Restricted to PhD candidates in the history of art for completion of dissertation research. Candidates must be US citizens or matriculated at a US institution.
Level of Study: Predoctorate.
Purpose: To facilitate advanced dissertation research in association with a selected art historical institute in Florence, Jerusalem, Leiden, London, Munich, Nicosia, Paris, Rome or Zurich.
Type: Fellowship.
No. of awards offered: 4.
Frequency: Annual.
Value: US$18,000 per year.
Length of Study: 2 years.
Study Establishment: One of a number of art historical institutes in Florence, Jerusalem, Leiden, London, Munich, Nicosia, Paris, Rome or Zurich.
Country of Study: Outside USA.
Application Procedure: Applicants must be nominated by their art history department. Limit of one applicant per department.
Closing Date: November 30th.

SAN ANGELO SYMPHONY SOCIETY

PO Box 5922, San Angelo, TX, 76902, United States of America
Tel: (1) 915 658 5877
Fax: (1) 915 653 1045
Email: symphony@wcc.net
Contact: Ms Mercyla Shelburne, Manager

The San Angelo Symphony provides the only source of classical music in a 90-mile radius. Eight concerts, a summer pop concert, two children's concerts, and the International

Sorantin Competition comprise the annual season. The Symphony also support a 100-voice chorale, and a 300-member guild.

Sorantin Young Artist Award

Subjects: Piano performance, vocal performance and instrumental performance.
Eligibility: Open to instrumentalists and pianists under 28 years of age and vocalists under 31 years of age by November 19th in the year of the competition.
Level of Study: Postgraduate.
Purpose: To recognise and reward talent.
Type: Competition.
No. of awards offered: Varies.
Frequency: Annual.
Value: Overall Winner US$3,000 plus his/her division prize and a guest appearance with the San Angelo Symphony Orchestra; Division Winner US$1,000; Division Runner-Up US$400.
Country of Study: Any country.
Closing Date: Thirty days before the competition is held (in November).

SAN FRANCISCO CONSERVATORY OF MUSIC

1201 Ortega Street, San Francisco, CA, 94122, United States of America
Tel: (1) 415 759 3422
Fax: (1) 415 759 3499
Email: cmk@sfcm.edu
www: http://www.sfcm.edu
Contact: Office of Student Services

The Conservatory is a college of music and trains students for careers as professional symphony musicians, concert artists, opera singers, composers, conducters and teachers.

San Francisco Conservatory Performance Scholarships in Music

Subjects: Musical performance.
Eligibility: Open to US and foreign nationals who will be attending the Conservatory on a full-time basis. Candidates must have had considerable experience in musical performance.
Level of Study: Postgraduate, Undergraduate.
Purpose: To permit talented students to attend the Conservatory.
Type: Scholarship.
No. of awards offered: Varies.
Frequency: Varies.
Value: US$300-US$17,400.
Length of Study: 1 year; renewable.
Study Establishment: San Francisco Conservatory of Music.
Country of Study: USA.

Application Procedure: Candidates must complete both admission and scholarship applications, and must audition.
Closing Date: March 1st.

SCHOLARSHIP FOUNDATION OF THE LEAGUE OF FINNISH-AMERICAN SOCIETIES

Mechelininkatu 10, Helsinki, SF-0010, Finland
Tel: (358) 9 41 333 700
Fax: (358) 9 408 794
Email: sayl@sayl.fi
www: http://www.sayl.fi
Contact: Ms Sisko Rauhala, Culture and Youth Programmes

Scholarship Foundation of the League for Finnish-American Societies

Subjects: All subjects.
Eligibility: Open to Finns only.
Level of Study: Doctorate, Postdoctorate, Postgraduate.
Purpose: To enable Finns to study in the United States.
Type: Scholarship.
No. of awards offered: 2-3.
Frequency: Annual.
Value: US$3,000-US$5,000.
Length of Study: 1 academic year.
Study Establishment: University.
Country of Study: USA.
Application Procedure: Application form and references must be submitted.
Closing Date: First Monday in October.
Additional Information: The Scholarship Foundation also handles awards given to Finns by the American-Scandinavian Foundation and Thanks to Scandinavia Inc, both based in New York.

SCHOOL OF ORIENTAL AND AFRICAN STUDIES (SOAS)

University of London
Thornhaugh Street
Russell Square, London, WC1H 0XG, England
Tel: (44) 171 637 2388
Fax: (44) 171 436 4211
Email: dgi@soas.ac.uk
www: http://www.soas.ac.uk
Telex: 262433 W6876
Contact: Mrs Deirdre Goodman, Assistant Registrar

SOAS Bursary

Subjects: Oriental and African studies in archaeology area studies, economics, ethnomusicology, geography, history, law, languages, linguistics, phonetics, politics, religious

studies, social anthropology, development studies.
Eligibility: There are no eligibility restrictions; open to nationals of any country.
Level of Study: Postgraduate.
Purpose: To provide financial assistance to study for a Master's or postgraduate diploma.
Type: Bursary.
No. of awards offered: 6.
Frequency: Annual.
Value: £6,855.
Length of Study: 1 year (not renewable).
Study Establishment: SOAS.
Country of Study: United Kingdom.
Application Procedure: Application form (obtainable from Registrar, SOAS) must be completed and submitted with two references plus 500 word submission.
Closing Date: March 31st.

SOAS Research Student Fellowships

Subjects: Languages and cultures of East Asia, Southeast Asia, South Asia, Near and Middle East and Africa, anthropology and sociology, art and archaeology, economics, geography, history, law, linguistics, political studies, study of religions, development studies, ethnomusicology.
Eligibility: There are no eligibility restrictions.
Level of Study: Doctorate.
Purpose: To support research study at SOAS.
Type: Fellowship.
No. of awards offered: 5.
Frequency: Annual.
Value: £5,400 plus remission of home /EU fees.
Length of Study: 3 years.
Study Establishment: SOAS.
Country of Study: United Kingdom.
Application Procedure: Application form must be completed (obtainable from Registrar, SOAS) and submitted with two references plus 500 word submission, plus five photocopies.
Closing Date: March 31st.

SCOTTISH OFFICE EDUCATION DEPARTMENT

Gyleview House
3 Redheughs Rigg
South Gyle, Edinburgh, EH12 9HH, Scotland
Tel: (44) 131 244 5846
Fax: (44) 131 244 5887
Contact: Ms Anne Hampson, Team Leader

To administer the students' allowance scheme, the postgraduate students' allowance scheme, the Scottish studentship scheme and the nursing and midwifery bursary scheme.

Scottish Studentship Scheme

Subjects: Arts and humanities.
Eligibility: Open to students ordinarily resident in Scotland, who are in their final year of undergraduate study at a UK university or who have already graduated and also to nationals of the European Union. Applicants should normally be under 35 years of age.
Level of Study: Doctorate, Postgraduate.
Purpose: To assist advanced postgraduate studies in the arts and humanities.
Frequency: Annual.
Value: Varies.
Length of Study: 1-3 years, depending on the award.
Country of Study: United Kingdom. Only in exceptional circumstances will studentships be offered for study outside United Kingdom.
Application Procedure: Applications for all studentships must be submitted to the Department through universities.
Closing Date: May 1st of the year in respect of which application is made.
Additional Information: These awards correspond to those made by the British Academy on behalf of the Department for Education under the State Studentship Scheme and the same requirements as to age, academic qualifications and UK residence apply; they are also of the same annual value.

SCOTTISH OPERA

39 Elmbank Crescent, Glasgow, G2 4PT, Scotland
Tel: (44) 141 248 4567
Fax: (44) 141 221 8812
Email: 101776.3172@compuserve.com
Contact: Ms Margaret Sloan, Auditions Secretary

John Noble Bursary Award

Subjects: Singing.
Eligibility: Minimum entry age is 18, there is no upper age limit but the competition is intended for singers at the early stage of their professional careers. Scottish connections are required through birth, training, residency, or two years of permanent residence in Scotland before the closing date of entry.
Level of Study: Professional development.
Purpose: To encourage and help young singers with Scottish connections at the early stage of their professional careers.
Type: Bursary.
No. of awards offered: 1.
Frequency: Every two years.
Value: £2,000.
Country of Study: United Kingdom.
Application Procedure: Application form and other relevant documents to be submitted.
Closing Date: February 1st.

THE SCOULOUDI FOUNDATION

c/o The Institute of Historical Research
University of London
Senate House, London, WC1E 7HU, England
Tel: (44) 171 636 0272
Fax: (44) 171 436 2183
Email: g-younan@sas.ac.uk
Contact: Secretary

Scouloudi Foundation Historical Awards

Subjects: History or a related subject.
Eligibility: Open to graduates of UK universities who possess a relevant honours degree or UK citizens with a similar qualification from a university outside the UK. These awards are not made for study or research towards a postgraduate qualification.
Level of Study: Doctorate, Postdoctorate, Postgraduate.
Purpose: To provide subsidies towards the cost of publishing a book or article in the field of history, incorporating an academic thesis or other scholarly work already accepted by a reputable publisher or learned journal; or to pay for special expenses incurred in the completion of advanced historical work (except theses for higher degrees) such as the cost of fares and subsistence during visits to libraries or record repositories.
Type: Varies.
No. of awards offered: Varies.
Frequency: Annual.
Value: £100-£1,000. Applicants should not ask for more than their minimum requirements for the year concerned.
Country of Study: Any country.
Application Procedure: Application form to be completed.
Closing Date: March 1st.

SHASTRI INDO-CANADIAN INSTITUTE

Room 1402 Education Tower
2500 University Drive NW, Calgary, AB, T2N 1N4, Canada
Tel: (1) 403 220 7467
Fax: (1) 403 289 0100
Email: sici@acs.ucalgary.ca
www: http://www.uclagary.ca/~sici
Contact: Mr Lozi Mudrick-Donnon, Programme Officer

The Shastri Indo-Canadian Institute (SICI) is a unique educational enterprise that promotes understanding between Canada and India, mainly through facilitating academic activities. The Institute funds research, links institutions in the two countries, and organises seminars and conferences.

India Studies Fellowship Competition

Subjects: Subjects relating to India in the social sciences and humanities (including education, law, and management), and the arts.

Eligibility: Applicants must be Canadian citizens or landed immigrants.
Level of Study: Doctorate, Postdoctorate, Postgraduate, Professional development.
Purpose: To support candidates wishing to undertake research or training in India.
Type: Fellowship.
No. of awards offered: Varies from year to year.
Frequency: Annual.
Value: Varies.
Length of Study: 3-12 months.
Study Establishment: Varies.
Country of Study: India.
Application Procedure: Please contact the Canada head office for application procedure.
Closing Date: June 30th.

Shastri Indo-Canadian Institute Language Training Fellowship

Subjects: Social sciences and humanities (including education, management and law), with a substantial India studies or developmental studies component.
Eligibility: Open to Canadian citizens or landed immigrants.
Level of Study: Doctorate, Undergraduate.
Purpose: To support students in Canadian universities by offering training in the Indian language of choice.
Type: Fellowship.
No. of awards offered: 6.
Frequency: Annual.
Value: C$2,500.
Length of Study: Varies.
Study Establishment: Varies.
Country of Study: Canada.
Application Procedure: Please contact the Canada office for application procedure.
Closing Date: January 31st.

SIDNEY SUSSEX COLLEGE, CAMBRIDGE

Cambridge, CB2 3HU, England
Tel: (44) 1223 338800
Fax: (44) 1223 338884
Email: aga22@cam.ac.uk
www: http://www.sid.com.ac.uk
Contact: Tutor for Graduate Students

Founded in 1596, Sidney Sussex College admits men and women as undergraduates and graduates. The college presently has 150 graduate students, including 75 working for the PhD degree. The college has excellent sporting, dramatic, and musical facilities, and can house the majority of its graduate students in college rooms.

Sidney Sussex College Research Studentship

Subjects: All subjects.
Eligibility: Applicants must also apply for a postgraduate place at the University of Cambridge. Preference is for candidates under 26 years of age. Candidates must be or must become members of Sidney Sussex College.
Level of Study: Doctorate.
Purpose: To provide full support for one student to do three years of research leading to the degree of PhD at the University of Cambridge.
Type: Studentship.
No. of awards offered: 1.
Frequency: Every two years.
Value: £5,455 maintenance per year plus fees.
Length of Study: 3 years.
Study Establishment: University of Cambridge.
Country of Study: United Kingdom.
Application Procedure: Application form is available from the tutor for graduate studies.
Closing Date: March 1st.

SIR ERNEST CASSEL EDUCATIONAL TRUST

8 Malvern Terrace
Islington, London, N1 1HR, England
Tel: (44) 171 607 7879
Contact: Secretary

The Trust awards overseas research grants -through the British Academy - in the language, literature, or civilisation of any country. The Trust also awards the Mountbatten Memorial Grants to commonwealth students in their final years of study in the United Kingdom.

Mountbatten Memorial Grants to Commonwealth Students

Subjects: All subjects.
Eligibility: Open to Commonwealth students who are pursuing a course of study at undergraduate or postgraduate level at universities or other recognised institutions of higher education in the UK.
Level of Study: Postgraduate, Undergraduate.
Purpose: To assist overseas students from the Commonwealth who encounter unforeseen financial difficulties in their final year of study.
Type: Grant.
No. of awards offered: Varies.
Frequency: Annual.
Value: Up to £500.
Country of Study: United Kingdom.
Application Procedure: Applications in writing, including brief CV.
Additional Information: Grants are administered and awarded, on the Trust's behalf, by a number of universities and other institutions of higher education. Applicants should consult their university or college student welfare officer for

further information. The Trust does not sponsor or award scholarships, or pay fees. There are no grants for one-year courses.

Sir Ernest Cassel Educational Trust Overseas Research Grants

Subjects: Language, literature or civilization of any country.
Eligibility: Open to the more junior teaching members of faculties of universities and other recognised institutions of higher education in the UK, regardless of country of birth.
Level of Study: Unrestricted.
Purpose: To help towards the expenses of approved research abroad.
Type: Research Grant.
No. of awards offered: Varies.
Value: £100-£500.
Country of Study: Outside United Kingdom.
Application Procedure: Candidates should write to the British Academy at 20-21 Cornwall Terrace, London NW1 4QP.
Closing Date: September 30th, December 31st, February 28th, April 30th.
Additional Information: These Grants are administered by the British Academy.

SIR HALLEY STEWART TRUST

88 Long Lane
Willingham, Cambridge, CB4 5LD, England
Tel: (44) 1954 260707
Contact: Mrs Fawcitt

Sir Halley Stewart Trust Grants

Subjects: Medical, social or religious research.
Eligibility: There are no eligibility restrictions.
Level of Study: Unrestricted.
Purpose: To assist pioneering research in medical, social, educational and religious fields.
Type: Research Grant.
Frequency: Dependent on funds available.
Value: Salaries and relevant costs for young research students from PhD level to about £12,000 per year.
Length of Study: Limited to 2 or 3 years.
Study Establishment: Under the auspices of a charitable institution, for example a hospital, laboratory, university department or charitable organisation.
Country of Study: Any country.
Application Procedure: There is no application form. Please contact the Trust for further details.
Closing Date: Applications are accepted at any time.

SIR HENRY RICHARDSON TRUST

16 Ogle Street, London, W1P 7LG, England
Tel: (44) 171 636 4481
Fax: (44) 171 647 4307
Contact: Mrs Susan Dolton

Sir Henry Richardson Award

Subjects: Musical performance - repetiteurs in even-numbered years, accompanists in odd-numbered years.
Eligibility: Open to postgraduates of up to 30 years. Applicants should be British, Indian, Pakistani, or Bangladeshi nationals or have been resident in the UK for three years.
Level of Study: Postgraduate, Professional development.
Purpose: To assist accompanists and repetiteurs in alternate years.
No. of awards offered: 1.
Frequency: Annual.
Value: £8,000.
Country of Study: Any country.
Application Procedure: Selected students will be asked to audition.
Closing Date: End of April.

SIR ROBERT MENZIES CENTRE FOR AUSTRALIAN STUDIES

28 Russell Square, London, WC1B 5DS, England
Tel: (44) 171 862 8854
Fax: (44) 171 580 9627
Email: k.mcintyre@sas.ac.uk
Contact: Ms Kirsten McIntyre

The Sir Robert Menzies Centre for Australian Studies is at the Institute of Commonwealth Studies, University of London. There are six broad areas of activity which form the core of the Centre's operations - teaching, postgraduate seminars, public lectures, conferences, research and external lecturing, and its scholarships and fellowships programmes.

Australian Bicentennial Scholarships and Fellowships

Subjects: All subjects.
Eligibility: The scholarship is open to candidates registered as a postgraduate student at a British tertiary institution or eligible for registration at an Australian tertiary institution and usually resident in the UK. The fellowship is open to holders of a good postgraduate degree or relevant experience who are seeking to further their education or professional experience but not through taking a further degree.
Level of Study: Postdoctorate, Postgraduate.
Purpose: To promote scholarship, intellectual links, mutual awareness and understanding between the UK and Australia and to enable UK graduates to study in approved courses or undertake approved research in Australia and to enable Australian graduates to study in approved courses to

undertake approved research in the UK. To make allowance for disadvantaged persons.
Type: Scholarship and fellowship.
No. of awards offered: 1-4.
Frequency: Annual.
Value: Up to £4,000.
Study Establishment: Any approved Australian tertiary institution (UK applicants) or in any approved UK tertiary institution (Australian applicants).
Country of Study: Australia or United Kingdom.
Application Procedure: Application form and three references must be submitted plus a letter of acceptance from the proposed host institution.
Closing Date: June 7th for UK applicants; October 29th for Australian applicants.

Northcote Graduate Scholarship

Subjects: All subjects.
Eligibility: Open to applicants resident in the UK who are under 30 years old.
Level of Study: Postgraduate.
Purpose: To enable students to undertake a higher degree at an Australian University.
Type: Scholarship.
No. of awards offered: Up to 2.
Frequency: Annual.
Value: Allowance of A$17,427 per year, plus return economy air fare and payment of compulsory fees.
Length of Study: Up to 3 years.
Study Establishment: Any approved Australian tertiary institution.
Country of Study: Australia.
Application Procedure: Application form, two references, and letter of acceptance from Australian university must be submitted.
Closing Date: August 30th.

Visual Arts Fellowship

Subjects: Drawing and painting, sculpture, handicrafts, design.
Eligibility: Open to UK citizens only.
Level of Study: Postdoctorate, Postgraduate.
Purpose: For appropriately qualified UK candidates to take up a fellowship at the Western Australian Academy of Performing Arts, Edith Cowan University, Australia, and its regional centres.
Type: Fellowship.
No. of awards offered: 1.
Frequency: Annual.
Value: Up to £4,000.
Length of Study: A minimum of 3 months.
Study Establishment: WAAPA, Edith Cowan University, Western Australia.
Country of Study: Australia.
Application Procedure: Application form, three references, and six slides of work must be submitted.
Closing Date: June/ variable.

Additional Information: This award is run in conjunction with the Australian Bicentennial Scholarships & Fellowships scheme.

SISTER KENNY INSTITUTE

Abbott Northwestern Hospital
800 East 28th Street, Minneapolis, MN, 55407, United States of America
Tel: (1) 612 863 4463
Fax: (1) 612 863 8942
www: http://www.allina.com
Contact: Mrs Linda Paulson

Sister Kenny Institute is a rehabilitation centre located in Minneapolis. For 36 years the institute has sponsored an annual International Art Show - displaying and selling art produced by the disabled community in a month long show.

Sister Kenny Institute Encouragement Awards

Subjects: Drawing, sculpture, photography, mixed media, painting, watercolour, oils and acrylics.
Eligibility: There are no restrictions, except that applicants must be disabled physically or emotionally.
Level of Study: Unrestricted.
Purpose: To encourage artists to continue with their talents in the Arts.
No. of awards offered: Varies, in excess of 65.
Frequency: Annual.
Value: Varies US$25 -US$250.
Country of Study: Any country.
Application Procedure: An application form must be submitted.
Closing Date: March 15th.

Sister Kenny International Art Show by Artists with Disabilities

Subjects: Original art work in mediums including oils, acrylics, watercolors, graphic, sculpture, photography, mixed media.
Eligibility: Open to individuals having a physical or mental impairment which substantially limits one or more major life activity (such as caring for oneself, performing manual tasks, walking, seeing, hearing, breathing, learning and working).
Level of Study: Unrestricted.
Purpose: To provide an art selling forum for the creative talents of persons with disabilities; to give disabled artists an outlet to sell their work on a competitive basis; and to create an awareness and appreciation of the talents of disabled artists.
No. of awards offered: 67.
Frequency: Annual.
Value: US$50-US$500; awards of US$5,000 and sales of about US$12,000.
Country of Study: Any country.

Application Procedure: Application registration form accompanies artwork; please call 612 863 4463 for form.
Closing Date: March 22nd.
Additional Information: Artists may submit up to two pieces of art (one must be for sale) not exceeding 36 inches in length or width, including frame. The show is held for one month, from mid April to mid May.

SMITHSONIAN INSTITUTION

955 L'Enfant Plaza
Suite 7000
MRC 902, Washington, DC, 20560, United States of America
Tel: (1) 202 287 3271
Email: siofg@ofg.si.edu
www: http://www.si.edu/research+study
Contact: Office of Fellowships and Grants

Conservation Analytical Laboratory Materials Analysis Fellowship

Subjects: Research on problems in the application of techniques of the physical sciences to problems in art history, anthropology, archaeology, and the history of technology.
Eligibility: Open to all qualified individuals without reference to race, colour, religion, sex, national origin, condition of handicap or age. Pre and postdoctoral fellowships are available. Applications will also be accepted from persons with a degree or certificate of advanced training in the conservation of artefacts or art objects.
Level of Study: Doctorate, Postdoctorate, Postgraduate.
Type: Fellowship.
No. of awards offered: 1-2.
Frequency: Annual, if funds are available.
Value: US$15,000 for Predoctoral Fellows; US$27,000 for Postdoctoral Fellows.
Length of Study: 12 months.
Study Establishment: Smithsonian Institution.
Country of Study: USA.
Application Procedure: Please write for details.
Closing Date: January 15th.

For further information contact:

Conservation Analytical Laboratory
Smithsonian Institution, Washington, DC, 20560, United States of America
Contact: Ms Lambertus van Zelst, Director

Smithsonian Institution Postdoctoral Fellowships

Subjects: American social and cultural history, history of science and technology, history of art, anthropology, biological sciences, earth sciences, history of African art and culture.

Eligibility: Open to candidates of any nationality who have received the PhD or equivalent within seven years of the application date. Recipients must have completed the degree or certificate at the time the fellowship commences. Fluency in English is required.

Level of Study: Postdoctorate.

Purpose: To offer appointments to those who wish to pursue postdoctoral research training at the Smithsonian Institution in collaboration with a member of the professional staff of the Institution.

Type: Fellowship.

No. of awards offered: 3.

Frequency: Annual.

Value: US$27,000 per year, plus research and travel allowances.

Length of Study: 3-12 months, with the majority of appointments being for 1 year.

Study Establishment: Smithsonian Institution facilities, including museums on the Mall and elsewhere in Washington, DC, at its Astrophysical Observatory in Cambridge, Massachusetts, and at its Tropical Research Institute, Panama.

Country of Study: USA.

Application Procedure: Application form can be obtained from the Secretary. For further information please contact the Institution.

Closing Date: December 15th.

Smithsonian Institution Predoctoral Fellowships

Subjects: Anthropology, biological sciences, earth sciences, history of art, history of science and technology, American social and cultural history, history of African art and culture.

Eligibility: Open to students of any nationality who are enrolled in a university as candidates for the PhD or equivalent. At the time of appointment, the university must approve the undertaking of dissertation research at the Smithsonian Institution and indicate that requirements for the doctorate, other than dissertation, have been met. Fluency in English is required.

Level of Study: Postgraduate, Predoctorate.

Type: Fellowship.

No. of awards offered: Varies.

Frequency: Annual.

Value: US$15,000 per year, plus research and travel allowances.

Length of Study: 3-12 months.

Study Establishment: Smithsonian Institution facilities.

Country of Study: USA.

Application Procedure: Application form must be completed.

Closing Date: January 15th.

Additional Information: Projects proposed will be approved in advance by a Smithsonian staff member who will serve as the appointee's advisor. Projects must be related to the research and interest of the Institution's professional staff.

THE SOCAN FOUNDATION

41 Valleybrook Drive, Don Mills, ON, M3B 2S6, Canada
Tel: (1) 416 442 3815
Fax: (1) 416 442 3371
Email: foundation@socan.ca
www: http://www.socan.ca
Contact: Administrator

The SOCAN Foundation is an independent organisation guided by its own board of directors consisting of composers, songwriters and music publishers. Its programs are dedicated to fostering musical creativity, promoting a better understanding of the role of these creators in today's society and encouraging performance opportunities of Canadian music creators.

SOCAN Awards For Young Composers

Subjects: The Sir Ernest MacMillan Awards for orchestral compositions, The Serge Garant Awards for chamber music compositions, The Pierre Mercure Awards for solo or duet compositions, The Hugh Le Caine Awards for compositions realised on tape with electronic means, The Godfrey Ridout Awards for choral compositions of any variety.

Eligibility: Open to candidates under 30 years of age on the closing date of the competition. The competition is open to SOCAN members or to composers who are not members of a performing right society but are Canadian citizens. Works submitted must be original and unpublished.

Level of Study: Unrestricted.

Purpose: To support and encourage Canadian composers.

Frequency: Annual.

Value: Three prizes offered in each of five categories: C$2,000 (1st prize), C$1,000 (2nd prize) and C$500 (3rd prize).

Country of Study: Canada.

Application Procedure: Please write for details.

Closing Date: May 1st.

SOCIAL SCIENCE RESEARCH COUNCIL (SSRC)

810 Seventh Avenue, New York, NY, 10019, United States of America
Tel: (1) 212 377 2700
Fax: (1) 212 377 2727
Email: lastname@ssrc.org
www: http://www.ssrc.org
Contact: The Awards Committee

Abe Fellowship Program

Subjects: Research in the social sciences and humanities relevant to any one or combination of the following themes - global issues, problems common to advanced industrial societies, and issues that relate to improving US-Japanese relations.

Eligibility: Open to Japanese and American citizens, and other nationals, who can demonstrate serious and long-term affiliations in Japanese and/or American research communities. Applicants must hold a PhD or have attained an equivalent level of professional experience as evaluated in their country of residence. Applications from researchers in non-academic professions are welcome.

Level of Study: Postdoctorate.

Purpose: The programme seeks to develop a new generation of researchers who study policy-relevant topics of long-range importance and who will become members of bilateral and global research networks. The programme promotes a new level of intellectual co-operation between the Japanese and American academic and professional research communities concerned with and trained for advancing global understanding and problem solving.

Type: Fellowship.

Frequency: Annual.

Value: To include a base award and supplementary research and travel expenses as necessary for completion of the research project.

Length of Study: Up to 12 months.

Study Establishment: An appropriate American or Japanese institution.

Country of Study: USA or Japan.

Application Procedure: A reference is required; optional language evaluation form.

Closing Date: September 1st.

Additional Information: In addition to receiving fellowship awards, Fellows will attend annual conferences and other events sponsored by the program, which will promote the development of an international network of scholars concerned with research on contemporary policy issues. Funds are provided by the Japan Foundation's Center for Global Partnership.

ACLS/SSRC International Postdoctoral Fellowships

Subjects: The processes of immigration and settlement, and the outcomes for both immigrants and native-born Americans.

Eligibility: Applicants must be US citizens or permanent residents, or international scholars who are affiliated with a US academic or research institution during the time of the award. Applicants must hold a PhD or its equivalent in one of the social sciences (including history) or in an allied professional field.

Level of Study: Postdoctorate.

Purpose: To foster innovative research that will advance theoretical understandings of the origin of immigration to the United States.

Type: Fellowship.

No. of awards offered: 10.

Frequency: Dependent on funds available.

Value: The maximum amount to be awarded is US$20,000. Applicants are encouraged to seek supplemental funds from other sources to complete their budgets, but the SSRC reserves the right to reduce its award should the total funds raised exceed the project's budget.

Length of Study: 6-12 months.

Country of Study: USA.

Application Procedure: Further information will be available in mid-summer from the ACLS, 228 East 45th Street, New York, NY 10017-3398; fax: 212 949-8058; email: grants@acls.org.

Additional Information: The programme especially encourages applications from members of minority racial, ethnic, and nationality groups, and women.

The SSRC Eastern Europe Program: Dissertation Fellowships

Subjects: The social sciences and humanities relating to Albania, Bulgaria, the Czech Republic, the eastern part of Germany, Hungary, Poland, Romania, Slovakia and the former Yugoslavia. Proposals dealing with Germany should focus on the culture and society of the Communist period, its antecedents or consequences.

Eligibility: Open to US citizens or permanent legal residents.

Level of Study: Postgraduate.

Purpose: To fund dissertation research.

Type: Varies.

Frequency: Annual, if funds are available.

Value: Up to US$15,000, plus expenses.

Length of Study: 1 academic year.

Study Establishment: Any university or institution.

Country of Study: Outside Eastern Europe.

Application Procedure: This programme is administered by the American Council of Learned Societies (ACLS), therefore for further information contact them.

Closing Date: November.

Additional Information: The product of the proposed work must be disseminated in English.

For further information contact:

ACLS
Office of Fellowships and Grants
228 East 45th Street, New York, NY, 10017, United States of America

The SSRC Eastern Europe Program: East European Language Training Grants

Subjects: Any East European language (except the languages of the Commonwealth of Independent States).

Eligibility: US citizenship or permanent resident status is required. Applicants must hold at least a four-year college degree. Graduate students and postdoctoral scholars are eligible to apply. These awards are intended for people who will use the East European languages in their academic or other professional careers.

Level of Study: Postgraduate.

Purpose: To support summer language training for students and scholars who cannot receive such training at their home institutions.

Type: Varies.

Frequency: Annual.

Value: US$2,000 for first or second year study; US$2,500 for intermediate or advanced training.

Country of Study: USA for first or second year study; Eastern Europe for intermediate or advanced training.
Application Procedure: This programme is administered by the American Council of Learned Societies (ACLS), therefore for further information, please contact them.
Closing Date: February 1st.

For further information contact:

ACLS
Office of Fellowships and Grants
228 East 45th Street, New York, NY, 10017, United States of America

The SSRC Eastern Europe Program: Fellowships for Postdoctoral Research

Subjects: The social sciences and humanities relating to Albania, Bulgaria, the Czech Republic, the eastern part of Germany, Hungary, Poland, Romania, Slovakia and the former Yugoslavia. Proposals dealing with Germany should focus on the culture and society of the Communist period, its antecedents or consequences.
Eligibility: Applicants are required to be US citizens or permanent legal residents, and to hold the PhD or its equivalent as of the application deadline.
Level of Study: Postgraduate.
Purpose: To provide free time for research.
Type: Varies.
Frequency: Annual, if funds are available.
Value: Up to US$25,000. The funds may be used to supplement sabbatical salaries or awards from other sources, provided they would intensify or extend the contemplated research.
Length of Study: 6-12 months.
Country of Study: Outside Eastern Europe.
Application Procedure: This programme is administered by the American Council of Learned Societies (ACLS) Please contact them for further information.
Closing Date: November.
Additional Information: The product of the proposed work must be disseminated in English.

For further information contact:

ACLS
Office of Fellowships and Grants 228 East 45th Street, New York, NY, 10017, United States of America

The SSRC Eurasia Program: Dissertation Fellowships

Subjects: The humanities and social sciences relating to the former Soviet Union and its successor states.
Eligibility: Open to US citizens who have completed research for their doctoral dissertation and who expect to complete the writing of their dissertation during the next academic year.
Level of Study: Doctorate, Postdoctorate.
Purpose: To provide support to students who have completed research for their doctoral dissertations and expect to complete the writing of their dissertations during the next academic year.

Type: Fellowship.
Frequency: Annual.
Value: Up to US$15,000.
Length of Study: Up to 1 year.
Country of Study: Any country.
Application Procedure: Application form, three letters of recommendation, one official copy of all relevant post secondary study, language self evaluation, and a narrative statement must be submitted.
Closing Date: February 3rd.

The SSRC Eurasia Program: Postdoctoral Fellowships

Subjects: The social sciences and humanities relating to the Soviet Union and its successor states.
Eligibility: US citizens who have received their PhD~185~s after 1991 and are untenured. Applicants must have the PhD in hand at the time of application.
Level of Study: Postdoctorate.
Purpose: To improve the academic employment and tenure opportunities of new PhDs.
Type: Fellowship.
No. of awards offered: Varies.
Frequency: Dependent on funds available.
Value: A stipend of US$24,000 to provide two years of summer support plus one semester free of teaching for scholars.
Length of Study: 2 years.
Country of Study: Any country.
Application Procedure: Please write for details.
Closing Date: February 3rd.

SSRC International Predissertation Field Research Fellowships

Subjects: Social science and humanities.
Eligibility: The programme is open to full-time graduate students in the social sciences and humanities, regardless of citizenship, enrolled in doctoral programs in the United States. Applicants must have completed all PhD requirements except the field work component by the time the fellowship begins.
Level of Study: Postdoctorate.
Purpose: To provide support for social scientists and humanists to conduct dissertation field research in Africa, Central Asia and the Caucasus, China, Latin America and the Caribbean, the Near and Middle East, South Asia, and Southeast Asia.
Type: Fellowship.
No. of awards offered: 50.
Frequency: Annual.
Length of Study: 12 months.
Country of Study: Any country.
Application Procedure: Email angus@ssrc.org for more information.
Closing Date: November, contact the SSRC for exact details.
Additional Information: Application materials are available from the following 23 universities: University of California, Berkeley; University of California, Los Angeles; University of

California, San Diego; University of Chicago; Columbia University; Cornell University; Duke University; Harvard University; University of Illinois, Urbana-Champaign; Indiana University, Bloomington; Massachusetts Institute of Technology; Michigan State University; University of Michigan, Ann Arbor; University of Minnesota, Twin Cities Campus; University of North Carolina, Chapel Hill; Northwestern University; University of Pennsylvania; Princeton University; Stanford University; University of Texas, Austin; University of Washington; University of Wisconsin, Madison; and Yale University.

The SSRC Japan Program: Advanced Research Grants

Subjects: Social sciences and humanities.
Eligibility: Open to holders of the PhD or an equivalent degree who are US citizens or have been resident in the USA for at least three consecutive years at the time of application.
Level of Study: Postdoctorate.
Purpose: To encourage innovative research which is comparative and contemporary in nature, and has long-term applied policy implications, or which engages Japan in wider regional and global debates.
Type: Research Grant.
No. of awards offered: Varies.
Frequency: Annual.
Value: Grants are disbursed in dollars and/or yen depending on the location of the research.
Length of Study: 2-12 months.
Country of Study: Any country.
Application Procedure: For further information contact winther@ssrc.org.
Closing Date: December - contact the Research Council for confirmation.
Additional Information: Special attention will be given to Japanists who are interested in broadening their skills and expertise through additional training or comparative work in an additional geographic area; and to non-Japanists who use Japan as a case study or those who draw Japan into wider global debates.

The SSRC Japan Program: JSPS Postdoctoral Fellowship Program

Subjects: Social sciences and humanities.
Eligibility: Open to US citizens or permanent residents. Applicants will need proof of an affiliation with an eligible host research institution. For 12 to 24 months of study, scholars must have received the PhD no more than six years prior to April 1st of the year for which they are applying. For three to 11 months of study, scholars must have received the PhD no more than 10 years prior to April 1st of the year for which they are applying.
Level of Study: Postdoctorate.
Purpose: To provide qualified researchers in the social sciences and humanities with the opportunity to conduct research with leading universities and other research institutions in Japan.
Type: Fellowship.

No. of awards offered: 1.
Frequency: Annual.
Value: Round-trip airfare; insurance coverage for accidents and illness; monthly stipend of Y270,000; settling-in allowance of Y200,000; monthly housing allowance of Y100,000; monthly family allowance of Y50,000; eligibility for up to an additional Y1,500,000 annually for research expenses.
Length of Study: 1-2 years.
Study Establishment: Approved institution in Japan.
Country of Study: Japan.
Application Procedure: Please contact winther@ssrc.org for further information.
Closing Date: December. Please contact the SSRC for exact date.

The SSRC Near and Middle East Program: Advanced Research Fellowships in the Social Sciences and Humanities

Subjects: Doctoral dissertation research on the Near and Middle East (North Africa, the Middle East, Afghanistan, Iran and Turkey) in the humanities and social sciences. Research projects must be concerned with the period since the beginning of Islam. Researchers in disciplines previously underrepresented in this competition are especially encouraged; these include literature, economics, sociology, demographics, philosophy, religion, art history, and performance studies.
Eligibility: Open to citizens or permanent residents of the USA who are scholars whose competence for research on the area has been demonstrated by their previous work and who intend to make continuing contributions to the field.
Level of Study: Postdoctorate.
Purpose: To fund advanced research requiring fieldwork in the Middle East.
Type: Research Grant.
No. of awards offered: Varies.
Frequency: Annual.
Length of Study: 4-9 months.
Country of Study: One or more countries in the Near or Middle East.
Application Procedure: Please write for details.
Closing Date: December 1st.
Additional Information: Preference will be given to individuals without access to other major research support and to projects which are in the early stages of preparation and which require substantial field research.

The SSRC Near and Middle East Program: Dissertation Research Fellowships in the Social Sciences and Humanities

Subjects: Doctoral dissertation research on the Near and Middle East (North Africa, the Middle East, Afghanistan, Iran, and Turkey) in the humanities and the social sciences. Research projects must be concerned with the period since the beginning of Islam.

Eligibility: Open to graduate students working towards the PhD in the social sciences and humanities who are of American citizenship.
Level of Study: Postdoctorate.
Purpose: To help fund doctoral dissertation research.
Type: Fellowship.
Frequency: Annual.
Length of Study: 4-9 months.
Country of Study: One or more countries in the Near or Middle East.
Application Procedure: Please write for details.
Closing Date: November 1st.

The SSRC Southeast Asia Program: Vietnam Advanced Research Grants

Subjects: All aspects of the society and culture of Vietnam.
Eligibility: Open to holders of the PhD or an equivalent degree who are US citizens or have been resident in the USA for at least three consecutive years at the time of application.
Level of Study: Postdoctorate.
Purpose: To enable social scientists, humanists, and other professionals to conduct research or analyse previously gathered material on Vietnam.
Type: Research Grant.
No. of awards offered: Varies.
Frequency: Annual.
Value: Up to $30,000.
Length of Study: Either a single research visit for 12 months or 2 research trips, each lasting no less than 6 months.
Study Establishment: Research visits to Vietnam.
Country of Study: Vietnam.
Application Procedure: Please email rosenberg@ssrc.org for further details.
Closing Date: December 1st.

The SSRC Southeast Asia Program: Vietnam Dissertation Field Fellowships

Subjects: Doctoral dissertation research in the social sciences and humanities in Vietnam.
Eligibility: Graduate students enrolled full-time in PhD programmes in any of the social sciences or humanities at accredited universities in the US or Canada are eligible. Awards are subject to proof of completion of all departmental requirements other than the dissertation. There are no citizenship restrictions.
Level of Study: Doctorate.
Purpose: To help fund doctoral dissertation research.
Type: Fellowship.
Frequency: Annual.
Value: Up to $15,000.
Length of Study: 12-24 months.
Country of Study: Southeast Asia.
Application Procedure: Please write for details.
Closing Date: Please write for details.

The SSRC Soviet Union and Successor States Graduate Training Fellowships

Subjects: Eurasia area studies.
Eligibility: US citizens enrolled in accredited graduate programmes in any discipline of the social sciences or humanities.
Level of Study: Postgraduate.
Purpose: To support training in Eurasia Area Studies.
Type: Fellowship.
Frequency: Annual.
Value: Up to US$15,000.
Length of Study: 2 years.
Country of Study: Any country.
Application Procedure: Application forms; three letters of recommendation; one official copy of all relevant post-secondary study; language self evauation; description of programme of study.
Closing Date: February 3rd.

SOCIAL SCIENCES AND HUMANITIES RESEARCH COUNCIL OF CANADA (SSHRC)

350 Albert Street
PO Box 1610, Ottawa, ON, K1P 6G4, Canada
Tel: (1) 613 943 7777
Fax: (1) 613 992 1787
Email: fellowships@sshrc.ca
www: http://www.sshrc.ca
Contact: Fellowships & Institutional Grants Division

SSHRC is a federal agency responsible for promoting and supporting research and research training in the social sciences and humanities in Canada. SSHRC support research on the economic, political, social and cultural dimensions of human activity.

Social Sciences and Humanities Research Council of Canada Doctoral Fellowships

Subjects: Social sciences and humanities.
Eligibility: Open to persons who, by the time of taking up the fellowship, will have completed one year of graduate study or all the requirements for the Master's degree beyond the honours BA or its equivalent, and will be registered in a programme of studies leading to the PhD or its equivalent. Fellowships are available to Canadian citizens and nationals of other countries who have obtained permanent resident status.
Level of Study: Doctorate.
Purpose: To develop research skills and to assist in the training of highly qualified personnel.
Type: Fellowship.
No. of awards offered: Approx. 600 new Fellowships.
Frequency: Annual.
Value: Up to C$15,000 per year.

Length of Study: A full 48 months, or a shorter period of not less than 6 months.
Country of Study: Canada, or elsewhere under certain conditions.
Application Procedure: Application form must be completed.
Closing Date: Completed application forms must be mailed to the Council by November 15th for applicants not registered at a Canadian university and by January 15th for applicants registered at Canadian universities. Each Canadian university must submit applications for students registered at their university.

Social Sciences and Humanities Research Council of Canada Postdoctoral Fellowships

Subjects: Social sciences and humanities.
Eligibility: Open to Canadian citizens or permanent residents of Canada who have been awarded a doctoral degree no earlier than three years prior to the competition deadline (or who have fulfilled all requirements for a doctorate before the Fellowship period), and who intend to engage in full-time postdoctoral research for at least one year while affiliated with a recognised university or research institute.
Level of Study: Postdoctorate.
Purpose: To support the most promising new scholars and to assist them in establishing a research base at an important time in their research career.
Type: Fellowship.
No. of awards offered: Approx. 100.
Frequency: Annual.
Value: Up to C$28,428, plus a research allowance of up to C$5,000.
Length of Study: A full 24 months.
Country of Study: Any country, under certain conditions.
Application Procedure: Application form must be completed.
Closing Date: October 1st.

Social Sciences and Humanities Research Council of Canada Research Grants (Major)

Subjects: Social sciences, humanities.
Eligibility: Open to career scholars who are Canadian citizens or permanent residents of Canada affiliated with a Canadian university, or a recognised post-secondary institution.
Level of Study: Postgraduate.
Purpose: To support large-scale advanced research and editorial projects and programs.
Type: Research Grant.
No. of awards offered: Varies.
Frequency: Annual.
Value: A minimum of C$100,000 for one year; C$250,000 for three years; C$400,000 for five years. The ceiling is C$500,000 in any given year.
Length of Study: 5 years maximum.
Study Establishment: An approved institution.
Country of Study: Any country.

Application Procedure: Please contact Pierrett Tremblay for details. Tel: 613 992 3145 Fax: 613 992 1787 email pierrette.tremblay@sshrc.ca.
Closing Date: October 15th.

Social Sciences and Humanities Research Council of Canada Research Grants (Standard)

Subjects: Social sciences, humanities.
Eligibility: Open to career scholars who are Canadian citizens or permanent residents of Canada affiliated with a Canadian university or a recognised post-secondary institution.
Level of Study: Postgraduate.
Purpose: To support advanced research.
Type: Research Grant.
No. of awards offered: Varies.
Frequency: Annual.
Value: Less than C$100,000 per year or less than C$250,000 over a three year period. A minimum of C$5,000 in at least one of the years is required unless the applicant is at an institution not receiving a General Research Grant.
Length of Study: Grants in support of research programs will ordinarily be expected to cover 3 year periods.
Study Establishment: An approved institution.
Country of Study: Any country.
Application Procedure: Please contact Pierrett Tremblay for details. Tel: 613 992 3145 Fax: 613 992 1787 email pierrette.tremblay@sshrc.ca.
Closing Date: October 15th.

Social Sciences and Humanities Research Council of Canada Strategic Research Grants, Research Networks, Research Workshops, Partnership Development Grants

Subjects: Any subject relevant to the current five themes - Women and Change; Education and Work in a Changing Society; Applied Ethics; Managing for Global Competitiveness; Science and Technology Policy in Canada; mature themes are replaced after a period of five years.
Eligibility: Open to teams headed by career scholars who are Canadian citizens or permanent residents of Canada and who are affiliated with an eligible post-secondary institution in Canada.
Level of Study: Postgraduate.
Purpose: To support research projects and research related activities in areas of national importance.
Type: Research Grant.
No. of awards offered: Varies.
Frequency: Annual.
Value: Up to C$100,000 for one year or C$250,000 for three years (Strategic Research Grants); up to C$40,000 per year (Research Networks); up to C$15,000 per event (Research Workshops); up to C$5,000 (Partnership Development).
Length of Study: Up to 3 years (Strategic Research Grants); normally 3 years (Research Ne2rks); for single events held in Canada only (Research Workshops); 1 year or less (Partnership Development).
Study Establishment: An appropriate institution.
Country of Study: Canada.

Application Procedure: Please contact Susan Snyder for details. Tel: 613 992 3145 Fax: 613 992 1787 email susan.snyder@sshrc.ca.
Closing Date: October 15th; Partnership Development, any time.
Additional Information: An applicant may be principal investigator on only one Strategic Research Grant but may also participate in a Network or Workshop. Research Networks should be centred in Canada but may include non-Canadian members. Only the Canadian participants' expenses will be supported by the SSHRC.

SSHRC Institutional Grants

Subjects: Social sciences, humanities.
Eligibility: Open to Canadian universities.
Level of Study: Postgraduate.
Purpose: To enable Canadian universities to meet modest research requirements of their teaching staff.
Type: Research Grant.
No. of awards offered: Varies.
Frequency: Every three years.
Value: Varies: calculated on the number of faculty in each university. Universities may award not more than C$5,000 to individual researchers to help cover small research expenses, cost of travel to conferences and other similar costs.
Country of Study: Any country.
Application Procedure: Application form must be completed.
Closing Date: December 1st.

SOCIETY FOR THE PROMOTION OF HELLENIC STUDIES

Senate House
Malet Street, London, WC1E 7HU, England
Tel: (44) 171 862 8730
Fax: (44) 171 862 8731
Email: hellenic@sas.ac.uk
www: http://www.sas.ac.uk/icls/hellenic/
Contact: The Secretary

Dover Fund

Subjects: Greek language and papyri.
Eligibility: Open to currently registered research students, and, within the first five years of their appointment, to lecturers, teaching fellows, research fellows, postdoctoral fellows and research assistants.
Level of Study: Doctorate, Postdoctorate, Postgraduate.
Purpose: To further the study of the history of the Greek language in any period from the Bronze Age to the 15th century AD, and to further the edition and exegesis of Greek texts, including papyri and inscriptions, from any period within those same limits.
Type: Grant.
No. of awards offered: Varies.
Frequency: Annual.

Value: Grants will be made for such purposes as books, photography (including microfilm and xeroxing), and towards the costs of visits to libraries, museums and sites. The sums awarded will vary according to the needs of the applicant, but most grants will be in the range £50-£250; larger grants may be made from time to time at the discretion of the awards committee.
Study Establishment: Society for the promotion of Hellenic Studies.
Country of Study: Any country.
Application Procedure: Application form (including section for a referee) available from the Society. Mark applications 'FAO Dover Fund' and send them to the main address.
Closing Date: February 14th of the year in which the award is sought.

Dover Fund Grant

Subjects: Classical Greek.
Eligibility: Open to currently registered research students, lecturers and postdoctoral Fellows in their first five years of appointment.
Level of Study: Doctorate, Postdoctorate, Postgraduate.
Purpose: To further the study of the history of the Greek language, from the Bronze Age to the 15th century AD.
Type: Grant.
No. of awards offered: Approx. 3.
Frequency: Annual, if funds are available.
Value: Usually £50 - £250.
Application Procedure: Please request an application form from the Society.
Closing Date: February 14th.

SOCIETY FOR THE PROMOTION OF ROMAN STUDIES

Senate House
Malet Street, London, WC1E 7HU, England
Tel: (44) 171 862 8727
Fax: (44) 171 862 8728
Email: romansoc@sas.ac.uk
www: http://www.sas.ac.uk/icls/roman/
Contact: Dr Helen M Cockle, Secretary of Society

Promoting the study of history, architecture, literature and the art of Italy and the Roman Empire, from the earliest times to about 700 AD.

Hugh Last and Donald Atkinson Funds Committee Grants

Subjects: Italy and the Roman Empire - history, archaeology, literature and art.
Eligibility: Open to applicants of postgraduate or postdoctoral status or the equivalent, usually of UK nationality.
Level of Study: Postdoctorate, Postgraduate.

Purpose: To assist in the undertaking, completion or publication of work that relates to any of the general scholarly purposes of the Roman Society, which promotes the study of the history, archaeology, literature and art of Italy and the Roman Empire, from the earliest times down to about AD 700. In addition, postgraduate students may apply for small grants for visits to conferences and for other research purposes.
Type: Grant.
No. of awards offered: 20.
Frequency: Annual.
Value: Varies, but usually £200-£1,200.
Country of Study: Not specified, but usually a country formerly in the Roman Empire.
Application Procedure: Completion of application form is not essential, but all applicants must ensure that two references are sent directly to the Society.
Closing Date: January 15th.
Additional Information: Grants for the organisation of conferences colloquial and symposia will be considered only in exceptional circumstances.

THE SOCIETY FOR THE SCIENTIFIC STUDY OF SEXUALITY (SSSS)

PO Box 208, Mount Vernon, IA, 52314-0208, United States of America
Tel: (1) 319 895 8407
Fax: (1) 319 895 6203
Email: thesociety@worldnet.att.net
www: http://www.ssc.wisc.edu/ssss
Contact: Mr Howard J Ruppel, Executive Director

The Society for the Scientific Study of Sexuality is an international organisation dedicated to the advancement of knowledge about sexuality. The Society brings together an interdisciplinary group of professionals who believe in the importance of both production of quality research and the clinical, educational, and social applications of research related to all aspects of sexuality.

SSSS Student Research Grant Award

Subjects: Related to the field of human sexuality from any discipline - psychology, anthropology, social work, biology, theology, medical research, etc.
Eligibility: Open to students of any nationality who are enrolled in a degree granting programme.
Level of Study: Unrestricted.
Purpose: To support research in the field of human sexuality.
Type: Grant.
No. of awards offered: 3.
Frequency: Twice a year.
Value: US$750.
Study Establishment: An appropriate institution.
Country of Study: Any country.

Application Procedure: Please send SASE for further details and application packet.
Closing Date: February 1st, September 1st.
Additional Information: The purpose of the research can be a Master's thesis or doctoral dissertation, but this is not a requirement. Funds to support these grants are provided by the Foundation for the Scientific Study of Sexuality.

SOCIETY FOR THE STUDY OF FRENCH HISTORY

History Department
Keele University, Keele, Staffordshire, ST5 5BG, England
Tel: (44) 1782 583199
Fax: (44) 1782 583195
Email: hia10@keele.ac.uk
Contact: Dr Malcolm Crook, Secretary

The Society for the Study of French History was established to encourage research into French history. It offers a forum where scholars, teachers and students can meet and exchange ideas. It also offers bursaries for research and conferences to postgraduates registered in the UK undertaking research into French history.

Society for the Study of French History Bursaries

Subjects: Any aspect of French history.
Eligibility: Open to postgraduate students registered at a UK university.
Level of Study: Postgraduate.
Purpose: To enable postgraduates to complete research in French history.
Type: Bursary.
No. of awards offered: 2.
Frequency: Annual.
Value: £500.
Length of Study: Dependent on project for which the award is given.
Country of Study: France.
Application Procedure: Applications, giving details of the research being pursued and the use to which the money would be put, should be sent to the address shown, together with the names of two referees.
Closing Date: June 30th.
Additional Information: Preference will be given to those applicants who are in later stages of research.

Society for the Study of French History Research Bursaries

Subjects: Any aspect of French history.
Eligibility: Open to postgraduate students registered at a UK university.
Level of Study: Postgraduate.
Purpose: To attend conferences related to research.
Type: Bursary.
No. of awards offered: 5.

Frequency: Annual.
Value: Up to £100 each.
Country of Study: France.
Application Procedure: Applications, giving details of the research being pursued and the use to which money would be put, should be sent to the address shown, together with the names of two referees.
Closing Date: June 30th.

THE SOCIETY FOR THEATRE RESEARCH

c/o The Theatre Museum
1E Tavistock Street, London, WC2E 7PA, England
Email: e.cottis@btinternet.com
www: http://www.unl.ac.uk/str
Contact: Research Awards Sub-Committee Chairman

The Society for Theatre Research was founded in 1948 for all interested in the history and technique of British theatre. It publishes annually one or more books, newsletters, and three issues of the journal 'Theatre Notebook', and holds lecture-meetings and other events; and gives an annual book-prize as well as grants for theatre research.

Society for Theatre Research Awards

Subjects: Research substantially concerned with the history and practice of the British theatre, including music hall, opera, dance and other associated performing arts, exclusively literary topics are not eligible.
Eligibility: Applicants should normally be aged 18 or over but there is no other restriction on their status, nationality, or the location of the research.
Level of Study: Unrestricted.
Purpose: To aid research into practice and history of British theatre.
No. of awards offered: 2 major awards and a number of lesser awards.
Frequency: Annual.
Value: From a total of approximately £4,000: major awards normally £1,000 - £1,500; other awards normally £200 - £500. Payment for undergraduate course fees is not eligible.
Country of Study: Any country.
Application Procedure: Please write to the Chairman of the Research Awards Sub-Committee after October 1st in the year previous, for an application form and guidance notes. All applications and enquiries must be made by post to the Society's accommodation address.
Closing Date: February 1st.
Additional Information: While applications will need to show evidence of the value of the research and a scholarly approach, they are by no means restricted to professional academics. Many awards, including major ones, have previously been made to theatre practitioners and 'amateur' researchers, who are encouraged to apply. The Society also

welcomes proposals which in their execution extend methods and techniques of historiography. In coming to its decisions, the Society will consider the progress already made by the applicants and the possible availability of other grants.

SOCIETY OF ARCHITECTURAL HISTORIANS (SAH)

1365 North Astor Street, Chicago, IL, 60610-2144, United States of America
Tel: (1) 312 573 1365
Fax: (1) 312 573 1141
Email: info@sah.org
www: http://www.sah.org
Contact: Ms Angela Fitzsimmons, Assistant Director

A national, non-profit, membership organisation established in 1940, the Society of Architectural Historians promotes discussion among those interested in architecture and its related disciplines, encourages scholarly research in the history of architecture and the history of architecture and the built environment, and supports preservation of architectural monuments worldwide.

Edilia and François-Auguste de Montequin Fellowship in Iberian and Latin American Architecture

Subjects: Spanish, Portuguese or Ibero-American architecture, including colonial architecture produced by the Spaniards in the Philippines and what is today the USA.
Eligibility: Open to SAH members who are junior scholars, including graduate students, or senior scholars.
Level of Study: Doctorate, Postdoctorate, Postgraduate.
Purpose: To fund travel for research on Spanish, Portuguese, or Ibero-American architecture.
Type: Fellowship.
No. of awards offered: 2.
Frequency: Annual.
Value: US$2,000 for junior scholars, US$6,000 for senior scholars (offered every 2 years).
Country of Study: Any country.
Application Procedure: Application forms are available on request. Write to SAH for application guidelines.
Closing Date: November 15th.

Keepers Preservation Education Fund Fellowship

Subjects: Historic preservation.
Eligibility: Open to members of any nationality who are currently engaged in study in historic preservation.
Level of Study: Postgraduate.
Purpose: To enable a graduate student to attend the annual meeting of the Society, held each April.
Type: Fellowship.
No. of awards offered: 1.
Frequency: Annual.

Value: All fees and charges connected with the meeting itself are waived; plus reimbursement for travel, lodging, and meals directly related to the meeting, up to a combined total of US$500.
Country of Study: Any country.
Application Procedure: Write to SAH for application guidelines.
Closing Date: Applications are due November 15th.
Additional Information: Application materials are available on request.

Rosann Berry Fellowship

Subjects: Architectural history or an allied field (eg. city planning, landscape architecture, decorative arts or historic preservation).
Eligibility: Open to persons of any nationality who have been members of SAH for at least one year prior to the meeting, and who are currently engaged in advanced graduate study (normally beyond the Master's level) that involves some aspect of the history of architecture or of one of the fields closely allied to it.
Level of Study: Postgraduate.
Purpose: To enable a student engaged in advanced graduate study to attend the annual meeting of the Society.
Type: Fellowship.
No. of awards offered: 1.
Frequency: Annual.
Value: All fees and charges connected with the meeting itself are waived; plus reimbursement for travel, lodging, and meals directly related to the meeting, up to a combined total of US$500.
Country of Study: Any country.
Application Procedure: Application forms are available on request. Write to SAH for application guidelines.
Closing Date: November 15th.

SAH Architectural Study and Tour Scholarship

Subjects: Architectural history.
Eligibility: Open to SAH members who are students engaged in graduate work in architecture, or architectural history, city planning or urban history, landscape or the history of landscape design.
Level of Study: Postgraduate.
Purpose: To enable an outstanding student to participate in the annual SAH domestic tour.
Type: Scholarship.
No. of awards offered: 1.
Frequency: Annual.
Value: A surcharge on non-student participants' registrations is applied toward such tour scholarships to defray the cost of the tour itself.
Country of Study: Any country.
Application Procedure: Write to SAH for SAH guidelines.
Closing Date: The date changes each year.
Additional Information: Application forms are available on request.

Sally Kress Tompkins Fellowship

Subjects: Architectural history, historic preservation.
Eligibility: Open to architectural history students.
Level of Study: Doctorate, Postgraduate.
Purpose: To enable an architectural history student to work as a summer intern on an historic American buildings survey project, during the summer.
Type: Fellowship.
No. of awards offered: 1.
Frequency: Annual.
Value: US$7,500.
Country of Study: USA.
Application Procedure: Applications should include a sample of work, a letter of recommendation from a faculty member, and a US Government Standard Form (171 available from HABS or most US Government personnel offices). Applications should be sent to The Sally Kress Tompkins Fellowship, c/o HABS/HAER, National Park Service, PO Box 37127, Washington, DC 20013-7127, USA. Applicants not selected for the Tomkins Fellowship will be considered for other HABS summer employment opportunities. For more information, please contact E. Blaine Cliver, Chief, HABS/HAER.
Closing Date: January 13th.

Spiro Kostof Annual Meeting Fellowship

Subjects: Architectural history.
Eligibility: Open to doctoral candidates only.
Level of Study: Doctorate, Predoctorate.
Purpose: To enable an advanced graduate student in architectural history to attend the annual meeting of the Society of Architectural Historians.
Type: Fellowship.
No. of awards offered: 1.
Frequency: Annual.
Value: US$500.
Application Procedure: Please write for an application form, available after June 1st.
Closing Date: November 15th.

SOCIETY OF ARCHITECTURAL HISTORIANS OF GREAT BRITAIN

St John's College, Cambridge, Cambridgeshire, CB2 1TP, England
Tel: (44) 1223 339 360
Fax: (44) 1223 740 399
Email: djh1000@hermes.cam.ac.uk
Contact: Dr Deborah Howard, Chairman

The Society of Architectural Historians of Great Britain encourages the study and enjoyment of architectural history. It was founded in 1956. Through its membership, the Society provides a forum for the interchange of ideas and information, acting as a valuable link between architectural historians both in Great Britain and abroad. Membership is open to all who are interested in architecture and its history.

Ramsden Bursaries

Subjects: The topic in the application may relate to any aspect of the history of architecture.

Eligibility: Awards are open to members of the Society of Architectural Historians of Great Britain in any category. (For details on membership, please contact the Membership Secretary: Laurence Kinney, Brandon Mead, Old Park Lane, Farnham, Surrey, GU9 0AJ.) Candidates may apply for a second award, but in cases of equal merit, priority will be given to the first-time applicant. No one may receive more than two awards.

Level of Study: Postgraduate.

Purpose: To support postgraduate research in the field of architectural history.

Type: Bursary.

No. of awards offered: Up to 5 awards twice per year.

Frequency: Twice a year.

Value: To support the following research expenses: travel, building survey, photography, conference attendance. They are not awarded for maintenance at home, purchase of books or equipment, secretarial help, tuition fees. Value does not normally excees £500. Maximum £1,000.

Length of Study: Project normally to be completed within 1 year.

Country of Study: Applicants must either be resident in the British Isles, or working on the history of British Architecture.

Application Procedure: Applications should include: title and description of project, CV, detailed estimated costs, date of start of project and estimated completion date, and two letters of recommendation to be sent directly by referees to the Secretary (applicants are responsible for asking their referees to write). Five copies of the application should be submitted to the Hon Secretary of the Society with a stamped addressed envelope if acknowledgement is requires.

Closing Date: April 30th and October 31st each year.

Additional Information: The award decisions will be made annually in May and November, and announced in the Society's Newsletter. Payments to successful applicants will only be made after documentary evidence of each major item of expenditure has been supplied. This may be in receipt or invoice, or confirmation of travel booking or conference enrolment. The Society must be acknowledged in any published work arising out of the application. Copies of books, or in the case of shorter publications, an offprint or photocopy should be sent to the Hon Secretary of the Society. A brief report of the use made of the grant must be submitted to the Hon Secretary within a year of its receipt and, if the work extends beyond twelve months, a second report should be submitted on its completion.

For further information contact:

115 Henderson Row, Edinburgh, EH3 5BB, Scotland
Contact: Dr Deborah Mays, Hon Secretary of the Society

Stroud Bursaries

Subjects: The topic in the application may relate to any aspect of the history of architecture.

Eligibility: Awards are open to members of the Society of Architectural Historians of Great Britain in any category. (For details on membership, please contact the Membership Secretary, Laurence Kinney, Brandon Mead, Old Park Lane, Farnham, Surrey, GU9 0AJ.) Candidates may apply for a second award, but in cases of equal merit, priority will be given to the first-time applicant. No one may receive more than two awards.

Level of Study: Unrestricted.

Purpose: To support publication in the field of architectural history.

Type: Bursary.

No. of awards offered: Up to 5 twice per year.

Frequency: Twice a year.

Value: Subsidy to defray publication costs, cost of purchase of illustrations, payment of copyright fees, contribution to the costs of mounting an exhibition. Amount does not normally exceed £500, maximum £1,000.

Length of Study: Project normally to be completed within 1 year.

Country of Study: Applicants must either be resident in the British Isles, or working on the history of British Architecture.

Application Procedure: Applications should include: title and description of project, CV, detailed estimated costs, date of start of project and estimated completion date, and two letters of recommendation to be sent directly by referees to the Secretary (applicants are responsible for asking their referees to write). Five copies of the application should be submitted to the Hon Secretary of the Society with a stamped addressed envelope if acknowledgement is required.

Closing Date: April 30th and October 31st each year.

Additional Information: The award decisions will be made annually in May and November, and announced in the Society's Newsletter. Payments to successful applicants will only be made after documentary evidence of each major item of expenditure has been supplied. The Society must be acknowledged in any published work arising out of the application. Copies of books, or in the case of shorter publications, an offprint or photocopy should be sent to the Hon. Secretary within a year of receipt and, if the work extends beyond twelve months, a second report should be submitted on its completion.

For further information contact:

115 Henderson Row, Edinburgh, EH3 5BB, Scotland
Contact: Dr Deborah Mays, Hon Secretary of the Society

SOCIETY OF CHILDREN'S BOOK WRITERS AND ILLUSTRATORS (SCBWI)

345 North Maple Street, Beverly Hills, CA, 90210, United States of America
Tel: (1) 859 9887
Fax: (1) 859 4877
www: http://www.scbwi.org
Contact: Mr Stephen Mooser, President

The Society of Children's Book Writers and Illustrators is an organisation of 11,000 writers, illustrators, editors, agents, and publishers of childrens books, television, film, and multimedia.

Barbara Karlin Grant

Subjects: Children's picture-books.
Eligibility: Open to both full and associate members of the Society who have never had a picture-book published. The grant is not available for a project on which there is already a contract.
Level of Study: Unrestricted.
Purpose: To assist picture-book writers in the completion of a specific project.
Type: Grant.
No. of awards offered: 1.
Frequency: Annual.
Value: US$1,000.
Country of Study: Any country.
Application Procedure: Please write for details.
Closing Date: May 15th.

Don Freeman Memorial Grant-in-Aid

Subjects: Children's picture-books.
Eligibility: Open to both full and associate members of the Society who, as artists, seriously intend to make picture-books their chief contribution to the field of children's literature.
Level of Study: Unrestricted.
Purpose: To enable picture-book artists to further their understanding, training and work in the picture-book genre.
Type: Grant.
No. of awards offered: 2.
Frequency: Annual.
Value: US$1,000.
Country of Study: Any country.
Application Procedure: Application to be submitted to the Society. Receipt of application will be acknowledged.
Closing Date: Application requests June 15th; completed application February 10th.

SCBWI General Work-in-Progress Grant

Subjects: Children's literature.
Eligibility: Open to both full and associate members of the Society. The grant is not available for projects on which there

is already a contract. Recipients of previous US$1,000 SCBWI Grants are not eligible to apply for any further SCBWI Grants.
Level of Study: Unrestricted.
Purpose: To assist children's book writers in the completion of a specific project.
Type: Grant.
No. of awards offered: 1 full grant and 1 runner-up grant.
Frequency: Annual.
Value: Full grant: US$1,000; runner-up grant: US$500.
Country of Study: Any country.
Application Procedure: Please write for details.
Closing Date: May 1st.

SCBWI Grant for a Contemporary Novel for Young People

Subjects: Children's literature.
Eligibility: Open to both full and associate members of the Society. The grant is not available for projects on which there is already a contract. Recipients of previous US$1,000 SCBWI Grants are not eligible to apply for any further SCBWI Grants.
Level of Study: Unrestricted.
Purpose: To assist children's book writers in the completion of a specific project.
Type: Grant.
No. of awards offered: 1 full grant and 1 runner-up grant.
Frequency: Annual.
Value: Full grant: US$1,000; runner-up grant: US$500.
Country of Study: Any country.
Application Procedure: Please write for details.
Closing Date: May 1st.

SCBWI Grant for Unpublished Authors

Subjects: Children's literature.
Eligibility: Open to both full and associate members of the Society who have never had a book published. The grant is not available for a project on which there is already a contract. Recipients of previous SCBWI Grants are not eligible to apply for any further SCBWI Grants.
Level of Study: Unrestricted.
Purpose: To assist children's book writers in the completion of a specific project.
Type: Grant.
No. of awards offered: 1 full grant and 1 runner-up grant.
Frequency: Annual.
Value: Full grant: US$1,000; runner-up grant: US$500.
Country of Study: Any country.
Closing Date: May 1st.

SCBWI Non-Fiction Research Grant

Subjects: Children's literature.
Eligibility: Open to both full and associate members of the Society. The grant is not available for projects on which there is already a contract. Recipients of previous US$1,000 SCBWI Grants are not eligible to apply for any further SCBWI Grants.

Level of Study: Unrestricted.
Purpose: To assist children's book writers in the completion of a specific project.
Type: Grant.
No. of awards offered: 1 full grant and 1 runner-up grant.
Frequency: Annual.
Value: Full grant: US$1,000; runner-up grant: US$500.
Country of Study: Any country.
Application Procedure: Please write for details.
Closing Date: May 1st.

SOROPTIMIST INTERNATIONAL OF GREAT BRITAIN AND IRELAND

127 Wellington Road South, Stockport, Cheshire, SK1 3TS, England
Tel: (44) 161 480 7686
Fax: (44) 161 477 6152
www: http://titan.glo.be/~bea/sieorg.htm
Contact: The Chairman

Soroptomist International of Great Britain and Ireland Golden Jubilee Fellowship

Subjects: Any subject, but preference is given to women seeking to train or retrain for a business or profession as mature students. However all applications will be considered by the Committee.
Eligibility: Open to women residing within the boundaries of Soroptimist International of Great Britain and Ireland, who need not be Soroptimists. The countries are Anguilla, Antigua and Barbuda, Bangladesh, Barbados, British Virgin Islands, Cameroon, Gambia, Grenada, Guernsey, India, Isle of Man, Jamaica, Jersey, Republic of Ireland, Malawi, Malta, Mauritius, Nigeria, Pakistan, Seychelles, Sierra Leone, South Africa, Sri Lanka, St Vincent and the Grenadines, Thailand, Trinidad and Tobago, Turks and Caicos Islands, Uganda, United Kingdom, and Zimbabwe.
Level of Study: Unrestricted.
Type: Fellowship.
No. of awards offered: Approx. 40.
Frequency: Annual.
Value: Normally within range £100-£500 per year, from a fund of £6,000.
Study Establishment: Any agreed institution, providing the residential stipulation is met.
Country of Study: Any country.
Application Procedure: Please enclose SAE or IRCs for details.
Closing Date: April 30th for the academic year beginning the following autumn.

SOROS FOUNDATION - HUNGARY

Bolyai u 14, Budapest, H-1023, Hungary
Tel: (36) 1 315 0315
Fax: (36) 1 315 0201
Email: office@soros.hu
www: http://www.soros.hu (in Hungarian)
Contact: Ms Judit Ronai, Public Relations Manager

Bologna Program

Subjects: Archaeology, fine and applied arts, philosophy, medicine, law, and natural sciences.
Eligibility: Open to Hungarian nationals with Italian language.
Level of Study: Postgraduate.
Purpose: To participate in the international science world.
Type: Grant.
No. of awards offered: 4-8.
Frequency: Annual, if funds are available.
Value: 1,200,000 lire per month scholarship, plus travel costs.
Length of Study: 2-4 months.
Country of Study: Italy.
Application Procedure: Please write for an application form.
Closing Date: March 15th.

Leuven Program

Subjects: Humanities and social sciences.
Eligibility: Open to Hungarian nationals with English, French, German, or Flemish language.
Level of Study: Postdoctorate, Postgraduate.
Purpose: To participate in the international science world.
No. of awards offered: 10-12.
Frequency: Annual.
Value: Accommodation, scholarship, travel costs and living expenses.
Length of Study: 3-9 months.
Study Establishment: A university.
Country of Study: Belgium.
Application Procedure: Please write for an application form.
Closing Date: January 31st.
Additional Information: In the case of excellent achievement there is a possibility for a PhD course.

Soros Foundation General Program

Subjects: Natural sciences, humanities and social sciences.
Eligibility: Open to Hungarian nationals only.
Level of Study: Postgraduate.
Purpose: To participate in the international science world.
Type: Grant.
No. of awards offered: 10-12.
Frequency: Annual, if funds are available.
Value: US$800 - US$1200 per month.
Length of Study: 3-9 months.
Country of Study: Western Europe or USA.
Application Procedure: Please write for an application form.
Closing Date: January 31st.

SOROS FOUNDATION - LATVIA

Raina bulv 19
Room 243, Riga, LV-1586, Latvia
Tel: (371) 782 0385
Fax: (371) 782 0385
Email: dvisnola@lanet.la
Contact: Mr Dace Sinkevica, Director of EAC

The Soros Foundation was created by George Soros with a view to building and supporting free and open societies. The Foundation hopes to achieve its aim by supporting a wide range of programs in education; media and communications; civil society; science and medicine; arts and culture; economic restructuring; and legal reform.

Soros Foundation (Latvia) Support Programme for Studies Abroad

Subjects: All subjects.
Eligibility: Open to Latvian nationals and residents only.
Level of Study: Doctorate, Postgraduate.
Purpose: To support Latvian students who are studying abroad.
Type: Grant.
No. of awards offered: 20.
Frequency: Annual.
Value: An average of US$1,000, with a maximum of US$3,000.
Length of Study: A minimum of 1 semester.
Study Establishment: Any university.
Country of Study: Outside Latvia.
Application Procedure: Application package consists of application forms, description of the study programme, CV and other documentation. Please write for further details.
Closing Date: July 1st, November 1st.
Additional Information: The awards are not to be used to cover study fees, accommodation or living expenses.

SOUTH AFRICAN ASSOCIATION OF UNIVERSITY WOMEN

PO Box 642, Parklands, 2121, South Africa
Tel: (27) 11 836 2027
Fax: (27) 11 784 1338
Email: bell@newaa.co.sa
Contact: Mrs J A Bell, National President

Edna Machanick Award

Subjects: All subjects.
Eligibility: Open to South African women of all races who have successfully completed one year of a course of study and are in need of financial assistance to complete their studies towards a non-degree qualification (diploma or certificate) at the tertiary education level.

Level of Study: Postgraduate.
Purpose: To provide assistance to women at tertiary institutions, other than a university.
Type: Award.
No. of awards offered: 3-4.
Frequency: Annual.
Value: R500 per year.
Study Establishment: Any institution of tertiary education.
Country of Study: Any country.
Application Procedure: Write for application forms.
Closing Date: October 31st.
Additional Information: The awards are generally made by the institutions concerned. SAAUW provides the funding.

Isie Smuts Research Award

Subjects: All subjects.
Eligibility: Open to members of the South African Association of University Women.
Level of Study: Postgraduate.
Purpose: To assist postgraduate women in research.
Type: Award.
No. of awards offered: 1.
Frequency: Annual.
Value: R1,000.
Study Establishment: Any South African university.
Country of Study: South Africa.
Application Procedure: Write for application to Miss V Henley at the main address.
Closing Date: October 31st.

SAAUW International Fellowship

Subjects: Any subject - postgraduate research.
Eligibility: Open to members of the International Federation of University Women.
Level of Study: Postgraduate.
Purpose: To assist members of the International Federation of University Women, who wish to study in South Africa.
Type: Fellowship.
No. of awards offered: 1.
Frequency: Annual.
Value: R1,000.
Length of Study: Not less than 6 months.
Country of Study: South Africa.
Application Procedure: Write for application forms to the address below.
Closing Date: August 31st.
Additional Information: The award is made when a suitable applicant applies.

For further information contact:

21 Templeton Drive, Grahamstown, 6140, South Africa
Contact: Miss V Henley

SOUTH PLACE SUNDAY CONCERTS

Fernside
Copthall Green
Upshire, Waltham Abbey, Essex, EN9 3SZ, England
Contact: Mr Raymond Cassidy, Honorary Secretary

Clements Memorial Prize

Subjects: Musical composition.
Eligibility: There are no restrictions on eligibility.
Level of Study: Unrestricted.
Purpose: To encourage the composition of chamber music.
Type: Prize.
No. of awards offered: 1.
Frequency: Every two years.
Value: £750.
Country of Study: Any country.
Application Procedure: Conditions and entry forms are available on request from the Honorary Secretary. Please always send a self addressed stamped envelope for the entry form.
Closing Date: October 1st in the year of the award (2000).
Additional Information: Entries should be for three to eight unmodified non-electronic musical instruments and should not have been publicly performed or have won a prize in any other competition. The winning composition will remain the copyright of its author.

SOUTHDOWN TRUST

Hillbarn Cottage
10 Nepcote
Findon, Near Worthing, West Sussex, BN14 0SD, England
Contact: Mr J G Wyatt, Secretary

The Southdown Trust is a small charity which gives limited help to individuals.

Southdown Trust Awards

Subjects: All subjects except medicine, law, drama and music, dance and journalism, sociology, women's studies, Business studies, arts, sport, IT, counselling.
Eligibility: Open mainly to UK citizens but other nationalities are considered.
Level of Study: Postgraduate.
Purpose: To encourage personal initiative and concern for others.
No. of awards offered: Varies.
Frequency: Varies, depending on funds available.
Value: Varies, but limited; ranges between £25-£200.
Country of Study: United Kingdom.
Application Procedure: No application form. Applicant must write in giving full details.
Closing Date: May 1st, November 1st.

Additional Information: Stamped addressed envelopes must always be enclosed.

SOUTHERN URAL STATE UNIVERSITY

International Affairs Office
76 Lenin Avenue, Chelyabinsk, 454080, Russia
Tel: (7) 3512 65 65 04
Fax: (7) 3512 347 408
Email: dmitry@irex.urc.ac.ru
www: http://www.tu-chel.ac.ru/
Contact: Mr Dimitry Sherbakov

Southern Ural State University is a public institution of higher education and research accredited by the State Committee for Higher Education of the Russian Federation. The staff includes 1,500 teachers, 750 associate professors, 15,000 students and 15 faculties and the University award bachelors, engineering, candidate of science and doctor of science degrees.

SUSU Rector's Award

Subjects: Architecture and town planning; business administration and management; engineering; law; mathematics and computer science; transport and communications.
Eligibility: Open to citizens of any nationality. Applicants must be fluent in Russian.
Level of Study: Unrestricted.
Purpose: To give international students the opportunity to study in Chelyabinsk, Russia.
Type: Bursary.
No. of awards offered: 2.
Frequency: Annual.
Value: Two semesters of education at CSTU free of charge.
Length of Study: 2 semesters.
Study Establishment: Chelyabinsk State Technical University.
Country of Study: Russia.
Application Procedure: Application form must be completed. Available upon request.
Closing Date: March 1st.

SPALDING TRUSTS

PO Box 85, Stowmarket, Suffolk, IP14 3NY, England
Fax: (44) 1359 240739
Contact: Mrs T Rodgers, General Secretary

The Trust supports academic research on comparative inter-faith projects; consideration is also given to applications which are not academically oriented, provided that they will have a practical and beneficial effect on inter-religious understanding.

Spalding Trusts Grants-in-Aid of Research

Subjects: World religions other than that of the holder. Such study should be the principal, not a subsidiary, object.
Eligibility: Open to those engaged in academic studies or in study which will have practical benefit in promoting inter-religious understanding.
Level of Study: Doctorate, Postdoctorate, Postgraduate, Research.
Purpose: To promote a better understanding between the great cultures of the world by encouraging the study of the religious principles on which they are based.
Frequency: According to research project.
Value: Limited amounts in the form of grants for subsistence, purchase of books or for travel.
Length of Study: Short periods.
Country of Study: Any country.
Application Procedure: Candidates are requested to submit a research proposal, budget, reference (academic), and CV. Applications take 2-3 months to be considered. SAE appreciated.
Closing Date: Applications are considered throughout the year but major applications in April.
Additional Information: Trustees are particularly interested in research projects which are backed by professional ability to raise the standard of knowledge of religious principles and practices, and to interpret their relation to contemporary society.

ST ANDREW'S SOCIETY OF THE STATE OF NEW YORK

42 St Andrew Square, Edinburgh, EH2 2YE, Scotland
Tel: (44) 131 523 2049
Fax: (44) 131 557 9178
Telex: 72230 RBSCOT
Contact: Mr Tony Smith, Executive Assistant

St Andrew's Society of the State of New York Scholarship Fund

Subjects: All subjects.
Eligibility: Open to newly qualified graduates or undergraduates of a Scottish university or of Oxford or Cambridge. Candidates are required to have a Scottish background. The possession of an honours degree is not essential. Personality and other qualities will influence the selection.
Level of Study: Postgraduate.
Purpose: To support advanced study exchanges between the USA and Scotland by individuals with Scottish backgrounds.
Type: Scholarship.
No. of awards offered: 2.
Frequency: Annual.
Value: US$15,000 to cover university tuition fees, room and board, and transportation expenses.
Length of Study: 1 academic year.

Study Establishment: A University in the USA, restricted to a radius of 250 miles from New York City and only if there is an unusual reason and justification will the Society consider other locations for students who cannot find courses for their specialities within the boundaries outlined: thereafter, the scholar is expected to spend a little time travelling in America before returning to Scotland.
Country of Study: USA; restricted to a radius of 250 miles from New York City.
Application Procedure: Please write for further details.
Closing Date: Early January.
Additional Information: Each Scottish University will vet its own applicants and nominate one candidate to go forward to the Final Selection Committee to be held in Edinburgh in early March. Oxford and Cambridge applicants should apply directly to the Society.

ST ANDREW'S SOCIETY OF THE STATE OF NEW YORK

3 West 51st Street, New York, NY, 10019, United States of America
Tel: (1) 212 397 4849
Fax: (1) 212 397 4846
Email: standrewsny@msn.com
Contact: The Executive Director

St Andrew's Society of the State of New Yorks' constitution states -'For the relief of natives of Scotland and their descendants who might be in want or distress and to promote social intercourse among its members'.

St Andrew's Society of the State of New York Scholarship

Subjects: General, no field of endeavour requirement.
Eligibility: Students who have graduated from an American university, of Scottish-American descent, and New York area address (within a 250 mile radius).
Level of Study: Postgraduate.
Purpose: To promote cultural and intellectual interchange and goodwill between Scotland and the USA.
Type: Scholarship.
No. of awards offered: 2.
Frequency: Annual.
Value: US$10,000.
Length of Study: 1 year.
Study Establishment: Any university in Scotland.
Country of Study: Scotland.
Application Procedure: Application form, documentation of transcripts, and letters of recommendation; the President of each college or university must recommend one student only from that institution.
Closing Date: December 15th.

STATE HISTORICAL SOCIETY OF WISCONSIN

816 State Street, Madison, WI, 53706, United States of America
Tel: (1) 608 264 6464
Fax: (1) 608 264 6486
www: http://www.shsw.wisc.edu
Contact: Mr Michael E Stevens, State Historian

Alice E Smith Fellowship

Subjects: American history.
Eligibility: Open to women undertaking research in American history, with preference given to those applicants doing graduate research in the history of Wisconsin or the Middle West.
Level of Study: Doctorate.
Purpose: To encourage and support graduate research in American history, by women.
Type: Fellowship.
No. of awards offered: 1.
Frequency: Annual.
Value: US$2,000 paid in a lump sum.
Length of Study: 1 year; not generally renewable.
Country of Study: USA.
Application Procedure: Applicants should send four copies of a two page letter detailing their current research.
Closing Date: July 15th.
Additional Information: Usually awarded to candidates working on doctoral dissertations.

Amy Louise Hunter Fellowship

Subjects: American history.
Eligibility: Open to graduate students and beyond.
Level of Study: Doctorate, Postdoctorate.
Purpose: To promote research on topics related to the history of women and public policy, with preference given to Wisconsin topics or research using the collections of the State Historical Society.
Type: Fellowship.
No. of awards offered: 1.
Frequency: Every two years.
Value: US$2,500.
Length of Study: 1 year; not renewable.
Country of Study: USA.
Application Procedure: Applicants must submit four copies of a two-page letter describing their research and four copies of current résumé.
Closing Date: May 1st (even-numbered years).
Additional Information: Usually awarded to candidates working on doctoral dissertations or postdoctoral research.

John C Geilfuss Fellowship

Subjects: Wisconsin's business and economic history.
Eligibility: Open to graduate students and beyond.
Level of Study: Doctorate, Postdoctorate.
Purpose: To encourage research in Wisconsin's business and economic history.
Type: Fellowship.
No. of awards offered: 1.
Frequency: Annual.
Value: US$2,000.
Length of Study: 1 year; not renewable.
Country of Study: USA.
Application Procedure: Applicants must submit four copies of a two-page letter detailing their research, and four copies of a current résumé.
Closing Date: February 1st.
Additional Information: Usually awarded to candidates working on doctoral dissertations or postdoctoral research.

STATE LIBRARY OF NEW SOUTH WALES

Macquarie Street, Sydney, NSW, 2000, Australia
Tel: (61) 2 9273 1499
Fax: (61) 2 9273 1248
Email: jjones@slnsw.gov.au
www: http://slnsw.gov.au
Contact: Ms Jill Jones, Senior Project Officer

The State Library of New South Wales is the premier reference and research library in the state. The Library consists of the State Reference Library and the Mitchell Library which contains the famous Australian Research Collections pertaining to the history of Australia and the South West Pacific region.

C H Currey Memorial Fellowship

Subjects: Australian history.
Eligibility: Open to individuals of any nationality.
Level of Study: Unrestricted.
Purpose: To promote the writing of Australian history from original sources.
Type: Fellowship.
No. of awards offered: 1.
Frequency: Annual.
Value: Approximately A$20,000.
Country of Study: Australia.
Application Procedure: An application form is obtained by contacting the State Librarian.
Closing Date: July 31st.
Additional Information: Proposed work must conform to the purpose of the award.

Nancy Keesing Memorial Fellowship

Subjects: Australian history, literature, life and culture.
Eligibility: Open to researchers of any nationality.
Level of Study: Unrestricted.
Purpose: To encourage the use of the State Library's collections for original research.
Type: Fellowship.
No. of awards offered: 1.
Frequency: Annual.
Value: A$10,000.
Study Establishment: State Library of New South Wales.
Country of Study: Australia.
Application Procedure: Please write for application forms.
Closing Date: March 31st.

STATE SCHOLARSHIPS FOUNDATION

Greek Embassy
Cultural Department
1a Holland Park, London, W11 3TP, England
Tel: (44) 171 229 3850
Fax: (44) 171 229 7221
Contact: Dr Victoria Solomonidis, Cultural Attache

Scholarships for Postgraduate Studies in Greece

Subjects: All subjects.
Eligibility: Open to nationals of countries which are part of the Council of Europe who hold a graduate degree from a foreign university, have a good knowledge of English or French and are not more than 35 years of age.
Level of Study: Doctorate, Postdoctorate, Postgraduate.
Purpose: To fund postgraduate studies.
Type: Scholarship.
No. of awards offered: 10.
Frequency: Annual.
Value: 70,000 drachmas monthly plus 50,000 drachmas for initial expenses; up to 60,000 drachmas for typing of PhD dissertation, up to 60,000 drachmas to cover mandatory laboratory expenses; exemption from tuition fees; free medical care in case of emergency.
Length of Study: 1 academic year; renewable for 2 further years.
Study Establishment: Any university or institution of higher education.
Country of Study: Greece.
Application Procedure: Application forms may be requested from January.
Closing Date: March 31st.
Additional Information: Scholars are strongly recommended to acquire at least an elementary knowledge of Modern Greek.

STORY MAGAZINE

1507 Dana Avenue, Cincinnati, OH, 45207, United States of America
Tel: (1) 513 531 2690 ext 328
Fax: (1) 513 531 1843
Email: competitions@fwpubs.com
www: http://storymagazine.com
Contact: Ms Teeri Boes, Promotion Associate

Story Magazine's Carson McCullers Prize for the Short Story

Subjects: Writing competition.
Eligibility: Open to writers of any nationality.
Level of Study: Unrestricted.
Purpose: To encourage and award short story writing.
No. of awards offered: 24.
Frequency: Annual.
Value: Cash prizes for first to tenth place winners.
Country of Study: Any country.
Application Procedure: Contestants may enter as many manuscripts as they wish. Manuscripts will not be returned and each entry must be made on an official entry form, accompanied by a US$10 entry fee, drawn on a US bank. Entries must be original and unprinted, 3,500 words or less.
Closing Date: May 3rd.

Story Magazine's Short Story Competition

Subjects: Writing competition.
Eligibility: Open to writers of any nationality.
Level of Study: Unrestricted.
Purpose: To encourage and award short story writing.
No. of awards offered: 25.
Frequency: Annual.
Value: Cash prizes for first to tenth place winners.
Country of Study: Any country.
Application Procedure: Candidates may enter as many manuscripts as they wish. Manuscripts will not be returned and each entry must be made on an official entry form, accompanied by a US$10 entry fee, drawn on a US bank. Entries must be original and unprinted, 1,500 words or less.

SUDAN CIVIC FOUNDATION (SCF)

SCF House
37 Monkswell Road, Cambridge, CB2 2JU, England
Tel: (44) 1223 504393
Fax: (44) 1223 501125
Email: sudan21@yawmail.com
www: http://www.sudan21.net/equiano.html
Contact: Dr Salah Al Bander, Director

The SCF is an independent non-profit making group whose purpose is to contribute to public understanding of socio-economic and political issues through research, discussion and publications. It was established in 1996 to provide, among other things, a network for those who share a common concern for better race relations.

Equiano Memorial Award

Subjects: The promotion of race relations.
Eligibility: There are no eligibility restrictions.
Level of Study: Unrestricted.
Purpose: To support a person engaged in the study or promotion of better race relations, tolerance and peaceful co-existence between communities; aiming to supplement academic coursework with some research or practical field investigations, leading to a report, essay or dissertation.
Type: Research Grant.
No. of awards offered: 1.
Frequency: Annual.
Value: £2,000.
Length of Study: 1 year.
Study Establishment: An academic or professional establishment.
Country of Study: Any country.
Application Procedure: Application form must be completed. Please write for details.
Closing Date: March 31st.
Additional Information: Applicants must be registered at a recognised educational institution. The award is based on need as well as academic merit. The area of study must fit in with research priorities of the Foundation. Applicants who are awarded the grant may re-apply for a second year's funding.

SWEDISH INFORMATION SERVICE

1 Dag Hammarskjold Plaza
45th Floor, New York, NY, 10017-2201, United States of America
Tel: (1) 212 583 2550
Fax: (1) 212 752 4789
Email: swedeninfo@ix.netcom.com
www: http://www.swedeninfo.com/sis
Contact: The Awards Committee

SIS is the information section of the consulate general of Sweden in New York. The purpose of SIS is to provide a central resource for all persons and organisations seeking information about Sweden on subjects other than tourism and trade or business.

The Swedish Government 'SASS' Travel Grants

Subjects: Study of, or research in, Swedish language, literature or linguistics.
Eligibility: Open to members in good standing of the Society for the Advancement of Scandinavian Studies (SASS). Priority will be given to graduate students and untenured faculty. Applicants must be nationals or permanent residents of the USA.

Level of Study: Doctorate, Postdoctorate, Postgraduate, Professional development.
Type: Travel Grant.
No. of awards offered: Varies.
Frequency: Annual.
Value: A sum of US$6,000 will be divided among the grantees. Awards vary depending upon individual need.
Country of Study: Sweden or USA.
Application Procedure: Self-written application form must follow specific pattern. Project description is required in addition to two letters of recommendation.
Closing Date: March 15th to be taken up during the calendar year.
Additional Information: Graduate students in the social sciences may use the grants for intensive Swedish language study in Sweden. Otherwise grants may be used for projects either in North America or Sweden.

SWISS FEDERAL INSTITUTE OF TECHNOLOGY ZÜRICH

Eidgenössische Technische Hochschule Zürich
Austauschdienst
ETH Zentrum, Zurich, CH-8092, Switzerland
Tel: (41) 1 632 20 86
Fax: (41) 1 632 12 64
Email: doc.exchange@rektorat.ethz.ch
www: http://www.mobilitaet.ethz.ch
Contact: Grants Management Officer

Swiss Federal Institute of Technology Scholarships

Subjects: Architecture, engineering (civil, mechanical, electrical, production, rural and surveying), computer science, materials science, chemistry, physics, mathematics, biology, environmental sciences, earth sciences, pharmacy, agriculture, forestry.
Eligibility: Open primarily but not exclusively to nationals of Canada, Germany, Italy, Japan, Poland, Spain, the UK and the USA. Candidates should be 20-30 years of age, have had at least two years of university study, and have a good working knowledge of German.
Level of Study: Unrestricted.
Type: Scholarship.
No. of awards offered: 15.
Frequency: Annual.
Value: CHF1,300-CHF1,500 per month, plus tuition.
Length of Study: 1 academic year (October-July).
Study Establishment: The Institute.
Country of Study: Switzerland.
Application Procedure: Applications should be made to the following addresses, as appropriate: Canada - Université Laval, Faculté des études supéieures, Pavillon Jean-Charles Bonenfant, Quebec; Germany - German Academic Exchange Service, Post Office Box 200404, D-53134 Bonn. Italy - Ministero degli Affari Esteri, Direzione Generale delle Relazioni Culturali, Piazzale della Farnesia, 00194 Roma. Japan -

Foreign Student Office, Tokyo Institute of Technology, O-okoyama, Meguro-ku, Tokyo 152-8550. Poland - Warsaw University of Technology, Akademisches Auslandamt Noakowskiego 18/20 00-668 Warsaw. Spain - Consejo Superior de Investigaciones Cientificas, Dpto. De relaciones internacionales, Calle Serrano 117, 28006 Madrid. UK - Imperial College of Sciences Technology and Medicine, Assistant Registrar, Exhibition Road, London SW7 2AZ. USA - Exchange Co-ordinator, Rensselaer Polytechnic Institute, Troy, NY 12180; World Student Fund, 756 West Peachtree Street, Atlanta, GA 30308 (Georgia Institute of Technology); International Programs, Michigan Technological University, Houghton, MI 49931; Global Programs Office, Worcester Polytechnic Institute, Worcester, MA 01609; International Programs, Union College, Schenectady, NY 12308; University of Kansas, Lawrence, KS 66045; Office of International Programs, Kansas State University, Manhattan, KS 66506.
Closing Date: February 15th.

For further information contact:

Eidgenössische Technische Hochschule
Austauschdienst
ETH Zentrum, Zurich, CH-8092, Switzerland
Tel: (41) 1 632 2086
Fax: (41) 1 632 1264

SWISS NATIONAL SCIENCE FOUNDATION (SNSF)

Wildhainweg 20
PO Box 3001, Berne, Switzerland
Tel: (41) 31 308 22 22
Fax: (41) 31 301 30 09
www: http://www.snf.ch
Contact: Dr Benno G Frey, Office for Fellowship and Exchange Program

The Swiss National Foundation (SNSF) support scientific research at Swiss universities and other scientific institutions and award fellowships to scientists. The SNSF was established in 1952 as a private Foundation entrusted with the promotion of basic non-commercial research. While the SNSF supports research through grants given to established or promising researchers, it does not maintain its own research institutions. The main objectives of the SNSF are to support basic research in all areas of academic research and to support young scientists and researchers, with the intent of ensuring the continuing high quality of teaching and research in Swiss higher education. In addition to the general research funding, the SNSF is responsible for the National Research Programmes (NRP) and for four of the federal government's Swiss Priority Programmes (SPPs).

Athena Fellowships Programme

Subjects: Arts and humanities, social and behavioural sciences.

Eligibility: Applicants must have a number of outstanding publications to their credit and postdoctoral (or equivalent) qualifications and plan to pursue an academic career. Applicants must be between the ages of 35 and 45.
Level of Study: Postdoctorate.
Purpose: To promote highly qualified young researchers planning an academic career in the framework of research project.
Type: A variable number of Fellowships.
No. of awards offered: Varies.
Frequency: Twice a year.
Value: Varies.
Length of Study: Up to 3 years, with the option of renewal for a further 3 years.
Study Establishment: Swiss universities and academic institutions.
Country of Study: Switzerland.
Application Procedure: For details please contact Dr Benno Frey or Laurence Bohren at the Office for Fellowship Exchange Programmes of the SNSF.
Closing Date: March 1st and October 1st.

Fellowships for Advanced Researchers

Subjects: All subjects.
Eligibility: Postdoctoral (and possibly predoctorate) students under the age of 35, who have at least two years experience in active research and are Swiss nationals or permanent residents in Switzerland. An exception to the age restriction can be made for candidates who have interrupted their scientific career due to family obligations.
Level of Study: Predoctorate.
Purpose: To promote postdoctoral or postgraduate students who have at least two years experience in active research and are Swiss nationals or permanent residents in Switzerland.
Type: A variable number of Fellowships.
No. of awards offered: Varies.
Frequency: Annual.
Value: Varies.
Length of Study: Varies.
Study Establishment: Universities or academic institutions worldwide.
Application Procedure: Application forms are available from the Research Council of the Swiss National Science Foundation at the end of each calendar year.
Closing Date: February 1st.

Fellowships for Prospective Researchers

Subjects: All subjects.
Eligibility: Promising young scholars under the age of 33 who are Swiss nationals or permanent residents of Switzerland, hold an MA or PhD and can demonstrate at least one years experience in active research. An exception to the age restriction (to a maximum of two years) can be made for candidates from clinical disciplines, or candidates who have interrupted their scientific careers due to family obligations. The main condition for such an exception is that the

candidate has reached a high scientific level and will in the future pursue an active career in science and research. A high priority will be given to candidates who plan to return to Switzerland.

Level of Study: Postdoctorate, Predoctorate.

Purpose: To promote holders of MA or PhD degrees, who have had at least one year's experience in active research after the completion of their degree.

Type: A variable number of Fellowships.

No. of awards offered: Varies.

Frequency: Annual.

Value: Varies.

Length of Study: Varies.

Study Establishment: Universities worldwide.

Country of Study: Any country.

Application Procedure: Application forms are available from the Local Research Commission. Candidates with a degree from a Swiss university should contact the Research Commission of their institution. Candidates with Italian as their native language, who have completed their studies in a foreign country should contact the Research Commission for the Italian speaking part of Switzerland. Swiss candidates who are residents of foreign countries, hold a degree from a foreign university, but who have concrete of returning to Switzerland should contact the Swiss scientific academy responsible for their area of research.

Closing Date: Please write for details.

Additional Information: For further information please contact Benno Frey or Laurence Bohren at the Office for Fellowship and Exchange Programs, or refer to the website: http://www.snf.ch.

Grants for Short Term Research in Humanities and Social Sciences

Subjects: Arts and humanities, mass communication and information science, recreation studies, religion and theology, social and behavioural sciences.

Eligibility: Promising young researchers who are Swiss nationals or permanent residents of Switzerland.

Level of Study: Postdoctorate, Postgraduate, Predoctorate.

Purpose: To give financial assistance to young graduates wishing to pursue short term research abroad.

Type: Travel Grant.

No. of awards offered: Varies.

Frequency: Varies.

Value: Varies.

Length of Study: 2-8 weeks.

Study Establishment: Universities or academic institutions offering short term courses or summer schools.

Country of Study: Any country.

Application Procedure: Submission of an application for funding together with a letter from the course director offering the candidate a place on the course. Application forms and a list of potential courses are available from the SNSF. Please contact Corine Hamann or Dr Benno Frey, Fachstelle für Stipendien, SNSF.

Closing Date: Applications are accepted at any time.

SYBIL TUTTON TRUST

16 Ogle Street, London, W1P 7LG, England
Tel: (44) 171 636 4481
Fax: (44) 171 637 4307
Contact: Mrs Susan Dolton

Sybil Tutton Awards

Subjects: Musical performance - opera.

Eligibility: Open to opera students of 18-30 years who have been resident in the UK for three years.

Level of Study: Postgraduate, Professional development.

Purpose: To assist exceptionally talented opera students on a recognised course of operatic study.

Frequency: Annual.

Value: From a total of £15,000.

Country of Study: Any country.

Application Procedure: An application form must be completed and two references provided.

Closing Date: April.

Additional Information: Selected students will be asked to audition.

SYMPHONY ORCHESTRA ASSOCIATION OF KINGSPORT

Kingsport Symphony Orchestra
Renaissance Center
Box 13
1200 East Center Street, Kingsport, TN, 37660, United States of America
Tel: (1) 423 392 8423
Fax: (1) 423 392 8428
Email: ksorch@aol.com
Contact: Ms Lis M Baker, General Manager

Elizabeth Harper Vaughn Concerto Competition

Subjects: Three categories alternating annually in the following sequence - percussion, winds and brass, strings, piano.

Eligibility: Open to musicians, 26 years of age or under.

Level of Study: Postgraduate.

Type: Competition.

No. of awards offered: 1.

Frequency: Annual.

Value: US$1,000, plus a concert performance with the orchestra and accommodation.

Country of Study: Any country.

Application Procedure: Applications must be accompanied by a letter of recommendation from a qualified teacher, the entrance fee (US$20, make cheques payable to Kingsport Symphony Orchestra), and a cassette tape. The tape recording must be a concerto, or work of similar importance, written with orchestral accompaniment.

Closing Date: December 31st.

Additional Information: The Competition is held in March.

SYRACUSE UNIVERSITY

SU Graduate School
303 Bowne Hall, Syracuse, NY, 13244-1200, United States of America
Tel: (1) 315 443 4492
Fax: (1) 315 443 3423
Email: kmsciort@syr.edu
www: http://cwis.syr.edu
Contact: Ms Kristin Sciortino, Graduate Awards Co-ordinator

Syracuse University is a non-profit, private student research university.

Syracuse University Fellowship

Subjects: All subjects.
Eligibility: Open to nationals of any country.
Level of Study: Unrestricted.
Purpose: To provide a full support package during a student's term of study.
Type: Fellowship.
No. of awards offered: 101.
Frequency: Annual.
Value: US$27,597.
Length of Study: 1-6 years.
Study Establishment: Syracuse University.
Country of Study: USA.
Application Procedure: Application for fellowship is done through admission application.
Closing Date: July 2nd.

THE TEXTILE INSTITUTE

International Headquarters
10 Blackfriars Street, Manchester, M3 5DR, England
Tel: (44) 161 834 8457
Fax: (44) 161 835 3087
Email: tiihq@textileinst.org.uk
www: http://www.texi.org
Contact: Mrs Deborah Woodhouse, Qualifications Officer

The Textile Institute has an international membership covering almost 100 countries and spanning every sector and occupation relating to fibres and their uses. The mission of the Textile Institute is to promote professionalism in all areas associated with the textile industries - including clothing and footwear - worldwide.

Cotton Industry War Memorial Trust Scholarships

Subjects: Textile technology or design.
Eligibility: All candidates must undertake to be employed in and for the benefit of the UK textile industry.
Level of Study: Doctorate, Postdoctorate, Postgraduate, Undergraduate.

Purpose: To assist students to study full-time or on a sandwich course basis for the Associateship of The Textile Institute, or for a textile degree in technology or design, or to assist professionally qualified people and degree holders in textile technology or design, related sciences or other disciplines to undertake a full-time course for a Master's degree or PhD.
Type: Scholarship.
No. of awards offered: Varies.
Frequency: Annual.
Value: Up to £500.
Country of Study: United Kingdom.
Application Procedure: Application form must be completed.
Closing Date: Last Friday in July.

Lee 400 Educational Trust

Subjects: Textiles.
Eligibility: Open to textile students studying in the UK for postgraduate qualification associated with knitting or lace.
Level of Study: Postgraduate.
Purpose: To assist those studying in the UK for a postgraduate qualification associated with knitting or lace.
Type: Bursary.
No. of awards offered: Varies.
Frequency: Annual.
Value: Multiples of £400.
Country of Study: United Kingdom.
Application Procedure: Please submit CV with synopsis of work.
Closing Date: End of April.

Lord Barnby Foundation Bursaries

Subjects: Textile technology.
Eligibility: Open to UK nationals previously employed for at least two years in the UK textile industry.
Level of Study: Unrestricted.
Purpose: To assist those who have been employed in the UK textile industry for at least two years, and who are registered on a full-time or part-time course of study leading to a qualification.
Type: Bursary.
No. of awards offered: 2.
Frequency: Annual.
Value: Varies; up to £500.
Country of Study: United Kingdom.
Application Procedure: Applications must be made through the Head of Department.
Closing Date: Last Friday in July.

Textile Institute Scholarship

Subjects: Any textile-related subject.
Eligibility: Open to students or professionally qualified individuals wishing to undertake further study in the fields of textile technology or design.
Level of Study: Doctorate, Postdoctorate, Postgraduate, Undergraduate.

Purpose: To assist students to study full-time or part-time for the Associateship of The Textile Institute, or for a textile degree in technology or design, or to assist professionally qualified people and degree holders in textile technology or design, related sciences or other disciplines to undertake a full-time course for a Master's Degree or PhD.
Type: Scholarship.
No. of awards offered: Varies.
Frequency: Annual.
Value: Generally £100-£400, larger scholarships may be made in certain circumstances.
Country of Study: Any country.
Application Procedure: Application form must be completed.
Closing Date: Last Friday in July.

Weavers' Company Scholarships

Subjects: Any subject relevant to weaving, including design.
Eligibility: All candidates must undertake to be employed in and for the benefit of the UK textile industry. UK nationals only.
Level of Study: Doctorate, Postdoctorate, Postgraduate, Undergraduate.
Purpose: To assist students to study full-time or on a sandwich course basis for the Associateship of The Textile Institute, or for a textile degree in technology or design, or to assist professionally qualified people and degree holders in textile technology or design, related sciences or other disciplines to undertake a full-time course for a Master's degree or PhD.
Type: Scholarship.
No. of awards offered: Varies.
Frequency: Annual.
Value: Varies; up to £500.
Country of Study: United Kingdom.
Application Procedure: Application form must be completed.
Closing Date: Last Friday in July.

THOURON-UNIVERSITY OF PENNSYLVANIA FUND FOR BRITISH-AMERICAN STUDENT EXCHANGE

Thouron Awards
University of Glasgow, Glasgow, G12 8QQ, Scotland
Tel: (44) 141 330 3628
Fax: (44) 141 307 4920
Email: jmblack@mis.gla.ac.uk
www: http://www.upenn.edu
Contact: Mr J M Black, Secretary

The University of Glasgow is host to the UK operation of the Thouron Awards and organises the annual competition for the selection of UK graduates applying for awards tenable at the University of Pennsylvania, Philadelphia, USA.

Thouron Awards

Subjects: All subjects.
Eligibility: Open to British citizens who are graduates and unmarried. Postdoctoral candidates are ineligible unless their proposed study is in a field different from that in which they undertook their previous postgraduate study. No application will be considered from a student already in the USA.
Level of Study: Postgraduate.
Purpose: To promote better understanding between the people of the UK and the USA.
Type: Award.
No. of awards offered: Approx. 10.
Frequency: Annual.
Value: US$1,247 per month, plus tuition and fees.
Length of Study: 1 or 2 years.
Study Establishment: The University of Pennsylvania, Philadelphia.
Country of Study: USA.
Application Procedure: Two application forms with two passport size photographs and three referee forms must be submitted.
Closing Date: October 20th.
Additional Information: American citizens interested in studying in the UK should write to the University of Pennsylvania for further details.

TIBOR VARGA INTERNATIONAL COMPETITION FOR VIOLIN

Case postale 954, Sion, CH-1951, Switzerland
Tel: (41) 27 323 4317
Fax: (41) 27 323 4662
Email: festivargasion@vtx.ch
www: http://www.nouvelliste.ch/varga/tvarga.htm
Contact: Mr Pierre Gillioz, Administrator

The Tibor Varga International Competition for Violin organises a classical music festival called 'Festival Tibor Varga' which runs annually from the middle of July until the beginning of September, with more than 25 concerts.

Tibor Varga International Competition for Violin

Subjects: Violin - interpretive performance.
Eligibility: Open to violinists of any nationality aged 15-32.
Level of Study: Unrestricted.
Purpose: To help discover a new talent, to enrich the musical experience and practice of the participants, and to encourage and support prize winners in their future careers.
Type: Prize.
No. of awards offered: 4 prizes and several special prizes.
Frequency: Annual.
Value: 1st prize CHF10,000; 2nd prize CHF7,500; 3rd prize CHF5,000; 4th prize CHF2,500; special prizes totalling approximately CHF30,000.
Length of Study: 10 days.
Country of Study: Switzerland.

Application Procedure: Application form fully filled in, plus three passport photographs (4x5cm) and curriculum vitae, plus a receipt showing payment of entrance fee.

Closing Date: May 1st.

Additional Information: Participants will compete in Sion during August. Prize-winners are obliged to remain in Sion for the awards presentation at the end of the competition. They will also be expected to perform in the presentation concert. The first prize-winner will be presented as soloist with a symphony orchestra at the Festival. There is an application fee of CHF100.

For further information contact:

Tibor Varga International Competition for Violin
Case Postale 1429, Sion, CH 1951, Switzerland
Contact: Mr Pierre Gillioz

UCLA CENTER FOR 17TH AND 18TH CENTURY STUDIES AND THE WILLIAM ANDREWS CLARK MEMORIAL LIBRARY

310 Royce Hall
UCLA, Los Angeles, CA, 90095-1404, United States of America
Tel: (1) 310 206 8552
Fax: (1) 310 206 8577
Email: c1718cs@humnet.ucla.edu
www: http://www.humnet.ucla.edu/humnet/c1718cs
Contact: Fellowship Co-ordinator

The Center provides a forum for discussion of central issues in the field of early modern studies, facilitates research and publication, supports scholarship, and encourages the creation of interdisciplinary, cross-cultural programs that advance the understanding of this important period. The William Andrews Clark Memorial Library, administered by the Center, is known for its collections on 17th and 18th century Britain, Oscar Wilde and the 1890's, the history of printing, and certain aspects of the American West.

Ahmanson and Getty Postdoctoral Fellowships

Subjects: The theme for the year 2000-2001 will be announced in the fall of 2000.
Eligibility: Open to postdoctoral scholars who have received the PhD in the last six years.
Level of Study: Postdoctorate.
Purpose: To encourage participation (research and reading a paper) in the Center's annual interdisciplinary, cross cultural programmes.
Type: Fellowship.
No. of awards offered: Up to 4.
Frequency: Annual.
Value: US$18,400 for the two-quarter period.
Length of Study: 2 consecutive academic quarters.

Study Establishment: UCLA/William Andrews Clark Memorial Library.
Country of Study: USA.
Application Procedure: Applicants must submit an application form, proposal statement, a bibliography, and three letters of reference.
Closing Date: March 15th.

ASECS/Clark Library Fellowships

Subjects: The Restoration or the eighteenth century.
Eligibility: Open to members of ASECS who are postdoctoral scholars and hold a PhD or equivalent degree at the time of application.
Level of Study: Postdoctorate.
Type: Fellowship.
No. of awards offered: Varies.
Frequency: Annual.
Value: US$2,000.
Length of Study: 1 month.
Study Establishment: William Andrews Clark Memorial Library, UCLA.
Country of Study: USA.
Application Procedure: Please submit an application, a proposal, a bibliography, and three letters of reference.
Closing Date: March 15th.

For further information contact:

William Andrews Clark Memorial Library
2520 Cimarron Street, Los Angeles, CA, 90018-2098, United States of America
Contact: Fellowship Co-ordinator

Clark Library Short-Term Resident Fellowships

Subjects: Research relevant to the Library's holdings.
Eligibility: Open to scholars holding a PhD or equivalent degree who are involved in advanced research.
Level of Study: Postdoctorate.
Type: Fellowship.
No. of awards offered: Varies.
Frequency: Annual.
Value: US$2,000 per month.
Length of Study: 1-3 months.
Study Establishment: William Andrews Clark Memorial Library, UCLA.
Country of Study: USA.
Application Procedure: Please submit an application, proposal statement, and letters of reference.
Closing Date: March 15th.

For further information contact:

William Andrews Clark Memorial Library
2520 Cimarron Street, Los Angeles, CA, 90018-2098, United States of America
Contact: Fellowship Co-ordinator

Clark Predoctoral Fellowships

Subjects: Any area represented in the Clark's collections.
Eligibility: Restricted to advanced doctoral students at the University of California, whose dissertation concerns an area appropriate to the collections of the Clark Library.
Level of Study: Doctorate, Postgraduate.
Purpose: To support dissertation research.
Type: Fellowship.
No. of awards offered: Varies.
Frequency: Annual.
Value: US$6,000.
Length of Study: 3 months.
Study Establishment: William Andrews Clark Memorial Library, UCLA.
Country of Study: USA.
Closing Date: March 15th.

For further information contact:

William Andrews Clark Memorial Library
2520 Cimarron Street, Los Angeles, CA, 90018-2098, United States of America
Contact: Fellowship Co-ordinator

Clark-Huntington Joint Bibliographical Fellowship

Subjects: Early modern literature and history and in other areas where the sponsoring libraries have common strengths.
Level of Study: Postdoctorate, Professional development.
Purpose: To support bibliographical research.
Type: Fellowship.
No. of awards offered: 1.
Frequency: Annual.
Value: US$4,000.
Length of Study: 2 months.
Study Establishment: Clark Library and Huntington Library.
Country of Study: USA.
Application Procedure: Applicants must submit an application form, description of project, a bibliography, and three letters of reference.
Closing Date: March 15th.

For further information contact:

William Andrews Clark Memorial Library
2520 Cimarron Street, Los Angeles, CA, 90018-2098, United States of America
Contact: Fellowship Co-ordinator

UCLA CENTER FOR MEDIEVAL AND RENAISSANCE STUDIES

Box 951485, Los Angeles, CA, 90095-1485, United States of America
Tel: (1) 310 825 1880
Fax: (1) 310 825 0655
Email: cmrs@humnet.ucla.edu
www: http://www.humnet.ucla.edu/humnet/cmrs/default.html
Contact: Ms Karen Burgess, Programme Co-ordinator

Through its activities and programmes, the UCLA Center for Medieval and Renaissance Studies promotes interdisciplinary and cross-cultural studies of modern civilisation in its formative period from late antiquity to the middle of the 17th century.

UCLA Summer Fellowship

Subjects: Medieval and early modern history, culture, literature, philosophy and religion.
Eligibility: No restriction, except applicant must have a PhD or similar degree from a recognised and accredited university.
Level of Study: Postdoctorate.
Purpose: To defray expenses for a scholar doing research at UCLA during July, August or September. The scholar should have a particular need to use UCLA and surrounding resources.
Type: Stipend.
No. of awards offered: 1.
Frequency: Annual.
Value: US$500.
Length of Study: Not to exceed 3 months.
Study Establishment: UCLA.
Country of Study: USA.
Application Procedure: Curriculum Vitae, two page project description, Biography for Academic Personnel form available through the center, one letter of recommendation.
Closing Date: Early February; (for Summer).

UCLA INSTITUTE OF AMERICAN CULTURE/AMERICAN INDIAN STUDIES

Box 951548
3220 Campbell Hall, Los Angeles, CA, 90095-1548, United States of America
Tel: (1) 310 825 7315
Fax: (1) 310 206 7060
Email: aisc@ucla.edu
www: http://www.sscnet.ucla.edu/indian/
Contact: Ms Roselle Kipp

UCLA Institute of American Culture Postdoctoral/Visiting Scholar Fellowships

Subjects: Arts and humanities, education and teacher training, fine and applied arts, law.

Eligibility: Open to nationals of any country.

Level of Study: Doctorate, Postdoctorate.

Purpose: To enable PhD scholars wishing to work in association with the American Indian Studies Center to conduct research and publish books or manuscripts relating to American Indian Studies.

Type: Fellowship.

No. of awards offered: 1.

Frequency: Annual.

Value: US$25,000-US$30,000 stipend plus health benefits and up to US$3,000 in research support.

Length of Study: From 9 months to 1 year.

Country of Study: USA.

Application Procedure: Application form must be completed. Forms are available from the Institute.

Closing Date: December 31st.

Additional Information: The fellowship period is usually from July 1st to June 30th.

Type: Bursary.

No. of awards offered: 2.

Frequency: Annual.

Value: The Toni Saphra Bursary amount fluctuates according to the prevailing interest rates and the amount is divided between 2-3 applicants. The Backon Bursary remains static and is awarded to two students.

Length of Study: 1 year; renewable.

Study Establishment: A university.

Country of Study: South Africa.

Application Procedure: Applicants must apply in writing for the bursary in the year preceding their proposed year of study. An application form with an allocated reference number will be sent to the student for completion. Any photocopied application forms will be disqualified. Proof of acceptance by the university for the proposed course must be submitted.

Closing Date: Closing date for written applications: July 31st. All other relevant documentation: August 31st.

UNION OF JEWISH WOMEN OF SOUTH AFRICA

PO Box 87556
Houghton, Johannesburg, 2041, South Africa
Tel: (27) 11 646 3402
Fax: (27) 11 646 3424
Email: ujwexec@netactive.co.za
Contact: The Bursary Officer

The Union of Jewish Women of South Africa is committed to: the needs and ideals of the Jewish community; the enrichment of the peoples of South Africa; the promotion of the rights and status of women; the strengthening of links with Israel; and the maintenance of an affiliation to the International Council of Jewish Women.

The Toni Saphra Bursary and the Fanny and Shlomo Backon Bursary

Subjects: Those subject areas in which the graduate can make a positive contribution to the community and South African society.

Eligibility: Open to any female student who already holds an undergraduate degree and whose proposed postgraduate course of study will qualify her to render some form of social service in the South African community. Applicants who have not completed a first degree but are in the final year of study may also apply. These applicants will only be considered for the bursary once they have provided their final year marks. Applicants must be South African citizens.

Level of Study: Postgraduate.

Purpose: To enable women graduates to upgrade their qualifications in order to continue rendering service to their communities.

UNITED DAUGHTERS OF THE CONFEDERACY

328 North Boulevard, Richmond, VA, 23220-4057, United States of America
Tel: (1) 804 355 1636
Fax: (1) 804 353 1396
www: http://www.hqudc.org
Contact: Ms Sarah O Dunaway, Chairman of the Awards Committee

Mrs Simon Baruch University Award

Subjects: Southern US history in or near the period of the Confederacy or bearing upon the causes that led to secession and the War Between the States. The life of an individual, a policy or a phase of life may be eligible.

Eligibility: Open to individuals who have graduated with an advanced degree from a US university or college within the previous 15 years, or whose thesis or dissertation has been accepted by such institutions as part of graduation requirements. Book-length manuscripts should contain at least 75,000 words; monographs 25,000-50,000 words.

Level of Study: Postgraduate.

Purpose: To encourage research in Southern history and to assist scholars in the publication of their theses, dissertations and other writings on the Confederate period.

No. of awards offered: 1.

Frequency: Every two years (even-numbered years).

Value: US$2,000 to aid in defraying the costs of publication, US$500 to the author.

Country of Study: Any country.

Application Procedure: Please write for details.

Closing Date: May 1st of the award year.

UNITED STATES CENTER FOR ADVANCED HOLOCAUST STUDIES

United States Holocaust Memorial Museum
100 Raoul Wallenberg Place SW, Washington, DC, 20024-2126, United States of America
Tel: (1) 202 488 6585
Fax: (1) 202 479 9726
Email: eanthony@ushmm.org
www: http://www.ushmm.org
Contact: Fellowships Office

The United States Holocaust Memorial Museum is America's national institution for the documentation, study, and interpretation of Holocaust history, and serves as the country's memorial to the millions of people murdered during the Holocaust. The Center for advanced Holocaust Studies fosters research in Holocaust and genocide studies.

Center Research Fellowships

Subjects: Language and humanity subjects, as they relate to the study of the holocaust and genocide.
Eligibility: Applicants must be post doctoral researchers with recent degrees received from accredited American universities, PhD candidates preparing dissertations at accredited American universities, or senior scholars from accredited academic and research institutions worldwide.
Level of Study: Doctorate, Postdoctorate, Professional development.
Purpose: To enable research in holocaust and genocide studies.
Type: Fellowship.
No. of awards offered: Up to 3.
Frequency: Annual, if funds are available.
Value: Up to US$15,000 for research at the Center. The Museum will also provide office space, postage, and access to computer, telephone, facsimile machine, and photocopier. Cost sharing among other institutions is welcome.
Length of Study: 1 semester or more.
Country of Study: USA.
Application Procedure: Please contact Betsy Anthony, Programme Assistant, Center for Advanced Holocaust Studies for application forms and information.
Closing Date: October 31st.

Dissertation Award

Subjects: Holocaust and genocide studies.
Eligibility: Open to all PhD candidates completing their dissertations after January 1 1998 and before the application deadline.
Level of Study: Postdoctorate.
Purpose: To encourage the work of exceptional new scholars in the area of the holocaust and genocide studies. The fellowship also provides an opportunity for a new PhD to work at the Center on a conversion of the dissertation into a monograph or on a new post-dissertation holocaust-related research topic.

Type: Award.
No. of awards offered: 1.
Frequency: Annual.
Value: A stipend of up to US$15,000 for residence at the Center. The museum will also provide office space, postage, and access to a computer, telephone, facsimile machine, and photocopier.
Length of Study: 1 semester or more.
Study Establishment: United States Center for Advanced Holocaust Studies.
Country of Study: USA.
Application Procedure: Please contact Renee Taft, Director, Visiting Scholars Programme, or Betsy Anthony, Programme Assistant, Visiting Scholar Programme for more information and application forms. Dissertations should be nominated by the author's university department chair and accompanied by a letter of acceptance for the degree and a 250-word abstract of the dissertation's subject matter. Three copies of the dissertation should be submitted. A statement must be included giving the United States Holocaust Memorial Museum permission to produce the dissertation for copying purposes.
Closing Date: March 15th.
Additional Information: The Center's historian, fellows-in-residence, and publications staff will be available to assist the successful applicant.

For further information contact:

United States of America
Tel: (1) 202 314 0378
Fax: (1) 202 479 9726
Contact: Ms Renee Taft, Visiting Scholar Program Director

Matthew Family Programme for Israeli Scholars

Subjects: Holocaust and genocide studies.
Eligibility: Candidates must be citizens of Israel and should hold a PhD or equivalent professional/terminal degree or have equivalent recognised professional standing.
Purpose: To foster greater co-operation between Yad Vashem and other relevant Israeli institutions and the United States Holocaust Memorial Museum. The programme provides each year for an Israeli scholar to be in residence at the Museum for a period of four to six weeks to conduct research using the resources of the Museum and other collections in Washington DC.
Type: Fellowship.
No. of awards offered: 1.
Frequency: Annual.
Value: US$5,000 to cover housing, living, and travel expenses. The Matthew Fellow will also received office space, postage, and access to a computer, telephone, facsimile machine, and photocopier.
Length of Study: 4 - 6 weeks.
Country of Study: USA.
Application Procedure: Please contact Betsy Anthony at the Center for Advanced Holocaust Studies for an application from and further details.
Closing Date: October 31st.

Additional Information: The Fellow will be encouraged to participate in the Museum's broad array of scholarly and other programmes.

Miles Lerman Center for the Study of Jewish Resistance Research Fellowship

Subjects: Cultural studies, languages and humanities subjects, as they relate to the study of Jewish resistance.
Eligibility: Applicants must be post-doctoral researchers with recent degrees received from accredited American universities, PhD candidates preparing dissertations at accredited American universities, or senior scholars from accredited academic research institutions worldwide.
Purpose: To encourage exploration of aspects of Jewish resistance.
Type: Fellowship.
No. of awards offered: 1.
Frequency: Annual.
Value: A stipend of up to US$15,000 for residence at the Center for one semester or more. The Museum will provide office space, postage, and access to a computer, telephone, facsimile machine, and photocopier.
Length of Study: 1 semester or more.
Country of Study: USA.
Application Procedure: Please contact Betsy Anthony, Programme Assistant, Visiting Scholar Programme at the Center for Advanced Holocaust Studies for an application form and further information.
Closing Date: October 31st.
Additional Information: The Fellow will be encouraged to participate in the Museum's broad array of scholarly and other programmes. Cost sharing by home institutions or other relevant organisations will be encouraged to extend the residency of the applicant at the Museum or to make possible additional research at other institutions in the United States or abroad.

The Joyce and Arthur Schechter Fellowship

Subjects: Linguistics, cultural studies, and related subjects.
Eligibility: Applicants must hold a PhD or be an advanced PhD candidate (ABD) by the application deadline. Those candidates with equivalent professional/terminal degrees or recognised professional standing may also apply.
Purpose: To provide for a scholar to be in residence at the Museum for a period of six weeks to three months to conduct research using the vast resources of the Museum.
Type: Fellowship.
No. of awards offered: 1.
Frequency: Annual.
Value: A stipend of US$5,000 to cover housing, living, and international/domestic travel expenses. The Joyce and Arthur Schechter Fellow will also be provided with office space, postage, and access to a computer, telephone, facsimile machine, and photocopier. Cost sharing by the applicants home institution is welcome.
Country of Study: USA.
Application Procedure: A completed application form and supporting material is required for fellowship consideration. To request and application or additional information please

contact Renee Taft, Director, Visiting Scholars Program, at the Center for Advanced Holocaust Studies.
Closing Date: October 31st.
Additional Information: The Schechter Fellow is encouraged to participate in the Museum's broad array of scholarly and other programmes.

For further information contact:

United States of America
Tel: (1) 202 314 0378
Fax: (1) 202 479 9726
Contact: Ms Renee Taft, Visiting Scholar Program Director

The Pearl Resnick Post Doctoral Fellowship

Subjects: Cultural studies, languages and humanities subjects, as they relate to the study of the Holocaust.
Eligibility: Candidates must have a PhD or equivalent degree earned within the last ten years, and must hold the PhD by the application deadline.
Purpose: To provide young, promising scholars with a year in residence at the Center for Advanced Holocaust Studies.
Type: Fellowship.
No. of awards offered: 1.
Value: A stipend of US$40,000 for the academic year, office space, postage, and access to a computer, telephone, facsimile machine, and a photocopier. A travel supplement not to exceed US$3,500 for the Fellow and accompanying family members (spouse and dependent children) is also available.
Country of Study: USA.
Application Procedure: Please contact Betsy Anthony, Visiting Scholars Program, the Center for Advanced Holocaust Studies for an application form, or further details.
Closing Date: October 31st.
Additional Information: The Fellow will be encouraged to participate in the Museum's broad array of scholarly and other programmes.

UNITED STATES EDUCATIONAL FOUNDATION IN INDIA (USEFI)

Fulbright House
12 Hailey Road, New Delhi, 110001, India
Tel: (91) 11 3328944
Fax: (91) 11 3329718
Email: fulbright@usefid.ernet.in
Contact: Program Officer

USEFI Internships in Art History

Subjects: Art history - Asian and Western art.
Eligibility: Open to Indian citizens present in India at the time of the application and interview, who are permanently employed at an educational institution or museum and directly involved in teaching or research in art and art history.
Level of Study: Postgraduate.
Type: Internship.

Frequency: Annual.
Value: Stipend.
Country of Study: Any country.
Application Procedure: Requests for application forms must state the candidate's academic/professional qualifications, date of birth and present position, and should be accompanied by a large SAE.
Closing Date: Early July.
Additional Information: These Internships are currently being revised and details will be published after Board decision in April. Anyone wishing to apply should contact USEFI from April onwards.

USEFI Postdoctoral Travel-Only Grants

Subjects: Research or teaching assignments; faculty engaged in inter-institutional collaboration, with Indian government approval; candidates in the field of social sciences, humanities, fine arts and performing arts.
Eligibility: Open to Indian scholars present in India at the time of application. Candidates should be proficient in English and be in good health, and should not have been in the USA during the last four years to teach, to carry out research, or on a professional assignment. Research applicants must have a PhD or equivalent published work.
Level of Study: Postdoctorate.
Type: Travel Grant.
No. of awards offered: Limited.
Frequency: Twice a year.
Value: Return air fare.
Study Establishment: Travel only, for varying periods.
Country of Study: USA.
Application Procedure: Applicants should have letters of invitation/sponsorship and have secured financial support.
Closing Date: February 1st, August 1st.
Additional Information: These grants are currently being revised and details will be published after Board decision in April. Anyone wishing to apply should contact USEFI from April onwards.

UNITED STATES FOUNDATION

Fondation des États-Unis
15 boulevard Jourdan, Paris Cedex 14, F-75690, France
Tel: (33) 1 53 80 68 80
Fax: (33) 1 53 80 68 99
Contact: The Director

Harriet Hale Woolley Scholarships

Subjects: Art and music. Grants are for persons doing painting, printmaking, sculpture, and for instrumentalists, not for research in art history, musicology or composition, not for students of dance or of theater.
Eligibility: Open to US citizens, 21-29 years of age, who have graduated with high academic standing from an American college, university, or professional school of recognised standing. Preference is given to mature students who have already done graduate study. Applicants should provide

evidence of artistic or musical accomplishment. Applicants should have a good working knowlege of French, sufficient to enable the student to benefit at once from study in France; good moral character, personality and adaptability; and good physical health and emotional stability.
Level of Study: Postgraduate.
Type: Scholarship.
No. of awards offered: 4-5.
Frequency: Annual.
Value: A stipend of US$8,500, payable in French francs.
Length of Study: 1 academic year.
Country of Study: France.
Application Procedure: Please write for details.
Closing Date: January 31st.

UNIVERSAL ESPERANTO ASSOCIATION

Nieuwe Binneweg 176, Rotterdam, NL-3015 BJ, Netherlands
Tel: (31) 10 436 1044
Fax: (31) 10 436 1751
Email: uea@inter.nl.net
www: http://www.esperanto.net/info/index_en.html
Contact: Mr P Zapelli

Universal Esperanto Association Awards

Subjects: Esperanto.
Eligibility: Open to individuals of all nationalities who are between 18 and 29 years of age. A fluent knowledge of Esperanto, both written and spoken, is an essential prior qualification.
Level of Study: Unrestricted.
Purpose: To train young volunteer workers for the advancement of the language and literature of Esperanto.
Type: Award.
No. of awards offered: 1-2.
Frequency: Annual.
Value: A monthly stipend of 280 Euros, plus other expenses.
Length of Study: Up to 1 year; not renewable.
Study Establishment: The Head Office of the Association.
Country of Study: Netherlands.
Closing Date: All year round.

UNIVERSITA' PER STRANIERI DI SIENA

Via Pantaneto N 45, Siena, I-53100, Italy
Tel: (390) 577 240 111
Fax: (390) 577 283 163
Email: info@unistrasi.it
www: http://www.unistrasi.it
Contact: Ufficio Assistenza

The University of Siena for Foreigners is a state institution of higher education which carries out didactic activity and scientific research. The aim is to spread knowledge of the Italian language and culture. The university is in the historical centre of Siena and offers courses for students and teachers.

Unstra Grants - PVS Grants-Cils Grants

Subjects: Italian language and culture.
Eligibility: P.V.S Students from developing countries, Cils and Unstra - world students with a general certificate of education.
Level of Study: Postgraduate.
Purpose: To support study at regular courses.
Type: Grant.
Frequency: Dependent on funds available.
Value: Unstra - cover the course fees, P.V.S and Cils grants - cover fees and lodging.
Length of Study: 2 or 3 months.
Study Establishment: University of Siena for Foreigners.
Country of Study: Italy.
Application Procedure: Students must fill out the enrolment form and enclose: two passport sized photographs, a copy of an identity document, a translated and authenticated copy of a degree or diploma valid for admission to universities, the receipt for payment of the first insallment of course fees.
Closing Date: Enrolment applications must be received by the Student Secretariat of the University at least 20 days prior to the first day of the course.

UNIVERSITY FOR FOREIGNERS (ITALY)

Universita' per Stranieri
Palazzo Gallenga
Piazza Fortebraccio 4, Perugia, I-06100, Italy
Tel: (390) 75 57461
Fax: (390) 75 574 6213
Contact: Rector

University for Foreigners Scholarships

Subjects: Italian language and culture.
Eligibility: Open to foreign citizens and Italians resident abroad. Preference is given to students of Italian, at schools and universities abroad, and to teachers of the Italian language.
Level of Study: Postgraduate.
Type: Scholarship.
No. of awards offered: Varies.
Frequency: Annual.
Value: To cover one month's study and living expenses.
Study Establishment: The University.
Country of Study: Italy.
Application Procedure: Application for scholarships must be made through the Italian Institutes of Culture in the country of residence. Direct application to the University for Foreigners may be made only by applicants residing in countries where there are no Italian Institutes of Culture or, independently of this, applicants holding particular qualifications who intend to

specialise in linguistic, literary, historical or artistic studies begun in their own countries and applicants who have attended courses at the University for Foreigners for at least three months in the past. special scholarships are awarded to the best qualified applicants wishing to attend the Course for Teachers of Italian abroad. Applications must be made before September 30th for the winter course/January; March 31st for the summer course/August. Forms containing details about qualification requirements and application procedures may be requested from the University for Foreigners or the Italian Institutes.
Closing Date: At least four months before the start of the course.

UNIVERSITY OF ALBERTA

Faculty of Graduate Studies & Research
105 Administration Building, Edmonton, AB, T6G2M7, Canada
Tel: (1) 403 492 3499
Fax: (1) 403 492 0692
Email: grad.mail@ualberta.ca
www: http://www.ualberta.ca/~graduate/graduate.html
Contact: Ms T J Retson-Spalding, Graduate Awards Assistant

Opened in 1908, the University of Alberta has a long tradition of scholarly achievements and commitment to excellence in teaching, research and service to the community. It is one of Canada's five largest research-intensive universities, with an annual research income from external sources of more than C$112 million. It participates in all fourteen of the Federal Networks of Centres of Excellence which link industry, universities and government in applied research and development.

Izaak Walton Killam Memorial Postdoctoral Fellowships

Subjects: All subjects.
Eligibility: Open to candidates of any nationality who have recently completed a PhD programme or will do so in the immediate future. Applicants who have received their PhD degree from the University of Alberta, or who will be on sabbatical leave, or who have held (or will have held) postdoctoral fellowships at other institutions for two years are not eligible. Tenable at the University of Alberta.
Level of Study: Postdoctorate.
Purpose: To attract scholars of superior research ability who have graduated within the last three years.
Type: Fellowship.
No. of awards offered: 5.
Frequency: Annual.
Value: C$35,000 per year. A non-renewable, one-time research grant of C$3,000 accompanies the award, plus incoming and return airfare.
Length of Study: 2 years.
Study Establishment: University of Alberta.
Country of Study: Canada.

Application Procedure: Application information is available from university departments.
Closing Date: January 2nd.

Izaak Walton Killam Memorial Scholarships

Subjects: All subjects.
Eligibility: Open to candidates of any nationality who are registered in, or are admissible to, a doctoral programme at the University. Scholars must have completed at least one year of graduate work prior to beginning the Scholarship. Applicants must be nominated by the department in which they plan to pursue their doctoral studies.
Level of Study: Doctorate, Postgraduate.
Type: Scholarship.
No. of awards offered: Approx. 13.
Frequency: Annual.
Value: C$16,200 per year, a non-renewable, one-time C$1,500 research grant, plus tuition and fees.
Length of Study: 2 years (from May 1st or September 1st); subject to review after the first year.
Study Establishment: University of Alberta.
Country of Study: Canada.
Application Procedure: Application information is available from university departments.
Closing Date: February 1st for submission of nominations from departments. Check with the department for internal deadline.

Province of Alberta Graduate Fellowships

Subjects: All subjects.
Eligibility: Open to Canadian citizens or permanent residents at the date of application who have completed at least one year of graduate study and are registered in a full time doctoral programme at the University of Alberta.
Level of Study: Doctorate, Postgraduate.
Type: Fellowship.
No. of awards offered: Approx. 35.
Frequency: Annual.
Value: C$10,500 (May commencement); C$7,000 (September commencement).
Length of Study: 1 year (from May 1st or September 1st).
Study Establishment: University of Alberta.
Country of Study: Canada.
Application Procedure: Applicants must be nominated by the department in which they plan to pursue their doctoral studies.
Closing Date: February 1st for submission of nominations from departments. Check with the department for internal deadline.
Additional Information: Recipients must carry out a full-time research programme during the summer months.

Province of Alberta Graduate Scholarships

Subjects: All subjects.
Eligibility: Open to Canadian citizens or permanent residents at the date of application who are entering or continuing in a full-time Master's programme at the University of Alberta. Applicants must be nominated by the department in which

they plan to pursue their studies. Students registered as qualifying graduate students are not eligible.
Level of Study: Postgraduate.
Type: Scholarship.
No. of awards offered: Approx. 38.
Frequency: Annual.
Value: C$9,300 (May commencement); C$6,200 (September commencement).
Length of Study: 12 months (from 1 May) or for 8 months (from September 1st); partial awards may be recommended at a reduced value and the award may be terminated earlier by either the student or the university and the amount reduced proportionately.
Study Establishment: University of Alberta.
Country of Study: Canada.
Application Procedure: Application forms are available from university departments.
Closing Date: February 1st for submission of nominations from departments. Check with the department for internal deadline.

UNIVERSITY OF AUCKLAND

Private Bag 92019, Auckland, 1000, New Zealand
Tel: (64) 9 373 7999
Fax: (64) 9 373 7400
Email: appointments@auckland.ac.nz
www: http://www.auckland.ac.nz
Contact: Mr M V Lellman, Assistant Registrar

The University of Auckland has a commitment to conserving, advancing and disseminating knowledge through teaching of the highest standard provided by scholars who are among the foremost researchers in New Zealand. The University aims to be a university of high international standing and a leader in the Asia-Pacific region.

UARC Postdoctoral Fellowships

Subjects: Any academic discipline represented at this University.
Eligibility: Applicants must have completed a PhD not more than four years previously. Open to any suitably qualified applicant who has been the holder of a doctorate from an institution other than the University of Auckland for not more than four years.
Level of Study: Postdoctorate.
Purpose: To foster research.
Type: Fellowship.
No. of awards offered: 4 or 5.
Frequency: Annual.
Value: NZ$46,250 per year, plus allowance for air fare of up to NZ$4,000.
Length of Study: 2 years; not renewable.
Study Establishment: Auckland University.
Country of Study: New Zealand.
Application Procedure: All vacancies are advertised and application details are given in the advertisement.
Closing Date: Around June.

Additional Information: Fellowships are assigned to university staff members on a competitive basis. Graduates of the University of Auckland are not eligible for the Fellowships.

University of Auckland Foundation Visiting Fellowships

Subjects: Any subject offered by the University.
Eligibility: Open to suitably qualified scholars of high academic standing.
Level of Study: Postdoctorate, Professional development.
Purpose: To bring visiting scholars of high standing in their academic field, to the University of Auckland.
Type: Fellowship.
No. of awards offered: Up to 15.
Frequency: Annual.
Value: Varies, up to NZ$5,000.
Length of Study: Variable periods of up to 1 year.
Study Establishment: University of Auckland.
Country of Study: New Zealand.
Application Procedure: Recipients must be nominated by a staff member at the University of Auckland.
Closing Date: June 30th.

University of Auckland Literary Fellowship

Subjects: Creative writing.
Eligibility: Open to writers of proven merit who are New Zealand residents. Not available to staff of the University of Auckland.
Level of Study: Unrestricted.
Purpose: To foster New Zealand writing.
Type: Fellowship.
No. of awards offered: 1.
Frequency: Annual.
Value: NZ$45,750.
Length of Study: 1 year.
Study Establishment: Auckland University.
Country of Study: New Zealand.
Application Procedure: A 'method of application' is detailed when the vacancy is advertised, there is no specific application form.
Closing Date: As advertised, usually in September/October.
Additional Information: Appointee must reside in Auckland for the duration of the award.

UNIVERSITY OF BATH

Graduate Office
Claverton Down, Bath, BA2 7AY, England
Tel: (44) 1225 826826
Fax: (44) 1225 826366
Email: grad-office@bath.ac.uk
www: http://www.bath.ac.uk/
Contact: Dr Lisa Isted, Graduate Office Administrator

The University, which occupies a beautiful greenfield site just outside the world hertitage city of Bath, specialises in engineering and design, science, humanities and social

sciences, and management. The University of Bath came sixth in the 1996 research assessment exercise, with 12 out of 21 units achieving grade 5.

University Research Studentships

Subjects: All subjects offered by the University.
Eligibility: Open to candidates of any nationality with a first or good second class honours degree or equivalent. Candidates must have applied, or been accepted, for study for a research degree.
Level of Study: Doctorate, Postdoctorate.
Purpose: To provide funds for well-qualified candidates to pursue full-time research leading to a research degree.
Type: 1 Scholarship.
No. of awards offered: Approx. 20.
Frequency: Annual, if funds are available.
Value: Home fees plus maintenance at level equivalent to research councils.
Length of Study: Up to 3 years.
Study Establishment: University of Bath.
Country of Study: United Kingdom.
Application Procedure: Those wishing to be considered should state this when applying for a higher degree and should contact the appropriate academic department or the graduate office.
Closing Date: August 1st.
Additional Information: Other studentships are available at the University of Bath. Please contact the graduate office for further details.

UNIVERSITY OF BIRMINGHAM

Scholarships Office
Edgbaston, Birmingham, West Midlands, B15 2TT, England
Tel: (44) 121 414 3344
Fax: (44) 121 414 3907
www: http://www.bham.ac.uk
Telex: 333762 UOBHAM G
Contact: Ms Anne Baker, Scholarships Officer

The University of Birmingham is a leading research institution, offering a wide range of programmes, high teaching and research standards, and excellent facilities for academic work.

Neville Chamberlain Scholarship

Subjects: Humanities subjects. Preference will be given to studies focussing on modern political, social and economic history, especially concering Great Britain and its 19th century sphere of influence.
Eligibility: Open to (preferably) non-UK students with a good honours degree who have been offered (either conditionally or unconditionally) and have accepted admission to study for a higher degree in a humanities subject.
Level of Study: Postgraduate.
Purpose: To provide financial assistance to students wishing to study for a higher degree in a humanities subject.

Type: Scholarship.
No. of awards offered: 1.
Frequency: Annual, if funds are available.
Value: Supplement to student's resources should these be inadequate for taking the degree. An award may be given towards both tuition fees and maintenance but normally should not exceed £7,000 per annum.
Length of Study: 1 year; renewable as funds permit.
Study Establishment: University of Birmingham.
Country of Study: United Kingdom.
Application Procedure: Applicants should should tell the School of the University of Birmingham in which they intend studying that they would like that School to nominate them for this scholarship.
Closing Date: Mid June.
Additional Information: Proficiency in English is essential.

UNIVERSITY OF BRISTOL

Student Finance Office
Students Union
Queen's Road, Bristol, BS8 1LN, England
Tel: (44) 117 954 5886
Fax: (44) 117 923 9085
Email: judith.tyler@bristol.ac.uk
www: http://www.bristol.ac.uk
Contact: Ms J Tyler, Overseas Recruitment & Liaison Director

University Postgraduate Scholarships

Subjects: Any research topic which is covered in the work of the Department within the University.
Eligibility: New research students with normally at least an upper second class honours degree or equivalent. Full-time students or part-time students who are not in full-time employment. All University scholars must be registered and in attendance for a research degree at the University.
Level of Study: Postgraduate.
Purpose: To help the University to recruit high quality research students.
Type: Scholarship.
No. of awards offered: 90.
Frequency: Annual.
Value: £5,455-£7,910 plus home tuition fees of £2,610.
Length of Study: 3 years.
Study Establishment: University of Bristol.
Country of Study: United Kingdom.
Application Procedure: Students must apply on the appropriate form to the Department of their field of interest.
Closing Date: Normally May 1st.
Additional Information: Overseas students need to find the difference between home and overseas fees. To do this they can apply for an overseas research scholarship.

For further information contact:

Postgraduate Admissions
University of Bristol
Senate House
Tyndall Avenue
Clifton, Bristol, BS8 1TH, England

UNIVERSITY OF BRITISH COLUMBIA

Faculty of Graduate Studies
180-6371 Crescent Road, Vancouver, BC, V6T 1Z2, Canada
Tel: (1) 604 822 4556
Fax: (1) 604 822 5802
Email: gradawards@mercury.ubc.ca
www: http://www.grad.ubc.ca/awards/top.htm
Contact: Graduate Awards Officer

The University of British Columbia is one of North America's major research universities. The faculty of Graduate Studies has 6,500 students and is a national leader in interdisciplinary study and research, with 88 departments, 17 research centres, 6 graduate programmes, 2 residential colleges and a school.

Izaak Walton Killam Postdoctoral Fellowships

Subjects: All subjects.
Eligibility: Open to candidates who show superior ability in research and have obtained, within two academic years of the anticipated commencement date of the Fellowship, a doctorate at a university other than the University of British Columbia. Graduates of the University of British Columbia are not normally eligible.
Level of Study: Postdoctorate.
Purpose: To support all areas of academic research.
Type: Fellowship.
No. of awards offered: 8.
Frequency: Annual.
Value: C$32,000.
Length of Study: 2 years, subject to satisfactory progress at the end of the first year.
Study Establishment: UBC.
Country of Study: Canada.
Application Procedure: Application form, academic transcripts and three reference letters must be submitted to the appropriate department.
Closing Date: November 15th.
Additional Information: Candidates are responsible for contacting the appropriate department at the University to ensure their proposed research project is acceptable and may be undertaken under the supervision of a member of the department. Travel/research grant of C$3,000 is available during the tenure of the fellowship. (Email: killam@mercury.ubc.ca).

Killam Predoctoral Fellowship

Subjects: Full-time study and/or research leading to a doctoral degree in any subject.
Eligibility: Open to students of any nationality, discipline, age or sex. This award is given at PhD level only and is strictly based on academic merit. Students must have a first class standing in their last two years of study.
Level of Study: Doctorate.
Purpose: To assist doctoral students to devote full time to their studies and research.
Type: Fellowship.
No. of awards offered: Approx. 20.
Frequency: Annual.
Value: C$22,000 per year.
Study Establishment: UBC.
Country of Study: Canada.
Application Procedure: Top-ranked students are selected from the University Graduate Fellowship competition. Application forms can be obtained from departments or the Faculty of Graduate Studies.
Closing Date: January 26th.
Additional Information: Students must submit their applications to the departments, not to Graduates Studies; please check for internal departmental deadlines.

University of British Columbia Graduate Fellowship

Subjects: Full-time study and/or research leading to a masters or doctoral degree in any discipline.
Eligibility: Open to students of any nationality, discipline, age or sex. This award is strictly based on academic merit. Students must have a first class standing in their last two years of study.
Level of Study: Postgraduate.
Purpose: To assist graduate students to devote full time to their studies and research.
Type: Fellowship.
No. of awards offered: Approx. 400.
Frequency: Annual.
Value: C$16,000 per year for full renewable UGFs; or C$8,000 for one-year UGF's.
Study Establishment: UBC.
Country of Study: Canada.
Application Procedure: Applicants are nominated by their departments based on academic merit. Students must submit their applications to the UBC Department, not to The Faculty of Graduate Studies.
Closing Date: End of January or mid-March.
Additional Information: Please check for internal departmental deadlines.

THE UNIVERSITY OF CALGARY

Earth Sciences Building
Room 720
2500 University Drive NW, Calgary, AB, T2N 1N4, Canada
Tel: (1) 403 220 5690
Fax: (1) 403 289 7635
Email: cbusch@acs.ucalgary.ca
www: http://www.ucalgary.ca
Contact: Ms Connie Busch, Graduate Scholarship Assistant

Alberta Art Foundation Graduate Scholarships in The Department of Art

Subjects: Major fields of study in the Department of Art.
Eligibility: Open to students entering the second year of the MFA programme in the specialisations of painting, printmaking, sculpture, drawing and photography.
Level of Study: Postgraduate.
Purpose: To support study.
Type: Scholarship.
No. of awards offered: 3.
Frequency: Annual.
Value: C$6,000.
Study Establishment: University of Calgary.
Country of Study: Canada.
Application Procedure: Apply through nomination by the Department of Art.
Closing Date: February1st.

Craigie (Peter C) Memorial Scholarship

Subjects: The humanities.
Eligibility: Open to full-time registrants from any country who are registered in and have completed one term of study in a programme of studies leading to an MA degree in a department of the Faculty of Humanities.
Level of Study: Postgraduate.
Type: Scholarship.
No. of awards offered: 1.
Frequency: Every two years.
Value: C$5,000.
Study Establishment: University of Calgary.
Country of Study: Canada.
Application Procedure: Applicants should apply to the faculty of Humanities in the first instance. Recommendations from the faculty will be submitted for consideration and approval by the University Graduate Scholarship Committee.
Closing Date: February 1st.
Additional Information: The recipient must have an outstanding scholastic record and will have been or be involved in activities contributing to the general welfare of the university committee.

Izaak Walton Killam Memorial Scholarships

Subjects: All subjects.
Eligibility: Open to qualified graduates of any university who are admissible to a doctoral programme at the University of Calgary. Applicants must have completed at least one year of graduate study prior to taking up the award.
Level of Study: Doctorate, Postgraduate.
Type: Scholarship.
No. of awards offered: 4-5.
Frequency: Annual.
Value: C$19,500. If approved, award holders may also receive up to C$2,100 over the full term of appointment for special equipment and/or travel in direct connection with the PhD research.
Length of Study: 1 year.
Study Establishment: University of Calgary.
Country of Study: Canada.
Application Procedure: Apply for application from The Graduate Scholarship Secretary at the university.
Closing Date: February 1st annually.
Additional Information: One year duration renewable once upon presentation of evidence of satisfactory progress. Further renewal in open competition.

Province of Alberta Graduate Scholarships and Fellowships

Subjects: All subjects.
Eligibility: Candidates for the scholarships or fellowships must be registered in or admissible to a programme leading to a Master's or Doctoral degree respectively. Eligible to Canadian citizens and landed immigrants.
Level of Study: Doctorate, Postgraduate.
Type: Fellowship, Scholarship.
No. of awards offered: 60-70.
Frequency: Annual.
Value: Scholarship: C$9,300 per year. Fellowship: C$10,500 per year.
Length of Study: 1 year.
Study Establishment: University of Calgary.
Country of Study: Canada.
Application Procedure: Application forms are available from the Directors of Graduate Studies of the regarded departments.
Closing Date: February 1st.
Additional Information: One year, renewable in open competition. Students whose awards begin in May are expected to carry out a full-time research programme during the summer months.

University of Calgary Dean's Special Entrance Scholarship

Subjects: All subjects.
Eligibility: Open to women admissible to the Faculty of Graduate Studies in a programme of study leading to either the Master's or Doctoral degree.
Level of Study: Doctorate, Postgraduate.
Type: Scholarship.
No. of awards offered: 4.

Frequency: Annual.
Value: C$8,000.
Length of Study: 1 year; not renewable.
Study Establishment: University of Calgary.
Country of Study: Canada.
Application Procedure: Candidates should apply to the chairperson of the Graduate Scholarship Committee, Room 720 Earth Sciences Building, The University of Calgary, using the Graduate Scholarship Application Form. In addition, the description of the family responsibilities, no longer than one page, must be appended to the application.
Closing Date: February 1st.
Additional Information: Applicants must be entering a first year of graduate work after an absence from full-time study at a university for a minimum of three years for the purposes of raising children, caring for elderly parents or other demanding family responsibilities. Applicants must include a description of those responsibilities.

University of Calgary Dean's Special Master's Scholarship

Subjects: Disciplines where the Master's degree is the terminal degree at the University of Calgary.
Eligibility: Open to candidates who are or will be registered in a full-time thesis-based MA programme in a discipline where the MA-degree is the terminal degree at the University of Calgary.
Level of Study: Postgraduate.
Type: Scholarship.
No. of awards offered: Up to 15.
Frequency: Annual.
Value: C$5,000.
Length of Study: 1 year.
Study Establishment: University of Calgary.
Country of Study: Canada.
Application Procedure: Candidates must apply to the regarded departments at the University of Calgary.
Closing Date: February 1st.
Additional Information: One-year duration, renewable in open competition.

University of Calgary Silver Anniversary Graduate Fellowships

Subjects: All subjects.
Eligibility: Open to qualified graduates of any recognised university who are registered in or admissible to a doctoral programme at the University of Calgary. Canadian residents only.
Level of Study: Doctorate.
Type: Fellowship.
No. of awards offered: Minimum of 2.
Frequency: Annual.
Value: Up to C$20,000 but in no case less than C$16,000.
Length of Study: 1 year.
Study Establishment: University of Calgary.
Country of Study: Canada.
Application Procedure: Candidates should apply to their department.

Closing Date: February 1st.
Additional Information: One year duration, renewable once upon presentation of evidence of satisfactory progress. Awards are granted on the basis of academic standing and demonstrated potential for advanced study and research.

UNIVERSITY OF CAMBRIDGE

University Registry
The Old Schools, Cambridge, CB2 1TN, England
Tel: (44) 1223 332 317
Fax: (44) 1223 332 332
Email: mrf25@admin.cam.ac.uk
Contact: Ms Melanie Foster, Scholarships Clerk

The University of Cambridge is a loose confederation of faculties, colleges and other bodies. The Colleges are mainly concerned with the teaching of their undergraduate students (through tutorials and supervisions) and the academic support of both graduate and undergraduate students, while the University employs Professors, Readers, Lecturers and other teaching and administrative staff who provide the formal teaching (in lectures seminars and practical classes). The University also administers the University Library.

Churchill College Research Studentships

Subjects: Any subject for which research supervision can be provided at the university.
Eligibility: Open to any person who has graduated from a university or, if not a graduate, can show evidence of exceptional qualifications for research.
Level of Study: Doctorate.
Purpose: To assist research for candidates who intend to register for the degree of PhD at the University of Cambridge.
Type: Studentship.
No. of awards offered: Varies, depending on funds available.
Frequency: Annual.
Value: University and college fees, plus maintenance (based on recommended rates).
Length of Study: 3 years.
Study Establishment: Churchill College.
Country of Study: United Kingdom.
Application Procedure: Application forms are available from the given address.
Closing Date: February 15th.

For further information contact:

Churchill College, Cambridge, CB3 0DS, England
Tel: (44) 1223 336157
Fax: (44) 1223 336177
Contact: Mr Henry Hurst, Tutor for Advanced Students

Clare Hall Foundation Fellowship

Subjects: All subjects.
Eligibility: Open to persons who already hold academic posts in their own country, have not previously studied in the UK or North America, and are able to demonstrate that a period of

study in Cambridge would be of special benefit. There is no restriction as to sex or age, although preference may be given to applicants under the age of 40.
Level of Study: Postdoctorate.
Purpose: To help a rising scholar from either a developing country, a centrally planned economy, or a country in transition to a market economy.
Type: Fellowship.
No. of awards offered: 1.
Frequency: Annual.
Value: Normally sufficient for three months residence in Cambridge.
Length of Study: 3 months; although by supplementing other funds the Fellowship would possibly permit a longer stay of up to 6 months.
Study Establishment: Normally Clare Hall, but probably attached to one of the university departments.
Country of Study: United Kingdom.
Application Procedure: Applications, accompanied by a curriculum vitae, should be addressed to the Chairman of the Fellowship Committee at the College, to whom three referees should write direct. One reference should be from a referee whose work is recognized in the UK.
Closing Date: Application are accepted at any time.
Additional Information: The Fellowship is awarded on the grounds of academic suitability.

For further information contact:

Clare Hall
Herschel Road, Cambridge, CB3 9AL, England
Tel: (44) 1223 332360
Fax: (44) 1223 332333
Contact: Ms Elizabeth Ramsden, College Secretary

Corpus Christi College Research Scholarships

Subjects: All subjects.
Eligibility: Open to holders of a first class honours degree or equivalent. Candidates eligible for UK state awards are not eligible.
Level of Study: Doctorate.
Purpose: To enable the successful candidate to pursue, as a member of the College, a course of study in any subject leading to a research-based higher degree, normally the PhD, at the University of Cambridge.
Type: Scholarship.
No. of awards offered: 1+.
Frequency: Annual.
Value: Awards are made usually in collaboration with the Cambridge Commonwealth and Overseas Trusts. The amount of the awards varies but substantial contributions (£6,000) towards fees or maintenance costs are made.
Length of Study: Usually 3 years.
Study Establishment: Corpus Christi College.
Country of Study: United Kingdom.
Application Procedure: All applications to the Board of Graduate Studies which name Corpus Christi College as their first preference on CIGAS Form A will be considered for these scholarships, provided they reach the College by the closing date. Separate application to the College is not required.
Closing Date: End of March.

For further information contact:

Corpus Christi College, Cambridge, CB2 1RH, England
Tel: (44) 1223 338038
Fax: (44) 1223 338057
Contact: Dr C J B Brookes, The Tutor for Advanced Students

Downing College Research Fellowships

Subjects: As advertised, but generally arts and science subjects in alternate years.
Eligibility: Open to graduates who have completed or are on the point of completing a PhD. Applicants must normally be under 30 on taking up the award, or if over 30, must normally not have completed more than 12 terms research as a registered research student.
Level of Study: Postdoctorate.
Purpose: To enable promising young scholars to undertake research, undistracted by other duties, to consolidate their reputations.
Type: Fellowship.
No. of awards offered: 1.
Frequency: Annually at present.
Value: Resident pre-PhD £11,443, resident post-PhD £13,893; living out allowance £2,000.
Length of Study: 3 years.
Study Establishment: Normally based in Cambridge.
Country of Study: United Kingdom.
Application Procedure: Application forms are available from the Senior Tutor, following advertisements.
Closing Date: As advertised.
Additional Information: Application form indicates that candidates must get referees to write to the college.

For further information contact:

Downing College, Cambridge, CB2 1DQ, England
Tel: (44) 1223 334811
Fax: (44) 1223 362279
Contact: Ms Jane Perks, Tutorial Office Manager

E D Davies Scholarship

Subjects: All subjects.
Eligibility: Open to graduates of any university who have been admitted to a course of research.
Level of Study: Doctorate.
Purpose: To enable graduates to undertake a course of research in any subject area.
Type: Scholarship.
No. of awards offered: 1.
Frequency: Annual.
Value: £1,250 per year. The award is designed to supplement funding from other sources.
Length of Study: 3 years.
Study Establishment: Fitzwilliam College.
Country of Study: England.
Application Procedure: Application forms are available on request.
Closing Date: June 13th.

For further information contact:

Fitzwilliam College, Cambridge, CB3 ODG, England
Tel: (44) 1223 332 035
Fax: (44) 1223 332 082
Contact: Dr W Alison, Tutor for Graduate Students

Fitzwilliam College Research Fellowship

Subjects: To be advised in further particulars.
Eligibility: Open to candidates who are carrying out research for a PhD at any British or Irish university, or who have recently completed their course of study for this degree. Candidates should not have completed four years of full-time research by the April preceding the commencement of the fellowship.
Level of Study: Doctorate.
Purpose: To enable scholars to carry out a programme of new research.
Type: Fellowship.
No. of awards offered: Varies.
Frequency: Annual.
Value: Varies. Non-stipendiary also offered.
Study Establishment: Fitzwilliam College.
Country of Study: United Kingdom.
Application Procedure: Please write for details.
Closing Date: Early September.
Additional Information: Fellowships are awarded for new research only, not to enable candidates to complete their PhD dissertation.

For further information contact:

Fitzwilliam College, Cambridge, CB3 0DG, England
Tel: (44) 1223 332 035
Fax: (44) 1223 332 082
Contact: Dr W Alison, Tutor for Graduate Students

Fitzwilliam College Shipley Studentship

Subjects: Theology.
Eligibility: Open to graduates of any university who have been admitted to a course of research in the Faculty of Divinity (or exceptionally a course of research on a theological topic in some other Faculty). The awards are only available to candidates who have applied for admission to the University through the Board of Graduate Studies (4 Mill Lane, Cambridge CB2 1RZ, England) and subsequently satisfied the conditions of admission made by the Board. Candidates should also place Fitzwilliam College as their first preference in their application.
Level of Study: Postgraduate.
Type: Studentship.
No. of awards offered: 1.
Frequency: Annual.
Value: £1,250 per year. The award is designed to supplement other funds.
Length of Study: 1 year.
Study Establishment: Fitzwilliam College.
Country of Study: United Kingdom.

Application Procedure: Application forms are available on request.
Closing Date: June 13th.

For further information contact:

Fitzwilliam College, Cambridge, CB3 0DG, England
Tel: (44) 1223 332 035
Fax: (44) 1223 332 082
Contact: Dr W Alison, Tutor for Graduate Students

Girton College Research Fellowships

Subjects: Arts and humanities; natural sciences.
Eligibility: Open to qualified graduates of any university who are able to provide evidence of outstanding research abilities. This award is highly competitive.
Level of Study: Postdoctorate.
Purpose: To provide the opportunity for graduate students to conduct research in their chosen field of study.
Type: Fellowship.
No. of awards offered: 2-4.
Frequency: Annual.
Value: £9,475 per year for predoctoral fellows; £11,895-£12,525 per year for postdoctoral Fellows, over three years. The stipend is reviewed annually.
Length of Study: Up to 3 years.
Study Establishment: Girton College.
Country of Study: United Kingdom.
Application Procedure: Candidates must submit a completed application form, which is available from Mrs Crofts.
Closing Date: Usually October 31st.

For further information contact:

Girton College, Cambridge, CB3 0JG, England
Tel: (44) 1223 338 951
Fax: (44) 1223 338 896
Contact: Mrs Irene Crofts, Bursar's Secretary

Gonville and Caius College Gonville Bursary

Subjects: Any offered by the University.
Eligibility: Open to candidates who have been accepted by the College through its normal admissions procedures, and who are classified as overseas students for fees purposes. A statement of financial circumstances is required.
Level of Study: Doctorate, Postgraduate, Undergraduate.
Purpose: To help outstanding students from outside the EC to meet the costs of degree courses at the University of Cambridge.
Type: Bursary.
No. of awards offered: Up to 6.
Frequency: Annual.
Value: Reimbursement of College fees.
Length of Study: Up to 3 years, (renewable dependent on satisfactory progress).
Study Establishment: Gonville and Caius College.
Country of Study: United Kingdom.

Application Procedure: There are no application forms. For further information please contact the admissions tutor.
Closing Date: The same as for the University's courses.

For further information contact:

Gonville and Caius College, Cambridge, CB2 1TA, England
Tel: (44) 1223 332447
Fax: (44) 1223 332456
Contact: The Admissions Tutor

Magdalene College Leslie Wilson Research Scholarships

Subjects: Any subject offered by the University.
Eligibility: Open to graduates from the UK and overseas who will be studying at Cambridge for a PhD degree. Consideration is normally restricted to those who have obtained, or who have a strong prospect of obtaining, a first class honours (Bachelor's) degree. Preference is given to those nominating Magdalene as their first choice college.
Level of Study: Doctorate.
Purpose: To assist study leading to the degree of Doctor of Philosophy.
Type: Scholarship.
No. of awards offered: 1.
Frequency: Annual.
Value: A maximum of £10,787 (1998-99 values) for a scholar who has no other sources of finance (maintenance grant £6,455, university fees £2,610, and college fees £1,772). Rented accommodation in or near Magdalene College will be made available during the first year of residence for unmarried scholars. Married scholars will be offered rented accommodation near to the college.
Length of Study: Up to 3 years.
Study Establishment: Magdalene College and the University of Cambridge.
Country of Study: United Kingdom.
Application Procedure: Leslie Wilson Scholarship applicants should obtain a CIGAS form from the Board of Graduate Studies, 4 Mill Lane, Cambridge. UK candidates are expected to apply, if eligible, for State or Research Council Studentships. Overseas candidates are expected to apply for UK government support as well as Overseas Student Bursaries awarded by the University of Cambridge and administered by the Board of Graduate Studies. In addition, all candidates should obtain a Leslie Wilson Research Scholarship form from the address below.
Closing Date: May 1st.

For further information contact:

Magdalene College
University of Cambridge, Cambridge, CB3 0AG, England
Tel: (44) 1223 332135
Fax: (44) 1223 462589
Contact: Admissions Tutor for Graduates

Pembroke College Graduate Awards

Subjects: Any subject offered by the University.

Eligibility: Open to candidates of any nationality who are accepted by Pembroke College, and who intend to register for a PhD degree at the University of Cambridge. Candidates must make Pembroke their first choice college.
Level of Study: Doctorate, Postgraduate.
Type: Studentship.
No. of awards offered: 1.
Frequency: Annual.
Value: Full support.
Length of Study: 3 years.
Study Establishment: Pembroke College.
Country of Study: United Kingdom.
Closing Date: April 1st.
Additional Information: There are also a number of scholarships (fees only) and bursaries available.

For further information contact:

Pembroke College, Cambridge, CB2 1RZ, England
Tel: (44) 1223 338115
Fax: (44) 1223 338163
Contact: Ms Jenny Davis, Graduate Admissions Tutor

Queen's College Research Fellowships

Subjects: Subjects announced each year.
Eligibility: Open to graduates of any university who should normally be under 30 years of age and who are well advanced in their doctoral research or who have recently begun postdoctoral research.
Level of Study: Postdoctorate.
Purpose: To provide the opportunity for postdoctoral research in various fields of study.
Type: Fellowship.
No. of awards offered: 2.
Frequency: Annual.
Value: Approximately £10,000.
Length of Study: 3 years.
Study Establishment: Queen's College.
Country of Study: United Kingdom.
Application Procedure: Application form must be completed and research proposal submitted. Written work will be requested from short-listed candidates.
Closing Date: Usually October 8th.

For further information contact:

Queens' College, Cambridge, CB3 9ET, England
Tel: (44) 1223 335601
Fax: (44) 1223 335522
Contact: Dr K J I Thorne, Senior Tutor

St John's College Benefactors' Scholarships for Research

Subjects: Any subject offered by the University.
Eligibility: Open to candidates of any nationality with a first class honours or equivalent degree.
Level of Study: Postgraduate.
Purpose: To fund candidates for the PhD and MPhil degrees.
Type: Scholarship.
No. of awards offered: 6.

Frequency: Annual.
Value: £5,295; plus approved college & university fees, book allowance of £310 and other expenses.
Length of Study: Up to 3 years.
Study Establishment: St John's College.
Country of Study: United Kingdom.
Application Procedure: For further particulars see the Cambridge University Graduate Studies Prospectus.
Closing Date: May 1st.

For further information contact:

St John's College, Cambridge, CB2 1TP, England
Tel: (44) 1223 338612
Fax: (44) 1223 766419
Contact: Tutor for Graduate Affairs

Westminster College Lewis and Gibson Scholarship

Subjects: Theology.
Eligibility: Open to graduates of a recognised university who are members of the United Reformed Church in the UK or of any church which is a member of the World Alliance of Reformed Churches and has a Presbyterian form of government. Applicants must have been recognised by their churches as candidates for the Ministry of Word and Sacrament, but should not yet have been ordained.
Level of Study: Postgraduate.
Purpose: To enable the scholar to study for a theology degree of the University of Cambridge as an integral part of his or her training for the ministry of a church in the reformed tradition which has a Presbyterian order.
Type: Scholarship.
No. of awards offered: 1-2.
Frequency: Annually, except when the current holder(s) is/are likely to have the award renewed for the following year.
Value: One scholarship of £6,000 or two scholarships of £3,000 (approximately).
Length of Study: 1 year; renewable for up to 2 further years.
Study Establishment: University of Cambridge.
Country of Study: United Kingdom.
Application Procedure: If it is the intention to study at the postgraduate level, an application should be made at the same time to the Board of Graduate Studies of the university. The scholar will study for one of the following degrees: BA or MPhil in theology; MLitt; or PhD. He or she will be a member of both Westminster College and one of the University's constituent colleges.
Closing Date: December 31st.
Additional Information: Scholars from outside the United Reformed Church have usually been theology graduates and have used the scholarship for postgraduate work.

For further information contact:

Westminster College, Cambridge, CB3 0AA, England
Tel: (44) 1223 350175
Fax: (44) 1223 300765
Contact: Reverend John Proctor, Director of Studies

UNIVERSITY OF CANTERBURY

Private Bag 4800, Christchurch, New Zealand
Tel: (64) 3 364 2808
Fax: (64) 3 364 2325
Email: nr.acad.appts@regy.canterbury.ac.nz
www: http://www.regy.canterbury.ac.nz.home.html
Contact: Staffing Assistant Registrar

The University of Canterbury offers a variety of subjects in a few flexible degree structures; first and postgraduate degrees in arts, commerce, education, engineering, fine arts, forestry, law, music and science. At Canterbury, research and teaching are closely related. While this feature shapes all courses it is very marked at postgraduate level.

University of Canterbury and the Arts Council of New Zealand Toi Aoteoroa Writer in Residence

Subjects: Creative writing - fiction, drama and poetry.
Eligibility: Open to authors of proven merit who are normally resident in New Zealand and to New Zealand nationals temporarily resident overseas.
Level of Study: Unrestricted.
Purpose: To foster New Zealand writing by providing a full-time opportunity for a writer to work in an academic environment.
Type: Fellowship.
No. of awards offered: 1.
Frequency: Annual, if funds are available.
Value: Emolument at the rate of NZ$46,500 per year.
Length of Study: Up to 1 year.
Study Establishment: At the university.
Country of Study: New Zealand.
Application Procedure: Send details only of published writings and work in progress, and proposal of work during appointment. Conditions of appointment are available from the university in August each year.
Closing Date: Usually October 31st.
Additional Information: The appointment will be made on the basis of published or performed writing of high quality. Conditions of appointment should be obtained from the Human Resources Registrar before applying.

UNIVERSITY OF DELAWARE

Department of History
University of Delaware, Newark, DE, 19716, United States of America
Tel: (1) 302 831 8226
Fax: (1) 302 831 1538
Email: patricia.orendorf@mvs.udel.edu
www: http://www.udel.edu
Contact: Ms Patricia H Orendorf, Administrative Assistant

The University of Delaware maintains more than 30 research centres which provide students with the opportunity to use state of the art equipment and computing facilities while conducting research at UD. A high proportion of full-time graduates receive financial assistance through fellowships, tuition scholarships and assistantships.

E Lyman Stewart Fellowship

Subjects: History.
Eligibility: Open to nationals of any country.
Level of Study: Doctorate, Postgraduate.
Purpose: To provide a programme of graduate study leading to a MA or PhD degree for students who plan careers as museum professionals, historical agency administrators, or seek careers in college teaching and public history.
Type: Fellowship.
No. of awards offered: 4-6.
Frequency: Annual.
Value: US$10,000 plus tuition.
Study Establishment: University of Delaware.
Country of Study: USA.
Application Procedure: University of Delaware application, transcripts, GRE scores, TOEFL where applicable, plus three letters of recommendation and a writing sample.
Closing Date: January 31st.

Fellowships in the University of Delaware - Hagley Program

Subjects: The history of industrialization, broadly defined to include business, economic, labour, and social history and the history of science and technology.
Eligibility: Open to graduate students of any nationality seeking degrees in American or European history or the history of science and technology.
Level of Study: Doctorate, Postgraduate.
Purpose: To provide a programme of graduate study leading to the MA or PhD degree for students who seek careers in college teaching and public history.
Type: Fellowship.
No. of awards offered: Approx. 2-3.
Frequency: Annual.
Value: US$10,000 for Master's candidates and doctoral candidates. All tuition fees for university courses are paid.
Length of Study: 1 year; renewable once for those seeking a terminal MA, and up to 3 times for those seeking the doctorate.
Study Establishment: University of Delaware, Newark.
Country of Study: USA.
Application Procedure: Fellows are selected upon GRE scores, recommendations, undergraduate grade index, work experience, and personal interviews.
Closing Date: January 31st.
Additional Information: This is an in-residence program.

UNIVERSITY OF DUNDEE

Dundee, DD1 4HN, Scotland
Tel: (44) 1382 23 181
Fax: (44) 1382 345 515
Email: j.e.nicholson@dundee.ac.uk
www: http://www.dundee.ac.uk
Contact: Postgraduate Office

The mission of the University is to provide education of the highest quality coupled with a leading contribution to the advancement of knowledge, thereby developing in its students the imagination, talents, creativity and skills necessary for the varied and rapidly changing requirements of modern life.

University of Dundee Research Awards

Subjects: Medicine, dentistry, science, engineering, law, arts, social sciences, environmental studies, town planning, architecture, management and consumer studies, nursing, fine art, television & imaging.
Eligibility: Open to holders of a first class or upper second class honours degree or equivalent.
Level of Study: Postgraduate.
Purpose: To assist full-time research leading to a PhD.
Type: Studentship.
No. of awards offered: Approx. 4-6 depending on funds available.
Frequency: Annual.
Value: £5,400 plus tuition fees at the home rate.
Length of Study: 1 year; renewable annually for up to a maximum of 2 additional years.
Study Establishment: University of Dundee, Tayside.
Country of Study: United Kingdom.
Application Procedure: Write for information.
Closing Date: February 26th.

UNIVERSITY OF EAST ANGLIA (UEA)

Norwich, Norfolk, NR4 7TJ, England
Tel: (44) 1603 592734
Fax: (44) 1603 593522
Email: v.striker@uea.ac.uk
www: http://www.uea.ac.uk
Contact: Director of Personnel & Registry Services

David T K Wong Fellowship

Subjects: Writing.
Eligibility: Open to any writer who wishes to produce a work of fiction in English which deals seriously with some aspect of life in the Far East.
Level of Study: Unrestricted.
Purpose: To support promising writers in producing a work of fiction set in the Far East.
Type: Fellowship.

No. of awards offered: 1.
Frequency: Annual.
Value: £25,000.
Length of Study: 1 year.
Study Establishment: University of East Anglia.
Country of Study: United Kingdom.
Application Procedure: Further information and application forms can be obtained by writing to the School of English and American Studies at UEA.
Closing Date: October 31st.
Additional Information: The Far East is defined as China, Hong Kong, Macau, Taiwan, Japan, Korea, Mongolia, Laos, Cambodia, Vietnam, Thailand, Burma, Philippines, Singapore, Malaysia, Indonesia, and Brunei.

UEA Writing Fellowship

Subjects: Creative writing.
Eligibility: Open to practising, published writers in fiction and poetry. Applicants must be English speaking.
Level of Study: Professional development.
Purpose: To enable a creative writer to work in a university atmosphere and with a regional arts board on a reciprocal basis.
Type: Fellowship.
No. of awards offered: 1.
Frequency: Annual.
Value: £7,000, plus free accommodation.
Length of Study: The spring semester of each academic year (January to June).
Study Establishment: University of East Anglia.
Country of Study: United Kingdom.
Application Procedure: Applicants should submit at least two examples of recent work, application form and CV.
Closing Date: October/November (for exact dates each year, see advertisements in the press, or telephone). Interviews take place in December.
Additional Information: A driving licence and access to a car would be an advantage.

For further information contact:

Personnel Office
University Plain, Norwich, Norfolk, NR4 7TJ, England
Tel: (44) 1603 592274
Fax: (44) 1603 507728
Contact: V Striker, Assistant to Dean

UNIVERSITY OF EXETER

Northcote House
The Queen's Drive, Exeter, Devon, EX4 4QJ, England
Tel: (44) 1392 263 263
Fax: (44) 1392 263 108
Email: pgao@exeter.ac.uk
www: http://www.ex.ac.uk/
Contact: Postgraduate Admissions Office

The University of Exeter is representative of the best of British University education. It combines research of international standing across all departments with excellence in education, and is one of the most popular in the country among applicants.

University of Exeter Postgraduate Scholarships

Subjects: Any subject offered by the university if the School has scholarship funding available. Graduate Teaching Assistantships and Graduate Research Assistantships may also be available in certain schools.
Eligibility: Open to candidates for research degrees who have obtained at least an upper second class honours degree or its equivalent.
Level of Study: Doctorate, Postgraduate.
Purpose: To study for a higher degree, ie. MPhil or PhD.
Type: Scholarship.
No. of awards offered: 5-20.
Frequency: Annual, if funds are available.
Value: Home fees plus maintenance at similar level to research council level awards.
Length of Study: Up to 3 years.
Study Establishment: University of Exeter.
Country of Study: United Kingdom.
Application Procedure: Those wishing to be considered should state this when applying for a higher degree and should contact the appropriate academic department direct.
Additional Information: The following named Scholarships are included in this scheme: Sir Arthur Reed Graduate Scholarship; Fuller Scholarship; Anning Morgan Bursary; Sir Henry Lopes Scholarship; Eden Phillpotts Scholarship; Exeter Research Scholarship; Devon Graduate Scholarship; St Cyres Scholarship; G T J James Postgraduate Scholarship; Wreford Clark Scholarship; Frank Southerden Scholarship; Andrew Simons Graduate Scholarship. Scholarships may not be held in conjunction with other major awards or sources of income. Not every scholarship is available every year.

UNIVERSITY OF GLASGOW

Glasgow, G12 8QQ, Scotland
Tel: (44) 141 330 4515
Fax: (44) 141 330 4413
Email: pgadmissions@mis.gla.ac.uk
Contact: Ms Hazel Sydeserff, Graduate Admissions Officer

The University of Glasgow is a major research-led university operating in an international context which aims to: provide education through the development of learning in a research environment; undertake fundamental, strategic and applied research; and to sustain and add value to Scottish culture, to the natural environment and to the national economy.

University of Glasgow Postgraduate Scholarships

Subjects: All subjects.
Eligibility: Open to candidates of any nationality who are proficient in English and who have obtained a first or an upper second class honours or equivalent degree.
Level of Study: Postgraduate.
Purpose: To assist with research toward a PhD degree.
Type: Scholarship.
No. of awards offered: 26.
Frequency: Annual.
Value: £6,456 maintenance allowance, plus home fees of £2,610.
Length of Study: 3 years; subject to satisfactory progress.
Study Establishment: University of Glasgow.
Country of Study: Scotland.
Application Procedure: Applicants should use the University's form, Application for Graduate Studies, which covers application for admission and for the scholarship. For the address to send the application form to please refer to Notes for Applicants booklet issued with the application form.
Closing Date: Faculties of Medicine and Science, January 31st; Arts, Divinity, and Veterinary Medicine, February 28th; Engineering, Law and Financial Studies, and Social Sciences, March 31st.
Additional Information: Scholars from outside the European Union will be expected to make up the difference between the home fee and the overseas fee.

William Barclay Memorial Scholarship

Subjects: Biblical studies, theology and church history.
Eligibility: Open to any suitably qualified graduate of theology from a university outside the UK.
Level of Study: Postgraduate.
Purpose: To provide an opportunity for a scholar from outside the UK to undertake research or graduate study.
Type: Scholarship.
No. of awards offered: 1.
Frequency: Annual.
Value: Up to £4,000 approximately.
Length of Study: 1 year, renewable.
Study Establishment: In the Faculty of Divinity, University of Glasgow.
Country of Study: Scotland.
Application Procedure: Applicants must request postgraduate study application material. The PG form is used for the Barclay application.
Closing Date: March 31st.

For further information contact:

Faculty of Divinity, Glasgow, G12 8QQ, Scotland
Tel: (44) 141 330 8855
Fax: (44) 141 330 4943
Contact: Mr R Macdonald

UNIVERSITY OF KENT

Canterbury, Kent, C2T 7NZ, England
Tel: (44) 1227 827 656
Fax: (44) 1227 762 811
www: http://www.ukc.ac.uk
Contact: Postgraduate Office

English Scholarship

Subjects: English.
Eligibility: Candidates are expected to hold an upper second class honours degree and be a national of one of the European Union countries.
Level of Study: Postgraduate.
Purpose: To support research.
Type: Research Grant.
No. of awards offered: 2.
Frequency: Annual.
Value: Home tuition fees and £2,500 stipend.
Length of Study: 3 years.
Study Establishment: University of Kent.
Country of Study: United Kingdom.
Application Procedure: Applicants should contact Anita Whitley, School of English, Rutherford College for further information. (Email: a.s.whitley@ukc.ac.uk).
Closing Date: June.
Additional Information: Holders of the scholarship are expected to undertake a small amount of teaching/research assistance each week.

Ian Gregor Scholarship

Subjects: English.
Eligibility: Candidates must be a citizens of one of the European Union countries. Please write for further details with regard to academic eligibility.
Level of Study: Postgraduate.
Purpose: To support the English coursework programme.
Type: Scholarship.
No. of awards offered: 1.
Frequency: Annual.
Value: Home fees plus £300.
Length of Study: 1 year.
Study Establishment: University of Kent.
Country of Study: United Kingdom.

Maurice Crosland History of Science Studentship

Subjects: History of science.
Eligibility: Open to qualified applicants of any nationality.
Level of Study: Postgraduate.
Purpose: To fund research to PhD level.
Type: Studentship.
No. of awards offered: 1.
Frequency: Annual.
Value: Home fees plus a maintenance bursary at the same rate as that provided by the Arts and Humanities Research Board.
Length of Study: 3 years.

Study Establishment: University of Kent.
Country of Study: United Kingdom.
Application Procedure: Please apply to Dr Crosbie Smith at the address shown.
Closing Date: May 1st.

For further information contact:

Centre for History and Cultural Studies of Science
Rutherford College
University of Kent at Canterbury, Canterbury, Kent, CT2 7NX, England
Tel: (44) 1227 764 000
Fax: (44) 1227 827 258
Contact: Dr Crosbie Smith

School of Drama, Film and Visual Arts Scholarships

Subjects: Various subjects.
Eligibility: Candidates are expected to hold an upper second class honours degree and be a citizen of one of the European Union countries.
Level of Study: Postgraduate.
Purpose: To support research.
Type: Research Grant.
No. of awards offered: 1.
Frequency: Annual.
Value: In the region of £1,000.
Length of Study: 3 years.
Study Establishment: University of Kent.
Country of Study: United Kingdom.
Application Procedure: Applicants should contact Jean Field, School of Arts and Image Studies, Rutherford College for further information. (Email: j.m.field@ukc.ac.uk).
Closing Date: June.
Additional Information: Some teaching may be required.

School of European Culture and Language Scholarships

Subjects: Various subjects from the School of European Culture and Languages.
Eligibility: Candidates are expected to hold an upper second class honours degree and be a citizen of one of the European Union countries.
Level of Study: Postgraduate.
Purpose: To support research.
Type: Research Grant.
No. of awards offered: Varies, up to 3.
Frequency: Annual.
Value: £1,500.
Length of Study: 3 years.
Study Establishment: University of Kent.
Country of Study: United Kingdom.
Application Procedure: Applicants should contact Professor Robin Gill, School of European Culture and Languages, Cornwallis West Building. (Email: r.gill@ukc.ac.uk).
Closing Date: June.
Additional Information: Some part-time teaching will be required.

UNIVERSITY OF LEEDS

Research Degrees & Scholarships Office, Leeds, West
Yorkshire, LS2 9JT, England
Tel: (44) 113 233 4007
Fax: (44) 113 233 3941
Email: rsdnh@central.admin.leeds.ac.uk
www: http://www.leeds.ac.uk
Contact: Mrs J Y Findlay

Iceland - Leeds University - FCO Chevening Scholarships

Subjects: All subjects.
Eligibility: Open to candidates who have obtained a first
degree of similar standard to at least a UK second class
honours degree. Candidates must be nationals of Iceland.
Level of Study: Postgraduate.
Type: Scholarship.
No. of awards offered: 1.
Frequency: Annual.
Value: To cover academic fees and living expenses, books,
equipment, arrival and departure allowance, economy return
airfares and production of dissertation.
Length of Study: 1 year taught mastership course.
Study Establishment: University of Leeds.
Country of Study: United Kingdom.
Application Procedure: By application form and acceptance
on to a taught course. Application forms are available from
the British Embassy in Ireland.
Closing Date: January 10th.

For further information contact:

British Embassy, Reykjavik, Iceland
Contact: HM Ambassador

Kulika-Leeds University FCO Chevening Scholarships

Subjects: All subjects.
Eligibility: Open to candidates who have obtained a first
degree of similar standard to at least a second UK second
class honours degree. Candidates must be a national of
Uganda.
Level of Study: Postgraduate.
Purpose: To provide postgraduate scholarships to students
of a high academic calibre.
Type: Scholarship.
No. of awards offered: 3.
Frequency: Annual.
Value: To cover academic fees and living expenses, books
equipment, arrival and departure allowance, economy return
airfares and production of dissertation.
Length of Study: 1 year taught mastership course.
Study Establishment: University of Leeds.
Country of Study: United Kingdom.
Application Procedure: By application form and acceptance
on to a taught course. Application forms are available from
the university.
Closing Date: To be announced.

For further information contact:

British Council in Uganda
IPS Building
Parliament Avenue
PO Box 7070, Kampala, Uganda

Tetley and Lupton Scholarships for Overseas Students

Subjects: All subjects.
Eligibility: Open to candidates liable to pay tuition fees for
Master's degrees and research degrees at the full-cost rate
for overseas students. Applicants must be of a high academic
standard.
Level of Study: Doctorate, Postgraduate.
Purpose: To provide awards to overseas students of high
academic calibre.
Type: Scholarship.
No. of awards offered: 70.
Frequency: Annual.
Value: £3,000 per year to be credited towards academic fees.
Length of Study: 1 year; may be renewed for second or third
year according to duration of course. May be held
concurrently with other awards except those providing full
payment of fees.
Study Establishment: University of Leeds.
Country of Study: United Kingdom.
Application Procedure: Apply for a course and then apply
for scholarship. Research candidates need to apply with
national ORS competition.
Closing Date: Postgraduates are required to submit
applications by March 1st; Research postgraduates by June
1st.

UNIVERSITY OF LONDON

Senate House
Malet Street, London, WC1E 7HU, England
Tel: (44) 171 636 8000
Fax: (44) 171 636 0373
www: http://www.qmw.ac.uk
Contact: Grants Management Officer

Queen Mary and Westfield College Research Studentships

Subjects: Arts (except French), sciences, engineering, social
sciences, law, medicine and denstistry.
Eligibility: Open to suitably qualified candidates who hold at
least an upper second class honours at first degree level.
Level of Study: Research.
Purpose: To provide the opportunity for full-time research
leading towards an MPhil or PhD.
Type: Studentship.
No. of awards offered: Approx. 50.
Frequency: Annual.

Value: Maintenance at the current research council rate, plus tuition fees at the home level (successful overseas apllicants must provide the difference).
Length of Study: 3 years full-time, subject to satisfactory academic report.
Study Establishment: Queen Mary and Westfield College.
Country of Study: United Kingdom.
Application Procedure: Please write to the Admission and Research Student Office for details.
Closing Date: June 25th.
Additional Information: These studentships are open only to research students commencing their studies in the 1999/200 session. They are not available to existing research students.

For further information contact:

Queen Mary and Westfield College
University of London
Mile End Road, London, E1 4NS, England
Tel: (44) 171 975 3657
Fax: (44) 171 975 5588
Contact: Mr Peter Smith, Admissions Assistant

UNIVERSITY OF MANCHESTER

Oxford Road, Manchester, M13 9PL, England
Tel: (44) 161 275 2736
Fax: (44) 161 275 2445
www: http://www.man.ac.uk
Contact: Office of the Academic Registrar

The University of Manchester is an international provider of quality research and graduate education across a wide variety of disciplines.

University of Manchester Research Studentships or Scholarships

Subjects: Any area of study within the purview of the Graduate Schools of Arts, Social Sciences, Education, Science, Engineering and Medicine.
Eligibility: Open to graduates of any approved university, or other suitably qualified persons, who can furnish satisfactory evidence of their qualifications to pursue research. Applicants must hold at least an upper second class degree to be eligible.
Level of Study: Postgraduate.
Purpose: To support postgraduate research, and provide funding for high quality UK, European and overseas graduates wishing to study for PhD.
Type: Studentship/Scholarship.
No. of awards offered: Up to 50.
Frequency: Annual.
Value: Varies. Some full studentships (maintenance and UK fees), also part scholarships.
Length of Study: Normally 3 years.
Study Establishment: Manchester University.

Country of Study: United Kingdom.
Application Procedure: Application forms available on request from Research and Graduate Support Unit.
Closing Date: May 1st.

UNIVERSITY OF MANITOBA

Faculty of Graduate Studies
500 University Centre, Winnipeg, MB, R3T 2N2, Canada
Tel: (1) 204 474 9836
Fax: (1) 204 474 7553
Email: ilse_krentz@umanitoba.ca
www:
http://www.umanitoba.ca/faculties/graduate_studies/awards
Contact: Ms Ilse Krentz, Awards Officer

University of Manitoba Graduate Fellowships

Subjects: Any discipline taught at the graduate level at the University.
Eligibility: At the time of application, students do not need to have been accepted by the Department/Faculty, but at the time of taking up the award must be regular full-time graduate students who have been admitted to and registered in advanced degree programmes (Master's or PhD, but not pre-Master's) in any field of study or Faculty of the University of Manitoba. Students beyond the second year in the Master's programme or beyond the fourth year in the PhD programme are not eligible to apply for or hold a University of Manitoba Graduate Fellowship. Students whose previous study at the Master's level has been part-time will be eligible for a University of Manitoba Graduate Fellowship for a period of one year from the date of registration as full-time students.
Level of Study: Doctorate, Postgraduate.
Purpose: To award academic excellence for graduate study.
Type: Fellowship.
No. of awards offered: 100-110.
Frequency: Annual.
Value: C$16,000 for PhD; C$10,000 for Master's.
Study Establishment: The University of Manitoba in either a Master's (not pre-Master's) or a PhD program.
Country of Study: Canada.
Application Procedure: Application forms may be requested from the department to which applicants are applying at the University of Manitoba and must be returned to that department. Forms are available from the beginning of December and can be requested either by phoning or writing or from the website at:
http://www.umanitoba.ca/faculties/graduate_studies/forms.
Closing Date: February 15th, with earlier departmental deadline.

UNIVERSITY OF MARYLAND

National Orchestral Institute School of Music - 2114 Tawes
University of Maryland, College Park, MD, 20742-1211,
United States of America
Tel: (1) 301 403 8370
Fax: (1) 301 403 8375
www: http://www.umcp.umd.edu
Contact: Mr Don Reinhold

International Music Competitions

Subjects: Major international competitions for piano (William
Kapell), cello (Leonard Rose) and voice (Marian Anderson).
Eligibility: Open to musicians of all nationalities: piano 18-33
years of age; cello 18-30 years of age; voice 21-39 years of
age.
Level of Study: Professional development.
Purpose: To recognise and assist the artistic development of
young musicians at the highest levels of achievement in
piano, cello, and voice.
Type: Competition.
No. of awards offered: 3 Finalist, 9 Semi-Finalist Prizes.
Frequency: Annually, in rotation: piano biennially (2000/2002);
cello every four years (2001/2005); voice every four years
(next in 1999).
Value: Finalist prizes US$20,000, US$10,000 and US$5,000;
Semi-Finalists US$1,000.
Study Establishment: University of Maryland.
Country of Study: USA.
Application Procedure: Applicants should submit application
form, fee, cassette recording, repertoire list, résumé, photos,
and letters of recommendation.
Closing Date: March 15th.
Additional Information: The competition is held in July.
Concurrent Festivals offer master classes, recitals and
symposia.

National Orchestral Institute Scholarships

Subjects: Orchestral performance.
Eligibility: Open to advanced musicians between 18 and 28
years of age. Primarily for students and postgraduates of
American universities, conservatories and colleges; others,
however, are welcome to apply but must appear at an
audition centre. String players, including harpists, who live
more than 200 miles away from an audition centre may
audition by tape.
Level of Study: Professional development.
Purpose: To provide an intensive three-week orchestral
training programme to enable musicians to rehearse and
perform under internationally acclaimed conductors and
study with principal musicians of America's foremost
orchestras in preparation for careers as orchestral musicians.

Type: Scholarship.
No. of awards offered: Approx. 90.
Frequency: Annual.
Value: Full tuition, room and board.
Length of Study: 3 weeks.
Study Establishment: University of Maryland.
Country of Study: USA.
Application Procedure: Applicants must submit application,
fee, resumé and letters of recommendation.
Closing Date: Before regional auditions.
Additional Information: Personal auditions are required at
one of the audition centers throughout the country.

UNIVERSITY OF MELBOURNE

Parkville, VIC, 3052, Australia
Tel: (61) 3 344 8747
Fax: (61) 3 349 1760
Email: postgrad@scholarships.unimelb.edu.au
www: http://www.unimelb.edu.au
Contact: Ms Janet White, Melbourne Scholarships Office

The University of Melbourne has a long and distinguished
tradition of excellence in teaching and research. It is the
leading research institution in Australia and enjoys a
reputation for the high quality of its research programs,
consistently winning the largest share of national competitive
research funding.

University of Melbourne Research Scholarships

Subjects: Any subject offered by the University.
Eligibility: Open to candidates from Australia and foreign
countries.
Level of Study: Doctorate, Postgraduate.
Purpose: To enable graduates to undertake research.
Type: Scholarship.
No. of awards offered: 232 (of which up to 50 may be
awarded to international students).
Frequency: Annual.
Value: A$15,600 per year, payable fortnightly.
Length of Study: Up to 2 years at the Master's level; up to 3
years at the PhD level, with the possibility of extension for an
additional 6 months.
Study Establishment: The University of Melbourne.
Country of Study: Australia.
Application Procedure: Application form must be
completed. Please contact the Melbourne Scholarships
Office.
Closing Date: October 31st for Australian citizens and
residents (main selection round); September 15th for
international students (a small number of scholarships may be
available throughout the year subject to availabilty).
Additional Information: Further information can be accessed
through the internet site.

UNIVERSITY OF NEW ENGLAND

Research Services, Armidale, NSW, 2351, Australia
Tel: (61) 2 6773 3571
Fax: (61) 2 6773 3543
Email: aharris@metz.une.edu.au
www: http://research.une.edu.au/home/
Contact: Postgraduate Scholarships Officer

The University of New England is Australia's oldest regional university. UNE has a reputation for quality research with students undertaking research in the arts, education, environmental engineering, health studies, rural science, and science. The UNE PhD is over 40 years old and has 550 PhD students currently enrolled.

University of New England Research Scholarships

Subjects: Arts, education, economics, sciences, social science, resource sciences, archaeology, and environmental engineering.
Eligibility: Open to candidates of any nationality having at least a Bachelor's degree with first class honours or equivalent, and English test for candidates from non-English speaking countries.
Level of Study: Postgraduate.
Purpose: To provide assistance toward the completion of a research Master's degree, PhD, or EdD.
Type: Scholarship.
No. of awards offered: 20.
Frequency: Annual.
Value: Approximately A$16,000.
Length of Study: 2 years (Master's degree) or for an initial period of 3 years which may be renewed for 6 months (PhD).
Study Establishment: University of New England.
Country of Study: Australia.
Application Procedure: Application form with certified copies of academic transcripts and academic referees.
Closing Date: October 31st.
Additional Information: Candidates who are not permanent residents or citizens of Australia must provide evidence of additional financial support of at least A$10,000. The research proposal must be approved by the head of the relevant department. Initial enquiries from overseas students should be directed to the International Students Officer at the university.

UNIVERSITY OF NOTTINGHAM

Graduate School
University Park, Nottingham, NG7 2RD, England
Tel: (44) 115 951 4664
Fax: (44) 115 951 4668
Email: graduateschool@nottingham.ac.uk
www: http://www.nottingham.ac.uk
Contact: Dr Richard Masterman, Director of Research Policy Administration

University of Nottingham Graduate Studentships

Subjects: Any subject from a prescribed list.
Level of Study: Postgraduate.
Purpose: To provide promising students with home and EU fees only studentships for one year full-time (or equivalent) taught Master's courses.
Type: Studentship.
No. of awards offered: Approx. 20.
Frequency: Annual.
Value: Home/EU fees only.
Length of Study: Usually 1 year full-time (or part-time equivalent).
Study Establishment: University of Nottingham.
Country of Study: United Kingdom.
Application Procedure: Applications must be submitted to the individual schools. Please contact schools offering studentships for details.
Closing Date: Applications are accepted at anytime.

University of Nottingham Postgraduate Scholarships

Subjects: Any subject offered by the University.
Eligibility: Open to graduates of all nationalities. The scholarships are allocated to schools/institutes, to whom students should apply for further information.
Level of Study: Postgraduate, Predoctorate.
Purpose: To promote research.
Type: Scholarship.
No. of awards offered: 75.
Frequency: Annual.
Value: £6,455 per year maintenance and payment of fees at home/EU rate.
Length of Study: 3 years leading to PhD submission given adequate academic progress.
Study Establishment: University of Nottingham.
Country of Study: United Kingdom.

Application Procedure: Please contact the individual schools for information.
Closing Date: Please contact the individual schools for information.
Additional Information: The scholarships are awarded internally to the schools and/or institutes that bid for them. It is then up to those schools receiving awards to advertise the scholarship and set an application deadline.

UNIVERSITY OF OSLO

International Summer School
University of Oslo
Box 3
Blindern, Oslo, N-0313, Norway
Tel: (47) 22 85 63 85
Fax: (47) 22 85 41 99
Email: iss@admin.uio.no
www: http://www.uio/iss/iss.html
Contact: Registrar

The International Summer School is a centre for learning in an international context, offering a wide variety of courses at both undergraduate and graduate levels.

University of Oslo International Summer School Scholarships

Subjects: General courses - Norwegian art; Nordic folklore; Norwegian language; history and literature of Norway; ScandiNorwegian music; Scandinavian literature; Norwegian economics, politics, culture and society; Norway and Scandinavia in international relations. Graduate courses - special education; peace research; international development studies; analysis and planning of investment projects; media studies; energy planning and sustainable development; international issues in health systems deveolpment.
Eligibility: Open to students with good academic records as evidenced by an official transcript (US students should have completed their sophomore year; non-US students must present evidence of matriculation at a recognised university in their own country or abroad); teachers with a good professional record as evidenced by a statement from the teacher's present supervisor, principal or headmaster; and members of graduate courses who have good professional records and/or other qualifications listed on the relevant application form.
Level of Study: Graduate, Postgraduate.
Purpose: To impart knowledge about various aspects of Norwegian and Scandinavian culture or topics of international interest, comparatively presented, and to increase international understanding.
Type: Scholarship.
No. of awards offered: 200-300.
Frequency: Annual.
Value: Normally covers room and board and incidental expenses. There is no tuition fee.
Length of Study: 6 weeks, from late June to early August.
Study Establishment: University of Oslo.

Country of Study: Norway.
Application Procedure: Submission of a completed application form. Application forms are available from the International Summer School or the Norwegian embassies in most countries. Candidates should return application forms directly to the International Summer School office or to the Norwegian embassy in their country. Prospective participants from the USA and Canada should make formal application for admission on special forms from Oslo International Summer School, North American Branch Office, Saint Olaf College, 1520 Saint Olaf Ave, Northfield, MN 55057-1098, USA.
Closing Date: February 1st.
Additional Information: All lectures, except Norwegian language classes, are given in English.

UNIVERSITY OF OXFORD

University Offices
Wellington Square, Oxford, OX1 2JD, England
Tel: (44) 1865 270 000
Fax: (44) 1865 270 708
www: http://www.oxford.ac.uk
Contact: Information Officer

Balliol College Dervorguilla Scholarship

Subjects: Arts or sciences.
Eligibility: Eligible to overseas students only.
Level of Study: Postgraduate.
Type: Scholarship.
No. of awards offered: 1.
Frequency: Annual.
Value: All fees (college and university), and full maintenance grant.
Length of Study: 2 years; renewable for a third year.
Study Establishment: Balliol College.
Country of Study: United Kingdom.
Application Procedure: Please write for details.
Closing Date: March.

For further information contact:

Balliol College, Oxford, OX1 3BJ, England
Contact: Tutor for Graduate Admissions

Brasenose Hector Pilling Scholarship

Subjects: All subjects.
Eligibility: Open to graduates of any Commonwealth university; preference will be given to applicants who are serving or who have served in the Royal Air Force or the Air Force of a Commonwealth country or to the children or dependents of such persons, but this qualification is not essential.
Level of Study: Postgraduate.
Type: Scholarship.
No. of awards offered: 1.
Frequency: Varies.

Value: Fees plus maintenance equal to a state maintenance grant, plus college room for the first year.
Length of Study: 1 year plus 2 further years.
Study Establishment: Brasenose College.
Country of Study: United Kingdom.
Closing Date: Please write for details.
Additional Information: Not available very year, the next time it will be available will be October 2000.

For further information contact:

Brasenose College, Oxford, OX1 4AJ, England
Contact: Tutor for Graduates

Brasenose Senior Germaine Scholarship

Subjects: All subjects.
Eligibility: Candidates must have graduated from a university or institution of similar standing in the UK, or be expected to graduate by October 1st in the year in which they make their application; candidates should normally be below the age of 27 on October 1st of the year in which they apply.
Level of Study: Postgraduate.
Type: Scholarship.
No. of awards offered: 1.
Frequency: Annual.
Value: Fees plus maintenance equal to the state maintenance grant, plus college room for the first year of the course.
Length of Study: 1 year; being annually renewable for a maximum of 2 further years.
Study Establishment: Brasenose College.
Country of Study: United Kingdom.
Application Procedure: Please write for details.
Additional Information: Not available every year, the next year it is available is 2000; check availability with the Tutor for Graduates.

For further information contact:

Brasenose College, Oxford, OX1 4AJ, England
Contact: The Tutor for Graduates

Chevening Oxford-Australia Scholarships

Subjects: All subjects.
Eligibility: Open to Australians.
Level of Study: Postgraduate.
Purpose: To assist Australians with overseas study.
Type: Travel Grant.
No. of awards offered: 2.
Value: £11,000.
Length of Study: 1 year.
Study Establishment: University of Oxford.
Country of Study: United Kingdom.
Application Procedure: Please write for details.
Additional Information: The alternative address can be contacted for details as can Oxford University International Office.

For further information contact:

Research school for Chemistry
Australian National University
GPO Box 414, Canberra, ACT, 2601, Australia
Tel: (61) 6 249 3637
Fax: (61) 6 249 4903

Christ Church Hugh Pilkinton Scholarship

Subjects: All subjects.
Eligibility: Open to graduate students from the European Union.
Level of Study: Postgraduate.
Type: Scholarship.
Value: £3,000 per annum.
Length of Study: 1 year.
Study Establishment: Christ Church.
Country of Study: United Kingdom.
Application Procedure: Please write to the Dean's secretary at Christ Church College for further information. Applications should be made when applying for admission.

For further information contact:

Christ Chutch College, Oxford, OX1 1DP, England
Contact: Dean's Secretary

Christ Church ODA Shared Scholarship

Subjects: All subjects.
Eligibility: Citizens of developing Commonwealth countries only.
Level of Study: Postgraduate.
Type: Scholarship.
No. of awards offered: 1.
Frequency: Annual.
Value: £7,000 per annum.
Length of Study: Up to 3 years.
Study Establishment: Christ Church.
Country of Study: England.
Application Procedure: Please write for details.

For further information contact:

University Offices
Wellington Square, Oxford, OX1 2JD, England
Contact: International Office

Christ Church Senior Scholarships

Subjects: All subjects.
Eligibility: Open to candidates who will have been reading for a higher degree in the University of Oxford for at least one year, but not more than two years, by October 1st of the year in which the award is sought.
Level of Study: Postgraduate.
Purpose: To enable graduate scholars to undertake some definite course of literary, educational, scientific or professional study or training.
Type: Scholarship.
No. of awards offered: 2.
Frequency: Annual.

Value: Rooms and maintenance at Research Council level.
Length of Study: 2 years; renewable for a further year.
Study Establishment: Christ Church, University of Oxford.
Country of Study: United Kingdom.
Application Procedure: Please write for details, Applications should be made in February.
Closing Date: The date is fixed each year, but usually during April.
Additional Information: Normally, the Scholarship is held in conjunction with an award from a government agency which pays the university fees.

For further information contact:

The Deanery
Christ Church, Oxford, OX1 1DP, England
Contact: The Dean's Secretary

Christ Church The American Friends Scholarship

Subjects: All subjects.
Eligibility: Open to graduate students from the USA only.
Level of Study: Postgraduate.
Type: Scholarship.
No. of awards offered: Varies.
Frequency: Annual.
Value: $7,000 per annum.
Length of Study: 1 year.
Study Establishment: Christ Church.
Country of Study: United Kingdom.
Closing Date: Please write for details.
Additional Information: Subject to deduction of grants from other sources.

For further information contact:

Christ Church, Oxford, OX1 1DP, England
Contact: The Senior Censor

Exeter College Usher-Cunningham Senior Studentship

Subjects: Alternately awarded for a graduate degree in medical science, or for any graduate from an Irish University studying for a graduate degree in medieval or modern history. Next available for modern history in 2000.
Eligibility: The Modern History Studentship is only open to graduates of Irish Universities. Enquiries should be addressed to the College Secretary.
Level of Study: Postgraduate.
Purpose: To support graduate study.
Type: Studentship.
No. of awards offered: 1.
Frequency: Every three years.
Value: Full fees plus maintenance up to the equivalent of a Research Council Studentship.
Length of Study: 1 year, renewable for up to 2 additional years.
Study Establishment: Exeter College.
Country of Study: United Kingdom.
Closing Date: Please write for details.

For further information contact:

Exeter College, Oxford, OX1 3DP, England
Tel: (44) 1865 279660
Fax: (44) 1865 279630
Contact: Tutor for Graduates

Felix Scholarships

Subjects: All subjects.
Eligibility: Indian nationals under 30 years of age and must have at least a first class Bachelor's degree from an Indian university or comparable institution. Those who already hold degrees from universities outside India are not eligible to apply.
Level of Study: Postgraduate.
Purpose: To enable Indian graduates accepted for entry to Oxford to read for taught graduate courses or for a Master's or DPhil degree by research, who would be unable, without financial assistance, to take up their place.
No. of awards offered: Up to 6.
Value: University and college fees and maintenance costs.
Length of Study: For 2 years in the first instance, with a possible extension for 3 years for those initially registered for a DPhil degree.
Study Establishment: University of Oxford.
Country of Study: United Kingdom.
Application Procedure: Candidates must apply separately for admission to Oxford through the Graduate Admissions Office. Please write for further details. Applicants for Felix Scholarships are expected to apply for an Overseas Research Students (ORS) award if the course they intend to take makes them eligible.
Closing Date: March 1st.

For further information contact:

International Office
University Offices
Wellington square, Oxford, OX1 2JD, England

Fulbright Oxford University Scholarships

Subjects: All subjects.
Level of Study: Postgraduate.
Value: Full funding (round trip travel, maintenance allowance and approved tuition fees). The value of bursaries will be determined according to individual need with a maximum of £3,245 (at 1999-2000 rates). A candidate gaining 3 awards (Fulbright, ORS and Oxford bursary) will have adequate funding for 2 years..
Length of Study: 2-3 years.
Study Establishment: University of Oxford.
Country of Study: United Kingdom.
Application Procedure: An application form must be completed.
Closing Date: October 23rd; those enrolled in US institutions must file applications with their Fulbright Programme Advisor by the deadline set by the campus advisor.

Additional Information: The course must lead to a higher degree and qualify for funding under the Overseas Research Students (ORS) award scheme. Candidates must apply for the ORS award.

For further information contact:

US Student Programs
Institute of International Education (IIE)
809 United Nations Plaza, New York, NY, 10017-3580, United States of America

Hertford College Senior Scholarships

Subjects: All subjects.
Eligibility: Restricted to students about to commence a new research degree course or those about to upgrade their current course.
Level of Study: Postgraduate.
Type: Scholarship.
Value: £500 per annum, plus priority for housing.
Length of Study: 2 years in the first instance renewable for a further year.
Study Establishment: Hertford College.
Country of Study: United Kingdom.
Application Procedure: Please write to the college for further details.

For further information contact:

Hertford College, Oxford, OX1 3BW, England
Contact: College Secretary

Hong Kong Oxford Scholarship Fund Bursaries

Subjects: All subjects.
Eligibility: National's of the People's Republic of China. It is a condition of the award that students should be planning to return to and to benefit their home country on completion of their studies.
Level of Study: Postgraduate.
Value: Up to £4,000.
Study Establishment: University of Oxford.
Country of Study: United Kingdom.
Application Procedure: Candidates must apply for admission to Oxford through the Graduate Admissions Office. Please write for further details.
Closing Date: July.

For further information contact:

International Office
University Offices
WellingtonSquare, Oxford, OX1 2JD, England

James Fairfax and Oxford-Australia Fund

Subjects: Oxford-Australia Fund scholarships are open to any discipline, James Fairfax Scholarships are intended for those wishing to study for a second undergraduate or a graduate degree in the arts or social sciences.
Level of Study: Postgraduate.
No. of awards offered: 2.

Value: University and college fees and living allowance of the order of A$11,000 per annum.
Length of Study: Oxford-Australia Fund scholarships- 2 years or in the case of MPhil, for 3 years; James Fairfax Scholarships will generally be 2 years duration.
Study Establishment: University of Oxford.
Country of Study: United Kingdom.
Application Procedure: Please write for details.
Closing Date: March 20th.
Additional Information: Candidates are also expected to apply for an Overseas Research Students (ORS) award if the course they intend to follow makes them eligible.

For further information contact:

International Office
University Offices
Wellington Square, Oxford, OX1 2JD, England

James Ingham Halstead Scholarship in Music

Subjects: Music.
Eligibility: Open to graduates of any university who intend to proceed to one of the university's advanced degrees in music (MLitt, MPhil or DPhil) or are intending to supplicate for the BMus or Dmus.
Level of Study: Doctorate, Postdoctorate, Postgraduate.
Purpose: To support graduates of any university who intend to proceed to one of the university's advanced degrees in music.
Type: Scholarship.
No. of awards offered: Varies.
Frequency: Annual.
Value: Normally £300 per year.
Length of Study: 1 year.
Study Establishment: University of Oxford, in the first instance.
Country of Study: United Kingdom.
Application Procedure: Applications must include: date of birth; brief statement of academic career; examples of original work (compositions, theses, essays, articles etc, whether published or not); brief statement of proposed research; and the names of two referees. If applicants submit pieces of research whose purpose and relationship to their main plan of research is not immediately clear, a short introduction should be included, if necessary, to set the work in context of larger aims.
Closing Date: March 1st.
Additional Information: Scholarships may be renewable for a maximum of 2 further years, subject to reports of satisfactory progress. Halstead scholars may qualify for awards supplementary to their financial circumstances and the state of the fund.

For further information contact:

Board of the Faculty of Music
University Offices
Wellington Square, Oxford, OX1 2JD, England
Tel: (44) 1865 270001
Fax: (44) 1865 270708
Contact: Secretary

Jesus College Graduate Scholarship

Subjects: Arts and social sciences.
Eligibility: Restricted to arts and social science candidates who have been accepted by Oxford University but have not obtained funding from any other source. Candidates must be from the United Kingdom or the European Union only.
Level of Study: Postgraduate.
Type: Scholarship.
Frequency: Varies.
Value: Fees and maintenance.
Length of Study: Up to 3 days.
Study Establishment: Jesus College.
Country of Study: United Kingdom.
Application Procedure: The scholarship is only advertised in years when it falls vacant, with an early September deadline.
Closing Date: Early September when award available.

Jesus College Old Member's Graduate Scholarship

Subjects: Arts.
Eligibility: Open to both home and overseas students.
Level of Study: Postgraduate.
Type: Scholarship.
No. of awards offered: Varies.
Frequency: Annual.
Value: £1,500.
Length of Study: 3 years.
Study Establishment: Jesus College.
Country of Study: United Kingdom.
Closing Date: March.

For further information contact:

Jesus College, Oxford, OX1 3BJ, England
Contact: Tutor for Graduates

Joanna Randall-MacIver Junior Research Fellowship

Subjects: Fine arts, music or literature of any nation - research.
Eligibility: Open to women candidates only.
Level of Study: Unrestricted.
Type: Fellowship.
No. of awards offered: 1.
Frequency: Annual.
Length of Study: 2 years in rotation; not renewable.
Study Establishment: Lady Margaret Hall, Somerville College, St Hugh's College, St Hilda's College and St Anne's College.
Country of Study: United Kingdom.
Application Procedure: Please contact for details.

For further information contact:

Oxford University, Oxford, OX2 6QA, England
Contact: Lady Margaret Hall, The Principal's Secretary

K C Wong Scholarships

Subjects: All subjects.
Eligibility: Residents of the People's Republic of China. (It should be noted that it is a requirement for the award of K C Wong Scholarships that candidates should currently be resident in the People's Republic of China).
Level of Study: Doctorate.
Purpose: To assist students studying at doctorate level.
No. of awards offered: 3.
Value: University and college fees and maintenance for a maximum of 3 years.
Study Establishment: University of Oxford.
Country of Study: United Kingdom.
Application Procedure: Please write for further details and an application form.
Closing Date: April 1st.
Additional Information: Applicants for the K C Wong scholarships are also expected to apply for an Overseas Research Students (ORS) award.

For further information contact:

International Office
University Offices
Wellington Square, Oxford, OX1 2JD, England

Karim Rida Said Foundation Scholarships

Subjects: All subjects.
Eligibility: Students from countries in the Arab League.
Level of Study: Postgraduate.
Purpose: To assist students from the Arab League with either a taught Master's degree, a Master's degree by research or for the DPhil degree.
No. of awards offered: Varies.
Value: University and college fees plus maintenance grant for the duration of the student's course.
Study Establishment: University of Oxford.
Country of Study: United Kingdom.
Application Procedure: Candidates must apply separately for admission to Oxford through the Graduate Admissions Office. Please write for further details.
Closing Date: July.

For further information contact:

International Office
University Offices
Wellington square, Oxford, OX1 2JD, England

Keble College Gwynne-Jones Scholarship

Subjects: All subjects.
Eligibility: Eligible to nationals of Sierra Leone, or among the Yoruba-speaking people of Nigeria.
Level of Study: Postgraduate.
Type: Scholarship.

No. of awards offered: Varies.
Frequency: Annual.
Value: Up to £4,000 per annum.
Length of Study: 2 years.
Study Establishment: Keble College.
Country of Study: United Kingdom.
Closing Date: Late May.

For further information contact:

Keble College, Oxford, OX1 3PG, England
Contact: Tutor for Graduates

Keble College Keble Association Graduate Scholarship

Subjects: All subjects.
Level of Study: Postgraduate.
Type: Scholarship.
No. of awards offered: At least 1.
Frequency: Annual.
Value: To the value of College fees.
Length of Study: Up to 2 years.
Study Establishment: Keble College.
Country of Study: United Kingdom.
Closing Date: Late February.

For further information contact:

Keble College, Oxford, OX1 3PG, England
Contact: Tutor for Graduates

Keble College Water Newton and Gosden Graduate Scholaraship

Subjects: All subjects.
Eligibility: Restricted to students admitted to study for a research degree in the University of Oxford and intending to seek ordination in a church or communion with the Church of England.
Level of Study: Postgraduate.
Type: Scholarship.
Value: Up to £5,000 per annum.
Length of Study: 2 years.
Study Establishment: Keble College.
Country of Study: United Kingdom.
Application Procedure: Contact the Tutor for Graduate, in the first instance at Keble College.
Closing Date: Late February.

For further information contact:

Keble College, Oxford, OX1 3PG, England
Contact: Tutor for Graduates

Kellogg College Kellogg Scholarships

Subjects: All subjects.
Eligibility: Restricted to those offered a place at Kellogg College, Oxford.
Level of Study: Postgraduate.
Type: Scholarship.
Value: Approximately £300 per annum.

Length of Study: 2 years or more.
Study Establishment: Keble College.
Country of Study: United Kingdom.
Application Procedure: Contact the Tutor for Admissions in the first instance at Kellog College.

For further information contact:

Kellogg College, Oxford, OX1 2JA, England
Contact: Tutor for Admissions

Korea Foundation Scholarship in Korean Studies

Subjects: Korean studies - Korean language, history or classical literature in the faculty of oriental studies. Candidates wishing to study the areas of economics, politics, anthropology or sociology may also be considered.
Eligibility: Students from the EU.
Level of Study: Postgraduate.
Purpose: To assist students wishing to study Korean studies.
No. of awards offered: 1.
Value: University and college tuition fees only.
Study Establishment: University of Oxford.
Country of Study: United Kingdom.
Application Procedure: Candidates must apply separately for admission to Oxford through the Graduate Admissions Office. Please write for further details.
Closing Date: March 1st.

For further information contact:

International Office
University Offices
Wellington Square, Oxford, OX1 2JD, England

Lady Noon/Oxford University Press Scholarship

Subjects: All subjects.
Eligibility: Nationals of Pakistan.
Level of Study: Postgraduate.
No. of awards offered: 1 partial award.
Value: Approx £10,500.
Study Establishment: University of Oxford.
Country of Study: United Kingdom.
Application Procedure: Candidates must apply separately for admission to Oxford through the Graduate Admissions Office. Please write for further details.
Closing Date: April 1st.

For further information contact:

International Office
University Offices
Wellington Square, Oxford, OX1 2JD, England

Linacer College Lloyd African Scholarship DFID Scholarships

Subjects: A subject which will be beneficial in aiding the economic and/or social development of the student's country.
Eligibility: Open to qualified graduate students from African universities.
Level of Study: Postgraduate.

Purpose: To enable a qualified graduate student from an African university to pursue a one or two year taught Master's course.
Type: Scholarship.
No. of awards offered: 2.
Frequency: Annually or bi-annual.
Value: University and college fees; stipend; return air travel.
Length of Study: 1 or 2 years.
Study Establishment: Linacre College.
Country of Study: England.
Application Procedure: Please write for details.

For further information contact:

Linacre College, Oxford, OX1 3JA, England
Contact: The Tutor of Admissions

Linacre College Domus Studentships

Subjects: All subjects.
Eligibility: Open to students with a good first degree, who intend to begin reading for a higher degree, or to current members of Linacre College.
Level of Study: Postgraduate.
Purpose: To assist postgraduate study.
Type: Studentship.
No. of awards offered: Varies.
Frequency: Annual.
Value: £250 per year.
Length of Study: Up to 3 years.
Study Establishment: Linacre College.
Country of Study: United Kingdom.
Closing Date: Please write for details.

For further information contact:

Linacre College
St Cross Road, Oxford, OX1 3JA, England
Tel: (44) 1865 271657
Fax: (44) 1865 271668
Contact: The Tutor for Admissions

Lincoln College Berrow Scholarship

Subjects: All subjects.
Eligibility: Open to graduates of the following Swiss universities: Berne, Geneva, Lausanne, Fribourg, Neuchâtel, or the Ecole Polytechnique Fédérale de Lausanne.
Level of Study: Doctorate, Postgraduate.
Purpose: To permit graduates of Swiss universities to undertake postgraduate study at Oxford.
Type: Scholarship.
No. of awards offered: 3.
Frequency: Annual.
Value: All university and college fees are covered, plus a generous maintenance allowance.
Length of Study: 2 years, with possible renewal for 1 year.
Study Establishment: Lincoln College, Oxford.
Country of Study: United Kingdom.
Application Procedure: Please write for details.
Closing Date: Please write for details.

For further information contact:

Lincoln College, Oxford, OX1 3DR, England
Tel: (44) 1865 279836
Fax: (44) 1865 279802
Contact: Tutor for Graduates

Lincoln College Dresdner Kleinwort Benson Senior Scholarships

Subjects: Any area of study.
Eligibility: Restricted to students from Studienstiftung des deutschen Volkes wishing to study at Lincoln. Such students come to Oxford as Visiting Graduate Students.
Level of Study: Postgraduate.
Type: Scholarship.
No. of awards offered: 2.
Frequency: Annual.
Value: Sufficient to cover College fees and proven academic supervision at a high level.
Length of Study: 1 year only.
Study Establishment: Lincoln College.
Country of Study: United Kingdom.
Application Procedure: Students form the Studienstiftong who place Lincoln College as first choice are eligible; no separate application is necessary.
Closing Date: Please write for details.

For further information contact:

Lincoln College, Oxford, OX1 3DR, England
Contact: Tutor for Graduates

Lincoln College Erich and Rochelle Endowed Prize in Music

Subjects: Music.
Eligibility: Open to graduate students of exceptional and proven musical ability. The successful candidate will be expected to play a prominent part in the musical life of the college and in particular to act, if requested, as organising secretary of the college's active Music Society.
Level of Study: Postgraduate.
No. of awards offered: 1.
Frequency: Annual.
Value: £1,000.
Length of Study: 1 year only.
Study Establishment: Lincoln College.
Country of Study: United Kingdom.
Closing Date: Please write for details.

For further information contact:

Lincoln College, Oxford, OX1 3DR, England
Contact: Tutor for Graduates

Lincoln College Keith Murray Senior Scholarship

Subjects: Varies from year to year.
Eligibility: Open to holders of a very good first degree, who are citizens of any country outside the EC.
Level of Study: Doctorate, Postgraduate.

Purpose: To permit students from outside the EU to undertake postgraduate study at Oxford University.
Type: Scholarship.
No. of awards offered: 1+, depending on funds available.
Frequency: Dependent on funds available.
Value: All university and college fees are covered, plus a generous maintenance allowance.
Length of Study: 2 years with the possibility of a 3rd year.
Study Establishment: Lincoln College, Oxford.
Country of Study: United Kingdom.
Application Procedure: Please write for details.
Closing Date: December of the year preceding commencement of study.

For further information contact:

Lincoln College, Oxford, OX1 3DR, England
Tel: (44) 1865 279836
Fax: (44) 1865 279802
Contact: Tutor for Graduates

Lincoln College Overseas Graduate Entrance Scholarship - The Paul Shuffrey Scholarship

Subjects: History of art and related subjects such as archaeology.
Eligibility: Restricted to those offered a place for graduate study at Lincoln College.
Level of Study: Postgraduate.
Type: Scholarship.
No. of awards offered: 1.
Value: £15,000.
Length of Study: 1 year only.
Study Establishment: Lincoln College.
Country of Study: United Kingdom.
Application Procedure: For further information contact the Tutor for Graduates, Lincoln College.

For further information contact:

Lincoln College, Oxford, OX1 3DR, England
Contact: Tutor for Graduates

Lincoln College Overseas Graduate Entrance Scholarships

Subjects: Crewe Scholarship may be held in any area of study, Paul Shuffrey Scholarship in history of art and related subjects, two EPA fund-supported scholarships are for medicine and the medical sciences.
Eligibility: Restricted to those offered a place at Lincoln College.
Level of Study: Postgraduate.
Type: Scholarship.
No. of awards offered: 4.
Value: £1,500.
Length of Study: 1 year.

Study Establishment: Lincoln College.
Country of Study: United Kingdom.
Application Procedure: For further information contact the Tutor for Graduates, Lincoln College.

For further information contact:

Lincoln College, Oxford, OX1 3DR, England
Contact: Tutor for Graduates

Magdalen College Hichens Scholarship

Subjects: All subjects.
Level of Study: Postgraduate.
Value: Cost of college accomodation.
Length of Study: 1 year.
Study Establishment: Mansfield college.
Country of Study: United Kingdom.
Application Procedure: For further information contact the Tutor for Graduates in the first instance at Magdalen College.

For further information contact:

Magdalen College, Oxford, OX1 4UA, England
Contact: Tutor for Graduates

Mansfield College Elfan Rees Scholarship

Subjects: Alternates between politics and theology.
Level of Study: Postgraduate.
Type: Scholarship.
No. of awards offered: Varies.
Frequency: Every four years; next award 2001 in theology.
Value: £2,000 per annum.
Length of Study: 2 years.
Study Establishment: Mansfield College.
Country of Study: United Kingdom.
Application Procedure: Please write for details.

For further information contact:

Mansfield College, Oxford, OX1 3TF, England
Contact: Tutor for Admissions

Merton College Graduate Entrance Scholarships

Subjects: Any subject accepted by the college.
Eligibility: Open to non-UK citizens.
Level of Study: Postgraduate.
Type: Scholarship.
No. of awards offered: 2.
Frequency: Annual.
Value: Fees; housing and maintenance.
Length of Study: 3.
Study Establishment: Merton College.
Country of Study: United Kingdom.
Closing Date: Late January.

For further information contact:

Merton College, Oxford, OX1 4JD, England
Contact: Assistant Tutorial Secretary

Merton College Greendale Senior Scholarships

Subjects: All subjects.
Eligibility: Open to nationals and permanent residents of Switzerland who have a degree from a Swiss university.
Level of Study: Postgraduate.
Type: Scholarship.
No. of awards offered: 1.
Frequency: Annual.
Value: Fees, housing and maintenance.
Length of Study: For length of course up to 3 years.
Study Establishment: Merton College.
Country of Study: United Kingdom.
Closing Date: Early December- please check with the college.

For further information contact:

Merton College, Oxford, OX1 4JD, England
Contact: Assistant Tutorial Secretary

Merton College Leventis Senior Scholarship

Subjects: Greek studies (from the Bronze Age to AD 1453).
Eligibility: Must be citizens of Greece or the Republic of Cyprus.
Level of Study: Postgraduate.
Type: Scholarship.
No. of awards offered: 1.
Frequency: Every two years.
Value: Fees, housing and maintenance.
Length of Study: 2 years; with possible renewal for a 3rd year.
Study Establishment: Merton College.
Country of Study: United Kingdom.
Closing Date: Mid-December.

For further information contact:

Merton College, Oxford, OX1 4JD, England
Contact: The Warden's Secretary

Merton College Senior Scholarships

Subjects: All subjects.
Eligibility: Candidates from any country may apply.
Level of Study: Postgraduate.
Type: Scholarship.
Frequency: Annual.
Value: Fees, housing and maintenance.
Length of Study: 2 years.
Study Establishment: Merton College.
Country of Study: United Kingdom.
Application Procedure: For further datils contact the Assistant Tutorial Secretary in the first instance at Merton College.
Closing Date: Beginning of April.

For further information contact:

Merton College, Oxford, OX1 4JD, England
Contact: Assistant Tutorial Secretary

Merton College Third World Graduate Scholarship

Subjects: All subjects except medicine.
Eligibility: Nationals of under-developed countries (decided on a rotational basis).
Type: Scholarship.
No. of awards offered: 1.
Frequency: Every two years.
Value: Fees, housing and maintenance.
Length of Study: 2 years.
Study Establishment: Merton College.
Country of Study: United Kingdom.
Application Procedure: Please write for details.
Closing Date: Early January.

For further information contact:

Merton College, Oxford, OX1 4JD, England
Contact: Assistant Tutorial Secretary

New Century Scholarships

Subjects: All subjects.
Eligibility: Nationals of Japan. Candidates should be completing or have completed a first degree course and should be between the ages of 21 and 30.
Level of Study: Postgraduate.
Purpose: To assist postgraduate study leading to a degree or for a one year period of study as a visiting student.
No. of awards offered: Varies.
Study Establishment: University of Oxford.
Country of Study: United Kingdom.
Application Procedure: Please write for further details.

For further information contact:

International Office
University Offices
Wellington Square, Oxford, OX1 2JD, England

Oriel College Graduate Scholarships

Subjects: Arts or sciences.
Eligibility: Open to all graduates in residence in the College reading for a higher degree.
Level of Study: Postgraduate.
Type: Scholarship.
Value: £1,250.
Length of Study: 2 years.
Study Establishment: Oriel College.
Country of Study: United Kingdom.
Application Procedure: For further information contact the Tutor for Graduates in the first instance at Oriel College.

For further information contact:

Oriel College, Oxford, OX1 4EW, England
Contact: Tutor for Graduates

OSHIRA (Oxford Research in the Scholarship and Humanities of Africa) Studentships

Subjects: Humanities.
Eligibility: Applicants may be candidates for admission, or already registered as graduate students. The successful applicant, if not already a member of an Oxford college, may be offered a place at St Antony's College or St Cross College.
Level of Study: Postgraduate.
Purpose: To support postgraduate study of Africa in the humanities. Particular subject area details are available from the Committee Secretary.
Type: Studentship.
No. of awards offered: 1.
Value: College and University fees plus maintenance allowance. University fees will normally be covered at home rate, although in exceptional circumstances supplemental grants may be made in order to meet (or to go some way towards meeting) the difference between home and overseas fee.
Length of Study: 2 years with the possibility of extension for 3 and very occasionally 4. Students may also apply for less than 2 years support and Dphil students who have completed their fee liability but who have run out of support to cover costs will also be eligible.
Study Establishment: University of Oxford.
Country of Study: United Kingdom.
Application Procedure: Please write to the Secretary of the Interfaculty Committee for African Studies for further details.
Closing Date: February 26th.
Additional Information: Candidates without any existing college association should name St Cross College as their first choice, and St Antony's as their second choice. For further information please contact the Secretary of the Inter-Faculty Committee, at the University Offices.

Overseas Research Student (ORS) Awards Scheme

Subjects: All subjects.
Level of Study: Postgraduate.
No. of awards offered: Varies.
Value: Equivalent to the difference between home and overseas fees.
Length of Study: Renewable for as long as a student is liable for University fees.
Study Establishment: University of Oxford.
Country of Study: United Kingdom.
Application Procedure: Please write for further details.
Additional Information: ORS awards can be held in conjunction with many other scholarships, and can be seen as an element of a package of financial support assembled by a prospective student. The degrees at Oxford which qualify as research courses for ORS support are: DPhil, MLitt, MSc by research, BPhil, MPhil (where an applicant intends to submit a dissertation), and those MSt's in Research or

Research Methods which are an integral part of a research programme in a particular subject. Therefore, students who are applying for admission as a Probationer Research Student (leading to a degree of DPhil, MLitt or MSc by research) or as a BPhil or MPhil are eligible to apply. Students applying for an MSt (other than the research MSt's defined above), MBA, MSc by coursework, MJur, BCL, Diploma or Certificate, or who will not submit a dissertation as part of an Mphil, are not eligible for an ORS award. Competition for ORS awards is severe, and candidates should be aware that acceptance for study at Oxford does not necessarily mean the University will nominate them for an ORS award, and that nomination by the University does not guarantee success in the national ORS competition. Candidates who gain an ORS award may take it up at any time in the academic year for which it is initially awarded, but cannot defer the award for a full academic year.

For further information contact:

International Office
University Offices
Wellington Square, Oxford, OX1 2JD, England

Pembroke College Australian Graduate Scholarship

Subjects: Classics, law, medicine, philosophy, theology.
Eligibility: Open to male graduates of Melbourne University.
Level of Study: Postgraduate.
Type: Scholarship.
No. of awards offered: Varies.
Frequency: Annual.
Value: £4,000 per annum.
Length of Study: 2 years.
Study Establishment: Pembroke College.
Country of Study: United Kingdom.
Application Procedure: Please write for details.

For further information contact:

Pembroke College, Oxford, OX1 1DW, England
Contact: Dean of Graduate Students

Pembroke College TEPCO Senior Studentship

Subjects: Japanese studies.
Eligibility: Open to nationals from any country.
Level of Study: Postgraduate.
Type: Studentship.
No. of awards offered: Varies.
Frequency: Annual.
Value: Fees and maintenance (where the holder has no other means of support).
Length of Study: 1 year; renewable for a further 2 years.
Study Establishment: Pembroke College.
Country of Study: United Kingdom.
Application Procedure: Please write for details.

For further information contact:

Pembroke College, Oxford, OX1 1DW, England
Contact: Dean of Graduate Students

Peter Jenks Vietnam Scholarship

Subjects: All subjects.
Eligibility: Nationals of Vietnam.
Level of Study: Postgraduate.
Purpose: To assist students studying for a taught Master's degree, a Master's degree by research, or the DPhil degree.
No. of awards offered: 1.
Value: University and college fees and maintenance costs for the duration of the student's course.
Study Establishment: University of Oxford.
Country of Study: United Kingdom.
Application Procedure: Candidates must apply separately for admission to Oxford through the Graduate Admissions Office. Please write for further particulars and an application form.
Closing Date: April 1st.
Additional Information: For further details please contact the International Office.

Pirie-Reid Scholarships

Subjects: All subjects.
Level of Study: Postgraduate, Undergraduate.
Purpose: To enable persons, who would otherwise be prevented by lack of funds, to begin a course of study at Oxford.
Type: Scholarship.
No. of awards offered: Up to 2.
Frequency: Annual.
Value: University and College fees plus maintenance grant; subject to assessment of income from other sources.
Length of Study: Renewable from year to year, subject to satisfactory progress and continuance of approved full-time study.
Study Establishment: University of Oxford.
Country of Study: United Kingdom.
Application Procedure: Please write for application forms.
Closing Date: May 1st.
Additional Information: Preference will be given to candidates applying from other universities i.e. not matriculated at Oxford, and to those domiciled or educated in Scotland. Candidates not fulfilling these criteria are unlikely to be successful. For further information please contact Mrs J M Brown, at the University Offices.

Prendergast Bequest

Subjects: All subjects.
Eligibility: Candidates must be men or women born in the Republic of Ireland whose parents are citizens of the Republic of Ireland.
Level of Study: Postgraduate, Undergraduate.
No. of awards offered: 1.
Frequency: Annual.
Value: Varies; in the region of £500 - £2,000 (means tested).

Length of Study: 1 year.
Study Establishment: University of Oxford.
Country of Study: United Kingdom.
Application Procedure: Applicants who intend to follow a postgraduate course must have been accepted by both a college and the faculty board concerned before a grant can be awarded. Please write for further information and application forms.
Closing Date: July.

For further information contact:

Prendegast Bequest
University Offices
Wellington Square, Oxford, OX1 2JD, England
Contact: The Secretary to the Board of Management

Queen's College Cyril and Phillis Long Studentship

Subjects: Varies.
Eligibility: Open to nationals of any country.
Level of Study: Postgraduate.
Type: Studentship.
No. of awards offered: 1.
Frequency: Annual.
Value: Full fees (college and university) plus equivalent of a Research Council maintenance grant.
Length of Study: 3 years; with a possibility of renewal for a fourth.
Study Establishment: The Queen's College.
Country of Study: United Kingdom.
Closing Date: Please write for details.

For further information contact:

The Queen's College, Oxford, OX1 4AW, England
Contact: The Tutor for Admissions

The Queen's College Hastings Senior Studentship

Subjects: All subjects.
Eligibility: For graduates (with first class Honours) of the Universities of Bradford, Hull, Leeds, Sheffield and York.
Level of Study: Postgraduate.
Type: Scholarship.
Value: £1,436 per annum (under review); assistance may be given with fees if holder not eligible for Research Council or British Academy Studentships.
Length of Study: 1 year, renewable for 2nd and 3rd years.
Study Establishment: The Queen's College.
Country of Study: United Kingdom.
Application Procedure: For further details contact the Tutor for Admissions, in the first instance, at Queen's College.

For further information contact:

Queen's College, Oxford, OX1 4AW, England
Contact: Tutor for Admissions

Queen's College Wendell Herbruck Studentship

Subjects: All subjects.
Eligibility: Preference given to residents of Ohio, although open to other US residents; no older than 26 when appointed.
Level of Study: Postgraduate.
Type: Studentship.
No. of awards offered: Varies.
Frequency: Annual.
Value: £1,425 per annum (under review).
Length of Study: 1 year; renewable for 2nd or 3rd year.
Study Establishment: The Queen's College.
Country of Study: United Kingdom.
Application Procedure: Please write for details.

For further information contact:

The Queen's College, Oxford, OX1 4AW, England
Contact: The Tutor for Admissions

Radhakrishnan/British Chevening Scholarships

Subjects: All subjects.
Eligibility: Nationals of India.
Level of Study: Postgraduate.
No. of awards offered: Varies.
Value: University and colleges fees and maintenance for the duration of the student's course.
Study Establishment: University of Oxford.
Country of Study: United Kingdom.
Application Procedure: Please write for further information and an application form.
Closing Date: April 1st.
Additional Information: For further details please contact the International Office.

Regent's Park College (Permanent Private Hall) Asheville Scholarship

Subjects: Theology.
Eligibility: Open to men and women from Baptist Seminaries in the USA.
Level of Study: Postgraduate.
Type: Scholarship.
No. of awards offered: Varies.
Frequency: Annual.
Value: Up to £1,000 per annum.
Length of Study: 2nd and 3rd years of course.
Study Establishment: Regents Park College (Permanent Private Hall).
Country of Study: United Kingdom.
Application Procedure: Please contact the college for further information.

Regent's Park College (Permanent Private Hall) Eastern European Scholarship

Subjects: Theology.
Eligibility: Open to students from Central and Eastern Europe, with a preference given (but not restricted to), members of the Baptist denomination.
Level of Study: Postgraduate.
Type: Scholarship.
No. of awards offered: 1.
Frequency: Annual.
Value: Up to £1,800 per annum.
Length of Study: Up to 3 years.
Study Establishment: Regent's Park College (Permanent Private Hall).
Country of Study: United Kingdom.
Application Procedure: Please contact the college for further information.

Regent's Park College (Permanent Private Hall) Ernest Payne Scholarship

Subjects: Theology.
Eligibility: Open to men and women resident in the UK preparing for Baptist ministry.
Level of Study: Postgraduate.
Type: Scholarship.
No. of awards offered: 1.
Frequency: Annual.
Value: Up to £1,500 per annum towards fees.
Length of Study: 2 years; extendable to 3.
Study Establishment: Regent's Park College (Permanent Private Hall).
Country of Study: United Kingdom.
Application Procedure: Please contact the college for further information.

Regent's Park College (Permanent Private Hall) Henman Scholarship

Subjects: Theology.
Eligibility: Open to overseas students.
Level of Study: Postgraduate.
Type: Scholarship.
No. of awards offered: Varies.
Frequency: Annual.
Value: Up to £1,800 per annum.
Length of Study: Up to 3 years.
Study Establishment: Regent's Park College (Permanent Private Hall).
Country of Study: United Kingdom.
Application Procedure: Please contact the college for further information.

Regent's Park College (Permanent Private Hall) J W Lord Scholarship

Subjects: Medicine or theology.
Eligibility: Open to men and women preparing to serve Christian churches in India, Hong Kong and China, or

otherwise in Asia, Africa, Central and South America and the Carribean; also available for in-service training or sabbatical study for similar candidates.
Level of Study: Postgraduate.
Type: Scholarship.
No. of awards offered: Varies.
Frequency: Annual.
Value: Up to £1,500 per annum.
Length of Study: Up to 3 years.
Study Establishment: Regent's Park College (Permanent Private Hall).
Country of Study: United Kingdom.
Application Procedure: Please contact the college for further information.

Regent's Park College (Permanent Private Hall) Organ Scholarship

Subjects: All subjects.
Eligibility: Open to suitably qualified candidates in any subject, but with preference to a graduate student in music.
Level of Study: Postgraduate.
Type: Scholarship.
No. of awards offered: Varies.
Frequency: Annual.
Value: £2,000 per annum.
Length of Study: Up to 3 years; renewable annually.
Study Establishment: Regent's Park College (Permanent Private Hall).
Country of Study: United Kingdom.
Application Procedure: Please contact the college for further information.
Additional Information: Includes duties as musical director at New Road Baptist Church.

Rhodes Scholarships

Subjects: All subjects.
Eligibility: Candidates must be between the ages of 19 and 25 (in Kenya the upper age limit is 27). Rhodes scholars must have graduated from a university and have resided for a number of years in their country of origin. Annual distribution of awards - Australia 9, Bermuda 1, Commonwealth Caribbean 2, Canada 11, Germany 4, Hong Kong 1, India 6, Jamaica 1, Kenya 2, Malaysia 1, New Zealand 3, Pakistan 2, Singapore 1, South Africa 9, USA 32, Zambia 1, Zimbabwe 2.
Level of Study: Postgraduate.
No. of awards offered: 88.
Value: University and college fees and maintenance stipend.
Length of Study: 2-3 years.
Study Establishment: University of Oxford.
Country of Study: United Kingdom.
Application Procedure: Rhodes scholars are chosen by local Selection Committees in each constituency. There is no formal written examination; scholars are chosen for their academic all-round qualities on the evidence of testimonials from responsible persons, and after personal interview (which is dispensible) by the Selection Committee concerned. Elections usually take place in November and December, and the Scholars come into residence the following October. After election, application is made on behalf of Scholars for admission to individual colleges and faculties in Oxford, and the election is not confirmed by the Rhodes Trustees until the Scholar-elect has been accepted for admission by the college.

Additional Information: All applications should be made to the Secretary of the local Selection Committee. A separate memorandum explaining the regulations in detail is published for each country and may be obtained from the local secretaries whose names and addresses are below: Australia: Professor G L Hutchinson, Civil and Environmental Engineering Department, University of Melbourne, Parkville, Victoria 3052. Bermuda: J C Collins Esq, c/o Conyers, Dill & Pearmen, Clarendon House, Church Street, Hamilton HM 11. Canada: A R A Scace Esq, QC, General Secretary Rhodes Scholarship Trust, PO Box 48, Toronto, Ontario, M5K 1E6. Commonwelath Caribbean & Jamaica: Mr Peter S Goldson, Secretary, Rhodes Scholarship Selection Committee, PO Box 417, Kingston 6. Germany: Herr T F M Böcking, Scherneck, Alteschlossstrasse 9, 8621 Untersiemau. Hong Kong: Mrs C Lee, Rhodes Scholarship Selection Committee, Office of Student Affairs, The Chinese University of Hong Kong, Shatin, NT, Hong Kong. India: Professor V S Chauhan, International Centre for Genetice Engineering and Biotechnology, Aruna Asaf Ali Marg, New Delhi 110067 Kenya: J D M Silvester Esq, PO Box 30333, Nairobi. Malaysia: Mr P Slinn, Scholarships and Training Officer, The British Council, Jalan Bukit Aman, PO Box 10539, 50916 Kuala Lumpur. New Zealand: The Scholarships Officer, The New Zealand Vice Chancellors' Committee, PO Box 11-915, Manners Street, Wellington. Pakistan: Rhodes Scholarship Selection Committee, PO Box 2939, Islamabad. Singapore: Dr Ong Teck Chin, c/o Department of Physiology, National University of Singapore, Lower Kent Ridge Road, Singapore 0511. South Africa: The General Secretary, Rhodes Scholarships in South Africa, PO Box 41468, Craighall, Tranvaal 2024. USA: Mr E F Gerson, The Rhodes Scholarship Trust, 700 14th St NW, Suite 500, Washington DC 20005-2010. Zambia: Professor A S Saasa, Director, Institute for African Studies, University of Zambia, PO Box 30900, Lusaka. Zimbabwe: Mr D L L Morgan, The Secretary of the Selection Committee, Rhodes Scholarships, PO Box 53, Harare.

Sir John Rhys Studentship in Celtic Studies

Subjects: Celtic studies.
Eligibility: Open to persons engaged in graduate research in Celtic Studies who need financial support in respect of living expenses or fees. The award is not intended for those who hold full-time university posts.
Level of Study: Postgraduate.
Purpose: To enable the successful candidate to complete a research programme on which he or she is already engaged.
Type: Studentship.
No. of awards offered: 1-2.
Frequency: Annual.
Value: Dependent on circumstances; normally similar to a graduate studentship from a UK research council.
Length of Study: 1 year; renewable only in exceptional circumstances.
Study Establishment: University of Oxford, normally Jesus College.

Country of Study: United Kingdom.
Application Procedure: Applications should be sent to the Secretary of the Taylor Institution, 37 Wellington Square, Oxford OX1 2JF, and should include: a CV; a brief outline of the research proposed; an indication of the size of grant required (i.e. any necessary expenses in addition to the normal living costs of a graduate student) and of other sources of financial support (if any); brief details of any other awards or appointments for which the candidate is applying; the names of two academic referees; and the candidate's address for the Easter period if different from the term-time address.
Closing Date: March 1st.
Additional Information: The successful applicant, if not already a member of the University of Oxford, would normally become a member of Jesus College and would be expected to reside in Oxford for the greater part of the academic year.

For further information contact:

37 Wellington Square, Oxford, OX1 2JF, England
Tel: (44) 1865 270753
Fax: (44) 1865 270757
Contact: Secretary of the Taylor Institution

Somerville College Graduate Scholarships

Subjects: Any subject offered at the College.
Eligibility: Open to students of any nationality who are reading for a higher degree.
Level of Study: Postgraduate.
Type: Scholarship.
No. of awards offered: 2.
Value: £1,500 per annum.
Length of Study: 2 years; with the possibility of renewal for a third year.
Study Establishment: Somerville College.
Country of Study: United Kingdom.
Application Procedure: Please contact the college Secretary in the first instance.

For further information contact:

Somerville College, Oxford, OX2 6HD, England
Contact: The College Secretary

Somerville College Levick Sisters Senior Scholarship

Subjects: Philosophy and/or philology (including Sanskrit and Old Norse).
Eligibility: For those reading for a higher degree.
Level of Study: Postgraduate.
Type: Scholarship.
Frequency: Annual.
Value: £1,500 per annum.
Length of Study: 1 year.
Study Establishment: Somerville College, Oxford.
Country of Study: United Kingdom.
Application Procedure: Please contact the college Secretary.

For further information contact:

Somerville College, Oxfordshire, OX2 6HD, England
Contact: College Secretary

Somerville College Oxford Bursary for American Graduates (Janet Watson Bursary)

Subjects: All subjects.
Eligibility: For those reading for a higher degree or diploma.
Level of Study: Postgraduate.
Type: Bursary.
Value: Approximately one quarter of total fees to a maximum of £3,500 per annum.
Length of Study: 2 years.
Study Establishment: Somerville College.
Country of Study: United Kingdom.
Application Procedure: Please contact the college Secretary.

For further information contact:

Somerville College, Oxford, OX2 6HD, England
Contact: College Secretary

Somerville College Ruth Adler Scholarship

Subjects: Philosophy, law or subjects related to social work.
Eligibility: For those reading for a higher degree.
Level of Study: Postgraduate.
Type: Scholarship.
Frequency: Annual.
Value: £1,500 per annum.
Length of Study: 1 year, in the first instance.
Study Establishment: Somerville College, Oxford.
Country of Study: United Kingdom.
Application Procedure: Please contact the College Secretary.

For further information contact:

Somerville College, Oxfordshire, OX2 6HD, England
Contact: College Secretary

St Anne's College Ethics Scholarship

Subjects: Philosophy.
Eligibility: Nationals of any country may apply.
Level of Study: Postgraduate.
Type: Scholarship.
No. of awards offered: 1.
Frequency: Annual.
Value: £1,500.
Length of Study: 1 year.
Study Establishment: St Anne's College.
Country of Study: United Kingdom.
Application Procedure: All graduate students with an interest in ethics who by June 30th have accepted a place at St Anne's to read for a higher degree in philosophy (of more than one year's duration) will automatically be considered without any further application being necessary. Enquiries should be directed to Dr R Crisp, St Anne's College.

For further information contact:

St Anne's College, Oxford, OX2 6HS, England
Contact: Dr R Crisp

St Anne's College Irene Jamieson Research Scholarship

Subjects: Any arts or social science subject offered by the University.
Eligibility: Open to men and women who are UK or EC citizens and who are graduates of any university, or individuals who can show some other proof of their ability to undertake advanced work. Candidates who are graduates of a British university must have obtained first or good second class honours. All candidates must be accepted by the University of Oxford to read for a higher degree of at least two years' duration, and by the college, by June 1st. Candidates for one year courses or for second BA's are not eligible.
Level of Study: Postgraduate.
Purpose: To fund graduate research.
Type: Scholarship.
No. of awards offered: 1.
Frequency: Annual.
Value: Equal to the College fee.
Length of Study: 1 year; renewable for a further year.
Study Establishment: St Anne's College.
Country of Study: United Kingdom.
Closing Date: June 30th.

For further information contact:

St Anne's College, Oxford, OX2 6HS, England
Tel: (44) 1865 274825
Fax: (44) 1865 274899
Contact: Registrar

St Anne's College Olwen Rhys Research Scholarship

Subjects: Medieval romance language and literature, medieval history.
Eligibility: Open to men and women who are UK or EC citizens and who are graduates of any university, or individuals who can show some other proof of their ability to undertake advanced work. Candidates who are graduates of a British university must have obtained first or good second class honours. All candidates must be accepted by the University of Oxford to read for a higher degree of at least two years' duration, and by the college, by June 1st. Candidates for one year courses and for second BA's will not be eligible.
Level of Study: Postgraduate.
Purpose: To fund graduate research.
Type: Scholarship.
No. of awards offered: 1.
Frequency: Annual.

Value: Equal to the college fee.
Length of Study: 1 year; renewable for a further year.
Study Establishment: St Anne's College.
Country of Study: United Kingdom.
Closing Date: June 20th.

For further information contact:

St Anne's College, Oxford, OX2 6HS, England
Tel: (44) 1865 274825
Fax: (44) 1865 274899
Contact: Registrar

St Anne's College Overseas Scholarship

Subjects: Any subject offered by the University.
Eligibility: Open to graduates of any university who are not UK or EC citizens. All candidates must be accepted by the University of Oxford to read for a higher degree of at least two years' duration, and by the college, by June 1st.
Level of Study: Postgraduate.
Purpose: To fund graduate research.
Type: Scholarship.
No. of awards offered: 3.
Frequency: Annual.
Value: Equal to the College fee.
Length of Study: 1 year; renewable for a further year.
Study Establishment: St Anne's College.
Country of Study: United Kingdom.
Closing Date: June 20th.

For further information contact:

St Anne's College, Oxford, OX2 6HS, England
Tel: (44) 1865 274825
Fax: (44) 1865 274899
Contact: Registrar

St Anne's College Research Scholarship

Subjects: Arts and social science subjects.
Eligibility: Candidates for one year courses will not be eligible.
Level of Study: Postgraduate.
Type: Scholarship.
No. of awards offered: 1.
Frequency: Annual.
Value: Equal to the College Fee.
Length of Study: 1 year; renewable for a further year.
Study Establishment: St Anne's College.
Country of Study: United Kingdom.
Application Procedure: All graduate students who have accepted a place at St Anne's will automatically be considered without any further application being neccessary. For further information contact the college secretary.
Closing Date: June 30th.

For further information contact:

St Anne's College, Oxford, OX2 6HS, England
Contact: College Secretary

St Catherine's College Overseas Graduate Scholarship

Subjects: All subjects (see the University Graduate Studies Prospectus).
Eligibility: Open to qualified individuals who are citizens of non EC countries.
Level of Study: Postgraduate.
Purpose: To assist graduates studying for a research degree, usually in their first year at the University of Oxford.
Type: Scholarship.
No. of awards offered: 1.
Frequency: Annual.
Value: £1,500.
Length of Study: 2 years in the first instance; current holders may reapply for a 3rd year.
Study Establishment: St Catherine's College, University of Oxford.
Country of Study: United Kingdom.
Application Procedure: Please write for details.
Closing Date: July 1st.

For further information contact:

St Catherine's College, Oxford, OX1 3UJ, England
Tel: (44) 1865 271732
Fax: (44) 1865 271768
Contact: Tutor for Graduates

St Cross College Major College Scholarships

Subjects: All subjects.
Eligibility: Open to students from Oxford or from other institutions of higher education who intend to study or are studying for a postgraduate degree.
Level of Study: Postgraduate.
Purpose: To support postgraduate study.
Type: Scholarship.
No. of awards offered: Up to 2.
Frequency: Annual.
Value: £1,675 per annum.
Length of Study: 1 to 3 year.
Study Establishment: St Cross College.
Country of Study: United Kingdom.
Closing Date: March.

For further information contact:

St Cross College, Oxford, OX1 3LZ, England
Tel: (44) 1865 278490
Contact: Tutor for Admissions

St Cross College Paula Soans O'Brian Scholarships

Subjects: All subjects.

Eligibility: Open to students from Oxford or from other institutions of higher education who intend to study or are studying for a postgraduate degree.
Level of Study: Postgraduate.
Purpose: To support postgraduate study.
Type: Scholarship.
Frequency: Varies.
Value: £1,675 per year.
Length of Study: 1-3 years.
Study Establishment: St Cross College.
Country of Study: United Kingdom.
Application Procedure: Forms are available from the Tutor for Admissions in January and February.
Closing Date: Please write for details.

For further information contact:

St Cross College, Oxford, OX1 3LZ, England
Tel: (44) 1865 278490
Contact: Tutor for Admissions

St Edmund Hall William R Miller Graduate Awards

Subjects: All subjects.
Level of Study: Postgraduate.
No. of awards offered: 3.
Frequency: Annual.
Value: Free accomodation.
Length of Study: 2 years.
Study Establishment: St Edmund Hall.
Country of Study: United Kingdom.
Application Procedure: Please contact the Tutor for Graduates, St Edmund Hall for further information.
Closing Date: May 1st.

For further information contact:

St Edmund Hall, Oxford, OX1 4AR, England
Contact: Tutor for Graduates

St Hilda's College Dame Helen Gardner Scholarship

Subjects: Humanities.
Eligibility: Open to women who have been accepted to read for a higher research degree at Oxford in the humanities.
Level of Study: Postgraduate.
Purpose: To support study in the humanities.
Type: Scholarship.
No. of awards offered: 1.
Frequency: Usually every three years.
Value: £5,000 per annum.
Length of Study: 3 years.
Study Establishment: St Hilda's College.
Country of Study: United Kingdom.
Application Procedure: Awards are advertised in January for the following October. Application forms will be sent after the candidates have been accepted by Oxford University.
Closing Date: August 1st.

For further information contact:

St Hilda's College, Oxford, OX4 1DY, England
Tel: (44) 1865 276815
Fax: (44) 1865 276816
Contact: Academic Office

St Hilda's College Graduate Scholarships

Subjects: Any subject offered by the University.
Eligibility: Open to women graduates from any country working for a higher research degree.
Level of Study: Postgraduate.
Type: Scholarship.
No. of awards offered: Normally 4.
Frequency: Annual.
Value: Up to £1,000 per year.
Length of Study: 1 year; renewable.
Study Establishment: St Hilda's College.
Country of Study: United Kingdom.
Application Procedure: Applicants must have been accepted by the relevant university faculty before applying for a scholarship.
Closing Date: August 1st.
Additional Information: The award amalgamates the previous Graduate Studentships and Overseas Bursaries.

For further information contact:

St Hilda's College, Oxford, OX4 1DY, England
Tel: (44) 1865 276815
Fax: (44) 1865 276816
Contact: Academic Office

St Hilda's College New Zealand Bursaries

Subjects: Any subject offered by the University.
Eligibility: Open to women students who are New Zealand citizens, who have been accepted for a graduate research degree.
Level of Study: Postgraduate.
Purpose: To enable women educated and resident in New Zealand to study at Oxford.
Type: Bursary.
No. of awards offered: Varies.
Frequency: Annual.
Value: Up to £1,700 per annum.
Length of Study: 1-3 years.
Study Establishment: St Hilda's College.
Country of Study: United Kingdom.
Application Procedure: Application forms will be sent after the candidates have been accepted by Oxford University.
Closing Date: August 1st.
Additional Information: Available for undergraduate or postgraduate degrees. The main criteria for the award is academic merit; financial circumstances are also considered. Applicants must show evidence of sufficient funding to complete their course.

For further information contact:

St Hilda's College, Oxford, OX4 1DY, England
Tel: (44) 1865 276815
Fax: (44) 1865 276816
Contact: Academic Office

St Hugh's College Bursaries for Students from PRC

Subjects: Any subject offered at the College.
Eligibility: Open to nationals of the People's Republic of China.
Level of Study: Postgraduate.
Type: Scholarship.
Value: £2,000 per annum.
Length of Study: 2 years, with the possibility of renewal for the fee-paying duration of the course.
Study Establishment: St Hugh's College.
Country of Study: United Kingdom.
Application Procedure: Please contact the College Secretary in the first instance.

For further information contact:

St Hugh's College, Oxford, OX2 6LE, England
Contact: The College Secretary

St Hugh's College Graduate Scholarships

Subjects: All subjects.
Eligibility: Open to British nationals and candidates from overseas.
Level of Study: Postgraduate.
Purpose: To provide financial support to graduates reading for a degree by research.
Type: Scholarship.
No. of awards offered: Up to 12.
Frequency: Annual.
Value: £2,000 per annum, plus accommodation and some dining rights.
Length of Study: For the fee-paying duration of the course.
Study Establishment: St Hugh's College.
Country of Study: United Kingdom.
Application Procedure: Please contact the College Secretary in the first instance.
Closing Date: March 1st.

For further information contact:

St Hugh's College, Oxford, OX2 6LE, England
Tel: (44) 1865 274918
Fax: (44) 1865 274912
Contact: The College Secretary

St Hugh's College The Dorothea Gray Scholarship

Subjects: Classics.
Eligibility: Open to candidates of any nationality.
Level of Study: Postgraduate.
Type: Scholarship.

Value: £2,000 per annum.
Length of Study: For the fee-paying duration of the course.
Study Establishment: St Hugh's College.
Country of Study: United Kingdom.
Application Procedure: Please contact the college Secretary in the first instance.

For further information contact:

St Hugh's College, Oxford, OX2 6LE, England
Contact: The College Secretary

St Hugh's College The Rawnsley Scholarship

Subjects: Czech, Slovak and Polish languages and literature.
Eligibility: Open to nationals of the Czech Republic, Slovakia and Poland.
Level of Study: Postgraduate.
Purpose: To foster the study of Czech, Slovak and Polish languages and literature.
Type: Scholarship.
Value: Equivalent to the current British Academy Awards.
Length of Study: 1 year; renewable for 1 year.
Study Establishment: St Hugh's College.
Country of Study: United Kingdom.
Application Procedure: Please contact the Tutor for Graduates in the first instance.

For further information contact:

University of Oxford, Oxford, OX2 6LE, England
Contact: The Tutor for Graduates

St Hugh's College The Yates Senior Scholarship

Subjects: Theology.
Eligibility: Open to candidates of any nationality.
Level of Study: Postgraduate.
Type: Scholarship.
Value: £2,000 per annum.
Length of Study: For the fee-paying duration of the course.
Study Establishment: St Hugh's College.
Country of Study: United Kingdom.
Application Procedure: Please contact the college Secretary in the first instance.

For further information contact:

St Hugh's College, Oxford, OX2 6LE, England
Contact: The College Secretary

St Hugh's College William Thomas and Gladys Willing Scholarship

Subjects: Modern languages.
Eligibility: Open to candidates of any nationality.
Level of Study: Postgraduate.
Type: Scholarship.
Value: £2,000 per annum.
Length of Study: For the fee-paying duration of the course.
Study Establishment: St Hugh's College.
Country of Study: United Kingdom.

Application Procedure: Please contact the college Secretary in the first instance.

For further information contact:

St Hugh's College, Oxford, OX2 6LE, England
Contact: The College Secretary

St John's College I Beeston Scholarships

Subjects: All subjects, but particularly Middle Eastern Studies.
Eligibility: Normally restricted to graduates with UK degrees, who have already begun research; advertised in November/December and tenable from following October; no deferment of commencement of scholarships is permitted.
Level of Study: Postgraduate.
Type: Scholarship.
Value: Fees and accomodation and equivalent of a Research Council grant when the candidate's grant expires.
Length of Study: Normally 2 years.
Study Establishment: St John's College.
Country of Study: United Kingdom.
Application Procedure: Please contact the Senior Tutor, St John's College in the first instance.

For further information contact:

St John's College, Oxford, OX1 3JP, England
Contact: Senior Tutor

St John's College North Senior Scholarships

Subjects: Theology.
Eligibility: Normally restricted to graduates with UK degrees, who have already begun research; advertised in November/December and tenable from the following October; no deferment of commencement of scholarships is permitted.
Level of Study: Postgraduate.
Type: Scholarship.
Value: Fees and accommodation and equivalent of a Research Council grant when the candidate's grant expires.
Length of Study: Usually 2 years.
Study Establishment: St John's College.
Country of Study: United Kingdom.
Application Procedure: Please contact the Senior Tutor in the first instance.

For further information contact:

St John's College, Oxford, OX1 3JP, England
Contact: The Senior Tutor

St Peter's College Leonard J Theberge Memorial Scholarship

Subjects: Any subject offered at the College.
Eligibility: Open to US citizens; preference is to mature students over 30, or those who have been employed for five years.
Level of Study: Postgraduate.
Type: Scholarship.

Value: A substantial contribution to maintenance and personal expenses.
Length of Study: 1-2 years.
Study Establishment: St Peter's College.
Country of Study: United Kingdom.
Application Procedure: Please contact the Tutor for Graduates in the first instance.

For further information contact:

St Peter's College, Oxford, OX1 2DL, England
Contact: Tutor for Graduates

Wadham College Norwegian Scholarship

Subjects: All subjects.
Eligibility: Open to registered students or graduates of Oslo University who are Norwegian citizens.
Level of Study: Postgraduate, Undergraduate.
Type: Scholarship.
Frequency: Annual.
Value: Fees and maintenance.
Length of Study: 1 year.
Study Establishment: Wadham College, Oxford.
Country of Study: United Kingdom.
Application Procedure: Applications in August of each year to the committee for the Norsk Oxford-Stipendium ved Wadham College at the University of Oslo.
Closing Date: August.

Wolfson College Department for International Development Shared Scholarship Scheme (formerly ODASSS)

Subjects: All subjects.
Eligibility: Developing Commonwealth countries only.
Type: Scholarship.
Value: Full fees and maintenance.
Length of Study: Normally 1 year.
Study Establishment: Wolfson College.
Country of Study: United Kingdom.
Application Procedure: Please write for details.

For further information contact:

International Office
University Offices
Wellington Square, Oxford, OX1 2JD, England

Wolfson College The Hargreaves-Mawdsley Studentship

Subjects: 18th-century Spanish history, preferably in relation to American colonies.
Level of Study: Postgraduate.
Type: Studentship.
No. of awards offered: 1 at any one time.
Frequency: Varies.
Value: Not less than £5,000 per annum.
Length of Study: 2-3 years.
Study Establishment: Wolfson College.
Country of Study: United Kingdom.

Application Procedure: Please contact the Academic Secretary in the first instance.

For further information contact:

Wolfson College, Oxford, OX2 6UD, England
Contact: Academic Secretary

UNIVERSITY OF PENNSYLVANIA

School of Arts and Sciences
16 College Hall, Philadelphia, PA, 19109-6378, United States of America
Tel: (1) 215 898 8220
Fax: (1) 215 573 2063
Email: tturner@mail.sas.upenn.edu
Contact: Ms Wendy Steiner, Co-ordinator, Penn Humanities Forum

The Penn Humanities Forum promotes interdisciplinary collaboration across Penn departments and schools and between the University and the Delaware Valley region. Each year, a broad topic sets the theme for a research seminar for resident and visiting scholars, courses and public events involving the cultural institutions of the area.

Mellon Postdoctoral Fellowships in the Humanities

Subjects: Humanities.
Eligibility: Open to younger scholars who, at the time of application, have received the PhD, but have not yet held it for more than eight years nor been granted tenure. Research proposals are invited in all areas of humanistic studies except educational curriculum building and performing arts. Preference is given to proposals that are interdisciplinary and directly related to the annual topic, and to candidates who have not previously utilised the resources of this university and whose work would allow them to take advantage of the research strengths of the institution and to make contribution to its intellectual life. The requirements are residency at the University of Pennsylvania, and the teaching of one course per semester.
Level of Study: Postdoctorate.
Purpose: To support research for younger scholars.
Type: Fellowship.
No. of awards offered: 5.
Frequency: Annual.
Value: US$32,000.
Length of Study: 1 academic year and possibly the summer term before or after; not renewable.
Study Establishment: University of Pennsylvania.
Country of Study: USA.
Application Procedure: Each applicant must complete an application.
Closing Date: Postmark no later than October 15th.
Additional Information: Fellows may not normally hold other concurrent awards.

For further information contact:

Penn Humanities Forum
116 Bennett Hall
3340 Walnut Street, Philadelphia, PA, 19104, United States of America
Tel: (1) 215 898 8220
Fax: (1) 215 573 2063
Contact: Ms Wendy Steiner, Penn Humanties Forum Director

THE UNIVERSITY OF QUEENSLAND

Office of Research and Postgraduate Studies, QLD, 4072, Australia
Tel: (61) 7 3365 2033
Fax: (61) 7 3365 4455
www: http://www.uq.edu.au
Contact: Ms Jan Massey, The Scholarships Officer

University of Queensland Postdoctoral Research Fellowship

Subjects: Any subject offered by the University.
Eligibility: Open to candidates of any nationality. An applicant must not have had more than five years' full-time professional experience since the award of a Doctoral degree as at June 30th of the year before the fellowship commences.
Fellowships may be offered to applicants who do not hold a doctoral degree provided that evidence is given that a doctoral thesis has been submitted by June 30th (for candidates from Australia, New Zealand or Papua New Guinea) or September 1st (for all other candidates), and that the selection committee is satisfied that the degree will be awarded by June 30th of the fellowship year.
Level of Study: Postdoctorate, Professional development.
Type: Fellowship.
No. of awards offered: Approx. 9.
Frequency: Annual.
Value: A$41,199-A$45,910 per year, plus excursion return air fare for the recipient only.
Length of Study: 2 years; sometimes extendable by 1 year.
Study Establishment: The University.
Country of Study: Australia.
Application Procedure: Application forms are available from the heads of the relevant departments or from the Director, Research Services. They can also be downloaded from the university website.
Closing Date: May 17th of the year preceding the award.

University of Queensland Postgraduate Research Scholarships

Subjects: All subjects.
Eligibility: Open to candidates of any nationality who are acceptable as full-time internal students for a postgraduate research degree at the University. Applicants should hold an Australian first class honours or Master's degree, or the equivalent. Candidates must have a sound knowledge of both written and spoken English.
Level of Study: Doctorate, Postgraduate.
Type: Scholarship.
No. of awards offered: Approx. 75.
Frequency: Annual.
Value: A$15,000.
Length of Study: 2 years for the Master's degree, and for up to 3 years for the PhD degree.
Study Establishment: The University.
Country of Study: Australia.
Application Procedure: International students must apply through the university's International Education Office, email ieoenquiries@mailbox.uq.edu.au; Australian students must apply through The Scholarships Officer, email m.schmidt@research.uq.edu.au.
Closing Date: September 30th.
Additional Information: To assist with tuition fee expenses international students may apply for the Overseas Postgraduate Research Scholarships (OPRS) which are administered through the International Education Office.

University of Queensland Travel Scheme for International Collaborative Research

Subjects: Any subject offered by the University.
Eligibility: Open to any suitably qualified scholar actively engaged in academic work at a university or internationally recognised research institution, who will be able to contribute substantially to research activity in the department to which he or she is attached at the University of Queensland.
Level of Study: Postdoctorate.
Purpose: To facilitate visits by scholars from institutions in other countries.
Type: Grant.
No. of awards offered: Approx. 15.
Frequency: Annual.
Value: Return economy air fare.
Length of Study: 8 weeks or longer during semester periods in the year of the award.
Study Establishment: The University.
Country of Study: Australia.
Application Procedure: Application forms are available from the head of the relevant department or from the Director, Research Services, at the University of Queensland. Details and application forms may also be downloaded from the university website.
Closing Date: August 1st of the year preceding the award year.

THE UNIVERSITY OF READING

Whiteknights
PO Box 217, Reading, Berkshire, RG6 6AU, England
Tel: (44) 118 931 8373
Fax: (44) 118 935 2063
Email: d.a.stannard@reading.ac.uk
www: http://www.rdg.ac.uk/
Contact: Mr D A Stannard, Senior Administrative Assistant

The University of Reading is one of the UK's foremost institutions of higher education. It offers undergraduate and postgraduate taught and research degree courses in all the traditional subject areas, except medical sciences. Many other, more vocational courses are also offered. Research work in many areas is of international renown.

The University of Reading Postgraduate Studentship

Subjects: There are no restrictions on subject area, subject to availability of appropriate supervision at the University.
Eligibility: Candidates must hold a first degree qualification.
Level of Study: Doctorate, Postgraduate.
Purpose: To enable students to obtain a doctoral degree.
Type: Studentship.
No. of awards offered: 4.
Frequency: Annual.
Value: Composition fee (at home standard rate), plus maintenance award as for Research Council Postgraduate Studentships, plus £1,000.
Length of Study: Up to 3 years.
Study Establishment: University of Reading.
Country of Study: United Kingdom.
Application Procedure: An application form (available from Mr D A Stannard) should be completed, and a confidential academic reference should also be submitted.
Closing Date: A date to be arranged in March of the year of entry.
Additional Information: At present the Studentships are awarded on the nomination of the Head of Department.

UNIVERSITY OF REGINA

Faculty of Graduate Studies & Research, Regina, SK, S4S
OA2, Canada
Tel: (1) 306 585 4161
Fax: (1) 306 585 4893
Email: grad.studies@leroy.cc.uregina.ca
www: http://www.uregina.ca/gradstudies/
Contact: Ms Chris Blair

Founded as Regina College and granted a provincial charter in 1911, the University of Regina became an affiliated junior college of the University of Saskatchewan in 1925, and acquired degree-granting status in 1959. The University achieved academic autonomy in 1974.

Regina Graduate Scholarships

Subjects: Any graduate programme offered at the University of Regina.
Eligibility: Applicants must be accepted by the Graduate Faculty as fully-qualified for admission to Master's or PhD degree programme at the University of Regina. Must be registered as full-time student and must not receive any other scholarship(s).
Level of Study: Doctorate, Postgraduate.
Purpose: These scholarships are awarded to students of high academic standing who wish to work full-time on programme requirements.
Type: Scholarship.
No. of awards offered: Approx. 120.
Frequency: Three times each year.
Value: Master's level: C$3,800 per semester; Doctoral level: C$4,000 per semester.
Length of Study: Varies.
Study Establishment: University of Regina.
Country of Study: Canada.
Application Procedure: Application forms are available from the Faculty of Graduate Studies and Research.
Closing Date: February 28th, June 15th, October 15th.

Regina Teaching Assistantships

Subjects: Any graduate programme offered at the University of Regina.
Eligibility: Candidates must meet appropriate qualifications to participate in the instructional programme in the assigned academic unit. Must be accepted by the Graduate Faculty at the University of Regina as fully qualified for admission to Master's or PhD degree.
Level of Study: Doctorate, Postgraduate.
Purpose: Teaching assistants to assist with the instructional programme of undergraduate courses or laboratories.
Type: Assistantship.
No. of awards offered: Approx. 88.
Frequency: Twice a year.
Value: Master's level: C$3,660 per semester; Doctoral level C$4,182 per semester.
Length of Study: Varies.
Study Establishment: University of Regina.
Country of Study: Canada.
Application Procedure: Application forms are available from the Faculty of Graduate Studies and Research.
Closing Date: June 15th, October 15th.

UNIVERSITY OF SHEFFIELD

85 Wilkinson Street, Sheffield, S10 2GJ, England
Tel: (44) 114 222 1404
Fax: (44) 114 222 1420
www: http://www.shef.ac.uk
Contact: Graduate Office

The University of Sheffield is a research led university offering research supervision, taught courses and professional training in engineering and physical sciences, biologies, environmental sciences, humanities, social sciences, medical and health sciences. Many departments have funding council accreditation and scholarships and bursaries may be available.

Hossein Farmy Scholarships

Subjects: Priority will be given to mining, expression of which shall include the geological, engineering, scientific, and technological aspects of mining, and the archaeological, economic, historical, legal and social aspects of mining and the mining industry.
Eligibility: Open to persons born in the UK. Candidates must hold a good honours degree from a recognised institution.
Level of Study: Postgraduate.
Purpose: To pursue a higher degree by research.
Type: Scholarship.
No. of awards offered: 4.
Frequency: Annual.
Value: Fees and maintenance at Research Council rates.
Length of Study: Up to 3 years.
Study Establishment: One of the departments of the University of Sheffield.
Country of Study: United Kingdom.
Application Procedure: Please write for details.
Closing Date: March 31st.

UNIVERSITY OF SOUTHAMPTON

Highfield, Southampton, Hampshire, SO17 1BJ, England
Tel: (44) 1703 594741
Fax: (44) 1703 593037
Contact: Academic Registrar

The University of Southampton was founded as the Hartley Institute in the mid 19th Century, and was granted its royal charter in 1952. Today, the university offers a range of postgraduate courses in 8 faculties: arts, engineering and applied science, law mathematics, medicine, health and biological science, science, social sciences and education.

University of Southampton Studentships

Subjects: All subjects offered by the University.
Eligibility: Open to candidates who hold a good honours first degree and are eligible for admission to the department in which they intend to study.
Level of Study: Postgraduate.
Purpose: To support postgraduate research study.
Type: Studentship.
No. of awards offered: Varies.
Frequency: Annual.
Value: Based on Research Council Studentship rates.
Length of Study: The duration of the course of study and research.
Study Establishment: University of Southampton.
Country of Study: United Kingdom.

Application Procedure: Initial enquiries should be directed to the head of the academic department in which research is to be undertaken.
Closing Date: Varies; enquiries should be made by January for the following October.

UNIVERSITY OF SOUTHERN CALIFORNIA (USC)

University Park
Mail Code 4012, Los Angeles, CA, 90089, United States of America
Tel: (1) 213 740 5294
Fax: (1) 213 740 8607
www: http://www.usc.edu/dept/las/faculty/mellon.htm
Contact: Mr Joseph Aonn, Dean of Faculty

Located near the heart of Los Angeles, the University of Southern California is a private research university. It maintains a tradition of academic strength at all levels - from the earliest explorations of the undergraduate to the advanced scholarly research of the postdoctoral Fellow.

Andrew W Mellon Postdoctoral Fellowships in the Humanities

Subjects: The humanities.
Eligibility: Open to Scholars who received their PhD within the past seven years and do not hold tenure at an academic institution.
Level of Study: Postdoctorate.
Purpose: To encourage junior scholars to develop their research.
Type: Fellowship.
No. of awards offered: 1-2.
Frequency: Annual.
Value: Approximately US$30,000, plus full faculty fringe benefits and modest research expense support.
Study Establishment: University of Southern California.
Country of Study: USA.
Application Procedure: Varies each year; information can be found on our website.

USC All-University Predoctoral Diversity Fellowships

Subjects: All subjects.
Eligibility: Consideration for a fellowship through the graduate school is contingent upon a completed application for admission to a PhD programme, and completion of a fellowship application. Open to incoming PhD applicants who are US citizens and members of the following under-represented minority groups: American Indians and Alaskan Natives (Eskimo or Aleut), Black/African Americans, US Hispanic/Latinos, and Native Pacific Islanders (Micronesians and Polynesians).
Level of Study: Postgraduate.

Purpose: The graduate school announces a programme of diversity fellowships for students aiming toward the PhD at USC and planning a career in university teaching and research.
Type: Fellowship.
No. of awards offered: Varies.
Frequency: Annual.
Value: US$14,000 per year, plus full tuition and mandatory fees.
Length of Study: 3 years eligibility, awarded annually with automatic renewal for a second and third year with continued superior performance.
Study Establishment: University of Southern California.
Country of Study: USA.
Application Procedure: A completed application must include: fellowship application form including statement of purpose; one transcript from each college or university; photocopy of scores from the Graduate Record Examination, and three academic letters of recommendation. Photocopies for all of the above are acceptable.
Closing Date: February 1st.

For further information contact:

University of Southern California
3601 Watt Way
GFS 315, Los Angeles, CA, 90089-1695, United States of America
Contact: The Graduate School

USC College Dissertation Fellowship

Subjects: Arts and humanities, natural sciences, social and behavioural sciences.
Eligibility: Open to outstanding all-but-dissertation students of any nationality, who present evidence of achievement and promise as scholars.
Level of Study: Postgraduate, Predoctorate.
Purpose: To provide financial assistance to students who are about to begin, or are in the process of, writing their doctoral dissertation in the College of Letters, Arts and Sciences at USC.
Type: Fellowship.
No. of awards offered: 29.
Frequency: Annual.
Value: US$14,500 plus 4 units of tuition and selected mandatory fees.
Length of Study: 1 year.
Study Establishment: The University of Southern California.
Country of Study: USA.
Application Procedure: Application dossier collated by department.
Closing Date: March 10th.

USC College of Letters, Arts and Sciences Merit Award

Subjects: Arts and humanities, natural sciences, and social/behavioural sciences.

Eligibility: Open to outstanding seniors and graduates of any nationality who present evidence of achievement and promise as scholars.
Level of Study: Postdoctorate.
Purpose: To provide an opportunity for students working towards a PhD degree who intend to pursue a career in university teaching and research.
Type: Fellowship.
No. of awards offered: 100.
Frequency: Annual.
Value: US$14,500 per year, plus full tuition.
Length of Study: Up to 5 years (2 years of fellowship, 3 years of teaching).
Study Establishment: University of Southern California.
Country of Study: USA.
Application Procedure: Application forms are available from the USC academic department to which the student is applying for admission.
Closing Date: February 1st.

UNIVERSITY OF ST ANDREWS

St Salvators College
Development Office
North Street, St Andrews, Fife, KY16 9AL, Scotland
Tel: (44) 1334 462 101
Fax: (44) 1334 462 030
Email: ec3@st-andrews.ac.uk
www: http://www.st-and.ac.uk/
Contact: Ms Shona M Hood, Secretary to the Special Lectureships Committee

The University of St Andrews' mission is to deliver high-quality education and research in a distinctive range of subjects in science, arts and divinity.

Gifford Research Fellowship

Subjects: Philosophy or natural theology.
Eligibility: Open to suitably qualified candidates having a doctorate in a relevant subject.
Level of Study: Postdoctorate.
Purpose: To pursue research in the areas of philosophy and natural theology.
Type: Fellowship.
No. of awards offered: 1.
Frequency: Generally every second year.
Value: £15,159 - £17,606.
Length of Study: 1 year; may be renewable for 1 further year.
Study Establishment: University of St Andrews.
Country of Study: United Kingdom.
Application Procedure: Please submit CV and an outline of proposed research, as advertised in the press.
Closing Date: January/February for appointment the following academic year.
Additional Information: When applications are required adverts usually appear in The Times, Church Times and The Tablet.

UNIVERSITY OF STIRLING

Research Office, Stirling, FK9 4LA, Scotland
Tel: (44) 1786 407041
Fax: (44) 1786 466688
Email: research@stir.ac.uk
www: http://www.stir.ac.uk/
Contact: Administrative Assistant

The University of Stirling offers postgraduate awards for research degrees on a full-time or part-time basis.

University of Stirling Research Studentships

Subjects: Awards are available in the arts and humanities, human sciences (applied, psychology and education) management studies including marketing, and natural sciences including aquaculture.
Eligibility: No restrictions.
Level of Study: Doctorate, Postgraduate.
Purpose: To support postgraduate study.
Type: Studentship.
No. of awards offered: 40.
Frequency: Annual.
Value: £6,500 per annum.
Length of Study: Up to 3 years.
Study Establishment: University of Stirling.
Country of Study: Scotland.
Application Procedure: Application forms for the individual faculties must be completed. The address to write to is the same as the main address including the name of the faculty being applied to.
Closing Date: Ongoing.

UNIVERSITY OF SUSSEX/ASSOCIATION OF COMMONWEALTH UNIVERSITIES

Postgraduate Office
Sussex House
Falmer, Brighton, East Sussex, BN1 9RH, England
Tel: (44) 1273 606 755
Fax: (44) 1273 678 335
Email: t.o-donnell@sussex.ac.uk
www: http://www.sussex.ac.uk
Contact: Ms Tina Wells

The University of Sussex is one of the top 12 UK universities for research. The University boasts a distinguished faculty that includes seventeen fellows of the Royal Society and four fellows of the British Academy. The University has over 10,000 students, twenty-five per cent of whom are postgraduates.

University of Sussex Overseas Research Studentships

Subjects: Arts and humanities, education science, English, law, mathematics and computer science, communication and information science, natural sciences, social sciences.
Eligibility: Open to students applying for research degrees (MPhil, DPhil) who are assessed as liable to the overseas rate of fee. Applicants are allowed to submit an award through only one institution.
Level of Study: Postgraduate.
Purpose: To assist overseas students of outstanding merit and research potential.
Type: Scholarship.
No. of awards offered: 15.
Frequency: Annual.
Value: Part of tuition fee.
Length of Study: Up to 3 years.
Study Establishment: University of Sussex.
Country of Study: United Kingdom.
Application Procedure: Application form must be completed with academic transcripts and references.
Closing Date: Early April.

THE UNIVERSITY OF SYDNEY

The Research and Scholarships Office
Main Quadrangle A14, Sydney, NSW, 2006, Australia
Tel: (61) 2 9351 3250
Fax: (61) 2 9351 3256
Email: scholars@reschols.usyd.edu.au
www: http://www.usyd.edu.au/rescols/welcome.html
Contact: Grants Management Officer

Australian Postgraduate Award (APA)

Subjects: All subjects.
Eligibility: Open to Australian citizens & permanent residents (resident in Australia continuously for 12 months prior to the closing date of each year).
Level of Study: Doctorate, Postgraduate.
Purpose: To enable candidates with exceptional research potential to undertake a higher degree.
Type: Scholarship.
No. of awards offered: Varies from year to year (147 in 1999).
Frequency: Annual.
Value: Stipend is A$16,135 (in 1999).
Length of Study: 2 year for Masters by research candidate; 3 years with possible 6 month extension for PhD candidate.
Study Establishment: University of Sydney.

Country of Study: Australia.
Application Procedure: Forms are available from the Scholarships Office between August and October. Can be downloaded from website or emailed on request.
Closing Date: October 31st.

University of Sydney International Postgraduate Research Scholarships (IPRS) and International Graduate Awards (IPA)

Subjects: All subjects.
Eligibility: Open to suitably qualified graduates from any country eligible to commence a higher degree by research. Australia and New Zealand citizens and Australian permanent residents are not eligible to apply.
Level of Study: Doctorate, Postgraduate.
Purpose: To fund study.
Type: Scholarship.
No. of awards offered: Varies from year to year.
Frequency: Annual.
Value: IPRS - tuition fees; IPA A$16,135 in 1999.
Study Establishment: University of Sydney.
Country of Study: Australia.
Application Procedure: Application forms are available between May and August from the International Office.
Closing Date: August 31st.

For further information contact:

International Office
Margaret Telfer Building K07, Sydney, NSW, 2006, Australia
Tel: (61) 2 9351 4161
Fax: (61) 2 9351 4013
Contact: Grants Management Officer

University of Sydney Postgraduate Award (UPA)

Subjects: All subjects.
Eligibility: Open to Australian citizens and permanent residents, and New Zealand citizens.
Level of Study: Doctorate, Postgraduate.
Purpose: To enable candidates with exceptional research potential to undertake a higher degree.
Type: Scholarship.
No. of awards offered: Varies from year to year (40 in 1999).
Frequency: Annual.
Value: A$16,135 per year (in 1999).
Length of Study: 2 years for Masters by research candidate; 3 years with possible 6 month extension for PhD candidate.
Study Establishment: University of Sydney.
Country of Study: Australia.
Application Procedure: Forms are available from the Scholarships Office between August and October. Can be downloaded from website or emailed on request.
Closing Date: October 31st.

UNIVERSITY OF TASMANIA

GPO Box 252-45, Hobart, TAS, 7001, Australia
Tel: (61) 2 6226 2766
Fax: (61) 2 6226 7497
www: http://www.research.utas.edu.au
Contact: Office for Research

Merle Weaver Postgraduate Scholarship

Subjects: All subjects.
Eligibility: Open to women graduates from South East Asia and the Pacific region.
Level of Study: Postgraduate.
Purpose: To fund research leading to a higher degree.
Type: Scholarship.
No. of awards offered: 1.
Frequency: Dependent on funds available.
Value: A$16,135 per year.
Length of Study: Up to 3 years.
Study Establishment: University of Tasmania.
Country of Study: Australia.
Application Procedure: Please write for details.
Closing Date: October 31st.

UNIVERSITY OF THE WITWATERSRAND

Private Bag 3, Wits, 2050, South Africa
Tel: (27) 11 716 1111
Fax: (27) 11 339 4387
www: http://www.wits.ac.za
Contact: Mr Haydn Johnson

Carnovski Postgraduate Scholarship

Subjects: African studies, African languages, social anthropology and African government, African literature.
Eligibility: Open to distinguished graduates of approved universities in South Africa.
Level of Study: Postgraduate.
Purpose: To assist with full-time honours degree studies.
Type: Scholarship.
Frequency: Annual.
Value: At the discretion of the Committee.
Length of Study: 1 year of full-time study.
Study Establishment: University of the Witwatersrand.
Country of Study: South Africa.
Application Procedure: Please write for details.
Closing Date: January 10th.

E P Bradlow/John Lemmer Scholarship

Subjects: All subjects.
Eligibility: Open to candidates showing appropriate academic merit. A student who accepts a scholarship shall

be required to remain in South Africa for a period of time equal to that for which the scholarship was held after completing all the requirements for the postgraduate degree.
Level of Study: Doctorate, Postgraduate.
Purpose: To assist with full-time Master's or PhD degree study.
Type: Scholarship.
Frequency: Annual.
Value: At the discretion of the Committee.
Study Establishment: University of the Witwatersrand.
Country of Study: South Africa.
Application Procedure: Please write for details.
Closing Date: January 10th.

Freda Lawenski Scholarship Fund Grants

Subjects: All fields of study offered at the University.
Eligibility: Open to distinguished graduates of approved universities in South Africa.
Level of Study: Postgraduate.
Purpose: To assist with full-time postgraduate studies.
Type: Scholarship.
Frequency: Annual.
Value: At the discretion of the Committee.
Length of Study: 1 year of full-time study.
Study Establishment: University of the Witwatersrand.
Country of Study: South Africa.
Application Procedure: Please write for details.
Closing Date: January 10th.

Henry Bradlow Scholarship

Subjects: Not restricted.
Eligibility: Open to distinguished graduates of approved universities in South Africa.
Level of Study: Postgraduate.
Purpose: To assist in postgraduate study towards a full-time Master's or PhD degree.
Type: Scholarship.
Frequency: Annual.
Value: At the discretion of the Committee.
Length of Study: 1 year of full-time study.
Study Establishment: University of the Witwatersrand.
Country of Study: South Africa.
Application Procedure: Please write for details.
Closing Date: January 10th.

Herbert Ainsworth Scholarship

Subjects: Modern history.
Eligibility: Open to distinguished graduates of approved universities in South Africa.
Level of Study: Postgraduate.
Purpose: To assist with study towards an honours degree.
Type: Scholarship.
Frequency: Annual.
Value: At the discretion of the Committee.
Length of Study: 1 year of full-time study.
Study Establishment: University of the Witwatersrand.
Country of Study: South Africa.

Application Procedure: Please write for details.
Closing Date: January 10th.

Raikes Scholarships

Subjects: Faculties of arts or sciences.
Eligibility: Open to distinguished graduates of approved universities in South Africa.
Level of Study: Postgraduate.
Purpose: To assist with full-time study towards an honours degree.
Type: Scholarship.
Frequency: Annual.
Value: At the discretion of the Committee.
Length of Study: 1 year of full-time study.
Study Establishment: University of the Witwatersrand.
Country of Study: South Africa.
Application Procedure: Please write for details.
Closing Date: January 10th.

UNIVERSITY OF WALES, ABERYSTWYTH

Old College
King Street, Aberystwyth, Ceredigion, SY23 2AX, Wales
Tel: (44) 1970 622 270
Fax: (44) 1970 622 921
Email: postgraduate-admissions@aber.ac.uk
www: http://www.aber.ac.uk
Contact: Dr Russell Davies, Marketing Manager

The University of Wales, Aberystwyth was established in 1872 and is situated in an area of outstanding natural beauty on the west coast of Wales, providing a rich academic and cultural environment. The postgraduate student population is about 800 and approximately thirty per cent of these are international students.

University of Wales (Aberystwyth) Postgraduate Research Studentships

Subjects: Any full-time research course (MPhil/PhD/LLM by research).
Eligibility: Open to UK/EU candidates who have obtained at least upper second class honours or equivalent in their degree examination and who wish to study full-time.
Level of Study: Doctorate, Postgraduate.
Purpose: To enable UK/EU students to undertake full-time postgraduate research at University of Wales, Aberystwyth.
Type: Studentship.
No. of awards offered: Usually 12.
Frequency: Annual.
Value: UK fees plus a subsistence allowance based on research council rates.
Length of Study: 1 year; usually renewable for up to 2 additional years, subject to satisfactory academic progress.
Study Establishment: The College.
Country of Study: United Kingdom.

Application Procedure: Completion of application form is required. Application forms are available from the Postgraduate Admissions Office.
Closing Date: March 1st.
Additional Information: For all enquiries, please contact the Postgraduate Admissions Office.

UNIVERSITY OF WALES, BANGOR

Academic Registry
College Road, Bangor, Gwynedd, LL57 2DG, Wales
Tel: (44) 1248 382025
Fax: (44) 1248 370451
Email: aos057@bangor.ac.uk
Contact: Dr John C T Perkins, Assistant Registrar

The University of Wales, Bangor is the principal seat of learning, scholarship and research in North Wales. It was established in 1884 and is a constituent institution of the Federal University of Wales. The University attaches considerable importance to research training in all disciplines and offers research studentships of a value similar to those of the research councils.

Mr and Mrs David Edward Roberts Memorial Award

Subjects: Any subject offered at University of Wales, Bangor.
Eligibility: Open to holders of relevant first or, exceptionally, upper second class honours degree, who are of any nationality classified as a home/EC student for fees purposes.
Level of Study: Doctorate, Postgraduate.
Purpose: To support doctoral studies in any subject area.
Type: Research Studentship.
No. of awards offered: 1.
Frequency: Dependent on funds available.
Value: No less than that of a Research Council or British Academy Research Studentship, including fees.
Length of Study: 1 year; renewable for a further 2 years if satisfactory progress is maintained.
Study Establishment: University of Wales, Bangor.
Country of Study: Wales.
Application Procedure: Application forms may be obtained from the Postgraduate Admissions Office at UWB.
Closing Date: June 1st.

University of Wales (Bangor) Postgraduate Studentships

Subjects: Any subject offered by the University.
Eligibility: Open to candidates classified as home/EC for fees payment purposes who have attained a first or exceptional upper second class honours degree (or equivalent).
Level of Study: Doctorate, Postgraduate.
Purpose: To fund research training to PhD level.
Type: Research Studentship.
No. of awards offered: 12-15.

Frequency: Annual.
Value: Equal to that of a British public-funded Research Studentship.
Length of Study: 1 year; renewable for up to 2 additional years.
Study Establishment: University of Wales, Bangor.
Country of Study: Wales.
Application Procedure: Expressions of interest should be made to the relevant department of proposed study. The department will nominate the most worthy eligible students.
Closing Date: June 1st.

University of Wales Bangor (UWB) Research Studentships

Subjects: All subjects covered within UWB.
Eligibility: Recent graduates classified at the lower (EU) rate, or for payment purposes hold a first or upper second class honours degree (or equivalent) in a relevant subject.
Level of Study: Postgraduate.
Purpose: To support students for the duration of a PhD programme.
Type: Studentship.
No. of awards offered: 10-14.
Frequency: Annual, if funds are available.
Value: Same basic value as a research council studentship.
Length of Study: 3 years.
Study Establishment: University of Wales, Bangor.
Country of Study: United Kingdom.
Application Procedure: An initial approach should be made to the Senior Postgraduate Tutor in the department of the proposed research programme. (See Postgraduate Prospectus).
Closing Date: 30th June. Those interested should make enquiries well before this date.
Additional Information: In exceptional circumstances and award may be made to an international student classified for the full cost fee. In such a case, the student would be required to pay the difference between the full cost fee and the home/EU fee.

UNIVERSITY OF WALES, CARDIFF

Postgraduate Registry
University of Wales College of Cardiff
PO Box 495, Cardiff, CF1 3XD, Wales
Tel: (44) 1222 874413
Fax: (44) 1222 874130
Contact: Senior Assistant Registrar

Cardiff University is one of Britain's major centres of higher education; its origins date back to 1883. The University currently has some 14,500 students of whom more than 3,000 are postgraduates. Cardiff is a research-led university, ranked 15th out of 102 UK universities for research activity, with 23 subject areas recognised as undertaking research of national and international excellence.

Cardiff University Postgraduate Research Studentships

Subjects: All subjects offered by the University.
Eligibility: Candidates must possess at least an upper second class honours degree from an approved university. For purposes of fee payment, applicants must be a home student ordinarily resident in the UK (or the European Community provided he or she is an EC national) throughout the period of three years immediately preceding the date on which the course of study is due to begin. Heads of department at the University select recipients from among the applicants for admission.
Level of Study: Postgraduate.
Purpose: To enable nominated students to pursue doctoral research to PhD level.
Type: Studentship.
No. of awards offered: 10.
Frequency: Annual.
Value: £2,610 (fees), plus up to £6,455 maintenance allowance.
Length of Study: 1 year; renewable annually to a maximum of 3 years.
Study Establishment: The University.
Country of Study: United Kingdom.
Application Procedure: Please write for details.
Closing Date: June 30th.

UNIVERSITY OF WESTERN AUSTRALIA

Nedlands, Perth, WA, 6009, Australia
Tel: (61) 9 380 2490
Fax: (61) 9 380 1919
www: http://www.uwa.edu.au
Contact: Ms Margaret Edwards, Senior Administrative Officer

University of Western Australia Postdoctoral Research Fellowship

Subjects: All areas covered by UWA departments. Please see UWA WWW home page for details.
Eligibility: Open to all nationalities. Applicants should hold a PhD for all appointments. The appointment of an overseas Fellow is subject to Australian Department of Immigration and Ethnic Affairs' approval of UWA's sponsorship for residence, and the Fellow's successful application for appropriate visa.
Level of Study: Postdoctorate.
Purpose: To provide a two-year appointment to a postdoctoral Research Fellow bringing special new expertise and a high level of relevant experience which is not otherwise available at the UWA department, to carry out a research project in a UWA department.
Type: Fellowship.
No. of awards offered: 3.
Frequency: Annual.

Value: A$37,345-A$40,087 per year salary plus A$3,500-A$5,000 per year fellowship support grant. A relocation allowance is also included.
Length of Study: 2 years.
Study Establishment: UWA.
Country of Study: Australia.
Application Procedure: Applications are accepted from UWA departments only.
Closing Date: Usually March 1st.

University of Western Australia Postgraduate Awards

Subjects: Any subject offered by the University.
Eligibility: Open to Australian citizens who are graduates with at least an upper second class honours degree, or a small number of overseas graduates who possess a first class honours or equivalent.
Level of Study: Postgraduate.
Purpose: To enable students to conduct research leading to a Master's or doctoral degree.
Type: Studentship.
No. of awards offered: Varies.
Frequency: Annual.
Value: A$15,100 per year (tax free); plus travel costs; relocation allowance within Australia of up to A$1,270; thesis allowance of A$400 (Master's) or A$800 (doctoral).
Length of Study: 1 year; renewable for 1 year (Master's) or for 2 years (doctoral).
Study Establishment: The University.
Country of Study: Australia.
Application Procedure: Please write for details.
Closing Date: August 31st for overseas applicants, October 31st for Australian applicants.
Additional Information: Scholarships may not be held concurrently with other awards of a similar nature. Employment is permitted to a maximum of 240 hours in a calendar year and no more than 8 hours in any one week.

UNIVERSITY OF WESTERN SYDNEY

Nepean Research Office
PO Box 10, Kingswood, NSW, 2747, Australia
Tel: (61) 2 4736 0052
Fax: (61) 2 4736 0013
Email: h.holmes@nepean.uws.edu.au
www: http://www.uws.edu.au
Contact: Ms Helen Holmes, Research Scholarships Officer

Nepean Postgraduate Research Award

Subjects: All subjects offered at the university.
Eligibility: Applicants must hold or be eligible for the award of B(Hons) Degree Class 1, from an Australian university, or an equivalent award.

Level of Study: Doctorate.
Purpose: To support students of high academic merit in undertaking postgraduate research degrees at UWS Nepean.
Type: Scholarship.
No. of awards offered: 10.
Frequency: Annual.
Value: A$16,135 stipend plus allowances.
Length of Study: 2 years for the Master's and 3 years for the doctorate.
Study Establishment: University of Western Sydney, Nepean.
Country of Study: Australia.
Application Procedure: Please submit application form, certified copies of all academic records and two academic referee reports (submitted by referees).
Closing Date: October 31st.

UNIVERSITY OF WOLLONGONG

Northfields Avenue, Wollongong, NSW, 2522, Australia
Tel: (61) 2 4221 3555
Contact: Ms Sharon Hughes

Wollongong sits between the dramatic Illawarra escarpment and the Pacific Ocean just one hour away from Sydney, Australia's largest city. The University of Wollongong enjoys a significant international research profile attracting more Australian Research Council funding per student in 1999 than any other Australian university. Over 3,000 postgraduate students are enrolled (30% overseas).

University of Wollongong Postgraduate Awards

Subjects: Any postgraduate research subject offered by the University.
Eligibility: Open to graduates with at least a second class honours degree.
Level of Study: Postgraduate.
Purpose: To provide financial support for full-time study leading to a Master's or PhD degree.
No. of awards offered: Varies.
Frequency: Annual.
Value: A$16,135.
Length of Study: 2 years for the Master's or 3 years for the PhD; renewable subject to satisfactory progress.
Study Establishment: University of Wollongong.
Country of Study: Australia.
Application Procedure: Application forms are available from the Office of Research in July/August each year.
Closing Date: October 31st.
Additional Information: Holders of the Award must pursue studies on a full-time basis and submit an annual report.

UNIVERSITY OF YORK

Graduate Schools Office
Heslington, York, YO1 5DD, England
Tel: (44) 1904 432 143
Fax: (44) 1904 432 092
Email: graduate@york.ac.uk
www: http://www.york.ac.uk/admin/gso/gsp/
Contact: Mr Philip Simison

The University of York offers postgraduate degree courses in archaeology, architectural and conservation studies, art history, biology, biochemistry, chemistry, computer science, economics, educational studies, electronics, english, environment, health sciences, health studies, history, language and linguistics, mathematics, medieval studies, music, philosophy, physics, politics, psychology, social policy, social work, sociology, and women's studies.

University of York Master's Scholarships

Subjects: All subjects.
Eligibility: Open to full-time candidates for Master's degrees (MA/MSc/MRes).
Level of Study: Postgraduate.
Purpose: To assist candidates of high academic standards to complete Master's degrees.
Type: Scholarship.
No. of awards offered: Approx. 10.
Frequency: Annual.
Value: Fee-waiver of up to £2,000.
Length of Study: 1 year.
Study Establishment: University of York.
Country of Study: England.
Application Procedure: Application forms are available from the Graduate Schools Office.
Closing Date: May 29th.

University of York Research Studentships/Scholarships

Subjects: All subjects.
Eligibility: Open to full-time candidates for research degrees (MPhil/DPhil).
Level of Study: Doctorate, Postgraduate.
Purpose: To assist candidates of a high academic standard to complete research degrees.
Type: Scholarship.
No. of awards offered: Approx. 24.
Frequency: Annual.
Value: Fees (at home/EU rate) plus up to £6,200.
Length of Study: Up to 3 years.
Study Establishment: University of York.
Country of Study: England.
Application Procedure: Application forms are available from Graduate Schools Office.
Closing Date: May 29th.

University of York Scholarships for Overseas Students

Subjects: Any full-time degree (graduate or undergraduate), diploma or certificate of the University.
Eligibility: Open to students who have been accepted for registration as a full-time student for a degree, diploma or certificate course of the University of York and are liable to pay tuition fees at the full-cost rate for overseas (non-EC) students.
Level of Study: Postgraduate, Undergraduate.
Purpose: To assist overseas candidates of high academic standard.
Type: Scholarship.
No. of awards offered: Approx. 30.
Frequency: Annual.
Value: One-third or one-sixth of the value of tuition fees.
Length of Study: Up to 3 years.
Study Establishment: University of York.
Country of Study: United Kingdom.
Application Procedure: Application form available for completion, contact the International office.
Closing Date: May 1st.

US ARMY CENTER OF MILITARY HISTORY

Building 35
103 3rd Avenue
Fort McNair, Washington, DC, 20319-5058, United States of America
Tel: (1) 202 685 2278
Fax: (1) 202 685 2077
Email: birtlaj@hqda.army.mil
www: http://www.army.mil/cmh-pg
Contact: Mr Andrew J Birtle

The US Army Center of Military History is the historical agency for the US Army.

US Army Center of Military History Dissertation Fellowships

Subjects: For the purposes of this program, the history of war on land is broadly defined, including such areas as biography, military campaigns, military organisation and administration, policy, strategy, tactics, weaponry, technology, training, logistics, and evolution of civil military relations.
Eligibility: Open to civilian graduate students of the USA who have completed by September all requirements for the PhD degree except the dissertation.
Level of Study: Doctorate.
Purpose: To support scholarly research and writing among qualified civilian graduate students preparing dissertations in the history of war on land, especially the history of the US Army.
Type: Fellowship.
No. of awards offered: 2.
Frequency: Annual.

Value: US$9,000 stipend, plus access to the Center's facilities and technical expertise.
Country of Study: Any country.
Application Procedure: Each applicant must submit a completed application form, a proposed plan of research, a statement of approval from the academic director of the dissertation, two other letters of recommendation, an official graduate transcript, and a writing sample 10-25 pages.
Closing Date: January 15th.
Additional Information: Fellows visit the Center at the beginning and end of the Fellowship period. On the first visit, the Fellow meets key individuals at the Center and is consulted on ways CMH can help him/her. On the second visit, the Fellow presents an oral report on his/her progress. A brief written report and a copy of the completed dissertation are also required. Candidates who have previously held or accepted an equivalent Fellowship from any other US Department of Defense agency are not eligible.

US DEPARTMENT OF EDUCATION

International and Graduate Programs
600 Independence Avenue SW, Washington, DC, 20202-5331, United States of America
Tel: (1) 202 401 9784
Fax: (1) 202 205 9489
Email: jose_martinez@ed.gov
www: http://www.ed.gov
Contact: Mr Jose L Martinez, Program Officer

US Department of Education International Research and Studies Program

Subjects: Arts and humanities, modern languages and literatures.
Eligibility: Open to US citizens or legal residents.
Level of Study: Postdoctorate, Independent Research.
Purpose: To conduct research and develop instructional materials in foreign languages, area and international studies; including studies and surveys to assess the use of graduates of programs supported under Title VI of the Higher Education Act, as amended.
Type: Grant.
No. of awards offered: 13-15.
Frequency: Dependent on funds available.
Country of Study: Any country.
Application Procedure: Application forms may be requested in August by writing to Jose L. Martinez at the address shown.
Closing Date: Late October or early November.
Additional Information: Funds awarded by this programme may not be used for the training of teachers or students.

US NAVAL HISTORICAL CENTER

901 M Street SE
Bldg 57 Wny, Washington, DC, 20374-5060, United States of America
Tel: (1) 202 433 3940
Fax: (1) 202 685 0132
Email: emarolda@nhc.navy.mil
www: http://www.history.navy.mil
Contact: Mr Edward J Marolda, Senior Historian

Rear Admiral John D Hayes Pre-Doctoral Fellowship in US Naval History

Subjects: US naval history.
Eligibility: Applicants must be US citizens, enrolled in a recognised graduate school, who have completed requirements for the PhD except the dissertation, and have an approved topic in the field of US naval history.
Level of Study: Doctorate.
Purpose: To assist scholars in research/writing of doctoral dissertations relating to US naval history.
Type: Fellowship.
No. of awards offered: 1.
Frequency: Annual.
Value: US$8,000.
Country of Study: USA.
Application Procedure: A completed and signed application with supporting data attached, including a copy of approved dissertation outline, must be submitted.
Closing Date: February 28th.

Vice Admiral Edwin B Hooper Research Grants

Subjects: US naval history.
Eligibility: Applicants must be US citizens and must hold a PhD from an accredited university, or equivalent attainment as a published author.
Level of Study: Postdoctorate.
Purpose: To assist scholars in research/writing of books or articles relating to US naval history.
Type: Research Grant.
No. of awards offered: 2.
Frequency: Annual.
Value: US$2,500.
Country of Study: USA.
Application Procedure: Applicants should send a letter stating the purpose and scope of the research project, including a proposed budget, and a completed application. In addition, two letters of recommendation from individuals familiar with the applicant's field of study will be required.
Closing Date: February 28th.

THE US-UK FULBRIGHT COMMISSION

Fulbright House
62 Doughty Street, London, WC1N 2LS, England
Tel: (44) 171 404 6880
Fax: (44) 171 404 6834
Email: education@fulbright.co.uk
www: http://www.fulbright.co.uk
Contact: Ms E Davey, Programme Director

The US-UK Fulbright Commission has a programme of awards offered annually to citizens of the UK and USA. The Commission's Educational Advisory Service deals with enquiries from the public on all aspects of US education.

Fulbright Calvin Klein Harvey Nichols Award in Fashion Design

Subjects: Fashion design.
Eligibility: Open to citizens normally resident in the UK. Applicants must hold the minimum of an upper second class honours degree, have at least 2-3 years' work experience, and be able to demonstrate leadership qualities.
Level of Study: Graduate.
Purpose: To enable a graduate student to further knowledge of their subject in the trans-atlantic country.
Type: Scholarship.
No. of awards offered: 1.
Frequency: Offered altenate years to British and American citizens.
Value: $4,000.
Length of Study: Minimum 3 months.
Study Establishment: Approved fashion school of the candidates own choice.
Country of Study: UK and USA.
Application Procedure: Application form and interview.
Closing Date: Usually November for British candidates and October for US candidates.
Additional Information: See the Commission's website for details.

Fulbright Graduate Student Awards

Subjects: All subjects. Some special funding exists for MBA or related studies. Other special funding available for software or electronic engineering, bioscience, teaching of English as a second language.
Eligibility: Open to US citizens, normally resident in the USA. Minimum GPA: 3.5; must demonstrate evidence of leadership qualities.
Level of Study: Postgraduate.
Purpose: To enable US students to follow postgraduate study or research in the UK.
No. of awards offered: Approx. 20.
Frequency: Annual.
Value: Maintenance allowance, approved tuition fees and round-trip travel are covered.
Length of Study: A minimum of 9 months.

Study Establishment: Any approved UK institution of higher education.
Country of Study: United Kingdom.
Application Procedure: Formal application is required, with four references and a telephone interview for shortlisted candidates.
Closing Date: October - to be confirmed.

For further information contact:

Institute of International Education
809 United Nations Plaza, New York, NY, 10017, United States of America
Tel: (1) 212 984 5466
Fax: (1) 212 984 5465
Contact: Student Program Division

Fulbright Scholar Grants

Subjects: Any subject, with particular interest in topics which address problems shared by the USA and UK.
Eligibility: Open to US scholars who took their first degree more than five years ago.
Level of Study: Postdoctorate.
Purpose: To enable US scholars to carry out lecturing and research in the UK.
No. of awards offered: 4 Distinguished Scholars.
Frequency: Annual.
Value: Distinguished Scholar: £15,000 (round trip travel inclusive).
Length of Study: 1 full academic year.
Study Establishment: Any approved UK institution of higher education.
Country of Study: United Kingdom.
Application Procedure: Application and four references should be submitted to the CIES.
Closing Date: August 1st.

For further information contact:

Council for International Exchange of Scholars
3007 Tilden Street NW
Suite 5M, Washington, DC, 20008-3009, United States of America
Tel: (1) 202 686 6245
Contact: Grants Management Officer

Fulbright-Robertson Visiting Professorship in British History

Subjects: British history.
Eligibility: Open to scholars of British History, with 1-2 years' experience of teaching undergraduates.
Level of Study: Professional development.
Purpose: To enable a British scholar to spend ten months at Westminster College, Fulton, Missouri, lecturing in British History.
Type: Professorship.
No. of awards offered: 1.
Frequency: Annual.
Value: Up to US$40,000 plus round-trip travel for grantee and up to four accompanying dependants.

Length of Study: 10 months.
Study Establishment: Westminster College, Fulton, Missouri.
Country of Study: USA.
Application Procedure: Please submit formal application and two references.
Closing Date: Usually December - to be confirmed.
Additional Information: Shortlisted candidates will be interviewed (usually March).

US-UK Fulbright Commission Postdoctoral Research Scholarship at De Montfort University

Subjects: All subjects offered by the University.
Eligibility: Open to US nationals only.
Level of Study: Postdoctorate.
Purpose: To enable a scholar to undertake postdoctoral research at De Montfort University, Leicester.
Type: Scholarship.
No. of awards offered: 1.
Frequency: Annual.
Value: £5,000 plus round-trip travel.
Length of Study: 12 months.
Study Establishment: De Montfort University.
Country of Study: United Kingdom.
Application Procedure: Application forms are available from: CIES, 3007 Tilden Street NW, Suite 5M, Washington, DC 2008-3009.
Closing Date: August 1st.

US-UK Fulbright Commission Postgraduate Student Awards

Subjects: All subjects.
Eligibility: Applicants must: be UK citizens normally resident in the UK; hold, prior to departure, a minimum of an upper second class honours degree; and demonstrate outstanding leadership qualities.
Level of Study: Postgraduate.
Purpose: To enable students to carry out postgraduate study or research in the USA.
No. of awards offered: 10-12.
Frequency: Annual.
Value: Tuition and maintenance for nine months and round-trip travel.
Length of Study: A minimum of 9 months.
Study Establishment: An approved US institution of higher education.
Country of Study: USA.
Application Procedure: Please submit a formal application with two references.
Closing Date: Usually early November - to be confirmed.
Additional Information: Shortlisted candidates will be interviewed.

US-UK Fulbright Commission Scholarship Grants

Subjects: All subjects - although subjects where there is an opportunity for collaborative innovation of international significance or a focus on Anglo-American relations are preferred.

Eligibility: Candidates must demonstrate academic or artistic excellence.
Level of Study: Postdoctorate, Professional development.
Purpose: To enable lecturers, junior and senior postdoctoral research scholars, to lecture or carry out research in the USA for a minimum of three months.
Type: Scholarship.
No. of awards offered: 3.
Frequency: Annual.
Value: £15,000; proof of additional dollar support is required.
Length of Study: 10 moths minimum.
Study Establishment: An approved US institution of higher education or similar.
Country of Study: USA.
Application Procedure: Please submit a formal application and two references.
Closing Date: March/April - exact date to be confirmed.
Additional Information: Shortlisted candidates will be interviewed (usually in April/May).

USIA FULBRIGHT PROGRAMMES

Institute of International Education
809 United Nations Plaza, New York, NY, 10017-3580, United States of America
Tel: (1) 212 984 5330
www: http://www.usia.gov
Contact: US Student Programs

USIA Fulbright Study and Research Grants for US Citizens

Subjects: Study and research in all fields, as well as professional training in the creative and performing arts.
Eligibility: Open to US citizens who have a Bachelor's degree or equivalent qualification. Candidates must have a high scholastic record, have an acceptable plan of study, demonstrate proficiency in the language of the host country, and be in good health. In some cases special language training is provided as part of a grant. Preference is given to persons who have not had prior experience of, or opportunity for, extended foreign study, residence or travel.
Level of Study: Postgraduate.
Purpose: To increase mutual understanding between the people of the USA and the people of other countries by means of educational and cultural exchange.
No. of awards offered: Varies.
Frequency: Annual.
Value: Full grants cover international transportation, language or orientation course (where appropriate), tuition, book, and maintenance allowances, and health and accident insurance. Travel grants will consist of travel expenses supplementing students personal funds or maintenance allowances and tuition scholarships which are granted to students by universities and other organisations.

Length of Study: 1 academic year.
Study Establishment: Institutions of higher learning.
Country of Study: Outside USA. A list of participating countries in a given year may be obtained from the Institute of International Education.
Application Procedure: Applicants enrolled in a college or university should apply to the Fulbright Programme Adviser on their campus. Applicants not enrolled in a college or university should apply to the Institute of International Education. Applications should be requested at least 15 days prior to the closing date.
Closing Date: October 23rd.

VERNE CATT MCDOWELL CORPORATION

PO Box 1336, Albany, OR, 97321-0440, United States of America
Tel: (1) 541 926 6829
Contact: Ms Emily Killin, Business Manager

The Verne Catt McDowell Scholarship only educates pastoral ministers of the Christian Church by providing supplementary financial grants to graduate theology students only. All scholarship candidates must be ministers who are ordained or who are studying to meet the requirements to be ordained as a minister in the Christian Church.

Verne Catt McDowell Scholarship

Subjects: Religion and theology; church administration.
Eligibility: All scholarship candidates must be ministers ordained or studying to meet the requirements to be ordained as a minister in the Christian Church (Disciples of Christ). Candidates must be a member of the Christian Church (Disciples of Christ) denomination. Preference given to Oregon graduates.
Level of Study: Postgraduate.
Purpose: To provide supplemental financial grants to men and women for graduate theological education for ministry in the Christian Church Denomination.
Type: Scholarship.
No. of awards offered: 4.
Frequency: Annual, if funds are available.
Value: US$400 per school month.
Study Establishment: A graduate institution of theological education, accredited by the general assembly of the Christian Church (Disciples of Christ).
Country of Study: USA.
Application Procedure: Candidates are required to complete an application form and provide details of qualifications, transcripts, three references and state where they obtained information about the scholarship. An interview will be requested.
Closing Date: May.

VICTORIA UNIVERSITY

Emmanuel College
75 Queen's Park Crescent East, Toronto, ON, M5S 1K7,
Canada
Tel: (1) 416 585 4539
Fax: (1) 416 585 4516
Email: ec.office@utoronto.ca
www: http://www.vicu.utoronto.ca/index.htm
Contact: Director for Advanced Degree Studies

Emmanuel College, set within Victoria University and the University of Toronto, is the United Church of Canada's largest theological college. The College offers four basic or first professional degrees and five advanced or graduate degrees. About 210 students are currently enrolled. Emmanuel College is one of seven member schools of the Toronto School of Theology.

Bloor Lands Entrance Scholarship

Subjects: Religion and theology.
Level of Study: Doctorate.
Purpose: To assit newly admitted ThD or PhD students with potential for excellence in scholarship demonstrated by high achievement in previous theological studies.
Type: Scholarship.
No. of awards offered: 1.
Frequency: Annual.
Value: C$9,000 for a two year period.
Length of Study: 2 years.
Study Establishment: Emmanuel College.
Country of Study: Canada.
Application Procedure: Admission to the Toronto School of Theology/Emmanuel College must first be granted. Application is then made c/o the Director of Advanced Degree Studies.
Closing Date: March 31st.

Graduate Student Assistantships

Subjects: Religion and theology. Graduate students are assigned to work with the Asian Centre and in the fields of christian education, church and society, ethics, field education, history of christianity, homiletics, new testament, old testament, pastoral theology, systematic theology, worship.
Level of Study: Doctorate.
Purpose: To provide funding for doctoral students.
Type: Scholarship.
No. of awards offered: 13.
Frequency: Annual.
Value: C$8,000 per year.
Length of Study: 2 years.
Study Establishment: Emmanuel College.
Country of Study: Canada.

Application Procedure: Admission to the Toronto School of Theology/Emmanuel College must first be granted. Application is then made c/o the Director of Advance Degree Studies.
Closing Date: February 28th.

Vernon Hope Emory Entrance Scholarship

Subjects: Religion and theology.
Level of Study: Doctorate.
Purpose: To support an outstanding newly admitted ThD or PhD student with preference given to United Church members who have undertaken their previous theological studies at institutions other than Emmanuel College.
Type: Scholarship.
No. of awards offered: 1.
Frequency: Annual.
Value: C$9,000 for a 2 year period.
Length of Study: 2 years.
Study Establishment: Emmanuel College.
Country of Study: Canada.
Application Procedure: Admission to the Toronto School of Theology/Emmanuel College must be first granted. Application is then made c/o the Director of Advanced Degree Studies.
Closing Date: March 31st.

VIRGINIA CENTER FOR THE CREATIVE ARTS

PO Box VCCA, Sweet Briar, VA, 24595, United States of
America
Tel: (1) 804 946 7236
Fax: (1) 804 946 7239
Email: vcca@vcca.com
www: http://www.vcca.com
Contact: Ms Suny Monk, Director

The Viginia Center for the Creative Arts is a year-round community that provides a supportive environment for superior national and international visual artists, writers, and composers, of all cultural and economic backgrounds, to pursue their creative work without distraction in a pastoral residential setting.

Virginia Center for the Creative Arts Fellowships

Subjects: Writing, musical composition, photography, art.
Eligibility: Open to artists with professional competence and promise, regardless of age, sex, citizenship or academic background. Writers, visual artists, composers, choreographers, photographers, film makers, interdisciplinary and multimedia artists are all eligible. Admission is through a jury selection process.

Level of Study: Unrestricted.

Purpose: To support literacy, musical and visual artists during the most crucial creative phase of their work.

Type: Fellowship.

No. of awards offered: Approx. 300 Fellowships in any given year.

Value: Subsidised residence at the Center. No cash stipends or travel allowances are provided.

Length of Study: 1-3 months each year; renewable.

Study Establishment: The Center.

Country of Study: USA.

Application Procedure: Application form, work samples, and letters of reference must be submitted (to one of three deadlines per year).

Closing Date: January 15th, May 15th, September 15th.

VOLZHSKY INSTITUTE OF HUMANITIES

Volgograd State University (VIH)
40 Let Pobedy Street, Volzhsky, Volgograd, 404132, Russia
Tel: (7) 8443 291778
Fax: (7) 8443 291778
Email: oboris@vgumi.vlink.ru
Contact: M M Guzev, Director

VIH is the leading scientific and cultural centre of the region on the left bank of the Volga with about 2000 students studying at three faculties. Highly qualified specialists lecture at the VIH, among them 15 doctors of sciences. VIH develops relations with universities abroad.

Volzhsky Institute of Humanities Awards

Subjects: Environmental management, management systems and techniques, applied mathematics, ecology, natural resources, statistics, criminal law, philosophy, computer science, econometrics, soil conservation, modern languages and literatures - English, French, German, Russian, comparative literature, foreign languages education, education of foreigners, higher education, teacher training, educational technology, modern history, business computing.

Eligibility: Applicants must be of at least postgraduate standard and have a sound knowledge of Russian.

Level of Study: Postgraduate, Professional development.

Purpose: To allow recipients to acquire new skills and undertake research.

No. of awards offered: 2 in each subject area.

Frequency: Dependent on funds available.

Value: Tuition fees.

Length of Study: 2-4 months.

Study Establishment: VIH.

Country of Study: Russia.

Application Procedure: Please contact the VIH for details.

Closing Date: November 30th.

W EUGENE SMITH MEMORIAL FUND, INC.

c/o International Center of Photography
1130 Fifth Avenue, New York, NY, 10128, United States of America
Tel: (1) 212 860 1777 ext 186
Fax: (1) 212 860 1482
Contact: Ms Helen Marcus, President

This Memorial Fund presents major grant to a photographer whose past work and proposed project follows in the humanistic tradition of Smith. The Funds' grant programme is financed by Nikon, Inc.

Smith (W Eugene) Grant in Humanistic Photography

Subjects: Photojournalism.

Eligibility: Open to outstanding photographers of any nationality.

Level of Study: Unrestricted.

Purpose: To support a photographer working on a project in the humanistic tradition of W Egene Smith, in order to continue to pursue the work.

Type: Grant.

No. of awards offered: 2.

Frequency: Annual.

Value: One grant for US$20,000, with a possible second grant for US$5,000.

Country of Study: Any country.

Application Procedure: For further information send a self addressed envelope to the given adddress.

Closing Date: July 15th.

THE WARBURG INSTITUTE

University of London
Woburn Square, London, WC1H 0AB, England
Tel: (44) 171 580 9663
Fax: (44) 171 436 2852
Email: warburg@sas.ac.uk
www: http://www.sas.ac.uk/warburg/
Contact: Miss A C Pollard, Secretary and Registrar

The Warburg Institute is concerned with the interdisciplinary study of the continuities between the ancient Mediterranean civilisations and the cultural and intellectual history of post-classical Europe before 1800 AD. Its collections are arranged to encourage research into the processes by which different fields of thought and art interact.

Albin Salton Fellowship

Subjects: Cultural contacts between Europe, the East and the New World in late medieval, Renaissance and early modern periods. To promote understanding of those elements of cultural and intellectual history leading to the formation of a new world view.

Eligibility: Applicants must normally be under 35 years of age on October 1st of the academic year prior to which the fellowship is taken up, and have completed at least two years' research towards a doctorate.
Level of Study: Doctorate, Postdoctorate.
Purpose: To promote research.
Type: Fellowship.
No. of awards offered: 1.
Frequency: Annual.
Value: £620-£1400.
Length of Study: 1-2 months.
Study Establishment: The Warburg Institute.
Country of Study: United Kingdom.
Application Procedure: Further information should be obtained from the Secretary and the Registrar.
Closing Date: Beginning of December.

Brian Hewson Crawford Fellowship

Subjects: The classical tradition.
Eligibility: Applicants must normally be under 35 years of age on October 1st of the academic year prior to which the fellowship is taken up, and have completed at least two years' research towards a doctorate.
Level of Study: Doctorate, Postdoctorate.
Purpose: To support research in any aspect of the classical tradition.
Type: Fellowship.
No. of awards offered: 1.
Frequency: Annual.
Value: £850-£1400.
Length of Study: 1-2 months.
Study Establishment: The Warburg Institute.
Country of Study: United Kingdom.
Application Procedure: Further information should be obtained form the Secretary and the Registrar.
Closing Date: Beginning of December.

Frances A Yates Fellowships

Subjects: Cultural and intellectual history.
Eligibility: Applicants must normally be under 35 years of age on October 1st of the academic year prior to which the Fellowship is taken up, and have completed at least two years of postgraduate study.
Level of Study: Doctorate, Postdoctorate.
Purpose: To promote research.
Type: Fellowship.
No. of awards offered: 1 long-term fellowship, 6-10 short-term fellowships.
Frequency: Annually. The long-term fellowship is not available every year.
Value: £14,000-£15,500 (long-term); £850-£2,000 (short-term).
Length of Study: 1-3 years (long-term fellowship, not normally renewable) or 1-3 months (short-term fellowships, not renewable).
Study Establishment: The Warburg Institute.
Country of Study: United Kingdom.

Application Procedure: Further information should be obtained from the Secretary and Registrar.
Closing Date: Early December.

Henri Frankfort Fellowship

Subjects: The intellectual and cultural history of the ancient Near and Middle East.
Eligibility: Open to individuals under 35 years of age on October 1st of the academic year prior to which the Fellowship is taken up, who have completed at least two years of postgraduate study.
Level of Study: Doctorate, Postdoctorate.
Purpose: To promote research.
Type: Fellowship.
No. of awards offered: 1.
Frequency: Annual.
Value: £620-£2,000.
Length of Study: 1-3 months.
Study Establishment: The Warburg Institute.
Country of Study: United Kingdom.
Application Procedure: Further information should be obtained from the Secretary and Registrar.
Closing Date: Early December.
Additional Information: This fellowship is not intended to support archaeological excavation.

Mellon Research Fellowships

Subjects: Humanities.
Eligibility: The fellowships are open to Bulgarian, Czech, Hungarian, Polish, Romanian and Slovak scholars. Candidates should not be permanently resident outside these countries. Fellows should have obtained a doctorate or have equivalent experience. The fellowships are intended for younger postdoctoral scholars. Preference will be given to those under 40 years of age.
Level of Study: Postdoctorate.
Purpose: To support Eastern European scholars in the study of the humanities.
Type: Fellowship.
Frequency: Annual.
Value: The sterling equivalent of $11,500.
Length of Study: 3 months.
Study Establishment: The Warburg Institute.
Country of Study: England.
Application Procedure: Applications should be made by letter to the Director. Applicants should include a CV, an outline of proposed research, particulars of grants received, if any, for the same subject, the names and addresses of two or three referees, and copies of published work (if possible).
Closing Date: April 5th.
Additional Information: Fellows will be expected to participate in the life of the Institute and to put their knowledge at the disposal of the Institute by presenting their work in a seminar and by advising the Library and Photographic Collection. Fellows will be required to present a brief written report at the conclusion of their appointment.

Nord/LB Warburg-Wolfenbüttel Research Fellowship

Subjects: History.
Eligibility: Applicants must normally be under 35 years of age on October 1st of the academic year prior to which the fellowship is taken up, and have completed at least two years of postgraduate study.
Level of Study: Doctorate, Postdoctorate.
Purpose: To promote research into the cultural and intellectual history of early modern Europe.
Type: Fellowship.
No. of awards offered: 1.
Frequency: Annual.
Value: £5,100 (DM14,800).
Length of Study: 2 months in the UK, 2 months in Germany.
Study Establishment: Warburg Institute/Herzog August Bibliothek Wolfenbüttel.
Country of Study: United Kingdom and Germany.
Application Procedure: Application information can be obtained from the Secretary and Registrar.
Closing Date: Early December.

WASHINGTON UNIVERSITY

Graduate School of Arts & Sciences
Campus Box 1187
1 Brookings Drive, St Louis, MO, 63130, United States of America
Tel: (1) 314 935 6821
Fax: (1) 314 935 4887
Email: c43000je@wuvmd.wustl.edu
www: http://www.artsci.wustl.edu/gsas
Contact: Ms Joyce Edwards, Graduate Student Affairs and Services Co-ordinator

Mr and Mrs Spencer T Olin Fellowships for Women

Subjects: Any graduate discipline or professional school in the University.
Eligibility: Open to female graduates of a baccalaureate institution in the USA who plan to prepare for a career in higher education or the professions. Applicants must meet the admission requirements of the graduate or professional school of Washington University. Preference will be given to those who wish to study for the highest earned degree in their chosen field, do not already hold an advanced degree, and who are not currently enrolled in a graduate or professional degree programme.
Level of Study: Doctorate, Postgraduate.
Purpose: To encourage women of exceptional promise to prepare for professional careers.
Type: Fellowship.
No. of awards offered: Approx. 6.

Frequency: Annual.
Value: Full tuition and, in some cases, a living expense stipend.
Length of Study: 1 year; renewable up to 4 years, or until completion of degree program, whichever comes first.
Study Establishment: Washington University in St Louis.
Country of Study: USA.
Application Procedure: Application form must be completed. Candidates must be interviewed on campus at the expense of the University. Applications should be addressed to Dr Nancy P Pope.
Closing Date: February 1st.
Additional Information: Candidates must also make concurrent application to the department or school of Washington University in which they plan to study.

Washington University Chancellor's Graduate Fellowship Programme for African Americans

Subjects: Any of Washington University's PhD or DSc programs in arts and sciences, business, engineering, or social work. The fellowship includes other Washington University programs providing final disciplinary training for prospective college professors.
Eligibility: Open to African-American doctoral candidates.
Level of Study: Doctorate.
Purpose: To encourage African Americans who are interested in becoming college or university professors.
Type: Fellowship.
No. of awards offered: 5-6.
Frequency: Annual.
Value: Doctoral candidates will receive full tuition plus US$16,000 stipend and allowances.
Length of Study: 5 years, subject to satisfactory academic progress.
Study Establishment: Washington University.
Country of Study: USA.
Application Procedure: Application form must be completed.
Closing Date: January 25th.

WHATCOM MUSEUM OF HISTORY AND ART

121 Prospect Street, Bellingham, WA, 98225, United States of America
Tel: (1) 360 676 6981
Fax: (1) 360 738 7409
Email: jacobs@cob.org
www: http://www.cob.org/cobweb/museum/jacobs.htm
Contact: Jacobs Research Funds Administrator

The Jacobs Research Fund is an enduring expression of a commitment to the collection and preservation of data documenting the languages, ethnography, and literature of indigenous peoples.

Jacobs Research Funds

Subjects: Grants are given for field research in language, social organisation, political organisation, religion, mythology, music, other arts, psychology, and folk science.
Eligibility: There are no eligibility restrictions.
Level of Study: Unrestricted.
Purpose: To support anthropological research (sociocultural or linguistic in content) on the indigenous peoples of Canada, mainland United States (including Alaska) and Mexico, with a focus on the Pacific Northwest.
Type: Grant.
No. of awards offered: Average of 16.
Frequency: Annual.
Value: Maximum of US$1,200.
Length of Study: 1 year.
Country of Study: Mainland USA, including Alaska, Canada and Mexico.
Application Procedure: Application form and guidelines by request via mail, phone, fax, email; or for personal viewing/printing via website address. Two letters of reference are also required.
Closing Date: February 15th.
Additional Information: Archival research is not ordinarily supported. Proposals which have as their goal only the application of anthropological knowledge, or which are for work in archaeology or biological anthropology will not be considered.

WILLIAM HONYMAN GILLESPIE SCHOLARSHIP TRUST

Messrs Tod Murray WS
66 Queen Street, Edinburgh, EH2 4NE, Scotland
Tel: (44) 131 226 4771
Fax: (44) 131 225 3676
Contact: Mr David William McLetchie, Trustee

William Honyman Gillespie Scholarships

Subjects: Theology.
Eligibility: Open to graduates in theology of any Scottish university.
Level of Study: Postgraduate.
Purpose: To allow recipient to engage full-time in an approved scheme of theological studies or research.
Type: Scholarship.
No. of awards offered: 1-2.
Frequency: Annual.
Value: £1,000 per annum.
Length of Study: 2 years.
Study Establishment: An approved university or similar institution.
Country of Study: Any country.
Application Procedure: Application guidelines are available from the Trust or the candidate's university department. Applications should be submitted through the Principal of the theological college of the Scottish university of which the applicant is a graduate.

Closing Date: May 15th.
Additional Information: The Trustees may vary the number of scholarships awarded.

THE WINGATE SCHOLARSHIPS

38 Curzon Street, London, W1Y 8EY, England
Tel: (44) 171 465 1521
Fax: (44) 171 499 2018
Email: reid@win-sch.demon.co.uk
www: http://www.win-sch.demon.co.uk
Contact: Ms Jane Reid, Administrator

Wingate Scholarships are awarded to individuals (over 24) of great potential or proven excellence who need financial support to undertake creative or original work of intellectual, scientific, artistic, social or environmental value, and to outstanding musicians for advanced training.

Wingate Scholarships

Subjects: Almost any subject, except fine arts and taught courses of any kind, including courses of drama, art or business, or courses leading to professional qualifications and electives.
Eligibility: Open to British, Commonwealth, Irish or Israeli and European Union country citizens provided that they are, and have been for at least five years, resident in the United Kingdom. Applicants must be over 24 years of age and resident in British Isles when applying. No qualifications are necessary.
Level of Study: Doctorate, Postdoctorate, Postgraduate.
Purpose: To fund creative or original work of intellectual, scientific, artistic, social or environmental value and advanced music study. Need is also taken into account.
Type: Scholarship.
No. of awards offered: Approx. 40.
Frequency: Annual.
Value: Costs of a project which may last for up to 3 years. Average of £6,500 total and the maximum in any one year is £10,000.
Length of Study: 1-3 years.
Study Establishment: Any or none.
Country of Study: Any country.
Application Procedure: Application forms available from the Administrator. Applicants must be: able to satisfy the Scholarship Committee that they need financial support to undertake the work projected; able to show why the propsed work (if it takes the form of academic research) is unlikely to attract Research Council, British Academy or major agency funding; citizens of the United Kingdom.
Closing Date: February 1st.
Additional Information: The scholarships are not intended for professional qualifications, taught courses or electives. Musicians are eligible for advanced training, but apart from that all applicants must have projects which are personal to them and involve either creative or orginal work.

WINSTON CHURCHILL MEMORIAL TRUST (AUS)

218 Northbourne Avenue, Braddon, ACT, 2612, Australia
Tel: (61) 6 2478333
www: http://sunsite.anu.edu.au/churchill_fellowships
Contact: Ms Margaret Bell, Finance Officer

The principal object of the Trust is to perpetuate and honour the memory of Sir Winston Churchill by the awarding of Memorial Fellowships known as Churchill Fellowships.

Churchill Fellowships

Subjects: All subjects.
Eligibility: Open to all Australian residents over the age of 18 years. There are no prescribed qualifications academic or otherwise for the award of most Churchill Fellowships. Merit is the primary test, whether based on past achievement or demonstrated ability for future achievements in any walk of life. Fellowships will not be awarded to enable the applicant to obtain higher academic or formal qualifications. The only criteria for the awarding of a Fellowship is that the applicant has gone as far as they can go in Australia and now needs to go overseas to obtain information not available in Australia.
Level of Study: Unrestricted.
Purpose: To enable Australians from all walks of life to undertake overseas study or an investigative project of a kind that is not fully available in Australia.
Type: Fellowship.
No. of awards offered: Approx. 100.
Frequency: Annual.
Value: Approximately A$15,000. Return economy air fare to country/countries to be visited. Living allowance plus fees if necessary.
Length of Study: 4-10 weeks (but this may be longer or shorter depending upon the project).
Country of Study: Any country.
Application Procedure: Application form must be completed. Please send a self address envelope to 'Application Forms' at the main address. Applications open on November 1st.
Closing Date: Last day of February.

WOLF FOUNDATION

56 Kidushei Ha'shoa Street
PO Box 398, Herzlia Bet, 46103, Israel
Tel: (972) 9 9557120
Fax: (972) 9 9541253
Email: wolffund@netvision.net.il
www: http://www.aquanet.co.il/wolf/
Contact: Ms Yaron Gruder, Director General

Wolf Foundation Prizes

Subjects: In science the fields are - agriculture, chemistry, mathematics, medicine and physics, and in the arts -

architecture, music, painting and sculpture.
Eligibility: There are no eligibility restrictions.
Level of Study: Postgraduate.
Purpose: To recognise the achievements of outstanding scientists and artists in the interest of mankind and friendly relations among people.
Type: Prize/honorarium.
No. of awards offered: 1 in each category.
Frequency: Arts awards are awarded every four years, whilst the Science awards are awarded annually.
Value: The prize in each field consists of a diploma and US$100,000.
Country of Study: Any country.
Application Procedure: Application forms will be sent on request.
Closing Date: August 31st.

THE WOLFSON FOUNDATION

8 Queen Anne Street, London, W1M 9LD, England
Tel: (44) 171 323 5730
Fax: (44) 171 323 3241
Contact: Executive Secretary

The aims of the Wolfson Foundation are the advancement of health, education, arts and humanities. Grants are given to act as a catalyst, to back excellence and talent and provide support for promising projects which may be underfunded, particularly for renovation and equipment. The emphasis is on science and technology, research, education, health and the arts.

Wolfson Foundation Grants

Subjects: Areas supported by the Trustees are - medicine and health care, including the prevention of disease and the care and treatment of the sick, disadvantaged and disabled; research, science, technology and education, particularly where benefits may accrue to the development of industry or commerce in the UK; arts and the humanities, including libraries, museums, galleries, theatres, academies and historic buildings.
Eligibility: Open to registered charities and to exempt charities such as universities. Eligible applications from registered charities for contributions to appeals will normally be considered only when at least 50% of that appeal has already been raised. Grants to universities for research and scholarship are normally made under the umbrella of designated competitive programmes in which vice-chancellors and principals are invited to participate from time to time. Applications from university researchers are not considered outside these programmes. Grants are not made to private individuals.
Level of Study: Postgraduate.
Type: Grant.
No. of awards offered: Varies.
Frequency: The trustees meet twice a year.

Value: The Trustees make several types of grant which are not necessarily independent of each other. Capital Projects: grants may contribute towards the cost of erecting a new building or extension, or of renovating and refurbishing existing buildings; Equipment Grants: the supply of equipment for specific purposes, and/or furnishing and fittings; Recurrent Costs: grants in this category are not normally provided unless they form part of a designated programme.

Country of Study: Any country.

Application Procedure: Before embarking on a detailed proposal, prospective applicants are encouraged to explore its eligibility by submitting in writing a brief outline of the project with one copy of the organisation's most recent audited accounts.

Closing Date: March 15th and September 15th.

THE WOLFSONIAN-FLORIDA INTERNATIONAL UNIVERSITY

1001 Washington Avenue, Miami Beach, FL, 33139, United States of America
Tel: (1) 305 535 2632
Fax: (1) 305 531 2133
Contact: Mr Joel Hoffman, Associate Director, Academic Programs

The Wolfsonian-Florida International University promotes the collection of art and design from the period 1885-1945. The University supports projects examining the aesthetics, production, use, and cultural significance of objects in its collection. Objects include rare books and periodicals, paintings, sculpture, posters, prints, drawings, and furniture.

Wolfsonian Fellowship Visiting Scholar Assoc Fellowship

Subjects: History and philosophy of art.

Eligibility: Wolfsonian Fellowships are granted on the basis of outstanding professional or academic accomplishment and are limited to those with at least a Master's degree. Doctoral candidates may apply for dissertation research related to the Wolfsonian collection.

Level of Study: Doctorate, Postdoctorate, Professional development.

Purpose: To conduct research on the Wolfsonian's collection of 70,000 objects from the period 1885-1945, including decorative arts, works on paper, books and ephemera.

Type: Fellowship.

No. of awards offered: Varies, approx. 6.

Frequency: Annual.

Value: Varies.

Length of Study: Approx. 6 weeks.

Study Establishment: The Wolfsonian - Florida International University.

Country of Study: USA.

Application Procedure: Application form must be completed and submitted with three recommendations. Contact the Programme Officer for details and application materials.

Closing Date: Applications are accepted at any time.

WOMEN'S STUDIO WORKSHOP

PO Box 489, Rosendale, NY, 12472, United States of America
Tel: (1) 914 658 9133
Fax: (1) 914 658 9031
Email: wsw@ulster.net
www: http://www.wsworkshop.org
Contact: Ms Ann Kalmbach

Women's Studio Workshop (WSW) is an artist-run workshop with facilities for printmaking, papermaking, photography, book arts and ceramics. WSW supports the creation of new work through an annual book arts grant programme and an ongoing subsidized fellowship programme. WSW offers studio-based educational programming in the above disciplines through its annual summer arts institute.

Women's Studio Workshop Artists' Book Residencies

Subjects: Art - books.

Eligibility: Open to women artists only.

Level of Study: Unrestricted.

Purpose: To enable artists to produce a limited edition of a book work at the Women's Studio Workshop.

Type: Residency.

No. of awards offered: Varies, usually between 3-5.

Frequency: Annual.

Value: A stipend of up to US$1,800, materials of up to US$450, and housing at the Women's Studio Workshop.

Length of Study: 4-6 weeks.

Study Establishment: Women's Studio Workshop.

Country of Study: USA.

Application Procedure: Applications should include a one-page description of the proposed project, the medium or media used to print the book, number of pages, page size, edition number, a structural dummy, a materials budget, a resumé, 6-10 slides and a SASE for return of materials. Applications are reviewed by past grant recipients and a WSW staff artist. Please write for an application form.

Closing Date: November 15th.

For further information contact:

UPS Federal Express Address:
722
Binnewater Lane, Kingston, NY, 12401, United States of America
or
Mail/Express Mail:
PO Box 489, Rosendale, NY, 12472, United States of America

Women's Studio Workshop Artists' Fellowships

Subjects: Intaglio, water-based silkscreen, photography, papermaking and ceramics.
Eligibility: Open to women artists only.
Level of Study: Unrestricted.
Purpose: To provide a time for artists to explore new ideas in a dynamic and co-operative community of women artists in a rural environment.
Type: Fellowship.
No. of awards offered: 10-20.
Frequency: Annual.
Value: US$200 per week, including housing.
Length of Study: 2-4 weeks between September and June.
Study Establishment: Women's Studio Workshop.
Country of Study: USA.
Application Procedure: Application form must be completed; please write for details.
Closing Date: May 15th and November 1st.

Women's Studio Workshop Internships

Subjects: Book arts, papermaking, printmaking, ceramics, photography.
Eligibility: Open to young women artists/students who are aged between 20 and 30.
Level of Study: Unrestricted.
Purpose: To provide opportunities for young artists to continue development of their work in a supportive environment while learning studio skills and responsibilities.
Type: Internship.
No. of awards offered: 9.
Frequency: Three times each year.
Length of Study: 3-5 months.
Study Establishment: Women's Studio Workshop.
Country of Study: USA.
Application Procedure: Please send resumé, 10-20 slides, three current letters of reference, letter of interest which addresses why an internship at WSW would be important, what applicants have to offer, and SASE.
Closing Date: Summer - March 15th; fall - July 1st; spring - November 1st.

Women's Studio Workshop Production Grants

Subjects: Art - books.
Eligibility: Open to all artists; there are no restrictions on eligibility.
Level of Study: Unrestricted.
Purpose: To assist artists working in their own studios with the creation and publication of a book work.
Type: Grant.
No. of awards offered: Varies.
Frequency: Annual.
Value: To cover production costs, up to US$750.
Country of Study: Any country.
Application Procedure: Applications should include a one-page description of the proposed project, the medium or media used to print the book, number of pages, page size, edition number, a structural dummy, a materials budget, a resumé, 6-10 slides and a SASE for return of materials.

Applications are reviewed by past grant recipients and a WSW staff artist. Please write for an application form.
Closing Date: November 15th.

THE WOODROW WILSON NATIONAL FELLOWSHIP FOUNDATION

CN 5281, Princeton, NJ, 08543-5281, United States of America
Tel: (1) 609 542 7007
Fax: (1) 609 542 0066
Email: charlotte@wwnff.org
www: http://www.woodrow.org
Contact: Ms Judith L Pinch

The Andrew W Mellon Fellowships in Humanistic Studies

Subjects: Humanistic studies.
Eligibility: Open to college senior or recent graduate US citizens or permanent residents entering into a programme leading to a PhD in the humanities. Must not be enrolled in graduate or professional study, or hold the MA degree.
Level of Study: Doctorate.
Purpose: To attract exceptionally promising students to prepare for careers of teaching and scholarship in humanistic studies by providing top level, competitive, portable awards, and to contribute to the continuity of teaching and research of the highest order in America's colleges and universities.
Type: Fellowship.
No. of awards offered: 80.
Frequency: Annual.
Value: US$14,000 plus tuition and mandated fees.
Length of Study: 1 year.
Country of Study: USA or Canada.
Application Procedure: The following must be provided by mail, phone, fax, or email: full name, current address and telephone and physical address in March 1998; details of undergraduate institution, major and year of graduation; intended discipline in graduate school; details of mailing address, US mail, or email.
Closing Date: Early December.

Charlotte W Newcombe Doctoral Dissertation Fellowships

Subjects: Topics of religious or ethical values in all fields.
Eligibility: Open to students enrolled in doctoral programmes in the humanities and social sciences at an American university. Students must have completed all pre-dissertation requirements by November 30th.
Level of Study: Doctorate.
Purpose: To encourage new and significant research.
Type: Fellowship.
No. of awards offered: 30-35.
Frequency: Annual.

Value: US$14,000.
Study Establishment: At any appropriate graduate school in the USA.
Country of Study: USA.
Closing Date: Early December.

WORLD UNIVERSITY SERVICE (WUS)

14 Dufferin Street, London, EC1Y 8PD, England
Tel: (44) 171 426 5800
Fax: (44) 171 251 1314
Contact: The Small Grants Programme

WUS Adaption Grants

Subjects: Subjects leading to professional requalification.
Eligibility: Open to refugees, including asylum seekers who wish to requalify in the UK.
Level of Study: Unrestricted.
Purpose: To assist refugees, including people with exceptional leave to remain and asylum seekers. WUS also offers an educational advisory service.
No. of awards offered: Varies.
Frequency: Dependent on funds available.
Value: A one-off payment not normally exceeding £500. Cheques will normally be made out in the name of the educational institution.
Country of Study: United Kingdom.
Application Procedure: Prospective applicants should visit WUS offices on Tuesdays and Thursdays between 10.00am-12.30pm.

WORLD WITHOUT WAR COUNCIL, INC.

Fellows Program Coordinator
1730 Martin Luther King Jr Way, Berkeley, CA, 94709-2140, United States of America
Tel: (1) 510 845 1992
Fax: (1) 510 845 5721
Email: pic@wwwc.org
www: http://www.wwwc.org
Contact: Mr Robert Pickus, President

The Council's aim is to make America a leader in progress towards a world that resolves political conflict wthout war, in ways which contribute to the well-being of our own, by building a wiser, richer, more effective and better linked independent sector at work for peace and freedom, and by advancing a perspective and policy proposals essential to progress towards a world without war.

Americans and World Affairs Fellows Program

Subjects: International law, human rights, religious studies, economics, political science and government, international relations, history of societies, development studies and area/cultural studies, American history and civic education.
Eligibility: Fellows are generally expected to have completed academic work for an MA or its equivalent. Individuals with a BA and demonstrated commitment to the goals and values of the programme will also be considered. Most fellowships require US citizenship.
Level of Study: Postgraduate, Professional development.
Purpose: To give participants a better understanding of the role non-governmental organisations play in shaping our engagements with the world, and of the competing perspectives in the field.
Type: Fellowship.
No. of awards offered: 2, but WWWC places 10 with other organisations. All require full-time work with one of our co-operating organisations.
Frequency: Annual.
Value: Fellows who work full-time may receive stipends ranging from US$3,600 to US$12,000 a year. Payments depend on the financial resources of the organization to which the fellow applies. Many Fellows receive only a small stipend, or no stipend at all, they have to use their own resources or hold a second, part-time job to support themselves.
Length of Study: 1 year; some may be of a shorter term.
Study Establishment: Training takes place in Berkley CA and Chicago IL.
Country of Study: USA.
Application Procedure: Application packets should be requested.
Closing Date: June 15th.
Additional Information: The Programme accomplishes its purposes by providing participating fellows with: work experience, seminars, encounters, individual study and skills training.

For further information contact:

(for Midwest)
WWWC
5441 S Ridgewood Court, Chicago, IL, 60615, United States of America

THE WORSHIPFUL COMPANY OF MUSICIANS

74-75 Watling Street, London, EC4M 9BJ, England
Tel: (44) 171 489 8888
Fax: (44) 171 489 1614
Contact: S F Waley, The Clerk

The Worshipful Company of Musicians supports young musicians particularly in the 'wilderness' years between graduating and setting out on their musical careers.

Allcard Grants

Subjects: Music.
Eligibility: Open to individuals wishing to undertake a relevant training or research programme. The grants are not available for courses leading either to a first degree at a university or to a diploma at a college of music, and only in exceptional circumstances will assistance towards the cost of a fourth or fifth year at a college of music be considered. Grants are not available towards the purchase of instruments.
Level of Study: Postgraduate.
Purpose: For advanced training for performers at home or abroad, or for significant projects of a special nature - eg. in the field of musicology.
Type: Grant.
No. of awards offered: A limited number.
Frequency: Annual.
Value: Up to £3,000.
Country of Study: Any country.
Application Procedure: Nominations must be made by any one of the following: principals or heads of music departments, Royal Academy of Music, Royal College of Music, Guildhall School of Music, Royal Northern College of Music, Royal Scottish Academy of Music and Drama, Welsh College of Music, Birmingham Consevatoire, Trinity College of Music, City University, Huddersfield University, Goldsmiths and other university departments.
Closing Date: Applications to be made after January 1st and before April 1st.
Additional Information: Applications have to be recommended by the Principal of a college of music.

Carnwath Scholarship

Subjects: Music.
Eligibility: Open to any person of either sex permanently resident in the UK and 21-25 years of age. The Scholarship is intended only for the advanced student who has successfully completed a solo performance course at a college of music.
Level of Study: Postgraduate.
Purpose: To support young pianists.
Type: Scholarship.
No. of awards offered: 1.
Frequency: Every two years.
Value: £3,000.
Length of Study: Up to 2 years.
Country of Study: United Kingdom.
Application Procedure: Nominations must be made by any one of the following: principals, Royal Academy of Music, Guildhall School of Music and Drama, Royal Northern College of Music, Royal Scottish Academy of Music, Trinity College of Music, London College of Music, Welsh College of Music and Drama, Birmingham School of Music; director, Royal College of Music. No application should be made directly to the Worshipful Company of Musicians.
Closing Date: June 1st in the year of the award.

John Clementi Collard Fellowship

Subjects: Music.
Eligibility: Open to professional musicians of standing and experience who show excellence in one or more of the higher branches of musical activity, such as composition, research, and performance (including conducting).
Level of Study: Postgraduate.
Type: Fellowship.
No. of awards offered: 1.
Frequency: Approximately every three years.
Value: £5,000 per year.
Length of Study: Up to 3 years.
Country of Study: United Kingdom.
Application Procedure: Nominations must be made by any one of the following: professors of music at Oxford, Cambridge or London Universities; director, Royal College of Music; principals, Royal Academy of Music, Guildhall School of Music and Drama, Royal Northern College of Music. No application should be made directly to the Worshipful Company of Musicians.
Closing Date: March 31st in the year of the award.

Maisie Lewis Young Artists Fund

Subjects: Musical performance.
Eligibility: Open to instrumentalists (including organists) up to 25 years of age and to singers of up to 30 years of age.
Level of Study: Postgraduate.
Purpose: To assist young artists of outstanding ability who wish to acquire experience on the professional soloist concert platform.
No. of awards offered: 6 half-recitals per year.
Frequency: Annual.
Value: Reimbursement of recitalists' expenses.
Country of Study: United Kingdom.
Application Procedure: Application forms are available from January 1st.
Closing Date: May 1st.
Additional Information: Auditions are normally held in September.

For further information contact:

6 Pembridge Crescent, London, W11 3DT, England
Contact: Mrs J Lowy

W T Best Memorial Scholarships

Subjects: Music.
Eligibility: Open to advanced students of the organ.
Level of Study: Postgraduate.
Purpose: To encourage organ music.
Type: Scholarship.
No. of awards offered: 1.
Frequency: Every three years (1999).
Value: £3,000 per year.
Length of Study: Up to 3 years.

Country of Study: United Kingdom.
Application Procedure: Nominations must be made by any one of the following: professors of music at Oxford, Cambridge or London Universities; directors, Royal College of Music and Royal College of Organists; principals, Royal Academy of Music, Guildhall School of Music and Drama, Royal Northern College of Music, and Royal Scottish Academy of Music and Drama; directors, Edinburgh, Cardiff and Belfast Universities. No application should be made directly to the Worshipful Company of Musicians.
Closing Date: June 1st in the year of the award.

WRITER'S DIGEST

1507 Dana Avenue, Cincinnati, OH, 45207, United States of America
Tel: (1) 513 531 2490 ext 328
Fax: (1) 513 531 1843
Email: competitions@fwpubs.com
www: http://www.writersdigest.com
Contact: Category Judge

Writer's Digest Writing Competition

Subjects: Creative writing - genre short stories and mainstream/literary works (up to 4,000 words), feature articles and personal essays (2,500 words), stage plays and television/movie scripts (the first 15 pages segment of script in standard script format) plus a one page synopsis, rhyming poetry and non-rhyming poetry (one poem up to 16 lines). Inspirational writing - 2,500 words maximum. Children's fiction - 2,000 words maximum.
Eligibility: Open to authors of any nationality; works must be written in English.
Level of Study: Unrestricted.
Type: Competition.
No. of awards offered: 1,001.
Frequency: Annual.
Value: Cash prizes for first to fifth place winners.
Country of Study: Any country.
Application Procedure: Contestants may enter as many categories and as many times in each category as they wish. Manuscripts will not be returned and each entry must be made on an official entry form and accompanied by a US$10 entry fee, drawn on a US bank. Entries must be original and unprinted.
Closing Date: May 31st.

YALE CENTER FOR BRITISH ART

PO Box 208280, New Haven, CT, 06520-8280, United States of America
Tel: (1) 203 432 2850
Fax: (1) 203 432 9628
Email: bacinfo@minerva.cis.yale.edu
www: http://www.yale.edu/ycba
Contact: Director

The Yale Center for British Art houses the most comprehensive collection of English paintings, prints, drawings, rare books, and sculpture outside Great Britain. Given to Yale University by Paul Mellon, the Center's resources illustrate British life and culture from the 16th century to the present.

Yale Center for British Art Fellowships

Subjects: British art from the Elizabethan period onwards.
Eligibility: Open to scholars in postdoctoral or equivalent research related to British art.
Level of Study: Postdoctorate.
Purpose: To allow scholars of either literature, history, the history of art or related fields, to study the Center's holdings of paintings, drawings, prints and rare books, and to make use of its research facilities.
Type: Fellowship.
No. of awards offered: 10-12.
Frequency: Annual.
Value: Cost of travel to and from New Haven, plus accommodation and a living allowance.
Length of Study: Normally 4 weeks.
Study Establishment: Yale Center for British Art.
Country of Study: USA.
Application Procedure: There is no application form. Please submit name, address, telephone number, CV listing professional experience, education and publications, three page outline of research proposal, and two confidential letters of recommendation.
Closing Date: January 15th.
Additional Information: Applications are also welcomed from museum professionals whose responsibilities and research interests include British art.

YALE UNIVERSITY PRESS

PO Box 209040, New Haven, CT, 06520-9040, United States of America
Tel: (1) 203 432 0960
Fax: (1) 203 432 2394
Email: richard-miller@yale.edu
www: http://www.yale.edu/yup
Contact: Mr Richard Miller

Yale Series of Younger Poets

Subjects: Poetry.
Eligibility: Writers must be US citizens under 40 years of age who have not yet published a book of poetry. Poems must be original, not translations.
Level of Study: Unrestricted.
Purpose: To select a book-length poetry manuscript for publication.
Type: Publication.
No. of awards offered: 1.
Frequency: Annual.
Country of Study: USA.
Application Procedure: There is no application form. Please write for more information on entry criteria.

Closing Date: Submissions must be postmarked between February 1st and the end of February.

YEHUDI MENUHIN INTERNATIONAL VIOLIN COMPETITION FOR YOUNG VIOLINISTS

8 St George's Terrace, London, NW1 8XJ, England
Tel: (44) 171 911 0901
Fax: (44) 171 911 0903
Email: kgaynor@msn.com
Contact: Ms Kim Gaynor

An international competition open to any nationality.

Yehudi Menuhin International Competition for Young Violinists

Subjects: Violin performance.
Eligibility: Open to violinists of any nationality. Maximum age of competitors is 22. Juniors must be under 16, seniors must be aged between 16 and 21 years.
Type: Prize.
No. of awards offered: 10.
Frequency: Every two years.
Value: Up to £4,000.
Country of Study: Any country.
Application Procedure: A completed application form, tape and two letters od redcommendation.
Closing Date: October 15th.
Additional Information: The competition is held in Folkestone and is sponsored by the Hattori family and supported by Shepway District Council. Competitors are accommodated by host families.

SUBJECT AND ELIGIBILITY
GUIDE TO AWARDS

SUBJECT CATEGORIES

ARCHITECTURE AND TOWN PLANNING
General
Structural architecture
Architectural restoration
Environmental design
Landscape architecture
Town and community planning
Regional planning

ARTS AND HUMANITIES
General
Interpretation and translation
Writing (authorship)
Native language and literature
Modern languages and literatures
  English
  French
  Spanish
  Germanic languages
  German
  Swedish
  Danish
  Norwegian
  Italian
  Portuguese
  Romance languages
  Modern Greek
  Dutch
  Baltic languages
  Celtic languages
  Finnish
  Russian
  Slavonic languages (others)
  Hungarian
  Fino Ugrian languages
  European languages (others)
  Altaic languages
  Arabic
  Hebrew
  Chinese

Korean
Japanese
Indian languages
Iranic languages
African languages
Amerindian languages
Austronesian and oceanic languages
Classical languages and literatures
  Latin
  Classical Greek
  Sanskrit
Linguistics and philology
  Applied linguistics
  Psycholinguistics
  Grammar
  Semantics and terminology
  Phonetics
  Logopedics
Comparative literature
History
  Prehistory
  Ancient civilisations
  Medieval history
  Modern history
  Contemporary history
Archaeology
Philosophy
  Philosophical schools
  Metaphysics
  Logic
  Ethics

FINE AND APPLIED ARTS
General
History and philosophy of art
  Aesthetics
Art management
Drawing and painting
Sculpture
Handicrafts
Music

Musicology
Music theory and composition
Conducting
Singing
Musical instruments (performance)
Religious music
Jazz and popular music
Opera
Drama
Dancing
Photography
Cinema and television
Design
  Interior design
  Furniture design
  Fashion design
  Textile design
  Graphic design
  Industrial design
  Display and stage design

RELIGION AND THEOLOGY
General
Religious studies
  Christian
  Jewish
  Islam
  Asian religious studies
  Agnosticism and Atheism
  Ancient religions
Religious education
Holy writings
Religious practice
Church administration (pastoral work)
Theological studies
Comparative religion
Sociology of religion
History of religion
Esoteric practices

ANY SUBJECT

Any Country

African Nations

Australia

GrantFinder - Arts

North Dakota Indian Scholarship, 244
Queen's College Wendell Herbruck
  Studentship, 348
Rhodes Scholarships, 349
Somerville College Oxford Bursary for
  American Graduates (Janet Watson
  Bursary), 350
The SSRC Soviet Union and Successor
  States Graduate Training Fellowships,
  294
St Andrew's Society of the State of New
  York Scholarship, 305
St Anne's College Overseas
  Scholarship, 351
St Catherine's College Overseas
  Graduate Scholarship, 352
St Peter's College Leonard J Theberge
  Memorial Scholarship, 354
US-UK Fulbright Commission
  Postdoctoral Research Scholarship at
  De Montfort University, 368
USC All-University Predoctoral Diversity
  Fellowships, 358
USIA Fulbright Study and Research
  Grants for US Citizens, 369

West European Countries

AAUW International Fellowships
  Program, 3
British-German Academic Research
  Collaboration (ARC) Programme, 61
Canon Foundation Visiting Research
  Fellowships/Professorships, 110
Christ Church Hugh Pilkinton
  Scholarship, 338
CIMO Bilateral Scholarships, 114
CIMO Nordic Scholarship Scheme for
  the Baltic Countries and Northwest
  Russia, 114
Clare Hall Foundation Fellowship, 325
Denmark-America Foundation Grants,
  132
Department of Education and Science
  (Ireland) Exchange Scholarships and
  Postgraduate Scholarships Exchange
  Scheme, 132
DoE (Ireland) Summer School Exchange
  Scholarships, 133
ERASMUS Grants, 120
Feodor Lynen Research Fellowships for
  German Scholars, 8
Japan Society for the Promotion of
  Science (JSPS) Research Fellowships,
  8

John Dana Archbold Fellowship
  Program, 245
Lincoln College Berrow Scholarship,
  343
Lincoln College Dresdner Kleinwort
  Benson Senior Scholarships, 343
Merton College Graduate Entrance
  Scholarships, 344
Merton College Greendale Senior
  Scholarships, 345
Mr and Mrs David Edward Roberts
  Memorial Award, 363
PEO International Peace Scholarship,
  185
Prendergast Bequest, 347
Scholarships for Postgraduate Studies
  in Greece, 307
Science and Technology Agency (STA)
  Research Fellowships, 9
St Anne's College Overseas
  Scholarship, 351
St Catherine's College Overseas
  Graduate Scholarship, 352
University of Wales (Bangor)
  Postgraduate Studentships, 363
Wadham College Norwegian
  Scholarship, 355

ARCHITECTURE AND TOWN PLANNING

GENERAL

Any Country

AIA College of Fellows Grant, 13
The AIA/AAF Scholarship for Advanced
  Study and Research, 13
Alexander S Onassis Programme of
  Research Grants, 7
Alexander S Onassis Research Grants,
  7
Board of Architects of New South Wales
  Research Grant, 56
Canadian Department of External Affairs
  Faculty Enrichment Program, 107
Canadian Department of External Affairs
  Faculty Research Program, 108
Canadian Department of External Affairs
  Institutional Research Program, 108
Center for Advanced Study in the
  Behavioral Sciences Postdoctoral
  Residential Fellowships, 112
CIB Developing Countries Fund, 182
Cotton Research Fellowships, 138

Foundation Praemium Erasmianum
  Study Prize, 150
George Pepler International Award, 281
Graham Foundation Grants, 162
Humanitarian Trust Awards, 171
JJR Research Grant, 204
Lemmermann Foundation Scholarship,
  205
M H Joseph Prize, 64
National University of Singapore
  Postgraduate Research Scholarship,
  234
Onassis Programme of Postgraduate
  Research Scholarships, 7
Paul Mellon Centre Grants, 259
Ramsden Bursaries, 300
RIAS Award for Measured Drawing, 275
RIAS John Maclaren Travelling
  Fellowship, 275
RIAS/Whitehouse Studios Award for
  Architectural Photography, 275
Rosann Berry Fellowship, 299
Royal Scottish Academy Annual
  Student Competition, 278
RSA Art for Architecture Award, 279

SAH Architectural Study and Tour
  Scholarship, 299
The Sir John Burnet Memorial Award,
  276
The Sir Robert Lorimer Memorial Award,
  276
The Sir Rowand Anderson Silver Medal,
  276
Stroud Bursaries, 300
SUSU Rector's Award, 304
The Thomas Ross Award, 276
Toro Industry Advancement Award, 205
UARC Postdoctoral Fellowships, 320
University of Auckland Foundation
  Visiting Fellowships, 321
University of Dundee Research Awards,
  330
University of Glasgow Postgraduate
  Scholarships, 331
University of Manchester Research
  Studentships or Scholarships, 334
University of Stirling Research
  Studentships, 360
Wolf Foundation Prizes, 375

African Nations

Friends of Peterhouse Bursary, 260
Fulbright Postdoctoral Research and Lecturing Awards for Non-US Citizens, 154
Merton College Third World Graduate Scholarship, 345

Australia

Byera Hadley Travelling Scholarship, Postgraduate Scholarship, Student Scholarship, 56
Friends of Peterhouse Bursary, 260
Fulbright Postdoctoral Research and Lecturing Awards for Non-US Citizens, 154
The Marten Bequest Travelling Scholarships, 39
Wingate Scholarships, 374

British Commonwealth

Canadian Commonwealth Scholarship Program, 181
Friends of Peterhouse Bursary, 260
RIBA Rome Scholarship in Architecture and Urbanism, 69
Sargant Fellowship, 70
Wingate Scholarships, 374

Canada

AIA/AHA Graduate Fellowship in Health Facility Planning and Design, 14
Friends of Peterhouse Bursary, 260
Fulbright Postdoctoral Research and Lecturing Awards for Non-US Citizens, 154
PRA Fellowships, 257
Swiss Federal Institute of Technology Scholarships, 308
Wingate Scholarships, 374

Caribbean Countries

Friends of Peterhouse Bursary, 260
Merton College Third World Graduate Scholarship, 345

East European Countries

CRF/RSE European Visiting Research Fellowships, 280
Friends of Peterhouse Bursary, 260
Fulbright Postdoctoral Research and Lecturing Awards for Non-US Citizens, 154
Merton College Third World Graduate Scholarship, 345
Swiss Federal Institute of Technology Scholarships, 308

Far East

ASEAN Graduate Scholarships, 234
Friends of Peterhouse Bursary, 260
Fulbright Postdoctoral Research and Lecturing Awards for Non-US Citizens, 154
Merton College Third World Graduate Scholarship, 345
Swiss Federal Institute of Technology Scholarships, 308

Indian Sub-Continent

Friends of Peterhouse Bursary, 260
Fulbright Postdoctoral Research and Lecturing Awards for Non-US Citizens, 154
Merton College Third World Graduate Scholarship, 345
Wingate Scholarships, 374

Middle East

Friends of Peterhouse Bursary, 260
Fulbright Postdoctoral Research and Lecturing Awards for Non-US Citizens, 154
Merton College Third World Graduate Scholarship, 345
Wingate Scholarships, 374

New Zealand

Friends of Peterhouse Bursary, 260
Fulbright Postdoctoral Research and Lecturing Awards for Non-US Citizens, 154

South Africa

Friends of Peterhouse Bursary, 260
Fulbright Postdoctoral Research and Lecturing Awards for Non-US Citizens, 154
Isie Smuts Research Award, 303

South America

Friends of Peterhouse Bursary, 260
Fulbright Commission (Argentina) Master's Program, 154
Fulbright Postdoctoral Research and Lecturing Awards for Non-US Citizens, 154
Merton College Third World Graduate Scholarship, 345
PRA Fellowships, 257

United Kingdom

Canada Memorial Foundation Scholarships, 104
Cardiff University Postgraduate Research Studentships, 364

CRF/RSE European Visiting Research Fellowships, 280

Frank Knox Fellowships at Harvard University, 151
Fulbright Postdoctoral Research and Lecturing Awards for Non-US Citizens, 154
Kennedy Scholarships, 196
The Martin Jones Memorial Scholarship and Award, 275
Research Grant, 130, 264
RIBA Rome Scholarship in Architecture and Urbanism, 69
Sargant Fellowship, 70
Swiss Federal Institute of Technology Scholarships, 308
Travel Grant, 130
Wingate Scholarships, 374

USA

AIA/AHA Graduate Fellowship in Health Facility Planning and Design, 14
Belgian-American Educational Foundation Graduate Fellowships for Study in Belgium, 53
British Schools and Universities Foundation, Inc. Scholarships, 71
Congress Bundestag Youth Exchange for Young Professionals, 112
Edith H Henderson Scholarship, 203
Friends of Peterhouse Bursary, 260
Fulbright Scholar Awards for Research and Lecturing Abroad, 130
Native American Scholarship Program, 235
Olivia James Traveling Fellowship, 31
PRA Fellowships, 257
Rotch Traveling Scholarship, 57
Samuel H Kress Fellowship, 23, 25
Samuel H Kress Joint Athens-Jerusalem Fellowship, 23, 26
Swiss Federal Institute of Technology Scholarships, 308
Thomas P Papandrew Scholarship, 204
William J Locklin Scholarship, 205

West European Countries

Belgian-American Educational Foundation Graduate Fellowships for Study in the USA, 54
Cardiff University Postgraduate Research Studentships, 364
CRF/RSE European Visiting Research Fellowships, 280
Friends of Peterhouse Bursary, 260
Fulbright Postdoctoral Research and Lecturing Awards for Non-US Citizens, 154
Janson Johan Helmich Scholarships and Travel Grants, 189

NAI Travel Grant, 244
Postgraduate Fellowships for Study in
the USA, 54
Scholarship Foundation of the League
for Finnish-American Societies, 284
Swiss Federal Institute of Technology
Scholarships, 308
Wingate Scholarships, 374

Swiss Federal Institute of Technology
Scholarships, 308

West European Countries

Swiss Federal Institute of Technology
Scholarships, 308
Wingate Scholarships, 374

USA

Asian Cultural Council Fellowship
Grants Program, 40

West European Countries

Wingate Scholarships, 374

STRUCTURAL ARCHITECTURE

Any Country

AIA College of Fellows Grant, 13
Alexander S Onassis Programme of
Research Grants, 7
Alexander S Onassis Research Grants,
7

Australia

Wingate Scholarships, 374

British Commonwealth

Gladys Krieble Delmas Foundation
Grants, 161
Wingate Scholarships, 374

Canada

Swiss Federal Institute of Technology
Scholarships, 308
Wingate Scholarships, 374

East European Countries

Swiss Federal Institute of Technology
Scholarships, 308

Far East

Swiss Federal Institute of Technology
Scholarships, 308

Indian Sub-Continent

Wingate Scholarships, 374

Middle East

Wingate Scholarships, 374

United Kingdom

Swiss Federal Institute of Technology
Scholarships, 308
Wingate Scholarships, 374

USA

Gladys Krieble Delmas Foundation
Grants, 161

ARCHITECTURAL RESTORATION

Any Country

AIA College of Fellows Grant, 13
Alexander S Onassis Programme of
Research Grants, 7
Alexander S Onassis Research Grants,
7
Center for Field Research Grants, 112
FAMSI Research Grant, 150
Keepers Preservation Education Fund
Fellowship, 298
NEH Senior Research Fellowship, 22
Onassis Programme of Postgraduate
Research Scholarships, 7
SAH Architectural Study and Tour
Scholarship, 299
Sally Kress Tompkins Fellowship, 299
University of Dundee Research Awards,
330

Australia

Wingate Scholarships, 374

British Commonwealth

Wingate Scholarships, 374

Canada

Wingate Scholarships, 374

Far East

Asian Cultural Council Fellowship
Grants Program, 40

Indian Sub-Continent

Wingate Scholarships, 374

Middle East

Wingate Scholarships, 374

United Kingdom

Wingate Scholarships, 374

ENVIRONMENTAL DESIGN

Any Country

AIA College of Fellows Grant, 13
Alexander S Onassis Programme of
Research Grants, 7
Alexander S Onassis Research Grants,
7
JJR Research Grant, 204
Peter Krueger-Christie's Fellowship, 127

Australia

Wingate Scholarships, 374

British Commonwealth

Wingate Scholarships, 374

Canada

Swiss Federal Institute of Technology
Scholarships, 308
Wingate Scholarships, 374

East European Countries

Swiss Federal Institute of Technology
Scholarships, 308

Far East

Swiss Federal Institute of Technology
Scholarships, 308

Indian Sub-Continent

Wingate Scholarships, 374

Middle East

Wingate Scholarships, 374

United Kingdom

Cardiff University Postgraduate
Research Studentships, 364
RSA Student Design Awards, 279
Swiss Federal Institute of Technology
Scholarships, 308
Wingate Scholarships, 374

USA

Swiss Federal Institute of Technology
Scholarships, 308

West European Countries

Cardiff University Postgraduate
Research Studentships, 364
RSA Student Design Awards, 279
Swiss Federal Institute of Technology
Scholarships, 308
Wingate Scholarships, 374

LANDSCAPE ARCHITECTURE

Any Country

AILA/Yamagani/Hope Fellowship, 203
Alexander S Onassis Programme of
Research Grants, 7
Alexander S Onassis Research Grants,
7
Dumbarton Oaks Fellowships and
Junior Fellowships, 139
JJR Research Grant, 204
Onassis Programme of Postgraduate
Research Scholarships, 7
Peter Krueger-Christie's Fellowship, 127
Raymond E Page Scholarship, 204

Australia

Wingate Scholarships, 374

British Commonwealth

Wingate Scholarships, 374

Canada

Ralph Hudson Environmental
Fellowship, 204
Wingate Scholarships, 374

Indian Sub-Continent

Wingate Scholarships, 374

Middle East

Wingate Scholarships, 374

United Kingdom

Martin McLaren Horticultural
Scholarship, 180
Wingate Scholarships, 374

USA

Hawaii Chapter/David T Woolsey
Scholarship, 204

Ralph Hudson Environmental
Fellowship, 204

West European Countries

Martin McLaren Horticultural
Scholarship, 180
Wingate Scholarships, 374

TOWN AND COMMUNITY PLANNING

Any Country

AIA College of Fellows Grant, 13
Alexander S Onassis Programme of
Research Grants, 7
Alexander S Onassis Research Grants,
7
George Pepler International Award, 281
JJR Research Grant, 204
Massey Doctoral Scholarship, 214
RICS Education Trust Award, 276
University of Dundee Research Awards,
330
University of New England Research
Scholarships, 336
University of Stirling Research
Studentships, 360

African Nations

African Dissertation Internship Awards,
270
Institute for Housing and Urban
Development Studies Fellowships for
Courses, 176

Australia

Wingate Scholarships, 374

British Commonwealth

Wingate Scholarships, 374

Canada

Swiss Federal Institute of Technology
Scholarships, 308
Wingate Scholarships, 374

Caribbean Countries

Institute for Housing and Urban
Development Studies Fellowships for
Courses, 176

East European Countries

Institute for Housing and Urban
Development Studies Fellowships for
Courses, 176
Swiss Federal Institute of Technology
Scholarships, 308

Far East

Institute for Housing and Urban
Development Studies Fellowships for
Courses, 176
Swiss Federal Institute of Technology
Scholarships, 308

Indian Sub-Continent

Institute for Housing and Urban
Development Studies Fellowships for
Courses, 176
Wingate Scholarships, 374

Middle East

Institute for Housing and Urban
Development Studies Fellowships for
Courses, 176
Wingate Scholarships, 374

South Africa

Institute for Housing and Urban
Development Studies Fellowships for
Courses, 176

South America

Institute for Housing and Urban
Development Studies Fellowships for
Courses, 176

United Kingdom

Cardiff University Postgraduate
Research Studentships, 364
Polish Embassy Short-Term Bursaries,
262
Swiss Federal Institute of Technology
Scholarships, 308
Wingate Scholarships, 374

USA

Swiss Federal Institute of Technology
Scholarships, 308

West European Countries

Cardiff University Postgraduate
Research Studentships, 364
NAI Travel Grant, 244
Swiss Federal Institute of Technology
Scholarships, 308
Wingate Scholarships, 374

REGIONAL PLANNING

Any Country

AIA College of Fellows Grant, 13
Alexander S Onassis Programme of
 Research Grants, 7
Alexander S Onassis Research Grants,
 7
George Pepler International Award, 281
JJR Research Grant, 204
Massey Doctoral Scholarship, 214
University of Dundee Research Awards,
 330
University of New England Research
 Scholarships, 336

African Nations

African Dissertation Internship Awards,
 270

Australia

Wingate Scholarships, 374

British Commonwealth

Wingate Scholarships, 374

Canada

Swiss Federal Institute of Technology
 Scholarships, 308
Wingate Scholarships, 374

East European Countries

Swiss Federal Institute of Technology
 Scholarships, 308

Far East

Swiss Federal Institute of Technology
 Scholarships, 308

Indian Sub-Continent

Wingate Scholarships, 374

Middle East

Wingate Scholarships, 374

United Kingdom

Cardiff University Postgraduate
 Research Studentships, 364
Swiss Federal Institute of Technology
 Scholarships, 308
Wingate Scholarships, 374

USA

Swiss Federal Institute of Technology
 Scholarships, 308

West European Countries

Cardiff University Postgraduate
 Research Studentships, 364
NAI Travel Grant, 244
Swiss Federal Institute of Technology
 Scholarships, 308
Wingate Scholarships, 374

ARTS AND HUMANITIES

GENERAL

Any Country

Adolfo Omodeo Scholarship, 187
AIATSIS Research Grants, 46
Albert J Beveridge Grant, 12
Alexander S Onassis Programme of
 Research Grants, 7
Alexander S Onassis Research Grants,
 7
American Society for Eighteenth-
 Century Studies, 239
Andrew W Mellon Postdoctoral
 Fellowships in the Humanities, 358
ARIT Humanities and Social Science
 Fellowships, 20
Arts Council of Northern Ireland Annual
 Award, 34
ASECS/Clark Library Fellowships, 313
Assistantships, 27
Audrey Lumsden-Kouvel Fellowship,
 240
Australian Academy of the Humanities
 Travelling Fellowships, 44
Australian National University Visiting
 Fellowships, 48
Balliol College Dervorguilla Scholarship,
 337
Banff Centre Scholarships, 53

Bass Ireland Arts Awards, 34
Bernadotte E Schmitt Grants, 13
British Academy Major International
 Conference Grant, 59
British Academy Overseas Conference
 Grants, 59
British Academy Small Personal
 Research Grants, 59
British Academy Visiting Professorships
 for Overseas Scholars, 59
Calouste Gulbenkian Foundation
 (International Department) Research
 Fellowships, 75
Camargo Fellowships, 75
Canadian Department of External Affairs
 Faculty Enrichment Program, 107
Canadian Department of External Affairs
 Faculty Research Program, 108
Canadian Department of External Affairs
 Institutional Research Program, 108
Canadian Friends of the Hebrew
 University Awards, 107
Center for Advanced Study in the
 Behavioral Sciences Postdoctoral
 Residential Fellowships, 112
Center for Field Research Grants, 112
Center for Renaissance Studies
 Fellowships, 240
Center for Renaissance Studies
 Seminar and Summer Institute
 Fellowships, 240

Clark-Huntington Joint Bibliographical
 Fellowship, 314
Concordia University Graduate
 Fellowships, 126
CQU University Postgraduate Research
 Award, 114
Craigie (Peter C) Memorial Scholarship,
 323
D'Arcy McNickle Center Frances C Allen
 Fellowships, 240
David J Azrieli Graduate Fellowship, 126
Downing College Research Fellowships,
 326
Equiano Memorial Award, 308
ERASMUS Prize, 150
European Enlightenment Project
 Fellowships, 175
Foundation Praemium Erasmianum
 Study Prize, 150
Frederico Chabod Scholarship, 187
Girton College Research Fellowships,
 327
Harold White Fellowships, 233
The Helen Wallis Fellowship, 67
Hosei International Fund Foreign
 Scholars Fellowship, 170
Howard Foundation Fellowships, 155
Humane Studies Fellowships, 177
Institute for Advanced Studies in the
 Humanities Visiting Research
 Fellowships, 175

Fulbright Postdoctoral Research and Lecturing Awards for Non-US Citizens, 154
Guggenheim Fellowships to Assist Research and Artistic Creation (US and Canada), 195
J W McConnell Memorial Fellowships, 126
Killam Research Fellowships, 104
Konrad Adenauer Research Award, 8
Margaret Dale Philp Award, 107
Mellon Postdoctoral Fellowships, 128, 241, 355
Shastri Indo-Canadian Institute Language Training Fellowship, 286
Sir Arthur Sims Scholarship, 279
Social Sciences and Humanities Research Council of Canada Doctoral Fellowships, 294
Social Sciences and Humanities Research Council of Canada Postdoctoral Fellowships, 295
Social Sciences and Humanities Research Council of Canada Research Grants (Major), 295
Social Sciences and Humanities Research Council of Canada Research Grants (Standard), 295
Social Sciences and Humanities Research Council of Canada Strategic Research Grants, Research Networks, Research Workshops, Partnership Development Grants, 295
SSHRC Institutional Grants, 296
Thompson (Homer and Dorothy) Fellowship, 105
Wingate Scholarships, 374

Caribbean Countries

CSD Grants for Foreign Research Fellows, 115
Friends of Peterhouse Bursary, 260
Guggenheim Fellowships to Assist Research and Artistic Creation (Latin America and the Caribbean), 194
Merton College Third World Graduate Scholarship, 345

East European Countries

Andrew W Mellon Foundation Fellowships, 24, 175
Andrew W Mellon Foundation Fellowships in the Humanities, 175
CSD Grants for Foreign Research Fellows, 115
Friends of Peterhouse Bursary, 260
Fulbright Postdoctoral Research and Lecturing Awards for Non-US Citizens, 154
Leuven Program, 302

Mellon Research Fellowship, 21
Mellon Research Fellowships, 372
Merton College Third World Graduate Scholarship, 345
Open Society Sofia Scholarships for Postgraduate Study Abroad, 249
SAFE Competiton for the Écoles Normales Superieures, 250
Soros Foundation General Program, 302
Soros Suplementary Grants Programme (SSGP), 250

Far East

Abe Fellowship Program, 290
ASEAN Graduate Scholarships, 234
Asian Cultural Council Fellowship Grants Program, 40
Chinese Fellowships for Scholarly Development, 12
Commonwealth Scholarships, Fellowships and Academic Staff Scholarships, 121
CSD Grants for Foreign Research Fellows, 115
Friends of Peterhouse Bursary, 260
Fulbright Postdoctoral Research and Lecturing Awards for Non-US Citizens, 154
Merton College Third World Graduate Scholarship, 345

Indian Sub-Continent

Commonwealth Scholarships, Fellowships and Academic Staff Scholarships, 121
CSD Grants for Foreign Research Fellows, 115
Friends of Peterhouse Bursary, 260
Fulbright Postdoctoral Research and Lecturing Awards for Non-US Citizens, 154
Merton College Third World Graduate Scholarship, 345
USEFI Postdoctoral Travel-Only Grants, 318
Wingate Scholarships, 374

Middle East

CSD Grants for Foreign Research Fellows, 115
Friends of Peterhouse Bursary, 260
Fulbright Postdoctoral Research and Lecturing Awards for Non-US Citizens, 154
Merton College Third World Graduate Scholarship, 345
Wingate Scholarships, 374

New Zealand

Commonwealth Scholarships, Fellowships and Academic Staff Scholarships, 121
CSD Grants for Foreign Research Fellows, 115
Friends of Peterhouse Bursary, 260
Fulbright Postdoctoral Research and Lecturing Awards for Non-US Citizens, 154
Nepean Postgraduate Research Award, 364

South Africa

Commonwealth Scholarships, Fellowships and Academic Staff Scholarships, 121
CSD Grants for Attendance at International Conferences, 115
CSD Prestige Scholarships for Doctoral Studies Abroad, 116
CSD Publication Grants, 116
CSD Research Grants, 116
CSD Scholarships for Doctoral/D-Tech Studies at Universities and Technikons in South Africa, 116
CSD Scholarships for Honours Degree Studies at Universities in South Africa, 117
CSD Scholarships for Master's Degree Studies/Studies for Master's Degree in Technology in South Africa, 117
Friends of Peterhouse Bursary, 260
Fulbright Postdoctoral Research and Lecturing Awards for Non-US Citizens, 154

South America

CSD Grants for Foreign Research Fellows, 115
Friends of Peterhouse Bursary, 260
Fulbright Commission (Argentina) Master's Program, 154
Fulbright Postdoctoral Research and Lecturing Awards for Non-US Citizens, 154
Guggenheim Fellowships to Assist Research and Artistic Creation (Latin America and the Caribbean), 194
Luis López Méndez CONICIT Cambridge Scholarships, 94
Merton College Third World Graduate Scholarship, 345

United Kingdom

Arts Council of England Combined Arts, 32
Arts Council of England Visual Arts, 32
British Conference Grants, 59

INTERPRETATION AND TRANSLATION

Any Country

WRITING (AUTHORSHIP)

Australia

Nepean Postgraduate Research Award, 364
Wingate Scholarships, 374

British Commonwealth

Wingate Scholarships, 374

Canada

Inuit Cultural Grants Program, 134
The Paul Sargent Memorial Linguistic Scholarship Program, 43
Wingate Scholarships, 374

East European Countries

CRF/RSE European Visiting Research Fellowships, 280
Open Society Sofia Long-term Grants, 249
Open Society Sofia Short-term Grants, 249

Indian Sub-Continent

Wingate Scholarships, 374

Middle East

Wingate Scholarships, 374

New Zealand

Nepean Postgraduate Research Award, 364

United Kingdom

BAAS Short Term Awards, 60
CRF/RSE European Visiting Research Fellowships, 280
English-Speaking Union Chautauqua Scholarships, 143
John Speak Trust Scholarships, 57
Research Grant, 130, 264
School of European Culture and Language Scholarships, 332
Travel Grant, 130
University of Wales (Aberystwyth) Postgraduate Research Studentships, 362
Wingate Scholarships, 374

USA

Adult Literature Award, Juvenile Literary Award, 152
IREX Grant Opportunities for US Scholars, 186
NEH Fellowship, 25
NEH Postdoctoral Research Award, 25

US Department of Education International Research and Studies Program, 366

West European Countries

CRF/RSE European Visiting Research Fellowships, 280
School of European Culture and Language Scholarships, 332
University of Wales (Aberystwyth) Postgraduate Research Studentships, 362
Wingate Scholarships, 374

ENGLISH

Any Country

Acadia Graduate Teaching Assistantships, 4
Ahmanson and Getty Postdoctoral Fellowships, 313
Alexander S Onassis Programme of Research Grants, 7
Alexander S Onassis Research Grants, 7
Andrew W Mellon Postdoctoral Fellowships in the Humanities, 358
ASECS/Clark Library Fellowships, 313
Barbara Thom Postdoctoral Fellowship, 171
Caroline Spurgeon Research Fellowship, 274
Clark Library Short-Term Resident Fellowships, 313
Clark-Huntington Joint Bibliographical Fellowship, 314
Eurocentres Scholarship, 149
Jubilee Research Fellowship, 274
Keele University Graduate Teaching Assistantships, 195
Lewis Walpole Library Fellowship, 207
Library Company of Philadelphia Research Fellowships in American History and Culture, 208
Massey Doctoral Scholarship, 214
Mellon Postdoctoral Research Fellowships, 12, 172
Onassis Programme of Postgraduate Research Scholarships, 7
Queen's University of Belfast Research and Senior Visiting Research Fellowships, 266
Thank-Offering to Britain Fellowships, 60
Theodora Bosanquet Bursary, 55
University of Dundee Research Awards, 330

University of Glasgow Postgraduate Scholarships, 331
University of Stirling Research Studentships, 360
University Postgraduate Scholarships, 322
USC College Dissertation Fellowship, 359
USC College of Letters, Arts and Sciences Merit Award, 359
Volzhsky Institute of Humanities Awards, 371
Writing Center Graduate Fellowships, 28

Australia

Wingate Scholarships, 374

British Commonwealth

Wingate Scholarships, 374

Canada

Wingate Scholarships, 374

Indian Sub-Continent

Wingate Scholarships, 374

Middle East

Wingate Scholarships, 374

United Kingdom

BAAS Short Term Awards, 60
Cardiff University Postgraduate Research Studentships, 364
English Scholarship, 332
Ian Gregor Scholarship, 332
Travel Grant, 130
University of Wales (Aberystwyth) Postgraduate Research Studentships, 362
University of Wales Bangor (UWB) Research Studentships, 363
Wingate Scholarships, 374

USA

National Endowment for the Humanities Fellowships, 172, 241

West European Countries

Cardiff University Postgraduate Research Studentships, 364
English Scholarship, 332
Ian Gregor Scholarship, 332
Scholarship Foundation of the League for Finnish-American Societies, 284
University of Wales (Aberystwyth) Postgraduate Research Studentships, 362

GERMANIC LANGUAGES

Any Country

Ahmanson and Getty Postdoctoral Fellowships, 313
Center Research Fellowships, 316
Clark Library Short-Term Resident Fellowships, 313
Clark-Huntington Joint Bibliographical Fellowship, 314
Hochschulsommersprachkurse at German Universities, 158
Miles Lerman Center for the Study of Jewish Resistance Research Fellowship, 317
The Joyce and Arthur Schechter Fellowship, 317
The Pearl Resnick Post Doctoral Fellowship, 317
University of Stirling Research Studentships, 360

Australia

Wingate Scholarships, 374

British Commonwealth

Wingate Scholarships, 374

Canada

Wingate Scholarships, 374

Indian Sub-Continent

Wingate Scholarships, 374

Middle East

Wingate Scholarships, 374

United Kingdom

Wingate Scholarships, 374

USA

Germanistic Society of America Fellowships, 160

West European Countries

Wingate Scholarships, 374

GERMAN

Any Country

Ahmanson and Getty Postdoctoral Fellowships, 313

Alexander S Onassis Programme of Research Grants, 7
Alexander S Onassis Research Grants, 7
Andrew W Mellon Postdoctoral Fellowships in the Humanities, 358
ASECS/Clark Library Fellowships, 313
Clark Library Short-Term Resident Fellowships, 313
Clark-Huntington Joint Bibliographical Fellowship, 314
Eurocentres Scholarship, 149
Hochschulsommersprachkurse at German Universities, 158
Jubilee Research Fellowship, 274
Keele University Graduate Teaching Assistantships, 195
Massey Doctoral Scholarship, 214
Onassis Programme of Postgraduate Research Scholarships, 7
University of Glasgow Postgraduate Scholarships, 331
University of New England Research Scholarships, 336
University of Stirling Research Studentships, 360
University Postgraduate Scholarships, 322
Volzhsky Institute of Humanities Awards, 371

Australia

Wingate Scholarships, 374

British Commonwealth

Wingate Scholarships, 374

Canada

Wingate Scholarships, 374

Indian Sub-Continent

Wingate Scholarships, 374

Middle East

Wingate Scholarships, 374

United Kingdom

Cardiff University Postgraduate Research Studentships, 364
University of Wales (Aberystwyth) Postgraduate Research Studentships, 362
University of Wales Bangor (UWB) Research Studentships, 363
Wingate Scholarships, 374

USA

Germanistic Society of America Fellowships, 160

West European Countries

Cardiff University Postgraduate Research Studentships, 364
University of Wales (Aberystwyth) Postgraduate Research Studentships, 362
University of Wales Bangor (UWB) Research Studentships, 363
Wingate Scholarships, 374

SWEDISH

Any Country

ASF Translation Prize, 28

Australia

Wingate Scholarships, 374

British Commonwealth

Wingate Scholarships, 374

Canada

Wingate Scholarships, 374

Indian Sub-Continent

Wingate Scholarships, 374

Middle East

Wingate Scholarships, 374

United Kingdom

Wingate Scholarships, 374

USA

The Swedish Government 'SASS' Travel Grants, 308

West European Countries

Wingate Scholarships, 374

DANISH

Australia

Wingate Scholarships, 374

British Commonwealth

Wingate Scholarships, 374

Canada

Wingate Scholarships, 374

Indian Sub-Continent

Wingate Scholarships, 374

Middle East

Wingate Scholarships, 374

United Kingdom

Wingate Scholarships, 374

West European Countries

Wingate Scholarships, 374

NORWEGIAN

Any Country

University of Oslo International Summer
School Scholarships, 337

Australia

Wingate Scholarships, 374

British Commonwealth

Wingate Scholarships, 374

Canada

Wingate Scholarships, 374

Indian Sub-Continent

Wingate Scholarships, 374

Middle East

Wingate Scholarships, 374

United Kingdom

Wingate Scholarships, 374

USA

Norwegian Emigration Fund of 1975,
245
Norwegian Information Service Travel
Grants, 245

West European Countries

Wingate Scholarships, 374

ITALIAN

Any Country

Ahmanson and Getty Postdoctoral
Fellowships, 313
Alexander S Onassis Programme of
Research Grants, 7
Andrew W Mellon Postdoctoral
Fellowships in the Humanities, 358
ASECS/Clark Library Fellowships, 313
Clark Library Short-Term Resident
Fellowships, 313
Clark-Huntington Joint Bibliographical
Fellowship, 314
Eurocentres Scholarship, 149
Jubilee Research Fellowship, 274
Onassis Programme of Postgraduate
Research Scholarships, 7
University for Foreigners Scholarships,
319
University of Glasgow Postgraduate
Scholarships, 331
University of New England Research
Scholarships, 336
University Postgraduate Scholarships,
322
Unstra Grants - PVS Grants-Cils Grants,
319
USC College Dissertation Fellowship,
359
USC College of Letters, Arts and
Sciences Merit Award, 359

Australia

Wingate Scholarships, 374

British Commonwealth

Balsdon Fellowship, 68
BSR Rome Awards in Archaeology,
History and Letters, 68
Rome Scholarships in Ancient, Medieval
and Later Italian Studies, 70
Wingate Scholarships, 374

Canada

Wingate Scholarships, 374

Indian Sub-Continent

Wingate Scholarships, 374

Middle East

Wingate Scholarships, 374

United Kingdom

Balsdon Fellowship, 68
BSR Rome Awards in Archaeology,
History and Letters, 68

Cardiff University Postgraduate
Research Studentships, 364
Rome Scholarships in Ancient, Medieval
and Later Italian Studies, 70
University of Wales (Aberystwyth)
Postgraduate Research Studentships,
362
Wingate Scholarships, 374

West European Countries

Cardiff University Postgraduate
Research Studentships, 364
University of Wales (Aberystwyth)
Postgraduate Research Studentships,
362
Wingate Scholarships, 374

PORTUGUESE

Any Country

University Postgraduate Scholarships,
322

Australia

Wingate Scholarships, 374

British Commonwealth

Wingate Scholarships, 374

Canada

Wingate Scholarships, 374

Indian Sub-Continent

Wingate Scholarships, 374

Middle East

Wingate Scholarships, 374

United Kingdom

Cardiff University Postgraduate
Research Studentships, 364
Wingate Scholarships, 374

West European Countries

Cardiff University Postgraduate
Research Studentships, 364
Wingate Scholarships, 374

ROMANCE LANGUAGES

Any Country

Ahmanson and Getty Postdoctoral
Fellowships, 313
ASECS/Clark Library Fellowships, 313
Camargo Fellowships, 75
Clark Library Short-Term Resident
Fellowships, 313
Clark-Huntington Joint Bibliographical
Fellowship, 314
Massey Doctoral Scholarship, 214
University of Glasgow Postgraduate
Scholarships, 331
University Postgraduate Scholarships,
322
USC College Dissertation Fellowship,
359
USC College of Letters, Arts and
Sciences Merit Award, 359

Australia

Wingate Scholarships, 374

British Commonwealth

Wingate Scholarships, 374

Canada

Wingate Scholarships, 374

Indian Sub-Continent

Wingate Scholarships, 374

Middle East

Wingate Scholarships, 374

United Kingdom

Wingate Scholarships, 374

West European Countries

Wingate Scholarships, 374

MODERN GREEK

Any Country

Alexander S Onassis Programme of
Research Grants, 7
Alexander S Onassis Research Grants,
7
Aristotle University of Thessaloniki
Scholarships, 31
Mary Isabel Sibley Fellowship, 260
NEH Senior Research Fellowship, 22

Onassis Programme of Postgraduate
Research Scholarships, 7
University of Glasgow Postgraduate
Scholarships, 331

Australia

Greek State Scholarships Foundation
Grants, 163
Wingate Scholarships, 374

British Commonwealth

Hector and Elizabeth Catling Bursary, 67
Macmillan-Rodewald Studentship,
School Studentship, Cary Studentship,
67
Wingate Scholarships, 374

Canada

Greek State Scholarships Foundation
Grants, 163
Thompson (Homer and Dorothy)
Fellowship, 105
Wingate Scholarships, 374

Far East

Greek State Scholarships Foundation
Grants, 163

Indian Sub-Continent

Wingate Scholarships, 374

Middle East

Wingate Scholarships, 374

United Kingdom

Hector and Elizabeth Catling Bursary, 67
Macmillan-Rodewald Studentship,
School Studentship, Cary Studentship,
67
Wingate Scholarships, 374

USA

Greek State Scholarships Foundation
Grants, 163

West European Countries

Greek State Scholarships Foundation
Grants, 163
Wingate Scholarships, 374

DUTCH

Australia

Wingate Scholarships, 374

British Commonwealth

Wingate Scholarships, 374

Canada

Wingate Scholarships, 374

Indian Sub-Continent

Wingate Scholarships, 374

Middle East

Wingate Scholarships, 374

United Kingdom

Wingate Scholarships, 374

West European Countries

Wingate Scholarships, 374

BALTIC LANGUAGES

Australia

Wingate Scholarships, 374

British Commonwealth

Wingate Scholarships, 374

Canada

Wingate Scholarships, 374

Indian Sub-Continent

Wingate Scholarships, 374

Middle East

Wingate Scholarships, 374

United Kingdom

Wingate Scholarships, 374

USA

The SSRC Eastern Europe Program:
East European Language Training
Grants, 291

West European Countries

Wingate Scholarships, 374

CELTIC LANGUAGES

Any Country

McCaig Bursaries and Postgraduate
Scholarships, 111
Queen's University of Belfast Research
and Senior Visiting Research
Fellowships, 266
Sir John Rhys Studentship in Celtic
Studies, 349
University of Glasgow Postgraduate
Scholarships, 331

Australia

Wingate Scholarships, 374

British Commonwealth

Wingate Scholarships, 374

Canada

Wingate Scholarships, 374

Indian Sub-Continent

Wingate Scholarships, 374

Middle East

Wingate Scholarships, 374

United Kingdom

Cardiff University Postgraduate
Research Studentships, 364
University of Wales (Aberystwyth)
Postgraduate Research Studentships,
362
University of Wales Bangor (UWB)
Research Studentships, 363
Wingate Scholarships, 374

West European Countries

Cardiff University Postgraduate
Research Studentships, 364
University of Wales (Aberystwyth)
Postgraduate Research Studentships,
362
University of Wales Bangor (UWB)
Research Studentships, 363
Wingate Scholarships, 374

FINNISH

Any Country

CIMO Scholarships for Advanced
Finnish Studies and Research, 114

Australia

Wingate Scholarships, 374

British Commonwealth

Wingate Scholarships, 374

Canada

Wingate Scholarships, 374

Indian Sub-Continent

Wingate Scholarships, 374

Middle East

Wingate Scholarships, 374

United Kingdom

Wingate Scholarships, 374

West European Countries

Wingate Scholarships, 374

RUSSIAN

Any Country

Andrew W Mellon Postdoctoral
Fellowships in the Humanities, 358
Keele University Graduate Teaching
Assistantships, 195
University of Glasgow Postgraduate
Scholarships, 331
University Postgraduate Scholarships,
322
USC College Dissertation Fellowship,
359
USC College of Letters, Arts and
Sciences Merit Award, 359
Volzhsky Institute of Humanities Awards,
371

Australia

Wingate Scholarships, 374

British Commonwealth

Wingate Scholarships, 374

Canada

Wingate Scholarships, 374

Indian Sub-Continent

Wingate Scholarships, 374

Middle East

Wingate Scholarships, 374

United Kingdom

Wingate Scholarships, 374

USA

IREX Grant Opportunities for US
Scholars, 186

West European Countries

Wingate Scholarships, 374

SLAVONIC LANGUAGES (OTHERS)

Any Country

Alexander S Onassis Programme of
Research Grants, 7
Alexander S Onassis Research Grants,
7
The Helen Darcovich Memorial Doctoral
Fellowship, 108
Kennan Institute Short Term Grants, 196
Marusia and Michael Dorosh Master's
Fellowship, 108
Neporany Research and Teaching
Fellowship, 109
University of Glasgow Postgraduate
Scholarships, 331

Australia

Wingate Scholarships, 374

British Commonwealth

Wingate Scholarships, 374

Canada

Wingate Scholarships, 374

East European Countries

St Hugh's College The Rawnsley
Scholarship, 354

Indian Sub-Continent

Wingate Scholarships, 374

Middle East

Wingate Scholarships, 374

United Kingdom

Polish Embassy Short-Term Bursaries,
262
Wingate Scholarships, 374

USA

IREX Grant Opportunities for US Scholars, 186
Kennan Institute Research Scholarship, 196
The SSRC Eastern Europe Program: East European Language Training Grants, 291
Year Abroad Programme at the Jagiellonian University in Krakow, 199

West European Countries

Wingate Scholarships, 374

HUNGARIAN

Australia

Wingate Scholarships, 374

British Commonwealth

Wingate Scholarships, 374

Canada

Wingate Scholarships, 374

Indian Sub-Continent

Wingate Scholarships, 374

Middle East

Wingate Scholarships, 374

United Kingdom

Wingate Scholarships, 374

USA

IREX Grant Opportunities for US Scholars, 186
The SSRC Eastern Europe Program: East European Language Training Grants, 291

West European Countries

Wingate Scholarships, 374

FINO UGRIAN LANGUAGES

Any Country

CIMO Scholarships for Advanced Finnish Studies and Research, 114

Australia

Wingate Scholarships, 374

British Commonwealth

Wingate Scholarships, 374

Canada

Wingate Scholarships, 374

Indian Sub-Continent

Wingate Scholarships, 374

Middle East

Wingate Scholarships, 374

United Kingdom

Wingate Scholarships, 374

West European Countries

Wingate Scholarships, 374

EUROPEAN LANGUAGES (OTHERS)

Any Country

Open Society Sofia Scholarships for Foreign Scholars, 249
Spidola Award and Scholarships, 205

Australia

Wingate Scholarships, 374

British Commonwealth

Wingate Scholarships, 374

Canada

Wingate Scholarships, 374

Indian Sub-Continent

Wingate Scholarships, 374

Middle East

Wingate Scholarships, 374

United Kingdom

Wingate Scholarships, 374

West European Countries

Wingate Scholarships, 374

ALTAIC LANGUAGES

Australia

Wingate Scholarships, 374

British Commonwealth

Wingate Scholarships, 374

Canada

Wingate Scholarships, 374

Indian Sub-Continent

Wingate Scholarships, 374

Middle East

Wingate Scholarships, 374

United Kingdom

Wingate Scholarships, 374

USA

ARIT Language Fellowships, 20
IREX Grant Opportunities for US Scholars, 186

West European Countries

Wingate Scholarships, 374

ARABIC

Any Country

King Faisal International Award for Arabic Literature, 197
SOAS Bursary, 284
SOAS Research Student Fellowships, 285

Australia

Wingate Scholarships, 374

British Commonwealth

Wingate Scholarships, 374

Canada

Wingate Scholarships, 374

Indian Sub-Continent

Wingate Scholarships, 374

Middle East

Wingate Scholarships, 374

United Kingdom

Wingate Scholarships, 374

West European Countries

Wingate Scholarships, 374

HEBREW

Any Country

SOAS Bursary, 284
SOAS Research Student Fellowships, 285
University of Glasgow Postgraduate Scholarships, 331

Australia

Wingate Scholarships, 374

British Commonwealth

Wingate Scholarships, 374

Canada

Wingate Scholarships, 374

Indian Sub-Continent

Wingate Scholarships, 374

Middle East

Wingate Scholarships, 374

United Kingdom

Wingate Scholarships, 374

West European Countries

Wingate Scholarships, 374

CHINESE

Any Country

Andrew W Mellon Postdoctoral Fellowships in the Humanities, 358
Massey Doctoral Scholarship, 214
SOAS Bursary, 284
SOAS Research Student Fellowships, 285
University of New England Research Scholarships, 336
USC College of Letters, Arts and Sciences Merit Award, 359

Australia

Wingate Scholarships, 374

British Commonwealth

Wingate Scholarships, 374

Canada

Canada-Taiwan Scholarships Programme, 42
Wingate Scholarships, 374

Indian Sub-Continent

Wingate Scholarships, 374

Middle East

Wingate Scholarships, 374

United Kingdom

Wingate Scholarships, 374

West European Countries

Wingate Scholarships, 374

KOREAN

Any Country

Andrew W Mellon Postdoctoral Fellowships in the Humanities, 358
Korea Foundation Fellowship for Korean Language Training, 198
Korea Foundation Fellowship for Korean Studies, 198
SOAS Bursary, 284
SOAS Research Student Fellowships, 285
USC College Dissertation Fellowship, 359
USC College of Letters, Arts and Sciences Merit Award, 359

Australia

Wingate Scholarships, 374

British Commonwealth

Wingate Scholarships, 374

Canada

Wingate Scholarships, 374

Indian Sub-Continent

Wingate Scholarships, 374

Middle East

Wingate Scholarships, 374

United Kingdom

Wingate Scholarships, 374

West European Countries

Wingate Scholarships, 374

JAPANESE

Any Country

Andrew W Mellon Postdoctoral Fellowships in the Humanities, 358
Massey Doctoral Scholarship, 214
Pembroke College TEPCO Senior Studentship, 346
SOAS Bursary, 284
SOAS Research Student Fellowships, 285
University of New England Research Scholarships, 336
University of Stirling Research Studentships, 360
USC College Dissertation Fellowship, 359
USC College of Letters, Arts and Sciences Merit Award, 359

Australia

Wingate Scholarships, 374

British Commonwealth

Wingate Scholarships, 374

Canada

Wingate Scholarships, 374

Indian Sub-Continent

Wingate Scholarships, 374

Middle East

Wingate Scholarships, 374

United Kingdom

Cardiff University Postgraduate Research Studentships, 364
Wingate Scholarships, 374

West European Countries

Cardiff University Postgraduate Research Studentships, 364
Wingate Scholarships, 374

INDIAN LANGUAGES

Any Country

Manipur University Scholarship, 211
SOAS Bursary, 284
SOAS Research Student Fellowships, 285

Australia

Wingate Scholarships, 374

British Commonwealth

Wingate Scholarships, 374

Canada

India Studies Fellowship Competition, 286
Shastri Indo-Canadian Institute Language Training Fellowship, 286
Wingate Scholarships, 374

Indian Sub-Continent

Wingate Scholarships, 374

Middle East

Wingate Scholarships, 374

United Kingdom

Wingate Scholarships, 374

West European Countries

Wingate Scholarships, 374

IRANIC LANGUAGES

Any Country

SOAS Bursary, 284
SOAS Research Student Fellowships, 285

African Nations

British School of Archaeology in Iraq Grants, 71

Australia

British School of Archaeology in Iraq Grants, 71
Wingate Scholarships, 374

British Commonwealth

British School of Archaeology in Iraq Grants, 71
Wingate Scholarships, 374

Canada

British School of Archaeology in Iraq Grants, 71
Wingate Scholarships, 374

Far East

British School of Archaeology in Iraq Grants, 71

Indian Sub-Continent

British School of Archaeology in Iraq Grants, 71
Wingate Scholarships, 374

Middle East

Wingate Scholarships, 374

New Zealand

British School of Archaeology in Iraq Grants, 71

South Africa

British School of Archaeology in Iraq Grants, 71

United Kingdom

British School of Archaeology in Iraq Grants, 71
Wingate Scholarships, 374

USA

IREX Grant Opportunities for US Scholars, 186

West European Countries

Wingate Scholarships, 374

AFRICAN LANGUAGES

Any Country

SOAS Bursary, 284
SOAS Research Student Fellowships, 285

Australia

Wingate Scholarships, 374

British Commonwealth

Wingate Scholarships, 374

Canada

Wingate Scholarships, 374

Indian Sub-Continent

Wingate Scholarships, 374

Middle East

Wingate Scholarships, 374

United Kingdom

Wingate Scholarships, 374

West European Countries

Wingate Scholarships, 374

AMERINDIAN LANGUAGES

Any Country

Jacobs Research Funds, 374
UCLA Institute of American Culture Postdoctoral/Visiting Scholar Fellowships, 314

Australia

Wingate Scholarships, 374

British Commonwealth

Wingate Scholarships, 374

Canada

Wingate Scholarships, 374

Indian Sub-Continent

Wingate Scholarships, 374

Middle East

Wingate Scholarships, 374

United Kingdom

Wingate Scholarships, 374

West European Countries

Wingate Scholarships, 374

AUSTRONESIAN AND OCEANIC LANGUAGES

Australia

Wingate Scholarships, 374

Open Society Sofia Short-term Grants, 249

Indian Sub-Continent

Wingate Scholarships, 374

Middle East

Wingate Scholarships, 374

United Kingdom

Cardiff University Postgraduate Research Studentships, 364
CRF/RSE European Visiting Research Fellowships, 280
ESRC Research and Advanced Course Studentships, 141
Research Grant, 130, 264
Travel Grant, 130
University of Wales Bangor (UWB) Research Studentships, 363
Wingate Scholarships, 374

USA

IREX Grant Opportunities for US Scholars, 186
NEH Fellowship, 25
The Swedish Government 'SASS' Travel Grants, 308
US Department of Education International Research and Studies Program, 366

West European Countries

Cardiff University Postgraduate Research Studentships, 364
CRF/RSE European Visiting Research Fellowships, 280
ESRC Research and Advanced Course Studentships, 141
NAI Travel Grant, 244
Scholarship Foundation of the League for Finnish-American Societies, 284
University of Wales Bangor (UWB) Research Studentships, 363
Wingate Scholarships, 374

APPLIED LINGUISTICS

Any Country

Andrew W Mellon Postdoctoral Fellowships in the Humanities, 358
Camargo Fellowships, 75
Massey Doctoral Scholarship, 214
Onassis Programme of Postgraduate Research Scholarships, 7

UCLA Institute of American Culture Postdoctoral/Visiting Scholar Fellowships, 314
University of Stirling Research Studentships, 360
Unstra Grants - PVS Grants-Cils Grants, 319

Australia

Wingate Scholarships, 374

British Commonwealth

Wingate Scholarships, 374

Canada

Wingate Scholarships, 374

Indian Sub-Continent

Wingate Scholarships, 374

Middle East

Wingate Scholarships, 374

United Kingdom

University of Wales Bangor (UWB) Research Studentships, 363
Wingate Scholarships, 374

West European Countries

University of Wales Bangor (UWB) Research Studentships, 363
Wingate Scholarships, 374

PSYCHOLINGUISTICS

Any Country

Andrew W Mellon Postdoctoral Fellowships in the Humanities, 358
Onassis Programme of Postgraduate Research Scholarships, 7
University of Stirling Research Studentships, 360

Australia

Wingate Scholarships, 374

British Commonwealth

Wingate Scholarships, 374

Canada

Wingate Scholarships, 374

Indian Sub-Continent

Wingate Scholarships, 374

Middle East

Wingate Scholarships, 374

United Kingdom

University of Wales Bangor (UWB) Research Studentships, 363
Wingate Scholarships, 374

West European Countries

University of Wales Bangor (UWB) Research Studentships, 363
Wingate Scholarships, 374

GRAMMAR

Any Country

Andrew W Mellon Postdoctoral Fellowships in the Humanities, 358
Camargo Fellowships, 75
Jacobs Research Funds, 374
Onassis Programme of Postgraduate Research Scholarships, 7
Writing Center Graduate Fellowships, 28

Australia

Wingate Scholarships, 374

British Commonwealth

Wingate Scholarships, 374

Canada

Wingate Scholarships, 374

Indian Sub-Continent

Wingate Scholarships, 374

Middle East

Wingate Scholarships, 374

United Kingdom

University of Wales Bangor (UWB) Research Studentships, 363
Wingate Scholarships, 374

West European Countries

University of Wales Bangor (UWB) Research Studentships, 363
Wingate Scholarships, 374

SEMANTICS AND TERMINOLOGY

Any Country

Andrew W Mellon Postdoctoral Fellowships in the Humanities, 358
Camargo Fellowships, 75
Jacobs Research Funds, 374
Onassis Programme of Postgraduate Research Scholarships, 7
Unstra Grants - PVS Grants-Cils Grants, 319

Australia

Wingate Scholarships, 374

British Commonwealth

Wingate Scholarships, 374

Canada

Wingate Scholarships, 374

Indian Sub-Continent

Wingate Scholarships, 374

Middle East

Wingate Scholarships, 374

United Kingdom

University of Wales Bangor (UWB) Research Studentships, 363
Wingate Scholarships, 374

West European Countries

University of Wales Bangor (UWB) Research Studentships, 363
Wingate Scholarships, 374

PHONETICS

Any Country

Andrew W Mellon Postdoctoral Fellowships in the Humanities, 358
Camargo Fellowships, 75
Onassis Programme of Postgraduate Research Scholarships, 7
Unstra Grants - PVS Grants-Cils Grants, 319

Australia

Wingate Scholarships, 374

British Commonwealth

Wingate Scholarships, 374

Canada

Wingate Scholarships, 374

Indian Sub-Continent

Wingate Scholarships, 374

Middle East

Wingate Scholarships, 374

United Kingdom

University of Wales Bangor (UWB) Research Studentships, 363
Wingate Scholarships, 374

West European Countries

University of Wales Bangor (UWB) Research Studentships, 363
Wingate Scholarships, 374

LOGOPEDICS

Australia

Wingate Scholarships, 374

British Commonwealth

Wingate Scholarships, 374

Canada

Wingate Scholarships, 374

Indian Sub-Continent

Wingate Scholarships, 374

Middle East

Wingate Scholarships, 374

United Kingdom

Wingate Scholarships, 374

West European Countries

Wingate Scholarships, 374

COMPARATIVE LITERATURE

Any Country

Adolfo Omodeo Scholarship, 187
Ahmanson and Getty Postdoctoral Fellowships, 313
Alexander S Onassis Programme of Research Grants, 7
Alexander S Onassis Research Grants, 7
Andrew W Mellon Postdoctoral Fellowships in the Humanities, 358
ASECS/Clark Library Fellowships, 313
British Academy Major International Conference Grant, 59
British Academy Overseas Conference Grants, 59
British Academy Small Personal Research Grants, 59
Camargo Fellowships, 75
Center for Advanced Study in the Behavioral Sciences Postdoctoral Residential Fellowships, 112
ChLA Research Fellowships and Scholarships, 119
Clark Library Short-Term Resident Fellowships, 313
Clark-Huntington Joint Bibliographical Fellowship, 314
CQU University Postgraduate Research Award, 114
Foundation Praemium Erasmianum Study Prize, 150
Frederico Chabod Scholarship, 187
Humane Studies Fellowships, 177
M Alison Frantz Fellowship in Post-Classical Studies at The Gennadius Library (formerly known as the Gennadeion Fellowship), 22
Mary Isabel Sibley Fellowship, 260
NHC Fellowships in the Humanities, 232
Onassis Programme of Postgraduate Research Scholarships, 7
Queen's University of Belfast Research and Senior Visiting Research Fellowships, 266
SOAS Bursary, 284
SOAS Research Student Fellowships, 285
UCLA Summer Fellowship, 314
University of Glasgow Postgraduate Scholarships, 331
USC College Dissertation Fellowship, 359
USC College of Letters, Arts and Sciences Merit Award, 359
Volzhsky Institute of Humanities Awards, 371

Australia

Nepean Postgraduate Research Award, 364
Quinn, Nathan and Edmond Scholarships, 65
Wingate Scholarships, 374

British Commonwealth

Quinn, Nathan and Edmond
Scholarships, 65
Wingate Scholarships, 374

Canada

Quinn, Nathan and Edmond
Scholarships, 65
Wingate Scholarships, 374

East European Countries

CRF/RSE European Visiting Research
Fellowships, 280
Open Society Sofia Long-term Grants,
249
Open Society Sofia Short-term Grants,
249

Indian Sub-Continent

Quinn, Nathan and Edmond
Scholarships, 65
Wingate Scholarships, 374

Middle East

Wingate Scholarships, 374

New Zealand

Nepean Postgraduate Research Award,
364
Quinn, Nathan and Edmond
Scholarships, 65

South Africa

Quinn, Nathan and Edmond
Scholarships, 65

United Kingdom

BAAS Short Term Awards, 60
Cardiff University Postgraduate
Research Studentships, 364
CRF/RSE European Visiting Research
Fellowships, 280
Quinn, Nathan and Edmond
Scholarships, 65
Research Grant, 130, 264
Travel Grant, 130
University of Wales Bangor (UWB)
Research Studentships, 363
Wingate Scholarships, 374

USA

IREX Grant Opportunities for US
Scholars, 186
Kennan Institute Research Scholarship,
196

West European Countries

Cardiff University Postgraduate
Research Studentships, 364
CRF/RSE European Visiting Research
Fellowships, 280
University of Wales Bangor (UWB)
Research Studentships, 363
Wingate Scholarships, 374

HISTORY

Any Country

AAS American Society for Eighteenth-
Century Studies Fellowships, 11
ABC-Clio America: History and Life
Award, 251
Adolfo Omodeo Scholarship, 187
Ahmanson and Getty Postdoctoral
Fellowships, 313
AIATSIS Research Grants, 46
Albert J Beveridge Grant, 12
Albin Salton Fellowship, 371
Alexander O Vietor Memorial
Fellowship, 192
Alexander S Onassis Programme of
Research Grants, 7
Alexander S Onassis Research Grants,
7
Alice E Smith Fellowship, 306
Amy Louise Hunter Fellowship, 306
Andrew W Mellon Postdoctoral
Fellowships in the Humanities, 358
ASECS/Clark Library Fellowships, 313
Avery O Craven Award, 251
Barbara S Mosbacher Fellowship, 192
Berkshire Summer Fellowship, 73
Bernadotte E Schmitt Grants, 13
British Academy Major International
Conference Grant, 59
British Academy Overseas Conference
Grants, 59
British Academy Small Personal
Research Grants, 59
BSA Fellowship Program, 55
C H Currey Memorial Fellowship, 306
Camargo Fellowships, 75
Center for Advanced Study in the
Behavioral Sciences Postdoctoral
Residential Fellowships, 112
Center for Field Research Grants, 112
Center for New World Comparative
Studies Fellowship, 192
Charles H Watts Memorial Fellowship,
192
Clark Library Short-Term Resident
Fellowships, 313
Clark-Huntington Joint Bibliographical
Fellowship, 314

Cotton Research Fellowships, 138
Council of the Institute Awards, 263
CQU University Postgraduate Research
Award, 114
DAAD Leo Baeck Institute Grants, 157
Dixon Ryan Fox Manuscript Prize of the
New York State Historical Association,
238
Edouard Morot-Sir Fellowship in
Literature, 174
Equiano Memorial Award, 308
The Erik Barnouw Award, 252
Exeter College Usher-Cunningham
Senior Studentship, 339
Fellowships in the University of
Delaware - Hagley Program, 329
Foundation Praemium Erasmianum
Study Prize, 150
Frances A Yates Fellowships, 372
Frederico Chabod Scholarship, 187
George A Barton Fellowship, 24
Gilbert Chinard Fellowships, 174
Graduate Institute of International
Studies (Geneva) Scholarships, 162
Hagley Museum and Library Grants-in-
Aid of Research, 165
Hagley/Winterthur Arts and Industries
Fellowship, 165
Harry S Truman Library Institute
Dissertation Year Fellowships, 166
Harry S Truman Library Institute
Research Grants, 166
Harry S Truman Library Institute
Scholar's Award, 166
Harvard-Newcomen Fellowship in
Business History, 167
The Helen Wallis Fellowship, 67
Helen Watson Buckner Memorial
Fellowship, 192
Henri Frankfort Fellowship, 372
Henry Bellin du Pont Fellowship, 165
Herbert Hoover Presidential Library
Association Travel Grants, 169
Humane Studies Fellowships, 177
Huntington Short-Term Fellowships, 172
IHS Summer Graduate Research
Fellowship, 177
Institute for Advanced Study
Postdoctoral Residential Fellowships,
176
Institute of European History
Fellowships, 178
Irish Research Funds, 187
The J B Harley Research Fellowships in
the History of Cartography, 188
J Franklin Jameson Fellowship, 13
Jane Addams/Andrew Carnegie
Fellowships in Philanthropy, 174
Jeannette D Black Memorial Fellowship,
193
John C Geilfuss Fellowship, 306

African Nations

Australia

British Commonwealth

Canada

East European Countries

Far East

Indian Sub-Continent

Middle East

New Zealand

South Africa

South America

United Kingdom

PREHISTORY

Wingate Scholarships, 374

ANCIENT CIVILISATIONS

Any Country

AIAR Annual Professorship, 23
Albert J Beveridge Grant, 12
Alexander S Onassis Programme of
  Research Grants, 7
Alexander S Onassis Research Grants,
  7
Andrew W Mellon Postdoctoral
  Fellowships in the Humanities, 358
ASCSA Fellowships, 21
ASCSA Summer Sessions, 22
ASOR Mesopotamian Fellowship, 24
Bernadotte E Schmitt Grants, 13
Center for Field Research Grants, 112
Center for Hellenic Studies Junior
  Fellowships, 113
Dover Fund, 296
Dumbarton Oaks Fellowships and
  Junior Fellowships, 139
FAMSI Research Grant, 150
Henri Frankfort Fellowship, 372
Hugh Last and Donald Atkinson Funds
  Committee Grants, 296
The J B Harley Research Fellowships in
  the History of Cartography, 188
J Franklin Jameson Fellowship, 13
Jacob Hirsh Fellowship, 22
Littleton-Griswold Research Grant, 13
Mary Isabel Sibley Fellowship, 260
NEH Senior Research Fellowship, 22
Onassis Programme of Postgraduate
  Research Scholarships, 7
Samuel H Kress Fellowship in Classical
  Art History, 23
Samuel H Kress Joint Athens-Jerusalem
  Fellowship, 23, 26

African Nations

British School of Archaeology in Iraq
  Grants, 71

Australia

British School of Archaeology in Iraq
  Grants, 71
Wingate Scholarships, 374

British Commonwealth

Balsdon Fellowship, 68
British School of Archaeology in Iraq
  Grants, 71
BSR Rome Awards in Archaeology,
  History and Letters, 68

Hector and Elizabeth Catling Bursary, 67
Hugh Last Fellowship, 69
Macmillan-Rodewald Studentship,
  School Studentship, Cary Studentship,
  67
Rome Scholarships in Ancient, Medieval
  and Later Italian Studies, 70
Wingate Scholarships, 374

Canada

ANS Fellowship in Roman Studies, 17
British School of Archaeology in Iraq
  Grants, 71
Wingate Scholarships, 374

Far East

British School of Archaeology in Iraq
  Grants, 71

Indian Sub-Continent

British School of Archaeology in Iraq
  Grants, 71
Wingate Scholarships, 374

Middle East

Wingate Scholarships, 374

New Zealand

British School of Archaeology in Iraq
  Grants, 71

South Africa

British School of Archaeology in Iraq
  Grants, 71

United Kingdom

Balsdon Fellowship, 68
British Institute of Archaeology at
  Ankara Research Grants, 66
British Institute of Archaeology at
  Ankara Travel Grants, 66
British School of Archaeology in Iraq
  Grants, 71
BSR Rome Awards in Archaeology,
  History and Letters, 68
Cardiff University Postgraduate
  Research Studentships, 364
Hector and Elizabeth Catling Bursary, 67
Hugh Last Fellowship, 69
Macmillan-Rodewald Studentship,
  School Studentship, Cary Studentship,
  67
Research Grant, 130, 264
Rome Scholarships in Ancient, Medieval
  and Later Italian Studies, 70
Travel Grant, 130
Wingate Scholarships, 374

USA

ANS Fellowship in Roman Studies, 17
Earthwatch Teacher Advancement
  Awards, 140

West European Countries

Cardiff University Postgraduate
  Research Studentships, 364
Merton College Leventis Senior
  Scholarship, 345
Wingate Scholarships, 374

MEDIEVAL HISTORY

Any Country

Albert J Beveridge Grant, 12
Alexander S Onassis Programme of
  Research Grants, 7
Alexander S Onassis Research Grants,
  7
Andrew W Mellon Postdoctoral
  Fellowships in the Humanities, 358
ASCSA Fellowships, 21
ASCSA Summer Sessions, 22
Barbara Thom Postdoctoral Fellowship,
  171
Bernadotte E Schmitt Grants, 13
Camargo Fellowships, 75
Clark-Huntington Joint Bibliographical
  Fellowship, 314
Dumbarton Oaks Fellowships and
  Junior Fellowships, 139
Isobel Thornley Research Fellowship,
  179
The J B Harley Research Fellowships in
  the History of Cartography, 188
J Franklin Jameson Fellowship, 13
Littleton-Griswold Research Grant, 13
Mary Isabel Sibley Fellowship, 260
Massey Doctoral Scholarship, 214
Mellon Postdoctoral Research
  Fellowships, 12, 172
NEH Senior Research Fellowship, 22
Neil Ker Memorial Fund, 60
Onassis Programme of Postgraduate
  Research Scholarships, 7
Royal History Society Fellowship, 179
Scouloudi Fellowships, 179
Spidola Award and Scholarships, 205
UCLA Summer Fellowship, 314
University of Oslo International Summer
  School Scholarships, 337
University of Stirling Research
  Studentships, 360
Yorkist History Trust Fellowship, 179

Australia

Wingate Scholarships, 374

British Commonwealth

Balsdon Fellowship, 68
BSR Rome Awards in Archaeology,
  History and Letters, 68
Hector and Elizabeth Catling Bursary, 67
Macmillan-Rodewald Studentship,
  School Studentship, Cary Studentship,
  67
Rome Scholarships in Ancient, Medieval
  and Later Italian Studies, 70
Wingate Scholarships, 374

Canada

Wingate Scholarships, 374

East European Countries

Open Society Sofia Central European
  University Scholarship, 249

Indian Sub-Continent

Wingate Scholarships, 374

Middle East

Wingate Scholarships, 374

United Kingdom

Balsdon Fellowship, 68
British Institute of Archaeology at
  Ankara Research Grants, 66
British Institute of Archaeology at
  Ankara Travel Grants, 66
BSR Rome Awards in Archaeology,
  History and Letters, 68
Cardiff University Postgraduate
  Research Studentships, 364
Hector and Elizabeth Catling Bursary, 67
Macmillan-Rodewald Studentship,
  School Studentship, Cary Studentship,
  67
Research Grant, 130, 264
Rome Scholarships in Ancient, Medieval
  and Later Italian Studies, 70
St Anne's College Olwen Rhys Research
  Scholarship, 351
Travel Grant, 130
University of Wales (Aberystwyth)
  Postgraduate Research Studentships,
  362
University of Wales Bangor (UWB)
  Research Studentships, 363
Wingate Scholarships, 374

USA

Earthwatch Teacher Advancement
  Awards, 140
National Endowment for the Humanities
  Fellowships, 172, 241
William B Schallek Memorial Graduate
  Fellowship Award, 268

West European Countries

Cardiff University Postgraduate
  Research Studentships, 364
St Anne's College Olwen Rhys Research
  Scholarship, 351
University of Wales (Aberystwyth)
  Postgraduate Research Studentships,
  362
University of Wales Bangor (UWB)
  Research Studentships, 363
Wingate Scholarships, 374

MODERN HISTORY

Any Country

Adelle and Erwin Tomash Fellowship in
  the History of Information Processing,
  118
Ahmanson and Getty Postdoctoral
  Fellowships, 313
Albert J Beveridge Grant, 12
Alexander S Onassis Programme of
  Research Grants, 7
Alexander S Onassis Research Grants,
  7
Alice E Smith Fellowship, 306
Amy Louise Hunter Fellowship, 306
Andrew W Mellon Postdoctoral
  Fellowships in the Humanities, 358
ASCSA Fellowships, 21
ASECS/Clark Library Fellowships, 313
Barbara Thom Postdoctoral Fellowship,
  171
Bernadotte E Schmitt Grants, 13
C H Currey Memorial Fellowship, 306
Camargo Fellowships, 75
Center Research Fellowships, 316
Clark Library Short-Term Resident
  Fellowships, 313
Clark-Huntington Joint Bibliographical
  Fellowship, 314
Dixon Ryan Fox Manuscript Prize of the
  New York State Historical Association,
  238
E Lyman Stewart Fellowship, 329
Elisabeth Barker Fund, 59
Fellowships in the University of
  Delaware - Hagley Program, 329

Hagley/Winterthur Arts and Industries
  Fellowship, 165
IEEE Fellowship in Electrical History,
  178
Institute of European History
  Fellowships, 178
Isobel Thornley Research Fellowship,
  179
The J B Harley Research Fellowships in
  the History of Cartography, 188
J Franklin Jameson Fellowship, 13
Jean Monnet Fellowships, 145
John C Geilfuss Fellowship, 306
John Treloar Grants-in-Aid, 49
Joyce A Tracy Fellowship, 11
Lewis Walpole Library Fellowship, 207
Library Company of Philadelphia
  Research Fellowships in American
  History and Culture, 208
Littleton-Griswold Research Grant, 13
Mary Isabel Sibley Fellowship, 260
Mellon Postdoctoral Research
  Fellowships, 12, 172
Miles Lerman Center for the Study of
  Jewish Resistance Research
  Fellowship, 317
Minnesota Historical Society Research
  Grant, 220
NEH Senior Research Fellowship, 22
Neville Chamberlain Scholarship, 321
Onassis Programme of Postgraduate
  Research Scholarships, 7
Queen's University of Belfast Research
  and Senior Visiting Research
  Fellowships, 266
Rockefeller Archive Center Research
  Grant Program, 270
Roosevelt Institute Grant-in-Aid, 151
Royal History Society Fellowship, 179
Scouloudi Fellowships, 179
Spidola Award and Scholarships, 205
Thank-Offering to Britain Fellowships,
  60
The Joyce and Arthur Schechter
  Fellowship, 317
The Pearl Resnick Post Doctoral
  Fellowship, 317
UCLA Institute of American Culture
  Postdoctoral/Visiting Scholar
  Fellowships, 314
UCLA Summer Fellowship, 314
University of Dundee Research Awards,
  330
University of Oslo International Summer
  School Scholarships, 337
University of Stirling Research
  Studentships, 360
Volzhsky Institute of Humanities Awards,
  371
Wolfsonian Fellowship Visiting Scholar
  Assoc Fellowship, 376

Australia

Wingate Scholarships, 374

British Commonwealth

Balsdon Fellowship, 68
BSR Rome Awards in Archaeology, History and Letters, 68
Hector and Elizabeth Catling Bursary, 67
Macmillan-Rodewald Studentship, School Studentship, Cary Studentship, 67
Rome Scholarships in Ancient, Medieval and Later Italian Studies, 70
Wingate Scholarships, 374

Canada

Wingate Scholarships, 374

East European Countries

Open Society Sofia Central European University Scholarship, 249

Indian Sub-Continent

Wingate Scholarships, 374

Middle East

Wingate Scholarships, 374

New Zealand

J M Sherrard Award, 110

United Kingdom

Balsdon Fellowship, 68
BSR Rome Awards in Archaeology, History and Letters, 68
Cardiff University Postgraduate Research Studentships, 364
Hector and Elizabeth Catling Bursary, 67
Macmillan-Rodewald Studentship, School Studentship, Cary Studentship, 67
Polish Embassy Short-Term Bursaries, 262
Research Grant, 130, 264
Rome Scholarships in Ancient, Medieval and Later Italian Studies, 70
Travel Grant, 130
University of Wales (Aberystwyth) Postgraduate Research Studentships, 362
University of Wales Bangor (UWB) Research Studentships, 363
Wingate Scholarships, 374

USA

Earthwatch Teacher Advancement Awards, 140

National Endowment for the Humanities Fellowships, 172, 241
Rear Admiral John D Hayes Pre-Doctoral Fellowship in US Naval History, 135, 367
Vice Admiral Edwin B Hooper Research Grants, 367

West European Countries

Cardiff University Postgraduate Research Studentships, 364
European University Institute Postgraduate Scholarships, 144
NAI Travel Grant, 244
University of Wales (Aberystwyth) Postgraduate Research Studentships, 362
University of Wales Bangor (UWB) Research Studentships, 363
Wingate Scholarships, 374

CONTEMPORARY HISTORY

Any Country

AIATSIS Research Grants, 46
Albert J Beveridge Grant, 12
Alexander S Onassis Programme of Research Grants, 7
Alexander S Onassis Research Grants, 7
Alice E Smith Fellowship, 306
Amy Louise Hunter Fellowship, 306
Andrew W Mellon Postdoctoral Fellowships in the Humanities, 358
Barbara Thom Postdoctoral Fellowship, 171
Bernadotte E Schmitt Grants, 13
Camargo Fellowships, 75
Centro de Estudios Politicos Y Constitutionales Grant, 117
Dixon Ryan Fox Manuscript Prize of the New York State Historical Association, 238
E Lyman Stewart Fellowship, 329
Elisabeth Barker Fund, 59
Fellowships in the University of Delaware - Hagley Program, 329
IEEE Fellowship in Electrical History, 178
Institute of European History Fellowships, 178
Isobel Thornley Research Fellowship, 179
J Franklin Jameson Fellowship, 13
Jean Monnet Fellowships, 145
John C Geilfuss Fellowship, 306

John Treloar Grants-in-Aid, 49
Littleton-Griswold Research Grant, 13
Mary Isabel Sibley Fellowship, 260
Massey Doctoral Scholarship, 214
Mellon Postdoctoral Research Fellowships, 12, 172
Minnesota Historical Society Research Grant, 220
Onassis Programme of Postgraduate Research Scholarships, 7
Queen's University of Belfast Research and Senior Visiting Research Fellowships, 266
Royal History Society Fellowship, 179
Scouloudi Fellowships, 179
Spidola Award and Scholarships, 205
University of Dundee Research Awards, 330
University of Oslo International Summer School Scholarships, 337
University of Stirling Research Studentships, 360

Australia

Wingate Scholarships, 374

British Commonwealth

Balsdon Fellowship, 68
BSR Rome Awards in Archaeology, History and Letters, 68
Hector and Elizabeth Catling Bursary, 67
Macmillan-Rodewald Studentship, School Studentship, Cary Studentship, 67
Rome Scholarships in Ancient, Medieval and Later Italian Studies, 70
Wingate Scholarships, 374

Canada

Wingate Scholarships, 374

East European Countries

Open Society Sofia Central European University Scholarship, 249

Indian Sub-Continent

Wingate Scholarships, 374

Middle East

Wingate Scholarships, 374

United Kingdom

Balsdon Fellowship, 68
BSR Rome Awards in Archaeology, History and Letters, 68
Cardiff University Postgraduate Research Studentships, 364
Hector and Elizabeth Catling Bursary, 67

Macmillan-Rodewald Studentship, School Studentship, Cary Studentship, 67

Polish Embassy Short-Term Bursaries, 262

Research Grant, 130, 264

Rome Scholarships in Ancient, Medieval and Later Italian Studies, 70

Travel Grant, 130

University of Wales (Aberystwyth) Postgraduate Research Studentships, 362

Wingate Scholarships, 374

USA

Beeler-Raider Fellowship, 212

National Endowment for the Humanities Fellowships, 172, 241

Rear Admiral John D Hayes Pre-Doctoral Fellowship in US Naval History, 135, 367

Vice Admiral Edwin B Hooper Research Grants, 367

West European Countries

Cardiff University Postgraduate Research Studentships, 364

European University Institute Postgraduate Scholarships, 144

NAI Travel Grant, 244

University of Wales (Aberystwyth) Postgraduate Research Studentships, 362

Wingate Scholarships, 374

ARCHAEOLOGY

Any Country

Adolfo Omodeo Scholarship, 187

AIAR Annual Professorship, 23

AIAR Islamic Studies Fellowship, 23

AIATSIS Research Grants, 46

Alexander S Onassis Programme of Research Grants, 7

Alexander S Onassis Research Grants, 7

ASCSA Fellowships, 21

ASCSA Research Fellow in Faunal Studies, 21

ASCSA Research Fellow in Geoarchaeology, 21

ASCSA Summer Sessions, 22

British Academy Major International Conference Grant, 59

British Academy Overseas Conference Grants, 59

British Academy Small Personal Research Grants, 59

CBA Grant for Publication, 129

Center for Advanced Study in the Behavioral Sciences Postdoctoral Residential Fellowships, 112

Center for Field Research Grants, 112

Center for Hellenic Studies Junior Fellowships, 113

Conservation Analytical Laboratory Materials Analysis Fellowship, 289

Cotton Research Fellowships, 138

Dover Fund, 296

FAMSI Research Grant, 150

Foundation Praemium Erasmianum Study Prize, 150

Frederico Chabod Scholarship, 187

George A Barton Fellowship, 24

Hugh Last and Donald Atkinson Funds Committee Grants, 296

J Lawrence Angel Fellowship in Human Skeletal Studies, 22

Jacob Hirsh Fellowship, 22

James A Swan Fund, 261

Kenan T Erim Award, 30

Kress/ARIT Graduate Fellowship, 20

Lemmermann Foundation Scholarship, 205

Mary Isabel Sibley Fellowship, 260

NEH Senior Research Fellowship, 22

NHC Fellowships in the Humanities, 232

Onassis Programme of Postgraduate Research Scholarships, 7

Prehistoric Society Conference Fund, 264

Prehistoric Society Research Fund Grant, 264

Research Grant Conference Award, 264

Samuel H Kress Fellowship in Classical Art History, 23

Samuel H Kress Joint Athens-Jerusalem Fellowship, 23, 26

SOAS Bursary, 284

SOAS Research Student Fellowships, 285

Spidola Award and Scholarships, 205

University of Glasgow Postgraduate Scholarships, 331

University of Manchester Research Studentships or Scholarships, 334

University of New England Research Scholarships, 336

University Postgraduate Scholarships, 322

African Nations

British School of Archaeology in Iraq Grants, 71

Australia

British School of Archaeology in Iraq Grants, 71

Wingate Scholarships, 374

British Commonwealth

Balsdon Fellowship, 68

British Institute in Eastern Africa Research Studentships and Graduate Attachments, 65

British School of Archaeology in Iraq Grants, 71

BSR Archaeological Fieldwork Support, 68

BSR Rome Awards in Archaeology, History and Letters, 68

Hector and Elizabeth Catling Bursary, 67

Macmillan-Rodewald Studentship, School Studentship, Cary Studentship, 67

Rome Scholarships in Ancient, Medieval and Later Italian Studies, 70

Wingate Scholarships, 374

Canada

Anna C and Oliver C Colburn Fellowship, 30

The Archchaeology Geology Division - Claude C Albritton, Jr Scholarships, 155

British School of Archaeology in Iraq Grants, 71

Harriet and Leon Pomerance Fellowship, 30

Thompson (Homer and Dorothy) Fellowship, 105

Wingate Scholarships, 374

East European Countries

Bologna Program, 302

CRF/RSE European Visiting Research Fellowships, 280

Open Society Sofia Long-term Grants, 249

Open Society Sofia Short-term Grants, 249

Far East

Asian Cultural Council Fellowship Grants Program, 40

British School of Archaeology in Iraq Grants, 71

Indian Sub-Continent

British School of Archaeology in Iraq Grants, 71

PHILOSOPHY

Any Country

Australia

British Commonwealth

Wingate Scholarships, 374

Canada

Wingate Scholarships, 374

East European Countries

Bologna Program, 302
CRF/RSE European Visiting Research
  Fellowships, 280
Open Society Sofia Long-term Grants,
  249
Open Society Sofia Short-term Grants,
  249

Indian Sub-Continent

Jawaharlal Nehru Memorial Fund
  Cambridge Scholarships, 90
Wingate Scholarships, 374

Middle East

Wingate Scholarships, 374

United Kingdom

Cardiff University Postgraduate
  Research Studentships, 364
CRF/RSE European Visiting Research
  Fellowships, 280
Research Grant, 130, 264
Travel Grant, 130
Wingate Scholarships, 374

USA

Americans and World Affairs Fellows
  Program, 378
IREX Grant Opportunities for US
  Scholars, 186
Kennan Institute Research Scholarship,
  196
NEH Fellowship, 25
NEH Postdoctoral Research Award, 25

West European Countries

Cardiff University Postgraduate
  Research Studentships, 364
CRF/RSE European Visiting Research
  Fellowships, 280
Scholarship Foundation of the League
  for Finnish-American Societies, 284
Wingate Scholarships, 374

PHILOSOPHICAL SCHOOLS

Any Country

Ahmanson and Getty Postdoctoral
  Fellowships, 313
Andrew W Mellon Postdoctoral
  Fellowships in the Humanities, 358
ASECS/Clark Library Fellowships, 313
Camargo Fellowships, 75
Clark Library Short-Term Resident
  Fellowships, 313
Clark-Huntington Joint Bibliographical
  Fellowship, 314
Gifford Research Fellowship, 359
Onassis Programme of Postgraduate
  Research Scholarships, 7
Spidola Award and Scholarships, 205
University of Dundee Research Awards,
  330

Australia

Wingate Scholarships, 374

British Commonwealth

Hector and Elizabeth Catling Bursary, 67
Macmillan-Rodewald Studentship,
  School Studentship, Cary Studentship,
  67
Wingate Scholarships, 374

Canada

Wingate Scholarships, 374

Indian Sub-Continent

Wingate Scholarships, 374

Middle East

Wingate Scholarships, 374

United Kingdom

Cardiff University Postgraduate
  Research Studentships, 364
Hector and Elizabeth Catling Bursary, 67
Macmillan-Rodewald Studentship,
  School Studentship, Cary Studentship,
  67
Wingate Scholarships, 374

West European Countries

Cardiff University Postgraduate
  Research Studentships, 364
Wingate Scholarships, 374

METAPHYSICS

Any Country

Andrew W Mellon Postdoctoral
  Fellowships in the Humanities, 358
Camargo Fellowships, 75
Gifford Research Fellowship, 359
Massey Doctoral Scholarship, 214
University of Dundee Research Awards,
  330

Australia

Wingate Scholarships, 374

British Commonwealth

Wingate Scholarships, 374

Canada

Wingate Scholarships, 374

Indian Sub-Continent

Wingate Scholarships, 374

Middle East

Wingate Scholarships, 374

United Kingdom

Wingate Scholarships, 374

West European Countries

Wingate Scholarships, 374

LOGIC

Any Country

Andrew W Mellon Postdoctoral
  Fellowships in the Humanities, 358
Camargo Fellowships, 75
Gifford Research Fellowship, 359
Massey Doctoral Scholarship, 214
University of Dundee Research Awards,
  330

Australia

Wingate Scholarships, 374

British Commonwealth

Wingate Scholarships, 374

Canada

Wingate Scholarships, 374

Indian Sub-Continent

Wingate Scholarships, 374

Middle East

Wingate Scholarships, 374

United Kingdom

Cardiff University Postgraduate
Research Studentships, 364
Wingate Scholarships, 374

West European Countries

Cardiff University Postgraduate
Research Studentships, 364
Wingate Scholarships, 374

ETHICS

Any Country

AIATSIS Research Grants, 46
Andrew W Mellon Postdoctoral
Fellowships in the Humanities, 358

Camargo Fellowships, 75
Center Research Fellowships, 316
Charlotte W Newcombe Doctoral
Dissertation Fellowships, 377
Gifford Research Fellowship, 359
Massey Doctoral Scholarship, 214
Miles Lerman Center for the Study of
Jewish Resistance Research
Fellowship, 317
The Joyce and Arthur Schechter
Fellowship, 317
The Pearl Resnick Post Doctoral
Fellowship, 317
University of Dundee Research Awards,
330

Australia

Wingate Scholarships, 374

British Commonwealth

Wingate Scholarships, 374

Canada

Social Sciences and Humanities
Research Council of Canada Strategic

Research Grants, Research Networks,
Research Workshops, Partnership
Development Grants, 295
Wingate Scholarships, 374

Indian Sub-Continent

Wingate Scholarships, 374

Middle East

Wingate Scholarships, 374

United Kingdom

Cardiff University Postgraduate
Research Studentships, 364
Wingate Scholarships, 374

USA

NEH Postdoctoral Research Award, 25

West European Countries

Cardiff University Postgraduate
Research Studentships, 364
Wingate Scholarships, 374

FINE AND APPLIED ARTS

GENERAL

Any Country

Adolfo Omodeo Scholarship, 187
Ahmanson and Getty Postdoctoral
Fellowships, 313
AIATSIS Research Grants, 46
Alberta Art Foundation Graduate
Scholarships in The Department of Art,
323
Alexander S Onassis Programme of
Research Grants, 7
Alexander S Onassis Research Grants,
7
Alice Berger Hammerschlag Trust
Award, 34
Arts Council of Northern Ireland Annual
Award, 34
ASECS/Clark Library Fellowships, 313
Banff Centre Scholarships, 53
Barbara Thom Postdoctoral Fellowship,
171
Bass Ireland Arts Awards, 34
British Academy Small Personal
Research Grants, 59
Camargo Fellowships, 75

Canadian Department of External Affairs
Faculty Enrichment Program, 107
Canadian Department of External Affairs
Faculty Research Program, 108
Canadian Department of External Affairs
Institutional Research Program, 108
Center for Field Research Grants, 112
Clark-Huntington Joint Bibliographical
Fellowship, 314
Concordia University Graduate
Fellowships, 126
David J Azrieli Graduate Fellowship, 126
Equiano Memorial Award, 308
European Enlightenment Project
Fellowships, 175
Foundation Praemium Erasmianum
Study Prize, 150
Frederico Chabod Scholarship, 187
Hagley/Winterthur Arts and Industries
Fellowship, 165
Hambidge Center Residency Program,
166
Harold White Fellowships, 233
Howard Foundation Fellowships, 155
Institute for Advanced Studies in the
Humanities Visiting Research
Fellowships, 175

Jesus College Old Member's Graduate
Scholarship, 341
Joanna Randall-MacIver Junior
Research Fellowship, 341
John W O'Brien Graduate Fellowship,
126
Jubilee Research Fellowship, 274
Keele University Graduate Teaching
Assistantships, 195
Lindberg Grants, 118
Logan Research Fellowships, 222
London Arts Board Awards and
Schemes for Artists, 208
Mellon Postdoctoral Research
Fellowships, 12, 172
MICA International Fellowship Award,
214
Monash Graduate Scholarships, 223
Monash University Partial Tuition
Postgraduate Research Scholarship
Scheme, 223
Monash University Silver Jubilee
Postgraduate Scholarship, 223
New York Fellowship, 35
Onassis Programme of Postgraduate
Research Scholarships, 7
Paul Mellon Centre Grants, 259
The Philip Brett Award, 16

African Nations

Australia

British Commonwealth

Canada

Caribbean Countries

East European Countries

Far East

Indian Sub-Continent

Middle East

CSD Grants for Foreign Research Fellows, 115
Friends of Peterhouse Bursary, 260
Fulbright Postdoctoral Research and Lecturing Awards for Non-US Citizens, 154
Merton College Third World Graduate Scholarship, 345
Wingate Scholarships, 374

New Zealand

Commonwealth Scholarships, Fellowships and Academic Staff Scholarships, 121
CSD Grants for Foreign Research Fellows, 115
Friends of Peterhouse Bursary, 260
Fulbright Postdoctoral Research and Lecturing Awards for Non-US Citizens, 154
Nepean Postgraduate Research Award, 364
Quinn, Nathan and Edmond Scholarships, 65

South Africa

Commonwealth Scholarships, Fellowships and Academic Staff Scholarships, 121
CSD Grants for Attendance at International Conferences, 115
CSD Prestige Scholarships for Doctoral Studies Abroad, 116
CSD Publication Grants, 116
CSD Research Grants, 116
CSD Scholarships for Doctoral/D-Tech Studies at Universities and Technikons in South Africa, 116
CSD Scholarships for Honours Degree Studies at Universities in South Africa, 117
CSD Scholarships for Master's Degree Studies/Studies for Master's Degree in Technology in South Africa, 117
Friends of Peterhouse Bursary, 260
Fulbright Postdoctoral Research and Lecturing Awards for Non-US Citizens, 154
Isie Smuts Research Award, 303
Quinn, Nathan and Edmond Scholarships, 65

South America

CSD Grants for Foreign Research Fellows, 115
Friends of Peterhouse Bursary, 260
Fulbright Commission (Argentina) Master's Program, 154

Fulbright Postdoctoral Research and Lecturing Awards for Non-US Citizens, 154
Guggenheim Fellowships to Assist Research and Artistic Creation (Latin America and the Caribbean), 194
Merton College Third World Graduate Scholarship, 345
PRA Fellowships, 257

United Kingdom

Arts Council of Wales Grants for Artists, 36
Canada Memorial Foundation Scholarships, 104
Commonwealth Scholarships, Fellowships and Academic Staff Scholarships, 121
CSD Grants for Foreign Research Fellows, 115
English-Speaking Union Chautauqua Scholarships, 143
Fulbright Postdoctoral Research and Lecturing Awards for Non-US Citizens, 154
George Campbell Travel Award, 34
Henry Moore Sculpture Fellowship at the BSR, 69
Portia Geach Memorial Award, 39
Quinn, Nathan and Edmond Scholarships, 65
Research Grant, 130, 264
Rome Scholarships in the Fine Arts, 70
Sargant Fellowship, 70
St Anne's College Irene Jamieson Research Scholarship, 351
Travel Grant, 130
University of Wales (Aberystwyth) Postgraduate Research Studentships, 362
Visual Arts Fellowship, 288
Visual Arts Project Fund, 38
Wingate Scholarships, 374

USA

Asian Cultural Council Fellowship Grants Program, 40
Belgian-American Educational Foundation Graduate Fellowships for Study in Belgium, 53
British Schools and Universities Foundation, Inc. Scholarships, 71
CSD Grants for Foreign Research Fellows, 115
Federal Chancellor Scholarship, 7
Fellowship of the Flemish Community, 148
Friends of Peterhouse Bursary, 260
Fulbright Scholar Awards for Research and Lecturing Abroad, 130

Guggenheim Fellowships to Assist Research and Artistic Creation (US and Canada), 195
Harriet Hale Woolley Scholarships, 318
Louise Wallace Hackney Fellowship, 17
National Endowment for the Humanities Fellowships, 172, 241
National League of American Pen Women Grants for Mature Women, 232
Native American Scholarship Program, 235
PRA Fellowships, 257
Richard Rodgers Awards for the Musical Theater, 10

West European Countries

Artflight Arts Council-Aer Lingus Travel Awards, 33
Arts Council of Ireland Travel Awards to Creative Artists, 33
Belgian-American Educational Foundation Graduate Fellowships for Study in the USA, 54
CSD Grants for Foreign Research Fellows, 115
Friends of Peterhouse Bursary, 260
Fulbright Postdoctoral Research and Lecturing Awards for Non-US Citizens, 154
George Campbell Travel Award, 34
The Macaulay Fellowship, 33
The Marten Toonder Award, 34
NAI Travel Grant, 244
Postgraduate Fellowships for Study in the USA, 54
Scholarship Foundation of the League for Finnish-American Societies, 284
St Anne's College Irene Jamieson Research Scholarship, 351
University of Wales (Aberystwyth) Postgraduate Research Studentships, 362
Wingate Scholarships, 374

HISTORY AND PHILOSOPHY OF ART

Any Country

Adolfo Omodeo Scholarship, 187
Ahmanson and Getty Postdoctoral Fellowships, 313
Albert J Beveridge Grant, 12
Alexander S Onassis Programme of Research Grants, 7
Alexander S Onassis Research Grants, 7

University of Wales (Aberystwyth)
Postgraduate Research Studentships,
362
Wingate Scholarships, 374

USA

Asian Cultural Council Fellowship
Grants Program, 40
Gladys Krieble Delmas Foundation
Grants, 161
Kennan Institute Research Scholarship,
196
Kress Fellowship in the Art and
Archaeology of Jordan, 24
National Endowment for the Humanities
Fellowships, 172, 241
NEH Fellowship, 25
NEH Postdoctoral Research Award, 25
Samuel H Kress Fellowship, 23, 25
Samuel H Kress Joint Athens-Jerusalem
Fellowship, 23, 26

West European Countries

Scholarship Foundation of the League
for Finnish-American Societies, 284
University of Wales (Aberystwyth)
Postgraduate Research Studentships,
362
Wingate Scholarships, 374

AESTHETICS

Any Country

Adolfo Omodeo Scholarship, 187
Andrew W Mellon Postdoctoral
Fellowships in the Humanities, 358
British Academy Major International
Conference Grant, 59
British Academy Overseas Conference
Grants, 59
Camargo Fellowships, 75
Frederico Chabod Scholarship, 187
Onassis Programme of Postgraduate
Research Scholarships, 7
Roswell Artist-in-Residence Program,
271

Australia

Wingate Scholarships, 374

British Commonwealth

Wingate Scholarships, 374

Canada

Wingate Scholarships, 374

Far East

Asian Cultural Council Fellowship
Grants Program, 40

Indian Sub-Continent

Wingate Scholarships, 374

Middle East

Wingate Scholarships, 374

United Kingdom

British Conference Grants, 59
Wingate Scholarships, 374

USA

Asian Cultural Council Fellowship
Grants Program, 40

West European Countries

Wingate Scholarships, 374

ART MANAGEMENT

Any Country

Lifchez/Stronach Curatorial Internship,
217
Metropolitan Museum of Art Six-Month
Internship, 217
Metropolitan Museum of Art Summer
Internships for College Students, 217
Metropolitan Museum of Art Summer
Internships for Graduate Students, 218
MICA Fellowship, 214
Muddy Waters Scholarship, 56

Australia

Wingate Scholarships, 374

British Commonwealth

Wingate Scholarships, 374

Canada

Wingate Scholarships, 374

East European Countries

Marcel Hicter Foundation Travel Bursary
Scheme, 211
Open Society Sofia Long-term Grants,
249
Open Society Sofia Short-term Grants,
249

Far East

Asian Cultural Council Fellowship
Grants Program, 40

Indian Sub-Continent

Wingate Scholarships, 374

Middle East

Wingate Scholarships, 374

United Kingdom

Wingate Scholarships, 374

USA

Asian Cultural Council Fellowship
Grants Program, 40

West European Countries

Marcel Hicter Foundation Travel Bursary
Scheme, 211
Wingate Scholarships, 374

DRAWING AND PAINTING

Any Country

Alberta Art Foundation Graduate
Scholarships in The Department of Art,
323
Alexander S Onassis Programme of
Research Grants, 7
Alexander S Onassis Research Grants,
7
Banff Centre Scholarships, 53
British School at Rome Fellowship, 34
Camargo Fellowships, 75
Chautauqua Institution Awards, 119
Don Freeman Memorial Grant-in-Aid,
301
The Elizabeth Greenshields Grant, 143
Fine Arts Work Center in Provincetown
Fellowships, 147
Foundation Praemium Erasmianum
Study Prize, 150
Gottlieb Foundation Emergency
Assistance Grants, 5
Gottlieb Foundation Individual Support
Grants, 5
Hambidge Center Residency Program,
166
House of Humour and Satire Prizes, 170
The John Kinross Memorial Fund
Student Scholarships, 278
MICA Fellowship, 214

SCULPTURE

Any Country

Henry Moore Sculpture Fellowship at the BSR, 69
Polish Embassy Short-Term Bursaries, 262
Rome Scholarships in the Fine Arts, 70
Sargant Fellowship, 70
Visual Arts Fellowship, 288
Wingate Rome Scholarship in the Fine Arts, 70

USA

Asian Cultural Council Fellowship Grants Program, 40
National Academy of Design Prizes for Sculpture in their Annual Exhibition Competition, 226
Olivia James Traveling Fellowship, 31

HANDICRAFTS

Any Country

Foundation Praemium Erasmianum Study Prize, 150
Haystack Scholarship, 168
MICA Fellowship, 214

Australia

Fulbright Postgraduate Student Award for the Visual and Performing Arts, 50
Wingate Scholarships, 374

British Commonwealth

Wingate Scholarships, 374

Canada

Wingate Scholarships, 374

Far East

Asian Cultural Council Fellowship Grants Program, 40

Indian Sub-Continent

Wingate Scholarships, 374

Middle East

Wingate Scholarships, 374

United Kingdom

Visual Arts Fellowship, 288
Wingate Scholarships, 374

USA

Asian Cultural Council Fellowship Grants Program, 40

West European Countries

Janson Johan Helmich Scholarships and Travel Grants, 189
Wingate Scholarships, 374

MUSIC

Any Country

Ahmanson and Getty Postdoctoral Fellowships, 313
Alexander S Onassis Programme of Research Grants, 7
Alexander S Onassis Research Grants, 7
Allcard Grants, 379
AMS 50 Dissertation Fellowship, 15
Arthur Rubinstein International Piano Master Competition, 31
Arts Council of England Music Grants, 32
Banff Centre Scholarships, 53
Boise Foundation Scholarships, 57
Brandon University Graduate Assistantships, 58
British Academy Small Personal Research Grants, 59
Camargo Fellowships, 75
Chautauqua Institution Awards, 119
Clark-Huntington Joint Bibliographical Fellowship, 314
Foundation Praemium Erasmianum Study Prize, 150
Fromm Foundation Commission, 153
Hambidge Center Residency Program, 166
Hinrichsen Foundation Awards, 170
The Howard Mayer Brown Fellowship, 15
International Beethoven Piano Competition, 180
International Jeunesses Musicales Competition, 191
International Music Competition of the ARD, 72
International Robert Schumann Competition, 186
James Ingham Halstead Scholarship in Music, 340
Joanna Randall-MacIver Junior Research Fellowship, 341
John Clementi Collard Fellowship, 379
Keele University Graduate Teaching Assistantships, 195
Kurt Weill Foundation Music Grant, 201
Kurt Weill Prize, 201
Leggett Awards, 265
Lincoln College Erich and Rochelle Endowed Prize in Music, 343

MacDowell Colony Residencies, 210
Manhattan School of Music Scholarships, 211
Manoug Parikian Award, 211
Muddy Waters Scholarship, 56
Muriel Taylor Cello Scholarship, 225
Onassis Programme of Postgraduate Research Scholarships, 7
The Paul A Pisk Prize, 16
Prize Winner of the International Music Competition of the ARD, 72
Royal Academy of Music General Bursary Awards, 273
Royal College of Music Exhibitions, 273
Royal College of Music Scholarships, 273
Ryan Davies Memorial Fund Scholarship Grants, 281
Sir Henry Richardson Award, 288
Sir James McNeill Foundation Postgraduate Scholarship, 223
SOAS Bursary, 284
SOAS Research Student Fellowships, 285
St Hilda's College Dame Helen Gardner Scholarship, 352
Sybil Tutton Awards, 310
University of Glasgow Postgraduate Scholarships, 331
University of New England Research Scholarships, 336
University of Oslo International Summer School Scholarships, 337
University of Stirling Research Studentships, 360
University Postgraduate Scholarships, 322
W T Best Memorial Scholarships, 379
Whittingham Award, 259
Yehudi Menuhin International Competition for Young Violinists, 381

African Nations

ESU Music Scholarships, 143
Royal Over-Seas League Music Competition, 277

Australia

AMF Award, 46
ESU Music Scholarships, 143
Fulbright Postgraduate Student Award for the Visual and Performing Arts, 50
The Marten Bequest Travelling Scholarships, 39
Nepean Postgraduate Research Award, 364
Royal Over-Seas League Music Competition, 277
Wingate Scholarships, 374

British Commonwealth

The Countess of Munster Musical Trust
Awards, 131
Wingate Scholarships, 374

Canada

Alfred Einstein Award, 15
ESU Music Scholarships, 143
Inuit Cultural Grants Program, 134
The Orford String Quartet Scholarship,
248
The Otto Kinkeldey Award, 16
Royal Over-Seas League Music
Competition, 277
Thompson (Homer and Dorothy)
Fellowship, 105
Wingate Scholarships, 374

Far East

Asian Cultural Council Fellowship
Grants Program, 40
ESU Music Scholarships, 143
Royal Over-Seas League Music
Competition, 277

Indian Sub-Continent

ESU Music Scholarships, 143
Royal Over-Seas League Music
Competition, 277
Wingate Scholarships, 374

Middle East

Sharett Scholarship Program, 10
Wingate Scholarships, 374

New Zealand

ESU Music Scholarships, 143
Nepean Postgraduate Research Award,
364
Royal Over-Seas League Music
Competition, 277

South Africa

ESU Music Scholarships, 143
Royal Over-Seas League Music
Competition, 277
SAMRO Bursaries Undergraduate for
General Music Study In Southern
Africa, 282
SAMRO Intermediate Bursaries for
Composition Study In Southern Africa,
282
SAMRO Overseas Scholarship, 282
SAMRO Undergraduate Bursaries for
School Music Teaching, 282

United Kingdom

Arts Council of Wales Awards for
Advanced Study in Music, 35
Carnwath Scholarship, 379
The Countess of Munster Musical Trust
Awards, 131
English-Speaking Union Chautauqua
Scholarships, 143
ESU Music Scholarships, 143
Francis Chagrin Award, 151
Polish Embassy Short-Term Bursaries,
262
Research Grant, 130, 264
Royal Over-Seas League Music
Competition, 277
Travel Grant, 130
University of Wales Bangor (UWB)
Research Studentships, 363
Wingate Scholarships, 374

USA

Alfred Einstein Award, 15
ASCAP Grants to Young Composers, 39
Asian Cultural Council Fellowship
Grants Program, 40
Harriet Hale Woolley Scholarships, 318
Margaret Fairbank Jory Copying
Assistance Program, 14
The Otto Kinkeldey Award, 16

West European Countries

Donatella Flick Conducting Competition,
138
Maisie Lewis Young Artists Fund, 379
Scholarship Foundation of the League
for Finnish-American Societies, 284
University of Wales Bangor (UWB)
Research Studentships, 363
Wingate Scholarships, 374

MUSICOLOGY

Any Country

Ahmanson and Getty Postdoctoral
Fellowships, 313
Alexander S Onassis Programme of
Research Grants, 7
Alexander S Onassis Research Grants,
7
ARIT Humanities and Social Science
Fellowships, 20
ASECS/Clark Library Fellowships, 313
British Academy Major International
Conference Grant, 59
British Academy Overseas Conference
Grants, 59

British Academy Small Personal
Research Grants, 59
British Academy Visiting Professorships
for Overseas Scholars, 59
Camargo Fellowships, 75
Center for Advanced Study in the
Behavioral Sciences Postdoctoral
Residential Fellowships, 112
Center for Field Research Grants, 112
Clark Library Short-Term Resident
Fellowships, 313
Clark-Huntington Joint Bibliographical
Fellowship, 314
Eastman School of Music Graduate
Awards, 141
Kurt Weill Foundation Music Grant, 201
Lemmermann Foundation Scholarship,
205
NHC Fellowships in the Humanities, 232
Onassis Programme of Postgraduate
Research Scholarships, 7
The Paul A Pisk Prize, 16
Royal College of Music Exhibitions, 273
Royal College of Music Scholarships,
273
Spidola Award and Scholarships, 205
UCLA Institute of American Culture
Postdoctoral/Visiting Scholar
Fellowships, 314
University of Oslo International Summer
School Scholarships, 337

Australia

Wingate Scholarships, 374

British Commonwealth

Wingate Scholarships, 374

Canada

Wingate Scholarships, 374

East European Countries

Mellon Research Fellowship, 21

Indian Sub-Continent

Wingate Scholarships, 374

Middle East

Wingate Scholarships, 374

United Kingdom

British Conference Grants, 59
Cardiff University Postgraduate
Research Studentships, 364
Frank Knox Fellowships at Harvard
University, 151
Kennedy Scholarships, 196

University of Wales Bangor (UWB)
Research Studentships, 363
Wingate Scholarships, 374

West European Countries

Cardiff University Postgraduate
Research Studentships, 364
University of Wales Bangor (UWB)
Research Studentships, 363
Wingate Scholarships, 374

MUSIC THEORY AND COMPOSITION

Any Country

Alexander S Onassis Programme of
Research Grants, 7
Alexander S Onassis Research Grants,
7
American Accordion Musicological
Society Music Competition Contest,
10
Arts Council of England Music Grants,
32
Arts Council of Wales Commissions to
Composers, 36
Camargo Fellowships, 75
Clements Memorial Prize, 304
Eastman School of Music Graduate
Awards, 141
Hambidge Center Residency Program,
166
International Jeunesses Musicales
Competition, 191
Mendelssohn Scholarship, 216
National Association of Composers
Young Composers' Competition, 226
Omaha Symphony Guild International
New Music Competition, 246
Onassis Programme of Postgraduate
Research Scholarships, 7
Queen Marie José Prize International
Prize for Musical Composition, 265
Ragdale Foundation Residencies, 267
Royal College of Music Exhibitions, 273
Royal College of Music Scholarships,
273
Royal Philharmonic Society
Composition Prize, 278
Ryan Davies Memorial Fund
Scholarship Grants, 281
San Francisco Conservatory
Performance Scholarships in Music,
284
Virginia Center for the Creative Arts
Fellowships, 370
Whittingham Award, 259

Yaddo Residency, 128

Australia

Paul Lowin Awards, 259
Wingate Scholarships, 374

British Commonwealth

Wingate Scholarships, 374

Canada

SOCAN Awards For Young Composers,
290
Wingate Scholarships, 374

Indian Sub-Continent

Wingate Scholarships, 374

Middle East

Sharett Scholarship Program, 10
Wingate Scholarships, 374

South Africa

SAMRO Intermediate Bursaries for
Composition Study In Southern Africa,
282

United Kingdom

Cardiff University Postgraduate
Research Studentships, 364
Francis Chagrin Award, 151
Francis Chagrin Fund Awards, 151
Frank Knox Fellowships at Harvard
University, 151
Kennedy Scholarships, 196
University of Wales Bangor (UWB)
Research Studentships, 363
Wingate Scholarships, 374

USA

ASCAP Grants to Young Composers, 39
Commissioning Music/USA, 215
Harvey Garl Composition Contest, 261
Margaret Fairbank Jory Copying
Assistance Program, 14
Meet the Composer New Residencies,
215

West European Countries

The Arts Council of Ireland Composers
Commission Scheme, 33
Cardiff University Postgraduate
Research Studentships, 364
University of Wales Bangor (UWB)
Research Studentships, 363
Wingate Scholarships, 374

CONDUCTING

Any Country

Alexander S Onassis Programme of
Research Grants, 7
Alexander S Onassis Research Grants,
7
Chautauqua Institution Awards, 119
Eastman School of Music Graduate
Awards, 141
Hungarian Television/Interart
Festivalcenter International
Conductors' Competition, 171
Onassis Programme of Postgraduate
Research Scholarships, 7
Prague Spring International Music
Competition, 263
Royal College of Music Exhibitions, 273
Royal College of Music Scholarships,
273
Ryan Davies Memorial Fund
Scholarship Grants, 281
San Francisco Conservatory
Performance Scholarships in Music,
284

Australia

Wingate Scholarships, 374

British Commonwealth

Wingate Scholarships, 374

Canada

Heinz Unger Award, 247
The Leslie Bell Scholarship Fund for
Choral Conducting, 247
Wingate Scholarships, 374

Indian Sub-Continent

Wingate Scholarships, 374

Middle East

Sharett Scholarship Program, 10
Wingate Scholarships, 374

United Kingdom

University of Wales Bangor (UWB)
Research Studentships, 363
Wingate Scholarships, 374

West European Countries

Donatella Flick Conducting Competition,
138
University of Wales Bangor (UWB)
Research Studentships, 363
Wingate Scholarships, 374

SINGING

Any Country

Alec Redshaw Memorial Awards, 164
Alexander S Onassis Programme of Research Grants, 7
Alexander S Onassis Research Grants, 7
Associated Board of the Royal Schools of Music Scholarships, 40
Boise Foundation Scholarships, 57
Chautauqua Institution Awards, 119
Eastman School of Music Graduate Awards, 141
Grand Prix Opera and Grand Prix Paul Derenne, 127
International Jeunesses Musicales Competition, 191
International Music Competition of the ARD, 72
International Music Competitions, 335
International Robert Schumann Competition, 186
John Noble Bursary Award, 285
Loren L Zachary National Vocal Competition for Young Opera Singers, 210
Marcella Sembrich Voice Competition, 199
Miriam Licette Scholarship, 220
Onassis Programme of Postgraduate Research Scholarships, 7
Paris International Singing Competition, 181
Queen Elisabeth International Music Competition of Belgium, 265
Richard Tauber Prize, 29
Royal College of Music Exhibitions, 273
Royal College of Music Scholarships, 273
Ryan Davies Memorial Fund Scholarship Grants, 281
San Francisco Conservatory Performance Scholarships in Music, 284
Sorantin Young Artist Award, 284

Australia

The Marten Bequest Travelling Scholarships, 39
Sir Robert Askin Operatic Travelling Scholarship, 39
Wingate Scholarships, 374

British Commonwealth

NFMS Award for Young Concert Artists, 231
Wingate Scholarships, 374

Canada

Montreal Symphony Orchestra Competitions, 224
Wingate Scholarships, 374

Indian Sub-Continent

Wingate Scholarships, 374

Middle East

Sharett Scholarship Program, 10
Wingate Scholarships, 374

South Africa

SAMRO Overseas Scholarship, 282

United Kingdom

Arts Council of Wales Awards for Advanced Study in Music, 35
NFMS Award for Young Concert Artists, 231
Wingate Scholarships, 374

West European Countries

Wingate Scholarships, 374

MUSICAL INSTRUMENTS (PERFORMANCE)

Any Country

Adeline Rosenberg Memorial Prize Competition, 149
Arthur Rubinstein International Piano Master Competition, 31
Associated Board of the Royal Schools of Music Scholarships, 40
Banff Centre Scholarships, 53
Boise Foundation Scholarships, 57
Brandon University Graduate Assistantships, 58
Budapest International Music Competition, 73
Chautauqua Institution Awards, 119
Chopin Piano Competition, 198
Clara Haskil Competition, 120
Eastman School of Music Graduate Awards, 141
Elizabeth Harper Vaughn Concerto Competition, 310
Emily English Award, 143
Eric Thompson Trust Grants-in-Aid, 144
F Busoni International Piano Competition, 146

Hambidge Center Residency Program, 166
Hattori Foundation Awards, 168
Ian Fleming Charitable Trust Music Education Awards, 173
International Chamber Music Competition, 181
International Frederic Chopin Piano Competition, 184
International Géza Anda Piano Competition, 161
International Harp Contest, 184
International Jeunesses Musicales Competition, 191
International Music Competition of the ARD, 72
International Music Competitions, 335
International Organ Competition 'Grand Prix de Chartres', 185
International Paulo Cello Competition, 181
International Robert Schumann Competition, 186
Jean Sibelius International Violin Competition, 190
Julius Isserlis Scholarship, 277
KPMG Scholarship, 200
Leeds International Pianoforte Competition, 205
Leggett Awards, 265
London International String Quartet Competition, 209
Manoug Parikian Award, 211
Martin Musical Scholarships, 200
Miriam Licette Scholarship, 220
Muriel Taylor Cello Scholarship, 225
Myra Hess Awards Trust, 224
National Orchestral Institute Scholarships, 335
Nicolo Paganini International Violin Competition, 243
Paloma O'Shea Santander International Piano Competition, 258
Prague Spring International Music Competition, 263
Premier Grand Prix Marguerite Long, Premier Grand Prix Jacques Thibaud, 185
Queen Elisabeth International Music Competition of Belgium, 265
RCO Grants and Travel Scholarships, 274
RCO Scholarships and Awards, 274
Royal College of Music Exhibitions, 273
Royal College of Music Scholarships, 273
Ryan Davies Memorial Fund Scholarship Grants, 281
San Francisco Conservatory Performance Scholarships in Music, 284

Sidney Perry Scholarship, 200
Sir Henry Richardson Award, 288
Sorantin Young Artist Award, 284
Sybil Tutton Awards, 310
Tibor Varga International Competition
for Violin, 312
Trevor Snoad Memorial Trust, 200
Whittingham Award, 259
Yehudi Menuhin International
Competition for Young Violinists, 381

African Nations

Royal Over-Seas League Music
Competition, 277

Australia

The Marten Bequest Travelling
Scholarships, 39
Royal Over-Seas League Music
Competition, 277
Wingate Scholarships, 374

British Commonwealth

NFMS Award for Young Concert Artists,
231
Wingate Scholarships, 374

Canada

Montreal Symphony Orchestra
Competitions, 224
Royal Over-Seas League Music
Competition, 277
Wingate Scholarships, 374

Far East

Royal Over-Seas League Music
Competition, 277

Indian Sub-Continent

Royal Over-Seas League Music
Competition, 277
Wingate Scholarships, 374

Middle East

Sharett Scholarship Program, 10
Wingate Scholarships, 374

New Zealand

Royal Over-Seas League Music
Competition, 277

South Africa

Royal Over-Seas League Music
Competition, 277
SAMRO Overseas Scholarship, 282

United Kingdom

Arts Council of Wales Awards for
Advanced Study in Music, 35
Cardiff University Postgraduate
Research Studentships, 364
NFMS Award for Young Concert Artists,
231
Royal Over-Seas League Music
Competition, 277
Shell LSO Music Scholarship, 209
University of Wales Bangor (UWB)
Research Studentships, 363
Wingate Scholarships, 374

West European Countries

Cardiff University Postgraduate
Research Studentships, 364
Maisie Lewis Young Artists Fund, 379
University of Wales Bangor (UWB)
Research Studentships, 363
Wingate Scholarships, 374

RELIGIOUS MUSIC

Any Country

Royal College of Music Exhibitions, 273
Royal College of Music Scholarships,
273
Ryan Davies Memorial Fund
Scholarship Grants, 281

Australia

Wingate Scholarships, 374

British Commonwealth

Wingate Scholarships, 374

Canada

Wingate Scholarships, 374

Indian Sub-Continent

Wingate Scholarships, 374

Middle East

Wingate Scholarships, 374

United Kingdom

Wingate Scholarships, 374

West European Countries

Wingate Scholarships, 374

JAZZ AND POPULAR MUSIC

Any Country

Arts Council of England Music Grants,
32
Banff Centre Scholarships, 53
Eastman School of Music Graduate
Awards, 141
Kurt Weill Foundation Music Grant, 201
Ryan Davies Memorial Fund
Scholarship Grants, 281
Whittingham Award, 259

Australia

Wingate Scholarships, 374

British Commonwealth

Wingate Scholarships, 374

Canada

Wingate Scholarships, 374

Indian Sub-Continent

Wingate Scholarships, 374

Middle East

Sharett Scholarship Program, 10
Wingate Scholarships, 374

South Africa

SAMRO Overseas Scholarship, 282

United Kingdom

Wingate Scholarships, 374

West European Countries

Wingate Scholarships, 374

OPERA

Any Country

Banff Centre Scholarships, 53
Camargo Fellowships, 75
Chautauqua Institution Awards, 119
Eastman School of Music Graduate
Awards, 141
Kurt Weill Foundation Music Grant, 201
Loren L Zachary National Vocal
Competition for Young Opera Singers,
210
Marcella Sembrich Voice Competition,
199

Foundation Praemium Erasmianum Study Prize, 150
Hambidge Center Residency Program, 166
Jacob's Pillow Dance Festival Dance Scholarships, 188
Onassis Programme of Postgraduate Research Scholarships, 7
Ryan Davies Memorial Fund Scholarship Grants, 281
Yaddo Residency, 128

Australia

Fulbright Postgraduate Student Award for the Visual and Performing Arts, 50
Lady Mollie Askin Ballet Travelling Scholarship, 38
The Marten Bequest Travelling Scholarships, 39
Nepean Postgraduate Research Award, 364
Wingate Scholarships, 374

British Commonwealth

Wingate Scholarships, 374

Canada

Wingate Scholarships, 374

Far East

Asian Cultural Council Fellowship Grants Program, 40

Indian Sub-Continent

Wingate Scholarships, 374

Middle East

Sharett Scholarship Program, 10
Wingate Scholarships, 374

New Zealand

Nepean Postgraduate Research Award, 364

United Kingdom

Wingate Scholarships, 374

USA

Asian Cultural Council Fellowship Grants Program, 40

West European Countries

Scholarship Foundation of the League for Finnish-American Societies, 284
Wingate Scholarships, 374

PHOTOGRAPHY

Any Country

Alberta Art Foundation Graduate Scholarships in The Department of Art, 323
Alexander S Onassis Programme of Research Grants, 7
Alexander S Onassis Research Grants, 7
Banff Centre Scholarships, 53
British Academy Small Personal Research Grants, 59
Camargo Fellowships, 75
Grand Prix International du Salon de la Recherche Photographique, 162
Hambidge Center Residency Program, 166
Library Company of Philadelphia Research Fellowships in American History and Culture, 208
Light Work Artist-in-Residence Program, 208
MICA Fellowship, 214
Roswell Artist-in-Residence Program, 271
Sister Kenny Institute Encouragement Awards, 289
Sister Kenny International Art Show by Artists with Disabilities, 289
Smith (W Eugene) Grant in Humanistic Photography, 371
Virginia Center for the Creative Arts Fellowships, 370
Women's Studio Workshop Artists' Fellowships, 377
Yaddo Residency, 128

Australia

Fulbright Postgraduate Student Award for the Visual and Performing Arts, 50
Wingate Scholarships, 374

British Commonwealth

Wingate Scholarships, 374

Canada

Wingate Scholarships, 374

Far East

Asian Cultural Council Fellowship Grants Program, 40

Indian Sub-Continent

Wingate Scholarships, 374

Middle East

Sharett Scholarship Program, 10
Wingate Scholarships, 374

United Kingdom

Polish Embassy Short-Term Bursaries, 262
Visual Arts Fellowship, 288
Wingate Scholarships, 374

USA

Asian Cultural Council Fellowship Grants Program, 40
Coca-Cola National Fellows Programme for the MFA in Studio for Art Educators, 214

West European Countries

Janson Johan Helmich Scholarships and Travel Grants, 189
Scholarship Foundation of the League for Finnish-American Societies, 284
Wingate Scholarships, 374

CINEMA AND TELEVISION

Any Country

Alexander S Onassis Programme of Research Grants, 7
Alexander S Onassis Research Grants, 7
Banff Centre Scholarships, 53
British Academy Small Personal Research Grants, 59
Don and Gee Nicholl Fellowships in Screenwriting, 4
Muddy Waters Scholarship, 56
Onassis Programme of Postgraduate Research Scholarships, 7
Ragdale Foundation Residencies, 267
University of Dundee Research Awards, 330
University of Glasgow Postgraduate Scholarships, 331
University of Stirling Research Studentships, 360
University Postgraduate Scholarships, 322
Yaddo Residency, 128

Australia

Fulbright Postgraduate Student Award for the Visual and Performing Arts, 50
Wingate Scholarships, 374

British Commonwealth

Wingate Scholarships, 374

Canada

Wingate Scholarships, 374

Far East

Asian Cultural Council Fellowship Grants Program, 40

Indian Sub-Continent

Wingate Scholarships, 374

Middle East

Sharett Scholarship Program, 10
Wingate Scholarships, 374

United Kingdom

Polish Embassy Short-Term Bursaries, 262
University of Wales (Aberystwyth) Postgraduate Research Studentships, 362
Wingate Scholarships, 374

USA

Asian Cultural Council Fellowship Grants Program, 40

West European Countries

Janson Johan Helmich Scholarships and Travel Grants, 189
Scholarship Foundation of the League for Finnish-American Societies, 284
University of Wales (Aberystwyth) Postgraduate Research Studentships, 362
Wingate Scholarships, 374

DESIGN

Any Country

Alexander S Onassis Programme of Research Grants, 7
Alexander S Onassis Research Grants, 7
Foundation Praemium Erasmianum Study Prize, 150
Hagley/Winterthur Arts and Industries Fellowship, 165
Hambidge Center Residency Program, 166
Peter Krueger-Christie's Fellowship, 127
University of Dundee Research Awards, 330

Wolfsonian Fellowship Visiting Scholar Assoc Fellowship, 376

Australia

Fulbright Postgraduate Student Award for the Visual and Performing Arts, 50
Nepean Postgraduate Research Award, 364
Wingate Scholarships, 374

British Commonwealth

Wingate Scholarships, 374

Canada

Frank Knox Memorial Fellowships at Harvard University, 42
Wingate Scholarships, 374

Indian Sub-Continent

Wingate Scholarships, 374

Middle East

Sharett Scholarship Program, 10
Wingate Scholarships, 374

New Zealand

Nepean Postgraduate Research Award, 364

United Kingdom

Lord Barnby Foundation Bursaries, 311
Polish Embassy Short-Term Bursaries, 262
RSA Student Design Awards, 279
Visual Arts Fellowship, 288
Wingate Scholarships, 374

West European Countries

Janson Johan Helmich Scholarships and Travel Grants, 189
RSA Student Design Awards, 279
Scholarship Foundation of the League for Finnish-American Societies, 284
Wingate Scholarships, 374

INTERIOR DESIGN

Any Country

ASID/Joel Polsky-Fixtures Furniture Academic Achievement Award, 26
ASID/Joel Polsky-Fixtures Furniture Prize, 26
ASID/Mabelle Wilhelmina Boldt Memorial Scholarship, 27
Peter Krueger-Christie's Fellowship, 127

University of Dundee Research Awards, 330

FURNITURE DESIGN

Any Country

Peter Krueger-Christie's Fellowship, 127
University of Dundee Research Awards, 330

FASHION DESIGN

Any Country

Adele Filene Travel Award, 128
Cotton Industry War Memorial Trust Scholarships, 311
CSA Travel Research Grant, 129
Lee 400 Educational Trust, 311
Peter Krueger-Christie's Fellowship, 127
Stella Blum Research Grant, 129
Textile Institute Scholarship, 311
University of Dundee Research Awards, 330

United Kingdom

Fulbright Calvin Klein Harvey Nichols Award in Fashion Design, 367
Lord Barnby Foundation Bursaries, 311
Weavers' Company Scholarships, 312

USA

Fulbright Calvin Klein Harvey Nichols Award in Fashion Design, 367

TEXTILE DESIGN

Any Country

Cotton Industry War Memorial Trust Scholarships, 311
CSA Travel Research Grant, 129
Hambidge Center Residency Program, 166
Lee 400 Educational Trust, 311
Peter Krueger-Christie's Fellowship, 127
Textile Institute Scholarship, 311
University of Dundee Research Awards, 330

Middle East

Sharett Scholarship Program, 10

United Kingdom

Lord Barnby Foundation Bursaries, 311
Weavers' Company Scholarships, 312

GRAPHIC DESIGN

Any Country

Hambidge Center Residency Program,
166
Peter Krueger-Christie's Fellowship, 127
Sister Kenny Institute Encouragement
Awards, 289
Sister Kenny International Art Show by
Artists with Disabilities, 289
University of Dundee Research Awards,
330

Australia

Nepean Postgraduate Research Award,
364

Middle East

Sharett Scholarship Program, 10

New Zealand

Nepean Postgraduate Research Award,
364

INDUSTRIAL DESIGN

Any Country

Peter Krueger-Christie's Fellowship, 127
University of Dundee Research Awards,
330

Australia

Nepean Postgraduate Research Award,
364

Middle East

Sharett Scholarship Program, 10

New Zealand

Nepean Postgraduate Research Award,
364

DISPLAY AND STAGE DESIGN

Any Country

Banff Centre Scholarships, 53
Peter Krueger-Christie's Fellowship, 127

Middle East

Sharett Scholarship Program, 10

RELIGION AND THEOLOGY

GENERAL

Any Country

Ahmanson and Getty Postdoctoral
Fellowships, 313
AIATSIS Research Grants, 46
Alexander S Onassis Programme of
Research Grants, 7
Alexander S Onassis Research Grants,
7
Andrew W Mellon Postdoctoral
Fellowships in the Humanities, 358
ARIT Humanities and Social Science
Fellowships, 20
ASECS/Clark Library Fellowships, 313
Bloor Lands Entrance Scholarship, 370
British Academy Overseas Conference
Grants, 59
British Academy Small Personal
Research Grants, 59
Camargo Fellowships, 75
Center for Advanced Study in the
Behavioral Sciences Postdoctoral
Residential Fellowships, 112
Center for Field Research Grants, 112
Center Research Fellowships, 316
Charlotte W Newcombe Doctoral
Dissertation Fellowships, 377

Clark-Huntington Joint Bibliographical
Fellowship, 314
Concordia University Graduate
Fellowships, 126
David J Azrieli Graduate Fellowship, 126
Episcopal Church Foundation Graduate
Fellowship Program, 144
Equiano Memorial Award, 308
European Enlightenment Project
Fellowships, 175
Exeter College Senior Scholarship in
Theology, 145
Fitzwilliam College Shipley Studentship,
326
Foundation Praemium Erasmianum
Study Prize, 150
Gifford Research Fellowship, 359
Graduate Student Assistantships, 370
Harvard University, Center for the Study
of World Religions, Senior Fellowship,
167
Hugh Le May Fellowship, 268
Humane Studies Fellowships, 177
Institute for Advanced Studies in the
Humanities Visiting Research
Fellowships, 175
Jane Addams/Andrew Carnegie
Fellowships in Philanthropy, 174
John W O'Brien Graduate Fellowship,
126
Logan Research Fellowships, 222

Mansfield College Elfan Rees
Scholarship, 344
Miles Lerman Center for the Study of
Jewish Resistance Research
Fellowship, 317
Monash Graduate Scholarships, 223
Monash University Partial Tuition
Postgraduate Research Scholarship
Scheme, 223
Monash University Silver Jubilee
Postgraduate Scholarship, 223
NHC Fellowships in the Humanities, 232
Onassis Programme of Postgraduate
Research Scholarships, 7
Sir Halley Stewart Trust Grants, 287
SSSS Student Research Grant Award,
297
St Hugh's College The Yates Senior
Scholarship, 354
St John's College North Senior
Scholarships, 354
Stanley G French Graduate Fellowship,
127
The Joyce and Arthur Schechter
Fellowship, 317
The Pearl Resnick Post Doctoral
Fellowship, 317
UCLA Summer Fellowship, 314
University of Glasgow Postgraduate
Scholarships, 331

Regent's Park College (Permanent
Private Hall) J W Lord Scholarship, 348
Research Grant, 130, 264
Travel Grant, 130
University of Wales Bangor (UWB)
Research Studentships, 363
Wingate Scholarships, 374

USA

Americans and World Affairs Fellows
Program, 378
ARIT/NEH Fellowships for the
Humanities in Turkey, 20
Belgian-American Educational
Foundation Graduate Fellowships for
Study in Belgium, 53
CSD Grants for Foreign Research
Fellows, 115
Federal Chancellor Scholarship, 7
Friends of Peterhouse Bursary, 260
Fulbright Scholar Awards for Research
and Lecturing Abroad, 130
Kennan Institute Research Scholarship,
196
NEH Fellowship, 25
PRA Fellowships, 257
Regent's Park College (Permanent
Private Hall) Asheville Scholarship, 348

West European Countries

Belgian-American Educational
Foundation Graduate Fellowships for
Study in the USA, 54
CSD Grants for Foreign Research
Fellows, 115
Friends of Peterhouse Bursary, 260
Fulbright Postdoctoral Research and
Lecturing Awards for Non-US Citizens,
154
NAI Travel Grant, 244
Postgraduate Fellowships for Study in
the USA, 54
Scholarship Foundation of the League
for Finnish-American Societies, 284
University of Wales Bangor (UWB)
Research Studentships, 363
Wingate Scholarships, 374

RELIGIOUS STUDIES

Any Country

Ahmanson and Getty Postdoctoral
Fellowships, 313
Alexander S Onassis Programme of
Research Grants, 7
Alexander S Onassis Research Grants,
7

Andrew W Mellon Postdoctoral
Fellowships in the Humanities, 358
ASECS/Clark Library Fellowships, 313
British Academy Small Personal
Research Grants, 59
Clark-Huntington Joint Bibliographical
Fellowship, 314
Foundation Praemium Erasmianum
Study Prize, 150
Harvard University, Center for the Study
of World Religions, Senior Fellowship,
167
Institute for Ecumenical and Cultural
Research Resident Scholars Program,
176
Institute of European History
Fellowships, 178
M Alison Frantz Fellowship in Post-
Classical Studies at The Gennadius
Library (formerly known as the
Gennadeion Fellowship), 22
Massey Doctoral Scholarship, 214
Onassis Programme of Postgraduate
Research Scholarships, 7
Regent's Park College (Permanent
Private Hall) Henman Scholarship, 348
SOAS Research Student Fellowships,
285
UCLA Summer Fellowship, 314
University of Glasgow Postgraduate
Scholarships, 331
University of Stirling Research
Studentships, 360
USC College Dissertation Fellowship,
359
USC College of Letters, Arts and
Sciences Merit Award, 359

Australia

Wingate Scholarships, 374

British Commonwealth

Wingate Scholarships, 374

Canada

Bishop Thomas Hoyt Jr Fellowship, 176
Wingate Scholarships, 374

East European Countries

CRF/RSE European Visiting Research
Fellowships, 280

Indian Sub-Continent

Wingate Scholarships, 374

Middle East

Wingate Scholarships, 374

United Kingdom

Cardiff University Postgraduate
Research Studentships, 364
CRF/RSE European Visiting Research
Fellowships, 280
Research Grant, 130, 264
Travel Grant, 130
University of Wales Bangor (UWB)
Research Studentships, 363
Wingate Scholarships, 374

USA

Bishop Thomas Hoyt Jr Fellowship, 176
Fellowship Programme for Émigrés
Pursuing Careers in Jewish Education,
191

West European Countries

Cardiff University Postgraduate
Research Studentships, 364
CRF/RSE European Visiting Research
Fellowships, 280
University of Wales Bangor (UWB)
Research Studentships, 363
Wingate Scholarships, 374

CHRISTIAN

Any Country

Ahmanson and Getty Postdoctoral
Fellowships, 313
Andrew W Mellon Postdoctoral
Fellowships in the Humanities, 358
ASECS/Clark Library Fellowships, 313
Bross Prize, 72
Clark-Huntington Joint Bibliographical
Fellowship, 314
Onassis Programme of Postgraduate
Research Scholarships, 7
University of Stirling Research
Studentships, 360

United Kingdom

Cardiff University Postgraduate
Research Studentships, 364
University of Wales Bangor (UWB)
Research Studentships, 363

West European Countries

Cardiff University Postgraduate
Research Studentships, 364
University of Wales Bangor (UWB)
Research Studentships, 363

JEWISH

Any Country

Ahmanson and Getty Postdoctoral
  Fellowships, 313
Andrew W Mellon Postdoctoral
  Fellowships in the Humanities, 358
ASECS/Clark Library Fellowships, 313
Center Research Fellowships, 316
Clark-Huntington Joint Bibliographical
  Fellowship, 314
International Fellowships in Jewish
  Studies, 215
International Scholarship Programme for
  Community Service, 216
Memorial Foundation for Jewish Culture
  International Doctoral Scholarships,
  216
Miles Lerman Center for the Study of
  Jewish Resistance Research
  Fellowship, 317
Onassis Programme of Postgraduate
  Research Scholarships, 7
Samuel H Kress Joint Athens-Jerusalem
  Fellowship, 23, 26
Scholarships for Post-Rabbinical
  Students, 216
SOAS Bursary, 284
The Joyce and Arthur Schechter
  Fellowship, 317
The Pearl Resnick Post Doctoral
  Fellowship, 317
University of Stirling Research
  Studentships, 360

Australia

Wingate Scholarships, 374

British Commonwealth

Wingate Scholarships, 374

Canada

Wingate Scholarships, 374

Indian Sub-Continent

Wingate Scholarships, 374

Middle East

Wingate Scholarships, 374

United Kingdom

Cardiff University Postgraduate
  Research Studentships, 364
Polish Embassy Short-Term Bursaries,
  262
University of Wales Bangor (UWB)
  Research Studentships, 363

Wingate Scholarships, 374

USA

Fellowship Programme for Émigrés
  Pursuing Careers in Jewish Education,
  191

West European Countries

Cardiff University Postgraduate
  Research Studentships, 364
University of Wales Bangor (UWB)
  Research Studentships, 363
Wingate Scholarships, 374

ISLAM

Any Country

Ahmanson and Getty Postdoctoral
  Fellowships, 313
Andrew W Mellon Postdoctoral
  Fellowships in the Humanities, 358
King Faisal International Award for
  Islamic Studies, 197
Onassis Programme of Postgraduate
  Research Scholarships, 7
SOAS Bursary, 284
University of Stirling Research
  Studentships, 360

United Kingdom

Cardiff University Postgraduate
  Research Studentships, 364

West European Countries

Cardiff University Postgraduate
  Research Studentships, 364
NAI Travel Grant, 244

ASIAN RELIGIOUS STUDIES

Any Country

Ahmanson and Getty Postdoctoral
  Fellowships, 313
Andrew W Mellon Postdoctoral
  Fellowships in the Humanities, 358
Onassis Programme of Postgraduate
  Research Scholarships, 7
SOAS Bursary, 284
University of Stirling Research
  Studentships, 360

United Kingdom

Cardiff University Postgraduate
  Research Studentships, 364

West European Countries

Cardiff University Postgraduate
  Research Studentships, 364

AGNOSTICISM AND ATHEISM

Any Country

Andrew W Mellon Postdoctoral
  Fellowships in the Humanities, 358

ANCIENT RELIGIONS

Any Country

Andrew W Mellon Postdoctoral
  Fellowships in the Humanities, 358
FAMSI Research Grant, 150
Mary Isabel Sibley Fellowship, 260
Onassis Programme of Postgraduate
  Research Scholarships, 7
Samuel H Kress Joint Athens-Jerusalem
  Fellowship, 23, 26
SOAS Bursary, 284

Australia

Wingate Scholarships, 374

British Commonwealth

Hector and Elizabeth Catling Bursary, 67
Macmillan-Rodewald Studentship,
  School Studentship, Cary Studentship,
  67
Wingate Scholarships, 374

Canada

Wingate Scholarships, 374

Indian Sub-Continent

Wingate Scholarships, 374

Middle East

Wingate Scholarships, 374

United Kingdom

Hector and Elizabeth Catling Bursary, 67

Macmillan-Rodewald Studentship, School Studentship, Cary Studentship, 67
Wingate Scholarships, 374

West European Countries

Wingate Scholarships, 374

RELIGIOUS EDUCATION

Any Country

Alexander S Onassis Programme of Research Grants, 7
Alexander S Onassis Research Grants, 7
All Saints Educational Trust Personal Awards, 9
Dempster Fellowship, 154
Equiano Memorial Award, 308
Onassis Programme of Postgraduate Research Scholarships, 7

United Kingdom

Research Grant, 130, 264
Travel Grant, 130
University of Wales Bangor (UWB) Research Studentships, 363

USA

Americans and World Affairs Fellows Program, 378
Fellowship Programme for Émigrés Pursuing Careers in Jewish Education, 191

West European Countries

University of Wales Bangor (UWB) Research Studentships, 363

HOLY WRITINGS

Any Country

Alexander S Onassis Programme of Research Grants, 7
Alexander S Onassis Research Grants, 7
SOAS Bursary, 284
SOAS Research Student Fellowships, 285

United Kingdom

Research Grant, 130, 264

Travel Grant, 130

RELIGIOUS PRACTICE

Any Country

Alexander S Onassis Programme of Research Grants, 7
Alexander S Onassis Research Grants, 7
SOAS Bursary, 284
SOAS Research Student Fellowships, 285

United Kingdom

Research Grant, 130, 264
Travel Grant, 130
University of Wales Bangor (UWB) Research Studentships, 363

USA

Fellowship Programme for Émigrés Pursuing Careers in Jewish Education, 191

West European Countries

University of Wales Bangor (UWB) Research Studentships, 363

CHURCH ADMINISTRATION (PASTORAL WORK)

Any Country

Alexander S Onassis Programme of Research Grants, 7
Alexander S Onassis Research Grants, 7

United Kingdom

Cardiff University Postgraduate Research Studentships, 364
Research Grant, 130, 264
Travel Grant, 130

USA

Verne Catt McDowell Scholarship, 369

West European Countries

Cardiff University Postgraduate Research Studentships, 364

THEOLOGICAL STUDIES

Any Country

Alexander S Onassis Programme of Research Grants, 7
Alexander S Onassis Research Grants, 7
Andrew W Mellon Postdoctoral Fellowships in the Humanities, 358
Foundation Praemium Erasmianum Study Prize, 150
Gifford Research Fellowship, 359
Institute of European History Fellowships, 178
Onassis Programme of Postgraduate Research Scholarships, 7
University Postgraduate Scholarships, 322

African Nations

The Evelyn Hilchie Betts Memorial Fellowship, 43

Indian Sub-Continent

The Evelyn Hilchie Betts Memorial Fellowship, 43

Middle East

The Evelyn Hilchie Betts Memorial Fellowship, 43

South America

The Evelyn Hilchie Betts Memorial Fellowship, 43

United Kingdom

Cardiff University Postgraduate Research Studentships, 364
Research Grant, 130, 264
Travel Grant, 130
University of Wales Bangor (UWB) Research Studentships, 363

USA

ELCA Educational Grant Program, 145

West European Countries

Cardiff University Postgraduate Research Studentships, 364
University of Wales Bangor (UWB) Research Studentships, 363

COMPARATIVE RELIGION

Any Country

Ahmanson and Getty Postdoctoral Fellowships, 313
Alexander S Onassis Programme of Research Grants, 7
Alexander S Onassis Research Grants, 7
Andrew W Mellon Postdoctoral Fellowships in the Humanities, 358
ASECS/Clark Library Fellowships, 313
Camargo Fellowships, 75
Clark-Huntington Joint Bibliographical Fellowship, 314
Foundation Praemium Erasmianum Study Prize, 150
Harvard University, Center for the Study of World Religions, Senior Fellowship, 167
Institute of European History Fellowships, 178
Mary Isabel Sibley Fellowship, 260
Onassis Programme of Postgraduate Research Scholarships, 7
SOAS Bursary, 284
SOAS Research Student Fellowships, 285
Spalding Trusts Grants-in-Aid of Research, 305
University of New England Research Scholarships, 336
University of Stirling Research Studentships, 360
University Postgraduate Scholarships, 322

Australia

Wingate Scholarships, 374

British Commonwealth

Wingate Scholarships, 374

Canada

Wingate Scholarships, 374

East European Countries

Open Society Sofia Central European University Scholarship, 249

Indian Sub-Continent

Wingate Scholarships, 374

Middle East

Wingate Scholarships, 374

United Kingdom

Research Grant, 130, 264
Travel Grant, 130
University of Wales Bangor (UWB) Research Studentships, 363
Wingate Scholarships, 374

USA

NEH Postdoctoral Research Award, 25

West European Countries

University of Wales Bangor (UWB) Research Studentships, 363
Wingate Scholarships, 374

SOCIOLOGY OF RELIGION

Any Country

Ahmanson and Getty Postdoctoral Fellowships, 313
Alexander S Onassis Programme of Research Grants, 7
Alexander S Onassis Research Grants, 7
Andrew W Mellon Postdoctoral Fellowships in the Humanities, 358
ASECS/Clark Library Fellowships, 313
Camargo Fellowships, 75
Clark-Huntington Joint Bibliographical Fellowship, 314
Foundation Praemium Erasmianum Study Prize, 150
Harvard University, Center for the Study of World Religions, Senior Fellowship, 167
Onassis Programme of Postgraduate Research Scholarships, 7
Queen's University of Belfast Research and Senior Visiting Research Fellowships, 266
SOAS Bursary, 284
SOAS Research Student Fellowships, 285
University of New England Research Scholarships, 336
University Postgraduate Scholarships, 322

East European Countries

Open Society Sofia Central European University Scholarship, 249

United Kingdom

Research Grant, 130, 264

Travel Grant, 130

West European Countries

NAI Travel Grant, 244

HISTORY OF RELIGION

Any Country

Ahmanson and Getty Postdoctoral Fellowships, 313
Albert J Beveridge Grant, 12
Alexander S Onassis Programme of Research Grants, 7
Alexander S Onassis Research Grants, 7
Andrew W Mellon Postdoctoral Fellowships in the Humanities, 358
ASECS/Clark Library Fellowships, 313
Bernadotte E Schmitt Grants, 13
British Academy Small Personal Research Grants, 59
Camargo Fellowships, 75
Center for Field Research Grants, 112
Clark-Huntington Joint Bibliographical Fellowship, 314
Foundation Praemium Erasmianum Study Prize, 150
Harvard University, Center for the Study of World Religions, Senior Fellowship, 167
Institute of European History Fellowships, 178
Onassis Programme of Postgraduate Research Scholarships, 7
SOAS Bursary, 284
SOAS Research Student Fellowships, 285
University Postgraduate Scholarships, 322

Australia

Wingate Scholarships, 374

British Commonwealth

Wingate Scholarships, 374

Canada

Wingate Scholarships, 374

East European Countries

Open Society Sofia Central European University Scholarship, 249

Indian Sub-Continent

Wingate Scholarships, 374

Middle East

Wingate Scholarships, 374

United Kingdom

Research Grant, 130, 264
Travel Grant, 130
University of Wales Bangor (UWB)
 Research Studentships, 363
Wingate Scholarships, 374

West European Countries

University of Wales Bangor (UWB)
 Research Studentships, 363
Wingate Scholarships, 374

ESOTERIC PRACTICES

East European Countries

CRF/RSE European Visiting Research
 Fellowships, 280

United Kingdom

CRF/RSE European Visiting Research
 Fellowships, 280
Research Grant, 130, 264
Travel Grant, 130

West European Countries

CRF/RSE European Visiting Research
 Fellowships, 280

INDEX OF AWARDS

A

AAS American Society for Eighteenth-Century Studies Fellowships, 11

AAS National Endowment for the Humanities Visiting Fellowships, 11

AAS Northeast Modern Language Association Fellowship, 11

AAUW Educational Foundation American Fellowships, 3

AAUW International Fellowships Program, 3

AAUW/IFUW International Fellowships, 62

Abbey Awards in Painting, 68, 173

Abbey Awards in Painting, 68, 173

Abbey Scholarship in Painting, 68, 173

Abbey Scholarship in Painting, 68, 173

ABC-Clio America: History and Life Award, 251

Abe Fellowship Program, 290

Aboriginal and Torred Strait Islander Scholarship, 47

Acadia Graduate Teaching Assistantships, 4

ACLS/SSRC International Postdoctoral Fellowships, 291

Adele Filene Travel Award, 128

Adeline Rosenberg Memorial Prize Competition, 149

Adelle and Erwin Tomash Fellowship in the History of Information Processing, 118

Adolfo Omodeo Scholarship, 187

Adult Literature Award, Juvenile Literary Award, 152

Africa Educational Trust Emergency Grants, 5

African Dissertation Internship Awards, 270

African Graduate Fellowship, 27

AFUW Georgina Sweet Fellowship, 62

AFUW Victoria Endowment Scholarship, Lady Leitch Scholarship, 44

The AFUW-SA Inc Trust Fund Bursary, 44

Ahmanson and Getty Postdoctoral Fellowships, 313

AIA College of Fellows Grant, 13

The AIA/AAF Scholarship for Advanced Study and Research, 13

AIA/AHA Graduate Fellowship in Health Facility Planning and Design, 14

AIAR Annual Professorship, 23

AIAR Islamic Studies Fellowship, 23

AIATSIS Research Grants, 46

AIEJ Honors Scholarships, 41

AIIS Senior Performing and Creative Arts Fellowships, 14

AILA/Yamagani/Hope Fellowship, 203

Albert J Beveridge Grant, 12

Alberta Art Foundation Graduate Scholarships in The Department of Art, 323

Albin Salton Fellowship, 371

Aldo and Jeane Scaglione Prize for Comparative Literary Studies, 220

Aldo and Jeane Scaglione Prize for Studies in Slavic Languages and Literatures, 221

Aldo and Jeane Scaglione Prize for Translation of a Scholarly Study of Literature, 221

Aldo and Jeanne Scaglione Prize for French and Francophone Literary Studies, 221

Alec Redshaw Memorial Awards, 164

Alexander Graham Bell Scholarship Awards, 6

Alexander O Vietor Memorial Fellowship, 192

Alexander S Onassis Programme of Research Grants, 7

Alexander S Onassis Research Grants, 7

Alexander von Humboldt 'Bundeskanzler' Scholarships, 156

Alexander von Humboldt Research Fellowships, 156

Alfred D Chandler Jr Traveling Fellowships in Business History and Institutional Economic History, 167

Alfred Einstein Award, 15

Alice Berger Hammerschlag Trust Award, 34

Alice E Smith Fellowship, 306

Alice E Wilson Awards, 106

All Saints Educational Trust Corporate Awards, 9

All Saints Educational Trust Personal Awards, 9

Allcard Grants, 379

America-Norway Heritage Fund, 244

American Accordion Musicological Society Music Competition Contest, 10

American Society for Eighteenth-Century Studies, 239

American-Scandinavian Foundation, 28, 244

Americans and World Affairs Fellows Program, 378

AMF Award, 46

AMS 50 Dissertation Fellowship, 15

Amy Louise Hunter Fellowship, 306

The Andrew W Mellon Fellowships in Humanistic Studies, 377

Andrew W Mellon Foundation Fellowships, 24, 175

Andrew W Mellon Foundation Fellowships in the Humanities, 175

Andrew W Mellon Postdoctoral Fellowships in the Humanities, 358

The Anglo-Danish (London) Scholarships, 29

Anglo-Jewish Association Bursary, 29

Anna C and Oliver C Colburn Fellowship, 30

ANS Fellowship in Roman Studies, 17

ANU Alumni Association Country Specific PhD Scholarships, 47

ANU Masters Degree Scholarships (The Faculties), 47

ANU PhD Scholarships, 47

APA Book and Article Prizes, 17

Arab-British Chamber Charitable Foundation Scholarships, 75

The Archchaeology Geology Division - Claude C Albritton, Jr Scholarships, 155

Aristotle University of Thessaloniki Scholarships, 31

ARIT Humanities and Social Science Fellowships, 20

ARIT Language Fellowships, 20

ARIT/NEH Fellowships for the Humanities in Turkey, 20

Artflight Arts Council-Aer Lingus Travel Awards, 33

Arthur Rubinstein International Piano Master Competition, 31

Arthur Weinberg Fellowship for Independent Scholars, 239

Arts Council Drama Grants, 32

Arts Council Independent Dance Project Grants, 32

Arts Council Literature Awards, 32

Arts Council of England Combined Arts, 32

Arts Council of England Music Grants, 32

Arts Council of England Visual Arts, 32

The Arts Council of Ireland Composers Commission Scheme, 33

Arts Council of Ireland Travel Awards to Creative Artists, 33

Arts Council of Northern Ireland Annual Award, 34

Arts Council of Wales Awards for Advanced Study in Music, 35

Arts Council of Wales Commissions to Composers, 36

Arts Council of Wales Grants for Artists, 36

Arts Council of Wales Grants to Dancers, 36

Arts for All, 36

ASCAP Grants to Young Composers, 39

ASCSA Fellowships, 21

ASCSA Research Fellow in Faunal Studies, 21

C

GrantFinder - Arts

T

INDEX OF AWARDING
ORGANISATIONS

A

AAUW Educational Foundation, *USA*, 3

Academy of Motion Picture Arts and Sciences, *USA*, 4

Acadia University, *Canada*, 4

Adolph and Esther Gottlieb Foundation, Inc., *USA*, 4

Africa Educational Trust, *England*, 5

Afro-Asian Institute in Vienna and Catholic Women's League of Austria, *Austria*, 6

Alexander Graham Bell Association for the Deaf, *USA*, 6

Alexander S Onassis Public Benefit Foundation, *Greece*, 6

Alexander von Humboldt Foundation, *Germany*, 7

All Saints Educational Trust, *England*, 9

America-Israel Cultural Foundation, *Israel*, 10

American Academy of Arts and Letters, *USA*, 10

American Accordion Musicological Society, *USA*, 10

American Antiquarian Society (AAS), *USA*, 11

American Council of Learned Societies, *USA*, 12

American Historical Association, *USA*, 12

American Institute of Architects (AIA), *USA*, 13

American Institute of Indian Studies(AIIS), *USA*, 14

American Music Center, Inc., *USA*, 14

American Musicological Society, *USA*, 14

American Numismatic Society (ANS), *USA*, 17

American Oriental Society, *USA*, 17

American Philosophical Association, *USA*, 17

American Philosophical Society, *USA*, 18

American Research Institute in Turkey (ARIT), *USA*, 20

American School of Classical Studies at Athens (ASCSA), *USA*, 21

American Schools of Oriental Research (ASOR), *USA*, 23

American Society of Interior Designers Educational Foundation, Inc (ASID), *USA*, 26

The American University in Cairo, *Egypt*, 27

The American-Scandinavian Foundation (ASF), *USA*, 28

Anglo-Austrian Music Society, *England*, 29

The Anglo-Danish Society, *England*, 29

Anglo-Jewish Association, *England*, 29

The Archaeological Institute of America, *USA*, 30

Aristotle University of Thessaloniki, *Greece*, 31

Arthur Rubinstein International Music Society, *Israel*, 31

The Arts Council of England, *England*, 31

Arts Council of Ireland, *Ireland*, 33

Arts Council of Northern Ireland, *Northern Ireland*, 34

Arts Council of Wales, *Wales*, 35

Arts Management, *Australia*, 38

Arts Management Pty Limited, *Australia*, 39

The ASCAP Foundation, *USA*, 39

Asian Cultural Council, *USA*, 40

Associated Board of the Royal Schools of Music, *England*, 40

Association of African Universities, *Ghana*, 41

Association of Commonwealth Universities, *England*, 41

Association of International Education, Japan (AIEJ), *Japan*, 41

Association of Rhodes Scholars in Australia, *Australia*, 42

Association of Universities and Colleges of Canada, *Canada*, 42

Atlantic School of Theology, *Canada*, 43

Australian Academy of the Humanities, *Australia*, 44

Australian Federation of University Women - Victoria, *Australia*, 44

The Australian Federation of University Women, South Australia, Inc Trust Fund (AFUW), *Australia*, 44

The Australian Government, *Australia*, 46

Australian Institute of Aboriginal and Torres Strait Islander Studies, *Australia*, 46

Australian Musical Foundation, *England*, 46

Australian National University, *Australia*, 47

Australian War Memorial, *Australia*, 48

Australian-American Educational Foundation, *Australia*, 49

Austrian Science Fund, *Austria*, 51

B

The Banff Centre for the Arts, *Canada*, 53

Beit Trust (Zimbabwe, Zambia & Malawi), *Zimbabwe*, 53

Belgian-American Educational Foundation, Inc., *USA*, 53

Beverly Hills Theatre Guild, *USA*, 54

BFWG Charitable Foundation (formerly Crosby Hall), *England*, 55

Bibliographical Society of America, *USA*, 55

Blues Heaven Foundation, Inc., *USA*, 56

Board of Architects of New South Wales, *Australia*, 56

Boise Foundation, *England*, 57

The Boston Society of Architects, *USA*, 57

Bradford Chamber of Commerce and Industry, *England*, 57

Brandon University, *Canada*, 58

Bread Loaf Writer's Conference, *USA*, 58

The British Academy, *England*, 58

British Association for American Studies (BAAS), *England*, 60

British Association for Canadian Studies (BACS), *Scotland*, 60

The British Council, *Germany*, 61

The British Council, *USA*, 61

British Federation of Women Graduates (BFWG), *England*, 62

British Institute in Eastern Africa, *Kenya*, 65

British Institute in Paris, *England*, 65

British Institute of Archaeology at Ankara, *England*, 66

The British Library, *England*, 66

British School at Athens, *Greece*, 67

The British School at Rome (BSR), *Italy*, 68

British School of Archaeology in Iraq, *England*, 71

The British Schools and Universities Foundation, Inc. (BSUF), *England*, 71

The Broadcasting Corporations of the Federal Republic of Germany, *Germany*, 72

The Bross Foundation, Lake Forest College, *USA*, 72

Budapest International Music Competition, *Hungary*, 73

BUNAC, *England*, 73

The Bunting Institute of Radcliffe College, *USA*, 73

C

The Caledonian Research Foundation, *Scotland*, 74

Calouste Gulbenkian Foundation (International Department), *Portugal*, 75

The Camargo Foundation, *France*, 75

Cambridge Commonwealth Trust, Cambridge Overseas Trust and Associated Trusts, *England*, 75

GrantFinder - Arts